The Complete Commentary by Śaṅkara on the Yoga Sūtra-s

A Full Translation of the Newly Discovered Text

Trevor Leggett

Trevor Leggett Adhyatma Yoga Trust

Postal Address of the Trust:
Trevor Leggett Adhyatma Yoga Trust
PO Box 362
KINGS LYNN
PE31 8WQ
United Kingdom

Website address of the Trust:
www.tlayt.org

Printed edition first published in 1990 by Kegan Paul International Ltd

Printed in the United Kingdom
ISBN - 978-1-911467-08-3

Trevor Leggett Adhyatma Yoga Trust

To the late Hari Prasad Shastri,
pandit and jñani of India,
translator of Śaṅkara's works and
a faithful follower of Śaṅkara
in his own original works,
this translation is reverently dedicated

Acknowledgements

I am grateful to Dr. Hajime Nakamura, Professor Emeritus of the University of Tokyo and founder of the Eastern Institute, Tokyo, for help with the translation of the First Part. For errors that remain I am entirely responsible.

The late Shankaracarya of Sringeri, H.H. Abhinava Vidyatirtha, showed much interest in this Vivaraṇa and encouraged the present translator to tackle this difficult text, which (he said) might be of great importance in the study of Śaṅkara.

The trustees of the Trevor Leggett Adhyatma Yoga Trust wish to express their grateful thanks to Dr Kengo Harimoto of Mahidol University, Thailand, who kindly agreed to write a Foreword to this edition of The Complete Commentary by Śaṅkara on the Yoga Sutras, translated by Trevor Pryce Leggett. Dr Harimoto's most valuable and interesting Foreword reviews and puts in context some of the comments that have been made on the author's translation since it was first published in London in 1990 and also on the authenticity of the Vivaraṇa as a work by Śaṅkara.

Contents

Foreword by Kengo Harimoto	xxiii
Introduction for the general reader	1
How to use this Book for Yoga Practice	21
Technical introduction	23

First Part: SAMĀDHI

1 Yoga theory

Sūtra I.1	Now the exposition of yoga	65
Sūtra I.2	Yoga is inhibition of the mental processes	76
Sūtra I.3	Then the Seer is established in his own nature	81
Sūtra I.4	Otherwise, it conforms itself to the mental process	82

2 Mental processes

Sūtra I.5	The mental processes are of five kinds; they are tainted or pure	88
Sūtra I.6	Right knowledge, illusion, logical construction, sleep, memory	90
Sūtra I.7	Right knowledge is either direct perception, inference, or authority	90
Sūtra I.8	Illusion is false knowledge based on an untrue form	111
Sūtra I.9	Logical construction is something that follows on verbal knowledge but has no real object	114
Sūtra I.10	The mental process which rests on the notion of non-existence is sleep	118

Sūtra I.11 Memory is not letting slip away an object experienced 120

3 Practice

Sūtra I.12 Their inhibition is by practice and detachment 123
Sūtra I.13 Practice is the effort at steadiness in it 123
Sūtra I.14 But practised for a long time, uninterruptedly and with reverence, it becomes firmly grounded 124
Sūtra I.15 Detachment is consciousness of self-mastery, of one who has no thirst for any object either seen or heard about 124
Sūtra I.16 It is the higher detachment when from knowledge of Puruṣa there is no thirst for (even) the guṇa-s 126

4 Samādhi

Sūtra I.17 It is cognitive because accompanied with verbal associations (vitarka), with subtle associations (vicāra), with joy (ānanda), and the form of I-am-ness (asmitā) 129
Sūtra I.18 The other (samādhi) follows on practice of the idea of stopping, and consists of saṃskāra-s alone 131
Sūtra I.19 It results from birth in the case of gods discarnate, and in the case of those who absorb themselves into prakṛti 132
Sūtra I.20 For the others, it comes after faith, energy, memory, (cognitive) samādhi, and knowledge 133
Sūtra I.21 For those who practise with ardent energy, it is near 134
Sūtra I.22 Even among the ardent, there is a distinction of mild or moderate or intense 135

5 God

Sūtra I.23 Or by special devotion to the Lord 136
Sūtra I.24 Untouched by taints or karma-s or their fruition or their latent stocks is the Lord, who is a special kind of Puruṣa 136
Sūtra I.25 In whom the seed of omniscience becomes transcendent 141

Sūtra I.26	This teacher of even the first teachers, because not particularized by time	164
Sūtra I.27	Of him, the expression is praṇava (OM)	168
Sūtra I.28	Repetition of it and meditation on its meaning	171

6 Obstacles

Sūtra I.29	From that, realization of the separate consciousness, and absence of obstacles	173
Sūtra I.30	Illness, apathy, doubt, carelessness, laziness, failure to withdraw, misconceptions, failure to attain a state, instability (in the state) – these distractions of the mind are the obstacles	174
Sūtra I.31	Pain, frustration, restlessness of the body, spasmodic breathing in or out are the accompaniments of these distractions	176
Sūtra I.32	To prevent them, practice on one principle	177

7 Special Practices

Sūtra I.33	The mind is made clear by meditation on friendliness towards the happy, compassion for the suffering, goodwill towards the virtuous, and disinterest in the sinful	187
Sūtra I.34	Or by expulsion and retention of prāṇa	188
Sūtra I.35	Or achievement of supernormal perception of a divine object brings the mind to steadiness	188
Sūtra I.36	Or a radiant perception beyond sorrow	190
Sūtra I.37	Or on a mind whose meditation is on freedom from passion	191
Sūtra I.38	Or meditating on the knowledge of dream and sleep	192
Sūtra I.39	Or by meditation on what appeals to him	192
Sūtra I.40	His mastery extends right to the ultimate atom and to the ultimate magnitude	193

8 Absorption

Sūtra I.41	Identification-in-samādhi (samāpatti) is when the mental process has dwindled and the mind rests on either the knower or the knowing process or a known object, and like a crystal apparently takes on their respective qualities	194
Sūtra I.42	The samādhi-identification is called sa-vitarka when it is mixed up with mental constructs of word, thing, and idea	198
Sūtra I.43	When there is purification from memories, (that samādhi) apparently empty of its own nature of knowledge, with the object alone shining forth, is nir-vitarka	201
Sūtra I.44	In the same way, when it is on subtle objects, it is called sa-vicāra (with subtle associations) and nir-vicāra (without subtle associations)	209
Sūtra I.45	The scale of (causal) subtlety of objects ends in pradhāna	211
Sūtra I.46	These are samādhi from-a-seed	212
Sūtra I.47	From skill in nir-vicāra, a clearness in the self	213
Sūtra I.48	In this, the knowledge is Truth-bearing	213
Sūtra I.49	This knowledge is of a particular thing, unlike knowledge from authority or from inference	214
Sūtra I.50	The saṃskāra produced by it inhibits other saṃskāra-s	216
Sūtra I.51	When that too is inhibited, everything is inhibited, and thus this samādhi is without-seed.	217

SECOND PART: MEANS

1 Yoga of action

Sūtra II.1	Tapas, self-study, devotion to the Lord, are the yoga of action	223
Sūtra II.2	To actualize samādhi and thin out the taints	226

2 Taints

Sūtra II.3	Ignorance, I-am-ness, desire, hate, instinctive self-preservation, are the taints	227
Sūtra II.4	Ignorance is the field of germination of the subsequent ones, whether dormant or thinned out or checked or active	229
Sūtra II.5	Ignorance is the conviction of permanence, purity, happiness and self in what are really impermanent, impure, painful and not self	236
Sūtra II.6	The single selfhood, as it were, of the powers of seer and seeing is I-am-ness	244
Sūtra II.7	Desire follows on (anujanma) pleasure	246
Sūtra II.8	Hate follows on (anujanma) pain	247
Sūtra II.9	With spontaneous momentum, instinctive even in a Knower, is self-preservation	247
Sūtra II.10	In their subtle state, they are to be got rid of by dissolution in their source	249
Sūtra II.11	Mental processes arising from them are got rid of by meditation	250

3 Karma

Sūtra II.12	Rooted in taints is the karma-stock to be felt in present or future lives	251
Sūtra II.13	While the root is there, it will bear the fruit of birth, life span and experience	254
Sūtra II.14	Their fruits are joy and suffering caused by virtue and sin	269

4 Pain

Sūtra II.15	Because of the sufferings caused by changes and anxieties and the saṃskāra-s of them, and from the clash of the guṇa-s, to the clear-sighted, everything is pain alone	270

5 Guṇa-s 278

6 Release

Sūtra II.16 What is to be escaped is the pain not yet come 285
Sūtra II.17 The Seer-Seen conjunction is the cause of what is to be escaped 286

7 Guṇa-s again

Sūtra II. 18 With a constant tendency towards light, action, and fixity, the Seen consists of the elements and the senses, being for the purpose of experience and transcendence 291
Sūtra II.19 What particularizes itself, and what does not, what goes (liṅga, the Great principle) and what does not (a-liṅga, pradhāna), are guṇa-implementers 298

8 Puruṣa

Sūtra II.20 The Seer is sight alone; though pure, he looks on at the thoughts 305
Sūtra II.21 The essence of the Seen is to be for the purpose of him alone 311

9 Seer-Seen

Sūtra II.22 For one whose purpose has been effected, it is ended, but not for others, because it is common 312
Sūtra II.23 The conjunction causes awareness of the natures of the two powers, the property and its possessor 314
Sūtra II.24 Its cause is Ignorance (a-vidyā) 320
Sūtra II.25 Without it, there is no conjunction, and that release is Transcendental Aloneness (kaivalya) of the power-of-sight 323

10 Release again

Sūtra II.26	Unwavering Knowledge-of-the-difference is the means of release	324
Sūtra II.27	Therein, the ultimate state of the Knowledge is seven-fold	326

11 Yoga

Sūtra II.28	From following up the methods of yoga, destruction of impurity and a growing light of knowledge up to Knowledge-of-the-difference	329
Sūtra II.29	Restraints, observances, posture, restraint of vital currents, dissociation, concentration, meditation, samādhi are the eight methods	333

12 Restraints

Sūtra II.30	Of these, harmlessness, truth-speaking, no stealing, brahmacarya, not holding possessions, are the restraints	334
Sūtra II.31	When practised universally without qualification of birth, place, time, or obligation, they are called the Great Vow	337

13 Observances

Sūtra II.32	Purity, contentment, tapas, self-study, and devotion to the Lord are the observances	338

14 Contrary ideas

Sūtra II.33	If there is obstruction by contrary ideas, meditation on their opposite	340

Sūtra II.34	The contrary ideas, violence and the others, done or caused to be done or approved of, preceded by greed, anger or delusion, mild, medium, or intense – all result in endless pain and Ignorance. This is the meditation on their opposite	342

15 Perfections

Sūtra II.35	With establishment of harmlessness, in his presence enmity is abandoned	345
Sūtra II.36	With establishment of truth, events confirm his words	345
Sūtra II.37	With establishment in non-stealing, all precious things come to him	346
Sūtra II.38	With establishment in brahmacarya, attainment of energy	346
Sūtra II.39	With firmness in not possessing property, clear knowledge of the conditions of birth	346
Sūtra II.40	From purity, distaste for his own body and no intercourse with others	347
Sūtra II.41	Purity of mind-sattva, cheerfulness, one-pointedness, conquest of the senses, and fitness for vision of the self	348
Sūtra II.42	From contentment, attainment of unsurpassed happiness	348
Sūtra II.43	From destruction of impurity by tapas, perfection of body and senses	349
Sūtra II.44	From self-study, communion with the deity of his devotion	349
Sūtra II.45	From devotion to the Lord, perfection in samādhi	350
Sūtra II.46	Posture is to be firm and pleasant	350
Sūtra II.47	By relaxing effort and by samādhi (samāpatti) on infinity	352
Sūtra II.48	From that, he becomes immune to the opposites	352
Sūtra II.49	Prāṇāyāma is to sit in the posture and cut off the flow of in-breath and out-breath	353
Sūtra II.50	The external, internal, and fixating operations, practised in terms of place, of time and of number, become long and fine	353

Sūtra II.51	The fourth prāṇāyāma comes when both external and internal fields have been felt into	355
Sūtra II.52	Thereby is destroyed the covering of the light	356
Sūtra II.53	Fitness of the mind for concentrations	357
Sūtra II.54	Dissociation is when the senses, disjoined from their respective objects, assume as it were the nature of mind itself	357
Sūtra II.55	From that, supreme mastery of the senses.	358

THIRD PART: GLORY

1 Inner Methods

Sūtra III.1	Dhāraṇā is binding the mind to a place	363
Sūtra III.2	Continuity of the mind there is dhyāna (meditation)	363
Sūtra III.3	That same (meditation – dhyāna), when it comes to shine forth as the object alone, apparently empty of its own nature as knowledge, is called samādhi	364
Sūtra III.4	The triad (held) at the one place is saṃyama	365
Sūtra III.5	From mastery of that, the light of knowledge (prajñā)	365
Sūtra III.6	Its application is by stages	366
Sūtra III.7	Compared to the previous means, this triad is the direct means	368
Sūtra III.8	Even that is an indirect means as regards unseeded (yoga)	368
Sūtra III.9	The inhibitive transformation of the mind is when extravertive saṃskāra is overcome and the saṃskāra of inhibition is predominant, and mind itself is in a temporary state of inhibition	370
Sūtra III.10	It has a peaceful flow, by reason of the saṃskāra-s	372
Sūtra III.11	The destruction of the mind's dispersiveness, and rise of its one-pointedness, is the samādhi transformation	372
Sūtra III.12	In that (samādhi) the sameness of the idea which has subsided and the newly risen idea in the mind is its transformation of one-pointedness	373

2 Change

Sūtra III.13	By (analogy with) that, are explained the transformations of dharma, time-phase, and basis (avasthā) in the elements and in the senses	375
Sūtra III.14	What conforms to the subsided, uprisen, and indeterminable dharma-s is the dharmin	390
Sūtra III.15	Difference of sequence causes the differences of the changes	394
Sūtra III.16	From saṃyama on the three changes, knowledge of what is past and future	398

3 Meaning-flash

Sūtra III.17	There is confusion from the mutual projection of word, meaning and idea on to each other. From saṃyama on their distinctness (comes) understanding of the cries of all beings	399

4 Glories

Sūtra III.18	From direct perception of the saṃskāra-s, knowledge of previous lives	420
Sūtra III.19	(From direct perception, through saṃyama) of his thought, knowledge of the mind of another	422
Sūtra III.20	But not the subject of those ideas, because that was not the field of the saṃyama	422
Sūtra III.21	From saṃyama on the form of the body, its potentiality of being seen is nullified. Being disjoined from the light of the eye, it disappears	423
Sūtra III.22	Karma is rapid or slow. From saṃyama on it, or on omens, there comes foreknowledge of death	424
Sūtra III.23	(From saṃyama) on friendliness and the others (compassion and goodwill, sūtra I.33) (there arise) powers	425
Sūtra III.24	Powers like the power of an elephant (come from saṃyama) on them	426

Sūtra III.25	By projecting the light of supernormal radiant perception (I.36) on to what is subtle, hidden or remote, (he comes to) knowledge of that	427
Sūtra III.26	From saṃyama on the sun, knowledge of the worlds	427
Sūtra III.27	(From saṃyama) on the moon, knowledge of the dispositions of the stars	430
Sūtra III.28	(From saṃyama) on the Pole Star, knowledge of their motions	430
Sūtra III.29	On the navel circle, knowledge of the plan of the body	431
Sūtra III.30	At the pit of the throat, cessation of hunger and thirst	431
Sūtra III. 31	On the tortoise nerve, rigid steadiness	432
Sūtra III.32	On the Light in the head, vision of the perfect ones	432
Sūtra III.33	By the prātibha supernormal knowledge too (he knows) everything	433
Sūtra III.34	On the heart, awareness of the mind	433

5 Knowledge

Sūtra III.35	Experience is an idea which does not distinguish between sattva and Puruṣa, though they are absolutely separate; by saṃyama on what-is-for-its-own-sake, (distinct) from what-is-for-the-sake-of-another, there comes knowledge of Puruṣa	434
Sūtra III.36	From that arise supernormal knowledge and hearing, touch, sight, taste, and awareness of events	436
Sūtra III.37	They are obstacles in samādhi, but perfections in the extravertive state	437

6 Glories (continued)

Sūtra III.38	From loosening of the cause of tying, and awareness of how the mind moves, the mind can enter another body	437
Sūtra III.39	By mastering the upgoing vital current (udāna), he passes untouched over water, mud, thorns and so on, and at death he takes the upward course	438
Sūtra III.40	From mastery of samāna, blazing light	439

Sūtra III.41	From saṃyama on the relation between hearing and space, divine hearing	440
Sūtra III.42	From saṃyama on the relation between the body and space, followed by identification-in-samādhi (samāpatti) with the lightness of a thread, he travels through space	441
Sūtra III.43	The Great Bodiless is a mental process (vṛtti) functioning exterior (to the body), and not imaginary; from this comes dwindling away of the covering of the light	442
Sūtra III.44	From saṃyama on their physical form, essential nature, subtle form, inherence, and purposefulness: conquest of the elements	443
Sūtra III.45	From it (the saṃyama) manifest a set of eight powers like becoming minute, and perfection of the body, with freedom from impediment for its (bodily) attributes	448
Sūtra III.46	The perfection of the body is grace, splendour, power, and diamond hardness	450
Sūtra III.47	From saṃyama on their perception, essential nature, I-am-ness, inherence, and purposefulness, (comes) conquest of the senses	450
Sūtra III.48	From that, speediness as of the mind, independence of physical organs, and conquest of nature	452
Sūtra III.49	Having simply the knowledge that (mind-)sattva and Puruṣa are different, one has omnipotence over all beings and is omniscient	453
Sūtra III.50	From indifference to that too, the seeds of imperfection are destroyed, and there is Transcendental Aloneness	454
Sūtra III.51	No reaction of attachment or pride in case of invitations from rulers of celestial realms, for undesirable consequences follow	455

7 Omniscience

Sūtra III.52	From saṃyama on the instant, and on the two sequences of instants, comes knowledge-born-of-discrimination	458

Sūtra III.53 From this (knowledge) there is clear knowledge of two things (seemingly) equivalent because they cannot be distinguished by class, characteristic, or position 461
Sūtra III.54 Knowledge-born-of-discrimination, having all, and all times, for its object, is called Transcendent 465
Sūtra III.55 When the (mind-)sattva is like Puruṣa in purity, there is Transcendental Aloneness. So it is. 466

FOURTH PART: TRANSCENDENTAL ALONENESS (KAIVALYA)

1 Perfections

Sūtra IV.1 Perfections (siddhi) arise from birth or from drugs or from mantra-s or from tapas or from samādhi 471
Sūtra IV.2 The transformation into another life is implemented by prakṛti 471
Sūtra IV.3 That cause is not the impelling drive itself, but it makes a breach in the retaining barrier of the natures, as does a farmer (for irrigation) 472
Sūtra IV.4 The minds are projected from bare I-am-ness 474
Sūtra IV.5 In the variety of activities, it is the one mind that impels the several minds 474
Sūtra IV.6 Of those (minds with perfections), the mind whose perfections arise out of meditation (dhyāna) has no karma-stock 475

2 Karma

Sūtra IV.7 The karma of the yogin is neither white nor black; of the others, it is of three kinds 476
Sūtra IV.8 Therefore their consequent manifestation is of those saṃskāra-groups (vāsanā) that are compatible with it 481

Sūtra IV.9	Because there is sameness of form of memory and saṃskāra-s, there is consequent succession between them, even though separated by class and place and time	483
Sūtra IV.10	They are beginningless, because hope is eternal	485
Sūtra IV.11	They are held together by cause-effect-repository-focal-point. When these cease, they too cease	488
Sūtra IV.12	What are past and future do actually exist, but there is difference of time-phase in their dharma-s	490

3 Time

Sūtra IV.13	They are manifest or subtle, and consist of the guṇa-s	495
Sūtra IV.14	A thing is what it is by the fact of a unitary change	497

4 Against Buddhism

(Sūtra IV. 14, continued)

Sūtra IV.15	Since there is difference of the minds, while the object is the same, the two must be distinct categories	500
Sūtra IV.16	It is not dependent on a single mind, for when it was not giving rise to valid cognition in that mind, what would it be?	504
Sūtra IV.17	According to whether the mind is coloured by it, a thing is known or unknown	507
Sūtra IV.18	To Him, the Lord, the mental processes are always known, from the fact of the unchangeability of Puruṣa	508
Sūtra IV.19	It (mind) is not self-illumining, because it is itself something perceived	510
Sūtra IV.20	They cannot both be clearly ascertained at the same time	513
Sūtra IV.21	If it is to be seen by another idea, further and yet further ideas will be required. And there will be confusion of memories	514
Sūtra IV.22	In assumption of its (the mind's) form on the part of the unmoving consciousness, is awareness of the idea of the self	517

5 Mind

Sūtra IV.23	Mind, coloured by Seer and seen, has the various purposes	519
Sūtra IV.24	Though it is a mélange of countless saṃskāra-groups, it must exist for the purposes of another, because it is a construct	522

6 Release

Sūtra IV.25	For him who sees that One apart, cessation of meditation on his own being	524
Sūtra IV.26	Then the mind is inclined to discrimination, and is borne on towards Aloneness	526
Sūtra IV.27	At intervals in it, other ideas arise from saṃskāra-s	526
Sūtra IV.28	The escape from these is like that described in the case of the taints	527
Sūtra IV.29	For one who is through and through a man of discriminative knowledge, but is not grasping over his meditation practice, there comes about the samādhi called Raincloud of Dharma	528
Sūtra IV.30	From that, cessation of taints and karma-s	529
Sūtra IV.31	Then, with the infinity of knowledge free from all veiling taint, the knowable comes to be but a trifle	529
Sūtra IV.32	With that, the guṇa-s have fulfilled their purpose, and the succession of their changes comes to an end	531
Sūtra IV.33	The succession is conjoined to each instant, (but) recognizable at the very end	531
Sūtra IV.34	Transcendental Aloneness is withdrawal of the guṇa-s, now without any purposes of Puruṣa; or it is the establishment of the power-of-consciousness in its own nature	536

(Salutations and colophon) 538

Foreword by Kengo Harimoto

When Trevor Leggett published *The Complete Commentary by Śaṅkara on the Yoga sūtra-s* in 1990, it was the first full translation of the sub-commentary on the Yogasūtras, variously called the Yogasūtrabhāṣyavivaraṇa or the Pātañjalayogaśāstravivaraṇa, etc., into a modern language. The Sanskrit text (henceforth the Vivaraṇa) had attracted some attention from Western scholars from the time it was published in Madras in 1952 as part of the Madras Government Oriental Series, especially because the editors of the edition ascribed it to one of the most famous of Indian philosophers, Śaṅkara.

Hajime Nakamura, by translating whose work from Japanese into English Leggett had become known among Indologists, was one of those who were interested in the Vivaraṇa. Nakamura wrote a few articles on the Vivaraṇa in the late 1970s, mainly concerned with its authorship. He also published a Japanese translation of its first chapter from 1979 to 1983. I imagine that Leggett's interest in the Vivaraṇa was inspired by Nakamura.

Despite Leggett's long-term relationship with him, I do not see any evidence of the direct indebtedness of his English translation to Nakamura's Japanese translation. For example, in the Vivaraṇa towards the beginning of the commentary on Yogabhāṣya 1.6, there is a question from an opponent: *atha svaviṣayasāmanyaviśeṣāvabhāsanasāmarthye śrotrādīnāṃ cittasya ca kiṃkṛtam viśeṣāvadhāraṇaprādhānyam iti.* Leggett translates this as "A sense like hearing, and the mind, can reflect both the universality (i.e. class) and the particularity of an object; why is this supposed to be concerned mainly with determining a particular?" Nakamura in Japanese translates in effect "Senses, such as hearing, etc., can...; why is the mind...?" The difference lies in how these two translators understood the function of the particle *ca* (and). This particle has various functions in Sanskrit. One is to combine two or more items (typically words) by being placed after the last word of the sequence. So, A, B, C *ca* means "A, B, and C". It can also serve to connect sentences by being placed after the first word or syntagma of the following sentence. Leggett read the particle *ca* in the sentence as a word connector, combining *śrotrādīnām* and *cittasya,* whereas Nakamura read it as a sentence connector. I think that Leggett's understanding of the particle's function here is preferable. Since such instances are frequent, I conclude that Leggett's translation was his own original work.

The whole translation is remarkable in that it was prepared by someone primarily known for his works related to Japan. I am amazed that Leggett learned Sanskrit on his own. He had apparently read quite a few other works in the original Sanskrit. This is evident from the references to Sanskrit works in the introduction.

After its publication two reviews appeared in academic journals. One was a review article entitled "Notes on an English Translation of the Yogasūtrabhāṣyavivaraṇa" by Tuvia Gelblum in the *Bulletin of the School of Oriental and African Studies,* University of London, vol. 55 (1992) and the other, which was by J. W. de Jong, came out in the *Indo-Iranian Journal* 37 (1994).

Since I find the "Notes" by Gelblum to be unjustifiably critical of Leggett's book, I would like to point out some of the problems in them in this Foreword.[1]

Gelblum appears to have misunderstood Leggett's position with regard to the authorship problem of the Vivaraṇa. He treats it as if Leggett was convinced of the identity of Śaṅkara with the author of the Vivaraṇa, and he is critical of this view. In particular, he seems convinced that Leggett follows Hacker's "conversion theory" (namely that Śaṅkara was a follower of the yoga tradition—whatever that means—but subsequently became a Vedāntin).[2] He even includes a digression mentioning a post-Biblical legend concerning Jethro's conversion. What I read in Leggett's text, however, is that, although he was very much inclined to accept that Śaṅkara and the author of the Vivaraṇa were one and the same, he still remained cautious about this. Leggett points out a swing towards Vedānta in the Vivaraṇa; if he had been thinking only of a single author's evolution from being a scholar of Yoga to becoming a scholar of Vedānta, he would have been concerned only with the Yoga elements in Śaṅkara's Vedānta works. That was what Hacker did. The fact that Leggett did not do this indicates that, while not committing himself to Śaṅkara's authorship of the Vivaraṇa, he did not preclude the possibility that Śaṅkara, a Vedānta scholar, wrote the Yoga commentary.

Gelblum's "Notes" include what he regarded as an example of a portion of the text of the Vivaraṇa where it could inform us of the existence of a superior original reading of the Yogabhāṣya (3.14). However, the place which he chose was not a good example. As Gelblum himself appears to be aware, the author of the Vivaraṇa was most likely proposing an emendation to the text, because he first refers to a reading close to, but not the same as, what is found in published editions of the Yogabhāṣya. The author shows a preference for another reading and explains why he prefers it. It seems to me as if the first reading was all he knew and he did not like it. If in fact he had had two readings before him, then he would have interpreted the preferred reading first and mentioned the alternative reading second. At least, when an author does this, we are less likely to doubt that he saw the alternative reading. The proposal by the author of the Vivaraṇa may or may not reflect the transmission history of the Yogabhāṣya (namely that its reading had changed), but there is no guarantee that the author of the Vivaraṇa saw the alternative preferred reading in a manuscript.

Furthermore, Gelblum seems to have overlooked the more complicated and nuanced nature of the textual problem he was discussing. When he introduces the portion of the text in question, he casually emends the text of the Vivaraṇa from *samanantarībhavati* to *samanantaro bhavati*. The original reading was not a simple typographical error made in the edition (in hand-written Devanagari, the diacritics for '*ī*' and 'o' could look similar), as Gelblum appears to have assumed. The reading *samanantarībhavati* is indeed found in two old Malayalam manuscripts that were mutually independent witnesses to the common source of all the known manuscripts of the Vivaraṇa. There the diacritics for *ī* and *o* are very distinct in the Malayalam script. Gelblum adjusted the reading of the Yogabhāṣya preserved in the Vivaraṇa to what he believed it should be! That the reading *samantarībhavati* was in the Vivaraṇa is supported by two more sentences in the same section, if we read further in the text according to manuscripts. The first of these two sentences is found in the alternative text which the author of the Vivaraṇa prefers. Unfortunately, this reading was silently changed in the 1952 edition to *samanantaro bhavati*. Having no access to the manuscripts, Gelblum of course was not aware of this reading. Finally, although the two expressions might not seem to make much difference in meaning, a sentence in the Vivaraṇa ("although *[atīta]* has no *samanantara,* it is said that only *anāgata* will become *samanantara* of *atīta')*[3]clearly differentiates them. And some semantic difference is expected, so that the text of the Yogabhāṣya does not contradict what was said earlier: "Therefore it *(atīta)* has no *samanantara* (*tasmān na tasyāsti samanantaraḥ*)."[4] So, the difference with which the author of the Vivaraṇa was concerned was not between *tad anāgata eva samanantaro bhavati vartamānasya* and *tad anāgata eva samanantaro bhavati atītasya* as Gelblum has it but between *tad anāgata eva samanantarībhavati vartamānasya* and *tad anāgata eva samanantarībhavati atītasya.* The author of the Vivaraṇa did not know the reading which is printed in the editions of the Yogabhāṣya (*samanantaro … vartamānasya*) at all. So, Gelblum's discussion misses the point. The discussion in the Vivaraṇa presupposes the reading *samanantarībhavati* and the perceived semantic difference between *samanantaro bhavati* and *samanantarībhavati.* Despite Gelblum's unequivocal support for the reading, *tad anāgata eva samanantaro bhavati atītasya*, he was in fact arguing in favour of a reading which never existed.

Gelblum goes on to express his regret that Leggett produced his translation without having consulted manuscripts of the text. This is ironic, considering the fact that Gelblum himself entered into a philological discussion without studying the manuscripts, as explained in the previous paragraph.

The "Notes" contain further criticisms of Leggett's translation. Some of the points which he raises are valid but there are other points of dubious relevance. Gelblum devotes much space to the word *dāruyantra* which is found in dictionaries. Leggett's translation of the compound containing this word is certainly incorrect, but the long discussion in which Gelblum admits his own ignorance of the word was gratuitous. The word means a wooden puppet, a marionette. *Dāruyantra* is often encountered as an example of an insentient object acting like a sentient object, being controlled by a sentient being. Śaṅkara's Brahmasūtrabhāṣya and the so-called bhāṣya on the Bṛhadāraṇyaka Upaniṣad ascribed to him are two examples where *dāruyantra* appears in such a context.

A more significant instance of an unfair criticism of Leggett's translation relates to his translation of the term *kaivalya.* Gelblum comments:

> On the other hand, e.g., in rendering *kaivalya* (lit. 'wholeness', the state in which the self is rendered whole, integrated, authentic—i.e. liberation) Leggett adopts the erroneous 'Aloneness' and 'transcendental Aloneness' (pp. 2, 37, 191, 212, 353 and passim).

This statement is accompanied by a footnote referring to Gelblum's earlier publications. Perhaps it was erroneous from Gelblum's standpoint, but the truth is that he is the only person who insists on this interpretation. I have not seen anyone else adopting his understanding of the term *kaivalya.* Obviously, like many other terms, it has not had only one meaning throughout its history. Labelling someone else's translation erroneous because it does not agree with one's own ideas is not really fair.

Gelblum takes issue with Leggett's views on the readings of the Yogabhāṣya on sūtra 3.36. Here, my assessment is that Yogasūtra 3.36, the Yogabhāṣya that accompanies it, and the Vivaraṇa on both the sūtra and the Yogabhāṣya, must be studied very carefully before any conclusions are drawn. I think that both sides have failed to understand the underlying philological problems properly. Their primary error was that both trusted the text of the 1952 edition of the Vivaraṇa. The text in question is printed as *vṛttau bhavaṃ vārtam* in the edition. Gelblum's interpretation/translation of this part:

> (The word) *vārtam* ("consisting of everyday activities or occurrences"), being an adjective derived from (the word) *vṛtti* ("occurrence")

is probably closer to what the author of the Vivaraṇa intended. However, I suspect there was some corruption since *vārtta* as an adjective does not have the meaning of "news," and it cannot be paraphrased with *lokasaṃvyavahārajñānam* (knowledge of world affairs) as the author of the Vivaraṇa has paraphrased it. He was thinking of the feminine word *vār(t)tā*.

The problem comes down to what the sūtra means and how the bhāṣya explains it. The core of the problem is the long compound in the sūtra: *prātibhaśrāvaṇavedanādarśāsvādavārtāḥ*. To avoid tedious technical discussions, there is the possibility that the author of the Vivaraṇa understood the whole compound to mean "mental, auditory, tactile, visual, and gustatory forms of knowledge."[5] This understanding of the word in fact makes the sūtra intelligible. Leggett and Gelblum disagree on which reading of the Yogabhāṣya is more original and which represents a later deliberate change. The reality is that, as far as concerns this text, we can only say that the author of the Vivaraṇa had quite a different understanding of the sūtra from that gained from other commentaries, and this probably had something to do with the text of the Bhāṣya which he knew but which we do not. Whether the reading was older or younger is another question. The problem with Gelblum's "Notes" is that on the basis of erroneous observations and implausible speculations about how different readings (assumed to be erroneous) arose, he reached the conclusion that the Vivaraṇa was later than Vācaspati. Gelblum also thought that the Vivaraṇa's suggestion of an alternative reading for Yogabhāṣya 3.14 (discussed above) was an indication of the Vivaraṇa's posteriority to Vācaspati because the rejected reading was the one known to Vācaspati (but as discussed above, the reading rejected in the Vivaraṇa was not even the one known to Vācaspati). This conclusion, I think, has contributed to the fact that Vivaraṇa studies have taken a wrong direction.

I have touched upon Gelblum's arbitrariness elsewhere[6] but it might be worth repeating. This arbitrariness is found in the observation regarding the readings *citiśaktiḥ* or *citiśakteḥ* in Yogasūtra 4.34. Somehow Gelblum believes that the Vivaraṇa may be later than Bhoja because the Vivaraṇa does not adopt the same readings as Bhoja but accepts another reading in fact the same reading which everyone else, including Vācaspati, accepts. Essentially it is being argued that Vivaraṇa is later than Vācaspati because it does not know the reading adopted by Vācaspati in one place, and that it is later than Vācaspati and Bhoja because it adopts the reading known to Vācaspati in another. This is not convincing. (The idea that Bhoja presupposed the reading *citiśakteḥ* in sūtra 4.34 rather than *citiśaktiḥ*—the reading presupposed by Vācaspati and by the author of the Vivaraṇa—at least needs to be investigated by going back to the manuscripts of Bhoja's commentary. The matter is not as clear as Gelblum represents it. One cannot conclude that the Yogabhāṣya, too, presupposed the reading *citiśakteḥ,* as Gelblum asserts, from the text of the Yogabhāṣya.)

It was unfortunate that the publication of the "Notes" in a prestigious academic journal set the tone for the perception of Leggett's translation in the following years. This review article, in fact, contains misunderstandings; there are also some questionable views and unfair criticisms.

De Jong's review published in 1994 expresses a regret that Leggett's translation was made before a critical edition was available and before even there was any sign of such an edition appearing soon. Much of the rest of his review is devoted to pointing out the translation's shortcomings. De Jong mentions "contradictions between the Sūtras and the Bhāṣya." In fact in his introduction Leggett noted places where the Vivaraṇa contradicts either the sūtra or the bhāṣya.

In 2001 T. S. Rukmani published another English translation of the whole of the Vivaraṇa in two volumes.[7] In her introduction (pp. ix–xi), Rukmani acknowledges the pre-existence of Leggett's translation and discusses the differences between his and her translations. Apart from criticisms of the interpretation of some passages, the merits which she claims for her translation come down to the presence of the Sanskrit text in the body of her work and the index at the end of the two volumes.

I have written a review of Rukmani's translation and pointed out problems in her treatment of the authorship problem elsewhere.[8] Her assessment of the date of the Vivaraṇa and the identity of its author has been taken from her earlier publications, which are included as appendices in the second volume of the translation.[9] My own opinion is that her position that the author of the Vivaraṇa was acquainted with Vācaspati's commentary on the Yogabhāṣya cannot be sustained.

In terms of its quality as a translation Rukmani's translation is not necessarily superior to Leggett's. One reason is that it is still based on the old edition. It had been some time since the call for a new edition had been made by Wezler. However, Rukmani was either unaware of it or ignored it despite the fact that other publications which she cites refer to it frequently. The translation of the opening stanzas of the Vivaraṇa, at the very beginning of the text, can serve as a touchstone of the differences between the two translations. The Sanskrit text reads:

> *yasmin na staḥ karmavipākau yata āstāṃ kleśā yasmai nālam alaṅghyā nikhilānām|*
> *nāvacchinnaḥ kāladṛśā yaḥ kalayantyā lokeśas taṃ kaiṭabhaśatruṃ pranamāmi||1||*[10]
> *yaḥ sarvavit sarvavibhūtiśaktiḥ vihīnadoṣopahitakriyāphalaḥ|*
> *viśvodbhavāntasthitihetur īśo namo 'stu tasmai grave guror api||2||*

Leggett translates these lines as:

> In whom are neither karma nor its fruition but from whom they come about,
> Whom the taints of humanity can never withstand nor touch,
> Whom the eye of Time that reckons all cannot encompass,
> That Lord of the world, slayer of the demon Kaiṭabha—
> to him I bow.
>
> Who is omniscient, all-glorious and all powerful,
> Who is without taint, and who requires actions with their fruits,
> The Lord who is the cause of the rise, end, and maintenance of everything,
> To him, that teacher even of teachers, be this bow.

And here is Rukmani's translation:

> I bow down to that lord of the world, the enemy of Kaiṭabha, in

> whom there is neither action nor the fruit of action though both emerge from Him. This is because the afflictions which are difficult to overcome for all people are incapable to overcome him and cease to exist (for him): (and) he is one who when thought about in terms of time is not delimited by it.
>
> I bow down to him who is the guru (preceptor) even of the gurus. He who is omniscient, who is all-powerful (who has all the *siddhis),* who is free from the fruit of action which is full of defects, (and) who is the Lord who is the cause of the rise, sustenance and destruction of the universe.

Both translate *āstām* as if it is in the present tense. In fact it is in the imperfect, and the tense is significant. The author is stating that either the so-called law of *karman*—what action bears what fruit—or the book that lays down the rules, i.e. the Vedas, originated from Īśvara (God, here Viṣṇu). My impression is that he meant both: namely that Īśvara established the rules because he was the author of the Vedas.

Leggett and Rukmani translate the next hemistich *(kleśā yasmai nālam alaṅghyā nikhilānām)* slightly differently. There does not seem to be anything fundamentally incorrect about their renderings. However, Rukmani has this mysterious "because" and "cease to exist (for him)." These words are not in the Sanskrit text, nor are they even implied, and the resulting translation is unintelligible to those who are unfamiliar with the Yogasūtra and the Yogabhāṣya. What she had in mind was the series *kleśa-karma-vipāka* ... (affliction, action, fruit, etc.) which appears in the Yogasūtra and the Yogabhāṣya. It describes the mechanism by which afflictions produce actions and actions produce fruits. Unless this is explained, the conjunction "because" which connects the two clauses does not make sense.

Rukmani translates *kāladṛśā* as "when thought about in terms of time." This ignores the personification of time as the deity, Kāla.

It was unfortunate that the two translators relied on the 1952 edition of the Vivaraṇa and that the reading *lokeśam* in the accusative case was not known. The 1952 edition prints the word in the nominative, and this is clearly reflected in Rukmani's translation.

Neither translator understood *yaḥ sarvavit sarvavibhūtiśaktiḥ* properly. This is a metrically inspired expression of *yaḥ sarvajñaḥ sarveśvaraḥ sarvaśaktiḥ* (the one who is omniscient, the lord of all, and omnipotent). The author of the Vivaraṇa refers to Īśvara as having these three aspects throughout the text. At least Leggett understood that this expression refers to three aspects of Īśvara. Rukmani's understanding of the words is incorrect on several levels. She thought that the *vibhūti* in *sarvavibhūtiśaktiḥ* referred to supernatural powers which a yogin acquires as a result of practising yoga, but the *siddhis* to which she refers in parentheses, are more specific: there are eight of them in the Yogasūtra/Yogabhāṣya, and they are not all the supernatural powers that a yogin acquires. Also, if we were to understand the *sarvavibhūti* part of the compound to mean "all the *vibhūtis,"* the only way to understand the whole compound would be to translate: "the one whose capabilities are all the *vibhūtis"* and this makes little sense. Can he not do anything else? One cannot extract the meaning "all-powerful" from this compound. Rukmani might have understood the compound to mean "the one who has all the *vibhūtis* and *śaktis"*, but the phrase in parentheses "who has all the *siddhis"* contradicts this. The word *vibhūti* here means the ruling power, sovereignty, such as a king might have. Arbitrary interpretations of Sanskrit compounds are prevalent in this translation.

Although I have my own interpretation of the next hemistich, I acknowledge that it allows of various interpretations. However, again, Rukmani's interpretation does not make good sense. The word *doṣa* in the compound is used as a synonym of *kleśa* that is found in the expression *kleśakarmavipākāśayair aparāmṛṣṭaḥ puruṣaviśeṣa īśvaraḥ* of Yogasūtra 1.24, which is alluded to in this portion of the opening stanza. Leggett was aware of this, since he uses the same word "taint", which he had used in translating *kleśa,* to translate the word *doṣa* here.

I have some issues with Rukmani over the translation of the word *viśva* (all) as 'the universe.' The term "all" might be tantamount to the universe, but extending the meaning of *viśva* so far does not seem to be justified. Seeing that translation, readers may expect that some other Sanskrit word than *viśva* lay behind it.

Thus, even if we look only at the translations of the opening stanzas, Rukmani's translation does not seem to be superior to Leggett's. One might even consider it to be inferior on the ground that in places it appears to contravene Sanskrit grammar and syntax.

After the publication of Rukmani's translation, academic interest in the Vivaraṇa appeared to have waned. As a result, Gelblum and Rukmani's position that the Vivaraṇa is a late work has become widely cited, even though their reasoning in favour of this view can be criticised.

Owing to a series of unfavourable publications by Sanskrit specialists, some of which were of questionable substance, Leggett's translation of the Vivaraṇa did not receive the attention it deserved when it first came out. Some of the points that he raised are well worth consideration in the context of the authorship problem, and his contribution to the debate should be recognized. Further, his book was the first full translation of the text. Admittedly it is not flawless but it is the work of someone who was not a full-time Sanskritist. Reissuing this book in an electronic format will serve to round out his life's work and at the same time to testify to his wide interests and to his intellect, determination and perseverance.

1 I have discussed the "Notes" by Gelblum in relation to the authorship problem of the Vivaraṇa to some degree in: Kengo Harimoto, *God, Reason, and Yoga,* published by the Department of Indian and Tibetan Studies, University of Hamburg, printed and distributed by Aditya Prakashan, Delhi, 2014, pp. 229-230.

2 Paul Hacker, "Śaṅkara der Yogin und Śaṅkara der Advaitin, Einige Beobachtungen," Wiener Zeitschrift für die Kunde Süd- und Ostasiens, 12-13 (Festschrift E. Frauwallner), pp. 119-148.

3 *asamanantaro 'py anāgata eva samanantarībhavaty atītasyety ucyate*

4 Gelblum obviously did not realize that saying "*anāgata* is *samanantara* of *atīta*" contradicted *atīta* having no *samanantara.* He understood the sentence *tasmān na tasyāsti samanantaraḥ* of the Yogabhāṣya to mean "Therefore, [*vartamāna*] is not *samanantara* of *atīta.*" This understanding comes from another oversight of the reading of the Yogabhāṣya known by the author of the Vivaraṇa. In the Yogabhāṣya the sentence *tasmān na tasyāsti samanantaraḥ* is the conclusion to the question raised earlier, which according to the Vivaraṇa reads: *kimartham atītasyānantarā na bhavanti* (What is the point of saying that there are no *(sam)anantaras* of *atīta?).* However, the widely available version of the Yogabhāṣya adds *vartamānāḥ* at the end of the question (hence *kimartham atītasyānantarā na bhavanti vartamānāḥ*), making it to mean: "What is the point of saying that *vartamānas* are not *(sam)anantaras* of *atīta?"*. And Gelblum apparently understood the question according to this reading, and his understanding of the conclusion of the answer was also based on this understanding of the question. This difference in the text of the Yogabhāṣya, whether the initial question is accompanied by the word *vartamānāḥ* or not, makes a significant difference in the nature of the following discussion of the Yogabhāṣya. Since the text of the Yogabhāṣya known to the author of the Vivaraṇa expressed the

view that *atīta* has no *samanantara*, saying anything is *samanantara* of *atīta* would be a contradiction.

5 Technically, this type of compound is called a *tatpuruṣa* compound.

6 Harimoto, 2014, pp. 229-30.

7 T. S. Rukmani, *Yogasūtrabhāṣyavivaraṇa of Śaṅkara, Vivaraṇa Text with English Translation and Critical Notes along with Text and English Translation of Patañjali's Yogasūtras and Vyāsabhāṣya, Volume 1, Samādhipāda and Sādhanapāda, Volume 2, Vibhūtipāda and Kaivalyapāda,* published by Munshiram Manoharlal, New Delhi, 2001.

8 Journal of the American Oriental Society, 126.1, pp. 176-180.

9 I have discussed those in Harimoto, 2014, pp. 230-241.

10 In my critical edition I have *lokeśam* instead of *lokeśas*.

Introduction for the general reader

The text translated here is an historical find: an unknown commentary on the Yoga sūtra-s of Patañjali by Śaṅkara, the most eminent philosopher of ancient India. Present indications are that it is likely to be authentic, which would date it about AD 700.

The many references to Yoga meditation in his accepted works have sometimes been regarded as concessions to accepted ideas of the time, and not really his own views. If he has chosen to write a commentary on Yoga meditation, it must have been a central part of his own standpoint, although he was opposed to some of the philosophical doctrines of the official Yoga school. One would expect a tendency to modify those unacceptable doctrines, if this text is really by Śaṅkara. This turns out to be the case.

For those familiar with yoga meditation, who want to go straight into the text, here is the method of presentation:

(1) The basic text, the Yoga sūtra-s of Patañjali (about AD 300), is displayed in large type thus:

sūtra I.1 Now the exposition of yoga

(2) Below each sūtra is a (mostly brief) commentary by Vyāsa (about AD 600). This is printed in italics, and set in from the left-hand margin. Sometimes this commentary is printed in separate paragraphs.

The word Now means that this is the beginning, and the topic now begun is understood to be an exposition of yoga

(3) Below each section of the Vyāsa commentary, and sometimes below the sūtra itself, is the newly discovered Śaṅkara sub-commentary (technically called a vivaraṇa), printed in roman type and not set in from the margin, thus:

No one will follow through the practices and restrictions of yoga unless the goal and the related means to it have been clearly set out, and the commentator first explains what they were in the mind of the sūtra author, so that people may be led to practice.

* * *

The structure of the Sanskrit text, which has to be followed in the translation, is that the words or phrases of the original sūtra, then of Vyāsa's bhāṣya commentary, have first to be quoted and glossed, in order. In this translation, the sūtra or bhāṣya words being glossed in the main Śaṅkara vivaraṇa are given in italics.

Example:

sūtra II.48 From that, he becomes
immune to the opposites

(Vyāsa) *When a posture has been mastered, he is not overwhelmed by opposites like heat and cold.*

(Śaṅkara) *From that, he becomes immune to the opposites. From that,* from becoming firm in a posture. He gives an example of what he means: *not overwhelmed by opposites like heat and cold.*

The text is in four Parts: I Samādhi (sustained trance-concentration); II Means; III Glory (supernormal powers, limited and limiting); and IV Transcendental Aloneness

Yoga

Yoga practice as a technique of meditation, under strict rules of morals, austerity and control of instinctive impulses, and generally with a religious background, is ancient in India. The aim is release from all limitations, including death. This is to be realized not by a physical or mental immortality, but by disentangling the true self- in this text called Puruṣa – from illusory identification with limitations. Then Puruṣa stands in its own nature, pure consciousness without the movement in consciousness called thought: this is release. In the philosophy of the Yoga school as it developed, it came to be called kaivalya or Transcendental Aloneness.

Such an ideal of release from the mind-cage is not appealing to the generality of mankind, who associate freedom with something like jubilation and triumphant states of mind. But the deepest tradition of what is now India always had a keen sense of the constriction of the body-mind complex. The yoga aspirant regards the man of the world, and also those aiming at supernormal enjoyments in some heaven, as prisoners simply wanting more prestige and space within the prison, or perhaps a better prison, but who have not realized that they are imprisoned. They are like the small children in a prison camp, who do not feel confined. Provided the food and affection hold up, and they are not frightened, their wishes do not go beyond immediate circumstances. They would not want to leave the place: it is home. But when they grow up, they feel the need to get out.

Still, the notion of a sort of mindless emptiness, which is the nearest most people can get to imagining consciousness absolute, is not attractive. Many yogic aspirants are thinking at the beginning of some of the supernormal powers and knowledge described in repetitive detail in the third part of these Yoga sūtra-s (with the warning that they are sources of inevitable pain). The powers are presented in the text not to invite people to practise them, but because some of them may occur spontaneously in anyone practising meditation on the true Self. Unless a practitioner has had some warning that one of these may come to him, and that they are all limited and limiting, and further that the disastrous excitement they cause may throw him back into the whirl of futile desires for a long time, he can be held up for years, or even a lifetime.

It is noteworthy that in this text, in his commentary on the five sūtra-s on God (I.23–28), Śaṅkara swings the whole trend of the practice towards oneness with God. He quotes the Gītā verse XI.55:

He who does works for Me, seeing Me as the supreme, devoted to Me,
Free from attachment, without hatred for any, he comes to Me, O Pāṇḍava

In the Gītā this is identification with the creator-Lord, also described at great length in the commentary to the five Yoga sūtras here. It is quite different from the Transcendental Aloneness of the official Yoga school (to which, however, elsewhere he gives formal allegiance as a commentator on a Yoga text).

Yoga texts

A tradition developed in India that any system of religious or mystical practice must have as a background some satisfactory theory of the true nature of the universe and of the soul, and of its own *modus operandi.* In the case of yoga, this demand was met by the rise of a Yoga school; it is usually regarded (as in the present text, for instance) as sharing most of its philosophical ideas with the Sāṅkhya school, except that Yoga proposed the existence of a god where Sāṅkhya put the question aside as not susceptible of proof. Both Sāṅkhya and the Yoga system are dualistic: Puruṣa or transcendental self, pradhāna or unmanifest nature which periodically manifests as mind and matter, are equally real and eternal.

The earliest substantial text now surviving on the Yoga school – there are fragments of others – is the Yoga sūtra-s of Patañjali, tentatively dated about AD 300. A book of sūtra-s was little more than a collection of headings, similar to those circulated by any teacher to pupils, to be filled out by oral instructions, without which many of them can hardly be understood. The oral traditions later came to be recorded in brief written commentaries; these in turn became fuller – sub-commentaries on the commentaries – and finally systematic presentations of the whole system, but still under the sūtra headings. This format occasionally necessitated long digressions from the ostensible subject-heading.

An important part of the presentation was refutation of objections, and there are long sections of debate against an opponent, who as fast as one position is refuted shifts his standpoint to another. Some of the objections are based on the views of philosophical schools which were elaborately worked out and could be strongly supported; where the opponent is simply raising one point, it may look rather feeble in isolation from the rest of the system.

The first commentary on Patañjali is that by Vyāsa. He is thought to have lived some time between AD 540 and 650. The next established commentary, on both the sūtra-s and on Vyāsa, is a long work by the famous Vācaspati, dated about AD 850. He was by conviction a follower of the Vedānta school, which teaches an omniscient god who projects, supports and withdraws the universe by his divine power called māyā, and who is also the real self of everything in it. Māyā has an element of illusion, and the universe, though it appears, is not as real as god. Ultimately there is no duality: only god exists.

In his commentary, however, Vācaspati adopted what had developed as the doctrine of the classical Yoga school: the universe is *real,* arising from unmanifest subtle matter (pradhāna) which has no intelligence of its own, and is not created by any intelligent god. There is a god, but he is mainly teacher and helper, and only one self (Puruṣa) out of many.

There were thus three works which laid the foundations of the Yoga philosophical school: Patañjali's Yoga sūtra-s about AD 300; Vyāsa's commentary, about AD 600; and the sub-commentary by Vācaspati, about AD 850. The Yoga sūtra-s have been translated many times, an early version being by Ballantyne in 1880; Vyāsa also has been translated many times. A masterly translation of Vācaspati was published by Professor J. H. Woods of Harvard in 1914.

The Śaṅkara sub-commentary (Vivaraṇa)

There has now appeared, unexpectedly, a sub-commentary which claims to be by Śaṅkara, the great commentator on the Upaniṣads and the Bhagavad Gītā, and the *de facto* founder of the non-dual Vedānta school. He lived about AD 700, and if this is genuinely by him it will precede Vācaspati's work by some 150 years, and thus be of great importance. It will be an unknown work, on the theory and practice of yoga, by India's greatest religious and philosophical genius.

The original Sanskrit text was published in 1952 as No. 94 in the Madras Government Oriental Series. It was based on a single surviving manuscript, which had to be re-arranged and considerably edited. This was done with great learning and patience by two pandits: P. S. Rama Sastri and S. R. Krishnamurti Sastri. Their judgement was, that this is a genuine lost work of Śaṅkara. It is certain that it existed in the fourteenth century, for it is quoted in a work of that date. Many of those who have worked on it are inclined to think it may well go back to Śaṅkara, about AD 700, and after working on it for a good time, I think it very probable. So far I have found nothing in it which would rule out the possibility, and quite a lot to support it. For the present purpose I shall assume it is by him.

The Yoga sūtra-s are in four Parts: I – Samādhi (trance in which the mental processes are inhibited partially or wholly); II – Means; III – Glory; IV – Kaivalya (Transcendental Aloneness). It is in the first Part, Samādhi, that he puts forward most of the original views, sometimes at great length, where he brings the thought into line with the Vedānta philosophy of which he was the leading representative. While ostensibly commenting on Vyāsa, he gives interpretations which are opposed to those of the Yoga school, at least as it developed. The most important passages come in the little group of sūtra-s on God, which total only five out of the fifty-one sūtra-s in this first Part. His remarks on these five sūtra-s take up nearly one-quarter of his commentary on the whole Part. Meditation on God, by the use of the syllable 'OM' in particular, has become the main practice of the yoga, whereas in Patañjali and in Vyāsa it is merely an alternative.

A Western reader may be surprised to find so much philosophical discussion in a text which claims to be a practical manual. But the view in India was that, as Śaṅkara explains at the beginning, people will not continue practice which demands their whole life unless they are intellectually satisfied about the goal and the means to it. This view is based on wide experience of human nature.

As a Western example, Dr Esdaile in Calcutta (1840) carried out hundreds of operations, including amputations, under hypnosis without pain to the patients, and modern surgeons who read the reports find them impressive; but he could give no account of how it worked, and his medical colleagues gave him no support. Lord Dalhousie, the Governor of Bengal, however, who knew prejudice when he saw it, backed Esdaile and put him in charge of a hospital in Calcutta. But when Dr Esdaile returned to Britain, he was far less successful with the patients in his native Aberdeen. They must have longed to be freed from pain, but because of their intellectual doubts could not give the full co-operation required. The Indian patients, on the other hand, could do so because there was justification in their own culture for the idea that mind could be separated from the operation of the senses. Soon after (1846), ether and chloroform were discovered, and the whole subject was dropped with relief. There is still no satisfactory account of hypnosis in Western intellectual terms, and this is undoubtedly a barrier to its further development; there is a justifiable unease about employing something not properly understood.

Śaṅkara stresses that intellectual conviction is supremely important in the early stages of yoga especially. Before there has been any direct experience, however small, it is all second-hand, as it were. After the first direct experience (as he explains in the commentary on sūtra I.35), there is an invigoration of the whole personality, and doubts no longer trouble the practitioner.

In the present text, for a long time Śaṅkara makes his explanations on the basis of inference and analogy; not till sūtra I.25 does he quote sacred authority for his statements about spiritual truths. Once he has begun to do so, however, he cites the Upaniṣads far more than Vyāsa or Vācaspati. This is a possible indication of the genuineness of the work, as Śaṅkara in his other works stresses the absolute necessity of the Upaniṣadic teaching for realization of truth.

A special feature of the sub-commentary is that it presents the regularities of the universe as consciously planned and directed. The arguments are developed at great length, and the author evidently thought them extremely important for yoga practice. The events of the world are indeed predictable, but in the sense that the notes are predictable in a performance by an expert musician, and not in a merely mechanical sense. God controls everything from within.

There are references to something like the 'anthropic principle' proposed recently, which shows that the evolution of any form of life in the universe depends rather delicately on apparent 'coincidences' among the physical constants.

It is interesting that Śaṅkara had an idea of gravity as a pull. Here it is proposed (sūtra I.25) that movements of heavenly bodies are controlled by something like magnetism, and elsewhere in his writings (Praśna Upaniṣad III.8; Taittirīya Upaniṣad II.2.1) he says that things are pulled down to earth. But there too it is stressed that this is a conscious action by the divinity of the earth, who controls it exactly. 'The deity of the earth by his grace keeps under control, by pulling down, the apāna (down-going) vital current of man; otherwise the body would fall because of its weight or would fly up into the sky if left free.'

There are certain principles which Śaṅkara holds as almost self-evident. One is, that anything that can be imagined or spoken of must be a knowable, and this means that it must be actually known either in the past or present or future. It would be meaningless to try to speak of something which is never known at any time.

The doctrine is extended, so that everything, in the past and future as well as the present, already is. Differences of time are merely of phase; essentially everything exists all the time. A similar view has been proposed by some modern cosmologists.

Śaṅkara assumes knowledge to be something like space: essentially unlimited. Their contents can be limited, and they seem to be limited by barriers. But in fact it is not so. God knows everything all the time.

Main points of the text

Part I. Samādhi

Following a rather disconcerting Indian tradition, the presentation begins with the expert. This Part is for one who already knows how to practise samādhi, sustained concentration in what could be called trance. To do this, he must be one who has greatly reduced the turmoil of illusory desires and fears. The orthodox account runs something like this: Puruṣa, pure consciousness-awareness, gives attention to prakṛti, describable as infinite unmanifest potentiality. As a result of his attention, it goes into world manifestation, as three conflicting elements – sattva (light), rajas (passion-struggle leading inevitably to pain), and tamas (darkness and inertia). Puruṣa is apparently caught up in prakṛti when he identifies himself with an element in it, in the erroneous belief that there is purity, happiness, and permanence to be had in experience of prakṛti. This illusion is called technically Ignorance (a-vidyā).

There is an omniscient god in the cosmos, but he is simply a special kind of Puruṣa, who is never deluded. He is not a creator or governor of the course of things, but confines himself to teaching, and removal of obstacles to release.

In the classical Yoga school, the illusion consists of being fascinated by prakṛti's displays, which are put on in accordance with the merits and demerits of the souls who experience them. Prakṛti is real enough, but Puruṣa enters it, so to speak, as a soul, under an illusion as to its quality. There is one illusion, and it is removed by reducing the mental processes, first to one, by meditation and detachment, and finally giving them up altogether. A reader might suppose that this would simply lead to sleep. But sleep too is a mental process, and it has to be inhibited like all the others. Then Puruṣa remains in His own transcendental nature. There are many Puruṣa-s.

The swing towards Vedānta

A feature of this text is that there is a consistent pull towards the Vedānta. For instance, the author will say that as all the Puruṣa-s are consciousness pure and alone, it is hard to see how they could be distinguished. If indistinguishable, they will be the same. This is against the official view of the Yoga school in the Yoga-sūtra-s.

Again, God is presented in this text, at great length, as the creator of the universe by his divine mind. In Vedānta too, God is the all-creating and ruling overlord of the universe, which he projects as a sort of magic show, also entering into it as the Inner Ruler of each thing in it. Release can be effected by worshipping him and repetition of his expressing word OM, leading to experience of the real Self as one with God who transcends the universe and all descriptions.

This text continually hints that the universe is unreal, not real as the orthodox view of Yoga would have it. Still, when his duty as a commentator requires it, Śaṅkara presents the formal Yoga view.

In the Vedānta view, there are two illusions, not just one. Puruṣa, the real Self, is fascinated by prakṛti's displays, under the illusion that happiness and other emotions are there where there is only suffering, and that a real self is there where there is only egoity: but more than that, the whole world-display is also an illusion, put on by the Lord who is within everything in it as the antaryāmin (inner ruler). So that at the very core of prakṛti there is the bliss of Brahman (God); only if the magic show is taken as absolutely real is there suffering. This final Upaniṣadic view is not expressed openly in the Vivaraṇa, but there are various indications of it, such as the references to the world-process as the complex plot of a drama. This is not the same as the Sāṅkhya-Yoga illustration of prakṛti as a dancing-girl.

In Śaṅkara's Vedānta, the Yoga system is accepted as an authority on meditation practice and some other things like ethics and renunciation. But Vedānta aims to go further, for instance to become aware of the intelligence behind the workings of prakṛti, which is discovered to be divine as set out here in the 17–page long commentary to sūtra I.25.

The total inhibition of mental processes is also described in the Upaniṣads and in the Gītā (for example, VI.25: 'let him not think of anything' – this is the highest yoga, comments Śaṅkara). Often the technical terms used are those of Patañjali's sūtra-s. But the object of meditation must be one recommended in the scriptures on Self-realization, just as here the Vivaraṇa restricts sūtra I.39, 'Let him meditate on what appeals to him', to prescribed objects and not to pleasures.

The techniques of samādhi are described. First is one-pointedness, concentration on some one of the prescribed objects – such as the sun, for instance. As the meditation is deeper and more sustained, associations are dropped off: name, concept, time, space, and finally all memories. Mind becomes so clear, pure, and still that the essence of the object of meditation blazes out as it is. When this is practised repeatedly on the same object, the knowledge becomes what is technically called Truth-bearing. In some cases it would correspond to what is called inspiration. The basis of the process is that mind is inherently omniscient, and the yogic practice simply removes its self-imposed limitations, and focuses the omniscience.

In such yogic practitioners, the mental processes are thinned and then reduced to one. The same process is applied to the roots of the mind, the seed-bed of dynamic seeds called saṃskāra, impressions left by actions and thoughts of a beginningless series of previous lives. When surface mental processes are in abeyance, the state consists of saṃskāra-s alone, and in an ordinary unpurified mind it manifests as dream or sleep. But the yogin's seed-bed of saṃskāra-s, purified by impressions of yogic practice which overcome the other latent impressions (because yoga based on truth will always in the end overcome illusion), supports samādhi for longer and longer periods.

Finally, as detachment from the illusions of worldly ideas becomes complete, all mental processes are inhibited without exception. By extended practice of this, there is no more mental confusion which has obscured the distinction between Puruṣa and prakṛti, and Puruṣa stands out alone as pure awareness. This is a foretaste of release, and soon becomes permanent.

In the first Part, which is about one-third of the whole, Śaṅkara is establishing certain key positions, and refuting key objections, some of them highly technical. The general reader might at his first reading begin from near the end of sūtra I.1, where the Vyāsa commentary says: *But the samādhi in the one-pointed mind makes clear the object as it is ...* Break at page 70, after reading sūtra 1.6 and sūtra 1.7, and come in again at sūtra 1.8: Illusion is false knowledge based on an untrue form.

Part II. Means

This is yoga presented for the man of the world, who must first clear, and then steady, his mind against the fury of illusory passions, and free his life from entanglements.

In sūtra 1, the means are first given collectively as the Yoga of Action (kriyā yoga). It consists of three elements: (1) Tapas: practising keeping the mind serene under the pressure of heat and cold, and other such opposites; (2) Self-study, which is study of the Upaniṣads, and also repetition of the sacred syllable OM; (3) Devotion to God.

These three means can by themselves remove the taints and bring about samādhi. It is noteworthy that when Śaṅkara defines the Yoga of Action (karma yoga) in his commentary to Gītā II.39, it is in the same three terms, and even similar wording.

In fact this is an expansion of the method given in the first Part, in sūtra 23, 'Or by devotion to the Lord'. It was there described as meditation on the classical indications of God such as the creation and maintenance of the world as explained in the Upaniṣad-s, and also repetition of OM as the expression of God. In this second Part of the yoga sūtra-s, devotion is analysed further. The study and meditation on the Upaniṣad-s, and repetition of OM, are a separate heading, namely Self-study. Devotion to God, which had included them, is now confined to consigning actions to the Lord, or else surrendering the fruits of actions to the Lord. (These are two stages explained in Śaṅkara's commentary to Gītā XII.10 and 11.)

The triple Yoga of Action will appear again at the end of the second Part, as the last three elements of the observances (sūtra-s II.32 and II.43–II.45). In that place, however, it is said again (sūtra 45) that from devotion alone comes perfection in samādhi. Nevertheless other methods, including the restraints such as harmlessness (ahiṃsā) are given, along with means such as posture. They are all, however, meaningful only as methods of thinning out the taints and helping to steady the mind. Any encouragements to practise such things as posture by promising long-lasting youth are against the spirit of the Yoga sūtra.

Nearly all the elements here are discussed by Śaṅkara in his Bhagavad Gītā commentary, and the arrangement of the restraints and observances of sūtra-s II.30 and II.32 is close to that in a group of verses in the Gītā, which is much older than Patañjali's sūtra-s:

Yoga sūtra II.30	*Gītā XVII. 14, 15*	
harmlessness (ahiṃsā)	Tapas of body:	harmlessness
not stealing		straightforwardness
brahmacarya (celibacy)		brahmacarya
not holding property		not holding property (VI. 10).
truth	Tapas of speech:	truth
sūtra II.32		
purity	Tapas of body:	purity
contentment		contentment (II.55)
tapas		tapas
self-study	Tapas of speech:	self-study
devotion to God		devotion to God (*passim*)

The Gītā is a textbook of yoga from the practical standpoint, and many of its verses are poetic paraphrases of Upaniṣadic declarations. It does not justify its statements with systematic reasoning, as does the Yoga sūtra. The two texts are complementary to some extent. There is nothing in the Gītā like the elaborate account of the operations of the guṇa-s which is given in the Vivaraṇa here, but the Gītā gives vivid examples of the guṇa-s operating in thought and action of particular kinds. Often these examples show deep insight; for instance, that there is a firmness with which some people cling to fear and depression and grief (XVIII.35).

Śaṅkara here explains the Self-study of sūtra II.1 as study of sacred texts on release, beginning with the Upaniṣad-s. Now the Gītā, though generally taken as a single word 'song', has for its fuller title 'the Upaniṣad sung (gītā) by the Lord', and Śaṅkara in his commentary on it says that it contains the essence of the Upaniṣad-s. Here in the Vivaraṇa the Gītā is quoted a number of times, and it is called more than once *āgama* or sacred scripture. Śaṅkara's Gītā commentary is a help in understanding the Yoga sūtra sub-commentary translated here. In the latter, for example, Śaṅkara modifies the analysis of experience into only lesser or greater pain by a sudden reference to Gītā XVIII.37, which speaks of happiness from inner purity produced by knowledge, non-attachment, meditation and samādhi (sūtra II.15). Again, on sūtra II.13 he refers to the distinction between Yoga and Sāṅkhya, a distinction discussed by him at great length in his Gītā commentary but not elsewhere.

The detailed exposition of the Taints elaborates the background, without which (as was said at the very beginning of the Vivaraṇa) people cannot be expected to sustain their practice. The fine distinctions such as dormant, checked, and scorched are not felt strange today. The comments on sūtra II.5 contain the first grammatical excursus, purely technical and to be passed over.

Then comes Sūtra II.13's long discussion of karma, on which there is a final apt comment: 'this course of karma is complicated and hard to know.' It is noteworthy that on sūtra II.13 the Vivaraṇa overrules Vyāsa by citing Manu, for whom Śaṅkara has always great reverence.

The following analysis of experience into greater or lesser pain is not spiritual hypochondria, but to make the yogin-s vividly aware of the constrictions of present experience. If they sink into an apathy of acceptance the efforts to escape will flag.

The description of the guṇa-s is further background; the practical application is found in Gītā XVII and XVIII.

Vital sections for practice are those on Release and the relation of Seer and Seen (II.20–29). Unless this becomes clear and firm in the yogin, he will never be able to make the final transfer of awareness from a mental idea to pure consciousness. The abandonment of mental ideas will feel like loss of everything, annihilation in fact.

It may be noted that the concept of Puruṣa as for-its-own-sake and all else as for-the-sake-of-another, illustrated with the example of a mirror, is prominent in *A Thousand Teachings,* one of Śaṅkara's other major works. It will come again under III.35.

The Part ends with introducing the eight steps of Yoga. Śaṅkara comments that their sole purpose is removal of the Taints, and attainment of samādhi. It is not expected that aspirants will become perfect in them before trying for samādhi. There is a certain lack of enthusiasm for the Restraints and Observances in the famous rush of modern life (when average TV viewing in many countries is over three hours daily), but in fact they are mostly negative: the last three of the Observances have been given already under the Yoga of Action at the beginning of the Part, as sufficient to take away Taints and bring samādhi. These are very positive.

The present sub-commentary on the Yoga sūtra is not a complete manual of practice. Some postures are merely named, leaving actual instruction to a teacher. More details on some points are to be found in the Gītā commentary, though there too a good deal is taken for granted. Take the process of prāṇāyāma. In this text and in the Gītā, exhaling to the limit and then checking the breath, and inhaling to the limit and then checking the breath, are separate practices, distinguished from suddenly holding the breath wherever it happens to be in mid-breath. In many later texts they were combined, and the breath was held only with the lungs full. Breathing with one nostril blocked is also a sign of later date.

Some of the practices of prāṇāyāma outlined in this text need expert direction. Śaṅkara knew the techniques, as shown by some original comments: for instance, on the inner sensations, and the 'up-stroke', a marked effect familiar to teachers of meditation. (It is referred to in Gītā VIII.9–13.) Modern yogin-s, such as Hari Prasad Shastri and Rama Tirtha, recommend simple exhalation (sūtra I.34) in a prolonged OM. This leads spontaneously to the 'up-stroke', as described by Swami Rama Tirtha in his essay called 'Praṇayama and Will-power'. It must always be remembered that prāṇāyāma is part of a whole discipline which includes worship of God and strict self-control.

At the end of this Part, the sūtra-s give a number of 'perfections' which arise automatically when a given discipline has been perfected. They are not the same as the special powers and knowledge which are aims of particular meditations in the third Part. He shows for some, and by implication for others, that a desire for them would prevent the perfection of the discipline.

Sūtra II.37 runs, 'With establishment in non-stealing, all precious things come to him.' This is not simply a rigid honesty, because, as he explains, the perfection consists of desirelessness. One who practised non-stealing, therefore, with the secret aim of attracting wealth by this perfection, would never in fact perfect it till he had abandoned the aim completely.

There is no question of Śaṅkara's own conviction of the reality of these effects. In his Brahma-sūtra commentary he quotes Yoga-sūtra II.44, From self-study, communion with the deity of his devotion', as proof that the sage Vyāsa could meet the gods face to face, and he adds, 'That yoga does, as tradition declares, lead to the acquirement of such powers ... is a fact which cannot be set aside by mere vehement denial.'

In the first Part, there were some notable shifts of the philosophical positions towards Vedānta, and there are a few more in this Part. The sub-commentary in various places in the second Part elaborates on Vyāsa's simile of yoga as like medical treatment. But on sūtra II.23 he takes it further, so that the treatment is not for any actual illness, but for a false auto-suggestion of having been poisoned, which causes symptoms of illness. Śaṅkara uses this simile of medical treatment in a number of places in his works, but this brings in a new and purely advaitic extension of it.

Part III. Glory

This begins with an analysis of the so-called inner limbs of Yoga, and the elements of samādhi. The description of the last is in terms of the highest stage of samādhi, when all memories have been transcended with other associations, and the object alone shines forth (sūtra I.43, 44).

There follow some long philosophical discussions on qualities and on time-phase, and then some of the supernormal knowledge and power resulting from samādhi practice taken to the limit. Śaṅkara gives some original comments which imply that he knew these practices. But though he describes a few in detail, most he dismisses briefly, and the long descriptions of heavenly realms in sūtra III.36 he ignores completely, whereas Vācaspati revels in the details.

(Incidentally it is not clear why saṃyama on the sun and moon should lead to knowledge of heavenly worlds and disposition of the stars respectively. The Chinese Taoist visions resulting from sun-meditation describe the interior of the sun – with equally surprising geography and inhabitants – and the stations of its orbit. Similarly those on the moon are more what one would expect.)

But Śaṅkara clearly takes literally the admonition of sūtra III.37 that these powers are perfections to the unpurified mind, but obstacles to samādhi, because they trigger off latent taints at the root of the mind.

Sūtra III.36 says that certain forms of supernormal knowledge arise from samādhi on Puruṣa, and Vyāsa comments: 'they always arise.' But Śaṅkara deliberately omits this comment of Vyāsa, and adds (under the next sūtra) that they do not arise in one who is detached. This direct contradiction of the sūtra, and of Vyāsa's comment, shows the great independence of mind of the Vivaraṇa author, and are another instance of the swing towards a Vedāntic view.

It may be noted that in the case of powers arising from samādhi made to acquire them, the exercise of them carries in it a sort of contradiction. To effect the samādhi, memory must have been purified of all associations (sūtra I.43, 44). But after a success, the excitement will rouse all the latent desires, and it will become increasingly difficult, and finally impossible, to free the memory from them. So the power will be lost, except in one who exercises it without any interest in it of pride or advantage. Śaṅkara in his Brahma-sūtra commentary says that all these powers are ultimately dependent on the Lord.

The very long debate on words and meanings under sūtra III.17 is entirely technical; it is of perhaps great historical importance, but of no significance for the general reader.

Sūtra III.35 is a central sūtra for those who seek release, as the Vivaraṇa remarks. It is closely connected with some important sections of Śaṅkara's *A Thousand Teachings,* on the switch from mental awareness of what can be only a 'reflection' of Puruṣa, to Puruṣa's ultra-cognitive awareness.

Sūtra III.52 has an interesting (and surprising) discussion on time. Time is not absolute, but operational. This will be elaborated in the next Part, sūtra IV.12 and 13.

Part IV. Transcendental Aloneness (kaivalya)

There is an account of the mechanism of powers. They are not *created* by samādhi, for instance, but are implementations of the infinite powers of prakṛti along a channel opened by samādhi. Prakṛti is a seething mass of potentialities, somewhat like the vacuum as envisaged by physicists, in which virtual particles are continuously appearing and annihilating one another.

The question of projection of several bodies by samādhi-power is touched on (sūtra IV.4, 5); the Brahma-sūtra bhāṣya on the same point (IV.4.15) refers to yoga scriptures as authority. The conclusion is the same, that there are several minds, but the Vivaraṇa does not refer to the Brahma-sūtra analogy of a lamp lighting other lamps.

There are further discussions on karma and time, and a long polemic against Buddhist doctrines (sūtra-s IV.13–14). This is elaborated vigorously by the Vivaraṇa, implying that Buddhism was still an opponent to be reckoned with at the time of writing.

The final sūtra-s show perfection of Knowledge-of-the-difference, and then turning away from all mental operations including even that Knowledge, so that Puruṣa stands in its own nature, pure awareness. The final turning away is the virāma-pratyaya or idea-of-stopping of sūtra I.18. It is illustrated in Śaṅkara's *A Thousand Teachings* I.19, which says at the beginning to the mind: 'O mind, make more efforts at tranquillization' and goes on to discard, on the basis of knowledge, the futile mental activity. It leads to nirvāṇa – the blowing out of a lamp, or the dying down of a flame as fuel is exhausted. This last simile is used in the Vivaraṇa to I.18: 'the idea of stopping is still an idea while coming to a stop and before it has ceased to be an idea at all ... as a fire, little by little going out, is still truly a flame until it finally becomes ashes.' Release is now final because the saṃskāra-s and all other aspects of the guṇa-s have fallen off. Puruṣa makes no more illusory identifications.

Cosmology

The cosmological doctrines of Sānkhya-Yoga are occasionally referred to in passing, and a few Sanskrit words have to be learnt. Some of them, like karma and nirvāṇa, are already familiar, and with the Western interest in yoga, it is likely that there will be a readiness to accept Sanskrit, just as the Italian terms were accepted in music.

The brief outline of the world according to Sānkhya-Yoga (but *not* followed always by Śaṅkara, as has been mentioned) would be something like the following:

There are two eternal principles: unconscious unmanifest matter (pradhāna or prakṛti), and Puruṣa, pure consciousness. Pradhāna is made up of three elements, sattva (light), rajas (passion-struggle) and tamas (dark inertia). They are explained in the commentary on sūtra II.15.

When Puruṣa gives attention to pradhāna, the latter goes into manifestation, as a play begins when the audience is ready. The manifestation first takes the form of a principle called the Great (mahat). Like everything else, it is made up of the three elements or gunā-s: sattva, rajas, and tamas. It is sometimes called Being Only. As it plays little part in the discussions, it is enough to know that it is the first manifestation. From it arises Ahaṅkāra, which could be loosely called the cosmic I. Neither of these two can be meditated upon in their fullness, as they are too great.

On the physical side, the next manifestation is what are called tanmātra-s; they are roughly speaking potentialities of sensations like smell and so on. They are not directly accessible to the senses, but can be experienced in the special concentration described in sūtra I.35. Less subtle than these, but still not within the grasp of the senses, are the atoms of various kinds. The aggregates of the atoms are the physical wholes of the world, perceived by the senses.

On the psychic side, the cosmic I produces the minds of all beings. They essentially consist of sattva, but become clouded and stained by the two other guṇa-s, namely rajas and tamas. The minds produce (or attract to themselves) senses, both of reception and of action.

Mental operations produce dynamic latent impressions called saṃskāra-s. These are the base of memory, and of impulse generally. In samādhi, mental operations are inhibited, partially or wholly. The inhibition lasts only for a time, because the urge of saṃskāra-s disturbs; however, inhibition produces a saṃskāra of its own, which is hostile to and overcomes the other saṃskāra-s which lie at the base of the mind. A great part of the yogic training consists in weakening unfavourable saṃskāra-s and reinforcing favourable ones.

Various words for mind are used rather indiscriminately in this text: antaḥ-karaṇa (inner organ), citta, manas, buddhi (sometimes distinguished as a higher mind), sattva. In the last case, the name of the guṇa of luminosity (sattva) is used for mind.

To follow the discussions on re-birth centred round II.13, it is useful to know that Nandīśvara was a poorly-off human, who through intense devotion was suddenly transformed into a divine being; Nahuṣa, a divine being, entertained a thought of lust and was on the spot changed into a snake.

The translation

The general reader of a text like this must be prepared for certain conventions. Sanskrit compounds of a basic text are often ambiguous, and one great responsibility of the commentator is to explain how they are to be understood. An example from English would be, 'a widely-read author'. The commentator has to say whether it means that the author has himself read widely, or that his words are read by many people. In translation, of course, the compound has already been resolved when it first occurs in the basic text (here Vyāsa), and the subsequent comment is only a repetition. Nevertheless, in a translation it has to be given, and occasionally an extra gloss is thrown in which does add something. But the reader should be warned of this apparently redundant wordiness.

In the free commentary, however, once the original words have been explained (and it was the convention that every one of them must be commented on), Śaṅkara is terse. He expects his readers to have an excellent memory, and to be able to follow the argument without repetitions. As the point sometimes requires a knowledge of an opponent's philosophical position, the general reader must accept that some passages will be obscure to him. I have not adopted the custom of putting in a series of parentheses to explain what I think he means.

This is a difficult text, and the conventional Sanskrit format makes translation occasionally awkward. The word in the basic text has to be followed immediately by its gloss, which means that sometimes the sentence has to be turned very artificially. Nevertheless, I hope that it will be found accessible to non-specialists, even at occasional cost to precision. In fact, the proper drive for precision can sometimes over-shoot into unreadability and even incomprehensibility.

I have hyphenated English plurals of Sanskrit words, to make them easy to distinguish from Sanskrit words in '-s' such as rajas or tamas. I have also split up compounds where feasible, to make the elements easier to recognize, and I have usually separated off the negative prefix 'a-'.

The Sanskrit words in parenthesis are mostly terms characteristic of Saṇkara, and important for the question of authenticity. They have no significance for the general reader who is primarily interested in Śaṅkara's yoga practice, on which this text throws a flood of light.

To facilitate reference, I have put headings to the sections of the text: they are only approximate, as the subject can change abruptly. No such headings are to be found in the text itself.

Authenticity

To examine and judge the likely authenticity of this text will require not only expert philological and historical knowledge. The ideas of the text also have to be compared with those of Śaṅkara's well-attested works. It is not enough to know the wording of the texts, however exactly. And ideas may be known without being understood.

A great scholar of Śaṅkara's works once remarked that Śaṅkara's mistake was to suppose that consciousness could only be one: Śaṅkara simply did not see that there could be two similar consciousnesses. The point was made as though it were obvious, and so it is, but only from a naïve standpoint. Erwin Schrödinger, Nobel Prize physicist and a philosopher of science, in his famous *What Is Life?* discussed this very point, and explicitly cited the Advaita view, which he confirmed. Schrödinger's support does not prove that Śaṅkara was right, only that his ideas are not to be dismissed out of hand.

The long arguments for an intelligent world-creator and ruler here in sūtra-s I.24 and 25 would, not very long ago, have been similarly dismissed as nursery teleology. Many of them are now acceptable, as massively evidenced for instance in *The Anthropic Cosmological Principle* by Barrow and Tipler (Oxford University Press, 1986).

The validity of yogic states, dismissed by Edgerton as 'self-hypnosis', is to be proved or disproved by experiment, not by pre-conceptions. In a sense, Japanese scholars have an advantage because they are familiar with a still-living stream of meditation practice, which is well attested historically to have freed many from the fear of death, and to have been a source of inspiration in many fields of culture. The life of the late Hari Prasad Shastri in London was equally convincing to his pupils.

How to use this Book for Yoga Practice

You have to know enough theory for a working basis; there is no need immediately to read the subtleties of the intellectual background.

THEORY

(1) Read the Introduction for the General Reader: at this stage pass over the Technical Introduction.
Then read the following passages of the sūtra and commentaries from part 1 only:-
(2) I.2 – I.6 then jump to
(3) I.12 – I.22
(4) I.23 – 26, God. Sūtra-s only – pass over the elaborate proofs. Take it as a working hypothesis to be confirmed by experiment.
(5) I.27 -32
(6) I.33 – 40
(7) I.41 – 49. Note the conditions for inspiration given in 1.43 and 1.47. Not all Samādhi-s are Truth-bearing.
(8) I.50 and I.51, and refer back to I.18.

Re-read these passages till you have a good idea of the basic pattern of the Yoga.

PRACTICE

(1) If you are cut off (say in solitary confinement) and the need is great, devote several hours a day to the basic practice of disentangling Seer from Seen (eg II.35). When this is established and comes of its own accord sometimes, practise giving up thoughts (I.18) in meditation. The yoga then takes over (I.50).

(2) If you are relatively free from obligations, with basic needs at hand, practise at least three hours a day. Patañjali hardly mentions a guru, but without some senior adviser few can keep going without changing the rules to suit themselves. This causes many failures. Capacity for devotion to God arises naturally in anyone who meditates with serious enquiry. When developed it gives direct vision (II.44) and perfection in Samādhi (II.45).

(3) If you have commitments, you must establish a do-or-die resolution to practise Yoga of Action (II.1,2). It requires some heroism. Evenness of mind in all concerns of daily life is the main tapas. Then there must be determination to set aside at least an hour-and-a-half every single day to the two other elements; self-study includes holy reading. The Gītā is a summary of the Upaniṣad-s in verse (Sir Edwin Arnold's Song Celestial is also in easily memorable verse.) Teachers today give meditations on avatars such as Rama and Jesus; they culminate in a vision which changes the whole life. It is essential to practise hard at the Yogic action, which must be energetic but free from a claim on results; it is given in detail in the early chapters of the Gītā.

Nearly all Yogis support themselves with the OM (I.28) and Maitri (I.33) practices. These also bring out hidden natural potentialities from the mind (I.29; III.33). But the so- called Glories are the delusive manipulations of the world-illusion and are mires of attachment.

When enthusiasm flags, read II.15 – 17; look around you and see how anxiety, pain and death are rushing towards us like an express train. Yoga is a way to escape them.

Technical introduction

The text

This is a pioneer translation of a text on Yoga, a vivaraṇa sub-commentary on the Vyāsa bhāṣya to Patañjali's Yoga sūtra, claiming to be by Śaṅkara Bhagavat-pāda (definable as the author of the Brahma sūtra bhāṣya). It came to notice as No. 94 in the Madras Government Oriental Series published in 1952, having been put together, with impressive scholarship and patience, from a single defective manuscript.

It has been unknown except for publication of a small portion in another context (Madras University Sanskrit Series, No. 6) in 1931, which context however seems to establish that it was already in existence in the fourteenth century. The editing, which involved rearranging, was done by two pandits: P. S. Rama Sastri and S. R; Krishnamurti Sastri, who judged that this was indeed a work by the great Śaṅkara.

In 1968, Paul Hacker published an influential article accepting the identification (though on somewhat different grounds), and further proposing that it was an early work by Śaṅkara, then a follower of the Yoga school, and only later an Advaita Vedāntin. Some others who have worked on it have found no absolute bar to Śaṅkara's possible authorship. A. Wezler has examined another manuscript, and the existence of still another is reported. He has pointed out that this Vivaraṇa contains some different, and sometimes superior, readings of the Vyāsa, when compared with Vācaspati's version in his Tattvavaiśāradī sub-commentary.

Wilhelm Halbfass, in an important 25–page appendix to his monograph *Studies in Kumārila and Śaṅkara* (No. 9 of Studien zur Indologie und Iranistik, Reinbek, 1983), compares some of the philosophical ideas of the Vivaraṇa with parallels in Śaṅkara's works, and finds striking resemblances. For example, the doctrine of 'lights' in the Vivaraṇa II.20 is close to the doctrine presented in the Bṛhadāraṇyaka Upaniṣad bhāṣya to IV.3.7. He concludes that some of the passages correspond to and supplement what is found also in 'mature', 'classical' works.

Two leading Japanese Vedānta scholars, H. Nakamura and S. Mayeda, are inclined to think it genuine. Nakamura has published what he calls a tentative translation of Part One, the samādhi pāda (in Japanese), in 36 successive issues of the Japanese Buddhist journal *Agama,* from December 1979. Nakamura remarks that it is not at all necessary to suppose that Śaṅkara must have been a Yoga school follower when he wrote this, and he points out in his notes some instances of advaita ideas strongly expressed in the Vivaraṇa. For instance, Puruṣa's experience is not real, as it is in orthodox Saṅkhya doctrine, but merely attributed as colours are attributed to a pure crystal; this last is an advaitic view. He also points out a number of places where the printed text is defective.

Sengaku Mayeda, who has analysed a number of works attributed to Śaṅkara and verified their authenticity, believes that the Vivaraṇa may well be by Śaṅkara. See, for example, his article on Śaṅkara in the *Encyclopaedia Britannica,* 15th edition: 'it is very probable that Śaṅkara is the author'. He gives some details in the notes to his translation of Śaṅkara's *A Thousand Teachings* (Tokyo University Press, 1979).

The swing towards Śaṅkara advaita

This text is on yoga practice, as the author says at the beginning, and comparisons with Śaṅkara's practice can also be made. (For instance, a corollary of the 'lights' doctrine forms the basis of a yogic practice under sūtra I.38, for calming the mind; it is in striking contrast to Vācaspati's interpretation.) This practice could be roughly summed up as throwing leggings and a stick to a nervous man trapped in a room by a coiled snake near the door. He puts them on and has confidence to walk out past the snake, which he then finds out to have been a rope all along. The thrower had told him this, but he was too nervous to put it to the test. So the thrower takes the snake as real for the moment, and provides the protection.

When the Vivaraṇa practice is examined along with the theory, it appears that the Vivaraṇa was written not by an orthodox Yoga school follower, but by an advaitin. The basis is the Śaṅkara bhāṣya to Brahma sūtra II.1.3, to the effect that the Yoga śāstra is authoritative as regards meditation, for śruti refers to it as such, but outside that, it shares with Sāṅkhya two defects: the doctrine of pradhāna (the principal defect, pradhāna-malla), and the doctrine of plurality of Puruṣa-s. These two defects the sub-commentator (henceforward V-Śaṅkara, or V-Ś) corrects, very forcibly in the case of the principal one, and more indirectly in the second case. He avoids head-on clashes with the main texts, and where necessary follows them on points which he has refuted elsewhere.

This is not a study, and I am simply pointing out a few indications noticed during the translating.

1 The philosophical swing

Pradhāna, in Yoga the unconscious and real cause of the manifestation of the universe, is declared as such in sūtra II.19, and this is not challenged there. But already the five sūtra-s on God (I.24–28) have entirely discarded it as the world-cause in favour of most elaborately supported arguments for an intelligent, omnipotent, omniscient, and purposeful divine mind. This section takes up nearly one-quarter of the whole Vivaraṇa on the Samādhi-pāda, itself the first third of the whole.

The arguments are teleological, ontological and analogical, and presented with confidence, originality and a large group of Upaniṣadic quotations.

As the pradhāna doctrine is the 'principal opponent' (punning pradhānamalla), which Śaṅkara attacks, the force of his presentation of the creative divine mind is significant. (It is interesting that the pradhāna-malla saying is quoted in the Vivaraṇa also.) Some of the main themes presented are expansions of ideas in Bṛhadāraṇyaka Upaniṣad bhāṣya III.8.9 and elsewhere.

There are a number of other places in the Vivaraṇa where pradhāna is replaced by Upaniṣadic conceptions, sometimes almost casually as it seems; see, for instance, the quotation under sūtra II.19: 'From that, from this Self, space was created' (Taittirīya Upaniṣad II.1).

The other point on which Śaṅkara rejects Sānkhya-Yoga doctrine is the plurality of Selves. It is correct in discerning a pure Self free from qualities, but fails to perceive the unity of that Self, as perceived by Manu.

The fact that in Yoga doctrine the Lord is distinguished as a particular Puruṣa (I.24) and that the Puruṣa of a yogin is only like the divine Puruṣa (Vyāsa to I.29) assumes distinction between them. However, V-Ś, though accepting this as it stands, elsewhere equivocates. The distinctions, after all, are made only on the basis of separate minds with which the Puruṣa-s are identified, and the identification is illusory.

Under I.41, he describes the released Puruṣa as ever freed, ever the Lord (sadaiva muktaḥ sadaiveśvaraḥ), which has been given by Vyāsa (on sūtra I.24) as part of the description of the Lord. Again, V-Ś remarks (on sūtra I.42) that the Puruṣa-s being attributeless cannot conceivably be different in their nature (svarūpeṇa bhedo duravabodha eva).

Then in the Vivaraṇa to I.28, speaking of what reveals itself to the yogin practising OM, he glosses the already slightly unexpected word paramātman in Vyāsa with a Vedic title for the creator-god, namely parameṣṭhin. This not very frequent compound comes in the Adhyātma-paṭala of the Āpastamba Lawbook (v. 10), on which there is a commentary by Śaṅkara likely to be genuine. He there glosses it as the creator Self Brahman standing in the space in the heart, and explains that from Him comes forth the whole world. This same verse is quoted in the Brahma sūtra bhāṣya, where it is explained as referring to the highest Self, the efficient as well as material cause of the world.

Here in the Vivaraṇa it refers to the Self of the yogin engaged in repeating and meditating on OM.

It cannot be said that V-Ś is necessarily out of line with Vyāsa in these places, inasmuch as Vyāsa himself (IV.22) quotes a verse, 'That hiding-place where the eternal Brahman lies concealed is not under the earth, nor a mountain cave, nor darkness, nor a cavern in the deep, but the mental process when not distinguished (from him) – so the sages declare.' Here Puruṣa is equated with Brahman: aham Brahmāsmi.

Śaṅkara occasionally compares his methods to medical treatment – for instance, in the introduction to his Māṇḍūkya Upaniṣad commentary, though there he takes the simile no further. In this Vivaraṇa, however, there is a continual edging in the direction of Śaṅkara's true attitude to the spiritual injunctions: the doctor gives a placebo to a panic-stricken man who wrongly believes he has been bitten by a snake, and who is sweating and writhing in painful cramps as a result. The doctor must give the placebo with intense seriousness: 'this will cure you'. The placebo has the same level of reality as the source of pain, and the doctor's statement is true: the sufferer is cured. At the beginning of Vivaraṇa II.23 it is shown how Knowledge-of-the-difference, though itself an idea, dissolves the false idea of conjunction with ideas, which is pain and bondage.

2 The swing in yoga practice

It is a fundamental principle of the Yoga sūtra that meditation taken to saṃyama produces side-effects, regardless of the intention of the meditator. For instance, when one practises meditation (bhāvanā) on Friendliness and so on (I.33) to steady the mind, if it comes to saṃyama, powers of friendliness arise (III.23). If one practises non-stealing till he is firm in it (explained as without contrary thought), 'from all directions precious things come to him' (II.37), which is certainly not his intention.

A central group of sūtra-s is III.35–37. Sūtra 35 says that from saṃyama on what-is-for-its-own-sake, comes knowledge of Puruṣa; the next sūtra says that from this saṃyama arise certain supernormal powers, such as sight of divine beings, the next sūtra says that these powers are obstacles to samādhi. Now the doctrine of what-is-for-its-own-sake is a major one for Śaṅkara, but in his advaita, knowledge of Self would not produce, of itself, supernormal powers, which would be in Ignorance. Self-knowledge dissolves illusions: it does not produce them. Here in the Vivaraṇa, V-Ś flatly contradicts sūtra 36, 'they arise', by saying at the end of his comment on sūtra 37: 'They do not arise in a concentrated mind (samāhita citta) which is detached.'

This is a striking swing of the Yoga sūtra doctrine, and Vyāsa, towards advaita of Śaṅkara. The conclusion, that appearance of supernormal phenomena is the result of latent desire, is in accord with the Vivaraṇa on I.35, where spontaneous appearances of a ray, or lights and so on are attributed not to skill (Vācaspati: vaiśāradya) but to unsteadiness (reading vaiṣamya). It may be possible to suppose that the alteration in the reading was made deliberately, as part of the drive towards Śaṅkara's own standpoint.

The Vivaraṇa to I.35 makes the striking comparison of the supernormal perceptions there with the smoke which appears when wood is being rubbed to create fire. Smoke is the opposite of what is wanted finally, but it marks a stage, and so gives confidence.

Two further remarkable examples are given later under Contrast with Vācaspati's Interpretation.

Variations in the sūtra text

There are a number of variations in the text of the sūtra-s as glossed by V-Ś. Four of them are given by V-Ś with the comment that others have a different reading, which he then gives. This different reading is that of Vācaspati's text. In most cases, however, V-Ś does not note any alternative reading.

Sūtra-s II.7 and 8 appear in the Vivaraṇa text of the sūtra, and in the Vivaraṇa itself, as sukhānujanmā rāgaḥ, and duḥkhānujanmā dveṣaḥ. In both places he glosses anujanmā as anuśayī, and notes under II.7: sukhānuśayī tathā duḥkhānuśayī anyeṣām pāthaḥ. In fact, when V-Ś himself quotes II.7 in the comments on IV.11, he gives it as sukhānuśayī.

The third and fourth variations occur in sūtra II.19, where two neuter plurals in the standard version appear as masculine plurals. The sūtra normally runs: viśeṣāviśeṣaliṅgamātrāliṅgāni guṇaparvāṇi, but the Vivaraṇa text goes: viśeṣāviśeṣaliṅgamātrāliṅgā guṇaparvāṇaḥ.

V-Ś does not read these masculines in the first instance as bahuvrīhi compounds, but justifies them at length as nouns of agency in the masculine formed correctly from verbs. At the end of his comments, however, he allows the possibility of bahuvrīhi, and he also notes the standard reading as keṣāmçid ayameva pāthaḥ.

Another variation is a reading of the standard ananta of sūtra II.47 as ānantya in the Vivaraṇa sūtra text and the Vivaraṇa itself, though the Vivaraṇa Vyāsa has ananta. The effect is to rule out the Hinduistic interpretation as Ananta the cosmic serpent, which Vācaspati and several other commentators adopt.

The alternative reading ānantya is, however, noticed in the Candrikā commentary for instance.

The remaining ones are all small, and mostly with only slight change of meaning.

Vācaspati sūtra	*Vivaraṇa sūtra*
I.26 Sa eṣa ...	Sa ...
I.51 ... samādhiḥ	... samādhiriti (the iti is glossed)
II.7,8 anuśayī	anujanmā
II.19 parvāṇi	parvāṇaḥ
II.41 sattvaśuddhau	sattvaśuddhi
II.47 ananta	ānantya
III.12 tataḥ punaḥ ...	tatra punaḥ
III.20 na ca tat sālambanam	na ca sālambanam
III.35 parāthatvāt	parārthāt
III.48 tato manojavitvam	tato manojavatvam
III.50 sthāny upanimantraṇe	sthāny upamantraṇe

III.55 kaivalyam	kaivalyam iti
IV.17 taduparāgāpekṣitvād asya vastu	taduparāgāpekṣatvāccittasya vastu
IV.18 puruṣasyāpariṇāmāt	puruṣasyāpariṇāmitvāt
IV.32 samāptir guṇānām	parisamāptir guṇānām

Variations in the Vyāsa text

There are far too many variations in the Vivaraṇa text from the Vyāsa text as commented on by Vācaspati to make a list here, and of course there are other Vyāsa texts which differ. M. Honda in his *Yoga-sho Chūkai* (Notes on the Yoga literature, published by Heirakuji Shoten, in Japanese, Kyōto, 1978) gives in passing in his notes some hundred variations. Many of them are simple omission of a word which does not materially alter the sense. But he was not listing them, and there are still more. For example:

1 The gloss on vārtā, in sūtra III.36. This word comes at the end of a list of supernormal perceptions: of sound (śabda), touch (vedana), sight (ādarśa), taste (āsvāda), and vārtā. Hypnotized by the conviction that this must complete the group of senses, Vyāsa renders it as 'fragrance' (gandha). Vācaspati follows him, adding that the Vyāsa comment is easy. Other commentators fall in with the interpretation by Vācaspati. There seems to be a tacit agreement not to mention that vārtā has nothing to do with fragrance. (Only Bhoja attempts a feeble justification.) Vārtā refers to events in the world – news, in fact. The Vivaraṇa gives its true meaning:

Vācaspati's Vyāsa	*Vivaraṇa*
vārtāto divyagandha vijñānam – ityetāni nityam jayante	Vārtātas saṃvyavahāratva rūpam yathāvat adhigacchati

It is interesting that Vijñāna Bhikṣu, in his free-wheeling exposition Yogasārasaṅgraha, has this word as vāta, which still does not have the sense of fragrance, though he glosses gandhagrahanam. (He could hardly do otherwise, as he commits himself to saying that the set consists of perfections of the senses.)

This is an example where the Vivaraṇa gloss is clearly better than the accepted text of Vyāsa, which is purely arbitrary.

2 The final comment of Vācaspati's Vyāsa: *etāni nityam jayante* 'these always arise', is deliberately omitted by the Vivaraṇa. Deliberately, because it would be contradicted by the Vivaraṇa to the next sūtra, which thus also contradicts sūtra 36 itself, at least partially. This is in accord with Śaṅkara's general line, that the supernormal powers are not inevitable accompaniments on the path to release.

3 In the discussion on fruition of karma, under sūtra II.13, Vyāsa instances cases of double fruition, namely experience and life span, giving the names of Nandīśvara and Nahuṣa. But the Vivaraṇa inserts a sentence which makes these cases of triple fruition. This has to be justified against the opponent.

Vācaspati's Vyāsa	*Vivaraṇa*
dvivipākārambhī vī āyurbhogahetutvāt, nandīśvaravat nahuṣavadveti	dvivipākārambhī vā āyurbhogahetutvāt trivipākārambhī vā janmāyurbhogahetutvāt nandīśvaranahuṣayoriva

(There are, however, editions of Vyāsa which give this same phrase.)

Some of the variations from Vācaspati's Vyāsa text are simple substitutions of a synonym like pravādiṣyāmaḥ for upapādiṣyāmaḥ. There are other cases where there is some change in meaning, such as sargādiṣu for sargāntareṣu (I.27). This last is also an example of the tendency of the scribe of the present Vivaraṇa text to amend the connected passages of the Vyāsa to what is now the standard text, while retaining the specific Vivaraṇa readings in the body of V-Ś's gloss. The effect is that in some cases V-Ś appears to be commenting on words which do not appear in the main Vyāsa text. In the present example, sargāntareṣu appears in the Vyāsa text, but V-Ś is glossing sargādiṣu. In such cases I have kept to the Vivaraṇa reading throughout.

Here are two cases in the Samādhi-pāda where the Vivaraṇa reading gives an entirely different meaning to the whole passage; in one case it is in fact the omission of a negative.

4 Vyāsa commentary to sūtra I.36: the Vivaraṇa reads *vaiṣamya* (uneven), but Vācaspati *vaiśāradya* meaning skill.

The Vyāsa commentary is referring to fixing attention on the heart-lotus, by which meditation the mind-sattva appears in its true nature like shining space. Then Vyāsa says, according to the accepted text followed by Vācaspati, 'By skill (vaiśāradya) in keeping stable in this, the perception becomes transformed into resplendent forms such as the sun or moon or a planet or a gem.' Vācaspati gives some references, presumably in connection with the 'skill', to the circle of the sun and of the moon and so on in the heart-lotus.

V-Ś, on the other hand, has not vaiśāradya but vaiṣamya, and he explains that the forms of sun and ray and so on appear because the meditation on the true form of shining space is still uneven. This view is in line with passages like Śvetāśvatara Upaniṣad II.11, and others in the Mahābhārata, to the effect that such shining forms are only forerunners.

In the text, the standard vaiśāradya appears in the Vyāsa passage, but in the actual Vivaraṇa the word is vaiṣamya, and V-Ś comments on it as such. Under sūtra 35 the Vivaraṇa refers again to the unsteadiness which produces the limited luminous forms like the sun, and the same word vaiṣamya is used there. This is quite different from Vācaspati's interpretation.

5 Vyāsa to sūtra I.47: Vivaraṇa has *anurodhi,* and Vācaspati *ananurodhi.*

This is a direct contradiction between Vācaspati who, reading 'not progressively' (ananurodhi), takes it that prajñā-knowledge is independent of any time sequence, and V-Ś who, reading 'progressively' (anurodhi), takes it to mean that the knowledge becomes progressively clearer as practice continues.

Later commentaries either directly quote ananurodhi as does the Vārttika, or paraphrase like Maṇiprabhā, which has akrameṇa. V-Ś had other texts of Vyāsa to compare (as we can tell from references to some alternative readings), so it seems the Vyāsa was not standardized in his time.

There are other occasions where the new reading reverses the sense. As I have noted in the translation, in the bhāṣya to II.4 the Vivaraṇa Vyāsa has in one place adagdha instead of dagdha, which does not fit in well with the sense.

In II.3, an important variation is the reading kāryakaraṇa (a much-favoured compound with Śaṅkara for body and senses) for kārya-kārana. This changes Vyāsa's description of the action of kleśa from 'increasing the current of effect and cause' to 'increasing the current in the body and senses', which V-Ś further glosses as activity of the body and senses such as the eye.

In the bhāṣya to II.19, at the end of the account of the unmanifest, the standard Vyāsa has a final nir-asat. It is not glossed or noticed in the Vivaraṇa. This nir-asat is one of the phrases interpreted by Vācaspati as ruling out a doctrine of illusion. There are other variations in this section of the text, and it is not clear whether V-Ś had it before him and deliberately ignored it, or whether it was already missing.

There are scribal errors affecting a single letter. At the end of the long explanations of karma in II. 13, the standard text, reproduced in the Vivaraṇa Vyāsa, runs: ihaiva te karma kavayo vedayante – 'here it is that the sages instruct you on karma'. But the Vivaraṇa itself glosses śarma instead of karma, so that the sentence now reads 'on (your) welfare' instead of 'on karma'. V-Ś explains śarma here as sukha and śānti. He would never have glossed karma as śānti, as they are polar opposites in his thought.

There are many small changes which do not affect the sense. In II.28, the samyagjñāna at the beginning of the Vyāsa and Vivaraṇa Vyāsa becomes samyagdarśana in the Vivaraṇa. We find changes like visrambhopagata for viśvopagata, and yo manyuḥ ujjihāsā for yah pratigho manyur jighāṃsā; uhyamāna (in II.15) 'borne away' is probably an improvement on the original vyuhyamāna, which may be a scribal error for vyuhyamāna (as in some of the editions).

In sūtra II.50, the śvāsa and praśvāsa have become switched round in the Vivaraṇa, so that checking the breath after expiration now becomes the internal operation. However, this is merely a matter of name, which does not recur, and V-Ś identifies them in the orthodox way by the alternative names given by 'others', namely pūraka and recaka, which he identifies as associated with apāna and prāṇa respectively, just as is done in the Gītā bhāṣya IV.29. This is one of the many places in the Gītā commentary where Śaṅkara uses the technical terms of yoga.

Sometimes, however, a new meaning is produced by a scribal error. The Vyāsa and Vivaraṇa Vyāsa to II.34 have vitarkāṇāṃ ca amum evāmanugatam; this becomes vitarkāṇāṃ chāyām ivānugatam, so that the sense of following like a shadow appears.

Śaṅkara and yoga

Śaṅkara refers in his commentaries to 'yoga śāstra' as an authority for things other than meditation, for instance for saṃnyāsa (Gītā bhāṣya introduction to VI), and on diet (Gītā bhāṣya VI.16). But it is most often cited as authoritative for meditation. In his Brahma sūtra bhāṣya he cites yoga for the ability of Vyāsa and other ṛṣi-s to converse with the gods (I.3.33), yoga as a means to vision of truth (atha tattvadarśanopāya) (II.1.3), on the mental processes (II.4.12), on meditation practice (II.1.3), on multiplication of bodies and other powers of the liberated in Brahmaloka (IV.4.15), on posture in meditation (IV.1.10).

Yoga śāstra at the time of Śaṅkara is generally assumed to refer to Patañjali's Yoga sūtra-s glossed by Vyāsa, but there are references in Ś to yoga śāstra-s that cannot be identified with the Yoga sūtra-s as we now have them. For instance, commenting on Taittirīya Upaniṣad I.6.2 he remarks that the channel called suṣumnā is well known from the yoga śāstra. But the word suṣumnā does not occur in either Patañjali or Vyāsa (nor in the Vivaraṇa, as a matter of fact). Other commentators on Vyāsa are referred to here in the Vivaraṇa, and these were presumably classed as yoga works (see for example commentary on sūtra I.24).

The 'atha tattvadarśanopāyaḥ yogaḥ' just mentioned is not in Vyāsa, nor is the direction on diet in Gītā VI.16 glossing 'moderate diet'

uktaṃ hi ardham aśanasya savyañjanasya tṛtīyam udakasya tu vāyoḥ sañcaraṇārthe tu caturtham avaśeṣayet ityādi.

There is nothing like this in Vyāsa, but Bhāskara evidently knew of this yoga-śāstra, as he mentions something similar in his comment on Gītā IV.30:

> *udarasyārdham annena pūrayet tṛtiyam bhagam udakena caturtho vāyuḥ saćarārthaḥ iti yogaśāstre darśitam.*

By the time it has reached Ānandagiri on Gītā VI.16, it has become a verse:

> *pūrayed aśanenārdham tṛtīyam udakena tu,*
> *vāyoḥ sañcaraṇārtham tu caturtham avaśeṣayet,*

There is a somewhat similar verse in Gheraṇḍa Saṃhita V.12, doubtless much later:

> *annena pūrayed ardham toyena tu tṛtīyakam udarasya*
> *turīyāṃśaṃ saṃrakṣed vāyucāraṇe.*

Śaṅkara makes a few references to yama-niyama as listed by Patañjali. Commenting on Praśna Upaniṣad V.l he has as necessary auxiliaries to OM meditation leading to release the following: satya, brahmacarya, ahiṃsā, aparigraha, tyāga, saṃnyāsa, śauca, santoṣa, amāyāvittva. This is very close to the first seven of the yama-niyama set in the Yoga sūtra (II.30, 32). Again, yama-niyama are cited as auxiliaries to an aspirant's partial saṃnyāsa in the introductory comments on Gītā VI.

Śaṅkara often speaks of the yogin-s in passing, and especially in connection with unusual powers, which he sometimes cites as examples. In the commentary to Gauḍapāda Kārika IV.9, for example, to gloss the word 'success' he instances successful yogin-s who have acquired the powers of becoming very small and so on. As an example of one and the same effect being produced by different causes, he says (Bṛhadāranyaka bhāṣya I.4.2): 'In the case of animals that see in the dark, the connection of eye with the object alone suffices, even without the help of light, to cause the perception. In the case of yogin-s, the mind alone is the cause of it. While with us there is a combination of causes such as connection of the eye with the object, and light, which again may vary, in quality or strength.' And on I.2.1, 'Another reason for supposing the pre-existence of the effect is the fact that the knowledge of the yogin-s concerning the past and future of a jar is infallible. Were the future jar non-existent, that perception of it would prove false. Nor is this perception a mere figure of speech.'

His remark that their precognition is an actual fact is repeated in the strong assertion (to Brahma sūtra I.3.33) that yoga does lead to acquirement of extraordinary powers, 'a fact which cannot be set aside by mere emphatic denial'. This is however what his pupil Padmapāda does in Pañcapādikā II.4 when he says that it is not found that meditation leads to perception of anything. There is a contradiction between his pupil and Śaṅkara, who here is apparently speaking from experience, for he cites in these places no other authority for his positive asseveration.

It may be remarked however that according to the Yoga-sūtra-s themselves, yogin-s who exercise such powers are creating obstacles in the way to release. Omniscience is a natural concomitant of the highest states of training, but sūtra III.37 says that the other powers are perfections to an extraverted mind but are obstacles to samādhi; the Vivaraṇa comments briefly on this, that they do not arise in a concentrated mind which is detached. They are limited and mostly have to be acquired by special meditations. They are possessed by an individual, and as such are quite different from the omniscience and godly power referred to in Brahma sūtra III.1.7 which become manifest when the self becomes free from the illusion of being connected with the body–mind aggregate, and realizes its identity with the Lord.

Śaṅkara presupposes skill in samādhi for his own spiritual practice: it is one of the qualifications (Upadeśa Sāhasrī I.17.23, Bṛhadāranyaka bhāṣya IV.4.23). In Gītā bhāṣya to II.39, samādhi is one of the elements of karma yoga, essential to purify the mind to receive knowledge; sometimes Ś singles out samādhi yoga as the means to this end (to Gītā IV.38). In this commentary, Ś more than forty times follows Vyāsa's gloss 'yoga is samādhi' by himself glossing yoga and its derivatives by samādhi and its derivatives. This is not dictated by the nature of the Gītā text, for Bhāskara commenting on the same text avoids the word.

This applies not only to the karma yoga passages, but to the jñānaniṣṭha passages such as Gītā V.8–9: here the truth-knower (tattvavid), who in the introduction is called ātmavid and samyagdarśin, is now directed solely to meditate with concentrated mind (samāhita cetas) on 'I do nothing at all', even during apparent actions like speaking and moving. This meditation is in fact natural to a truth-knower, Śaṅkara explains repeatedly: the practice is simply not to disturb it. It leads to Release, after which knowledge does not remain a second longer; if it did, duality would not have ceased (Māṇḍūkya bhāṣya VII). This is exactly the point in the Yoga sūtra doctrine that even discriminative knowledge (vivekajñāna), though the means to Release, is itself a creature of the guṇa-s and does not exist for Puruṣa-in-its-own-nature.

Śaṅkara makes samādhi one of the necessary means to release. In the philosophical texts he does not go into it in any detail: he simply assumes it. In Brahma-sūtra bhāṣya II.3.39 and 40, samādhi is recognized by him as taught in the Vedānta texts for Self-realization represented by the Upaniṣads: 'The Self indeed is to be seen, heard of, thought on, and deeply meditated on', 'The Self we must seek, must try to realize', and 'Meditate on the self as Om'. 'For the scripture does enjoin it (samādhi-vidhānāt).'

In his free composition, *A Thousand Teachings,* he says (I.17.22):

22. *When the mind becomes pure like a mirror, knowledge shines forth; (the mind should be purified) by abstention (yama), permanent rites, sacrifices and tapas (austerities).*
23. *The best tapas of the body etc., should be performed to purify the mind. The concentration of the mind etc. (samādhāna) and emaciation of the body in this and that (season) (should be performed).*

In similar terms he speaks of the means to knowledge: saṃnyāsa, śama, dama, uparama, titikṣā and samādhāna (Brahma sūtra bhāṣya IV.4.21). There are many such examples.

In the Brahma sūtra commentary to III.2.24 he confirms that the yogin-s see the Self referred to in the Upaniṣads in their profound meditation. He cites moreover Mahābhārata XII.47.55 that such yogin-s are sleepless, with breathing conquered (jitaśvāsaḥ), senses subdued (samyatendriya). (XII.46.55 begins with a description of Kṛṣṇa sitting like a statue, senses inoperative, and becoming aware in samādhi of the condition of the dying Bhīṣma.) Śaṅkara had no need to describe such details in his commentary, and it is a clearly approving reference to Patañjali-style trance meditation, applied to Brahman realization.

Similarly in his introduction to the Gītā, he describes Release in terms of an unmoving yogin: 'He is without merit and without sin, without good or evil – who is sitting in one posture, absorbed, silent, and thinking nothing (kiñcid acintayan)' (Anugītā). This last phrase is an echo of Gītā VI.25: 'settling the mind on Self, let him not think of anything (na kiñcidapi cintayet).' Śaṅkara cites this with approval as the highest yoga. It is the citta-vṛtta-nirodha of the Yoga sūtra-s, where mind is directed to Puruṣa and then dissolved.

The same phrase na kiñcidapi cintayet comes in the Gauḍapāda Kārikā I.24, and in 25 Śaṅkara glosses yuñjīta as samādadhyād. There are many references to samādhi practice in the commentary to the Muṇḍaka Upaniṣad. Niruddham manas comes also in the Kārikā comment on III.33.

Occasionally Śaṅkara sums up the Upaniṣadic doctrine by a single phrase. Four times in his Bṛhadāraṇyaka Upaniṣad commentary he cites 'one should meditate on it as the Self alone' as giving the whole Upaniṣad in a nutshell, or as a sūtra. And in his Gītā commentary on XIII.4 he selects this same phrase as the example of a Brahma sūtra 'well-reasoned and definite'.

Commenting on Bṛhadāraṇyaka Upaniṣad I.4.7, Śaṅkara denies that cittavṛttinirodha alone is a means to mokṣa apart from the Brahman-Self identity known from Vedānta. But he adds:

> *Na hi ātma-vijñāna-tatsmṛtisantāna vyatirekeṇa cittavṛttinirodhasya sādhanam asti. Abhyupagamyedamuktam, na tu brahmavijñana vyatirekeṇa. anya-mokṣa-sādhanam avagamyate. (For inhibition of the mental processes is not a means apart from Self-realization and the continuous remembrance of that. Admittedly it is mentioned, but it is not recognized as a means to Release apart from Brahman-realization.)*

In the same way, in the Brahma sūtra commentary to II.1.3, 'By that, the Yoga system is refuted', he points out that though it is authoritative on such things as meditation and renunciation, it is unacceptable on the two points already established against Sānkhya: the plurality of separate Puruṣa-s, and the unconscious pradhāna as source of the world. It is these two points in the Yoga system which the present Vivaraṇa apparently seeks to replace with Vedāntic views, in most places by hints and implications, but in sūtra I.25, for instance, with lengthy and unconcealed arguments on the inevitability of a creator-Lord. Elsewhere, by hints such as calling the successful yogin 'parameṣthin' (to I.28) or even 'parameśvara' (to III.45), he briefly indicates that the inner self is realized as the all-creator and the Self of all (as in Bṛhadāraṇyaka Upaniṣad IV.4.13).

The Brahma sūtra bhāṣya sums up Śaṅkara's standpoint on yoga practice. There is a clear distinction between the Yoga school, and those practising the yoga meditation methods on the basis of Upaniṣadic truths: either meditation with bhakti devotion to the Lord as such, namely with divine attributes, or meditations on the highest Self alone.

Sūtra II.1.3 rejects the philosophy of the Yoga school on the two grounds previously put forward against the Sānkhya: pradhāna, and plurality of Selves. The Yoga texts are, however, authoritative on meditation; yoga practice is mentioned in the Upaniṣad-s, even as to details. For example, Śvetāśvatara Upaniṣad II.8 describes meditation posture.

Bhāskara on the same sūtra takes a similar line, also quoting the verse of Śvetāśvatara Upaniṣad, though strangely altered.

Under sūtra II.1.3 Śaṅkara adds that the yoga taught in the Upaniṣad-s means meditation on Upaniṣadic truth, thus distinguishing it from many practices of the Yoga school. Finally, under sūtra III.2.5 he says that those who strenuously meditate on the Lord begin to acquire divine powers, but concludes that all such are dependent on the Lord (IV.4.18).

Contradiction of the Sūtra

Sūtra III.36 states that from saṃyama on Puruṣa come supernormal knowledge, and hearing, touch, sight, taste, and awareness of events. Śaṅkara does not deny this immediately, but he omits the reinforcing remark of Vyāsa: 'These always arise.' At the end of the Vivaraṇa comments on the next sūtra, he says: 'They appear from saṃyama on Puruṣa, but not in a concentrated mind (samāhita citta) which is detached.'

This is a contradiction of the sūtra, which had said that they do appear, and a total rejection of Vyāsa. But in Śaṅkara's Vedānta, samādhi on Self would not of itself lead to supernormal perceptions, which would be illusory like all things in Ignorance.

In most cases, the contradiction is not under the sūtra itself, but elsewhere. For instance a contradiction of the pradhāna doctrine comes in the commentary on sūtra II.19 where space is given as arising from ātman, according to the Upaniṣad.

The very long commentary on God implicitly contradicts the pradhāna doctrine; it says that the creation is intelligent, but does not say it is unreal. The doctrine of unreality does, however, come up in places – for instance, under IV.31 where the scriptural text about the blind man piercing the gem and other impossibilities are taken as examples of the world-process. The impossible happens, which can happen only in illusion. The interpretation is the same as that given in the Gītā bhāṣya to XIII. 14, on this same text which is quoted there by Śaṅkara.

The statement of sūtra I.24 that the Lord is a special kind of Puruṣa is contradicted by the later statement that the Puruṣa-s being attributeless cannot conceivably be different in their nature.

Contradiction of Vyāsa

The Vivaraṇa is written with great confidence. It does not hesitate to overrule Vyāsa, when he says that from one action there can be no more than one birth. The Vivaraṇa cites Manu as decisive authority that Brahmin-murder leads to many births in animal incarnations (sūtra II.13).

It has just been pointed out how the Vyāsa comment on III.36 'they always arise' is omitted, and the conclusion of Vyāsa and the sūtra itself rejected.

The gloss on 'vārtā' already referred to (earlier) is probably not really a variant of the Vyāsa reading, but a complete rejection of it, and substitution of a new, and far superior, gloss by the Vivaraṇa itself. It is possible to suppose that the missing word 'gandha' was accidently dropped from a very early Vyāsa manuscript, and its gloss got attached to 'vārtā', which then lost its own gloss.

There are a great number of places where the Vyāsa is modified without being overtly contradicted.

Contrast with Vācaspati's interpretations

There are many cases where the Vivaraṇa runs counter to Vācaspati. Here are a couple, on yoga practice, where the instructions are absolutely different. Vivaraṇa on I.38, *Or meditation on the knowledge of dream and sleep,* explains:

> *What the mind meditates on as its own being, that form indeed it becomes. In the dream state, there is knowledge without any physical objects like sound and so on, and the nature of that knowledge is pure illumination. Now he meditates on what that knowledge is. But not on the remembered objects themselves (appearing in the dream). For the mind can be caught by the bridle of an object even merely remembered.*

Compare Ś in the Brahma sūtra bhāṣya III.2.4

> *Moreover the topic of dream is introduced for revealing the self-effulgence of the witnessing self as a distinct fact. This is done because in the waking state we have the existence of the contact between the objects and the senses, and an admixture of the light of the sun etc., so that the self-effulgence of the self cannot be distinguished from them.*

Vācaspati's comment is altogether different:

> *When in his dream he adores the exalted Maheśvara's image which abides within a sequestered forest and seems as if it were sculptured out of the moon's orb; its members and limbs are soft as lotus stems; it is made of precious moonstone gems and festooned with garlands of exceedingly fragrant jasmine and lālatī flowers; it captivates the heart. When in the very act (of adoration) he awakens with mind in undisturbed calm; then, reflecting upon that same (image) which had become the object supporting the perception in his dream, while his mind is identical in form with it, his mind reaches a stable state in that very condition.*

This is the reverse of V-Ś's direction to meditate on the knowledge which illumines the dream, but never on any object of dream. Vācaspati's comment is one of several examples of the devotion to a form, elaborately described, which he recommends in his commentary, whereas nothing of the sort is found in the Vivaraṇa, or in Śaṅkara's writings even in the many passages on devotion in the Gītā bhāṣya. There are numerous other places where the two commentaries differ.

A typically different interpretation of a sūtra phrase appears in the respective sub-commentaries on sūtra III.38: 'From loosening of the cause of tying, and awareness of *how the mind moves,* the mind can enter another body.'

The words are pracāra cittasya, and Vyāsa does not feel a need to explain them, but Vācaspati glosses pracāra as:

> *cittasya gamāgamādhvāno nāḍyastasmin pracāre saṃyamāt (it means the nāḍī-s, the paths for the coming and going of mind).*

V-Ś is quite different, nothing to do with nāḍī practices:

> *'asminnimitte hṛṣyati muhyati lubhyati cānena kāraṇena' ity evamādi svacitta sañcaraṇasatattvavedanāñca (from this cause it thrills, or is deluded, or it is disturbed on account of that cause' – this sort of awareness of the movements and real state of the mind).*

Thus here Śaṅkara shows the same lack of enthusiasm for nāḍī practices as elsewhere, even when he has to comment on them (e.g. Gītā bhāṣya introduction to IX).

The Vivaraṇa and the Gītā

There are some interesting cross-correspondences between the Vivaraṇa and the Gītā bhāṣya. V-Ś frequently quotes from the Gītā, sometimes in paraphrase (sūtra I.25). In his Gītā commentary, which he himself calls a vivaraṇa, on verse II.39 he defines karmayoga (the first time this concept occurs in his commentary on the verses) as closely parallel with the kriyāyoga of Yoga sūtra II.1. The main points are almost the same:

Yoga sūtra Kriyāyoga	*Gītābh. Karmayoga*
Tapas, defined as *dvandva-sahatva*	*dvaṃdva-prahāṇa īśvarārādhanārthe*
īśvarapraṇidhāna, defined as *kriyāṇām ... īśvare samarpaṇa*	*karmānuṣṭhāna*
svādhyāya, defined as japa of *praṇava* and mokṣaśāstra beginning with upaniṣads	samādhi yoga

There is a remarkable intrusion of Gītā ideas, apparently quite out of context, in the Vivaraṇa on sūtra II.15's bhāṣya: 'To the vivekin, all is nothing but pain.' Vyāsa quotes the saying about a man caught up in the craving for pleasure, that he is 'like one running away from a scorpion who is bitten by a venomous snake' (quoted in Jacob, *Popular Maxims,* under Vṛiñcika bhita). Vācaspati sums up the passage with a verse of Manu (II.94) to the effect that gratification of desire only increases it, like ladling butter on to a fire, and he also cites the example of a man eating a sweet mixed with poison, whose pleasure is necessarily of only short duration. He quotes Gītā XVIII.38 (on rājasik happiness): 'The happiness arising from sense contacts with objects, like nectar at the beginning (agre), and in time (pariṇāme) like poison (visa).' Chocolates to a diabetic would be a modern example.

V-Ś on the same passage also quotes the Manu text, and makes the poisoned sweet example more telling by instancing a man who already knows that the food is poisoned. To him even the present pleasure of the sweet is pain.

But the Vivaraṇa unexpectedly changes the whole context by likening the lesser venom of the scorpion (which is of course real) with a merely *apparent* pain, escaping which a man falls into *real* calamity. He paraphrases (without acknowledging it) the Gītā verse which comes before Vācaspati's, on the happiness of sattva. It runs (XVIII.37): 'that which is poison as it were (*viṣam iva*) at first (*agre*),and in time (*pariṇāme*) like nectar, that happiness (*sukha*) is declared to be sāttvik, born of the purity of the self.' In his Gītā commentary to this verse he explains 'poison as it were at first' by 'attended by the trouble of acquiring jñāna, vairāgya, dhyāna and samādhi'. 'Born of the purity of the self he explains as 'ātmaviṣaya vā ātmāvalambanā vā buddhi ātmabuddhi, tatprasāda prakarṣād vājātam'. It is noteworthy that here Śaṅkara gives two yoga terms, dhyāna and samādhi, along with jñāna and vairāgya, as precursors of happiness. Now in the Vivaraṇa, the text runs: tathā ayam *agra-duḥkhābhāsāyāḥ pariṇāma-mahāsukhāyā* nivṛtto duḥkhabuddhyā bhīta. The key words are very alike.

This is a sudden irruption of the Vedānta teaching on the bliss of ātman in the middle of a passage saying that all is pain to the vivekin. However, Vyāsa does later follow sūtra II.42, and accepts that from santoṣa there arises unsurpassed happiness even in this world.

Another echo of yoga technique comes in Śaṅkara's bhāṣya to Gītā XVIII.33, which speaks of holding fast activities of thought, of prāna, and of senses, by firmness ever accompanied by yoga. Here, as so often in the bhāṣya, Śaṅkara glosses yoga by samādhi, and avyabhicāriṇya by nityasamādhyanuvatayā. This is the cittaikāgrya given by Vyāsa (II.55) as the true mastery of the senses, and identified as the view of Jaigīśavya.

Sūtras II.13, V-Ś cites two Mahābhārata texts (the first of which, XII.204.16a, he quotes also in Gītā bhāṣya to XIII.23 and Brahma Sūtra bhāṣya to III.3.32), to distinguish the way of release of Sāṅkhya and of yoga. This distinction, in these terms, of course comes everywhere in his commentary to the early chapters of the Gītā, but it is unexpected here.

There are a good many such assonances between the Vivaraṇa and Śaṅkara's Gītā bhāṣya. They are not the result of the nature of the Gītā as a yoga text, for Bhāskara, writing at about the same time as Śaṅkara, does not use the yoga terms to the same extent in his own commentary.

Citations from sacred authority

There are some unusual features in the use of sacred authority. In the first third of the Samādhi pāda, V-Ś cites Sāṅkhya masters quoted by Vyāsa, and some grammarians, but only one śruti text: Bṛhadāraṇyaka Upaniṣad II.4.4, on bringing a pupil's mind to concentration (samādhi).

Then in the middle of the very long sub-commentary to I.25, V-Ś suddenly begins to quote Upaniṣads (Muṇḍaka I.1.9 and Kaṭha 2.22); a little further on there is a whole group of them. All are texts used by Śaṅkara; one of them (Taittirīya Saṃhitā II.1.1), 'Vāyu is the swiftest god', is here used to make the same point as in Śaṅkara's Brahma sūtra bhāṣya I.3.33 – false statements are no praise.

The second Part has many quotations, but in the third and fourth they total only five.

There are a few texts not traced, as there are in Śaṅkara's authenticated works. He had access to Upaniṣadic texts not now extant, for example, the account of the answer of silence in his Brahma sūtra bhāṣya III.2.17. Similarly he knew of other works on yoga, not now available. For instance, in his Taittirīya Upaniṣad bhāṣya I.6.2 he refers to yoga śāstra for description of the nāḍī called suṣumnā, not however to be found in Patañjali, Vyāsa, or the present Vivaraṇa. A yoga śāstra, said to give details of nāḍī practice, is named here as Hairaṇyagarbha.

Five texts are untraced; they include two creation texts referring to Prajāpati. In a couple of places (in commentary on sūtras 1.25 and II.15) the Gītā is quoted without direct acknowledgment. The identified texts are: 23 śruti, and 34 smṛti. Those simply repeated from Vyāsa not included.

Śruti (Upaniṣad)		*Smṛti*	
Bṛhadāraṇyaka	8	Gītā	11
Chāndogya	3	other Mahābhārata	10
Taittirīya	3	Manu	10
Kaṭha	3	Gautama	2
Muṇḍaka	2	'a Purāṇa'	1
Praśna	1		
Mahānārayaṇa	1		
Śvetāśvatara	1		
Subāla	1		

The sources, and proportions, agree well with Śaṅkara's established preferences.

A smṛti 'bījānyagnyupadagdhāni' quoted without source in Brahma sūtra bhāṣya III.3.32 is here identified as from Vyāsa, and is in fact Mahābhārata XII.204.16a. The 'mirror' quotation on (sūtra IV.23) from Śānti Parva is also quoted in the Gītā bhāṣya III.4 by Śaṅkara, and by Bhāskara under III.1. The Gautama quote 'tataḥ śeṣena' is used by Śaṅkara in the introduction to Taittirīya Upaniṣad and elsewhere.

There is an interesting citation of Upavarṣa in the comment to sūtra III.16 here, though his contention is now rejected from the point of view of sphota. But he is still called 'bhagavān Upavarṣa'. His words (gakāraukāravisarjanīyaḥ) are those cited by Śabara, and not the 'varna eva tu śabdaḥ' of Brahma sūtra bhāṣya I.3.28.

An example of the use of Upaniṣadic texts as authority comes under sūtra II.19, when describing the development of the guṇa-s into elements such as space. An opponent is put up (in the commentary on sūtra II.19) to maintain that space is eternal, and this is met, in the first instance, with a phrase from the Taittirīya Upaniṣad (II.1) which meets the point but goes against the whole context: 'From that, from this Self, space was created.' This well-known text on creation refers to Brahman, and is out of place in a Sāṅkhya-style account of creation as development of guṇa-s. In sūtra II.1, texts on release are mentioned under svādhyāya, and the Upaniṣads are given as the first example.

It must be significant that the Gītā verse (XI.55) which Śaṅkara quotes in his presentation of worship of God is characterized by him in his Gītā bhāṣya as summing up the whole message of the Gītā.

Other commentators

The Vivaraṇa records a number of alternative readings, and also alternative interpretations, by 'others'. They are usually rejected. Not all of them are in the tradition represented by Vācaspati. See examples in the commentary on sūtras 1.24 and II.13.

The grammatical excursus

The first is under sūtra II.5, and pages 135, line 22 to 137, line 28 of the Sanṣkrit text. The passage is made more difficult by the fact that the text is corrupt: it seems necessary not only to amend the copyist's smṛti for vṛtti as the editors suggest, but also to change his nir- to ni-. The passage is set out in pūrvapakṣa-siddhānta form.

The phrase vrttyantarādau pratītiḥ (p. 135 last line) seems to echo the Nyāsa on Kāśikā II.ii.6, abrāhmaṇam ānayety ukte brāhmaṇa-sadṛśe kṣatriyādau pratītir bhavati. Further, the phrase (p. 137, penult, para.) asevitagrahaṇe punaḥ kriyamāne ca bahuvrīhīyyaṃ vijñāyate, avidyamāna-sevito 'sevita iti parallels Kāśikā VI.i.145, asevitagrahaṇe ... bahuvrīhir ayam ... vijñāsyate. avidyamānaṃ sevitam asminn iti bahuvrīhiḥ ... The author of the Nyāsa, Jinendrabuddhi, is now placed in the eighth century.

Comparing the siddhāntas of V-Ś and Vācaspati, Vācaspati's interpretation of agoṣpada as 'a big tract of land' (no mere puddle) seems simple and convincing on the face of it. But the Vivaraṇa interpretation has the merit of relating the meaning strictly to Pāṇini's interpretation (VI.i.145), as expressing a place impenetrable (asevita) to cows. And in considering the word asevita, which occurs in Pānini but not in Vyāsa, he quotes a phrase from the Nyāsa. (This meaning 'impenetrable to cows' appears in the new *Dictionary of Sanskrit,* Deccan College, Poona, whereas Vācaspati's does not.)

The second excursus comes under sūtra II.19, and has already been mentioned under variations of the sūtra text.

A third, very long, disquisition on grammar comes under III.17. In this, Upavarṣa is mentioned, and there is a remarkable example of humour where V-Ś quotes, refutes, and then re-writes verses of Kumārila with which he disagrees (from the sphoṭa standpoint).

Polemics

There are long polemical passages against Buddhist, Naiyāyika, and other schools. They mostly originate in the Vyāsa commentary, but some of them go well beyond it; the vigour of the attacks would imply that these were living opponents in the time of the Vivaraṇa author. As A. Wezler has illustrated, it may be that there are references in the Vivaraṇa arguments to works of these vanished schools which are no longer extant. The use of sūtra III.17 to mount a sustained and ironical attack on Kumārila, a great opponent of Śaṅkara, must be significant.

As to the Buddhists, in general the treatment follows that of Śaṅkara in the Brahma sūtra bhāṣya and elsewhere, by which the Vijñāna-vādin is allowed some reason for his belief, though erroneous, whereas the Śūnyavādin is summarily dismissed as knave or fool.

Examination of the debates would be a job for specialists. It would bear on the problem of authenticity, but not on the relevance today of the central theme of this text, which is yoga practice.

The experimental basis

If this text is genuine, it will establish the experimental and experiential basis behind Śaṅkara's view of revelation. Śruti is a revelation of truth, and a great point in the Upaniṣads is that this truth is confirmable today directly. Yoga experiences are not to be brushed aside as 'auto-hypnosis'; the yogin-s see the Self in their meditation, says the Brahma sūtra III.2.24. But he stresses in many places that final release is not a special mental state; it is in fact complete separation from buddhi.

Experimental results are not subject to criticism from a standpoint which takes no account of them. In the early nineteenth-century battle between the rival theories of the nature of light – waves which spread and may annihilate each other, or particles which cannot do so – the two positions were taken as fundamentally and irreconcilably opposed. The wave theory triumphed for a long time. But today the physicist reports light registering as particles, or as waves, depending on the nature of the experimental setup. He is not accused of inconsistency, nor is it supposed that his views must have changed between the experiments.

In the same way, it may not be necessary to suppose that Śaṅkara was inconsistent, or that his views changed during his career. The experiential results, confirmations of revelation, may be true, but inconsistent from a standpoint which has not performed the experiments.

Yoga technique

The author of this Yoga commentary was himself an expert: there are technical comments from time to time which show familiarity with the practices, and which are not derived from previous texts.

For instance, the experiential sensations during prāṇāyāma (sūtra II.50). The interesting comment on sa-vitarka samāpatti, that it is like ordinary concentrated attention except that it is absolutely unbroken, and descriptions of the buddhi experiences, show familiarity with them.

Similarly the Śaṅkara of the Gītā bhāṣya gives comments on details of the practices – for example, the nose-tip gaze (VI.13).

In both cases it is clear that the writer knew the Yoga techniques and practised them. In modern times, Dr. Hari Prasad Shastri, a close follower of Śaṅkara and who translated many of Śaṅkara's works, both practised and taught Patañjali's Yoga techniques, on which he gave many lectures, while pointing out the insufficiencies in the philosophy. He followed Śaṅkara in holding that only meditation on Upaniṣadic truths could give complete freedom.

Sūtra-s III.35–37

As an example of the relationship between this Vivaraṇa and Śaṅkara, take these central sūtra-s III.35–37, which sum up the main points of the whole Yoga sūtra, including the assertion and then depreciation of supernormal power.

> *35 Experience is an idea which does not distinguish between sattva and Puruṣa, though they are absolutely separate: by saṃyama on what-is-for-its-own-sake, (distinct) from what-is-for-sake-of-another, there comes knowledge of Puruṣa*
>
> *36 From that (saṃyama) arise supernormal knowledge and hearing, touch, sight, taste, and awareness of events*
>
> *37 They are obstacles in samādhi, but perfections in the extravertive state*

In these sūtra-s the yoga is summarized. Compare the way the points appear in the Vivaraṇa (II.19, II.20-21) and Śaṅkara's accepted works.

The opening sentence of sūtra 35 is rather similar to the opening of the Brahma sūtra bhāṣya:

> *Subject and object are opposed to each other as darkness and light … it is wrong to superimpose upon the subject, whose self is intelligence, the object … and vice versa … But from wrong knowledge, man fails to distinguish them, though they are absolutely distinct.*

The Self as what-is-for-its-own-sake distinct from what-is-for-the-sake-of-another, is a central theme of Śaṅkara's Upadeśa Sāhasrī II.2. For instance, the pupil comes to realize: *notions … cannot exist for their own sake, for like objects they are … perceived by a perceiver different in nature … . I have pure consciousness for my nature, so I exist-for-my-own-sake.*

In this whole section 2, Śaṅkara deliberately abstains from Upaniṣadic citations, so prominent in the previous section, and which he often states to be essential for release. However he is presenting Upaniṣadic truth by this concept of Atman's existence-for-itself. It parallels Yoga sūtra III.35, to which as a matter of fact Vyāsa supplies one of his very few Upaniṣadic citations: *By what, indeed, would one know the knower?* (Bṛhadāraṇyaka Upaniṣad 4.5.15). In Upadeśa Sāhasrī I.19.2 Śaṅkara mentions that this same doctrine is held also by 'others', namely Yogin-s, and it seems that here there are direct references to the Yoga sūtra III.35.

On meditation as the direct means (antaraṅga) to knowledge, though not to release, Upadeśa Sāhasrī II.1.5 refers to the twenty essential means to knowledge given in Gītā XIII.7–11. These begin with Humility, but go on to include other qualities which have nothing to do with humility, such as Sense-control, Detachment (vairāgya), Withdrawal (nirodha) from worldly involvements, unwavering Devotion to Me (God) in exclusive yoga (Śaṅkara glosses a-pṛthak-samādhi), Solitude, Steadiness in Self-knowledge, and end with Keeping in View the Goal of Knowledge (namely release). So these are not 'virtues like Humility', but 'beginning with Humility, the set ending with Keeping in View the Goal of Knowledge'. In his bhāṣya Śaṅkara concludes:

> *It is only when one perceives the goal of knowledge of truth, namely mokṣa, release, that one will endeavour to cultivate the qualities -from Humility to Keeping in View the Goal of Knowledge – which are the means of attaining that knowledge.*

Here, as in innumerable other places, he distinguishes knowledge-of-truth from release, just as does the Yoga sūtra and Vivaraṇa (III.50). A typical summarizing statement, which incidentally includes the Yoga śāstra as an authority, is in the Introduction to Gītā III: in *all the Upaniṣads, in the Itihāsas, in the Purāṇa, and in the Yoga śāstra, renunciation of all karma is enjoined on the seeker of mokṣa as an accessory to knowledge.* Meditation *per se* is not the means to release, but meditation on Upaniṣadic truth is the direct means to knowledge.

Knowledge, in steadiness (niṣṭhā) and with renunciation, both of which are natural consequences of knowledge and need only not to be disturbed, is the means to release (Bṛhadāraṇyaka Upaniṣad I.4.7, Gītā bhāṣya XVIII.55).

Meditation after knowledge is only to preserve the natural continuance of knowledge from disturbances due to memories (Bṛhadāraṇyaka Upaniṣad I.4.7) of illusion, caused by prārabdha karma, which may temporarily cloud over the knowledge (Upadeśa Sāhasrī I.4.3).

There is a striking parallel between the Vivaraṇa comments on sūtra III.35 ... *by saṃyama on what-is-for-its-own-sake, (distinct) from what-is-for-the-sake-of-another, there comes knowledge of Puruṣa,* and verses 6 and 7 of Śaṅkara's Upadeśa Sāhasrī I.12, which read in Mayeda's translation:

6. *A Yogin, seeing the notion (of the intellect) on which the reflection of the Seeing (= ātman) is mounted like the reflection of a face in a mirror, thinks that ātman is seen.*
7. *Only if he knows that the various deluded notions do not belong to the Seeing, is he beyond doubt the best of Yogin-s. No one else can be.*

This is very close to the Vivaraṇa here, sūtra III.35. The inferior yogin corresponds to the Opponent who says: 'But if Puruṣa is made the object of an idea, and Puruṣa is known by it, the Puruṣa ends up as for-the-sake-of-another.' The answer explains. '... As a mirror set before a face is changed to the form of the face, so the mind (citta) changed into the form of Puruṣa, a semblance of Puruṣa, is what is perceived by Puruṣa.' And the Vivaraṇa adds the interesting example that a face reflected in a sword appears long, though the face is not long – this proves the reflection is merely a semblance.

The point is, that knowledge-of-Puruṣa does not mean a mental operation by which Puruṣa is known as an object, though that is how it is understood by yoga practitioners at first. Properly it is bare awareness of a mentally constructed semblance of itself, and ultimately it is pure awareness, power-of-consciousness, the Seer, Puruṣa in its own nature. This is a technical point of meditation, said by teachers to be difficult to realize in practice. The fact that Śaṅkara picks it out shows that he was an expert.

As already pointed out, sūtra III.36 and Vyāsa are overruled, on the rise of supernormal powers from saṃyama on Puruṣa. This reflects Śaṅkara's general position, that such powers may arise from meditation on Brahman, but only if Brahman is meditated on in that way.

To sum up: each point in these three central sūtra-s is either found in Śaṅkara's works in a prominent position, or else has been swung, in the Vivaraṇa, towards Śaṅkara's doctrine, even at the cost of contradicting Vyāsa and the very sūtra itself. This points to an association between the two Śaṅkara-authors, and probably an identity.

Authenticity

To compare this text with authenticated works of Śaṅkara would be a tremendous task, and for specialists. I have not found anything which would, as far as my knowledge goes, absolutely rule out Śaṅkara as the author.

There are a number of striking parallels which could point to him. For instance:

(1) *Vivaraṇa* on sūtra III.52 (unreality of abolute time)
yathā ā godohanam svapiti ... paricchedakatvasya ca ā godohamāste ityādiṣu

Gauḍapāda kārikā bhāṣya II.14 (on same point)
yathā ā godohanamāste

(2) *Vivaraṇa* on sūtra III.52 (dream-time)
tathā svapnapi ghaṭikāmātreṇa buddhiparikalpitaṃ yojanasahasramaneka samvatsareṇaiva (gantavyam) gacchati

Gaudapāda kārikā bhāṣya II.2
dahadeśādyyojanaśatāntarite māsamātraprāye

Such cases are weak singly, but enough of them can be quite a strong indication.

Already in the 1968 Frauwallner Festschrift, Mayeda showed that the Vivaraṇa reflects Śaṅkara's view of perception (already indebted to Vyāsa's Yoga sūtra bhāṣya). He concludes: 'ātman's perceivership does not mean that ātman is the agent of perceiving action but that the reflection of self-effulgent ātman whose nature is perception is in the pratyaya of the buddhi. ātman does not do anything but simply exists as it is.' He cites Upadeśa Sāhasrī II.5.4 and other texts from the same work.

It is noteworthy that here in the Vivaraṇa, reflection of the face is shown to be unreal, by the striking illustration of a face reflected in a sword; though the face is not long, the reflection is long, and must therefore be unreal. (Lengthening of the reflected face has been verified by the present translator with an eighth-century Indian sword.)

A point in favour of Śaṅkara's authorship is that he does not follow Vācaspati, and it is hard to believe that if he had had that great work before him he would have so completely ignored it. Even in small points there are differences: for instance Vyāsa's compound prāṇāyāmānabhyasyato is read by Vācaspati as prāṇāyāmān abhyasyato, but by V-Ś as prāṇāyāma anabhyasyato, and the sentence turned accordingly.

Of course, the argument cuts both ways: if Śaṅkara did write this work, it is strange that Vācaspati does not know of it and mention it. There may be a parallel, more than superficial perhaps, with the suppression by the literary executors of George Fox of the book on Quaker miracles which had been so carefully compiled by him; its existence is now known only through a few chance references in other works.

The massive swing towards the creator-god idea has already been mentioned; the Vivaraṇa commentary on the five sūtra-s on God in Part I, the samādhi-pāda, takes up about 8 per cent of the whole Vivaraṇa text. (Vyāsa and Vācaspati would be 2–3 per cent). Other, much smaller, swings away from orthodox Yoga have also been noticed.

Samyagdarśana, a favourite word of Śaṅkara, which occurs more than 50 times in his Gītā bhāṣya, for instance, comes repeatedly in this Vivaraṇa but only twice in the Vyāsa.

The technical words adhyāsa and adhyāropa are used freely and interchangeably (for example, in the commentary to sūtras 1.7, I.41 and I.44). Other terms characteristic of Ś are parivijṛmbhita for creation, nityopalabdhṛ or one who is eternally aware, of Puruṣa. Others I have sometimes noted in brackets.

The definitions of adhyāsa in the Vivaraṇa accord closely with Śaṅkara's standard definition in the introduction to his Brahma sūtra bhāṣya: the apparent presentation to consciousness, of the form of a memory of something previously observed elsewhere (sūtra I.8).

Under II.23 here, avidyā is defined as viparyaya, as also in Upadeśa Sāhasrī I.10.6 by Śaṅkara, though not by his successors. The Vivaraṇa gives other identifications, such as avidyā as the vāsanā of viparyaya, and avidyā as mithyājñāna.

There is a generally realist standpoint against the Buddhists. But as against the traditional view that Puruṣa actually is the experiencer, V-Ś says that Puruṣa in its essence does not change; the apparent taking on of the forms is a projection (adhyāropa), as when something is placed against a crystal which then appears to take on the colour. This is a pure advaitic view. The illusion results from kleśa.

Kleśa is used in the sense of taint, and I have so translated it; elsewhere it often means affliction. In this text it means something like doṣa or defect, as it does in some of Śaṅkara's commentaries. There are a good many Vivaraṇa passages on it.

There are a certain number of places where V-Ś seems to say that *all* is illusory. On sūtra I.8 he remarks that inhibition of illusion must precede inhibition of all the other mental processes (which include right knowledge) since it is their root.

Vyāsa's commentary to sūtra IV.31 runs:

Then from the infinity of knowledge, the knowable is slight, no more than a firefly in the sky. On which point this has been said:

A blind man pierced a gem; one without fingers strung it on a thread; one without a neck put it on; a dumb man praised it. (Taittirīya āranyaka I.11)

Vācaspati does not know what to do with this extraordinary saying about the blind man; he refers it back to the previous sūtra, and takes it to mean that after impurities have been destroyed, rebirth would be as impossible as for a blind man to pierce a gem, and so on.

But Vyāsa has introduced it with the words: '*on which point* it has been said', so the saying must refer to the immediately preceding point, namely the littleness of the knowable. The Vivaraṇa keeps to this point: 'The firefly in the sky is simply not a knowable at all. In the state of the highest knowledge (paramārthajñāna) all the objects of knowledge disappear. The saying about the blind man is quoted to show that the whole relation of knowledge and knowable is only in the state of illusion (viparyaya).'

There are many assonances between the Ś Gītā commentary and the V-Ś Vivaraṇa. In the former kaivalya is used for mokṣa, just as here mokṣa and nirvāṇa are used for the yoga term kaivalya. The Gītā bhāṣya is full of Yoga terms, which Bhāskara commenting on the Gītā seems to avoid. Madhusūdana was not wrong in including a commentary on most of the sūtra-s of the Samādhi-pāda in his own Gītā commentary, avowedly an expansion of Śaṅkara. But he does not seem to know of the Vivaraṇa, which is presumably a point against its authenticity.

One of Śaṅkara's favourite words, samyagdarśana (here translated 'right vision'), has a central position in the Vivaraṇa exposition of yoga. See typically sūtras II.1, II.9, II.4, II.18, II.20. It occurs only twice in Vyāsa.

Hacker, Nakamura and Mayeda think that the vocabulary and use of words are similar to those in authenticated Ś commentaries. A number of those who have worked on this text think it likely that Śaṅkara is the author; Halbfass and Wezler think it merely a possibility.

A possible counter-indication would be, that especially in the first Part, V-Ś introduces the opponent with 'nanuca' far more frequently than with 'nanu'. It is something like 5 to 1, though the proportion drops in the later Parts. Nanuca is not common in works by Śaṅkara. However this may be merely a stylistic tic (or even a copyist's tic), correctible when pointed out by others.

Another slight counter-indication would be the possibility that the Nyāsa on Kāśikā is quoted in the grammatical excursus.

A third point is the great number of striking 'examples'. However Śaṅkara might have used these as substitutes for his normal reliance on śruti texts, which here are bunched together, though not lacking.

Under sūtra III.17, there is a possible obscure geographical reference. The Uddālaka-puṣpa-bhañjikā game is said to be played in eastern districts (Kāśikā: Monier-Williams).

Hacker pointed out in his original article that the fact that the colophons identify the author as Śaṅkara Bhagavat, and not as Saṅkarācārya, is a point in favour of authenticity.

Even more telling than the formal salutation to the creator-God with which the text opens, are passages like that under II.46, where the commentator almost unconsciously recommends salutation to parameśvara, Lord of all, and not to the limited īśvara of the orthodox yoga school, who is only a teacher and helper.

Similitudes

Another possible counter-indication of authenticity is the very great number of similitudes in this text. In a sense, they substitute for the very frequent citations of śruti and smṛti in Ś's other commentaries. There are relatively few of these here, and mostly concentrated around I.25.

As we do not have any other authenticated commentary by Śaṅkara on the doctrine of another school, it is hard to draw a conclusion. But the list which follows certainly forms an unusual feature of the text.

Some of them are brilliant, and as far as I can find out, original. For instance,

(1) yogic omniscience is illustrated by the example of an expert goldsmith who can accurately estimate the weight of a piece of gold by merely looking at it. He needs no scales, as the yogin needs no senses, for his knowledge; nevertheless the scales are of use in demonstrating the weight to his customers.

(2) sense-impressions are compared to a seal (mudrā) and the impress that it leaves (pratimudrā). Inquiries have produced no example of this analogy in the Indian literature, though it appears in the

Record of Linchi in China (ninth century), illustrating accurate transmission of realization.

(3) 'The fact of equality is the very thing that destroys it' – illustrated by the existence of two kings of equal power.

(4) Animal sacrifice is akin to rape.

(5) The very denial of a thing pre-supposes it – this argument comes repeatedly; Potter's *Indian Metaphysics & Epistemology* makes it original to Udayana (1050–1100), and dubs it Negative Ontology.

The list which follows, though lengthy, is not complete.

Sayings and similitudes

Part I

sūtra	page no.	
I.1	74	when main opponent is defeated, the others collapse (Brahma sūtra bhāṣya I.4.28, II.1.12)
I.1	74	when walking, there is a check at every step
I.4, I.7	83, 94	puruṣa as crystal (see also II.17)
I.4	94	agency by mere presence: king in council, sun shining a pot, though inert, is still called a 'cooker'
I.5	89	water and milk
I.7	90	sense impression like a seal (mudrā) and its impress (pratimudrā)
I.7	91	mirage not projected by someone who has never seen water
I.7, I.25	92, 145	omniscience inherent in sattva (Gītā bhāṣya IV.5)
I.7	97	sickle does not cut itself
I.7	98	torch even on distant peak still visible
I.7	101	vadhya-ghātaka: cat-and-mouse (Taittirīya vārttika II. 1.55)
I.7	104	101 are the meanings of the genitive (cp. Kāśikā: many are meanings of genitive)
I.7	106	crow's eye looks both ways (Śaṅkara on Adhyātma paṭala 5)
I.7	107	all pramāṇa-s can have 'semblances' (ābhāsa). (Bṛhadāraṇyaka Upaniṣad bhāṣya II.2.1; Naiṣkarmyasiddhi III.96)
I.10	119	awareness of time lapse on awakening from deep sleep

I.10	119	newborn child must have memory
I.11	120	memory of memory
I.11	121	mind as crystal (see also e.g. III.3)
I.11, I.25	121, 145	lamp in perforated jar (Bṛhadāraṇyaka Upaniṣad bhāṣya I.5.17; Bhāskara to Brahma sūtra I.1.1; Ātmabodha 51, Mānasollāsa III.6; Mahābhārata XII.194.15)
I.17, III.19	130, 422	telepathy need not taint the mind-reader (but see III.6 for opposite view)
		'I-am' (asmitā) is Ego (ahaṅkāra)
I.18	131	thought of 'stopping thought' is still a thought till it disappears, as a flame still a flame till fuel consumed entirely
I.20	134	kataka nut to clear water (Ātmabodha 5)
I.22	135	Yoga practice like racing for a prize
I.24	139	'what Manu said is medicine' (see also II.13, and Brahma sūtra bhāṣya II.1.1)
I.24	141	the fact of equality is the very thing that destroys it, e.g. two kings
I.25	143	sattva always overcomes rajas and tamas
I.25	143	a thousand repetitions of ignorance dispelled by one knowledge
I.25	142	knowledge of smoke is seed of knowledge of fire
I.25, I.26	141 164	anthropic cosmological principle (Brahma sūtra bhāṣya III.2.41; II.2.2; Bṛhadāraṇyaka Upaniṣad III.8.9)
		arguments from design, from regularities, from precision of control, from integration of complexity
I.25	144	everything inter-related, as actors by the plot of the drama
I.25	145	only taints impede omniscience (Gītā bhāṣya IV.5)
I.25	144	muncher of cake seen and heard at a distance
I.25	145	instructions on dharma like medical prescriptions
I.25	145	Lord manipulates beings like marionettes (Gītā XVIII.61 and bhāṣya)
1.25	146	things perishable because they destroy each other like armed men
I.25	146	astronomical movements like magnetic action
I.25	147	all natural movements like human movements, i.e. intelligent (Bṛhadāraṇyaka Upaniṣad bhāṣya III.8.9)

I.25	148-150	mention, even as denial, of thing pre-supposes its existence: 'negative ontology' (Potter: *Indian Metaphysics and Epistemology* attributes this to Udayana in eleventh century. Frequent in this Vivaraṇa e.g. III.17)
I.25	151	existence of a goatherd girl on a mountain cannot be denied because it is merely unevidenced
I.25	153	words cannot drive off a fact standing there like an elephant
I.25	157	no praise by describing what does not exist. 'Vāyu is the swiftest god' cannot mean that he is not
I.25	157	body as a house (Gītā V.13 and bhāṣya)
I.25	158	darkness is a thing (contrast Upadeśa Sāhasrī I.18.41)
I.25	159	dazzlement by lightning
I.25	159	snake immune to its own poison
I.25	160	one strong man lifts a weight that would require several ordinary men
I.25	160	skilled goldsmith can tell weight without scales
I.25	163	a cuckoo is not projected illusorily on to mother-of-pearl as silver may be
I.32	180	thought-stream like a line of red ants
I.32	183	ends of a balance rise and fall correspondingly
I.32	184	clay changes into jar, etc., like sorceress changing into many forms
I.32	186	no mirror needed to see what is on the hand
I.35	189	experience of divine sensations like first smoke in making fire by friction
I.36	191	buddhi as shining expanse. The Vivaraṇa takes this as the missing sānanda and sāsmita meditations which Vyāsa does not explain as he does explain sa-vitarka and sa-vicāra (cp. Gītā bhāṣya II.65)
I.41	196	everything must be known to someone at some time
I.41	197	self seen in self as in a clear mirror (Mahābhārata Śānti Parva 204.8, quoted also in Gītā bhāṣya III.4)
I.41	198	other Puruṣa-s inferred as reflected from a second mirror
I.43	203	snake and coils
I.43	204	crop-eared horse is not a new whole
I.49	215	plain facts ride on the king's highway

I.50	217	one not thirsty does not need a drink

Part II

II.1	225	worldly objects net the mind (cp. comm. to I.37, 38: 'Worldly objects put a bridle on the mind')
II.3	228	dye has no function without cloth
II.4	229	land supports grass and plants not separate from it
II.4	231	karma-already-in-operation like a shot arrow in the air (cp. Gītā bhāṣya to XIII.23)
II.4	232	Underground course of Sarasvatī river
II.4	233	eye which has looked at an elephant does not cease to exist because it is now looking at a jar
II.4	235	an enemy unborn or asleep is still to be feared; Indra cut up the embryo in Diti's womb, knowing this would be his future enemy
II.4	234	no bathing possible in a river intercepted
II.9	247	illogical fear of death by Knower also
II.10	249	unnecessary to grind what is already ground – piṣṭapeṣana (comm. on Kena Upaniṣad, Gītā II.21)
II.10	249	no fire necessary for what is already burnt cp. II.22 duty done is no longer a duty
II.12	252	many instances from Rāmāyana and Mahābhārata – cp. Upadeśa Sāhasrī I.18.100
II.12	253	Nandīśvara and Nahuṣa (and II.22)
II.12	253	fruiting depends on saṃskāra of seeds
II.13	255	taints husked or scorched
II.13	255	Yoga and Sāṅkhya different paths
II.13	256	Vyāsa overruled by Manu, citing scripture
II.13	257	saṃsāra without beginning
II.13	263	only compatible karmas co-operate to produce a life
II.13	261	karma like tent of wool
II.13	261	antelope sire kills newborn male

II.13	262	heaven and hell not mere subjective states of happiness or pain
II.13	263	owl's eye – light no help to it
II.13	263	conflicting seeds in a field
II.13	263	different kinds of death (Gītā VIII.6)
II.13	264	no action possible in embryo state or in dream
II.13	265	two antagonists fighting
II.13	266	Manu: disease of nails destroyed by penance
II.15	272	sweet mixed with poison (cp. II.23 imaginary contact with poison)
II.15	273	scorpion/snake
II.15	275	fist blow from the beloved not resented, nor fouling by a newborn son
II.15	276	eyeball and hard skin
II.15	277	even yogic powers are pain
II.15	279	darkness and light cannot be simultaneously in the same place
II.15	284	pradhāna's eternality not eternal (but I.45, II.19, etc.)
II.17	289	axe needs an object in order to function
II.18	291	Puruṣa compared to a crystal (also I.4, I.7)
II.18	291	drummer always tends to play a drum, not to be one
II.18	293	Mahat to clump of grass. Cp. II.28, Brahmā down to a post. Such pairings common in Śaṅkara, e.g. comm. to Gītā XIII.27, 'Brahmā down to the immovable'
II.18	294	where there is activity, some purpose always found (Brahma sūtra bhāṣya II.2.2)
II.18	296	dyer's work attributed to laundryman
II.19	300	excess of space is a symptom in medicine
II.19	301	from birds to serpents and plants, always a mouth
II.19	303	snake and coils, clay and pot
II.20	309	diamonds change internally
II.20	309	statements about sun's shining depend on presence or absence of objects
II.20	310	glowing iron seems on fire
II.22	313	many pradhāna-s (but later in II.22 and in III.53, only one)

II.22	313	many Puruṣa-s, because of distinctions of body and senses (kārya-karaṇa)
II.23	314	face and mirror; eye and mirror
II.23	315	false suggestion of poison causing actual illness: Śaṅka-viṣādnimitta-maraṇāḍī-kāryopalabdeḥ (Brahma sūtra bhāṣya II. 1.14)
II.23	317	when a thing has a purpose, that purpose is inevitably fulfilled
II.24	320	vāsanā of Ignorance called Ignorance
II.24	322	prārabdha karma:
		palaces remain after builders go
		broken branch does not at once lose leaves
		shot arrow
II.26	325	gold unrefined does not shine
II.27	325	scorched seeds do not germinate (Mahābhārata XII.204.16a, cited in Brahma sūtra bhāṣya III.3.32)
II.27	327	healed patient needs no more treatment
II.29	333	six-limbed yoga (Maitrī Upaniṣad VI.18; Bhāskara on Gītā IV.18)
II.30	335	Aśvatthāman: acting a lie
II.30	337	impossibility of obtaining things does not count as renunciation of them
II.32	339	Upaniṣads typical classics on release
II.34	343	actions done under orders
II.34	344	success in yoga directly perceptible in signs, unlike result of rituals, etc.
II.36	345	Kuṇḍadhārārādhi becomes righteous when the gods say so
II.36	345	Triśaṅku attains heaven when told by Viśvamitra
II.39	347	awareness of conditions of birth (past, present or future) is a foreshadowing of samyagdarśana
II.50	354	a ṛṣi could prolong breath for years

Part III

III.3	364	mind in samādhi like a crystal

III.6	367	telepathy a petty achievement causing confusion (but see under I.17,III.19,20)
III.6	368	steps in yoga like a blind man finding his way up a staircase
III.13	381	jar in an inner apartment still exists though hidden (IV.12)
III.13	381	when he halts, Devadatta's motion disappears but not the man
III.13	382	a living Devadatta not inside his house must be outside
III.13	382	Blind man gets himself a mirror
III.14	390	dharma-s like coils of a rope
III.17	403	letter-sounds like spokes of a wheel
III.17	405	whirling of the saṃsāra wheel is beginningless
III.17	406	denial of meaning-flash means its existence has been accepted: 'negative ontology', I.25
III.17	407	one man alone cannot carry a tree-trunk
III.17	407	digging a well
III.17	411	image of Viṣṇu, digits in decimal places, mere conventions (cp. Bṛhadāraṇyaka Upaniṣad bhāṣya I.3.1)
III.17	413	Anything signified by a word must exist. Cp. negative ontology p. 116
III.17	414	No one is old in only half the body (Bṛhadāraṇyaka Upaniṣad bhāṣya I.4.10)
III.17	415	(running to) mirage causes discovery (of what the real ground is like): so with digits and written letters
III.17	415	mistaking luminous cloud for moon
III.17	417	'frightener for children': frightener for grown-ups
III.33	433	ātman = īśvara
III.35	436	distorting mirror
III.38	438	mind as quivering struck bell, or scintillating charcoal bee-swarm
III.39	439	prāṇa-s move body as doves move their dovecot from within
III.41	440	space is visible within a transparent jewel
III.44	445	atom has a structure
III.44	446	black and white hair
III.52	459	time illusory
III.52	459	dream-time; meditation time

III.52	460	time dependent on some operation (boiling the rice, etc.)
III.52	460	jar on one potter's wheel not in sequence with clay on another's
III.53	464	not a plurality of pradhāna-s

Part IV

1V.2	472	from a 10–pala piece of iron an 80–pala spearhead cannot be fashioned
1V.7	477	animal sacrifice akin to rape
1V.7	479	animal sacrifice has dual causality, like eating (pleasure and sustenance) and bathing at sacred places (refreshment and blessing)
1V.7	479	sacrifices do always achieve their aim
1V.7	479	land traveller does not try to use a boat
1V.8	481	karma-fruition like a boy running after someone like his mother
1V.8	482	karma-fruition: near relatives touch us more closely than distant ones
1V.9	483	karma-fruition: mouth waters at seeing tamarind
1V.10	486	mind naturally omniscient (Śaṅkara Gītā bhāṣya IV.4)
1V.11	488	Ignorance like young driver making the chariot wheels whirl when lashings of the wheels give way, chariot collapses
1V.11	489	when the parasol goes, no shadow left
1V.12	492	making the curds manifest by churning
1V.12	494	jar in the future like a jar hidden in an inner apartment (compare III.13)
1V.14	497	light from opposites: oil, wick, and fire
1V.14	500	examples of objects of knowledge: good arguments and bad arguments
1V.15	501	body of the son appears differently to different outlooks: beloved, hateful, delusive, food for carnivores, corpse at funeral

1V.15	504	object in past and future: bare existence of a boy not his adulthood
1V.18	509	inner light and outer light (cp. I.7, I.25; Bṛhadāraṇyaka Upaniṣad bhāṣya IV.3.4)
1V.19	512	part of the mind can know another part, like hand scratching the body
1V.22	518	glowing iron has form of fire
1V.23	520	Indra-jala – Indra's net of illusion – catches Vaiśeṣika
1V.23	520	Vaināśika Buddhists merely pathetically deluded
1V.23	520	Materialists and Śunyavādin Buddhists are active deceivers
1V.23	520	in samādhi the object is reflected as in a spotless mirror

First Part:
SAMĀDHI

(Translation)

A sub-commentary (vivaraṇa) by holy Śaṅkara Bhagavatpāda to the commentary (bhāṣya) by Vyāsa on the Yoga sūtra-s of Patañjali

Sūtra I.1

Now the exposition of yoga

(Vyāsa) The word Now means here a beginning, and the topic now begun is understood to be an exposition of yoga.

(Śaṅkara:)
In whom are neither karma nor its fruition but from whom they come about,
Whom the taints of humanity can never withstand nor touch,
Whom the eye of Time that reckons all cannot encompass,
That Lord of the world, slayer of the demon Kaiṭabha – to him I bow.

Who is omniscient, all-glorious and all-powerful,
Who is without taint, and who requites actions with their fruits,
The Lord who is the cause of the rise, end, and maintenance of every thing,
To him, that teacher even of teachers, be this bow.

A sub-commentary is here begun on the yoga classic of Patañjali, from its first word *Now.*

No one will follow through the practices and restrictions of yoga unless the goal and the related means to it have been clearly set out, and the commentator first explains what they were in the mind of the sūtra author, so that people may be led to practise.

First as to the goal. A clarifying illustration is given from medicine. In classics of medicine, the exposition is under four heads: illness, cause of the illness, the healthy condition, the remedy. Medical science further explains these things in terms of prescriptions and restrictions.

So it is in yoga also. The sūtra (II.15) *Because of the sufferings caused by changes and anxieties and the saṃskāra-s (dynamic latent impressions) of them, and from the clash of the guṇa-s, to the clear-sighted everything is pain alone* corresponds to the first head (diagnosis of illness).

The parallel four-fold division of this work on yoga is as follows: *what is to be escaped* (= the illness) is saṃsāra full of pain; its *cause* is the conjunction of Seer and seen, caused by Ignorance (avidyā); the *means of release* is an unwavering (aviplava) Knowledge that they are different. When that Knowledge-of-the-difference (viveka-khyāti) appears, Ignorance ceases; when Ignorance ceases, there is a complete end to conjunction of Seer and seen, and this is the *release* called kaivalya.

Kaivalya (Transcendental Aloneness) here corresponds to the condition of health, and so it is release which is the goal.

(Opponent) What-is-to-be-escaped, and its cause, should not have been brought in: it is pointless to do so. The work is concerned with release, and it is only the means to that, namely Knowledge, which needs to be mentioned. When a thorn has pierced the sole of the foot, one should not busy oneself with questions of pain and what causes it, instead of getting it out.

(Answer) Not so: the means of release depends on what it is that is to be escaped from, and what is its cause. Without explaining both this wheel of saṃsāra which is to be escaped by that means, and also its cause, namely the conjunction of Seer and seen caused by Ignorance, one cannot explain the discriminative Knowledge which cancels Ignorance. In the one who is suffering from what-is-to-be-escaped and its cause, and looking for a means of release, we see a sick man searching for a remedy. And medical science is not taught without reference to particular illnesses and their causes.

Now the relation of the means to the goal. The desired end of Knowledge-of-the-difference (of Seer-seen) is release, and Knowledge is the sole means to release. The mutual relation between them is one of means and end exclusively. The medical parallel is: health alone is the desired end of the remedy, and the remedy is the sole means to health. This is the exclusive mutual relation between the two in medicine, as shown in its classics. Thus the exposition of yoga too includes the relation of the end and the means.

(Opponent) If release is the goal, and the means to it is that Knowledge, then it should have been said, 'Now the exposition of Knowledge'. So why does the sūtra say, *Now the exposition of yoga?*

(Answer) Because yoga is the means to Knowledge, and it is a means that has to be taught. For when means and ends are being set forth, the end has to have some means to it, and so the means must be described along with all its methods. When that is explained, all is explained.

(Opponent) How is yoga the means?

(Answer) Because the sūtra says: *From following up the methods of yoga, (there is) destruction of impurity and a growing light of knowledge, up to Knowledge-of-the-difference (II.28).* Again, *From skill in nir-vicāra (samādhi without subtle associations), a clearness in the self (I.47),* and *In this, the knowledge is truth-bearing (I.48).* In the same way here, the commentator is going to say: *(but the samādhi) in the one-pointed mind makes clear an object as it really is,* and Knowledge-of-the-difference is awareness of things as they really are (bhūtārtha). Therefore it has been rightly said in the first sūtra *Now the exposition of yoga,* because that is the means to Knowledge.

(Opponent) But if Knowledge-of-the-difference comes from following up the methods of yoga, it should be 'Now the exposition of yoga methods'.

(Answer) No, because the result is being stated first. As yoga is the result of applying the means to yoga, it is right to begin with the word yoga.

(Opponent) Then it should begin with the word release.

(Answer) No, because that is a goal – release is a goal only. Yoga is a goal of the yoga methods, but it is also a means, and more properly the means to Knowledge than to supernormal powers such as becoming very small. For a result should conform to its means.

There is also the sense of the next sūtra. For if it had been 'Now the exposition of the methods of yoga', it would not have been logical to go on to say that yoga is inhibition of the mental process, for in that case sūtra II.29, listing restraints, observances, posture, prāṇāyāma, dissociation, concentration, meditation and samādhi, would be the one to mention.

(Opponent) Yes, that should have come next.

(Answer) No, because the sūtra I.2 declares *Yoga is inhibition of the mental processes* in order to show the relation of means and result in regard to Knowledge: Knowledge is what is aimed at by yoga, but is the means to release, its result.

(Opponent) How does the sūtra go to show this relation? It simply gives a definition of seedless samādhi.

(Answer) True, but it does that only to show the relation between release and the means to it. For release is not something different from the samādhi of total inhibition (nirodha). There is some distinction in so far as after nirodha samādhi there is recurrence of active mental processes (pravṛtti), whereas release is a final cessation (nivṛtti) of them. But in that samādhi as such, there is no distinction from release. So the sūtra has said, *Then the seer is established in his own nature* (sūtra I.3), and it will also be said that being established in its own nature is release: *or it is the establishment of the power-of-consciousness in its own nature* (IV.34). So it is incontestable that the sūtra means to say that release is only by seedless (nirbīja) samādhi.

(Opponent) There is a view that seeded (sa-bīja) samādhi is a means to release.

(Answer) It is not. What is, then? Knowledge-of-the-difference alone is the means, by way of cessation of Ignorance. For bondage gets its power from Ignorance. Though the sūtra says only *exposition of yoga,* still since yoga aims at Knowledge, it does show that the relation of Knowledge to release is by way of yoga, and very clearly the connection with the later sūtra-s. So it is rightly said: *exposition of yoga.*

Though the teaching also gives means to limited results for people aiming at them, and instruction on those means for those desiring to practise them, that is not its purpose; there it is merely pointing out (in passing) what would be the results of various methods.

The exposition of yoga. A student is taught by setting out particular activities and abstentions and restrictions; so here the exposition of yoga, the particular end, involves the means with all its methods and restrictions like those of sūtra II.29. Exposition is instruction, and the work is an exposition of yoga because yoga is taught by it or so to say in it.

The word *Now* means that this is a new topic (adhikāra). The tradition of the learned lays it down that the word Now (atha) means a new topic, a beginning (ārambha), an introduction (prastāva).

(Opponent) But the learned traditionally give the meaning 'following on' to the word Now. So Śabara says (on Mīmāṃsā sūtra 1.1.1), 'Yet we see that the word Now normally has a meaning of something immediately following on some event.'

(Answer) No, because it always has the meaning of a beginning. It is (of course) implied that it does follow on (whatever went before); just so when the word 'son' is spoken, it is implied that there must be a father, though the meaning of 'son' is not 'father'. Here, it is a beginning alone that is specified, though there is an implication of following on.

That is why Śabara said, 'We see that the word Now normally has a meaning of something immediately following on some event.' If it had been the bare meaning of sequence, he would have said, 'the meaning normally is immediately following on some event.' But his expression is '*something* following on', which must mean a thing which immediately follows (and therefore begins).

In grammar too it is said: 'An indeclinable has either mainly the sense of a case-inflection, or mainly that of action. Uccais (above), nīcais (below) and so on have mainly the sense of a case; hiruk (away), pṛthak (apart), etc. have mainly that of action.' These are the only possible senses of indeclinables (such as atha, Now). Of the two possibilities, the word Now, even allowing the meaning of bare following on, could not reasonably be taken in the sense of a case, since the main thing there is a state-of-being; but taken in the sense of the action of beginning, it has not the unreasonable case-sense, since the principal thing now is not a state-of-being.

Therefore the word Now must be taken simply as introducing the new topic. The word is self-explanatory, as when a man says 'cow'. Moreover the word Now is often pronounced at the beginning for concentrating (samādhāna) a pupil's mind; this is a principle well-known in the holy texts, for instance, 'I will explain to you and do you meditate on my explanation' (Bṛhad. Up. 2.4.4).

Yoga is samādhi. It is a quality (dharma) of the mind in all the five mental states: impulsive, dull, changeable, one-pointed, inhibited.

What then is the yoga, whose exposition is introduced? The commentator says, *Yoga is samādhi.* Since the word samādhi is in apposition to it, yoga is not to be taken as from the root yuj- in the sense of joining together, but in the sense of sam-ā-dhā, set together. Yoga is samādhāna (= samādhi), complete concentration.

(Opponent) By saying that yoga is samādhi he has completely explained the sūtra. He should not have added that it is in all the states, for this is irrelevant.

(Answer) Not so. Samādhi is mentioned, which means that there is something to be concentrated, and there are many things which might be concentrated. Is it the self (ātman) that is concentrated, or the body, or again the senses? There are many possibilities. Samādhi has to be defined in some way, and the natural question is, whose is it and what is its special nature? So he says:

It is a quality of the mind in all the mental states. It is a quality of the mind, not of self or anything else. And it is the mind which concentrates itself, since there is no reference to any other who concentrates it.

What then are the mental states? *Impulsive, dull, changeable, one-pointed* and *inhibited.*

The *impulsive (kṣipta)* state comes about as it were of itself, like an (overfull) granary spontaneously bursting apart. The impulsive state holds steady as long as it does not encounter something undesired.

The *dull (mūḍha)* state is absence of discrimination.

The *changeable (vi-kṣipta)* state is impelled (kṣipta) in various (vi-) directions. It too comes about as it were of itself. The occasional discrimination in this state does not last long, because it gets distracted.

The *one-pointed (ekāgra)* state is a stream of similar thoughts.

The *inhibited (nirodha)* state is a mind empty of thoughts.

(Opponent) It is the quality (dharma) of the states themselves that he wishes to describe: why is he now talking of impulsive and so on, which refer to their possessor (dharmin)?

(Answer) There is no mistake, for a quality is displayed by its possessor. The possessor is the field of the qualities. Asked about the distinguishing marks of the cow nature, the answer is: something with horns, with a hump, and with a hairy tail at the end. Thus the qualities are explained by their possessor. So the sense here is, that impulsiveness and so on are the states of the mind, namely its qualities.

(Opponent) If the states are mental qualities, the state of samādhi must be one too. Why then the phrase *It is a quality of the mind in all the mental states,* which makes it out to be the support of the others, and so having all of them?

(Answer) Because samādhi is common to all, whereas the other states are distinct from each other. We say that now there is the impulsive state, now there is dullness, now changeability, and now one-pointedness; all these states, while they last, have the common character of persisting. And persistence (sthiti) is samādhi. So it is the common feature which exists as each one comes to predominate.

The form of the Sanskrit compound sārva-bhauma (in all the states) in the commentary is one of the compounds (Pāṇini 5.1.41) which by the grammatical rule (7.3.20) take the vṛddhi strengthening in both elements.

There are some who declare that the states are the external and internal objects of saṃyama (samādhi on a chosen object). But if that were so, the next sentence *(of the commentary): 'in the changeable state of the mind'* would not be referring to the same thing. How should the commentator contradict himself like that? The impulsive state is that in which the mind is impelled; the dull is that in which it is confused. These therefore cannot be objects of saṃyama, in which state there is no possibility of impulsiveness or dullness, since it comes about in the one-pointed state.

Then in the changeable state, there is no attempt at steadiness and so on, so no idea of firmness to support it. Nor can saṃyama exist in the inhibited mind, since there would be no mental process, and so nothing to effect saṃyama. In inhibition the mind is not restricted to a particular object, for there is no subject for an object.

Nor would the listing of just five items be logical, for the impulsive and others being only five, could not be the objects of saṃyama, which are infinitely many.

(Opponent) Some would make yoga out to be otherwise. They say:

> Pleasure and pain arise from contact of senses and mind with objects;
> when that contact is not formed,
> when mind abides in self (ātman),
> there is neither pleasure nor pain for the embodied one;
> yoga is the inner union (samyoga) arising from control of prāṇa and mind.

This is the view, further explained as follows: The cause of pleasure and pain is the contact of self, mind, and senses, with objects. By not forming it, there is neither pleasure nor pain. How can this be brought about? By the mind's abiding in self and not abiding in the senses. The phrase 'embodied one' means that he still preserves a body. Then on the principle that without the cause there will be no effect, when there is no connection with objects there will be no pleasure or pain. In that state there is this union (saṃyoga) by the mind with the all-pervading self (vibhorātman). The union as described depends upon holding fast prāṇa and mind, and is called yoga.

(Answer) To speak of the mind abiding in self (ātman) is not logical, because mind always abides in self.

(Opponent) Abiding in self means that the senses and mind do not engage in contact with objects.

(Answer) Then just to say that they do not so engage would be perfectly clear, and it is pointless to add 'when the mind abides in self.

Furthermore it would follow that the released one would still be practising yoga, since his mind abides in self, and there is no sense-contact with objects. Since he is all-pervading, and the mind is eternal, it must always abide in self.

Again, self has no location, so it is meaningless to speak of abiding *in* self. Nor could union with a self given a figurative location be a basis for a yoga of highest truth (paramārtha yoga), because anything figurative is illusory (mithyā).

Further, since it is a principle (on your view) that mind can have no direct contact with objects, it is unnecessary to make separate mention of the senses.

(Opponent) Without the sense, there is no contact of mind with objects; it could not reach them. So a prohibition (without mentioning the senses) against such contact by the mind would be illogical, because it would be impossible.

(Answer) Not so. Without the senses there is no contact of mind with objects (as you say). So by making the prohibition against engaging in them, it would be implicitly declared that reaching the objects is by way of the senses (which therefore need not be mentioned separately).

Moreover it is well known that pleasure and pain are experienced in all living beings from the contact of senses and mind with objects, and since the relation with self is invariable, it should have been enough to say that yoga is the eternal relation with the self and absence of pleasure and pain; nothing more was needed.

(Opponent) Still, just to say that yoga is absence of pleasure and pain, without mentioning contact of the senses and mind with objects, would mean that the released one too would be practising yoga, because for him there is no pleasure or pain either. The extra statement was rightly made, to rule this out.

(Answer) No, because the released never has pleasure or pain, and a process of negation can only be of something which is already possessed. That yoga is in negation of pleasure and pain applies only to one who does now have pleasure and pain, so it is proper to disallow the supplementary remark. Moreover, if we accept that he is embodied, why would he have returned from the state of release? There would be no motive for it, since he is already released. If yoga is merely absence of pleasure and pain, the present body would have no purpose because it would not serve for any result, and without some result, there would be no distinction between those released and those not.

Again, the statement about controlling prāṇa (vital currents) and mind is not right. The restraining effort of will is supposed to be inherent in the self, even without any activity of the mind, but without some contact with the senses it cannot effect control of mind and prāṇa. And if the mind *is* to be connected with the senses, then it is wrong to say that yoga is not engaging with them. And with the mind busy holding fast the prāṇa, there will be non-engagement with it. The prāṇa cannot be held fast without contact of senses and vital airs, and without holding fast the prāṇa, there is no yoga. Restraint of prāṇa is caused by a mental activity deriving from a restraining effort inherent in self.

(Opponent) Well then, what we mean by yoga is, (the separate state of) samādhi.

(Answer) That will not do. Self is actionless and always in samādhi. As we have said, steadiness (sthiti) is samādhi. Rightly has the commentator said, it is a quality of the mind in all the states.

In the changeable state of the mind, the samādhi is subject to this changeability, and is not classed as yoga.

(Opponent) If yoga is to be samādhi, and that is a quality of the mind in all the states, the efforts of all living beings must be already fulfilled, for samādhi must accompany the changeable and other states. Since therefore it is already accomplished without efforts at breath control and so on, it follows that means to achieve it are useless, and this present exposition of yoga is also useless.

(Answer) *In the changeable state of the mind, the samādhi is subject to this changeability, and is not classed as yoga.* What is accompanied by impulsiveness or dullness or changeability is not accepted as yoga. For a samādhi accompanied by them cannot reveal things as they are (bhūtārtha), because they are predominating in it. By dismissing changeability the states of impulse and dullness are dismissed also, on the principle that when the main opponent is defeated, the others collapse. That the samādhi of changeability should be the most important is appropriate to the context, for the mind then can be led to anything desired without any special preference, but a mind impelled by the attractiveness of an object, or dulled by separation from what it wants, cannot be led in another direction.

not classed as yoga: though there is a samādhi, it is not classed as yoga because it does not have any effect. When a man is walking, at every step there is a (momentary) stopping still (sthiti), but it is not called one because it does not have the effect of a stopping. The samādhi is subject to change, and he is simply pointing out that there is a samādhi in that state of changeability. The main thing is, that a samādhi does appear in each of the states, the common point being that the mental process is steady for a time in all of them.

(Opponent) If being subject to something is a reason for its not being classed as yoga, then in the one-pointed state too there is a subjection, namely to one-pointedness, so that should not be classed as yoga either.

But the samādhi in the one-pointed mind makes clear the object as it is, destroys the taints, loosens the karma-bonds, and brings the state of inhibition into view; it is called cognitive.

(Answer) *But the samādhi in the one-pointed mind:* in one-pointedness where there is no subjection to a state. Why not? Because the taints and karmas are weakened. When taints and karmas are weakened, changeability and dullness and impulsiveness do not arise.

The samādhi in the state of one-pointedness *makes clear* brings to experience *the object as it is.* For one not a yogin, the knowledge of things will have a trace of 'not-as-it-is' – this being the force of the word bhūta, meaning as-it-is.

It destroys makes an end of the *taints* which are five-fold, Ignorance and the others. *It loosens* makes slack *the karma-bonds* bonds being purely karmic, produced by actions good, bad and mixed, which bind to life-and-death. *It brings the state of inhibition clearly into view,* This is technically called by the teachers cognitive (sam-prajñāta).

It follows on meditations with verbal associations (vitarka), meditations with subtle associations (vicāra), meditations accompanied with joy, and meditations accompanied with I-am-ness; and we shall speak of it later.

Here the commentator remarks that it is better to have the definition of ultra-cognitive (a-sam-prajñāta) samādhi here, rather than to take the definition of the cognitive first. So he says, *We shall speak of it later.*

Accordingly the definition of ultra-cognitive samādhi is now to be given here to show that it is independent of the cognitive, being perfected by the two practices of highest detachment (para-vairāgya) and the idea of stopping (virāma-pratyaya, 1.18). If the definition of the cognitive were given here, and that of the other one later, there would be some suspicion that only through the cognitive is there qualification for ultra-cognitive samādhi. (This is not so and) thus he says that he will speak of the cognitive one later.

But the ultra-cognitive (samādhi) is when there is inhibition of all mental processes. The next sūtra is presented to give a definition of it.

But the ultra-cognitive is when there is inhibition of all mental processes. The word *But* has the meaning of restriction. *the next sūtra is presented to give a definition of it,* of the pure ultra-cognitive samādhi thus described. So it is right that the sūtra now states:

Sūtra I.2

Yoga is inhibition of the mental processes

(Opponent) If the sūtra has been presented to give this definition, it should have been 'Yoga *has* inhibition of the mental processes'; to put them in apposition is not right, for a definition should not be simply the thing defined. Or at any rate it should have been said, 'The definition is, inhibition of the mental processes.'

(Answer) A definition is projected (adhyas) on to the thing defined. When we say 'This person is Devadatta' there is a projection (adhyāsa) of the definition on to the thing defined. So there is no fault.

The omission of the word All shows that the cognitive (samādhi) too is yoga.

(Opponent) (The commentator's previous gloss) *But the ultra-cognitive is when there is inhibition of all mental processes* is also a definition of it, so the sūtra should have been 'Yoga is inhibition of *all* mental processes.' This has not been said and the definition is too wide.

(Answer) As to why the word All is omitted from the sūtra, he says that if All were put in, it would be denying that the cognitive samādhi, which comes about by restricting the processes to a single point, is yoga at all. To prevent that, the word All is left out.

(Opponent) If so, the cognitive and ultra-cognitive have the same definition and are not in fact distinguished.

(Answer) The subject is yoga, as we see from the repetition of the word (in the first two sūtra-s). And unless he did intend a distinction, there would have been no point in putting into the definition the word yoga (which is well known to include meditation on objects).

(Opponent) The word yoga is of minor importance for actual exposition; it would suit the purpose of exposition if the definition just said 'Inhibition of the mental processes' without the word yoga at all.

(Answer) Not so, because what was introduced was an exposition of yoga, and it is exposition of yoga that has been begun, not exposition of non-yoga. The proposed definition could have too many contexts and would not be connected to the meaning of the words 'exposition of yoga'. For the idea of an exposition of yoga does not follow from the words 'inhibition of mental processes'.

(Opponent) Why then should the word yoga lead to a definition of the ultra-cognitive samādhi alone, and not to a definition of the cognitive, if there is no such distinction in the word itself?

(Answer) Because it applies exactly. What applies loosely is not a definition of a thing. The definition as inhibition applies exactly to the ultra-cognitive samādhi, but only loosely to the cognitive. Having horns is not the mark of cow-ness, because it applies also to buffaloes and other animals.

(Opponent) Neither is inhibition exact as a definition of the ultra-cognitive; (it is too loose) because there is inhibition in the cognitive too, namely inhibition of the undesired mental processes.

(Answer) True, but the ultra-cognitive cannot be defined by anything else except inhibition. Inhibition alone is its definition because nothing else is there, whereas the cognitive is definable in terms of special characteristics like verbal associations. As a parallel case, when tangibility is cited as a defining mark, it is the element Air alone that is defined by the fact of tangibility, which is regarded as special to it, though in fact tangibility is found also in the other elements in the descending order from Fire (to Water and then Earth).

Thus the word yoga is simply a corroboration (anuvāda), and so it is that All has not been put in the sūtra. It is settled that the ultra-cognitive is defined by the bare word 'inhibition', and if 'All (the mental processes)' were included, it would deny that the cognitive also is yoga. Therefore this is the definition of ultra-cognitive alone, and the commentator will sum up later in these words: *Ultra-cognitive (a-sam-prajñāta) in the sense that in it no thing is cognized (sam-prajñāyate): this yoga is inhibition of the mental process.*

What is the nature of that mind, inhibition of whose processes is called yoga? To explain mind and its processes and their inhibition, the commentator says:

> *Now mind always tends towards illumination, activity, or stasis (sthiti); so it consists of the three guṇa-s.*

Mind is said to consist of the three guṇa-s, because it is always tending towards illumination, activity, or stasis. Illumination is making known, bringing to light, that being characteristic of sattva guṇa. Activity is motion and operation, that being characteristic of rajas. Stasis is being stationary, limitation, and resistance, such being characteristic of tamas. These are the invariable tendencies of the guṇa-s, and as mind is always tending towards one of them, it is true to say that it is continual transformation of the three guṇa-s.

To the objection that illumination and the others have not been established as causes, he says:

> *For mind-sattva is by nature illumination.*

The word *For* means that this is something generally accepted; it is well known in the world and from scripture how mind makes everything manifest. So mind *is* sattva, and is therefore called mind-sattva, because its main transformation is that of sattva.

Or again, mind can be pointed out clearly as pure knowledge (khyāti) having other mental processes mutually combining and separating. So it is that he says *For mind-sattva is by nature illumination.*

> *Mingled with rajas and tamas, mind is drawn towards power and possessions. Pervaded by tamas, it becomes subject to a-dharma, Ignorance, attachment and helplessness. That same mind, when the covering of illusion (moha) has dwindled, pervaded by a measure of rajas, is endowed with dharma, knowledge (jñāna), detachment and power. When the last trace of the stain of rajas is removed, the mind is grounded in its own nature, becoming simply the*

Knowledge (khyāti) that sattva and Puruṣa are different, and it is endowed with the Rain-cloud of Dharma, which the meditators call the highest prasaṅkhyāna (continuous meditation on Knowledge).

Now he explains the conflicting varieties of mental processes which arise from relative dominance or subordination of rajas and tamas. When sattva is predominant, but mingled with rajas and tamas, they being equally strong, mind becomes fond of power and possessions, and this fondness for them is passion. The meaning is, that thoughts arise concentrated on the passion for power and possessions.

When that mind, which is illumination by nature, is pervaded by tamas, with rajas subordinate in it, then tainted thoughts arise of a-dharma and the other three (Ignorance, passion, and helplessness).

That same mind, when the covering of illusion has dwindled, when tamas has been overcome, as when the rain-cloud passes away the darkness is at an end and the sun-disc illumines everything *pervaded by a measure* by a trace *of rajas,* is endowed with dharma, etc. (knowledge, detachment, and power), and pure thoughts of dharma and the others arise.

When the last stain of the trace of rajas is removed, the mind is grounded in its own nature in its own nature as illumination and that alone. *It becomes simply the Knowledge that sattva and Puruṣa are different.* Mind is sattva, and Puruṣa is the experiencer (bhoktṛ); discriminating them as different is Knowledge (khyāti) of them, awareness of them. The word *simply* indicates that it is free from taints or any other things (than Knowledge). *It is endowed with the meditation called Rain-cloud of Dharma,* this being the samādhi of that name.

The mind overcomes rajas and tamas by power of prasaṅkhyāna, which is meditation (dhyāna) established in the perception of the nature of Puruṣa alone, pure Knowledge itself, *which the meditators* the yogins *call the highest prasaṅkhyāna (continuous meditation on Knowledge).*

The power-of-consciousness is unchangeable, does not engage with objects, has the objects shown to it, is pure and infinite.

Having explained what the mental process is in itself, he shows how it is to be inhibited. *The power-of-consciousness (citi-śakti) is unchangeable:* consciousness alone is power, so it is called power-of-consciousness. Powers which blossom out only in births appropriate to the possession of those powers are not inherent power, but consciousness is inherent power, dependent on nothing else. It is therefore eternally established. The apposition of the word *consciousness (citi)* meaning pure consciousness (cinmātra) and the word *power (śakti)* is to show that the subjective consciousness is of unvarying nature. This being so, it is something unchanging. When in an abiding possessor-of-qualities (dharmin), one quality (dharma) gives way to a different one, that is called change. Since this consciousness never changes, it is unchanging. For just this reason, *it does not engage with objects.* For it is only things like mind, which do change, that are found to engage with objects.

So the various *objects are shown to it:* an object is shown to it through the mind (antaḥ-karaṇa). Therefore it is *pure* and therefore in space and in time it is *infinite.* (In this explanation which has been given) each fact is to be understood as the cause of the next one.

> *Opposed to pure consciousness is Knowledge-of-the-difference (viveka-khyāti), whose nature is sattva-guṇa. Therefore the mind, turning away from even that Knowledge, inhibits it.*

An example of the contrary is mind and senses. *Opposed to pure consciousness is Knowledge-of-the-difference, whose nature is sattva-guṇa.* Sattva-guṇa means pure sattva, and its essence is that alone. To say that its nature is sattva means that its nature is essentially to illumine. Again, it is said to be essentially sattva-guṇa because this thought is not concerned with any object of the world.

Again, Knowledge is bound by the very fact of being Knowledge, just because it is essentially sattva. This Knowledge being thus distinct from, and opposed to, the characteristics of the power-of-consciousness described, does have changes and so on.

Being associated with qualities like change, it is inferior to the supreme Puruṣa which is free from them. *Therefore* because it sees the defect (doṣa) in its own nature, *the mind, turning away from* giving up *even that Knowledge, inhibits it.*

> *In this state what remains is saṃskāra-s, and it is the seedless (nirbīja) samādhi. There is no cognition of anything in it, so it is ultra-cognitive. This yoga is inhibition of the mental processes.*

In this state the state of inhibition *what remains is saṃskāra-s;* only saṃskāra-s are left. *This samādhi* in this state of inhibition is the *seedless.* The meaning is, that here the seed is gone; in this all the seeds of taint and so on are gone.

To show this very mark of the ultra-cognitive samādhi, he quotes the sūtra, *This yoga is inhibition of the mental processes.*

> *What is Puruṣa, the cognizer of buddhi (buddhi-bodhātman), in that state when there is no object for him?*

Sūtra I.3

Then the Seer is established in his own nature

> *Then the power-of-consciousness rests in its own nature, as in the state of release. But when the mind is extraverted, though it is so, it is not so.*

It has been said that yoga is inhibition of the mental processes, by which inhibition the true being of Puruṣa as the cognizer (boddhṛ) is realized. In which case some might suppose that with inhibition of the thoughts of objects, there would be inhibition of the subject, the cognizer, the Puruṣa, also. Then they would assume that it would not be sensible to try to attain Knowledge-of-the-difference, the means to release, and that the exposition of yoga, which aims at that Knowledge, would be futile. To show that inhibition of the mental process is not inhibition of Puruṣa, and to point directly to the result of Knowledge, the commentator says: *What is Puruṣa, the cognizer of buddhi, in that state when there is no object for him? Then the seer is established in his own nature.* When the mental process has been inhibited, *then the power-of-consciousness rests in its own nature.*

In that state, in the state of inhibition, *when there is no object for him* since the object, the mental process, is not there, *what is* the nature of *Puruṣa, the cognizer of buddhi?* Puruṣa is the cognizer of buddhi in the sense that he is aware of buddhi in its transformations as the forms of the mental processes. The nature of Puruṣa is simple awareness of them; the one who is aware is not different from the awareness. If the one who is aware were different from the awareness itself, he would be changeable and then would not be a mere witness who has objects shown to him. So his awareness and subjectivity are spoken of figuratively as if conforming to a mental process. But the sūtra will say, *The Seer is sight alone (II.20).*

Here it is being asked, what is the real being of that Puruṣa, the cognizer of buddhi (buddhi-bodhātman)? The compound buddhi-bodhātman means that his nature is pure awareness of buddhi. Is it a perishable nature? Or if it is real being (sad-bhāva), what sort of real being is it, and how does it come about?

Then the Seer is established in his own nature: when the mental process has been inhibited, *then the power-of-consciousness rests in its own nature. Rests in its own nature* means that it is like release. He is going to speak of that real being later (IV. 19) when he says *Mind is not self-illumining, because it is itself something perceived.* The phrase about resting in its own nature has been used in order to clear up any doubt as to what is its real being.

(Opponent) The sūtra is in definite terms, and it must follow that at some other time the power-of-consciousness is *not* so established, for otherwise the specification *Then* would be meaningless. And if at this other time it is not established in its own nature, there is the objection that it will be subject to change, because it will then have become associated with a different condition.

(Answer) *But when the mind is extraverted, though it is so, it is not so.* The first phrase *though it is so* shows that even in this time of extraversion, the power-of-consciousness is established in its own nature, *it is not so* shows that the specification of the time of extraversion has some meaning.

How can this be? It is because objects are displayed to it.

Sūtra I.4

Otherwise, it conforms itself to the mental process

In the extraverted state, whatever the process in the mind, Puruṣa has a process not distinguished from it. As a sūtra says: There is only one sight, and the sight is knowledge alone.

(Opponent) If *though it is so* means that power-of-consciousness does rest in its own nature even when mind is extraverted, and *not so* denies that it so rests, there is the contradiction that the same thing both is so and is not so, and our side asks in bewilderment, *How can this be?*

(Answer) The answer from our side is, *Otherwise, it conforms itself to the mental process.*

(Opponent) Well, why does it conform to it?

(Answer) Because objects have been displayed to it. Though in the two cases there is no distinction as to the resting in its own nature, still there is a distinction according to whether it conforms to the mental processes or not, and so it is not a contradiction between being so and being not so.

(Opponent) Connection with conformity to a mental process is connection with a different state, and must entail defects like changeability.

(Answer) The answer lies in the fact that objects have been displayed to it. The apparent change is not intrinsic but projected (adhyāropita), like a crystal's taking on the colour of something put near it.

In the extraverted state outside the inhibited state *whatever the process in the mind* tainted or untainted, there is a process *not distinguished from it,* like it, which is natural to this one (Puruṣa). Without a process in the mind, and without this nature (of Puruṣa), there would be no process in Puruṣa. There is always something known to Puruṣa, so no change is involved in him.

There is a sūtra by an earlier teacher (ācārya): *There is only one sight, and the sight is knowledge (khyāti) alone.* There is only one sight (darśana) of buddhi and of Puruṣa. What does this mean? *The sight is knowledge alone.* Sight is a process of the mind (buddhi). It is a knowledge in the sense that it is known by Puruṣa; it is also knowledge in the sense that by it the nature of buddhi and of Puruṣa is known. It is an instrument in that the form of the object is apprehended by it, and it is an object inasmuch as it is apprehended by its own nature as knowledge; similarly, it is a sight in that it is seen, and also sight in that things are seen by it; it is knowledge (jñāna) in that it is known and also that things are known by it. This is how it is all to be understood.

(Opponent) But mind itself is the knowing agent (khyātikartṛ); it is that which is known and which knows. There is no need to suppose any other knowing.

(Answer) That we shall refute when we come to the sūtra, *(Mind) is not self-illumining because it is something perceived (IV.19).*

(Opponent) If all this is simply manifested (parivjṛmbhita) by mind, and Puruṣa sits apart, how can he be the experiencer (bhoktṛ)?

(Answer) Why not? Agents (kāraka) are of various kinds. Some are operational, and some are effective by mere proximity without any operation. When we say that one cooks, the man active in putting things on the fire and so on is called the agent; the pot, though not performing any operation by its holding and supporting the food, is still called a 'cooker'. The space in the pot itself does provide a place for the food, but we do not take this to be an operation by it.

Again, there is the king who is an agent by merely appearing (at the council), whereupon all the (ministerial) agencies become agents carrying out their own operations. The sun does not look to some external instrument for his shining, nor does he perform any operation. He does not produce some previously non-existent shining as he comes and goes. It is simply that shining is his nature. So he is said to illumine by proximity alone, manifesting jars and so on as bright forms.

In our present case too, the mental processes, pervaded by his nature as consciousness (cid-ātman), are seen by Puruṣa who is pure sight.

To show how Puruṣa is the seer he now says:

Mind is like a magnet.

Even the philosopher who holds that knowledge (jñāna) arises from a conjunction of the self (ātman) and mind (manas), calls the self the knower (jñātṛ), as pervading the known object by knowledge, not as performing an operation. Knowledge too, being (in his view) an attribute (guṇa) of the self, is without action; it is simply its nature to show objects. It cannot be maintained that a man cannot be said to know without some action, for a man is said to know when he pervades the object with knowledge.

If, however, new knowledge is assumed from conjunction of the self and mind, that knowledge belongs to self and not to the mind, for it is said that *he* knows, and not that his mind knows. Why?

(Opponent) Admitted, but the reason is that the self is what we call the inherent cause (samavāyī-kāraṇa, having knowledge as an attribute).

(Answer) That has not been established. Just as what had to be demonstrated was, why the knowledge should belong to the self (and not to the mind), so it would have to be demonstrated why self should be the inherent cause, and not mind, inasmuch as you maintain that mind is not itself the self, and that knowledge arises from conjunction of the two.

(Opponent) Let it be because of the recollection in memory of the saṃskāra, laid down by the knowledge, of the self as the sole agent.

(Answer) No, for that too would have to be demonstrated. In that case also it has to be shown why the saṃskāra of knowledge and the recollection of the memory should relate only to the self and not to the mind.

(Opponent) Let us say that it is because desire (icchā, an attribute of self in our system) and its fulfilment are (referred to) the same place.

(Answer) No, again it is the same thing. Once (it is accepted that) they are produced by a conjunction, it cannot be shown why the results and the desire should pertain to self alone and not to mind.

Moreover, this knowledge too is accepted (by you) to be a knowable object, so an infinite regress will follow. And it cannot be that one knowledge should be known by the instrument of another knowledge, and that by another, and that by another, endlessly.

To avoid the regress, one might say that at some point there is a knowledge which is primary, perceived not by some other knowledge but spontaneously by itself alone. But this would imply that (other) objects too should be able to perceive themselves spontaneously, just as knowledge is held to do.

(Opponent) Let us say that knowledge itself shines, and it makes others shine, being naturally luminous like a lamp, and so there is no defect in the argument, because nothing else is naturally luminous.

(Answer) Then even things like lights would never be known.

(Opponent) Well, knowledge knows spontaneously because it is an attribute of the self, and is luminous by nature as well, whereas things like lights which shine outwards are of opposite character to knowledge. So the argument holds.

(Answer) Not that either. If to be an attribute of the self and also luminous by nature were a cause for spontaneous knowing by knowledge, everyone would be omniscient.

(Opponent) There also has to be some knowable form.

(Answer) Not even that. (For knowledge to know itself) the cause of one knowledge would be the fact of the form of another knowledge, and in the same way, the form of the first knowledge as a knowable would cause yet another knowledge, and so the regress would be unavoidable.

Furthermore, no example is found to instance anything being subject and object for itself; even a light needs an eye to be known. Nor (can it be said that there) are two parts in knowledge, since it has no parts.

Even if it had, since they would both be luminous, they could not be subject and object to each other, any more than two lights.

Furthermore, if being both subject and object were accepted of knowledge, it could never be the real nature of the self.

Therefore knowledge of objective forms, and memory, and its recall, and effort and desire and so on, are all essentially not-self, because they are objects of knowledge like outer forms, and because they exist-for-another (parārtha) as is shown by their dependence on the body-mind aggregate for the manifestation of their forms and other qualities. So because they have dependence, and are impermanent, and are accompanied by effort – for these and similar reasons it is certain that they are essentially not-self.

Mind is like a magnet, serving by mere proximity, by the fact of being seen. It is the property of its owner, Puruṣa. There is a beginningless relation, and this is the cause of Puruṣa's awareness of the mental processes.

Mind is as it were a magnet. As a magnet serves to pervade with itself the iron, by merely being placed near it, so the mind serves to pervade with itself the self (ātman) which is pure consciousness, by the fact of being seen by it. It is spoken of as like a dancing-girl, because it puts on a display, by means of the inner-organ (antaḥkaraṇa – thought, emotion and so on). Here mind (citta) is the one who puts on the display, and Puruṣa is the one who sees it.

(Opponent) How does this distinction come about?

(Answer) It comes about as the relation of a thing to its owner.

(Opponent) But how does the relation of thing and owner come about?

(Answer) It is the nature of each.

(Opponent) What is this nature?

(Answer) Mind is comparable to a magnet.

(Opponent) What is the cause of Puruṣa's being aware of the mind process?

(Answer) A magnet serves by mere proximity, the mind by the fact of being seen. There is a beginningless relation, and this is the cause of Puruṣa's awareness of the mental processes.

There are many of them in the mind, and they are to be inhibited.

Sūtra I.5

The mental processes are of five kinds; they are tainted or pure

The tainted are caused by the five taints (kleśa); they become the seed-bed for the growth of the accumulated karma seed-stock. The others are pure and are the field of Knowledge. They oppose involvement in the guṇa-s. They remain pure even if they occur in a stream of tainted ones. In gaps between tainted ones, there are pure ones; in gaps between pure ones, tainted ones. It is only by mental processes that saṃskāra-s corresponding to them are produced, and by saṃskāra-s are produced new mental processes. Thus the wheel of mental process and saṃskāra revolves. Such is the mind. But when it gives up its involvement, it abides in the likeness of self (ātman) or else dissolves.

The mental processes are to be inhibited, though they are many. In the extraverted state, Puruṣa conforms to them as has been explained. Why are they to be inhibited? The sūtra says, *They are tainted or pure.*

(Opponent) They are too many to be inhibited.

(Answer) To this the sūtra says, *They are of five kinds.* Though there is an infinity of them, tainted and pure, still they are of only five kinds, of five classes, five groups. Only by recourse to practice and detachment, which oppose them en bloc, does inhibition succeed; their mere number does not make inhibition impossible, though there is no effective means of inhibiting them one by one.

The tainted are caused by the five taints, for mind, impelled by Ignorance and the other four taints, again and again invites the self, and *they become the seedbed for the growth of the accumulated karma seed-stock.* Karmas are favourable, unfavourable, and mixed, and they are referred to as karma seed-stock inasmuch as they have a latent drive towards producing fruits. The mass of them is held together, each sometimes predominating and sometimes auxiliary to others. With that mass of karma seed-stock as cause, Ignorance and the other taints become the seed-bed for tainted mental processes. When these last appear, the karma seed-stock is near to ripening.

The pure are the field of Knowledge, they are the seats (āspada) of Knowledge. *They oppose involvement* activity of the saṃskāra-s *with the guṇa-s* sattva, rajas, and tamas. It is because they are directed towards the field of Knowledge that they are pure, since Knowledge brings about release (apavarga).

When pure thoughts arise in the midst of a mass of tainted ones, do they themselves become tainted – like drops of water thrown into a pot of milk? And do the tainted, caught in a current of pure ones, themselves become pure? What would follow if they did? If pure ones that happened to be in a current of tainted ones were to become tainted, it would mean that memory, which conforms to the saṃskāra of the thought which produced it, and on whose accuracy life in the world depends, would be unreliable, for the thoughts would be inherently uncertain. So he says *In gaps between tainted ones, there are pure ones* which remain pure, and *in gaps between pure ones, the tainted* are still tainted. And this being so, *it is only by mental processes (vṛtti) that saṃskāra-s* corresponding to them *are produced.* Though the taints and so on do set up saṃskāra-s, it happens only through the medium of mental processes, and this is the force of the word *only.* And by saṃskāra-s, mental processes corresponding to them are produced; so *the wheel of process and saṃskāra continuously* incessantly *revolves.*

Such is the mind, characterized by having processes and saṃskāra-s each causing the other; but *when it has given up its involvement (adhikāra)* when the activity caused by Ignorance has ceased and it rests in the causal state alone *it rests in the likeness of self (ātman)* in the likeness of Puruṣa, as pure Knowledge alone, for a time conforming to the remainder of the saṃskāra-s which have already begun to function (prārabdha), *or else dissolves* when the saṃskāra-s have come to an end.

The mental processes, tainted or untainted, are of these five kinds:

Sūtra I.6

Right knowledge, illusion, logical construction, sleep, memory

Sūtra I.7

Right knowledge is either direct perception, inference, or authority

> *The right knowledge called direct perception is the process when the mind is coloured by an external thing through a sense-channel, and takes as its field the determination mainly of the particular nature of the thing, which has however also the nature of a universal.*

What then are the five kinds of mental process, tainted or pure? They are *right knowledge, illusion, logical construction, sleep, memory.* All the mental processes are included in these.

Right knowledge is either direct perception, inference, or authority. The process called right knowledge (pramāṇa, also proof) is divided into just these three, the first division of right knowledge being direct perception. Now the definition of direct perception is given. It is put first because the other two presuppose it.

By a sense channel: the sense referred to is one of the five senses of perception like hearing, not one of the senses of action (e.g. speech) which produce actions but not thoughts. The word could mean either but here he wishes to explain mental processes, so he is referring only to senses like hearing, which produce them. When mind is transformed by a thought, in verbal or some other form, the sense (by which the form is received) is the channel, the gateway. So the mind, through that gateway of sense, is transformed into the form of an external thing, which is both a universal and a particular, and is coloured by it. As a result of that colouring of the mind, the mental process receives an impression (prati-mudrā) as if from a seal (mudrā); the impression is of a thing which is both a universal and a particular, but it is determined mainly by the particular aspect, and this is called direct perception.

(Opponent) A sense like hearing, and the mind, can reflect both the universality (i.e. class) and the particularity of an object; why is this supposed to be concerned mainly with determining a particular?

(Answer) Because rejection and acceptance are concerned with particulars. It is not that the universal is not recognized, but it is taken as secondary. When it is said 'blue colour', the main thing is to specify blue, but it is the colour (universal) which is blue, this being a secondary meaning. So 'the word pain', 'the word happiness', and 'the word dull', and the mental process (of perception) are concerned mainly with a particular.

Moreover, perception of universals includes cases of doubt and illusion. Perceiving a universal, one may doubt whether this is indeed the particular he is seeking. Illusion, again, arises from memory of a different instance of the universal he is now perceiving. But doubt and illusion cannot maintain themselves when one has come to know the particular rightly, and so it is said that direct perception is concerned mainly with determining a particular.

Even where one wishes only to determine a universal, whether for instance this is a cow or a horse, inasmuch as one alternative is discarded and the other is settled on, the main thing is determination of which particular universal it is. Everything is both a universal and a particular in relation to other things.

(Opponent) But a universal is only something unreal (a-vastu), projected (adhyāropita) like mirage water on desert ground, and not an object of the senses.

(Answer) If so, there would be no regularity in the universals projected. Nothing can be projected unless perceived before. Someone who has never seen water does not project mirages in the desert.

(Opponent) He might project (adhyāropayet) something he did not remember.

(Answer) If so, one might project (adhyasyet) a quality of sound on to what had colour (i.e. anything could be projected on to anything).

(Opponent) Colour and sound are fields of different senses, so no such projection (adhyāsa) can take place.

(Answer) No; you have said they are unreal (a-vastu), so they can not be distinct particulars. Once you admit distinct particulars, they must be real. Again, unless we accept direct perception with its distinctions of place, time and other circumstances, practical life will collapse. There would be no memories 'I saw this on that occasion and that at that time, and so I can make out what it is'. There can be no memory of subjects and their predicates unless they have been directly perceived. No one in fact lives by fantasy (kalpanāpodha) remote from the field of practical life. There it is proper to accept perception only as it is generally recognized.

(Opponent) The yogic vision from trans-conceptual (nir-vikalpa) samādhi does not fit into the definition *through a sense-channel*. Furthermore, the knowledge of happiness, passion and so on has not previously passed through a sense-channel; so some other means of right knowledge must be supposed for them, unless they are to be called direct perception (and the definition amended).

(Answer) The difficulty is avoided by observing that direct perception is an idea (pratyaya) in Puruṣa, there being no mental process of direct perception which is not an idea. It is only as arising from an idea in consciousness (caitanya) that it has the power of perception at all. So it is now going to be said by the commentator, *The result is an awareness by Puruṣa of the mental process not distinguished from it.* This being so, in the case of the knowledge of happiness or passion etc., whether tainted or pure, it comes down to an idea in Puruṣa not distinguished from these things, so it is certain that they are cases of direct perception.

When it is said that perception is through a sense-channel, this is (not a definition but) merely a corroboration (anuvāda) of what happens in ordinary perception in the world. Otherwise, the knowledge possessed by the yogin, and by the Lord, which does not depend on sense-organs, would not come under direct perception. But in fact, when the limitation of the taints has been removed, there is simultaneous perception of all things, however subtle or remote, by the mind-sattva, which goes to all objects and all fields. It will be said (sūtra III.54) *Knowledge-born-of-discrimination, having all, and all times, without sequence, for its object, is called Transcendent (tāraka).* So the definition of direct perception is not to be restricted to what comes through sense-channels.

Coloured by an external thing is to rule out illusion.

Doubt is ruled out by the fact that right knowledge is concerned mainly with *ascertaining a particular.*

The result is an awareness by Puruṣa of the mental process, not distinguished from it.

(Opponent A) Some say that right knowledge (pramāṇa, also proof) is its own result.

(Opponent B) But others maintain that the result is not right knowledge, but something else, namely a development of right knowledge. As for instance the result of the right knowledge which perceives a jar is an idea (buddhi) of putting it aside, or picking it up, or disregarding it altogether. Since these ideas of picking it up, or disregarding it altogether and so on, are concerned with good points of the jar, or its defects, or absence of either, they are quite distinct from the bare perception of the jar which is the right knowledge of it. Therefore the result of the right knowledge relating to an object is something different, namely a development of the right knowledge, and it relates to a different object.

(Answer to Opponent B) It is not reasonable to say that the result of chopping up a khadira tree is the picking up or throwing away of the khadira wood. For the picking up or throwing away are themselves results of connection or separation, and one cannot speak of the result of a result – that would be dividing the result into two, and there would be a gap.

If results were to have results, it would mean that actions would not be needed, inasmuch as action is something done with a view to a result. If a previous result is going to bring about a result even without action, people will not engage in action needed to bring to fulfilment anything needing much effort. Nor would they search for means, because they would not be needing action.

(Answer to Opponent A) Nor can the result be the action (for instance perception or inference) itself. For (if it were) action would never come to an end. Action leads to the result, and if the result were no more than the action itself, results would not be desired, because action is inherently troublesome.

(Answer to both opponents) Therefore the result is not simply the right knowledge itself, nor is it some other kind of right knowledge different from it. So he says, *The result is an awareness by Puruṣa of the mental process, not distinguished from it.*

Not distinguished from it, not distinguished from that mental process called right knowledge; it is similar to it, being of its form.

Awareness by Puruṣa, this is Puruṣa's awareness, for it is Puruṣa's taking on the form of the process.

A result is not merely the material as it is, independent of any action. On the contrary, the result is the taking on by that material of a definite other state; it is produced by an action and appears with the cessation of the action, arising as the action attains its end. For only with fulfilment in the result does action come to its end. The awareness by Puruṣa of the mental process, not distinguished from it, is the main result. But side-effects – the (changes in a) substance resulting from an action apart from the main action, or some (further) action resulting from the (changed) substance – may allowably also be figuratively called results, since they bring out clearly the main result, by mutual reinforcement.

(Opponents) What you call the result is all purely figurative like that, for you accept as the result something not distinguished from the mental process. Puruṣa is pure, and so its assumption of that form is unreal. When a piece of red lac is put against a crystal, the crystal does not really become red.

(Answer) True. But still the main result is that alone, for it is seen to be so, and we do not see any other main result. Result means all that is produced by actions and agent, and it all ends in this. So it is defined as the result.

(Opponent) If the principal result, namely taking the form of the mental process, is only something unreal (mithyā-bhūta), there would be no desire for it.

(Answer) True. And experience *is* a purely illusory conformity to the mental process (mithyā-bhūta-vṛtty-anugata). So it will be said (sūtra III.35):

Experience is an idea which does not distinguish between sattva and Puruṣa, though they are absolutely separate. And the commentator will say (close to II.6), *When there is awareness of the true nature of these two, how would there be experience?* For this reason, right vision (saṃyag-darśana) is followed by complete cessation of the mental process.

But those who believe results to be real will not come to investigate them through right vision; there will be no release for them, because the requisite detachment will be absent. And release is not a consummation of action, because that would mean it would be impermanent.

We shall describe later (under II.17) how Puruṣa is the witness (pratisaṃvedin).

(Opponent) It is not established that there is any cognizer (boddhṛ) of buddhi, or (if there is) that it is Puruṣa.

(Answer) *We shall describe later how Puruṣa is the witness* of buddhi. Now those who suppose that direct perception is a conjunction (saṃnikarśa) of a sense with its object are wrong in their supposition, because any conjunction is the result of some action. Conjunction is a coming together (saṃyoga) and that is stated in their school to be produced by action. What produces a thing is proof (pramāṇa) of it; what is produced is the result of the producer (and not a proof).

(Opponent) Though it is a result, still as regards knowledge, the conjunction is proof.

(Answer) Not so. For when the topic is the (enlightening) proof which makes a thing known (jñāpaka pramāṇa), it is not proper to bring in a (creating) proof which produces a thing (kāraka pramāṇa). As your conjunction is, on your showing, the cause of producing knowledge (jñānasya utpādaka), it is not what makes that knowledge known. Direct perception and so on are brought forward to explain cognition of the knowable object (prameya), not as a cause for the rise of knowledge. The latter would introduce something irrelevant into the context.

(Opponent) But knowledge is itself something to be known (prameya), and when it arises, it is known; so the conjunction which makes it rise (utpattikāraṇa) *is* what makes it known (jñāpaka).

(Answer) No, for you yourself admit that knowledge is known only by knowledge, and a conjunction is not itself knowledge, for you have stated it to be what causes the rise of knowledge.

(Opponent) As providing the occasion for it, the conjunction is a cause of the knowledge of knowledge, so it is right knowledge (pramāṇa).

(Answer) Then the opening of the eyes and so on, and the inscrutable will of the Lord (as destiny), could not be refused the status of right knowledge, because they too provide the occasion for knowledge. If knowledge is to be itself known, the only way to avoid an infinite regress is to accept consciousness as the very nature of self (ātman).

(Opponent) The knownness of knowledge is simply as being an attribute inherent in the self, so no other knowledge which would involve a regress is needed.

(Answer) You still need a further knowledge, a direct perception, of the inherence of the knowledge in the self, because that fact is not accessible to the senses. Moreover, since your conjunction is supposed to be what produces knowledge as its result, the production will take time, so that knowledge would not be immediate.

If the knowledge is to be immediate, it can not be the result of a conjunction. And we have already pointed out that such ideas as rejecting are not results of simple knowledge of forms and so on.

Also there is the uncertainty. As when there arises in a number of men the same knowledge of the body of a beautiful woman, in one of them there is the idea of possessing her, in another the idea that she should be avoided, and in yet another neither of these ideas. There is no certainty whether the idea of possessing or the idea of avoiding will arise, though in both cases the knowledge is the same; and in the one who is indifferent, neither of the ideas appears. What is uncertain in its relation to another, cannot be the result of it.

Again, the indifference of the third man is simply a negative, inasmuch as it is no more than absence of avoiding and possessing, and the result of a positive right knowledge should not be a negative. The pair of ideas, taking and rejecting, are from the pair love and hate. Following the maxim 'no effect without a cause', without the latter pair there will be no idea of avoiding or taking; but there is still the consciousness of right knowledge, and that is what is called indifference. Since therefore there is this uncertainty about them, the ideas of avoiding and so on cannot be the result of right knowledge.

Furthermore, the ideas of taking and so on being the results of love or hate or absence of either, it would follow that love and hate or indifference would themselves be right knowledge.

(That would be a contradiction) but there is no contradiction when we take the result to be awareness by Puruṣa of the mental process.

(Opponent) It has not been shown how the mental process can itself be a knowable, for what is an instrument cannot be the object – the sickle is not cut by itself.

(Answer) The explanation is, that an action is of a different character from the instrumentalities which bring it to fulfilment. The instrumentalities, united for the completion of the action, operate reciprocally as object and subject for each other. But where a so-called action causes the result by its mere existence, its instrumentality is only figurative and not like that of a true agent. For to say that acting is the same as causing to act would be making the 'action' (by mere existence) into an instrumentality, and what is past is not to be described as future.

Further it entails a regress. If action were an instrument, there ought to be another action by which it would be impelled. Without this other action, no instrumentality would be possible for it. This other action would also be the instrument of still another action, and that of another, and so on. Since the chain of actions would never cease, it would never accomplish its result. If it is said that a final one could cause the result without needing any further action, then why not the first one?

But it is not objectionable that the mental process should be knowable, because of the very fact that it is a revealer.

We see that revealers, such as light, are instruments just because of their inherent knowability, and so it is with the mental process too.

(Opponent) The eye and other sense-organs also are revealers, but they are unreliable, because (sometimes) they do not perceive.

(Answer) The reason is, that there is a mingling of two things of the same kind. The senses are physical, and since there is the light of the eye which appears simultaneously with the external light which is of a physically similar kind, there is confusion as to which it is that is being perceived. When the light of several lamps appears simultaneously, it cannot be made out which is the light of which. And so with the ears and other senses.

(Opponent) Then in the case of the inner sense, which is not physical, it is a revealer of the same kind as the mental process, since that too is a revealer. So the mental process will not be perceived.

(Answer) Not so. Thanks to the consciousness (caitanya) with which it is endowed, it is not separate or distanced (from consciousness). Self (ātman) is all-pervading, and being subtle and extremely pure, has perception of the mental process because the mind is not distanced from it. Therefore it is established that Puruṣa, taking on the form of that very mental process of right knowledge, is aware of it. It is that being known which is the result.

Some maintain that a mental process is not directly knowable and there is no means to perceive any result (of right knowledge). For a result to be perceived, some unknown (means of) knowledge must be presumed. (They have to say that) no result is perceived, because they accept no proof that could operate to perceive it. And if one were accepted, there would be a regress. A right knowledge assumed to perceive the result (of right knowledge) will itself have a result, for which another right knowledge will be needed in proof, and there will be no end of the chain.

On their view, since there is no right knowledge of it, it must follow that this result does not exist, because there is no proof. Where means of proof which would reveal some existence do not go into operation, we assume that the thing is not there.

(Opponent) There could still be a right knowledge of the result though not itself perceived.

(Answer) No, because that would go against its character of being a revealer. Though seen to be revealing, your revealer would not (itself) be perceived. But a torch, even on the peak of a mountain, never loses its innate character (of being visible).

(Opponent) The right knowledge, being simply a revealer, reveals its result also.

(Answer) That confirms what we are maintaining. For one has perceptions of love and hate as particular mental processes. 'I love' and 'I hate' are each a particular process of the I-idea (aham-pratyaya); the perception of the mental process of love and so on is by perceiving oneself as having or not having them. Otherwise there would indeed be necessary some other means of knowledge to know them, as if they were external forms. And then there would be a regress.

So refusal to recognize that right knowledge has a result (i.e. being witnessed by Puruṣa) is arrogant obstinacy and should be disregarded as vain argument.

Inference is the mental process which has as its field the relation of inclusion of what is to be inferred among things of a like class, and exclusion of it from those of a different class. It is mainly concerned with determining a universal.

What is to be inferred, all about what one seeks to know; *inclusion,* as being like them in characteristics and nature, *and exclusion,* since it is not found there. *Relation:* what is this relation, and what two things does it relate? For a relation does not relate without two things to be related, as is clear from the sentence beginning with the relative pronoun *which.*

(Opponent) This inference is well known to be simply a relation between an indicatory mark and its possessor.

(Answer) No, for that would not suffice for drawing a conclusion (gamaka). A mere relation does not in itself lead to a conclusion. The relation with the mark has to be one of exclusion or inclusion. This is a question of the mark; it is no more than having or not having the mark, and that does lead to a conclusion.

(Opponent) But the mark alone is not thus conclusive without reference to a possessor of it. If a mark is to be taken as conclusive without reference to a relation between it and its possessor, then anything at all would be conclusive; so the relation should have been specified as relating these two.

(Answer) He has specified it, in the words *which has as its field inclusion among things of a like class to what is to be inferred.* Unless it were connected with what is to be inferred, namely the possessor of the mark, it would not be included among things of a like class, or excluded from things of an opposite class. So the clause beginning *which* confirms the generally accepted relation.

A mental process having as its field the things related and their relation, specified positively and negatively (anvaya-vyatireka), *mainly concerned with determining a universal,* a universal possessing the indicatory mark.

> *As having motion is inferred in the moon and stars, from their getting to another place, as with the man Caitra.*

The matter is clear merely from the definition. But to give instances and counter-instances demonstrates very plainly that there are actual examples of it. When it is said that the moon and stars have motion, it means that having motion is to be inferred in them. A corresponding (universal, namely) getting to another place, appears in things of like class which have motion, such as the man Caitra, and this excludes the stationary things of a different class, such as the Vindhya range. The relation is certain, because having motion is constant (in the examples of getting to another place).

So a relation, invariably in the particular class, can inform one of another thing related, as in the case of cat and mouse (vadhya-ghātaka, hunter and prey) in causal relation.

(Opponent) Allowing that between things which are not mutually exclusive there can be a permanent relation such as getting to another place, which leads to a conclusion, but there is no relation between cat and mouse, which are incompatibles, so how can you say there is anything to lead to a conclusion?

(Answer) The argument holds because there is a permanent relation between them (though invisible). Even in the case of the heavenly bodies, the feature of 'getting there' is not directly manifest to us (being too slow): if it were, the conclusion that they have motion would not be a case of inference (sāmānyato dṛṣṭa) at all. It is not in the moon and stars that the indicatory relation of getting there is directly perceived (though it is perceived in the case of the man).

(Opponent) If a relation can be conclusive even though not directly perceived, then everything would be conclusive as to everything, for there is nothing which is not related to everything else, since they are all in universal space.

(Answer) That is why the relation, in the field of inference, is only what suffices to cause the rise of the idea bringing the desired conclusion (gamya-gamaka). With the cat and mouse, from seeing one of them, one concludes the absence of the other, which is a pure inference. From seeing that a thing is not in its usual place, it is concluded that it is somewhere else, just as from the sight of the cat one infers absence of the mouse. There is the familiar example, 'when Caitra, a living man, is seen not to be at home, he is out.'

(The discussion now becomes technical. The opponent wishes to show that besides the three mentioned in the sūtra there are other means of right knowledge. One of these is cognition of absence, and a classical example referred to several times is this: a man looking for a jar glances into a bare room and concludes, 'the jar is not here'. The opponent calls this direct cognition of absence of the jar. Śaṅkara brings it under an inference from the sight of the bare floor, making it an idea and not a direct perception.)

(Opponent) Surely these are (the proofs postulated by some schools called) cognition of absence (a-bhāva) and presumption (arthāpatti), and not inference, for they do not depend on indicatory features like the horns of a cow for instance.

(Answer) No, because they do have indicatory features, namely the ones stated. The relation between cat and mouse has the feature of mutual exclusion. Wherever the cat may be, the mouse is never there – this is the invariable connection. The presence of the cat invariably means absence of the mouse, so also presence of the mouse means absence of the cat; it is like the presence of smoke and the inferred presence of fire.

(Opponent) How does the idea of the absence of the mouse from its usual haunts come to be known from the mere sight of the cat there? The operation of the means of right knowledge of existent things is in regard to the cat alone, and not to the mouse.

(Answer) From the mere right knowledge operating in regard to the cat's presence, the idea of the absence of the mouse arises, as from the mere right knowledge operating in regard to the presence of smoke there arises an idea of the presence of fire. Right knowledge operating as regards the specific characteristics of the cat gives rise to the idea of the absence of the specific characteristics of the mouse, just as the idea of the specific characteristics of fire arises from right knowledge operating in regard to the specific characteristics of smoke.

But for the one who argues for absence as a right knowledge, that knowledge of absence which he claims could never be specific; following up the sight of one of the incompatibles (like the cat) does not give actual sight of the absence of the other one (the mouse). Whereas to follow up a particular indicatory mark is as it were sight of the particular possessor of the mark. There is nothing specific about *absence* of the operation of right knowledge capable of revealing existent things, through which an idea could be formed of anything specific.

(Opponent) There is a specific thing which one wishes to know (for instance, whether the jar is there or not, and one knows it) from absence of any right knowledge of it.

(Answer) No; a non-existent can have nothing to do with associations of memory or will. What is non-existent like a hare's horn is never found producing an effect by association.

(Opponent) We find it now.

(Answer) No; the two things are on quite a different footing and it is not an example.

(Opponent) Well, there is a similarity.

(Answer) No, because in the case of the jar we see that it is real.

Nor is it reasonable that absence, which does not function because it is not a thing, should exist as a means of right knowledge. For in the world, what has no function is never found bringing about an effect. Therefore the *idea* of the absence of a knowable object, arising from a right knowledge capable of revealing it, is a knowable object like the idea of a jar; and because it is a fact, it causes some action or cessation of action. A counter-example is a non-existent like a hare's horn. A right knowledge of absence, supposed to be produced by absence, would not in fact come into existence at all, for we see from the examples given that a thing is like what is known to be its cause.

By the fact of being present, the sight of the cat is the indicatory mark for the idea of the absence of the mouse, and like the idea of smoke which causes the idea of fire, it dispels any doubt. Or one could say that the idea of the absence of the mouse, arising from the indicatory mark of the cat there, has a quality of certainty, like the idea of fire (from the indicatory mark of smoke).

(Opponent) The assertion 'the jar is not here' is not an inference, because it is not arrived at from an inferential relation of indicatory mark and its possessor. For the idea of fire is a following-up of an indication like smoke, but when it is said 'the jar is not here', there is no following-up of any such indication, because the idea is already there without it.

(Answer) Our position is not wrong. It is an idea in the form 'here' that is the indicatory mark. Following up the indication does not have to be from a previous idea of it. The mental impression in the form 'here' is the indicatory mark for the idea of the absence of the jar, the affirmative impression being excluded. Just as with the idea of the cat, here too the relation is one of exclusion. Where the things that cause the impression are not mutually exclusive, there is the idea 'it is'. It is because of this invariable relation that we say that what is called presumption (arthāpatti) is in fact merely inference.

In the case where the absence of a living man, Devadatta, in the house, means his presence outside, there is an inference both ways: when he is in, then he is not out, and when he is seen outside, this is his not being in – that is the pattern. The cause of the perception of absence is thus explained as the fact that something which could impress the mind is not impressing it.

The knowledge of powers like burning in fire, is mere inference. For in experience, we find in ourselves an unvarying relation of result and what causes it. It is seen in our own self: 'I can effect this result' or 'I cannot', which is a cognition of power specific to oneself as possessed by the self (ātman). The result is the exercise of the power of burning (or the latent powers in oneself), and this is certainly an inference.

(Opponent) Some give this instance of direct perception of something not there: Suppose that an object lit by some light is being viewed with the help of a mirror (placed behind it), though not of course as a unitary whole. Now what is seen (in the mirror) is not actually *there,* so that the same illuminating direct perception of what is there (the front of the object) also illumines what is not there.

They give this case also: someone is told, 'Fetch the robe which has no pattern on it.' On going to the store-room he finds a robe with a pattern next to one with no pattern. Seeing the patterned one, he knows by direct perception the robe distinguished by not having a pattern, and brings it. In this case there is no other means of right cognition except absence (through which he could know the robe).

(Answer) Not so; that would be to deny that objects are known through the mind's taking on their form. And it is generally accepted that whatever the mind takes the form of, that is known as it is by direct perception. In the case of a blue thing's being yellow (to vision affected by jaundice), the idea of the relation of the characteristic and its possessor turns out to be illusory (mithyā). In the same way, when it is said that the jar is not here, the idea of a relation of non-existence of the jar to the location Here is an idea of an unreal relation; no relation either acquired or inherent is conceivable between the absence of the jar and the location Here. Whereas when it is said that Devadatta is here, there is a relation. Therefore the idea of absence, like the blue thing's looking yellow, must be illusory as an idea, even though there is a notion of a relation of characteristic and its possessor.

If (you still say that) there is a relation between the absence of the jar and the location Here, then with a thing which is not blue, you will have a relation of non-existence of blueness, referring to an idea of a relation of blueness between the two things. But a relation is something that actually exists, and it is a contradiction to have this ambiguity about it, for you admit that absence is not an actual thing.

(Opponent) It is said by the grammarian, 'One hundred and one are the meanings of the genitive case' (as in absence *of* the jar, for instance).

(Answer) But then relationships could not be only of the two kinds called inherence and conjunction (as your school holds).

(Opponent) Let us say that the hundred and one relations of the genitive (including absence of the jar) can be subsumed under these two.

(Answer) No, for in the case of absence, it cannot belong to either.

Further, when it is said 'Here in the sky there is no flower', we get a relation of the sky which is invisible, and the absence of the sky-flower which is also invisible. It is all invisibility alone, and like the absence of flowers falling from the sky, so in the location Here on earth, the absence of the jar is invisible. It has to be said how it would be distinguished.

(Opponent) (The cause of the anomaly is) because space is not visible (whereas earth is).

(Answer) Not so. For if a flower does fall in space, we see that it exists. So the reason cannot be that space is not visible. Just as the invisibility of space cannot be a cause of the real existence of a falling flower, so it cannot be a cause of perception of the opposite of real existence.

(Opponent) The cause is simply the invisibility of space.

(Answer) Then the invisibility of anything concealed, though unrelated, would also have to be a cause.

(Opponent) The absence of sky-flowers is directly seen.

(Answer) That would mean that the connection of sense with its object would be unnecessary (for perception), and if so, it would follow that everyone would have extra-sensory perception and be omniscient.

(Opponent) Well, we admit that absence of sky-flowers is a case of inference (but not absence of the jar).

(Answer) As with the absence of the sky-flower, there is no distinguishing feature of 'absence of a jar here'; so it is certain that it is a matter of inference. Even for the proponent of absence as a means of right knowledge, the absence, for instance, of fire in waters concealed or remote must be a matter of inference; so the absence of a jar here, being of the same class, is knowable only by inference. This is the reasonable conclusion.

The Vindhya range has no movement because it does not get anywhere.

Another case of it is, that the Vindhya range has no movement because it does not get anywhere. The assertion is, that the Vindhya has no motion; the reason is, because it does not get anywhere. Taken with the case of Caitra, inference is shown working both ways, like the one-eyed crow (traditionally able to look all round). The relation is positive in the case of the moon and the stars having motion, and negative in the case of the Vindhya's not getting anywhere. It is thus demonstrated by both agreement in presence (anvaya) and agreement in absence (vyatireka), and the definition is complete.

Again, these applications show that illusion is ruled out (from the definition), and demonstrate that the definition has no defect because it applies equally to a different mark and its possessor.

When someone competent communicates by word something seen or inferred by him, with the intention of conveying to the other his own knowledge, the mental process whose object is the meaning obtained from the word, is authority for the hearer.

Someone competent motivated by goodwill to the other free from any defect (doṣa), his object being to tell *something seen or inferred by him, intending to convey to the other* to that particular hearer *his own knowledge* his own experience; *by word:* this here means a sentence, from which the particular meaning emerges. It is from the sentence that it is conveyed. The mental process whose object is the meaning of the sentence is mainly concerned with determining a universal, as in the case of inference.

Authority for the hearer: this sort of knowledge has been preceded by the original knowledge of the thing possessed by the speaker, for whom it is not authority, since he has in mind something seen or inferred by himself, so that his own knowledge has come through the senses or from some indication. Authority is not direct perception because it is not something within the field of the senses, and it is not inference because it does not depend on any such relation of indication and indicated as described above. For the knowledge arising from the meaning of the (scriptural) words 'heaven', 'apūrva' (the invisible power of the sacrifice which produced a later effect), and 'divinity' (of the sacrifice) does not come from some previously established relation of indication and indicated.

But as always with right knowledge, the result is an awareness of the mental process by Puruṣa.

When a speaker says questionable things, neither seen nor inferred by himself, this is fallacious authority. But if an original speaker has seen or inferred it, the authority is not suspect.

When a speaker says questionable things: when from his utterance, the mental process called authority arises, the result brought about by the operative statement is as before. The reference is to what is merely lacking in proof (i.e. not seen or inferred by the speaker himself), but that is not meant to exclude what is actually untrue, the operation of the statement being the same in both cases.

The authority of what is said by a speaker of something questionable is, however, to be distinguished. What is this something questionable which he speaks? It is something neither seen nor inferred by that speaker – for instance a Buddha or Arhat, since their teaching is other than what is well known to informed people (śiṣṭa). For a mind which is not infected with the taint of passion and so on will not describe otherwise what is well known (as true). *This is fallacious authority* being only a semblance (ābhāsa).

Though he has not spoken in so many words of semblance in the cases of direct perception and inference, by now pointing out that authority can in some cases be only a semblance, he implies that semblance is to be recognised as possible also in the previous cases of direct perception and inference, when their presentations are contrary to fact.

But if an original speaker has seen or inferred it: if it derives from the Lord as the first speaker, there is no reason to doubt, for his authority as a speaker of truth is unquestionable.

(Now the discussion turns to analogy (upamāna) which in some schools is rated as an independent means of knowledge. Śaṅkara denies this, to follow the sūtra which does not mention it.)

Analogy (upamāna, also comparison and resemblance) presupposes words, and therefore is not a separate means of right knowledge but comes under authority.

It occurs when having heard from a forest man 'a buffalo is like a cow', one sees a buffalo in the forest. Analogy is simply the memory of the similarity learnt from the previously heard sentence, and nothing more. The fact of similarity must have been previously learned from the words of the forest man.

Analogy is not simply learning the relation of name and named, though it too is grasped only from some sentence about it. One might see a buffalo in the forest and think 'it is a cow', because until he has come to know the word buffalo, he is not aware of the relation of name and named so as to think 'this is a buffalo'. The very word buffalo must refer back to some sentence about it: (in the case of analogy now discussed, the sentence was) 'a buffalo is like a cow.' It is clear to him only when he has previously heard a sentence about it.

(Opponent) But he has had no previous idea of what a buffalo is.

(Answer) You seem to be suffering from an inability to grasp the thrust of the argument – cornered like some wretched dog. *(This sentence has been heavily amended by the editors and is perhaps corrupt – Tr.)*

To insist that there must have been some previous experience would entail many different cases of resemblance, differing by closer or remoter association with various times and places and circumstances.

(Opponent) Let it be so.

(Answer) A previous idea of the thing is not the mass of associations formerly perceived; they are not the thing itself. For when the word 'cow' is spoken, one can always understand the meaning from the word itself without specifications of place and time and so on. The mere knowledge of the relation of name and named is not analogy, for analogy is something by which things are compared, being a knowledge of similarity. In comprehending the relation of name and named, no comparison of anything is being made; that comes afterwards. It is after hearing about the resemblance (from the sentence of the forest man) that he too makes the judgement, 'this is a buffalo'. So this (suggestion that analogy is nothing but the relation of name and named) fails.

(Opponent) Analogy could be an independent means of right knowledge, not consequent on words; the townsman, on seeing a buffalo in the forest, has the idea 'this is like a cow'.

(Answer) Not so, because there is no object which it is sought to know (prameya). It is when something is being sought that the appropriate means of right knowledge go into operation to reveal something existent. But there is in fact no one similarity covering the points of resemblance and difference of cow and buffalo.

(Opponent) There is the idea of resemblance, and this must have some basis.

(Answer) True, and it is here that a distinction has to be made: (a) is this like the notion (pratyaya) of a collection, such as a forest? or (b) is it like the idea (buddhi) of a thing like a jar?

Suppose it is like the notion of a forest, where the individual trees making up the pattern of growth are the causes of the notion 'forest', which does not exist apart from them. Just so the members (of the patterns) 'cow' and 'buffalo', through memories of the separate herds that have been seen, are the cause of determining a similarity, which does not exist apart from them. Therefore we arrive at something unreal.

Then let it be that there is here a factuality and demonstrability like the notion of a jar. It is now to be asked: what sort of fact this is. (There are these possibilities:)

Is it a single similarity, conforming to cow and buffalo, but distinct from cow-ness and buffalo-ness?

Or if they are distinct from each other

If (there are two similarities) distinct from each other, located in cow and buffalo but apart from them, are these qualified or not qualified by each other?

Is it that an individual has characteristics of the other class?

Is it that a class has characteristics of an individual of the other side?

Or is (the similarity) a class with characteristics of individuals of both sides?

Again, still further relations between them ought to be postulated with either one being the qualified and the other one the qualifier.

Of these cases, if there is a single similarity applying to both sides, then there is nothing to be compared, because it is just a single thing, as if one should say 'a cow is like a cow'.

(Opponent) By the similarity, one of two individuals may be compared.

(Answer) Not so: that would be referring to itself, as in 'like a cow because of cow-ness'.

(Opponent) One individual may be compared with another like it.

(Answer) Not that either, for cow-ness is not a basis for likening a young calf with half horns and a hornless cow.

(Opponent) By considering where their characteristics differ, the similarity can be made a basis for the idea of comparison.

(Answer) Then the similarity perishes. If a differing characteristic is to be the basis of the idea of comparison, you have proposed a destroyer of the similarity.

Furthermore there would be alternatives, such as whether a characteristic under consideration is single, having similarity to both sides, or divided, and there is just the same impossibility as before.

(Opponent) Let us say that the similarity is divided.

(Answer) The very assumption of a division refutes it: a horse is not like a cow. If things are taken one by one, the innumerable considerations become unmanageable. The previously proposed relations between class and individual are refuted in the same way.

Now take the hypothesis that similarity is an imaginary abstraction consisting of bringing out one idea by ignoring any opposing ideas. In that case, how is it that the notion of the spaces in the forest, in front of the trees and to their right and left, is not taken – by ignoring everything else – as a *thing* (as the trees are taken as a forest, in disregard of the spaces)?

(Opponent) Let it be that the idea of the forest is merely the trees which cause the idea of it.

(Answer) If so, 'a cow is similar to a buffalo' is merely an illusory notion (mithyā-pratyaya), as the idea of a forest is.

(Opponent) Well, if as you have said opposites cannot be compared, how is it that a horse is likened to a cow (as a domestic animal, for instance)?

(Answer) Both sides have parts, opposite or corresponding, in themselves which are causes of the idea of analogy, and it comes to the same thing as the notion of a forest.

The point need not be laboured too much: these many parts observed on both sides are the cause of the idea of similarity, as the trees cause the idea of a forest, and so it is established that there is no independent means of right knowledge called analogy (but it is included under authority).

(Reverting to the general point of authority as a means of right knowledge:) Nor should we imagine that since what is knowable is of just two kinds (perceptible or imperceptible), the means of right knowledge must be of just two kinds also (perception and inference, as Buddhists hold). Why not? Because an object is known as determined by the right knowledge, and it is not to be supposed that the object determines the right knowledge. If each object determined the knowledge of it, then everyone would be omniscient. In (the sacred declaration) 'From worship in the temple comes heaven', the idea of worship as the cause of attaining heaven is not in the field of perception or of inference, and it would be illusory unless one supposed a separate right knowledge for it.

(Opponent) This idea could be a corollary of an inference.

(Answer) If it is only a corollary, it would not itself be in the class of a right knowledge; in that case, the same would apply to the idea of what is referred to in the (sacred Buddhist) Three Refuges and so on.

In any case, the purpose here is not to analyse right knowledge. The main thing is to point out the accepted means of right knowledge, and other mental processes, with a view to inhibit them. The author of the sūtra-s, therefore, did not make further sūtra-s on them, and the commentator merely added something to confirm what is generally accepted. What objection can there be to following him?

Sūtra I.8

Illusion is false knowledge based on an untrue form

Illusion (viparyaya) is false knowledge (mithyā-jñāna) based on an untrue form.

Having explained right knowledge, now is described the mental process called *illusion:* it *is false knowledge based on an untrue form.*

(Opponent) Our subject is inhibition, and furthermore the release which comes from it, and furthermore the bondage to be escaped from, and furthermore the Ignorance (avidyā) which is the root of bondage. Ignorance is illusion, so this is the main thing to be inhibited. For it is the cause of bondage, and when the cause is inhibited, it follows that its effect is inhibited also. So illusion is the principal thing and should have been explained before right knowledge.

(Answer) Certainly illusion is the first thing as regards needing inhibition. But human efforts at inhibition are based on knowledge of what is correct and what is faulty, and that knowledge of the correct and faulty must be right knowledge. Without right knowledge, the evils of illusion would not be realized, nor would one know about inhibition and the means leading to it. So it was proper to take the mental process of right knowledge first. What is correct and what is erroneous are known by right knowledge; illusion is described immediately afterwards, as more important than any of the remaining mental processes. The reason is that inhibition of illusion must precede that of the others, since it is their root.

Illusion is false knowledge, they are synonyms, *based on an untrue form,* is the definition. The form of a thing is the true form, and what is not its form is an untrue form of it, an experience of a semblance of it (yad-ābhāsam vijñānam); the basis of the experience is that on which it rests.

Illusion is an idea which has merely a common element with something of which the particular is not now being perceived, which is aided with the memory of another thing experienced previously, associated with the definite form of it, and arising with an appearance of certainty.

Doubt has the form 'there is this similarity between the two things', and it arises in the mind of one who seeks to know, when seeing the similarity, which of the two things it is; doubt is classed purely as memory. The doubt 'Is this a post or a man?' arises only from the memory of the previously perceived individual things. Not so illusion, for there just one of the memories becomes conclusive. In a place where a post has been set up at some time, there arises the definite idea 'this is a man', coming from the memory of a man aroused by perception of something of the appropriate height and breadth and so on.

Although illusion is in the main like something perceived by way of the senses, it is not right knowledge because it is based on a memory of something not now there.

Why is it not right knowledge? Because it is negated by right knowledge. The object of right knowledge is a thing as it is, and the fact of not being right knowledge is shown by the fact that right knowledge cancels it. For instance, seeing the moon as double is negated by seeing that it is in fact a single moon.

Because it is negated by right knowledge: it is no more than a memory and its object is not an actual thing. For an object which is merely remembered is not there now.

(Opponent) So it turns out to be no more than a memory.

(Answer) No, because it distinctly appears. A memory is caused by a thing having been perceived in another place, and appears in the form 'this is how it was experienced'. An illusion is not like that. The illusion-idea arises when there is what amounts to a memory, possessing a close similarity and conformity in time and place etc. to some thing (now being perceived), and appearing distinctly as 'this'. Thus illusion has neither the character of right knowledge, nor that of memory, and is a separate kind of mental process.

Now the commentator gives an example to show how what is not right knowledge is negated by right knowledge. *Just as seeing the moon as double is negated by seeing that it is in fact a single moon.*If diseased vision sees things otherwise than as they are, sees (for instance) the moon as double, then by apprehending what it really is, the thing as it is, a single moon, the false view is negated. It is negated by means of the memory of the knowledge that the apparent second moon is really non-existent.

(Opponent) On a grammatical point: dvi-candra-darśanam (seeing a double moon) is a dvigu compound of the same class as dvipūlī (two bundles) or pañcapūlī (five bundles), as we learn from the Pāṇini sūtra 2.4.1, which teaches that where the last element ends in the letter 'a', the compound preferably takes the feminine form (i.e. the final 'a' becomes 'ī'). The word dvi-candra is a dvigu compound ending in 'a', and ought to have had the 'ī' ending.

(Answer) The form is not wrong because Pāṇini allows exceptions, for pātra etc., and the word etcetera there refers to a whole class. This class retains the final 'a' and is in accordance with the usage of the learned, and the compound dvi-candra should be taken as included in it. It is the type of compound called bahuvrīhi, and means the seeing in which there are two moons. It is unquestionable that the compound eka-candra (one-moon) is never a dvigu.

And this is the Five-fold Ignorance (avidyā), namely the taints (kleśa): Ignorance, I-am-ness, passion, hate, clinging to life. These have technical names: darkening, delusion, great-delusion, darkness, blind darkness. They will be discussed later, under defilements of the mind.

This illusion is Ignorance, of which there are five parts. As to what they are, they will be listed (in sūtra II.3): Ignorance, I-am-ness (asmitā), passion (rāga), hate (dveṣa), and clinging to life (abhiniveṣa). Ignorance and the others are taints which are each distinguished by a special technical name, defined in other classics as darkening (tamas) and the others, and they will be described in the second part as associated with the impurities of the mind.

Sūtra I.9

Logical construction is something that follows on verbal knowledge but has no real object

This (vikalpa) does not amount to right knowledge.

Now he describes logical construction. Verbal knowledge means knowledge from words, and *something that follows on verbal knowledge* means something whose nature is to follow from the verbal knowledge, good or bad, which comes from the fixed relation between words and their meanings; *but has no real object* means that nothing is actually expressed, inasmuch as there is no actual (yathābhūta) thing as the meaning of those words from which that knowledge follows. Logical construction is thinking without reference to any actual thing.

(Opponent) If it follows on verbal knowledge, it should be taken as authority.

(Answer) *It does not amount to right knowledge.* It does not fall under authority because it has no real object. Authority does arise from verbal knowledge, but it relates to actual things. So authority has a real object, indicated by the words, whereas logical construction, having no real object, is not right knowledge.

Moreover, logical construction is the same in the speaker and the hearer; in both of them the idea of the logical construction has arisen from words. Not so authority, which is such for the hearer alone; for the speaker it is what he has seen or inferred.

Again, for one in the samādhi without verbal associations (nir-vitarka), logical construction ceases, but not authority. Therefore it does not amount to a right knowledge.

Nor does it amount to illusion. Though its object is non-existent, it is by the prestige of verbal knowledge that worldly life is upheld wholly. As for example when it is said 'consciousness is the nature of Puruṣa', since Puruṣa is consciousness alone, what is being described here, and by what? Yet an idea does arise by way of description, as in the case of the words 'Caitra's cow'.

(Opponent) Since its object does not exist, it should be included under illusion.

(Answer) *Nor does it amount to illusion.* Why not? Because it follows on verbal knowledge. Illusion – though its object too is non-existent – has no reference to verbal knowledge; it has been defined as false knowledge based on an untrue form. But logical construction is an extension of ideas determined by a right knowledge. Illusion is in the end removed, because it contradicts everything else; not so, logical construction, because that conforms to ideas from a right knowledge.

So the expressions *whose object is non-existent* and *following on verbal knowledge,* taken together, point to a separate mental process, logical construction, which is distinct both from right knowledge and from illusion, though it has a trace of each of them about it. Inasmuch as there is this trace of them about it, logical construction is introduced immediately after them instead of memory, because memory is based simply upon something experienced formerly.

(Opponent) No such mental process can be established, because it has no real form.

(Answer) *Though its object is non-existent, it is by the prestige of verbal knowledge that worldly life is upheld wholly.* The word *wholly* is intended to make it clear that there is no other cause apart from verbal knowledge. To the demand for an example he says, *consciousness is the nature of Puruṣa.* As the power-of-consciousness has been defined as unchanging, Puruṣa is simply consciousness. That being the thing itself, there is no difference between them, and the words 'the consciousness of Puruṣa' do not amount to a description, which always presupposes some difference somewhere.

To make this point, the grammarian says in his work Vārttika, 'A thing is established by bringing out a secondary element (in the description).' In the present case, 'Caitra's cow' assumes a difference, and 'Puruṣa's consciousness' is just like it in form; but Puruṣa is not something different from consciousness, so the words cannot be descriptive, whereas Caitra's difference from his cow is the basis of a description. Nor is consciousness anything different from Puruṣa, which could make for a description. And yet, the idea does appear that 'consciousness is the nature of Puruṣa' is somehow a description, implying relation between different things.

> *'Puruṣa is actionless' is a denial that it has the property of a thing. Similarly, when it is said 'the arrow stops' or the arrow has stopped', we understand cessation of movement and the thing as itself alone. So 'Puruṣa does not come to have properties' means simply the absence of properties coming to be for him, not that Puruṣa does have a property – of not coming to be. Thus the properties, by which the life of the world goes on, are imagined logical constructs.*

Vastu-dharma means the property (dharma) of a thing or fact (vastu); pratiśiddha-vastu-dharmā means that the fact of having a property is denied of him. As Pāṇini says (sūtra 5.4.124) *dharmādanic kevalāt-* the word dharma becomes dharman and hence dharmā by the change called samāsānta at the end of a compound which is to be taken as a whole.

The word *thing* indicates the guṇa-s like sattva, and their properties are denied of Puruṣa.

It is not that the very denial would mean that the properties of sattva and the others must be possible in Puruṣa. The meaning is simply this: they do not exist in any Puruṣa so that they could be described as 'his'. But even so, just as there is an idea of description in the words 'the spotted cows are his', so there is an idea of description in the words 'the properties are denied of him'.

Again, to say 'action has gone from him' implies a previous connection with action, as when we say 'action has gone from Caitra' (an idiom for 'Caitra is taking a rest'). Action is impossible in Puruṣa, so it is impossible for action to go from Puruṣa. Still, the sentence 'Puruṣa is without action' does give an idea of description.

Puruṣa does not come to have properties means that the coming-into-existence of properties is not found in him, as has been said. The commentator explains: *it means simply the absence of properties coming to be for him.* For instance, he is without guṇa-s, pure, without parts. Giving the various examples in regard to the self (ātman) is to define by exclusion what the self really is.

The arrow stops, the arrow will stop, the arrow has stopped. A well-known example from life is given to resolve any remaining doubt. *Stops* is cessation of movement, absence of movement. There is no conjunction of an absence with any of the three periods of time, nor of an arrow as a substance regardless of function, nor any connection of the cessation of movement, which is an absence, with an arrow which is a thing. Thus the three examples are given: the arrow stops, will stop, has stopped.

(Opponent) The bare meaning of the root 'stop' is cessation of motion. What subject can there be for a predicate like cessation of motion?

(Answer) This is why other examples are given. Unless they are distinct, neither subject nor predicate can exist. There is a verbal root having the sense of cessation of motion, and an idea of description is aroused by the designative power of the words, implying a relation between an existent subject and existent predicate. This is how the object of a logical construction is produced, as demonstrated in the various examples.

Sūtra I.10

The mental process which rests on the notion of non-existence is sleep

This is a special notion arising from the recollection on waking in the form of 'I slept well; my mind is calm and has cleared up my understanding', or else 'I slept badly, my mind is dull and wanders aimlessly' or again 'I slept sunk in stupor; my limbs seem heavy and my mind is limp and faint, as if some force had seized control of it.' There would be no recollection on waking unless caused by an experience; without an experience there would be no memories based on it and corresponding to it. Therefore sleep is a particular notion, and like all the others it is to be inhibited in samādhi.

Now the sūtra describes sleep: *The mental process which rests on the notion of nonexistence is sleep (nidrā).* Right knowledge, illusion, and logical construction, which have just been explained, are in the waking condition, and sleep begins when they cease; so sleep is now described, immediately after them.

Non-existence means absence of the waking state, not absolute non-existence, because there could be no notion of that. The *notion of non-existence* means that there is a notion about non-existence. The mental process of which this is the support is one which rests on the notion of non-existence, and that is sleep (nidrā), a dreamless state (suṣupta-avasthā).

(Opponent) The dreaming state (svapna-avasthā) also must be included in sleep.

(Answer) It does not come under sleep as defined here, because the sūtra (I.38) will distinguish them: *Or by meditation on the knowledge of dream (svapna) and sleep (nidrā).* There sleep (nidrā) refers only to dreamless sleep. It is only dreamless sleep that rests on the notion of non-existence. Dreaming does not rest on that notion, but on memory, and memory is of something experienced. The commentator illustrates this point about memory when he says that in dream, things remembered become actualized (comm. to sūtra I.11).

It is evident that dream is a mental process, and there is no doubt about that. But the question does arise about dreamless sleep, and so the commentator says, *Dreamless sleep is a special notion arising from the recollection on waking.* Unless there had been a notion, there could hardly be a recollection. And when one wakes, one does recall, 'I have slept well' and so on. The recollection itself is a reflection of the notion that I have experienced something; unless there had been some experience, that reflection would not be there, nor could there reasonably be any memories about it. If dreamless sleep were not a notion, there would not be any effects or notional experiences such as *my mind has cleared up my understanding (of a problem)*, where mind is active.

Again, there is the experience *I slept badly, my mind is dull,* static, ineffective; or again *My limbs seem heavy (guruguru)* – following the sūtra 8.1.12 of the grammarian, the repetition of the word indicates some resemblance, so that the meaning is that they feel heavyish; *my mind is limp, as if some force had seized control of it* out of my possession, as it were. There are these various memories, effects and recollections, and the commentator has presented three of them by which it is established that sleep is a particular notion.

Again, a man who has been asleep in an inner room, without any hint from outside however slight, has recollected immediately on waking 'I have slept a long time', and this would otherwise be inexplicable.

(Opponent) These are not memories, because a memory must be of some particular thing which one has experienced, whereas on waking from dreamless sleep one does not remember any definite thing.

(Answer) In the infant as soon as he is born, we see the desire for union with the breast, which he has never experienced in this life. It is not something automatic; purposeful activity is always consequent on some memory, as we see in adults. So here, the recollection whose object is dreamless sleep must follow from some notion just because it is a recollection, like recollections of what has been perceived in the waking state. The heaviness of limb and so on of a man waking from dreamless sleep is an effect, preceded by some experience of discomfort or the like; the heaviness is an effect in its field, the limb. Just as it is certain that this effect has been preceded by some experience of discomfort, so it is certain that sleep is a special notion.

Sūtra I.11

Memory is not letting slip away an object experienced

Now he explains memory. *Memory is not letting slip away an object experienced.* Memory is described at the end because it is the effect of all the other mental processes, beginning with right knowledge.

The compound *object-experienced* means both what has been experienced and a particular object. That alone is the object which has been experienced, but what has been experienced is not necessarily an object. Otherwise a memory of another memory would be no memory, because a memory has no qualities like sound (as objects have). And since memory is intelligible to itself, it is necessary to have also memory of other memories. *Not letting slip away* means that there is no stealing away or disappearance (of any of it). Though the object itself is not present, memory is, by reason of similarity to it, an appearance as if the object were being perceived.

> *Is it the object, or the thought of it, that the mind remembers? The thought, coloured by the thing known, shines out in the forms both of the thing and the knowledge of it, and sets up a saṃskāra of the same kind. That manifests in accordance with its manifesting cause. The saṃskāra gives rise to a memory also consisting of the thing known and the knowing experience. A thought has primarily the form of the knowing experience; memory has primarily the form of the thing known.*

Thought and memory are equally appearances in the form of their object, so wherein lies the difference? To show the distinction between them he begins, *Is it the object, or the thought of it, that the mind remembers?* Though there is a distinction by the fact that (in memory) the object must have been experienced, but (in thought it is only that it) is not being experienced now, still there is a confusion because of their similarity, and he clears it up to show that there is a cause-and-effect relation between the two. Here the Vaināśika Buddhists, who do not admit anything external, say that the only cause is thought (buddhi). Well, is it an object or a thought that the mind remembers? (As objects of the verb of remembering, both words are in the genitive case in the text.) *Mind remembers:* he rules out any agency of Puruṣa, showing that it is only memory and thought that are agents. For the agency of thought, or agency of memory, are not from Puruṣa, because thoughts are simply objects perceived by Puruṣa. It will be shown later how things like jars must, by the very fact of being seen, be other than their perceiver.

Now, if mind remembers the *object,* then since the latter is also the object of the thought, memory would be no different from a thought. Yet if it is the *thought* that mind remembers, it would not accord with the sūtra which refers to a perceived object. For then the sūtra should have said 'not letting slip away an experience of perception'. So he says *coloured by the thing known;* resting on the thing known, it is coloured by it, like a crystal coloured by red lac placed behind it. *shining out in the forms both of the thing and the knowledge of it:* appearing as the form of the jar, which is perceived as having a wide base and so on, and in its own luminous aspect as knowledge, and so shining out in both forms.

The thought arises, and then while dying away lays down a saṃskāra in its possessor, the thinker. The saṃskāra corresponds to its cause and so has the two forms. *That manifests in accordance with its manifesting cause (sva-vyañjaka-añjana).* The manifesting cause is the karma which is the cause of the thought that lays down the saṃskāra, whose result is another action of a similar kind, which appears directly to produce its own result. And so he will say (sūtra IV.8), *Therefore their consequent manifestation is of those saṃskāra-group s (vāsanā) that are compatible with it (the fruition of their karma).* Or (one could say that) what is set up by the karma is a representation of a similar kind. Manifesting in accordance with its manifesting cause means, that it is made to appear as what manifests it.

The saṃskāra gives rise to a memory also consisting of the thing known and the knowing experience. Otherwise there would be no maturing of the karma which is its manifestor.

Of these, the thought has primarily the form of the knowing process. The knowing process is acceptance – pure receptivity precedes any knowing (of a particular thing). For one is not aware of a particular thing until there is first some (general) knowing process, desired or undesired; it is as when a light has been lowered into a jar (with perforations, see sūtra 1.25) and then the net of radiance comes out (by the holes).

Memory has primarily the form of the thing known, because it refers to something that has been experienced. If memory were primarily of a knowing process it would be like an idea and would not have reference to something experienced. But it does have that reference. So in memory it is the thing known, the object, which comes first, not the knowing process. Still, it comprises both, inasmuch as the memory and the saṃskara have the same (double) form. If one of them (the form of the object or of the knowing process) were excluded, memory would be impossible. And so it is said to be retention of an experienced object. The memory and the thought may be of the same object, and in both of them there is a knowing process, but there is no fallacy of equivocation (in the above account).

> *The latter (i.e. memory) is of two kinds: where the things remembered are actualized, and where they are not. In dream the things remembered become actual, but at the time of waking such things are not actualized. All memories arise from experience of right knowledge, of illusion, of logical construction, of sleep, or of other memories, and all these are essentially pleasure and pain and delusion. Pleasure and pain and delusion are to be explained as taints: Desire is the consequence of pleasure (II.7), Hate is the consequence of pain (II.8), while Delusion is Ignorance (II.5). All these mental processes are to be inhibited. When they are inhibited there is either cognitive or ultra-cognitive samādhi.*

Memory is of two kinds. What two? *Where the things remembered are actualized and where they are not. Actualized* (bhāvita) means that the thing has a reality because it is continuously brought into being – as a stream of oil is continuously brought into being out of some different substance. Because it is continuously actualized it does not need any further effort of attention etc. (to sustain it).

A case where the thing remembered does not need any further effort of attention is the memories actualized in dream. But in the waking state it is the reverse; there is need of further efforts of attention (to sustain memory). *All memories arise from experiences of right knowledge* and the other mental processes, *and all these are essentially pleasure and pain and delusion* which are the nature of saṃsāra. Pleasure and pain and delusion are to be explained as taints by the sūtra-author when he will say: *to the clear-sighted, everything is pain alone (II.15).* Here, however, he is merely saying where they abide.

Therefore the mental processes are to be inhibited, because they are essentially pleasure and pain and delusion. What then? *When they are inhibited, there is either cognitive or ultra-cognitive samādhi.*

> *Now what means are there for their inhibition?*

Sūtra I.12

Their inhibition is by practice and detachment

Flowing both ways, the so-called stream of the mind flows to good or flows to evil. When it is borne on to release, down into the field of discrimination, that is the flow towards good: when it is borne on to saṃsāra, down into the field of failure to discriminate, that is the evil flow. By detachment the current towards objects is dammed, and by practice of discriminating vision the auspicious current of discrimination is made to flow. Thus inhibition of the mental process depends on both.

He explains the means for their inhibition: *Their inhibition is by practice and detachment.* The characteristics of practice and detachment will be described in the coming sūtra-s. By these two the mental processes already described are inhibited, because they are opposed to them. Inhibition (nirodha) means cessation (upaśama). To show discrimination as the object of practice and detachment, the commentary explains the mind-stream.

The men of saṃsāra are always carried by the mind, as by a stream, towards objects. They are *borne on to saṃsāra,* ending up in saṃsāra, which is like an ocean, *dammed up:* held back, *made to flow*: set in movement, by making an opening. The form udghāṭyate is an optional retention of the long vowel in the causative, which otherwise would be short according to the Pāṇini sūtra 6.4.92.

So *it depends on both,* it is dependent on both practice and detachment.

Sūtra I.13

Practice is the effort at steadiness in it

Steadiness is the tranquil flow of the mind without mental processes. Practice is the effort thereto, the vigour, the enthusiasm, in undertaking the discipline to that end.

To explain the practice for it, he says, *Practice is the effort at steadiness in it. in it* means in their inhibition. The word *steadiness* is in the locative case, to show causality. The steadiness which is the cause of the inhibition of the mind is the result of effort, and the effort which is its cause is practice, *the tranquil flow* as it were of a stream free from mud is a transformation into a pure form *of a mind without mental processes,* which have been inhibited.

Effort: vigour, enthusiasm, are synonyms.

Practice is undertaking the discipline, the yoga discipline of restraints and observances and the others listed in sūtra II.29, *to that end.*

Sūtra I.14

But practised for a long time, uninterruptedly and with reverence, it becomes firmly grounded

Practised for a long time, practised uninterruptedly, practised with reverence – carried through with austerity, with brahmacarya, with knowledge and with faith, in reverence, it becomes firmly grounded. The meaning is that the purpose is not suddenly overwhelmed by an extravertive saṃskāra.

But how does this become firm? He says, *Practised for a long time, uninterruptedly.* Unless it is for a long time, and unless it is uninterrupted, the practice does not become firmly grounded, and therefore both are mentioned. The practice is also specified as to be done with reverence. He explains that *firmly grounded* means that it is not overwhelmed by an extravertive saṃskāra *suddenly* in a rush.

Sūtra I.15

Detachment is consciousness of self-mastery, of one who has no thirst for any object either seen or heard about

Detachment is the consciousness of self-mastery of one who has no thirst for any object either seen or heard about. It is that consciousness in one who is unmoved by visible objects like women, food and drink, or power, who is without thirst for objects heard about such as attainment of heaven or the state of the gods or of those absorbed into prakṛti, is inwardly aware of the defects in them by the power of his meditation, and who is wholly impassive – that consciousness of self-mastery which has nothing to avoid and nothing to accept, is detachment.

To describe detachment (vairāgya) he says, *Detachment is the consciousness of self-mastery of one who has no thirst for any object either seen or heard about.* The word *object* has to be taken twice: without thirst for any object seen, and without thirst for any object heard about.

Visible objects means what are both objects and directly perceived. What would they be? He illustrates with the examples of women, food and drink, and power. Though there is an infinity of objects, yet the principal impulse of passion is to possess women, food and drink, and power. In these cases passion is at its most powerful and is to be opposed with corresponding effort. So with *objects heard about,* which here means those described in the scriptures – the attractions of going to heaven, the joy of being dissolved into prakṛti, or the pleasure of the discarnate state of the gods.

(Opponent) Detachment (vairāgya, without rāga or passion) is simply freedom from thirst, for it will be said (comm. to sūtra II.7), *Passion is thirst, is greed.*

(Answer) No, for there are four distinct stages in the state of detachment: (1) awareness of striving, (2) awareness of transgressions, (3) awareness of mind alone, and (4) awareness of mastery. The awareness common to these four is detachment. So the commentator says that it is absence of thirst for visible objects or objects heard about, but it is the fourth one, to which the other three are preliminary, which he means, not a detachment which is merely freedom from thirst (perhaps temporary, in the absence of the objects or perhaps without knowledge that they exist).

He explains, *he who is inwardly aware of the defects in them* – seeing the defects causes detachment from objects, whereas seeing good points in them causes passion;

by the power of his meditation by practising meditation on seeing their defects; *who is wholly impassive* wholly unresponsive to objects *even when right in front of such things,* earthly or heavenly. As a crystal does not in fact take the colour of objects beside it, so his mind is in a state free from passion for them.

that consciousness of mastery, consciousness that they can be mastered. It is the state when all that is called desirable is recognized to be capable of being mastered, the state when it is realized that the senses have been mastered, or when the mastery becomes conscious.

Sūtra I.16

It is the higher detachment when from knowledge of Puruṣa there is no thirst for (even) the guṇa-s

One who is aware of the defects in objects visible or heard about is detached from objects, but one who from practising the vision of Puruṣa has his mind pure like it and clear-seeing, is detached from even the guṇa-s, with their qualities manifest or unmanifest. Thus detachment is of two kinds.

The second, higher one is nothing but pure Knowledge. When it rises, the yogin in whom this Knowledge has dawned thinks, 'Attained is what was to be attained, destroyed are the taints which were to be destroyed; broken is the continuous chain of the cycle of being, bound by which men born will die, and having died will be born.' Detachment is the highest peak of Knowledge: it borders on Transcendental Aloneness.

Detachment is of two kinds, higher or lower according to what it refers to. The lower has been described, now the higher is stated: *It is the higher detachment when from knowledge of Puruṣa there is no thirst for even the guṇa-s. It* refers to detachment. *higher* means that it comes at a later time than the first-mentioned one, or again that its object and cause are higher than the cause and object of the first one, or again that it is highest and supreme because it is nearest to release.

What is its cause? Its cause is Knowledge of Puruṣa. What is its object? There is no thirst for even the guṇa-s, sattva and the other two. *One who is aware of the defects in objects visible or heard about is detached from objects:* with this sentence he reminds us of the previous detachment with its cause and object, in order to make clear the different object and cause of the higher one. *From practising the vision of Puruṣa* as cause, *one has his mind pure like it and clear-seeing;* here *it* refers back to the vision of Puruṣa, which is pure because it is free from the impurity of the taints. Or it may refer to the purity of Puruṣa itself which makes clear-sighted the vision which rests on it as an object of meditation. The mind of that yogin is made clear-sighted.

detached from even the guṇa-s: this means that the higher detachment is from the guṇa-s, whereas the previous one was detachment from actual objects seen or heard about. This one is from even the guṇa-s, which are the cause of those objects, *with their qualities manifest or unmanifest:* in the state of the Great principle for example, they have manifest qualities, and in the state of pradhāna, they are unmanifest in qualities. He is detached from them.

Detachment, then, is of the two kinds, the previous one and this one, and the latter, being caused by the vision of Puruṣa and being detached from even the guṇa-s, *is nothing but pure Knowledge,* inasmuch as it is supreme clarity of the vision of Puruṣa alone.

The seer of Puruṣa becomes one who is free from rejecting or accepting anything, as it says (sūtra IV.29), *For one who is through and through a man of discriminative knowledge, but is not grasping over his meditation practice, there comes about the samādhi called Raincloud of Dharma.*

When it rises when detachment rises *(the yogin) in whom this Knowledge has dawned* the vision has appeared, *'Attained is what was to be attained'* and so on. *For it borders on Transcendental Aloneness* because that does not need any other means.

Detachment being nothing but pure Knowledge, there is no difference between detachment (vairāgya) and knowledge (jñāna), and there can therefore be no difference at all between their two opposites, passion (rāga) and Ignorance (a-jñāna). It is right that passion should be a particular state of Ignorance, for it will be said (II.8) that Ignorance (a-vidyā) is five-fold (including passion).

(Opponent) That contradicts the classical division of buddhi-states into eight. *(Note: the eight-fold classification is into pairs: Knowledge-Ignorance; detachment-passion; dharma-a-dharma; power-helplessness.* Tr.)

(Answer) No, because we accept a distinction within Knowledge (and Ignorance) which brings the six-fold up to eight. We are saying that detachment is extreme clearness of Knowledge (jñāna). In the same way, passion is a special particular state of Ignorance.

(Opponent) But there are several other different states of Knowledge and Ignorance, so the number will still not come out as eight.

(Answer) It will, because they are defined by their fruitfulness or the reverse. The members of the quartet of Knowledge-states are defined according to the differences of their results, and the quartet of Ignorance-states are defined by the fact of being their adversaries, namely a quartet of a-dharma and so on. So a total of eight is reached. It is the pairs of opposites like dharma and a-dharma which are being defined as the qualities; it is not simply a question of divisions of Ignorance (a-jñāna).

> *How is the samādhi defined which is called cognitive and which follows when the mental process has been inhibited by these two means?*

It has been said by the commentator (sūtra 1.1) that cognitive samādhi, accompanied with verbal associations and so on, will be spoken of later. The occasion has now come, *when the mental process has been inhibited by these two means'*, by detachment, higher and lower, and by practice, which is also to be understood to have two forms. What are the two forms of practice? The other remaining form, namely the practice for ultra-cognitive samādhi, will be given in sūtra I.18: *It follows from the practice of the idea of stopping.* From the wording, it is clear that there must have been a previous practice on an object of meditation. Furthermore he will say later (I.32), *To prevent (the obstacles), practice on one principle.*

The commentator has also said, (I.12), *By detachment the current towards objects is dammed and by practice of discriminative vision the auspicious current of discrimination is made to flow.* He has not said that cognitive samādhi is putting down the mental process entirely. The power to inhibit the whole mental process comes only after the withdrawal of its functioning first in regard to undesired objects; cognitive samādhi is still accompanied by certain mental objects. That is why in the second sūtra, inhibition was not given as the definition of cognitive samādhi.

Sūtra I.17

It is cognitive because accompanied with verbal associations (vitarka), with subtle associations (vicāra), with joy (ānanda), and the form of I-am-ness (asmitā)

The first (with vitarka) is an experience of something physical as the mind's object of meditation. It is with subtle associations (vicāra) when the object of meditation is subtle. Joy means delight. I-am-ness is the feeling of being an individual self.

It was explained under the second sūtra that inhibition is not the definition of cognitive samādhi. When the mental process has been inhibited by the two means described, namely practice and detachment, how is the resulting samādhi to be described? *It is cognitive, because accompanied with verbal associations, with subtle associations, with joy, and the form of I-am-ness.* The word *accompanied* goes with each of them, so it means that it is accompanied with experience of the physical, with experience of the subtle, with experience of joy, and accompanied with the form of I-am. The word *form* in this last has the implication of 'alone', so that it means that the three previously mentioned qualities, of physical experience and so on, have ceased. The samādhi accompanied with verbal associations is experience of something physical as the object of the mind's meditation. This experience is a confused meditation, the mind being transformed into the first form of meditation where it is mixed up with the physical. In the experience of the subtle, it relates to something subtle. Still more subtle is the third experience which is characterized by joy. 'I-am' is the bare thought of individual selfhood, when he is in samādhi on 'I-am' as his own nature. He will give an example (under I.36): *Having discovered the self which is subtle as an atom, he should be conscious of I-am alone.*

(Opponent) But he is going to put I-am-ness (asmitā) among the taints when he says: *The single selfhood, as it were, of the powers of seer and seeing is I-am-ness* (II.6). How should samādhi be associated with a taint like I-am?

(Answer) It is a reasonable point, but there is no reason why the samādhi should not be in the form of I-am, because this is meditation on its most refined cause, with everything else gone. Though there may be Ignorance in the *object* of meditation as I-am, this is not Ignorance in the yogin's thought. For example, telepathy does not involve taking on the Ignorance of the thought of the other party. One reading the thought of another mind does not himself become ignorant from some defect of Ignorance in the thought of the other mind on which he is meditating.

Again, taint (kleśa) is something invariably characterized by illusion (viparyaya), as in the ideas 'I go' or 'I am thin'. Not so the yogin's mind, because rajas and tamas have been subdued in it.

> *Of these, the first samādhi – with verbal associations, sa-vitarka – is associated with all four. The second – with subtle associations, sa-vicāra – is without the verbal associations of the first. The third- with associations of joy, sa-ānanda – is without the subtle associations of the second. The fourth, being pure I-am, is without the association of joy. All these samādhi-s rest on an object.*

In this sequence of four, an earlier one is associated with the qualities of all the later ones, and a later one is without the qualities of any earlier one. The purpose of the sūtra, then, is to define samādhi-s in terms of being associated with members of this set of four qualities. This is the normal way of defining a thing, by the special qualities which go with it, as 'cow' is defined as having a dewlap, etc.

Lest from the expression I-am it might be supposed that among these samādhi-s there is one without an object, he says, *All these rest on an object.*

It might be thought that I-am is something without any idea in it. But it is not so, for the established meaning of the expression I-am is ego (ahaṅkāra). And so he will say later, *I-am is a feeling.*

> *Now what is the means to ultra-cognitive samādhi, and what is its nature?*

Ultra-cognitive samādhi was defined in the words *Yoga is inhibition of the mental processes.* Having defined it, then *what is the means to it,* what is the discipline by which it can be approached? *and what is its nature,* what is it in itself, what sort of state is it? To show how its nature is connected to the particular discipline for it, the sūtra now says:

Sūtra I.18

The other (samādhi) follows on practice of the idea of stopping, and consists of saṃskāra-s alone

The words *follows on practice of the idea of stopping* show the relation to the discipline, but *consists of saṃskāra-s alone* explains its nature. They both go with *The other,* which therefore follows on the practice, and consists of saṃskāra-s alone. It is the seed-less ultra-cognitive samādhi, which is other than the cognitive samādhi which has just been defined in the previous sūtra.

> *When all the mental processes have stopped and only saṃskāra-s remain, the samādhi of the mind thus inhibited is ultra-cognitive. The means to it is the higher detachment. No meditation on an object can be a means to it, so the meditation is made on the idea of stopping, which is absence of anything. It is void of any object. The practice of this finally leads to a state as it were of absence of objects: this is the samādhi without seed which is ultra-cognitive.*

stopping is ceasing. The compound *idea-of-stopping (virāma-pratyaya)* means: stopping and the idea of it; the form of the idea is simply stopping, so it is called the idea of stopping. It still has the form of an idea at the time of ceasing from everything, while it is still coming to a stop and before it has ceased to be an idea at all. In the same way a flaming fire which is little by little going down as its fuel is used up, is still truly flame until it finally becomes ashes.

The practice of this idea of stopping finally leads to a state, which must have been preceded by this practice, where *only saṃskāra-s remain:* with the stopping of the ideas, what remains is only the saṃskāra-s of them. The meaning is that when the mind has withdrawn from ideas of objects, there remain saṃskāra-s alone. *The means to it is the higher detachment:* the further degree of detachment is the means to this samādhi.

(Opponent) It should have been said, the higher detachment *also,* because it has just been said that the means to inhibition is by practice and detachment both.

(Answer) Not so. There could be no question that practice is one of the means, because the sūtra itself says *practice of the idea of stopping.* But there might have been a doubt about detachment, which was not mentioned, and in merely supplying that, it is not necessary to say 'also'.

(Opponent) Well then, why is there no mention of detachment in the sūtra itself?

(Answer) It has been mentioned already.

(Opponent) Why was it mentioned there (and not here)?

(Answer) Because detachment was the context there, and it was mentioned in connection with the further (higher) detachment as distinct from the earlier one. The earlier detachment is confined to the field of the cognitive samādhi, and the remaining and higher detachment is a discipline with a different field, concerned only with the samādhi without seed (nir-bīja). So the sūtra did not use the word 'detachment', but the commentator indicates what is necessarily implied, because it has been declared, *Their inhibition is by practice and detachment (I.12).*

No meditation on an object can be a means to it, because that would be incompatible with this samādhi which has no object, whereas *the idea of stopping, which is absence of anything* is compatible with the samādhi with no object, and the meditation is on it. *This is the samādhi without seed,* with only saṃskāra-s remaining, *which is ultra-cognitive.*

This is of two kinds: the result of a means, or the result of birth. Of these, it is the one resulting from a means that is for yogin-s.

Sūtra I.19

It results from birth in the case of gods discarnate, and in the case of those who absorb themselves into prakṛti

In the case of the gods free from a physical body, they experience a state of seeming release by the mental experience of their own saṃskāra-s alone. And they pass beyond this state when the saṃskāra-s causing it have finished maturing. So also those who merge themselves into prakṛti; a commitment still remains in their mind in spite of the absorption, and though they experience a state of seeming release, it is only so long as their mind is not set whirling again by the force of that commitment.

This without-seed samādhi *is of two kinds: the result of a means, or the result of birth.* The first is a result of, is attained by, a means, and it is for yogin-s. Though the gods discarnate are indeed yogin-s, here the reference is only to those who are engaged now in the yoga discipline beginning with restraints (sūtra II.29). Their samādhi is attained by way of faith, energy, and memory (sūtra I.20).

The gods discarnate do have an eight-fold elemental body. *by mental experience of their own saṃskāra-s alone,* the remainder of the saṃskara-s laid down by detachment and practice, *they experience a state of seeming release.* But when from the dropping away of sattva-guṇa *the saṃskāra-s causing it have finished maturing* they fall away from it.

As to the ones merged in prakṛti, there is a commitment which has not been fulfilled. Inasmuch as they have not attained the Knowledge-of-the-difference between (sattva) guṇa and Puruṣa, the mind has still a commitment which has not been carried out, so mind in this state experiences only a seeming release, as in the case of the gods, *it is only so long as their mind is not set whirling again by the force of the commitment* by the force of the compulsion to acquire Knowledge (vidyā), so long they experience the seeming release.

Sūtra I.20

For the others, it comes after faith, energy, memory, (cognitive) samādhi, and knowledge

The one resulting from a means is for yogin-s. Faith is a settled clarity of the mind: like a good mother, it protects a yogin. When he has that faith, and is seeking knowledge, there arises in him energy. When energy has arisen in him, his memory stands firm. When memory stands firm, his mind is undisturbed and becomes concentrated in samādhi. To the mind in samādhi comes knowledge by which he knows things as they really are. From practice of these means, and from detachment from the whole field of mental process, arises ultra-cognitive samādhi.

The ultra-cognitive samādhi resulting from a means is that of the yogin-s, and it follows from faith, energy, memory, samādhi, and knowledge (prajñā).

What is called faith is a settled clarity of the mind in regard to attaining release, and to what he hears about the means to it; it is like the settled clarity of the water after the application of the kataka nut (which traditionally clears muddy water). *Like a good mother, it protects a yogin,* it defends him against adversities. *When he has that faith, and is seeking knowledge,* that is, when his goal is right vision (saṃyag-darśana), *there arises energy* enthusiasm for practising the yoga training. *When energy has arisen in him, his memory is firm,* memory of such things as the scriptural knowledge becomes very powerful. The qualification 'in the case of a seeker of knowledge' is to be read into each step. *When memory stands firm, his mind is undisturbed and becomes concentrated in samādhi.*

To the mind in samādhi comes extreme clarity of knowledge (prajñā), which has the power of illumining everything. He explains it further: *by which he knows things as they really are,* he knows facts like the self (ātman) as they really are (yathā-bhūta).

From practice of these means: as has been said, from the practice of the idea of stopping, there is vision of the self (ātman), and *from detachment from the whole field of mental process, arises ultra-cognitive samādhi.*

> *Yogin-s are of nine kinds, according to the methods which they follow, either mild or moderate or intense, and then sub-divided according to the energy – mild, moderate or ardent – with which they practise these respective methods. A mild method may be practised with mild or moderate or ardent energy, and so with the moderate method. Of those who practise intense methods,*

Sūtra I.21

For those who practise with ardent energy, it is near

> *They soon attain samādhi and the fruit of samādhi.*

The yogin-s, who practise the four methods beginning with faith, are of nine kinds. As he explains, they are divided *according to the methods which they follow, either mild or moderate or intense.* Each of these classes is sub-divided into three. Progress in the application of the method may be slow, or it may be moderate, or it may be energetic, and so it is with each of the three methods without exception. For those who practise the intense methods with ardent energy, samādhi and the fruit of samādhi are near at hand.

Sūtra I.22

Even among the ardent, there is a distinction of mild or moderate or intense

They may be mild or moderate or intense in their ardent energy, and so there is a further distinction. For the mildly ardent it is near: for the moderately ardent it is nearer: for the intensely ardent yogin who is practising intense methods, samādhi and the fruit of samādhi is nearest of all.

Even among these ardent yogin-s there are distinctions corresponding to whether their progress is slow or moderate or ardent, and this is a distinction of the saṃskāra-s created by their previous practice of the discipline. For the highest of them, the attainment of samādhi is nearest at hand.

The purpose of the sūtra is to fortify the enthusiasm of yogin-s in their practice. It is as in the world, where the prize goes to the one who runs fastest in the race. But again, by making it clear that (all) yogin-s whether slow or not do attain their aimed-at goal, it should arouse an undepressed spirit in them; those, on the other hand, who have become over-anxious as a result of fatigue from intense efforts, might lose heart (unless told the goal is near).

Is this the only way by which samādhi is soon attainable, or is there perhaps some other means?

Sūtra I.23

Or by special devotion to the Lord

As a result of the special devotion which is bhakti (love of God), the Lord bends down to him and rewards him according to what he has meditated on. If the yogin has meditated on it, the attainment of samādhi and its fruit is near at hand.

He explains that there is another way, *Or by special devotion to the Lord.* The meaning of the word Lord will be given later; here he describes devotion. It is the *devotion which is bhakti, and the Lord bends down to him and rewards him.* The Lord comes face to face with him and gives his grace to the yogin who is fully devoted to him, according to what the yogin has meditated upon; the grace is effortless, by the mere omnipotence of the supreme Lord. By that grace of the Lord, samādhi and its fruit are soon attainable.

Who is this Lord who is neither pradhāna nor Puruṣa?

Sūtra I.24

Untouched by taints or karma-s or their fruition or their latent stocks is the Lord, who is a special kind of Puruṣa

The taints are Ignorance, I-am-ness, desire, hate, and clinging to life. Karma-s are good and bad. Their fruition is the results they bring. The corresponding latent impulses (vāsanā) are the latent stocks. All these exist in the mind but are attributed to Puruṣa, for he is the experiencer of their results. It is as when victory or defeat, which are events on the battle-field, are attributed to the ruler. Untouched by such experience is the Lord, who is a special kind of Puruṣa.

Who is this Lord who is neither pradhāna nor Puruṣa? In the Sāṅkhya classics no proof of God is given, and one asks for some proof of the Lord, that he really exists, and again what is the special nature of this Lord who necessarily is not directly known. He gives the answer to these points in the sūtra, *Untouched by taints or karma-s or their fruition or their latent stocks is the Lord, who is a special kind of Puruṣa.*

Ignorance and the others are taints, because they cause defilement. They have been caused by previous karma-s, good and bad; this phrase *good and bad* implies that there are also some which are a mixture of good and bad. Their *fruition* is the experience of birth and life. These taints, karma-s, and fruitions lie latent (but dynamic) until they are absolutely dissolved and these are the *latent stocks;* the phrase can be taken to mean simply the whole mass of taints, karma-s, and fruitions.

They exist in the mind because they are mental processes (mano-vṛtti) *but are attributed to Puruṣa.* How so? *He is the experiencer of their results.* As victory and defeat, which are events of battles, are attributed to the king, because the result relates to the king.

Untouched by such experience is the Lord, who is a special kind of Puruṣa. No reference to tense is intended, because the implication is that he is not touched by it, nor will be touched by it, nor has been touched by it. The meaning is: never bound to taints of karma-s or their fruition or accumulation.

> *Is he then one of those who have attained their release? There are many who have done so. (No,) untouched by such experience is the Lord, who is a special kind of Puruṣa. Others have attained release by cutting the three bonds, but for the Lord such bondage never was nor will come to be, as it will for one who has absorbed his mind into prakṛti. But the Lord is ever freed, ever the Lord. His eternal perfection is from perfect sattva.*

To clarify the meaning of the sūtra he says *Is he then one of those who have attained their release? There are many who have done so.* For it is possible that being untouched by taints and karma-s might be only for some particular time. There are many who *have* been released: are they too Lords? No, because of the potentiality of contact, they are not absolutely untouched by taints etc. For them, there are both contact (in the past) and freedom from contact (now), but the Lord is never touched. The word *untouched* is not of itself unrestricted as to time, and it must be applied by extension to cover all times. So he alone is here called untouched who is absolutely never touched.

The others attained release after cutting the three bonds. The three bonds are those of the unmanifest prakṛti, those of manifest principles, and those connected with sacrifices; having destroyed them by right vision (saṃyag-darśana) they attained release, *but for the Lord, bondage,* by taints and karma-s, *never was.* It is not as in the case of a released one, where previous bondage must have existed, just because he does come to attain a state of release. For release (mukti) is release from some previous bondage. *nor will it come to be, as it will come to be for one who has absorbed his mind into prakṛti.* For him, a future mass of bondage, of the saṃsāra which has not yet come into operation, is inevitable. Then the (ordinary) man whose saṃsāra has begun to operate already, and whose mind is not absorbed into prakṛti, is subject to both past and future masses of bondage. What we have said is to show that *untouched* has no reference to time. *He is ever freed, ever the Lord.*

It has been said in the sūtra that the Lord is a special Puruṣa. The Puruṣa of the Lord will have no character of divine power, because power pertains to the mind; transcendent (niratiśaya) power must be connected to a perfect (prakṛṣṭa) mind. He confirms this conclusion in order to lead on to what follows: *That eternal perfection of the Lord is from his perfect sattva.* The perfection is the possession of the powers of omniscience and omnipotence, eternal and transcendent.

> *This perfection – does it have a cause or is it without a cause? The cause is holy scripture. Then what is the cause of scripture? The cause is the perfection (of the divine mind).*

To clarify what is being said, he begins with this question: is there any cause for it or is it causeless? The word nimitta means karaṇa (cause). So the point is, is it caused or uncaused? Now what is the object of the question?

(Opponent) If in the first place it is taken to have a cause, then it was illogical to say *ever the Lord,* because his perfection would not be eternal (if it had been caused). Again, if without a cause, it would follow that the perfection, which is an effect, would never come to exist at all. For no effect is ever found without a cause.

(Answer) It is not uncaused, because holy scripture is its cause. Scripture here means knowledge (jñāna); the perfection has a cause, because scripture is its cause. Scriptural knowledge is universal and eternal, and rests in a transcendent self-sufficient principle apart from ordinary postulates and proofs.

(Opponent) Knowledge has to be known by someone, and before that, it would have been imperfect. So what is the cause of scripture? If scriptural knowledge appears spontaneously (svābhāvika), it would be caused by imperfection like the ideas of a man drunk or mad (which arise suddenly from nowhere). But then again, if it has a cause, prior to the operation of that cause the scripture would have been defective.

(Answer) It is not causeless, in so far as it has perfection of sattva as its cause, which is to say that it rests on perfect sattva; and this is why there is no defect of knowledge spontaneously appearing (svābhāva jñāna- associated by the opponent with madness).

Furthermore, even if it were (taken as) spontaneously appearing knowledge, it is not like the ideas of madmen, because it rests on sattva and so is always free from Ignorance and other taints. Just as there is a beginningless relation, like that of seed and sprout, between knowledge, saṃskāra, and memory, related as they are as mutually cause and effect, just so there is a beginningless and endless relation between scripture and his perfection in the mind of the Lord, a relation which is ever active. The perfection of the Lord is simply the effect of the omniscience which is its cause.

There is an explanation by others, to the effect that the word nimitta (normally 'cause') here means 'proof.'

Scripture is its cause would then mean that it is the proof of it, for the Lord's perfection is proved by scripture. Then what proves scripture? The proof of it is the pure sattva of the Lord. For the authoritativeness of scripture is because it was composed out of pure sattva, as in the case of Manu and others. Thus scripture says, 'Whatever Manu said is medicine' (Taitt. Sam. 2.2.10.2). So in ordinary life, what is declared by a teacher is authoritative.

> *Between those two – scripture and perfection – present in the divine sattva, there is a beginningless relation.*

Scripture and perfection are eternally related, as proof and proved.

(Opponent) But the scripture which is supposed to prove perfection is not now in the divine sattva.

(Answer) It is, because since the sattva produced it, scripture is still present in it. Scripture arose from it, but is still present in it, just because it is omniscient. In ordinary life we see that what originates from something is in fact still present in it, as a cloth is present in the threads that compose it.

That scripture originates from the sattva is known from inference and authority. So the proof of the perfection is scripture, and the proof of scripture is the Lord; there is no fallacy of mutual dependence because they depend on different things.

(Opponent) If the authority of the Lord is based on scripture, but the scripture derives its own authority from the divine authority, then there *would* be the circle of mutual dependence.

(Answer) The authority of the Lord is established by inference, so there is no such fallacy.

> *Thus it is that he is ever and always the Lord and ever and always freed. That divine power of his is without any equal or superior.*

Thus it is – how so? The relation, in the form of mutual cause and effect, between the divine repository of perfect sattva, and the perfection and transcendent knowledge, is eternal; because it is eternal, *he is ever and always the Lord and ever and always freed.* That Lordship is without any equal or superior. This is the conclusion of the proofs to be given now. Or again, it is a summing up of the sūtra. Now he explains how the power of the Lord is unsurpassed:

> *For to begin with, it is not surpassed by any other power, because whatever other power would surpass it, would be that itself*

It is not surpassed by any other power. Why not? *because whatever other power* one might suppose *would surpass it, would be that itself*- the power which we are explaining, since whatever other surpassing power there is, that power is the Lord. There is no power equal to it, because perfection cannot be equalled.

Where the summit of power is attained, there is the Lord, and there can be no power equal to his. Why not? Suppose there were two equal Lords, and something which was the object of a wish by both, one of them wanting it to be new and the other wanting it to be old. Then if one succeeded, the other would be demeaned by frustration of his will. Nor could two equals possess the same thing at the same time, because that would be impossible. Therefore he who has power neither equalled nor surpassed, he alone is the Lord. And he is a special Puruṣa.

For there cannot be two kings in one kingdom, nor one king in two kingdoms. And so he explains, *Suppose there were two equal Lords, then …* one of them could not have his way without overriding the will of the other. If the two wanted the same thing, they could not both achieve it; there would be a battle for supremacy over the desired object. The fact of equality would be the very thing to destroy it.

And the conflict might be undeclared: an overt superiority on one side and a hidden superiority on the other are still in opposition. The point is that things which seem the same have relative superiorities (along with their apparent equality).

Therefore this Lord is one whose power has none to equal or surpass it, and it is established that the Lord is a special Puruṣa apart from pradhāna and Puruṣa-s.

Sūtra I.25

In whom the seed of omniscience becomes transcendent

All certain knowledge, of past or future or present or a combination of them, or from extra-sensory perception, whether that knowledge be small or great, is the seed of omniscience. He in whom it becomes transcendent is omniscient. The seed of omniscience attains the ultimate, because it is something which has degrees, like any measurable. He in whom knowledge attains the ultimate, is omniscient. And he is a special Puruṣa.

A proof is added in demonstration of the Lord who has been described: *In whom the seed of omniscience becomes transcendent. In whom* in that Lord as described, it is proper that it should become transcendent. What should become transcendent? *All certain knowledge* whether from perception or from inference, with its field *the past,* with its field *the future,* or with its field the *present,* or with its field a *combination of them,* or with its field what is beyond the senses. As the past and future are part of what is beyond the senses, those perceptions are all called *extra-sensory.* This extra-sensory perception is three-fold: with its field the subtle, with its field what is concealed, and with its field what is distant. The well-known limited knowledge, *whether small or great,* can increase by the very fact that it has degrees, so it is the seed of omniscience, as the knowledge of smoke (is the seed) of the knowledge of fire.

He verily *is omniscient in whom the supreme limit is reached.* It is said *in whom* because knowledge abides in a knower, so a knower is implied, and it is in that knower.

So with power too. It has degrees and so increases, and the one in whom it attains the limit is omnipotent. By this it is established that there is a creator, controlling the maintenance and withdrawal of the world also. He in whom the increase of power reaches the ultimate is the supreme Lord. And the perfection is the absence of the defect (doṣa) of illusions (viparyaya) like powerlessness.

(Opponent) If so, then in that Lord there will be perfection of ignorance (a-jñāna) too, increasing till perfect in its own nature by reaching the limit.

(Answer) Not so, because ignorance is opposed to knowledge, and these two opposites cannot coexist in a single being. For where knowledge is preeminent, ignorance is impossible. Where light increases, darkness can only be lessened.

(Opponent) The reverse should hold too.

(Answer) Not so, because when there is light, we do not see darkness. When darkness is there, it is removed by a light, but when there is a light it is never overcome by darkness.

Even in the rainy season when the sun does not appear because it is covered by clouds, that is merely a screening of the vision; the light itself is not overcome, as darkness is (by light).

Therefore ignorance cannot exist where there is increase of knowledge, any more than darkness can exist in the sun; for the material cause (upādāna) of knowledge is sattva, which always and altogether overcomes the other guṇa-s, rajas and tamas.

Further, there cannot be an increase in ignorance as such, because its object is not a real thing; whereas there can be growth of knowledge, whose object is knowable (real) things. If ignorance had a real thing as its object, it would be knowledge.

(Opponent) One might say that ignorance attains its perfection in inanimate things.

(Answer) But that cannot be called perfection, but a complete absence of knowledge (and that is all). If there were a perfection of ignorance, then a thousand repetitions of ignorance would not be dispelled by a single knowledge (as they are). It ought to require knowledge arising the corresponding number of times to dispel the ignorance. Therefore by its very nature, ignorance can have no 'perfection'.

Anything that has degrees increases till the ultimate is attained; the limited measure of things like fruits ends up in the vastness of space. And so the seed of omniscience can reach a highest limit. It is a direct perception by one entity of the whole and the parts of the total aggregate of things, which are all knowables like jars.

It is because things are knowables that men seek for them, as they look for jars for instance. Again, the earth is something produced, for it has parts like a jar.

So the world has been constructed by One who knows the separate classes of living beings, of their karma and its means and its results, and he provided the world as an appropriate place for these to be experienced, as one might build a palace for people to live in. The earth is created by One who has the knowledge of what is to be experienced by the many living beings, like rice and barley (cultivated by a farmer for others to eat).

These two examples show that the abode of all the living beings, the earth with its mountains and rivers, has been created by a single conscious master craftsman, adapted so that those who live in it can have the appropriate experiences.

The sun is created by one Knower who has power to control the light in which the many beings share, for its essence is light, like a lamp. The sun's course, rising and setting at fixed times, is ordered by One who knows its purpose, for it goes according to fixed times as if pulled along. The course of sun, planets, moon and stars is controlled by one intelligent Lord; for to keep to fixed times is inherently difficult, as it is for a punctilious student or servant.

The waxing and waning of the moon is controlled by a single Knower of the times of the lunar month, etc., for there is accurate discrimination of the divisions of time, as with a clock. The moon has been created by one who knows those discriminations of time, because its waxing and waning are controlled to the minute.

The world has a single Lord who is intelligent; just as when there are many groups of living beings each with its appointed leader and with conflicting interests, the whole tribe has a single sovereign.

There must be a supervision by some one entity of the whole complex of occupations with their means and ends, as in the example of war, for instance, where mutually opposing or co-operating interests must subserve a single purpose. There must be a supervision because it is complex, as in the operations of a potter. This is our position.

Everything is simultaneously overseen by One, because there are mutual relations between many things, and relations too are well known to be of more than one kind.

When a means like the fire rite (agnihotra) is to be undertaken, it is overseen by someone, because it is essentially a means to effect a purpose, like the satisfaction of hunger from eating.

All powers are overseen by some one, because of the fact that they are things, like jars. When there is no intervening obstacle, everything material is perceived by someone, since there is a relationship with that thing's attributes of sound and so on; as the sound is clearly heard when a man is munching a large cake, even apparently very far off.

Inherently everything is known directly by somebody by the very fact that it *is* a knowable, as in the case of a drama. In the absence of obstacles, everything is known by someone, inasmuch as everything is related to everything else, as the actors are bound together in the plot of the drama.

The omniscient (Lord) is free from saṃsāra because he has no Ignorance – in that like a released self; he is apart from taints, etc. because his knowledge is unobstructed – in that like a perfect yogin.

By the fact of that freedom from Ignorance and obstruction by taints, etc., it is certain that he has perfect knowledge of every object without the mediation of senses like the eye; the all-pervading mind of the supreme Lord is in simultaneous contact with every object, and so can perceive everything. For there can be no reason for his not perceiving the totality of things.

Nor can there be any obstruction by solid forms any more than by space, for his mind is in contact with all things. There being infinity of objects, there is infinity of their appearances and disappearances, of memories and purposes; but the process of that mind is like the light of the sun, for it grasps them in their forms as objects.

His mind-sattva is not impeded by any covering of taints and so on arising from contact with a-dharma. Sattva, all-pervading and in-all-things, does have also a dependent perception (in ordinary men) through the gates of the senses, where its innate mode of activity overcomes the limiting obstructions of a-dharma, etc. For instance, a lamp set in a perforated jar illumines what is outside through the openings of the holes in its enclosure; but this same lamp, when its enclosing covering has been shattered, illumines everything without being dependent on holes for a path. Just so the sattva of the Lord, being untouched by the covering of taints, etc., has perception of absolutely everything at the same time, for there is no cause which could suppress any particular object. So there is no question of transcending or failing to transcend (some limitation).

The world, then, must have a single Lord by whom everything is perceived, because there are many different kinds of things for which he stands as the protector, as in the familiar case of a kingdom.

The wise have taught the performance of duties of caste, stage of life and so on, with their respective agents, experiencers, action, discipline and the related results. These are to be performed by those seeking the results, or by those who are fearful of committing sins. So it is like applying medical remedies. The teachings are like medical prescriptions in that it is for the sake of others that they are taught, in that they are relied on by informed people, and in that they deal with things which the ordinary man would not come to know without being taught.

The sole efficient cause for the fashioning of body and senses is someone knowing all their purposes, for they are means of bringing about definite actions and states, like the machine which works the marionettes in a dolls'-house show. (Gītā XVIII.61).

They have a definite arrangement, as it has.

And the senses, as instruments, are comparable to a plane for paring wood fine.

Again, they all make up the occasion for definite effects, the purposes of the human experiencer and the means for his experiences, as a jar does. These are the reasons for their existence.

Earth is perishable because it is of middling dimensions, liable to be destroyed by various causes, a basis on which experience can take place, with forms which are means for producing the results of actions; in some places it is piled up, in others reduced, or increased or taken away or burnt or split.

Things like the body, composed of earth and other elements, are perishable, because they have the power of destroying each other, as armed men have.

And on the other side, in every way the opposite to man, there is space, with its properties of creation and destruction. It makes things manifest, as the receptacle which holds the external sense-objects with their properties, like a jar.

Therefore it is established that there is a supreme Lord (parameśvara) whose lordship is unlimited in power and knowledge.

(Opponent) The meaning of the word 'Lord' is not 'omniscient', because all that can be known is individual things denoted by words, whose knowers must depend on some means to know them, just as we do.

The word 'Lord' does not imply any connection with unlimited knowledge. It is a word, like the word jar, and the world has no omniscient Lord of all, for it consists of independent beings in mutual confrontation like princes and kings. In the past and future as in the present, no living beings experience omniscience, just because they are living beings like ourselves. There is no omniscient Lord of all as you imagine, for none such is known, any more than the horn of a hare.

He could not be omniscient and a Lord if he were incorporeal like a released self. Again, if he is supposed to have a body, then his embodiment would be in accordance with dharma and a-dharma and he would be a being of this world (saṃsārin) just like ourselves. If he is to be without a body, then he will not be the creator of the world who blesses his devotees; he will be simply a released self.

We admit that the particular ordering of the world is adapted to give particular experiences, but that is purely natural like the sharpness of thorns, or the opening and closing of waterlilies and lotuses. The going and staying of sun, moon, and stars also is natural to them, like the action of magnets.

(Answer) If it were merely natural, there would not be the order in the earth and elsewhere. Nor is there any example of anything accomplished of itself; it is generally accepted that the sharpness of thorns is not merely from their nature (but has a cause).

(Opponent) Heat and so on are, so to say, the very nature of fire; in the same way, order in the world is caused by the qualities of the things.

(Answer) Then the order in palaces too would be from the mere qualities of the things, and the argument would be too wide.

(Opponent) Let this too be from their nature.

(Answer) That is not right, because it is apparent that the order in the world is connected with the aim of giving experience of the results of dharma and a-dharma. It will subsequently control the states of the agent and his dharma and a-dharma.

Therefore the order in the world is not natural, because it has a purpose, namely to provide experience for living beings, like the order in a palace. The movement of the moon and stars is not natural, just because it is a movement, like the movement of us human beings.

(Opponent) Let us say that our movements too are natural.

(Answer) No, because then they ought always to be the same, like the heat of fire. The heat of fire being natural, there is nothing to produce any drive to attain something for itself, because there is no subject there. But in the order of action and result, there is a drive to attain something for oneself (as in building a palace), arising from a definite cause, and it is not merely natural.

(Opponent) Let the definite cause of the drive be the nature of the order in palaces.

(Answer) Allowing that the nature could be of this kind, then the order in the world too will embody a drive from that same definite cause as with the palaces. Therefore your argument is not at all a clearing up of the weak point, namely that there is dependence on an outside agent, and in fact it proves the opposite.

Your inferences are no proofs because they go against ordinary experience, against proper inference, and against authority. First there are the contradictions in the inference from the standpoint of having degrees (sātiśaya, as opposed to the transcendence or niratiśaya of the sūtra). Then the contradiction with sacred authority is established by such texts as 'he who is all-knowing, omniscient' (Muṇḍ. Up. 1.1.9) and 'One ruler' (Kaṭh. Up. 5.12).

But there is also contradiction of common experience. Everyone, including women and cowherds, does turn to God, under names like Śiva and Nārāyana. Even when they are being disobedient or distracted in their minds, running wild into fields prohibited by him, they still bow their heads before the Lord and worship him with offerings of lotus garlands. By this they hope to attain their ends.

(Opponent) The only contradiction is between two propositions: one declares the non-existence of omniscience, and the other is your own inference.

(Answer) That proposition of yours is no true inference. Why not? From the first, it is faulty. When you begin by saying that the meaning of the word 'Lord' is not 'omniscient', your very statement has referred to the Lord, so you are making an issue of something already established (siddha-sādhyatā).

(Opponent) It is only the Lord as proposed by us. ...

(Answer) Then it is the fallacy of specifying something uncertain.

(Opponent) What we are saying is, that the Lord is not omniscient.

(Answer) As before, you are making an issue of what you have already established (by your own words – siddham sādhyate).

And it contradicts your own position. How so? With the development of the seeds (potentialities) of power and omniscience, an ultimate must be reached, as with any measure. The word 'Lord' means that power has attained its ultimate, and 'omniscient' means that knowledge has similarly attained. The attainment of the ultimate means unlimitedness. As with all measures, the limitations of the measure come to an end in the self or in universal space or the like.

In fact you are referring to the meaning of the words while at the same time their meaning – that the Lord is the attainment of the ultimate – is supposed to have been rejected. If a word has part of its meaning rejected, it is not being meaningfully used.

(Opponent) Well, we do not admit that for all measures there is a final unlimitedness.

(Answer) That is opposed to your own doctrine. For if there is no all-pervadingness of self and space and so on, they will have the defects of limited measure and of transience.

(Opponent) The all-pervadingness of the self means simply that it shows itself in all places by its effects (as individual selves).

(Answer) Then the inference (sāmānyato-dṛṣṭa) would have to be drawn that the selves of birds should exist in the bodies of men. Here too inference cannot be contradicted.

(Opponent) You have not shown that our conclusion does contradict inference.

(Answer) The contradiction of inference comes in saying that self and space must be perceptible things, like elements such as earth. No such contradiction of inference can be allowed, because it would mean that inference would cease to exist (as a proof).

(Opponent) Let us do without inference.

(Answer) Then there could be no confidence in perception either.

(Opponent) Perception is valid because it produces confirmable ideas.

(Answer) The ideas from inference are equally certain, so that too should have validity.

(Opponent) Inference (for instance, of fire) is only when there is a perceived relation with the (seen) object, namely smoke.

(Answer) In that case inference would cease to exist. (Proposition) this place which has smoke does not have fire; (reason) because no relation with fire is known by direct perception; (example) as in places known to be without fire.

(Opponent) In such cases where the relation is not seen, the apparent force of inference comes from the fact that it agrees with some other means of proof.

(Answer) Then direct perception – inasmuch as it is a proof just like inference – would be a proof only because of agreeing with yet another proof. It would turn out to be no more of a proof than inference, because there would be no further proof to confirm it. Therefore the authoritativeness of inference cannot be impugned, in view of the fact that it produces ideas which are certain.

Further, one who does not accept the force of inference should have no fear of snakes and the like, because he has never actually perceived any personally fatal relation with them. He would not make use of medicines to cure disease, because he would have no fear of death. And as he would have had no experience of birth, he would think that his body had never been born. And he would not reject or take up or use things. Therefore inferring from the general case that what is measurable has increasing degrees, it is established that there is a knowledge which is unlimited – the knowledge possessed by the Lord.

Moreover, in the very statement that there is not a divine omniscience, we find a recognition that it exists, because it is impossible to deny what has no meaning. The word 'not' by itself has no sense. When it is said that the Lord is not omniscient, in those words the fact of an omniscience somewhere has been accepted.

As when it is said that there is no horn on a hare, or that there is no son of a barren woman, or there are no flowers in space – things like horns and sons and flowers do exist somewhere; the denial of them is only as related to the hare and the barren woman and space. So here too. When it is said 'the Lord is not omniscient', by the denial of any relation between what is meant by 'Lord' and what is meant by 'omniscience', an omniscience is being accepted, of someone other than the Lord. For unless the related things have been accepted as existent, their relationship can not be denied. Their existence thus proved, is now denied by you and made out to be unproved. Which is mere futility, for there can be no denial of the universally accepted meanings of the words 'Lord' and 'omniscient'. To deny the universally accepted infinite extent of space with the words 'there is no space of infinite extent', and then to propose that it exists in the limited measure of things like jars, is not reasonable.

When the Lord and omniscience are denied, the position is self-refuting by its own words, for it accepts the Lord and omniscience as the established meanings of the words 'Lord' and 'omniscience'. It cannot be that fire is not the meaning of the word 'fire'.

(Opponent) The words 'Lord' and 'omniscience' are not of established meaning.

(Answer) Even so, it is not reasonable to deny that they refer to something. One cannot take up a position as to something which is not established at all. One is not entitled -just because the matter is not established – to *deny* that there is a goatherd girl on this mountain. The denial would have no basis because it would refer to something uncertain.

(Opponent) Between the words 'Lord' and 'omniscient', with (allowably) established referents, and unlimited Lordship and omniscience, which have *not* been established as existing, the relation is simply imagined by certain people, like the imagination of flowers in the sky. It should be denied.

(Answer) There too, since a meaning has been accepted and then denied, the proposition is self-refuting.

Because you admit that the words 'Lord' and 'omniscient' mean universals, manifesting more than one lord and omniscient one, namely some with degrees and others transcendent.

It is well known that the two words give rise to the idea of something with more than one manifestation, in that they are connected with ideas of superior and inferior. For it is not that when the head of a village is called the lord of it, the heads of two or three villages will not be even greater lords, or that one who is the head of a single household should not be lord of it. This is the ordinary sense of the word.

In grammar, the word omniscient is always connected with the idea of degrees (i.e. knowing about every fact in one or more particular fields). 'Lord' and 'omniscient', with limits or without limits, must be accepted as the things referred to by the two words. So a proposition which denies them is contradicting what has been accepted, like denying that the meaning of the word 'great' is the greatness of Self or of space and so on.

(Opponent) There is no unlimited Lord or omniscient one, for none such is ever perceived; there is no Lord, any more than there is a man with two heads.

(Answer) Still, since it is admitted that the words do refer to something, the proposition contradicts what has been admitted. Inferring from the fact that lordship and omniscience are potentialities which increase by degrees, the fact of unlimited Lordship and omniscience can be known. Like anything measurable, they go to infinity, and they are not uncertain just because they are not directly perceived.

(Opponent) The word 'Lord' as it stands does not mean omniscient, because omniscience has to be demonstrated as a fact, like any other knowledge.

(Answer) That would be a proposition opposed to all proofs, which all establish that the settled meaning of the word 'Lord' is the omniscience which we are discussing.

Now let us see what he would say who maintains that the meaning of the word 'Lord' is not 'omniscient' because omniscience must be demonstrated factually like a jar-

(Opponent) There is no omniscient one in this world. Neither in time or direction or space or habitations of living beings, nor in living beings themselves, is there omniscience. Nor does any proof demonstrate anyone who is omniscient. True knowers never meet anyone omniscient.

(Answer) Such statements deny any unlimited Lord or omniscient one, and they are contrary to the accepted meanings of the words, so they must be said to be unsound as propositions.

(Opponent) Why then, the proposition that the son of a barren woman does not exist because no living being ever meets him anywhere in the world at any time, and no living being is the son of a barren woman, would be subject to the same unsoundness!

(Answer) Not so, because the words denying the existence of the barren woman's son do not refer to any established meaning, as do the words 'Lord' and 'omniscient'. All you have done is to deny a meaning which is merely an idea produced by stringing the words together; there is no acceptance of the existence of a barren woman's son. So the denial is not self-contradictory.

(Opponent) What the negation 'the Lord is not omniscient' is rejecting is simply an idea that had been accepted; of course it could never reject an actual fact, like a mahout driving away an elephant. If by a 'not' one could drive away a fact, then by a simple 'not' one would drive off the ideas of the theist (īśvara-vādin). What is being rejected here is a mere idea; this is a standard form of refutation, and there is no defect in our position.

(Answer) Yes, but there is a distinction. The idea of an established thing may get denied at some other particular time, being based on the universal of the thing, as in the sentence 'there is no jar (here and now)'. Another idea, of something imaginary, induced by verbal associations and without any real content at all, is also rejected, as in 'there is no son of a barren woman'.

But where there is rejection of a true fact established by some means of right knowledge, such rejection of what is admitted to exist must be wrong, as in the sentence, 'the meaning of the word Lord is not omniscient'. The statement that the transcendent omniscience of the Lord is the meaning of the words 'the Lord's omniscience' is generally accepted, and by that indicatory mark it is established that an unlimited Lordly omniscience does exist, just as words like 'great' and 'many' imply an infinite extent.

These words like 'great', carrying as they do the sense of the normal corresponding universals of degrees of greatness and so on, are indications pointing to the existence of an unlimited universal greatness, etc., manifesting in those degrees. The manifestation of unlimited greatness has the power of pervading the universals of greatness, etc., in the corresponding manifestation of limited degree. Whenever there is the limited degree, that unlimited pervades it. But the latter, being unlimited, is not something that can be pervaded by something else, so in infinity the pervading universal comes to an end, since that always depends on the existence of something which it can pervade. Thus it is established by right knowledge that the refusal of any meaning to the words 'Lord' and 'omniscience', which has been urged, is a rejection of a demonstrated fact; as such, it is a false position.

Nor can it be made out that the words 'Lord' and 'omniscience' do not have these meanings, or have some other meanings. From the gradually increasing degrees of power, omniscience and lordship among men, (we infer) a principle which is unlimited, and to labour to deny it is a position contradicting inference. Moreover in denying the Lord 'imagined by the other side', they end up basing themselves on a (telepathic) perception of the minds of others.

(Opponent) It is only from the words (of those others) ...

(Answer) No, because their words accord (with what we are saying), inasmuch as they show that the fact of degrees is a conclusive indication proving the existence of absolute omniscience. In denying such meaning to the words, you deny what you have accepted, and as before it is contrary to inference.

Again, without omniscience there is no certainty about the (limited) knowability of things. Why? Because that depends on having accepted the absolute knowledge and power which we have described. Now let him willingly accept what is similar (to what he has already accepted), and then there is the certainty of omniscience, from what has been already accepted.

To deny what is similar to what one has accepted comes to saying, 'a pot is not a pot, because it is a thing, like a cloth'; it would be like that here too.

Unless an unlimited principle is accepted, there would be no certain basis for the postulated characteristics of the knowability of objects. And when it is accepted, what needs to be proved further? He who would say to a satisfied man, 'Do not eat the food', what would he have accomplished?

(Opponent) Well then, accepting the Lord beyond limitations, I deny that he possesses omniscience.

(Answer) This is not reasonable, because omniscience too has no limits. Lordship and omniscience which have degrees are in the field of superiority and inferiority, and therefore indefinite, so they cannot be the principal meanings of the words 'Lord' and 'omniscient'. Words like 'great' are not being used in their primary sense when used to describe things like jars, because jars are of indefinite size, as against things like space. So here too, infinite Lordship and omniscience, which are not indefinite, are the principal meanings of the words. Rejecting the principal meaning of words leads nowhere.

You reject the omniscience of the Lord on the assumption that he must have the character of a knowable object; but it would similarly follow that if he were a knowable object like a jar he should be unconscious, because it is the same argument. As knowability would involve non-omniscience, so it would involve unconsciousness.

(Opponent) That contradicts perception.

(Answer) Here again, how is it that you do not even glance at your own contradiction of inference and sacred authority?

Nor can it be that somewhere there has been something illusorily projected, for or against. For among the knowables, the actual things always exist; a delusion is not classed as a knowable thing.

(Opponent) He is not omniscient because he is a self.

(Answer) It would follow that your gods would not have knowledge, any more than a released self.

(Opponent) That contradicts perception.

(Answer) You yourself are contradicting inference and authority, as before. As to the point that neither in the past nor in the future does anyone know of any Lord, which throws doubt on any knowledge of gods at the present time, inasmuch as living beings are the same now as in the past and future: the answer is, that living beings of the past and future know through indicatory marks such as having degrees, and as inquirers they are conversant with the means of right knowledge, so that they are like ourselves (and will reach the same conclusion).

(Opponent) The Lord has no body, so he is no more omniscient than the released selves, or space for example.

(Answer) Not so, because he has a body.

(Opponent) Since manifest and unmanifest (principles) are all without a body, we must conclude that such a Lord would not be eternal, because having a body he would then be connected with dharma and a-dharma.

(Answer) No, because he is without a body.

(Opponent) It is a contradiction that he both has a body and has not.

(Answer) No, for there is the example of the same self which when released has no body, but while in the process of releasing himself, has one.

(Opponent) In that particular case there is no contradiction because the times are different.

(Answer) Here too we accept difference of time. Furthermore just because he is the Lord, he has the double potentiality of simultaneously having instruments and being without them. So the holy texts say, 'Without a body, in all the bodies' (Kath. Up. 2.22), 'Who stands in all beings' (Bṛhad. Up. 3.7.15), and 'Who is all-knowing, omniscient (Muṇḍ. Up. 1.1.9) and others.

(Opponent) The holy texts of the Veda aim at giving injunctions and prohibitions, and not ideas about the Lord.

(Answer) Not so, for the holy texts (just cited) are not ancillary to anything else. For indications and so on from texts that are ancillary would not give right knowledge of something else (but these do).

(Opponent) They are merely ancillary, for rites like the full moon sacrifice contain the injunction to study of the scriptures on the Self and repetition of Om (svādhyāya).

(Answer) No, because there are other injunctions such as the soma rite, with separate instructions for them, and they could not each be ancillary to the other. So when holy texts say for instance 'He is to be thought on, to be meditated upon', it is proper that they have their own field, and are not ancillary to rites like agnihotra.

(Opponent) There is no result (from pure self-realization).

(Answer) There is, for it is shown in statements of the holy texts like 'He attains all worlds and all desires who has sought that self and realized it' (Chānd. Up. 8.12.6).

(Opponent) These texts are merely supplements to injunctions to worship (upāsanā), and they are simply praise.

(Answer) There cannot be praise by describing what does not exist at all. For the sense of the text 'Vāyu is the swiftest god' (Taitt. Saṃ. 2.1.1) cannot be that Vāyu is not the swiftest.

(Opponent) There could be praise by referring to something that does not exist in certain places.

(Answer) No, because here we are concerned with something established by inference (as all-pervading).

(Opponent) As he is conjoined with all bodies and sense organs, the Lord must be affected by the happiness and pain of all living beings.

(Answer) No, because there are other auxiliary causes for them. Dharma and a-dharma are the causes responsible for the embodiment and experience of living beings. Dharma and a-dharma are the causes which bring them to pain and other experiences, and there is no dharma or a-dharma in the Lord. What connects the effects of body and so on with their cause is the absolute omnipotence; it is like a house (built by the Lord) and the one who has entered it (the living being).

(Opponent) There is no perception of everything (by the Lord) because perception needs sense-organs (which are limited), as we find in our own experience.

(Answer) No, because there is no cause to obstruct those (such as the Lord or perfect yogin-s) who have the capacity to perceive all things. Any restriction of the field (of knowledge) is made by the covering up, by dharma and a-dharma, of sense-organs which are (inherently) all-pervasive. Where the veiling by the obstacles of dharma and a-dharma is not found, there is nothing to prevent the sense-organs from having as their field everything without exception.

Or again, the Lord experiences everything through the sense-organs of all the living beings, into which the inmost self, itself without sense-organs, has entered as into a house. There is nothing without the living Inner Dweller;

the holy texts 'Who is abiding in earth', 'Who is abiding in water' (Bṛhad. Up. 3.7.3 and 4) and others teach us of the Lord as the Inner Dweller in all.

And again, his perfect sattva, endowed with the Lordliness of eternal power and knowledge, going everywhere like space, is in touch with everything; it illumines every object because it is directed to everything, and it is never obstructed because it has no association with dharma or a-dharma and so on. Therefore, though the Lord has no body and no sense-organs, he is perfect in omniscience.

(Opponent) A mind can only come into touch with forms and so on by means of sense-organs like the eye.

(Answer) No, for this holds only in the absence of divine power or the dharma (which gives special power).

And it is found in the world that sometimes objects of vision are not perceived by the eye. When the object of vision is total blackness, it is known even with closed eyes by an attentive inner organ, and that same complete blackness is not apprehended even with eyes wide open when the mind has wandered off. It is the same with the light apprehended in space.

(Opponent) But darkness is simply absence of light; it is not a thing.

(Answer) It is, for an absence could not conceal things.

(Opponent) It is simply from absence of light, the cause of perception, that things like jars are not seen; it is not that darkness conceals them.

(Answer) Not so, because there is a light of the eye itself, and it is not that it depends on another light to help it. To the extent that there is nothing else of a different nature to conceal the things, just so much of them will be lit up by the light of the eye. For a light does not depend on another light to second it in lighting up things. If it did depend for help on some other light, then even at night, seconded by the light of the moon, it should perceive forms as clearly as in daylight, since there would be no cause of obstruction.

Again, if darkness were merely an absence, then it should not appear as a weak darkness in brilliant moonlight at night; it ought to be destroyed by that all-pervading light in whose brightness it stands. With an actual thing in the brightness, it is natural that it should have distinctions of weakness and intensity and so on, but not with an absence, for that can have no such distinctions.

(Opponent) Without assistance, the eye cannot perceive, and there is no cognition.

(Answer) This too is not invariably so. In the case of a flash of forked lightning, there is indeed light but it is so intense that the sight does not perceive anything by it. It is not however reasonable that the dazzlement which is seen as a result of connection with lightning should be an absence of perception, for it is not opposed to perception.

Again, in the medical texts, the shadow (of the patient) is said to be sweet, or to be cold. But there can be no sweetness or coldness of what is not a thing. And they call darkness good or bad for certain eye conditions: but an absence could not be so characterized.

Furthermore, a shadow is perceived as from a light. If darkness were a non-existent, how could there be – within the circle of illumination – a shadow caused by the light?

(Opponent) If we take it as a real thing, there is the difficulty that the two are opposites (co-existing).

(Answer) No; it is possible as with the snake and its poison. Poison is deadly, but not to the snake, and so with the light and its shadow.

Therefore darkness is a real thing, being intense or faint like light, excluding what is opposed to it like a jar, and making a distinguishing line for the perceiver, like a boundary.

Thus it is possible for the mind (antaḥkaraṇa) to perceive a sense-object even without recourse to the senses. Even when the ears are covered by bowls, there is awareness of the singing in them. Nor can it be supposed that the bowls would constitute another ear; if bowls are put over the ears of a deaf person, he cannot hear with them.

Again, we find that forms and so on are perceived, without need of senses, also through the knowledge of statements.

Further (if perception depended absolutely on the co-operation of the senses) nothing would arise from the memory, whereas we know that there is some degree of perception in the mind without the senses, for in a dream the memories stand out clearly as forms and other objects (like sounds).

If perception of an object is effected only by an accompanying conjunction of senses and mind, then in sleep, when they are separated, it would be inhibited. But this is not so.

Moreover it is everywhere agreed that the mind is independent in perception of pleasure and pain.

Therefore the senses are illumined by the mind, which is purely independent and spontaneous in its perception of objects. So it was said *through a sense-channel* (comm. to I.7) and there is the holy text 'By the mind alone he sees, by the mind he hears' (Bṛhad. Up. I.5.3).

(Opponent) As the senses have recourse to light, so the mind is a perceiver only when it has recourse to the help of the senses.

(Answer) No, because even the example is not invariably so. Nocturnal animals, for instance, see things by a second kind of faint light, as if it were full day. And even in the light of day, an owl does not see anything at all.

Further, take the case of weighing gold. We see that an expert can tell the amount of it by merely looking, without using any means of finding out the weight (such as using the scales).

(Opponent) Then the eye and other senses serve no purpose.

(Answer) The senses are like the scales, in that they are useful for the others. Just as a man who has very fine discrimination in the field of weighing has the skill to determine the quantity of gold without using any scales, so there is the possibility of the mind's perceiving an object, through its own great purity, even without calling on the aid of senses like the eye.

For a result which is normally accomplished by several men may still be accomplished by one; for example, a stone which would take more than one to lift may be seen to be lifted single-handed by some strong man.

So it is that the objects which are perceived by the mind of others only with the aid of the senses are perceived by the mind-sattva of the supreme Lord by its simple regard, without their having to be observed through an eye and so on. There is perfection of pure power and glory in Him, where they reach their peak.

But because of the inferiority of the saṃsārin-s (beings of the world) in power and knowledge, due to the taint of Ignorance, their mind depends on the aid of the senses, as when weak people combine to lift a stone.

Now there are certain worldly beings, like Buddha and Ṛṣabha, who become lords, but they do not achieve the transcendent power, knowledge and glory. Because there is the fact that they are limited by time; even those who are devoted to their religion admit that the Buddhas are limited by time.

So their Lord is limited in time. It can only be inferred, from the evidences of their being in time and having a beginning in time, that the sovereignty and so on of the Buddhas is not complete and has degrees. At one time they did not have it, at one time they do not have it, at one time they will not have it – these are the three indications for the inference. It is thus the opposite of transcendence.

Since their perfection is time-dependent, the earlier Buddhas would have had the advantage of time, but there could not be unlimited power and glory and omniscience in them, because it would be opposed by that of later ones.

(Opponent) They have equal power and knowledge and sovereignty, but their equal sovereignty and rulership is not at the same time.

(Answer) Still, since that would mean frustration of a desire of some Buddha from a different time to come into touch with things of this time, he could not have absolute sovereignty. For inasmuch as desire has no bounds, one Buddha will some time desire to overrule another Buddha and to come into his sphere; if he does not do it, his omnipotence would be impaired.

(Opponent) Another Buddha has no need of his grace. And there is no passion in him, so he will have no desire to enter the sphere of another Buddha.

(Answer) Formerly he had the desire for the condition of Buddhahood at some time, and that must come to fulfilment in the time of some Buddha or other. And there are other living beings to whom he could give his grace, so it is reasonable that he should wish to dwell in that other time. Not all the living beings of that time will have been given grace by the future Buddha.

Though it is suffering for his Buddhahood, yet in order to give his grace to living beings, from his Buddhahood he will come to be in that other time, according to his wish.

And the Buddhists admit that their perfect one's state of Buddha-nature and freedom from pain was formerly associated with Ignorance, so that transcendent power, knowledge and glory do not pertain to Buddha or to Ṛṣabha or any other tīrthakara.

But these defects do not apply to our Lord, for he is not limited in time. His power, knowledge and sovereignty are unlimited, and so we infer that no defect of having degrees or uncertainty can be suspected of him who is as it were like space.

> *Inference comes to an end in determining a universal and it cannot pronounce on individual cases. Particulars like names are to be known from sacred authority. He himself needs no grace; his purpose is to give grace to living beings, by teaching knowledge and dharma. At the dissolution at the end of the aeon, and at the great dissolution, he resolves, 'I will save them, caught as they are in saṃsāra.' So it is said: The First Knower, assuming a created mind out of compassion, as the exalted highest seer declared the doctrine to the inquirer Āsuri.*

Inference comes to an end in determining a universal and it cannot pronounce on individual cases. In determining the universal of the existence of a special Puruṣa with transcendent power, knowledge and sovereignty, the inference exhausts itself, because it goes only so far. The example of inference which was given (sūtra 1.7) was, that if there is getting to a place, there must be movement. Inference has no capacity to determine individual qualities or names, etc., of the Lord, though they exist, because these are not in the field of a pure universal.

To sum up: inference cannot tell us about individual qualities, because all it does is to reveal universals. How should inference reveal things absolutely inaccessible to it, outside its field, matters where it has no power or knowledge, questions of dharma and a-dharma and limitation and so on? So it does not reveal what is outside its field.

(But in its field) the inference that omniscience exists does not need the failure of the inference that omniscience does not exist. For inference is not something which has to wait for confirmation by another; when fire is inferred from the sight of smoke one does not wait for a statement by a third party.

He himself needs no grace because there is nothing which he lacks for himself; *his purpose is to give his grace to living beings* sunk in the mire of Ignorance. There is no other to give the teaching which is a boat by which they can cross over the sea of saṃsāra, and he teaches knowledge and dharma to those who take sole refuge in him.

Nor is the fact whether he is or is not omniscient to be arbitrarily taken as self-evidently doubtful, because we do not hold that the true being of the omniscient one is self-evident like a jar. Until it is settled that it is truly a hare, one cannot doubt whether or not the hare has horns.

(Opponent) What comes from another is dubious.

(Answer) It may come from another, but if you yourself do not know the true nature of the Lord, why should you doubt it?

(Opponent) He might be under an illusion.

(Answer) If no universal (of omniscience) is ever perceived, it cannot be a cause of illusion. For no one erroneously sees a cuckoo in the mother-of-pearl (in which they do sometimes erroneously see silver, which they must have seen existing somewhere else). So he says, *Particulars like names are to be known from sacred authority.* They are to be looked for in scriptures like the Veda, Itihāsa, Purāna, and books on yoga and dharma.

by teaching knowledge and dharma to those who take refuge in none other, who have entrusted themselves to him entirely, *at the dissolution at the end of the aeon and at the great dissolution* when the particular knowledge from the scriptures, which were received from the grace of the Lord, and the teachers of that knowledge, are all destroyed, again and again compassion rises to fill him – 'I will save them'. And likewise it has been said, *The First Knower, assuming a created mind out of compassion, as the exalted highest seer declared the doctrine to the inquirer Āsuri.* The First Knower means the one who in the beginning knows the knowledge which is not affected by rajas or tamas. Or the word *first* may refer to the fact that knowledge and dharma are at the beginning and the teaching begins with them, and that beginning is this Knower. He created a mind by his mere intention, a yogic mind, and entered into possession of it, in order to give the teaching.

as the exalted highest seer (ṛṣi): that he is the highest is known from scripture (āgama). Ṛṣi means, according to the root, on the one hand 'seeing' (from ṛṣ to see) and on the other hand 'condition' (from ṛ to go). The Lord alone, the highest ṛṣi, under the names Kapila or Nārāyana and so on, taught the inquirer Āsuri.

Therefore the Lord has been ascertained to be other than pradhāna or Puruṣa, and to be the source of grace for all living beings through his knowledge of their states and the ripening of the fruits of their karma. It is not to be objected that this does not show how the Lord endowed with the wealth of perfect sattva does create, or how he grants his grace, and so on, for it has been said, *From scripture it is to be sought.* There are things outside the range of inference to which it cannot reach, since it does not extend to particulars and their relationships.

Sūtra I.26

This teacher of even the first teachers, because not particularized by time

The first teachers are particularized by time. But with the Lord, time as a measure does not apply to him who is the teacher of even the first teachers. It is to be understood that as he is proved to be in the state of perfection at the beginning of this creation, so too at the beginning of past creations.

This highest Lord who has been described is *the teacher of even the first teachers,* those who teach all the related means and ends for material results and for the highest bliss (niḥśreyasa). The meaning is that he creates the knowledge and instruction which they give. For all the kinds of knowledge arise from him, as sparks of fire from a blaze or drops of water from the sea.

We have mentioned that he is the first knower, *since he is not particularized by time.* Other teachers are so particularized; they are qualified by past or future, or by being present now. But this Lord is inferred by them, and so by us, to be the eternally freed Lord.

(Opponent) Since he is a teacher like the others, how is it that he is not particularized by time?

(Answer) *time as a measure does not apply to him* to whom no measure can apply. A measure with its various sub-divisions may determine the limits of all that changes, but cannot make the Lord an object of its operations.

(Opponent) The perfect sattva of the Lord is an effect of pradhāna, and any effect of pradhāna must be particularized by time. So why not the divine sattva? It is only Puruṣa, and nothing else, which is not particularized by time, and that is because Puruṣa does not change. You might, of course, suppose that the Lord has no connection with any sattva, like the Lord in some other doctrines.

(Answer) No, because it is accepted by us that he is endowed with perfect sattva.

(Opponent) You could suppose that it is only the effect produced by the Lord's sattva which time particularizes, and not the sattva itself.

(Answer) That is not right either, because anything which is manifest can be measured, and the sattva of the Lord is manifest.

(Opponent) You might say that the divine sattva exists only in the latent state of pradhāna.

(Answer) That will not do, because then there would be no knowledge from it.

(Opponent) Well then you might say that you accept the doctrine that the effect *is* the cause, so that the sattva is the latent pradhāna state of knowledge.

(Answer) This is not satisfactory either, because it has to be available for ordinary life. And if it were so, it would mean that the knowledge of different people could not be distinct, because it would all be in a state of mere being, without any separate relations.

(Opponent) Or you could say that in the state of manifestation, some of the effects are distinguishable by time, and not others.

(Answer) That is contrary to reason.

(Opponent) You could meet that objection by saying that it is proved by scripture that the divine sattva transcends time.

(Answer) Not so, because scripture only makes facts clear (but does not create them).

(Opponent) You might argue that it is only the fact of the now manifesting sattva transcending time, unknown as that fact is, which scripture makes clear.

(Answer) Not that even, for it has its cause in the states of inhibition, which would be limited by time on this view; but as it is perfectly pure (in those states too) it could not be limited; so there would be a contradiction.

So the conclusion is, that in view of the perfect purity of the divine sattva, it is proper that it should transcend time.

(Opponent) The perfection of purity of other teachers transcends time because it is caused by their being endowed with yoga and dharma and so on, but this is not so with the Lord.

(Answer) The sattva of the Lord is pure sattva, and in it rajas and tamas are always subdued, so that it is independent of dharma, etc., as a cause; the knowledge which rises in it is purely illuminative and transcends time.

And the supremacy which is its effect also transcends time. As the heat and light of fire are not delimited by time in the fire, so the purity, knowledge and perfection of the divine sattva attain the state transcending time. So the commentator states *with the Lord, time as a measure does not apply,* and this is said just of these effects.

His role as teacher has no limits. *he is proved to be in the state of perfection* in knowledge and purity *at the beginning of this creation, and so at the beginning of other creations as well.* It is proved by inference from the fact of creation of beings, and also made known by the scriptures. *so too at the beginning of past creations* of the beings of those former times. In the same way inference and scripture establish it for future times as well.

The purport of the sūtra is this: Just as seen guru-s are continuously served, in their capacity as teachers of knowledge and dharma and other things, by pupils who depend on them exclusively, so this Lord who is the teacher of all teachers should be meditated upon in the worshipper's heart, by those devoted to him alone under his various names like Nārāyana.

Just as the human teachers turn their face towards the wholly devoted pupil and give him their favour, so this supreme teacher gives his favour when there is pure contemplation on him. The holy text says:

He who has supreme devotion to the Lord, and to his teacher as to the Lord, is a mahātmā, and from him shine forth these glories which have been related
(Śvet. Up. 6.23)

and tradition says:

He who does works for me, seeing me as the supreme, devoted to me, Free from attachment, without hatred for any, he comes to me, O Pāṇḍava

(Gītā II.55)

Sūtra I.27

Of him, the expression is praṇava (OM)

What is expressed by praṇava is the Lord.

It has been said *Or from devotion to the Lord (sūtra I.23).* How should one perform devotion to him, and what is the means of that devotion? To explain the form in which the devotee contemplates on him, the sūtra says *Of him, the expression is praṇava (OM).* Of the Lord who has been described, the *expression* the expressing word, *is praṇava.* In the same way the word cow expresses something which has a dewlap and horns and so on. Now the word praṇava is variously explained etymologically:

pra stands for *pra*karśena, perfectly;
nu (= nava) stands for *nū*yate, he is praised;
praṇava the word OM, praises (*praṇau*ti) the Lord;
the Lord is devoutly worshipped (*praṇi*dhīyate) through it by his devotees; they bow down (*praṇam*) to him through it;
through it they worship *(praṇi*dhā) the Lord mentally; here the extra -dhā stands for the final -va (of praṇava).

Mental devotion for things known only indirectly is through a word, as with the worship of the sacred mountain Meru or the god Indra. It is the Lord who is expressed by the word OM; the sound of the word accords with its meaning.

From the termination *-ava* is understood *ava*ti, he favours. The meanings like 'protection' are excluded from this word here. He brings out his devotees from saṃsāra, he leads those in saṃsāra to nirvāṇa, he brings to a devotee unsurpassed joy, he grants him samādhi to lead him to the highest truth. But all these meanings are associated with the most intense love of the Lord.

Does the power of expression of this syllable OM arise from conventional usage, or is it something fixed, like the relation between a lamp and its light?

The relation of what is to be expressed here, and its expressive word, is fixed. But conventional usage directs attention to what has been established by the Lord. Thus the relation of father and son is a fixed one, but it is made clear by conventional usage in the form 'He is that man's father; that man is his son'.

When the Lord is continuously worshipped in the mind by means of this syllable OM, he gives his grace. There are many sacred texts such as 'Om kham brahman' (Bṛhad. Up. 5.1.1) 'Brahman called Om' (Taitt. Up. 1.8.1) and the traditions 'Om tat sat' (Gītā 17.23) 'Om Viṣṇu is all' (first name of the Thousand Names of Viṣṇu). The grammarians declare that OM, ending as it does in 'm', is an indeclinable which does not take inflections.

(Opponent) Granted that the Lord, or someone, set up at some time this convention for common usage, in the form 'let this (OM) be the name of that (Lord)'. But before the convention was set up, thus giving devotees an option whether to worship by OM as the name of the Lord or by some other name, they would have used one of the other names. So let it be now; why should OM be singled out (as his expressive word)?

(Answer) The relation is *fixed like that between a lamp and its light.* So even at a first hearing, the Lord is understood, like the sun by its light.

(Opponent) If there is already a fixed relation, it is pointless to have a convention about it too. Unless the convention is established from the first, it is only a useless reiteration.

(Answer) *The relation of what is to be expressed here and its expressive word is fixed.* Whether the word be taken as permanent or transient, the conventional usage makes luminously clear that very fixed relation.

(Opponent) If the relation is fixed, people ought to understand it the first time they hear it.

(Answer) The relation of word and meaning is a relation of idea and what causes the idea, and though it is fixed, it is not perceptible to the senses, any more than the relation between a sense and its object. The capacity to express, and the capacity to be expressed, are not directly perceptible things.

(Opponent) Well, the meaning can be inferred from the word by which it is spoken.

(Answer) That is not so, because the relation is not perceptible. It depends on the usage of others, and an inference does not depend on the usage of others (so this cannot be an inference).

> *The convention is established exactly in accordance with the relation of the capacity of expression and the capacity for being expressed at the beginning of creations. The scriptural sages affirm that the relation of word and meaning is permanent, inasmuch as it is permanently accepted.*

(Opponent) An object can be inferred from a relation which is itself inferred.

(Answer) You will have to explain how a relation of word and meaning can be inferred.

(Opponent) Having ascertained the meaning from seeing the effect of the word (on its hearers), he understands the relation between them, just as when one knows a form through the eye, that is the visual relation.

(Answer) There is this refutation: definite knowledge comes from the word alone, without any inference. And when one has achieved his object by cooking food in one way, what would he gain by cooking it in another way?

(Opponent) A relation is perceived from seeing the conjunction of the two things several times, as with the relation between fire and smoke.

(Answer) We do not agree, for even in a hundred conjunctions, the relation of word and meaning is never directly perceived, as is perceived the relation between fire and smoke even at the beginning. And it is the same thing with a sentence and its meaning.

Therefore the conventional usage makes clear the relation between the Lord who is expressed and praṇava (OM) which expresses him, which is a fixed relation like the fixed relation of father and son. Since there is a convention as the means, the meaning is not recognized at the first hearing, any more than an object in darkness is recognized by the eye.

(Opponent) A word is something passing, and how can there be a permanent relation when one of the things related is passing? There is no permanent relation between a rope and a pot, which are passing things.

(Answer) In the cases of proof and proven, sense-organ and its object, action and its agencies, there is a fixed relation although the things related are passing. So too here the relation is ever-fixed, because it never varies; *the convention is in accordance with the relation of the capacities of expression and being expressed at the beginning of creations.*

Just as there is creation of form and eye, in accordance with the capacity of being perceived and of perceiving in the previous creation, so in this case conventional usage is established in accordance with the capacity of being expressed and of expressing.

Since it is invariably accepted, and there is the growing chain of traditional use of one thing to make another understood, the consensus is permanent and not otherwise; so *the scriptural sages (āgamin)* expounders of the Veda (veda-vādin) *affirm.* And the relation of word and meaning is based on that consensus, so they tell us.

Therefore it comes to this: whether from the standpoint of the traditionalists or from the other standpoint, in any case the relation is fixed, like that of father and son, and it is made manifest by the conventional usage.

If there were not the fixed relation between this expressive word and what it expresses, it would not be true that through the form of praṇava, OM, the Lord is met face to face. In the same way it would not be proper to take a fire as the means of cooking unless there were a fixed relation between the raw food and what cooks it. But since there is the fixed relation between this expression and what it expresses, it is proper to employ OM as a means for practising worship of God, and this is the purport of the whole commentary.

When the yogin has recognized the power of OM to express its meaning (the Lord), he should undertake -

Sūtra I.28

Repetition of it and meditation on its meaning

Repetition (japa) of it and meditation (bhāvanā) on the Lord who is signified by OM. When the yogin thus repeats OM and meditates on its meaning, his mind becomes one-pointed. So it has been said:

After OM repetition, let him set himself in yoga,
After yoga, let him set himself to repetition.
When OM repetition and yoga come to perfection
The supreme self (paramātman) shines forth.

When the yogin has thus understood the relation of the expression OM and its meaning, how does he attract the grace of the supreme Lord? The sūtra says, *Repetition of it and meditation on its meaning.*Practice of repetition of OM, which is the expression of the Lord, taken as consisting of three-and-a-half measures (mātra) or of three measures, is called japa; the repetition is either mental or in a low voice (upāṃśu).

meditation on its meaning the meditation is setting the heart on the Lord, the meaning, who by the word OM has been recalled and brought into the mind. The words *he should undertake* are to be supplied at the beginning of the sūtra. Yogin-s who are doing both attain one-pointedness of mind. He illustrates how the one-pointedness is the result of that worship by quoting the verse.

After OM repetition after repetition of the praṇava syllable, his mind bowed before the Lord, *let him set himself in yoga* let him meditate on the Lord, its meaning. When his mind becomes unwavering from meditation on the Lord, the meaning, *let him set himself to repetition* let him repeat OM mentally. Mental repetition is recommended because it is closer to meditation (than is verbal repetition). The sense is that the mind must not run towards objects. *When OM repetition and yoga come to perfection* when he is not disturbed by other ideas contrary to them, he is perfect in repetition and in yoga; by that perfection in repetition and meditation on the supreme Lord (parameśvara) *the supreme self (paramātman)* who stands in the highest place (parameṣṭhin) *shines forth* for the yogin.

And what happens to him?

Sūtra I.29

From that, realization of the separate consciousness, and absence of obstacles

As a result of devotion to the Lord, there are none of the obstacles like illness, and he has a perception of his own true nature. As the Lord is a Puruṣa, pure, radiant, alone, and beyond evil, so the Puruṣa in him, witness of the buddhi, knows himself to be.

The commentary introduces this sūtra with the words *And what happens to him?* The word *And* refers to the fact that one result, namely attainment of one-pointedness of mind, has already been mentioned in the previous sūtra. And is there some other result for him, or is it perhaps one-pointedness alone? The sūtra now says *From that, realization of the separate consciousness and absence of obstacles.* From that devotion to the Lord, there is realization of the separate consciousness: it is conscious of its own buddhi as separate, and so the self (ātman) is called the separate consciousness. The realization of it is awareness of one's own nature as it really is.

(Opponent) The Puruṣa is already realized in everyone in the feeling 'I am happy' or 'I am sad'. This is a well-known fact; why the special mention of it?

(Answer) True, but it is not seen as distinct by the thought in the mind. In 'I am happy' or 'I am sad', the 'happy' and 'sad' have the same common referent, the idea 'here I am', and they are in the field of mental processes, so they are certainly merely ideas of Ignorance.

He realizes: *As the Lord is a Puruṣa, pure* free from the stains (mala) of the taints, etc., and therefore
radiant clear, and therefore
alone (kevala) without the three guṇa-s, and therefore
beyond evil without the three kinds of suffering, a perfect being, who is
witness, so this too, my own Puruṣa, is pure, radiant, alone, beyond evil, and
witness of the buddhi.

With the words *As* and *so,* which point to an example and something like that example, he announces that there is a difference between the

Lord and the individual selves (kṣetrajña). This is because they (unlike the Lord) are subject to bondage and release, and also because pradhāna serves their purposes (first experience and then release). For these reasons too the kṣetrajña-s differ among themselves.

Now what are the obstacles? They are what distracts the mind. Which are they, and how many are they?

Sūtra I.30

Illness, apathy, doubt, carelessness, laziness, failure to withdraw, misconceptions, failure to attain a state, instability (in the state) – these distractions of the mind are the obstacles

There are nine obstacles which distract the mind. They appear only in conjunction with the mental processes described previously, and without the obstacles, the latter do not arise.

Illness is loss of balance in the humours (dhātu), secretions (rasa) or organs. Apathy is mental ineffectiveness. Doubt is an idea embracing both alternatives, in the form 'This might be so, or it might not be so'. Carelessness is lack of devotion to the means to samādhi. Laziness is inertia from heaviness physical and mental. Failure to withdraw is a hankering caused by past addiction to objects. Misconceptions are illusory knowledge (viparyaya jñāna). Failure to attain a state is not attaining any stage of samādhi. Instability is when a state has been attained but the mind is not established in it. It is an obstacle because in true attainment of samādhi the mind would be established there.

These distractions are explained as the blemishes, adversaries and obstacles of yoga.

In number they are nine, and they consist of illness and the rest. *Illness* is loss of balance in the humours, secretions or organs. The humours are air, bile, and phlegm; when the harmony between them is lost they become out of balance, and this happens when there is habitual excess (of one or two of them). Medicine teaches that an increase of a humour may be spontaneous or caused by something else.

The secretions are particular transformations of the food eaten. They are of seven kinds, and they are called secretions (rasa) because they are effects of the food-essence (rasa). Technically they are named rasa, blood, fat, flesh, bone, marrow and semen (śukla) and they become out of balance when there is excess or loss.

Disorder of the *organs* is blindness, deafness, etc.

Apathy is mental ineffectiveness a sort of paralysis.

Doubt is an idea which touches two contradictory alternatives, for instance, 'Is it a post or a man?'

Carelessness is lack of devotion to the means to samādhi a lack of persistence.

Laziness is *inertia from heaviness physical and mental.*

Failure to withdraw means either actual contact with the objects, or *hankering* the desire or thirst *caused by past addiction.*

Misconceptions are illusory knowledge deluded ideas about the yoga methods or the path itself.

Failure to attain a state not attaining any stage of samādhi; the stages such as vitarka have been mentioned as particular qualities of the mind, and will be discussed later (sūtra I.41–44).

Instability is when a stage of samādhi has been attained but it is unstable. Then by some means he should try to re-establish his unsteady mind in it. If this attempt is not successful, it is called instability.

These are the nine obstacles (antarāya). They are called antarāya because they move (āya) towards or create, an interval (antara), a gap, a break. They are known as the distractions, adversaries or blemishes in the achievement of yoga.

They appear only in conjunction with the processes of the mind described previously. They are distractions of mind because they distract it with various objects, and they appear only in conjunction with the processes of the mind of the five kinds, the two groups being reciprocally impelling and impelled. *without the obstacles* in the absence of illness and the other obstacles, the aforesaid mental processes like right knowledge do not arise, because there is no power to support them. As inevitably causing processes in the mind, the mental distractions are all classed as equally unfavourable.

Sūtra I.31

Pain, frustration, restlessness of the body, spasmodic breathing in or out are the accompaniments of these distractions

> *The pain is that proceeding from the self, or proceeding from living creatures, or proceeding from the gods. Pain is that by which living beings are struck down, and which they struggle to end. Frustration is the mental agitation when a desire is obstructed. Restlessness of the body is what makes it unsteady and trembling. Spasmodic breathing is inhaling the air from outside, or exhaling the abdominal air. These are the accompaniments of the distractions; they occur in one whose mind is distracted, and do not occur in one whose mind is concentrated in samādhi.*

Pain is that by which living beings are struck down, and to end which they struggle, they strive. It is of three kinds, the first being that *proceeding from the self (ādhyātmika).* What is related (adhy) to self (ātman) is adhyātma, and what arises from that is ādhyātmika. The pain is physical or mental. Physical is caused by disharmony of the humours, etc., and mental is caused by frustration of desires. The second is that *proceeding from living creatures (ādhibhautika).* Adhibhūti is what relates to (adhi) creatures (bhūta), and what is caused by them is ādhibhautika. And it is what comes about from domestic or wild animals, such as deer and other creatures. The third is that *proceeding from the gods (ādhidaivika).* Adhideva is what relates to (adhi) the gods (deva), and what comes about from them is ādhidaivika, for instance what is caused by rain and wind. The change of the vowels in these cases is by the rule of grammar that compounds like adhyātma, when they take the -ika suffix, undergo the vṛddhi strengthening in both their parts.

Pain is only one – of the nature of rajas – but it is here classified under the different causes.

Frustration is the mental agitation when a desire is obstructed; it is a baffled moving about.

Restlessness of the body is what makes it unsteady and trembling.

Spasmodic breathing in or out means in the first case drawing in the air in deep gasps but exhaling it slowly, while the second is the reverse.

These are the accompaniments of the distractions in that they are concomitants of distraction. *They do not occur in one whose mind is concentrated:* to the extent that it is concentrated, to that extent they do not occur.

These distractions which are antagonistic to samādhi are to be inhibited only by that pair, practice and detachment.

The distractions can be inhibited or extinguished only by the pair, practice and detachment. Distractions are unaffected by any other counter-measures. When it is said, in the commentary to I.29, *From devotion to the Lord, realization of the separate consciousness and absence of obstacles,* that obstacles are inhibited also by a previous devotion to the Lord, it is implied that there is no capacity to become devotees of the Lord without practice and detachment.

He sums up the content of practice in the following sūtra:

Sūtra I.32

To prevent them, practice on one principle

To prevent the distractions, let the mind practise meditation on one principle.

It has been said that they are inhibited by detachment and practice; the first has been described, and now he deals with practice. *To prevent them,* these distractions *practice on one principle,* on a single truth.

(Opponent) That one principle cannot be the object of meditation practice, because it is a real thing, and the fullness of real things like self (ātman) cannot even be spoken. They are established in their own greatness and not simply mental. He is going on to deny that such real things have any dependence on the mind, for instance in sūtra IV.16, *A thing is not dependent on a single mind.*

(Answer) With this doubt in mind the commentator says, *let the mind practise meditation on one principle.* Here he is showing how to understand what the sūtra says about practice on one principle.

But for one who (like a Buddhist) holds that mind is something momentary, no more than the (succession of) ideas determined by each object in turn – for him mind must be invariably one-pointed, and can never be distracted.

(Opponent) There is no one enduring mind which could hold an idea resting on a single principle. The mind *is* simply the ideas, each determined by an object in turn and each perishing each moment. There is no stability in the ideas which could be known as a self. Nor is any mind perceived as an enduring possessor of the ideas, apart from them. Even the idea of I as 'I' is only a relation of similarity because it too is only a flow (of ideas). It is as with a lamp-flame, which is nothing more than the hairs of the wick.

(Answer) This would mean that the possessor of the successive I-notions would be itself different for each one, because it would be identical with the ideas, which are absolutely distinct from each other. The possessor would have as its object the idea of the 'I' then present, and so be different from the possessors of the I–notions which are past or to come, because they would have other notions for their objects, different as a cloth from a jar, or rather, differentiated by time as a jar now present is different from one that has been broken or one not yet made. All the I-notions would be separate mental objects, just because they are notions, like notions of a jar and a cloth and other things.

He points out, moreover, that the view would contradict the (Buddhist's own) scripture: *for one who holds that mind is something momentary … mind must be invariably one-pointed,* just because there could be no distraction there. And since the mind could only be one-pointed and without distraction, the teaching of the scripture about removing distraction would be meaningless. There is the teaching (in Buddhist scripture also) of meditation on friendliness, etc., for training the mind, and to hold the mind to be as he maintains, would contradict the scripture.

(Opponent) Neither is there distraction if we accept your theory of something which possesses the successive ideas (vṛtti), because it is not separate from them; so the teaching about removing distraction would be pointless for you too.

(Answer) Not so, because we maintain that it possesses idea after idea. If indeed the ideas were produced separate from each other, independent and absolutely separate from their possessor, and determined each by its object, there would be this difficulty. But we do not admit this.

What then is our position? In its nature as possessor of the ideas, mind is a unity which has many objects; it is apart from the field of its objects, the ideas, and is steady, since we do not accept the illusion of its being both existent and non-existent. And so the commentator shows that the theory of self (ātman) is correct.

It is a fact that mind is withdrawn from all quarters and concentrated in samādhi on one object (in Buddhism also) and is then one-pointed. It follows that it is not something determined by successive objects.

If this mind runs in various directions because of the change of ideas, then for you (the Buddhist), just as if you were a follower of Sāṅkhya and yoga, it is *withdrawn* restrained *from all quarters* from all objects *and concentrated in samādhi* made steady *on one object* such as the self (ātman) *and is then one-pointed.* The sense is that this is something which is a proper goal of human effort.

So the teaching of scripture about training the mind is logical. *It follows that it is not something determined by successive objects:* from his own scriptural teaching about training the mind, the advocate of momentariness has already assumed, like the follower of Sāṅkhya and yoga, a mind which is a unity but with many objects, and not determined by successive objects. Otherwise he would be contradicting his own scripture.

If one (a Buddhist) holds that a mind is one-pointed as a stream of similar thoughts, one-pointedness being a property of the stream-mind, then the stream-mind, being composed of momentary instants, cannot be a unity.

(Opponent) A stream of similar thoughts is the one-pointed mind. It is a stream of thoughts which are similar, alike, and as that single series, the mind is one-pointed. The opposite, a stream of thoughts which are dissimilar, is distraction. One-pointedness is attained by ruling out distraction, and that is the purpose of the teaching, so where is there any contradiction of our scripture?

(Answer) There is, for the Buddhist does not admit that a stream of mind is a single thing to be possessor of qualities. For he does not accept a stream-mind which is a single thing possessing the qualities of the ideas past, present and future. If he did accept it, he would have to give up his own position. How so? Because the stream-mind, not being momentary, cannot be a single thing (which in the Buddhist system must be momentary) which could have the quality of one-pointedness. For all he accepts is ideas, closely following on one another like a line of red ants.

(Opponent) Let us suppose that even if it is not a single thing, there can still be a quality of one-pointedness of the totality of the ideas as streams of similar ideas, as it were the illumination consisting of all the rays of a lamp.

(Answer) Not so; for things which rise and perish at different times cannot form a combination. And the example does not demonstrate the point; the many rays do not make up one illumination, because they are different from one another. The illumination is not one single quality of the rays.

> *It may be maintained that it is as a member of the stream that an idea has the quality of one-pointedness; but since each idea is determined by its object, whether the stream be of similar or dissimilar ideas, each must be one-pointed and there will never be distraction. Therefore there has to be some enduring mind, one but with many objects. How could ideas be produced, inherently independent and not linked to a single mind? For one idea would remember what had been seen by another idea, and one idea would have experiences in accordance with the karma-s accumulated by other ideas.*

(Opponent) *It may be maintained that it is as a member of the stream that an idea has the quality of one-pointedness,* as in a line of red ants, each single ant is red.

(Answer) That involves the same defect as before. Each idea is a member of the stream, whether that is of similar or dissimilar ideas, and as before, it follows that it can only be one-pointed, since it is determined by its object; as a result there will never be distraction. And so if the training of the mind is to be taught by the scripture, some enduring mind has to be accepted, one but with many objects.

How could ideas be produced, inherently independent and not linked to a single mind as their cause? You must answer this. For it would mean that one would remember something seen by another – Yajñadatta would be remembering what had been seen by Devadatta.

And one idea would have experiences in accordance with the karma-s accumulated by other ideas. An unborn son ought not to come to enjoy the fruit, heaven or the like, of accumulated karma performed by his father (for himself).

(Opponent) For the purpose of the particular consciousness of the future son, the active consciousness as it perishes lays down some saṃskāra in the seed-bed consciousness (ālaya-vijñāna).

(Answer) Not so; because the seed-bed consciousness and the active consciousness are entirely distinct, and moreover are not real (vastu).

If the active consciousness is not different from the seed-bed consciousness, then they are one and the same thing and there is a difference only in name, so there would not be a memory connected with the laying down of a saṃskāra. If however they are different, in that case the separate active consciousness, just because it is separate, will not register as a saṃskāra in this particular seed-bed consciousness any more than in the seed-bed consciousness of some other stream.

Even if we allow that it does lay down a saṃskāra, still the seed-bed consciousness, being the saṃskāra-s laid down by the active consciousness, is not relevant to another place and time. And since it is accepted (by the Buddhist) as momentary, inasmuch as it perishes instantly, it cannot serve to help any other consciousness. If we allow that it can help even though separated by time and space, then it will also have to help in the production of yet other separate series.

If it remains as it is into another time, then momentariness is abandoned; if it stays for another moment, why should it not stay for a long time?

(Opponent) The first seed-bed consciousness perishes after it has laid down a saṃskāra of the future seed-bed consciousness, which is similar to itself, of the particular saṃskāra of the active consciousness which is to exist in the future time.

(Answer) Not that either. Because there is no other saṃskāra. If there were one, it would entail an infinite regress. If there is no substratum, then how can the idea of a seed-bed consciousness of the active consciousness help for laying down a saṃskāra? If a seed-bed consciousness is to lay down the saṃskāra of the future seed-bed consciousness which is to arise in the future and which does not exist yet, let the active consciousness itself lay down the saṃskāra of the future active consciousness which is to arise, but which does not exist yet, without looking to a seed-bed consciousness.

There is no example of something perishing laying down a saṃskāra of something else which is in the future and not yet existent. Nor can it make a saṃskāra in what is merely future. It is a contradiction to say that a future thing is being impressed with a saṃskāra by a previous thing, and at the same time to say that it is future. If a future thing, not existent at the time, is to be so impressed, what sense would it have to speak of the series as being the same or not the same? No definite connection being there, anything could be impressed by anything.

It cannot be a simultaneous disappearance of the perishing one and rise of the future one, because that would entail non-momentariness.

(Opponent) Let it be like the ends of a balance – one goes down as the other comes up. It *is* a simultaneous perishing of the previous one and rise of the following one, of two momentary things (vastu).

(Answer) No, for that goes against your premise. For the one who holds this position (Vaināśika Buddhist) does not accept any other agency apart from the action of rise and destruction.

When action and agent are separate, inasmuch as the production of the action by the agent has to be something enduring, the doctrine of momentariness has to be abandoned. If there is nothing enduring, then the purpose of the action which is its motive would become no purpose.

If the action alone is the agency, and the agent is action, then the words 'action' and 'agent' would be synonyms. By the same reasoning, because a sprout is born and Devadatta is born, 'sprout' and 'Devadatta' should be synonyms. For in both cases there would be mere action of birth.

(Opponent) One action of birth is particular to Devadatta, and the other is particular to the sprout.

(Answer) Then distinction of agency is admitted, for there is no distinction in the fact itself.

(Opponent) One action of production is in itself distinct from another action of production, as the forms characterizing them are distinct.

(Answer) No, because that would entail the oneness of existence and nonexistence. 'Here a sprout is born: the sprout dies' – that which is born is that which dies. In this case when it is said 'birth' and 'death', it is sprout-birth and sprout-death. For the sprout is said to be the action or agent.

(Opponent) Still, the action of sprout-death is separate from the action of sprout-birth.

(Answer) Then the sprout-birth would be permanent, because the death is something separate from it.

(Opponent) It can be a combination of destruction and production.

(Answer) That would mean that a non-existent could be a combination. Why so? On your theory, there is no agent apart from the action itself; destruction itself has birth and destruction, and birth itself has birth and destruction. That non-existent (agency) cannot have attributes like being a combination, for what is non-existent has no attributes; thus you blur the distinction between existent and non-existent, and your assumption cannot be justified through perception or inference.

As to the example of the rise and fall respectively of the two ends of a weighing balance, the two ends of the balance are there at the same time, and the fall of one is due to the addition of something else, a weight, and so is the rise of the other. But here it is the destruction and production of two consciousnesses, one present and one future, and as in the case of the cause of the movement of the balance, unless there is some third thing as an outside cause, they will not happen at the one time. One cannot say that what is merely perishing produces a consciousness similar to itself; it would be absurd that Devadatta in the act of dying should by his death produce a son like himself.

(Opponent) As the lump of clay perishes in causing the production of a jar, so here.

(Answer) No, because that is simply the parts of the clay changing into the form of the jar. It is like one sorceress that possesses the many qualities, of lump of clay, of jar, and of others.

As to the case when seeds have made a dynamic-impression (vāsanā) on something else, the so-called conforming to the impressing thing by the thing impressed is still not a case of causation, because both the thing impressed and the impressor are enduring. For it is only enduring things, like the sprouts in the seeds, which are impressed by the dynamic-impressions of the seeds. There are also subtle parts of the impressing substance which do not at all enter into the process. Therefore it is logical that it is only presently existent sprouts, etc., which are impressed by the dynamic-impressions of the seeds. For there is no production of non-existent things like the horns of a hare. If it were a non-existent thing which is produced, then since the impressed and the impressor would both have perished, and what is not presently existing has nothing to distinguish it, it would not conform to the impressing substance, and would not arise. Or else, it might turn out to be something else, like a hand.

Or if absolute non-existence is to be produced, like the horn of a hare, then something defined as non-existent in the three periods of time would have to be in the impressed seed. Therefore an enduring agency, in conjunction with the several mental processes of present and future, has to be admitted.

To try to force this argument is to exemplify the fallacious argument that cow-dung, as being also a product of the cow, can make a milk dish.

And to suppose the mind to be a stream of different things would be to deny one's own experience. When it is said 'What I saw, that I am touching', and 'What I touched, that I remember', though there is difference in the ideas, there is no difference in the notion of the 'I' as the common subject which has those ideas. This common self, the notion 'I', has as its field a single possessor of the ideas; how could it refer to a possessor of the ideas which is present as a mere similarity in absolutely separate minds? The idea of this identical 'I' is grasped in one's own experience.

The man who seeks to maintain otherwise, namely that mind is no more than momentary ideas, exemplifies *the fallacious argument that cow-dung, as being also a product of the cow, can make a milk dish.* However energetically one may argue with many reasons, such as the fact that they are both products of the cow, one cannot make cow-dung out to be milk, and neither can he make memory and so on possible for a mind consisting of moments.

To suppose the mind to be a stream of different things would be to deny one's own experience; if the mind is to be no more than ideas, it denies one's own experience, in that one does not remember what has been seen by someone else.

If a (Buddhist) witness were asked, 'What did you see?' he would have to say 'I did not see', for on his theory what was seen was seen by another. How can there be such a denial of experience? *What I saw, that I am touching* and I alone; *what I touched, that I am remembering* and I alone. It is when there is one single subject of both the idea and the memory that knowledge presents a jar in the form 'this is that', otherwise it would be in the form 'what someone resembling me saw is what I, who resemble him, am touching'. The idea 'I' in every man is present as one single subject of memory and of ideas, and it is directly perceived in ideas like 'I am seeing', 'I am touching' and 'I am remembering' as the one subject of those ideas, established as the identical possessor of the ideas.

(Opponent) The object of an idea is quite different from the memory of it, and even in regard to the same thing, the 'I' of the thinking would not be the 'I' of the remembering, by the simple fact that the words 'thinker' and 'rememberer' are different.

(Answer) No, because we see it directly, as he shows: *The idea of this identical 'I' is grasped in one's own experience.*

> *And the supremacy of direct perception cannot be challenged by other means of right knowledge, because it is only by virtue of direct perception that they find any application.*

(Opponent) 'Thinker' and 'rememberer' are different words and different ideas, so the I-notion is to be inferred as applying to different things.

(Answer) *The supremacy of direct perception* its authoritativeness, as of what is before the very eyes, *cannot be challenged* cannot be impugned from the side of inference.

This I-notion is a matter of right knowledge by direct perception, not something existing as a single subject only by similarity between ideas and memories of it. If what is proved by direct perception were to be challenged by inference, then the authoritativeness of inference itself would be lost, because inference is itself based on perception. So he points out that it is only by virtue of direct perception that other means of right knowledge find their application as such. The opponent, by his denial of direct perception, with the (consequent) denial of inference, is exposed to the fallacy of undermining his own position.

What holds (ādhāra) the saṃskāra of the idea of the present moment is no different from what holds the saṃskara-s of the past and future ideas; there is something which illumines them, as of the nature of self, as belonging to the same stream.

The substratum (āsraya) of the saṃskāra of the idea of the present moment is no different from the substratum upholding the saṃskāra-s of the past and future ideas; there is something which illumines them, from its nature as the self, as belonging to the same stream.

The present possessor of the I-notion is not separate from the past and future possessors of it; they have the idea as from their very nature, being joined to the same stream.

The idea now present is not separated from the possessors of the idea in the past and future, because there is something which illumines them, by nature coloured by the self, as belonging to the same stream.

The present possessor of the idea is not separated from the ideas past and future, because there is something which illumines them, as of the nature of self, as belonging to the same stream.

Since it is not found that separate streams mutually confound their memories, and memory is only observed in the individual stream, it is certain that there is a single subject in each. It is known to be so by the proof of direct perception, of all proofs the weightiest, so there is nothing left to be demonstrated by inference. No one takes a mirror to look at a mark on the palm of his hand.

Even so, some who will not accept the collapse of the inferences presented by the Vaināśika Buddhists, still produce plausible counter-inferences, and so he sums up: Therefore the mind is something enduring, one and with many objects, and it is for such an enduring mind that the training (parikarman) is prescribed by the teaching (śāstra). He is showing that the teaching is meaningful.

Therefore it is established that the mind is one, with a number of objects. The method of training this mind is now to be given.

Sūtra I.33

The mind is made clear by meditation on friendliness towards the happy, compassion for the suffering, goodwill towards the virtuous, and disinterest in the sinful

Let him practise friendliness towards all beings experiencing happiness, compassion to those in pain, goodwill to the habitually virtuous, and disinterest in habitual sinners. Such devoted meditations produce pure dharma, and thereby the mind becomes clear. When it is clear, it attains steadiness in one-pointedness.

How is the mind to be trained? Practice on one principle has been taught; what is the one principle which is to be the object of the practice? He says, *meditation on friendliness towards the happy, compassion for the suffering, goodwill towards the virtuous, and disinterest in the sinful.*

Friendliness is meditation on being a friend, one who rejoices in happiness when he sees it without anything like envy. So towards suffering, a kindly sympathy, and to the righteous he feels goodwill. It is added that he should practise disinterest in regard to the doings of the habitually sinful.

Practice of this all the time produces pure dharma, which does no injury to living beings; this dharma makes the mind clear. *When it is clear, it attains steadiness in one-pointedness;* the meaning is that by one-pointedness it is concentrated in samādhi, as the Gītā says, 'The mind of the pure-hearted soon becomes steady' (II.65).

(Opponent) Disinterest cannot produce dharma because it is not an action, so why is it included?

(Answer) If indifference were not mentioned, the mind would become engaged with those habitually sinful, and from the taint arising from dealings with them, it would not be fit for meditations on friendliness and the others. Disinterest is mentioned only in the context of steadying the mind so that there should be no a-dharma arising from casual dealings involving habitual sinners. The great thing here is steadiness of the mind.

When he has thus engaged his mind in meditation on one principle in this way, the mind will come to samādhi and no obstacles will then arise.

Sūtra I.34

Or by expulsion and retention of prāṇa

Expulsion is emission of the abdominal air through the two nostrils by a conscious effort; retention refers to the process of prāṇāyāma. By these two means one can attain steadiness of the mind.

The word *Or* means an alternative, so this is a means to steadiness other than meditations on friendliness, etc. The sense is that one should attain steadiness by some one of the means beginning with meditation on friendliness; a number of means are given, with the idea that one of them will be easier to a particular person and time and place.

Expulsion and retention separately or together. The first is emission of the abdominal air up to the limit through the nostrils, not by the mouth. Retention is the full process of prāṇāyāma, to the limit. Though prāṇa is to some extent restrained even by expulsion (alone), its function of going out has not been inhibited, and so retention is added, meaning prāṇāyāma.

Sūtra I.35

Or achievement of supernormal perception of a divine object brings the mind to steadiness

When one makes a concentration (dhāraṇā) on the tip of the nose, he will have a sensation (saṃvit) of divine fragrance; on the palate, of colour; on the middle of the tongue, of touch; and on the root of the tongue, of sound. These supernormal perceptions arising hold the mind in steadiness, remove doubts, and become a means to samādhi cognition (samādhi-prajñā).

In the same way experiences like the moon, sun, a planet, a jewel, a light or a ray, are to be known as supernormal perceptions of actual objects.

Although what is understood from the scriptures and inferences from them, and from instruction by a teacher, are real facts, since these are qualified to describe things as they really are, still until some one part of it has been known directly for oneself, it is all second-hand as it were, and does not produce a firm

> *conviction about release and other subtle things. Therefore some one definite thing has to be directly experienced in confirmation of what has been learned from scripture and inference and the teacher.*

Or a supernormal perception of a divine object brings the mind to steadiness. This is a yogic perception, of some object like fragrance, for example, when that has been made the object of the meditation. There is a direct awareness (saṃvedana) of that fragrance.

For the yogin who is practising yoga which is to give face-to-face experience, the perception is the first direct awareness, and it gives him confidence, creating enthusiasm for the practice of yoga; it is like the appearance of smoke when wood is being rubbed together to create fire. Such a perception fills him with joy because of the confidence it creates, and brings his mind to steadiness.

When one makes a concentration on the tip of the nose, he will have a sensation (saṃvit) of fragrance an experience of delightful fragrance arises and continues, as if by the ordinary sense contact. This is the perception of fragrance. So with the tongue and others; they are the locations of concentration. *These perceptions hold the mind in steadiness, remove doubts, and become a means to samādhi-cognition.*

The forms of a ray, moon, sun, planet, or a light and so on, appearing to one who is concentrating his mind on them, or spontaneously when the meditation on the lotus of the heart is unsteady (vaiṣamya), *are to be known as perceptions of actual objects.*

Although what is understood from the scriptures and inferences from them and from instruction by a teacher, are real facts, and there is no uncertainty about them, inasmuch as there is no contradictory teaching, *still until some one part of it has been known directly for oneself until* there is a direct perception (pratyakṣa) of at least one thing taught by them *it is all second-hand, as it were, and does not produce a firm conviction about such subtle things as release. Therefore some specific thing has to be directly experienced, to reinforce what has been so learnt.*

> *When some one thing out of what has been taught has been directly perceived, everything else is firmly believed', including such subtle matters as release, and this is why the yogin is directed to train the mind in this way.*
>
> *As regards the concentrations of the mind which have not been mastered, when the consciousness of mastery has arisen in regard to the objects (so far practised), he will be able to perceive directly (and thereby master) all the others. Then faith, energy, memory and samādhi will come to him without hindrance.*

When some one thing out of what has been taught has been directly perceived, everything else is firmly believed, including such subtle matters as release, and this is why the yogin is directed to train the mind in this way, beginning with *friendliness and compassion* (sūtra I.33) up to *mastery, from the ultimate atomic particles up to ultimate magnitude* (sūtra I.40); the training is set out in the section beginning with restraints, observances, posture and so on (sūtra II.29).

To sum up: by undertaking one of the practices taught in this section, some one thing is directly perceived; by this, doubt is removed and faith firmly established in the teachings right up to such subtle things as release, the extravertive mental processes are calmed, and the detachment called consciousness of mastery is accomplished. Then he will be capable of experiencing directly any of the things taught in the third chapter, beginning with the three transformations (past, present and future), whether to attain knowledge or powers. This is the purpose of teaching this mental training here, as the commentator has explained.

Sūtra I.36

Or a radiant perception beyond sorrow

> *The words 'brings the mind to steadiness' are to be supplied from the previous sūtra. When one concentrates on the heart-lotus, there is direct awareness of the buddhi. The buddhi-sattva is like shining space, but while the concentration is still wavering in stability, the perception takes the luminous form of a sun, or a moon, planet, or gems.*
>
> *When the mind reaches samādhi on I-am-ness, it is like the still ocean, serene and infinite, I-am alone. On which it has been said: Having discovered the self which is subtle as an atom, he should be conscious of I-am alone.*
>
> *There are thus the two sorrowless perceptions, one of divine objects, and one of self alone, by which the mind of the yogin attains steadiness.*

The sūtra has to be completed from the context, so that it runs: 'Or where a radiant perception, beyond sorrow, is attained, it brings the mind to steadiness.' As a perception in which light is experienced, it is called radiant, and as it causes sorrow to pass away, it is beyond sorrow. How is it produced? *When one concentrates on the heart-lotus, there is a direct awareness of the buddhi* an experience of its true nature. What then is this nature of the buddhi-sattva? *Like shining space,* ever radiant and all-pervading. But because there in that buddhi-sattva there is *still wavering (vaiṣamya) in the stability,* because the concentration has not come to complete likeness of the buddhi-sattva as it is in itself, *the radiant perception* of the yogic concentration on the heart-lotus *takes the luminous form of a sun or moon, planet or gems.*

When the mind reaches samādhi on I-am-ness, on 'I' (ahaṅkāra), which happens when the buddhi-sattva approximates to its own true nature, *it is like a still ocean, serene and infinite, I-am alone. On which it has been said* as regards this samādhi *Having discovered* having attained *the self* the ātman of I-am-ness (asmitā) which is being explained, *which is subtle as an atom* being so subtle *he should be conscious of I-am alone.* He should be conscious only of the likeness of the object of the meditation. As the true form of the I alone, it is seen as distinct from what has coloured it, like a crystal taking on the colour of what it is laid on.

There are these two sorrowless perceptions, one of divine objects and one of self alone. All of them, from the perception of fragrance to I-am-ness, are entirely without sorrow. But the radiant perception is different from the group of five beginning with the experience of fragrance. The ones connected with an object are preliminary to the pure I-am, and as such, there is a difference in their fields. *By which* sorrowless radiant perception *the mind of the yogin attains steadiness.*

Sūtra I.37

Or on a mind whose meditation is on freedom from passion

> *Coloured by meditation on a mind free from passion, the mind of the yogin attains steadiness.*

He from whose thinking all passion has gone, is *free from passion,* namely dispassionate. It is well known what dispassion is: there must be freedom from desire even in the case of a naturally passionate man in the presence of objects of desire, for instance women or possessions. Let him practise with this idea in mind. But actual objects should not be part of the meditation, because of the evils in them. *Thus coloured by meditation on a mind free from passion, the mind of the yogin attains steadiness.* For a mind, once the bridle of passion has been set on it, runs like a horse driven by another.

Sūtra I.38

Or meditating on the knowledge of dream and sleep

Either on the knowledge of dream or on the knowledge of sleep; the yogin's mind in that form attains steadiness.

Meditating, *either on the knowledge of dream or on the knowledge of sleep,* the mind becomes of that form alone. What the mind meditates on as its own being, that form indeed it becomes. In the dream state, there is knowledge without any physical objects like sound and so on, and the nature of that knowledge is pure illumination. Now he meditates on what that knowledge is, but not on the remembered objects themselves (which appear in the dream). For the mind can be caught by the bridle of an object even merely remembered. But the meditation on the knowledge of deep sleep, which is essentially non-perception of any particular objects, rests on the idea of non-existence, and is peaceful, infinite, and characterized by an experience of immutability. When the mind rests on that, it is natural that it attains steadiness.

Sūtra I.39

Or by meditation on what appeals to him

Let him meditate on whatever appeals to him. Having found some one thing on which he can steady his mind, he will be able to steady it on other things also.

Let him meditate on whatever appeals with the aim of steadying the mind, for steadying the mind is the purpose here. It must not be to secure pleasures and so on, for there is the prohibition 'Even if one should obtain objects, let him never dwell on them in any way'. *Having found something* which is a proper object for meditation *on which he can steady his mind, he will be able to steady it on other things also,* the things specifically prescribed for the training.

Sūtra I.40

His mastery extends right to the ultimate atom and to the ultimate magnitude

> *When he concentrates on it, he can steady his mind on anything subtle, right down to the ultimate atom; when he concentrates on it, he has steadiness of mind on anything substantial, up to the ultimate magnitude. When one can take his practice to either at will, it is full mastery; when he has full mastery, he does not require further practice in training.*

The words *right to* are to be taken with both the extremes. When he concentrates on something subtle, in the course of his practice the mind experiences things progressively smaller and smaller till he comes to the ultimate atom. By practice he becomes able to remain steady in that experience.

When he can take his practice to either limit at will, it is full mastery. He has complete mastery who is not obstructed by any opposing thought in his experience of either the very small or the very great. The earlier practices are (part of) the highest (mastery), but there is this distinction: *when he has full mastery he does not require further practice in training,* whereas those in the early stages do require some more training.

There is, then, a three-fold concentration (dhāraṇā): the contracted which touches the limit of minuteness, the extended which touches the limit of greatness, and the third which experiences both of the limits. The sūtra implies all three.

> *Now when the mind has attained steadiness (sthiti), what sort of samādhi does it have, and on what objects?*

When the mind has attained steadiness by one or more of the methods given *what sort of* samādhi *does it have and on what objects?* The following sūtra has been given to answer this question.

Sūtra I.41

Identification-in-samādhi (samāpatti) is when the mental process has dwindled and the mind rests on either the knower or the knowing process or a known object, and like a crystal apparently takes on their respective qualities

(Opponent) He is going to speak about the objects of samādhi in the Third Part (sūtra III.35): *by saṃyama on what-is-for-its-own-sake, (distinct) from what-is-for-the-sake-of another, there comes knowledge of Puruṣa.* There he is going to explain the nature of identification-in-samādhi, namely the nature of saṃyama, by the resultant effect, so the present sūtra is superfluous.

(Answer) Not so, because here he wishes to show the purpose of mastering the methods that have just been described. They have been properly mastered when the mind, identified in samādhi with the knower or with the process of knowledge or with a known object, assumes the appearance of it. Sūtra I.17 has already said that samādhi is cognitive when it is accompanied with vitarka (verbal associations), vicāra (subtle associations), ānanda (joy), and asmitā (I-am-ness), and now it has to be explained what they are. He cannot describe what they are without reference to samādhi, because they are properties of it.

When the mental process has dwindled means, when the ideas have died down.

The ideas, of right knowledge of external things and so on, have died down.

(Opponent) The ideas must have died out altogether. Only when they have all ceased does the commitment of the mind end, and there must be no dependence on anything physical or subtle.

(The answer is that Vyāsa in his commentary has explained that the cognitive states, where there is still one idea remaining, are preliminary to the other samādhi which is ultra-cognitive – Tr.)

The illustration is given of a flawless jewel. As a crystal, according to the different things set near it, becomes tinged with their colours and appears in their respective forms, so the mind is coloured by the object of meditation, and in samādhi on the object appears in the form of that object. Coloured by a physical object, it appears to have the nature of a physical object; coloured by meditation on a subtle object, identified in samādhi with a subtle object, it appears to have the nature of a subtle object. Coloured by any particular thing, identified with that thing in samādhi, it appears as that particular form.

So also with the senses, which are the process of knowledge. Coloured by meditation on the process of knowledge, identified in samādhi with it, mind appears to have the nature of the process of knowledge.

So also, coloured by meditation on Puruṣa as knower, identified in samādhi with Puruṣa as knower, it appears to have the nature of Puruṣa as knower. And coloured by meditation on Puruṣa released, identified in samādhi with Puruṣa released, it appears to have the nature of Puruṣa released.

(No Vivaraṇa comment on first two paragraphs – Tr.)

Identified with Puruṣa as knower means Puruṣa in its nature as causing buddhi to know (buddhi-bodhaka); concentrated on that, mind appears in the form of the knower; *identified with Puruṣa released*when this very knower of buddhi is no longer a knower of ideas of objects, then its state is the bare knowledge that sattva and Puruṣa are distinct.

When it is said that in this detachment the Puruṣa is released, the sense is that the mind is released from all taints. Freedom of the mind from taints is what is called 'release' of Puruṣa. This is why in the sūtra it says only *knower.* And here *Puruṣa released* means only the knower aspect of Puruṣa, otherwise he would have said just *Puruṣa.* When the highest consciousness of mastery in detachment has arisen, there is never again any involvement with saṃsāra. So it has been said: though there be still a bare connection with mind, if there is no connection with taints, 'he is ever freed, ever the Lord' *(comm.*to I.24).

Therefore it is said *coloured by meditation on Puruṣa released, identified in samādhi with Puruṣa released, it appears to have the nature of Puruṣa released.* Here it would be wrong to think that by meditating on mere cessation of any connection with mind one will be identified in samādhi with Puruṣa released and will appear in the form of Puruṣa released, because that would mean that the mind itself would have been dissolved. Puruṣa is at the limit of subtlety. Pradhāna is equally subtle, and mind is an effect of an effect of an effect of it. Mind, identifying itself in samādhi with Puruṣa or pradhāna, could not maintain itself when making the identification, any more than a jar can be identified with the jar-form without giving up its previous condition of clay-form.

(Opponent) But it is said that the Great principle (mahat) and the cosmic I (ahaṅkāra) are knowable to the mind of the yogin, even though it is an effect of them.

(Answer) As to whether they are knowable or not, there is a distinction according to how far the knowledge is to go. If they are to be knowablc, there has to be some special relation involving a knower whose nature is apart (from them). They are both manifest, so a special relation is not inconceivable; they could be known by a special relation in the same way that it is known by a special mental idea that one's own Puruṣa is a knower and is released. But they cannot be known as the self (ātman) of all, because that would be too great to comprehend. They would be the self of the very mind which sought to know them as the self of all, and as such they could not be known as an object by it. Pradhāna and Puruṣa, however, are essentially absolutely unmanifest, and there can be no perception of them in their own nature, or of any relation between them.

(Opponent) If pradhāna and Puruṣa and the relation between them are not to be directly perceived, it would mean that the Lord is not omniscient.

(Answer) There is no question that everything other than pradhāna and Puruṣa and the relation between them is capable of being perceived, for it is universally accepted that the range of direct perception is unrestricted; what is not within the range of our perception is knowable to the Lord. If there is a knowable then certainly somehow or other someone must know it; without a knower, it would not be a knowable.

Now if prakṛti (= pradhāna) and Puruṣa are to be knowable as objects in their own nature, they would be things experienced, like the mind. Then (being objects) they would exist-for-another, and that other would have to be supposed to be beyond them.

(Opponent) The Puruṣa-s could know each other, without supposing any further knower.

(Answer) Not so; the Puruṣa-s being identical, there would be nothing to determine which was subject and which was object. And two lamps can not each be subordinate to the other.

Moreover if Puruṣa is going to be known, it implies that there is happiness and so on in his nature, and this would involve many further difficulties, such as the fact that the happiness, etc., would not be dependent on pradhāna as cause.

(Opponent) But he does speak of Puruṣa as directly perceived (in sūtra III.35): *by saṃyama on what-is-for-its-own-sake, (distinct) from what-is-for-the-sake-of-another, there comes knowledge of Puruṣa.*

(Answer) Yes, and it is rightly said. This is why we said that Puruṣa does not become an object in its own nature. In the commentary there it says, *It is not* that Puruṣa is seen by any idea of Puruṣa, which – because it is an idea – would be essentially mind. It is Puruṣa that sees the idea resting on his own self. And so it has been said: 'By what indeed would one know the knower?' (Bṛhad. Up. II.4.13)

(Opponent) The mind coloured by resting on Puruṣa is an object for Puruṣa, so in fact Puruṣa *is* directly perceived, for when an idea coloured by resting on a jar is perceived by Puruṣa, that is what is called the jar's being perceived.

(Answer) The cases are not parallel. For Puruṣa is not pervaded by the mind, as the jar is. A thing like a jar is external and pervaded by the mind; not so Puruṣa, for it is infinite.

The limited mind, which would take Puruṣa as its object, cannot pervade that which is the infinite subject. If it could pervade Puruṣa, it should be able to pervade pradhāna too (which is impossible as it is only a remote effect of pradhāna).

Therefore, as the face is perceived in a mirror in the form of a reflection, so it is an idea transformed into the form of a reflection of Puruṣa which is seen by Puruṣa. Thus Vyāsa says, 'As in the clearness of a mirror, one sees the self in the self (Mahābh. Śānti Parva 204.8).

There is no possibility of the mind's taking on the form of some other released Puruṣa; though it might be the form of the other one, still it would be seen as one's own. For it is nothing else than a transformation of the mind; it is only the mind which Puruṣa sees transformed into his own form. The possibility of the transformation is when there is a relation to the form of Puruṣa its owner, of whom the mind is the property.

(Opponent) Then how can it ever be known that any other Puruṣa even exists, when that other would not be related as owner?

(Answer) As another face can be seen by means of another mirror, so Puruṣa sees his own mind transformed into the form of another mind, corresponding to the second mirror, and so knows another Puruṣa.

But the distinction 'This is his self, this is mine' is known by inference alone, by the indication of the special attributes of a mind different from one's own, for minds being composed of the three guṇa-s inevitably have attributes special to themselves. But Puruṣa-s being attributeless cannot conceivably be different in their own nature.

In this way the mind, like a flawless jewel, rests on and is coloured by the knower, or knowing process, or object of knowledge – Puruṣa, senses, or thing – and when it has become established in one of them, it takes on its form. This is called identification-in-samādhi (samāpatti).

It rests on the knower or on the knowing process or on an object, and it is coloured according to which one it rests on. When established there, it takes on that form.

The identification (sam-āpatti) is a complete assumption (samyag-āpatti) of the likeness in the form of an idea devoid of anything else. Though there are such identifications in the extravertive mind also, they are not very complete, because the mind is then predominantly under the control of rajas and tamas.

Sūtra I.42

The samādhi-identification is called sa-vitarka when it is mixed up with mental constructs of word, thing, and idea

We see for instance that the process of knowing takes place without discriminating between the word Cow and the thing Cow and the idea Cow, though they are on different levels, for there are some properties distinguished as belonging to words and others to things, and still others to ideas.

When a yogin makes the identification on a thing like a cow, if it arises in his samādhi-knowledge and manifests there full of mental constructs of word, thing, and idea, that confused identification is called sa-vitarka.

There are four of the samādhi-identifications. The sūtra explains the first of them: *the identification is called sa-vitarka when it is mixed up with mental constructs (vikalpa) of word, thing, and idea.*

There are verbal constructs, and constructs relating to things, and constructs relating to ideas. When it is mixed up and confused with mental constructs relating to what is being meditated upon, so that the thoughts interpenetrate each other, that is a confused identification.

(Opponent) Words and things and ideas are mutually exclusive. The yogin is supposed to meditate on just one thing, so let him take *either* a word, *or* a thing, *or* an idea; why should there be any confusion of mental constructs of words *and* things *and* ideas?

(Answer) This is just the point; ordinary knowledge is based on not distinguishing them. So it is that the normal usage has simply 'cow' to represent all three, and in knowing one of the three there is memory of the other two, not realized to be distinct from it.

(Opponent) Make the meditation simply on 'that thing as it is'.

(Answer) No, because the conventional association of the word for that thing will inevitably follow.

(Opponent) Let him choose some word which is a universal, and before he has any association (by experience of any individual of the class).

(Answer) No, because it still involves the knowledge that there are the other things.

there are some properties distinguished as belonging to words. The letter 'g' (in the word gau, cow), the vowels with intonation rising or falling, and short medium or long, are ways of knowing for the ear, but they are not properties of things or of ideas. The properties of things are of another kind: the dewlap of the cow, its tail, hump, hoof, horn, appearance, touch, and so on. Then the properties of ideas are of still another kind: that their nature is to be knowable to Puruṣa, that they are essentially appearances, that they cause saṃskāra-s, and so on. These are not the properties of words or of things. In reality there is not the faintest possibility of confusion. Thus *they are on different levels.*

When a yogin makes the identification on one of them *if it rises and manifests in his samādhi-knowledge full of mental constructs of word, thing, and idea,* if it is thus interpenetrated by conventional associations of word and thing and memories of them, then *that confused identification is called sa-vitarka* (with illusory projections relating to a physical thing).

> *But when there is purification from memories of verbal conventions, in a samādhi-knowledge empty of mental constructs of ideas heard or inferred, the object stands out in the form of its real nature alone, and limited to just that form. This is nir-vitarka identification, and it is the higher direct perception. It is the germ of authority and inference; from it, they have their being. That perception is not associated with any knowledge from outer authority or inference. The yogic perception, unmixed with any other source of right knowledge, arises out of this nir-vitarka samādhi. It is defined in the sūtra which follows.*

Now he speaks of nir-vitarka identification. *But when there is purification from memories of verbal conventions:* a verbal convention is the general consensus 'this is the expression for that, and that is what is expressed by this', and the memory produced by it is the memory of the verbal convention. Purification from this memory means that it ceases, from (the recognition of) its illusoriness, when rajas and tamas have been overcome.

Knowledge from authority means scriptural (āgamika) knowledge, and knowledge from inference means knowledge from indicatory marks. These two, knowledge from inference and from scripture, relate only to universals, whereas the mental construct arising from them is an illusory projection (adhyāropa) of a particular, made by a superimposition (adhyāsa).

In the samādhi-knowledge of the yogin *empty of the mental constructs of ideas heard of or inferred,* free from illusory superimpositions (adhyāsa) of inferential or conventional verbal knowledge, *the object stands out in the form of its real nature* alone. This is knowledge of the thing as it is; the object, free from such associations as direction and location and time and past experience, stands vividly in its own qualities alone. It manifests in the form of its real nature; the samādhi-knowledge of the yogin is limited to the real nature of that object, and does not reveal anything of place or time, etc., apart from that object.

The knowledge is not even aware of itself as a process of knowing, because of its extreme transparency. It appears as the object alone, and this as described is the nir-vitarka samādhi. Nir-vitarka means that vitarka has gone from it, vitarka being illusory projection (adhyāropa) which is not really there.

It is the higher direct perception (pratyakṣa) perfect, pure. The lower perception is common to all, and must have come through a previous mental process as has been mentioned; this higher one is for a yogin alone. *It is the germ of inference and authority.* It is stated to be the germ of authority and inference, but these its effects may themselves sometimes be uncertain. There is however no uncertainty in what they have received from direct perception in nir-vitarka samādhi, and so he says *from it authority and inference have their being. And that perception is not associated with any knowledge from outer authority or inference,* because it has a different sort of object, namely a particular, whereas the knowledge they give is of universals.

Sūtra I.43

When there is purification from memories, (that samādhi) apparently empty of its own nature of knowledge, with the object alone shining forth, is nir-vitarka

Purified from memories, which are mental constructs of verbal associations, or knowledge from authority or inference, the samādhi-knowledge coloured by the object as it is, having given up seemingly its own nature of pure perception, is identified with the object, the nature of the thing alone. That identification is what is described as nir-vitarka (samādhi).

When there is purification from memories of mental constructs of verbal association, authority, inference the mental construct of verbal association, the mental construct of ideas from authority, the mental construct of ideas from inference – this it is which is the memory, by which an alien quality from something else is illusorily projected (adhyāropyate). For a thing cannot in reality be projected into another thing.

(Opponent) How can what has merely been heard of or inferred be projected as a direct perception?

(Answer) It is well known that it is; what one has heard of, what one has inferred, one now sees as 'this'.

(Opponent) One may see it, but in fact it is only something one has inferred or heard about.

(Answer) No, because of the difference between a universal and a particular. What is heard of or inferred is a universal, but the object of direct perception is a particular thing. It is well known that there is sometimes illusory projection (adhyāsa) on to a thing of a universal similar to it.

The samādhi-knowledge of the yogin *coloured by the object as it is, having given up seemingly its own nature of pure perception, is identified with the object, the nature of the thing alone.* This word *seemingly* (iva) is used to show that its essence as cognition is not destroyed. For a crystal does not lose its inherent transparency by its proximity to the object placed against it. What is being said is, that the knowing process is unnoticed, and something different from it, an object, is there.

This as described is the nir-vitarka identification. In this a true object, apprehended as a unity such as a cow or a jar, though essentially a particular aggregation of atoms, is the whole world. It is apprehended as a unity, namely determined by a single idea (buddhi). It is a true object, in that it is something whose nature it is to be known by another.

> *The whole world consists of such true objects, apprehended as a unity like a cow or a jar, though essentially a particular aggregation of atoms. The special arrangement, a quality in which all the subtle elements take part, appears with an existence of its own (ātma-bhūta), inferred from its visible results, manifest in accordance with the causes of its manifestation.*

The object is something like a cow or a jar, for instance; the object is not (as some Buddhists hold) no more than a knowledge in the form of a cow, etc. *It is essentially a particular aggregation of atoms.* A cow or jar is a thing which is a particular arrangement of atoms, which are themselves made up of the subtle elements (tanmātra), and the mind rests on one such thing. The object is a particular arrangement of these subtle things so arranged.

So he says, *an existence of its own,* as *a quality in which all the subtle elements take part,* not apart from them, any more than the winding coils are apart from the snake.

(Opponent) Some hold that an effect is not the cause but quite apart from it.

(Answer) But they cannot explain the dependence of the effect on its cause. A thread depends on the filaments which make it up, as a cloth depends on its threads. Where two things are absolutely separate, one does not depend on the other; neither cloth nor threads, for instance, depends on a lump of clay (as a bowl does). If there are two absolutely separate things and one is destroyed, there is no corresponding destruction of the other; when a bowl is destroyed, a cloth does not disappear along with it.

(Opponent) What is called the cause is a relation. There is a relation of the threads to the cloth, and of the filaments to the thread, which is the cause (hetu), causing (karaṇa) both the dependence (when the cause operates) and the consequent destruction (when it ceases).

(Answer) A relation would include the relation between Caitra and his field; the fact of the particular relation would mean that Caitra would depend on his field and would be destroyed with it.

(Opponent) Well then, let us confine the word cause to a relation of inherence (samavaya).

(Answer) No, because a relationship, not being a particular, is not causal (between two things). Of two things related, the relation inhering in one side would not cause dependence, etc., in the other one; so even with a relationship defined as inherent, it is not clear which one would be caused to inhere in which. Nor do inherences of action, universals or particulars, exist without a substance, because dependence and so on exist only between substances. So there too a mere relation cannot have causality. Furthermore, if inherence is to be the cause of making one of the two things related to be dependent on the other, there would have to be a new inherence of the first inherence, and of that too another, and the result would be an infinite regress. And if an inherence relation among qualities is to make substances dependent, another inherence will have to be supposed to make the abstract inherence apply to the substances and make one of them dependent, and for that another and for that another – again an infinite regress.

If the effect does not exist before it originates, it can have no relation with the cause; there is no difference between the non-existence of hare's horns and that of a jar. It has to be explained why there should be a causal relation with the jar (which does appear) and not with things like the horns of a hare.

What was non-existent before can not come into being, any more than a hare's horns. What is different from threads cannot originate from threads, just because it *is* different from them; a jar, for example, cannot originate from threads.

(Opponent) What is existent already cannot originate either, because it already exists, like a jar present now. What is not different from something cannot originate from it, because it is already there, it is its very nature so to say.

(Answer) But to say that the existent does not come into being would mean that what does exist now never came into being, and this would be making an issue of something already established (siddha-sādhyatā). Nothing would ever manifest at all, and the conclusion could never be exemplified.

(Opponent) What I said was, that what is not different from something cannot originate from it.

(Answer) That is the same fallacy, and cannot be demonstrated. A thing is manifested out of its very nature; if there were no nature to manifest, even a thousand manifesting agencies could not effect the manifestation.

Furthermore the view (that a thing previously non-existent comes into being) would be the end of ordinary life. How so? Suppose Devadatta's cow or horse is seen early in the morning complete with ears and tail, and then wanders into the forest where someone crops its ears and tail. With the separation of its former parts, it will – on your view – have been destroyed, but a new one with cropped ears and tail will have been born, which is ownerless and can therefore be possessed by that someone. Then everywhere things would be having parts cut from them, and because there would be no settled rule as to who owned what, it would be the complete destruction of worldly life.

(Opponent) The new whole, with cropped ears and tail, comes into being from the parts it still possesses.

(Answer) Not so, for new wholes with cropped ears and tail, re-created in an instant without father and mother and so on, are not seen in life.

Moreover it should belong only to the one on whose land it was born, and not to the one who owned the previous parts, as grass and leaves belong to the owner of the land on which they grow. If seeds in one field are carried away by flood-water to another field, the corn from these seeds is reaped only by the owner of the latter field, and not by the former owner of the seeds, who cannot object on the ground that he knows the corn has grown from his seeds and so he should take it. In the same way the owner of the field would take the crop-eared animal, and could not be prevented on the grounds that the whole had arisen from parts formerly possessed by another.

Again when the crop-eared horse has been produced and the man who sees that it is in his field has then taken it, the one who did the cutting comes and says that as the cutter he has a greater claim and should therefore take it himself. To let him lawfully take it would be the end of social life, and also contrary to scripture.

So the conclusion is, that a whole is one, and not different from the parts which cause it, being their effect.

(Opponent) It *is* different, because the words and ideas and qualities applicable to the cause are different from those applied to the effect.

(Answer) That is not convincing; we see cases where the thing is the same in spite of differences in words and ideas and qualities. Hasta, kara and pāṇi are different words for the same thing, namely a hand; fatherhood and sonhood are different ideas which may be about the same person; bound and freed, fixed and gone away are differences as to time; power to burn and power to cook are differences of quality. Differences such as direction and location, moreover, are inconclusive (for establishing otherness). So the commentator has said: *with an existence of its own.*

And it is *inferred from its visible results* such as the capacity for carrying and holding water in the case of a jar. Something whose effect is a manifest result must certainly exist.

From different points of view it is spoken of either in terms of its common cause or else in terms of its powers. It is itself fully perceptible, but it is inferred that it has been an unmanifest, now made manifest as an effect called (for instance) a jar, by the operation of agencies such as the potter and his staff and his cord, and which existed formerly in the state of the clay, and is now manifested in accordance with the causes, the staff and other agencies.

> *It appears, and disappears when another quality arises. This, with such qualities, is called a whole. It is one, large or minute, tangible, with the quality of action, and not permanent. The life of the world is carried on in terms of such wholes.*

It appears, and disappears when another quality (dharma) arises. This, with such qualities, is called a whole. Now as atoms are imperceptible, in relation to them appearance and disappearance are meaningless. But these two do occur. So what comes to appear, and disappears when incompatible with a different quality which arises, and what for its manifestation requires manifesting agencies, that is called a whole. Such a whole is different from atoms.

There are also these factors which make the nature of a whole: *it is one, large or minute, tangible, with the quality of action, and not permanent.* These are factors separate from one another.

In the expression 'one jar', what is expressed by the word jar refers to the same thing as the oneness. There is the common reference: what this is, is one. But in the case of many atoms, there is nothing which can refer also to oneness.

As to *large or minute* there is nothing associated with the tiny atom which can refer equally to the quality of being large. So also with relative smallness, for the atoms are not small in comparison with other atoms, inasmuch as they are all atomic. They are called minute not in relation to other atoms, but from their being minute in comparison with other things.

And then, *that whose quality is action,* which is the reading of the compound kriyā-dharmaka. A whole is said to have fruitful function and activity, whereas there is no such fruitful functioning and activity in the case of atoms, for they are not utilizable by beings like us. A whole is *impermanent* whereas atoms are not taken to be so. Further it is visible whereas atoms are not seen, and it is *tangible,* for it can be left alone or acquired or held and so on. *The life of the world is carried on in terms of such wholes* but not in terms of atoms.

> *If one says that the particular aggregate is not real, and that no subtle cause is perceived for it, so that there is no whole apart from a mental construct and it is all false knowledge and not grounded in reality, then for him almost everything would turn out to be false knowledge.*

If someone (like a Buddhist) says that the whole is not real – although its existence is so well demonstrated by proofs – and that no subtle causes like atoms are perceived, *for him almost everything would turn out to be false knowledge (mithyā-jñāna),* that is to say all knowledge of objects would be false.

For such a Buddhist everything is knowledge, appearing in the form of sound and other sense perceptions, in the form of happiness and other inner perceptions, and in the form of the knowledge of both of them. Sounds and so on are imagined wholes producing the knowledge-forms, but not accepted as real. Happiness and other feelings also, being objective, come into the same category of imagined wholes. The very knowledge of them, whose essence is to produce (unreal) knowledge-forms, is therefore illusory also; so everything turns out to be illusory knowledge.

Even direct perception and inference will turn out to be only appearances (ābhāsa), since their objects are illusions such as sound.

And even the knowledge of the Buddhist's Omniscient One, that all is passing, painful, void, and without a self, and so on, will end up as false knowledge, since there is no object for it. Thus the free-thinking (sva-tantra) Buddhist (tīrthakara) has no credibility, and it has to be accepted that he and his doctrine would not exist (on his view), because they are no different from sound and other objects of knowledge.

> *Then what would be right knowledge, when there are no objects for it? Whatever is perceived is in fact taken as being a whole; the whole exists, accepted in life as large or small and so on, and becoming the object of nir-vitarka identification.*

The corollary is this: *what would be right knowledge, when there are no objects for it?* In any case (on the Buddhist view) knowledge would be simply providing a form by itself. What itself provides the form cannot be accepted (as right knowledge of anything), so knowledge would all be of itself alone, and no more than illusion.

Then what would be the right knowledge, against which other knowledge is adjudged illusory? If one denies the existence of wholes, established though they are by all right knowledge and all proofs, no object for right knowledge can be produced, and if it cannot, then how can all knowledge be adjudged false? Illusory knowledge is only such when compared with some right knowledge; right knowledge and illusory knowledge presuppose each other.

(Opponent) Let us say that right knowledge is knowledge without an object.

(Answer) Since it could not know its own nature, its existence could not be established. If known, it would be an object, and therefore (on your view) an illusion like all wholes; it being illusion, the knowledge of it would be illusion too, and the knowledge of that fact too would be illusion. Everything would be illusion, as before.

Again, allowing that right knowledge is knowledge without an object, now since the existence of objects is not accepted (by the Buddhist), all knowledge will be without an object, and so would have to be right knowledge. In which case, all knowledge being right knowledge, it must be said what illusory knowledge would be.

(Opponent) Illusory knowledge is what *appears* as if it had an object, whereas right knowledge is what is absolutely without any object.

(Answer) There too it can only be said that there is no proof of its existence. So it has to be accepted inescapably that the objects of right knowledge are wholes: *the whole exists, accepted in life as large or small and so on, and becoming the object of nir-vitarka identification.*

Sūtra I.44

In the same way, when it is on subtle objects, it is called sa-vicāra (with subtle associations) and nir-vicāra (without subtle associations)

Of these two, the sa-vicāra identification refers to subtle elements, whose qualities are manifest, with a particular location, time, cause and experience as their features.

The object of the meditation is the subtle elements, and then it is called sa-vicāra and nir-vicāra. The subtle elements (tan-mātra) are those of sound, etc. In the Sanskrit compound deśakālanimittānubhavāvacchinneṣu, the word for 'particularized' applies to each element separately, so the meaning is: featured by a particular location, a particular time, a particular cause, and a particular experience.

For purposes of ordinary life, everything is taken as having a particular location and so on, as related to the knower of that object, its subject. Such being the case, sa-vicāra is when the mental-constructs (vikalpa) of location and the others are associated with the object.

It is clear that on this point there is no difference between sa-vitarka and sa-vicāra, because in both there are illusory projections (adhyāsa). But there is this distinction, that in sa-vitarka there are all the illusory projections of verbal convention and object and idea, as well as projections of location, time, cause and experience, whereas in this sa-vicāra, since the tan-mātra subtle elements have no established verbal associations, the subtle object receives illusory projections of location and the other three, but no projection of any distinctive name. This is a clear distinction from sa-vitarka.

The object of the meditation is the subtle elements, grasped as one single idea, characterized by the qualities which are now manifest, and it presents itself to knowledge in the samādhi.

A subtle object, grasped as one single idea, *characterized by the qualities which are now manifest* the above-mentioned location, time, cause and experience, or manifest qualities in general, is the object of the meditation, so it is not bare unparticularized knowledge; *and it presents itself to knowledge in samādhi.*

> *But what is called nir-vicāra samādhi is on the subtle elements as in all ways and by all means free from particularization by any qualities dormant, manifest, or indeterminable, yet corresponding to the qualities and being the essence of all qualities. The subtle element, in its true form alone, by being meditated upon as such, colours the knowledge in the samādhi with its true form.*

Nir-vicāra samādhi is on the subtle elements as in all ways in every manner *and by all means* everywhere *free from particularization by any qualities dormant, manifest, or indeterminable.*

Dormant means that having performed its function, it has ceased from it; *manifest* means that it has come up into function; *indeterminable* means that it is neither dormant nor manifest nor a visible cause producing something. The unseen powers of a lump of gold to produce many unpredictable forms would be indeterminable qualities. The subtle elements are free from particularization by qualities, *yet they correspond to all qualities* because there is no object separate from the subtle elements. This is called nir-vicāra; all the features in the definition of nir-vitarka are applicable here to nir-vicāra.

The subtle element in its true form alone as free from particularizations of location, time, cause and experience, as the essence of all and as corresponding to all qualities *being meditated on as such colours the knowledge in samādhi.*

> *It is when the samādhi-knowledge is seemingly empty of its own nature, with the object alone shining forth, that it is called nir-vicāra. Sa-vitarka and nir-vitarka are concerned with physical objects and sa-vicāra and nir-vicāra with subtle objects. The distinction between nir-vicāra and sa-vicāra is made clear by what has been said about nir-vitarka.*

It is when the samādhi-knowledge is seemingly empty of its own nature, with the object alone shining forth, that it is called nir-vicāra: in this respect nir-vicāra has the same feature as nir-vitarka. He now shows where they differ: *the sa-vitarka and nir-vitarka are concerned with physical objects* with things of substantial size. The compound 'thing of substantial size' means an identity, like the compound 'head of Rāhu' (which is all head). It is the vitarka pair which have this kind of object; the vicāra pair have subtle objects. The vicāra pair is to be understood after the pattern of the vitarka pair; in the second one of each pair, mental constructs disappear. The first ones of the pairs also are to be understood by their common features. And the distinction between the two pairs has also been stated.

It has been said that the sa-vicāra and nir-vicāra have subtle objects. Now the further point is considered: what is the limit of subtlety?

Sūtra I.45

The scale of (causal) subtlety of objects ends in pradhāna

In the case of an atom of earth, the subtle element (tan-mātra) of odour is a subtler (causal) object (for the vicāra meditations); in the case of water it is the subtle element of taste; in the case of fire, light; in the case of air, touch; of space, it is the subtle element of sound. Subtler than these is the cosmic I (ahaṅkāra), and subtler than that is the Great Principle (liṅga); more subtle than that is pradhāna (a-liṅga – uncreated nature). There is nothing more subtle beyond pradhāna. (But) surely Puruṣa is at the limit of subtlety? Indeed it is, but it is not a subtle cause of the Great Principle in the same way that pradhāna is. Puruṣa is not the cause which produces it; it is only a cause which sets in motion. Hence the limit of subtlety is described as pradhāna (the ultimate cause).

In the case of an atom of earth, the subtle element of odour is a subtler (causal) object. When the atom of earth is analysed, it is found that the subtle element (tanmātra) of odour alone is its very essence. And the essence of the subtle element of odour has the liṅga, the principle called the Great, as its subtle cause.

The word liṅga (literally, having origination, and therefore destruction) carries the meaning that the subtle elements, which together with the cosmic I (ahaṅkāra) have come forth from the pure liṅga, the Great, go (ga) to dissolution (li) in it, and again that they come back from dissolution, from the pradhāna. Pradhāna, on the contrary, being a-liṅga (without liṅga or origination) neither goes to dissolution in anything else nor comes back. Of the Great, the pure liṅga, the subtle cause is pradhāna, the a-liṅga.

(Opponent) *Surely Puruṣa is at the limit of subtlety* too, so where does it come in this progression of ever more subtle causes?

(Answer) This objection is raised on the basis of a certain theory that Puruṣa too is a cause, but our position is not touched by it. The subtlety of the a-liṅga lies in the fact that it has no liṅga or origin but is the cause of the origin of the liṅga or Great principle. The point is that whatever is the cause of some effect is relatively more subtle than that effect. The objection raised is, that Puruṣa too is essentially without liṅga or origin. This is true, but Puruṣa is not more subtle than the liṅga in this special sense of being the cause of it. Puruṣa, though it is indeed without liṅga, is not the material cause of the liṅga principle, the Great, which is thus not its effect. Pure consciousness (caitanya) cannot be correlated with any effect.

If it could be so correlated, Puruṣa would necessarily also be something experienced, and would thus be for-the-sake-of-another, and would be essentially pleasure and pain and delusion. Moreover pradhāna would no longer be the cause of everything. This would go against all the evidence, and so he says that Puruṣa is only a cause (hetu) in the sense that its presence as experiencer sets pradhāna in motion. This is the meaning of the statement that subtlety reaches the limit with pradhāna.

Sūtra I.46

These are samādhi from-a-seed

> *These four samādhi-identifications have external things as their seed, so the samādhi is from-a-seed (sa-bīja). When it is a physical object, the samādhi is sa-vitarka or nir-vitarka; when a subtle object, it is sa-vicāra or nir-vicāra. So the four categories of samādhi have been described.*

They are from-a-seed because their objects are external things. The samādhi is from-a-secd, namely cognitive, as was explained under sūtra I.17: 'cognitive because accompanied with verbal associations (vitarka), subtle associations (vicāra), joy (ānanda), and the form of I-am-ness (asmitā)'. *When it is a physical object, the samādhi is sa-vitarka or nir-vitarka: when a subtle object, it is sa-vicāra or nir-vicāra. So the four categories of samādhi have been described.*

Sūtra I.47

From skill in nir-vicāra, a clearness in the self

When the mind-sattva whose nature is light, is freed from rajas and tamas, and has a clear steady flow, without any veiling contamination of impurity, that is the skill in nir-vicāra. When this skill in nir-vicāra appears, there is an inner clearness in the self of the yogin, which is a progressively (anurodhi) clearer and brighter light of knowledge of the object as it really is.

The *veiling impurity* is a sort of contamination, consisting of the taints, etc. *clearness in the self is* the knowledge which can distinguish such things as the self (ātman). It is of this that it is now said that it is *knowledge of the thing as it really is (bhūlārtha); it is a progressively clearer* stage by stage corresponding to the progressive destruction of the taints *and brighter* very distinct *light of knowledge* the nature of samādhi-knowledge being extreme purity. The light is the knowledge, for by it one knows the thing as it is (yathāvastu). *So it is said:*

As a man on a crag sees those in the plain, so the man of knowledge,
High on the palace of knowledge beyond sorrow, looks on all the beings in their pain.

Sūtra I.48

In this, the knowledge is Truth-bearing

The knowledge which appears in that clearness of the mind in samādhi has the special name of Truth-bearing, in the literal sense that it brings truth alone, and there is no trace of erroneous knowledge in it. So it is said:

By scriptural authority, by inference, and by zest for meditation practice – In these three ways perfecting his knowledge, he attains the highest yoga.

In this in the light of knowledge, the inner *clearness of the mind in samādhi, the knowledge which appears* born of discrimination (viveka) *has the special name of Truth-bearing, in the literal sense that it brings truth alone and there is no trace of erroneous knowledge in this,* which is born of discrimination. For it appears in the one in whom all taint of error has been destroyed, and being born, it dispels the obscurities associated with the object of knowledge. *So it is said:*

By scriptural authority, by inference, and by zest for meditation practice – In these three ways perfecting his knowledge, he attains the highest yoga. Knowledge is a component part of yoga, and it has three degrees. The first is, to follow the instructions of the scriptures and the teachers; the second is mainly concerned with removing, by reason (yukti) and inference, objections to the authoritative teaching which is being studied, and so rightly establishing it; but the third is eagerness for constant practice of meditation on what has thus been established by the scriptures and by inferences from them. Perfecting his knowledge in these three ways, the yogin attains yoga.

Sūtra I.49

This knowledge is of a particular thing, unlike knowledge from authority or from inference

Authority means the scripture, and that deals only with universals – scripture cannot point to individual things. Why not? Because an individual does not have the conventional association with a word. Inference too has only universals for its object. The example of inference has been given, that where there is getting to another place, there is motion, and where there is no such getting to another place, there is no motion. And the conclusion is reached by inference by means of a universal. So the object of authority or inference is never a particular thing.

Ordinary perception gives no knowledge at all of some subtle or remote or hidden thing, but we cannot assert that the latter is not demonstrable and has no existence. A particular relating to subtle elements or to Puruṣa is perceptible by samādhi-knowledge alone.

The object of the Truth-bearing knowledge is a particular, and not any universal conceived by man, as the sūtra says. Its object is a particular; there is an infinity of particular objects, and there cannot be a separate word for each one, so the conventional association with a word is only for a universal. Even where there is a word for a particular (e.g. an individual name), that word cannot identify or communicate that particular to one who does not already know it.

Inference too has only universals for its objects. As said before (comm. to I.7), it is mainly concerned with determining universals. *The example of inference has been given, that where there is getting to another place, there is motion, and where there is no such getting to another place, there is no motion. And the conclusion is reached by inference by means of a universal.* and that is all that inference can give. *So the object of authority or inference is never a particular.*

(Opponent) But this particular, relating to subtle elements or to Puruṣa, cannot be known by ordinary perception either, and apart from the three accepted means of right knowledge there is no other means by which we could know it.

(Answer) *Ordinary perception gives no knowledge of some subtle or remote or hidden thing, but we cannot assert that the latter is not demonstrable and has no existence.* For what is proved by experience does exist – it rides on the king's highway, as it were. *A particular relating to subtle elements or to Puruṣa is perceptible by samādhi-knowledge alone.*

(Opponent) You claim that these particulars relating to subtle things are known by direct perception (only in samādhi). But everything is made known by the Lord (in scripture). You may say that as they are facts, they must be known (or they could not be spoken of); then they are known from scripture and inference, but only in the sense that we can say 'they exist'. There is no rule that all particulars must be knowable by direct perception. Not all the particulars are known even of something held out on the hand.

(Answer) Not so, because we infer that particulars related to anything at all are in principle knowable by direct perception. How so? The idea is this: a particular is something which is an effect, and as such the particulars, even those relating to subtle elements, must be directly perceptible to someone, like the particulars of what is held on one's own hand. Therefore this knowledge has an object other than the knowledge deriving from authority or from inference, because its object is a particular.

When the yogin has attained samādhi-knowledge, a fresh saṃskāra made by the knowledge is produced.

Sūtra I.50

The saṃskāra produced by it inhibits other saṃskāra-s

The saṃskāra produced by truth-bearing knowledge removes the accumulated deposit of saṃskāra-s of extraversion. When the extravertive saṃskāra-s are overcome, no ideas arising from them appear. With inhibition of extravertive ideas, samādhi becomes habitual. Then there is knowledge from that samādhi; from that, more saṃskāra-s are laid down of knowledge, and so a fresh deposit of saṃskāra-s is built up. From that again knowledge, and from that more saṃskāra-s of it.

When the yogin has attained samādhi-knowledge, a fresh saṃskāra made by the knowledge is produced. Knowledge must set up a saṃskāra. Each time the knowledge is renewed, its special saṃskāra is reinforced. But the renewal of the knowledge is from again taking up meditation on the object, different from itself. *The saṃskāra produced by Truth-bearing knowledge removes the* other *accumulated deposit (āśaya) of saṃskāra-s of extroversion:* it can do this because it is produced by a different object, namely the thing as it really is (yathārtha). The accumulated deposit (āśaya) is so called because it 'lies there' (ā-śi) till release.

When the extravertive saṃskāra-s are overcome when the saṃskāra deposit of extraversion has been overcome by the saṃskara of samādhi-knowledge, *no ideas arising from them* from the extravertive saṃskāra-s *appear.*

With inhibition of ideas inhibition of extravertive ideas, *samādhi* namely the cognitive samādhi *becomes habitual* to the yogin. *Then there is knowledge from that samādhi: from that, more saṃskāra-s are laid down of knowledge, and so* in this way *a fresh deposit of saṃskāra-s is built up. From that again knowledge, and from that more saṃskāra-s of it.*

Why would not this new accumulation of saṃskāra-s draw the mind into involvement with it? It is because saṃskāra-s of knowledge cause the destruction of the taints, and so do not constitute anything that would involve the mind. In fact they make the mind cease its activity, for the exertions of mind come to an end in knowledge (khyāti).

(Opponent) The new accumulation of saṃskāra-s produced by samādhi-knowledge will set up movements which will involve the mind, because they will produce thoughts, as did the former accumulation of saṃskāra-s of extraversion, for they are equally saṃskāra-s of thought. And so the commentator expresses the doubt: *Why would not this new accumulation of saṃskāra-s draw the mind into involvement with it?* – mind which has the saṃskāra-s.

(Answer) The objection does not hold because they are saṃskara-s of inhibition. These saṃskāra-s *cause destruction of the taints, and so do not constitute anything that would involve the mind.* It is taints like Ignorance which cause saṃskāra-s producing thoughts of extraversion, and supply the drive for those saṃskāra-s to appear in the mind. But the saṃskara-s of ideas arising from samādhi will have produced ideas which inhibit the others, and they do not cause any mental involvement to appear to it.

They make the mind cease desist *from its activity* from mental processes arising from saṃskāra-s. For the exertions of mind come to an end in Knowledge. The birth of Knowledge of Puruṣa, and the existence of saṃskāra, is a contradiction. For one who is completely free from thirst will not desire to take a drink. In the same way, as regards Puruṣa there is nothing that has to be done by the mind, and no one feels he should do as a duty what is already done.

Sūtra I.51

When that too is inhibited, everything is inhibited, and thus this samādhi is without-seed.

This suppresses not only samādhi-knowledge, but also the saṃskāra-s of it. For the saṃskāra of inhibition suppresses the saṃskāra-s produced by samādhi. That there is a saṃskāra formed in the mind by inhibition is to be inferred from the experience that the inhibition remains steady for progressively longer periods.

And then *when that too is inhibited, everything is inhibited, and thus this samādhi is without-seed.* The word *thus* carries the sense of a conclusion. *When that too is inhibited,* the new saṃskāra produced by samādhi-knowledge. The word *too* shows that the samādhi-knowledge, which caused the saṃskāra, has also been inhibited. As has been said earlier (sūtras I.12, 18) the means to inhibition is two-fold: supreme detachment, and the practice of the idea of stopping.

What is the *everything* which is to be inhibited? The extraverted state, samādhi-knowledge, and the saṃskāra-s of both of them. Thence, everything being inhibited, it is samādhi without seed.

The saṃskāra produced by Truth-bearing knowledge inhibits that Truth-bearing samādhi-knowledge. And furthermore in the same way, it itself suppresses the saṃskāra-s of like nature to it and produced, like it, by knowledge which is its cause.

How so? *The saṃskāra formed in the mind by inhibition:* inasmuch as when samādhi-knowledge and the saṃskāra produced by it are inhibited, a saṃskāra is produced by that inhibition, which has not come from samādhi-knowledge. This comes about when samādhi-knowledge and the saṃskāra-s produced by it are removed. The saṃskāra of inhibition, then, suppresses the saṃskāra-s born of samādhi.

(Opponent) How is it known that this saṃskāra born of inhibition exists? Or if it does exist, that it represses everything else?

(Answer) To this the commentator says: *from the experience that the inhibition remains steady for progressively longer periods.* The inhibition holds steady for a time, and that time is experienced as progressively longer, increasing with each repetition. From that experience of the lengthening time of the steadiness of the inhibition, it is inferred that there is a saṃskāra produced by mind in the state of inhibition.

> *The mind, together with the saṃskāra-s of samādhi on outer objects, and the saṃskāra-s of the samādhi of inhibition which have promoted the release, is dissolved in its own original basis (prakṛti). Thus the saṃskāra-s do not cause the mind to continue to exist, but prevent its involvement with anything. The mind, no longer involved, ceases to exist, along with the saṃskāra-s which have promoted release. When mind ceases, Puruṣa abides in his own nature alone, and is therefore called pure, alone, and released.*

Thus ends the First Part, on Samādhi, of the Commentary by holy Vyāsa, compiler of the Vedas, on the Yoga-sūtra-s of holy Patañjali.

The mind, no longer involved with anything, is ended, together with the saṃskāra-s which have promoted the release, being dissolved in its cause, I-am-ness (asmitā) or egoity (ahaṅkāra) which is its original basis (prakṛti). Those saṃskāra-s, inasmuch as they are born of knowledge and of inhibition, prevent its involvement with anything, and do not cause it to continue to exist.

Consequently the mind, no longer involved with anything, with its purpose fulfilled in regard to that Puruṣa, *ceases to exist, along with the saṃskāra-s which promoted release. When it ceases, Puruṣa abides in his own nature alone and is therefore called alone and released,* release being simply cessation of the mental process.

Thus ends the first Part, on Samādhi, of the commentary on the Yoga sūtra-s of Holy Patañjali, as explained in the vivaraṇa written by Holy Lord Śaṅkara (Śrī Śaṅkara Bhagavat), a teacher who is a paramahaṃsa and parivrājaka, and a disciple of holy Lord Govinda whose feet are worshipped.

Second Part: MEANS

(Vyāsa) The yoga for a concentrated mind has been described; now he turns to how one of extravertive mind may become steady in yoga.

(Śaṅkara:)

Now the Second Part, on the means, is begun. Right vision (samyagdarśana) is the means to Transcendental Aloneness (kaivalya). The yogic means are only means to right vision through yoga, and as this Part is mainly concerned with them, it is called the Part of the Means.

Then the Third Part, concerned mainly with the glories which attend on one who has been devoted to the practice of the yogic means, is called the Part of Glory.

The Fourth Part, which deals mainly with Transcendental Aloneness, attained by the one who is detached from all yogic powers and glories in total renunciation, is called the Part of Transcendental Aloneness.

The First Part, which at the beginning explained samādhi principally, was called the part of Samādhi.

In this connection the commentator says: *The yoga for a concentrated mind has been described,* meaning one unconcerned with action. The seedless samādhi was described, attained through higher detachment and practice of the idea of stopping, by a yogin who has already attained steadiness by practising the various means such as meditation on friendliness and compassion (I.33 and following). *(Now he turns to) how one of extravertive mind may become steady in yoga.* The sūtra-s now turn to how even one of changeable (vikṣipta, I.1) mind may become capable of samādhi.

Sūtra II.1

Tapas, self-study, devotion to the Lord, are the yoga of action

> The means are listed: *Tapas, self-study (svādhyāya), devotion to the Lord, are the yoga of action.*

(Opponent) But tapas, self-study, and devotion to the Lord are going to be given among the observances (II.32); why are they mentioned here?

(Answer) The purpose is as has been said: to show how one of extravertive mind may become steady in yoga.

(Opponent) Not so, because that purpose is declared along with the list of observances. And do not say that it is also taught here that they thin out the taints, because that too is taught in that place. 'From following up the yoga methods, destruction of impurity' (II.28), and impurity means such things as the taints. As to (the other effect mentioned here namely) that they take him towards samādhi meditation, that too will be given as the result of a yoga method: 'From devotion to the Lord, perfection in samādhi' (IL45). So to have instruction on tapas and the other two in this place is meaningless.

(Answer) No, it has meaning. It shows that yoga practice, being the means to right vision (samyagdarśanopāya), comes before right vision. All the yoga methods are means to right vision and therefore precede it in time. From among them, some of the observances are here mentioned to illustrate the point that all the means must come first. Obviously the means must come first, but the point should thus be clear.

(Opponent) If they come before right vision, the latter should be mentioned immediately afterwards (instead of the taints, in II.3).

(Answer) No, because right vision is the direct adversary of the taints, etc., since Ignorance (the first taint) is the root of all evil, and Ignorance is destroyed when directly confronted by right vision.

(Opponent) Then one may ask: are tapas and the other two the direct opponent of Ignorance, or is that opponent right vision alone?

(Answer) In a work on right vision, first of all its field has to be stated, and that is: Puruṣa overcome by the mass of taints and karma-s and their fruition, as the man suffering from illness is the field of a medical work. Now the field and the subject of the field (viṣaya, viṣayin) should be defined by a mention immediately after tapas, etc., otherwise it will not be clear what is the field and what the subject of the field.

Moreover the teaching on the means to right vision at the beginning of this Part shows its connection with the First Part. There the yoga of the already concentrated (samāhita) mind was set out, and here it is shown how the extravertive mind, by tapas, etc., may become steady in yoga.

Now it has to be explained that the purpose of tapas and the others is samādhi meditation and thinning out the taints.

(Opponent) It is going to be said later on, 'From devotion to the Lord, perfection in samādhi' (II.45) and 'From destruction of impurity by tapas, perfection of body and senses' (II.43), so that a perfection is going to be stated for each means separately.

(Answer) Not so; what will be said there is only a statement in praise of the means, supplementary to the perfections given here, where the sūtra says, 'to actualize samādhi and thin out the taints' (II.2). What is said later on will be added in praise of the means.

Now the words of the sūtra are explained. The compound tapas-self-study-devotion-to-God means tapas *and* self-study *and* devotion to God. It is these which are yoga in the form of action, so this is yoga of action. Tapas and the others are actions, and as their aim is yoga, they are themselves called yoga. Yoga is the mental state of samādhi, and this yoga of action aims at that; he who practises it is a yogin.

> *In one without tapas, the yoga does not succeed. Tapas is taught because impurity, coloured from time without beginning by karma-s and taints and saṃskāra-complexes, a net of sense contacts, is not destroyed without tapas. And they hold that it is to be practised without the calm of the mind being upset by it.*

Self study is repetition of purifying (mantra-s) like OM, or study of the scriptures on release. Devotion to the Lord is consigning all actions to the Lord the supreme teacher, or letting go their fruits.

Tapas is fasts like kṛcchra and cāndrāyana, and endurance of pairs of opposites like heat and cold; *self-study (svādhyāya)* is repetition of OM, and the purifying scriptures on release (mokṣa-śāstra), beginning with the Upaniṣads; *devotion to the Lord* is consigning actions to the Lord, the supreme teacher, or else letting go their fruits and surrendering them to the Lord.

(Opponent) What has tapas got to do with yoga? It is concerned with the body and its impurities and so on, and remote from mental concentration, whereas self-study and devotion to the Lord are relevant to yoga because they are inner means.

(Answer) This is why he says, *In one without tapas, the yoga does not succeed.* One will not succeed in yoga whose attitude is to cherish the body and bodily things, whose habit is to avoid discomfort of body, senses and mind, who sees the body absolutely as his self and thinks of it as very delicate. This is why tapas is taught.

Impurity, coloured from time without beginning ... by saṃskāra-complexes (vāsanā), formed of complexes of saṃskāra impressions of sense contacts from time without beginning, and so variegated, *a net of sense contacts*; the objects of present time are a net, by which net of the present objects the mind is caught like a fish in a net; this *is not destroyed without tapas.* And how can there be samādhi for a mind whose impurity has not been destroyed?

And they the yogas *hold that it* tapas *is to be practised without the calm of the mind* the inner means to samādhi *being upset by it.* Since the goal is calmness of mind, if one should upset that by tapas, the very purpose would be frustrated.

This yoga of action is –

Sūtra II.2

To actualize samādhi and thin out the taints

Practised hard, it actualizes samādhi, and thins out the taints. When the taints have been thinned out, it will by the fire of meditation practice make them like scorched seeds, inherently infertile. Then the subtle realization, the knowledge of the utter difference between sattva and Puruṣa, no more caught up in taints because they have been thinned out, its involvement at an end, tends towards dissolution.

What is the purpose of this yoga of action? To explain its final purpose he says: *To actualize samādhi and thin out the taints.* How it comes to have the two-fold purpose, the commentator explains: *practised hard, it actualizes samādhi;* when it is combined with the other yogic methods it actualizes samādhi *and thins out the taints.* As he will say: 'With the destruction of impurity from following up the yoga methods, light of knowledge up to Knowledge-of-the-difference' (II.28).

He says on this: *When the taints have been thinned out, it will by meditation practice (prasaṅkhyāna)* by constancy in right vision (samyagdarśana) arising from the thinning out of the taints *make them like scorched seeds* like seeds whose fertility has been destroyed by being scorched, and which are therefore *inherently infertile,* infertile because they are not found to have any power to propagate, and inherently so because that is now their quality. This yoga will make the taints without the power of propagation.

Then the subtle realization, knowledge of the utter difference between sattva and Puruṣa, no more caught up in taints because they have been thinned out, and with its involvement at an end, will tend towards dissolution; it will tend no more to turn to the course of the world.

Even if the Knowledge (khyāti) that sattva and Puruṣa are wholly different should be produced by instruction of the scripture and teacher without practice of the yoga methods, still as the taints and a-dharma and so on will not have been removed at all, it will not produce the realization (prajñā) with involvement at an end; again and again there will be re-involvement with them. This the commentator shows by the phrase *no more caught up in taints.*

Now what are the taints? And how many are there?

Sūtra II.3

Ignorance, I-am-ness, desire, hate, instinctive self-preservation, are the taints

The word 'taints' means five illusions.

What are the taints by nature *and how many are they* in number? The sūtra has been given to explain their number and nature. *Ignorance, I-am-ness, desire, hate, instinctive self-preservation, are the taints.*Their individual characteristics are to be given in the sūtra-s following, and the present sūtra makes no attempt to do more than list them.

(Opponent) Right knowledge, illusion, logical construction, and the other mental processes have been distinguished from one another, but there is no differentiation of the taints from illusion. Why not?

(Answer) Because they are themselves different forms of illusion. They exist only when illusion is there, and so the commentator says, *The word means five illusions.*

(Opponent) In the sūtra-s which distinguished the classes of mental process, it was said, 'Right knowledge is either direct perception, inference, or authority' (I.7), making a division into three; so why did it not there also give the division of this illusion into five in the same way? It was said that illusion is indeed a mental process, and it has been stated, 'seeing the moon as double is negated by seeing that it is in fact a single moon' (comm. to I.8).

(Answer) There is no inconsistency, because the taints are not mental processes. For taints are not merely ideas, whereas mental processes are merely ideas. Taints are impurities of the mind, as the disease timira is of the eye. It is from absence of illusory ideas that there is freedom from the impurity of taints.

Now if illusion were no more than an idea, then when taints were suppressed, there would still be illusion in the yogin just as much as ideas of memory or right knowledge. But there is no illusion in those whose taints have dwindled away. So what is called illusion is impurity of the idea, causing distorted perception of things, as in the case of impurity of the eye.

It cannot however be found or spoken of apart from some idea, and so it is described as an idea itself: illusion is a mental process. Again, mental processes were previously divided into tainted or pure (I.5), so a distinction was made there in terms of taints. It would not be reasonable to differentiate mental processes solely in terms of the processes themselves. Further it was declared 'caused by the taints' (comm. to I.5), and it would not be logical that what causes mental processes should be itself only a mental process.

As the taints are thus not mental processes, they have not been presented there (in I.8) as divisions of a mental process.

Again it was said, 'They will be discussed later under impurity of the mind' (comm. to I.8), showing that taints are not mental processes but only impurities of them. Still, in so far as they relate to the same thing they are figuratively treated as not distinct, as when it is said (Gītā II.38, 39) that as smoke by its impurity covers fire, and as also an embryo and a mirror are covered (by womb and dust respectively) so is knowledge covered by this (Ignorance). It is just the same here.

> *Quickening to life, these confirm the involvement with the guṇa-s, impose change, stimulate the currents in the body and senses by mutually reinforcing each other, and bring on fruition of karma.*

He explains how the ideas are illusory: *quickening to life, these* ... This means that they appear vividly by way of an idea, for they have no action by themselves, any more than a dye without the clothes. They *confirm the involvement with the guṇa-s:* the involvement is an activity, the fact of something to be done, and they strengthen that. For when they are quickened, the mind is never without something which it has to do.

They *impose change* inasmuch as they are continually causing change. They *stimulate the currents in the body and senses:* they heighten the current of activity of the body and of the senses such as the eye. How does this come about? *by mutually reinforcing each other:* Ignorance and the others become mutually cause and effect in regard to one another.

And they *bring on the fruition of karma* which is three-fold; they bring on its fruition as birth, life-span and experience.

Sūtra II.4

Ignorance is the field of germination of the subsequent ones, whether dormant or thinned out or checked or active

Here Ignorance is the field, the place of germination, of I-am-ness and the other subsequent ones, which can be in one of four states: dormant, thinned, checked or active.

What is their dormant state? When implanted in the mind as a mere potentiality, reduced to the condition of a seed. It awakens when it confronts its object.

Ignorance is the field of germination of the subsequent ones, which can be either dormant or thinned or checked or active. The sūtra itself shows how it is that I-am-ness and the others are called illusion. Ignorance is the field for their germination, where they produce themselves; like a piece of land supporting grass, creepers, bushes and plants not separate from itself, it is the field for I-am-ness and the others, not separate from Ignorance, from illusion. And the four of them are individually either dormant or thinned or checked or active.

For the ideas of illusion produce themselves by means of this; it is Ignorance that transforms itself into I-am-ness and the others of the set of four.

What is their dormant state? What is called the dormant state relates to I-am-ness and the others, not to Ignorance; because Ignorance is their cause which accompanies all the alternative states of I-am-ness and the others, and is therefore always aroused, not dormant. For in sleep there is no activity. When I-am-ness or one of the others is dormant there has to be something different as a basis, otherwise there could be no rise of another taint. And so the alternatives of the four states of dormancy, etc. relate to I-am-ness and the other three alone.

(The dormant state is) *When implanted in the mind as a mere potentiality* which he explains as *reduced to the condition of a seed.* As the seed is there in the ground though it has not become a sprout, so in the mind, I-am-ness and the others are established as potentialities with the sprout of their true nature not manifest.

It awakens when it confronts its object: the revival of a taint like I-amness is when it confronts its object, the cause which makes it manifest (sva-vyañjaka-añjana).

(Opponent) In that case, there will always be taints in seed state, and their arousal under certain conditions.

> *For one who has attained meditation on truth (prasaṅkhyāna), in whom the seeds have been scorched (reading dagdha not a-dagdha, Tr.), even when confronted with the objects, the taints do not come again into manifest being. When the seeds have been scorched (in ovens) how should they revive? When his taints have dwindled away, he is said to be skilful and in his final incarnation. In him alone and not in others is there the fifth state of the taints, that of scorched seed. Of his remaining taints, the seed potentiality is then scorched, and even when confronting their objects they are not aroused. This is the description of the dormant state and the non-arousal of scorched seeds.*

(Answer) He replies: *For one who has attained meditation on truth (prasaṅkhyāna)* the yogin practising right vision (samyagdarśana), *in whom the seeds have been scorched (reading dagdha not a-dagdha), the taints* which have been reduced to the state of seed *do not come again into manifest being, even when confronted with their objects. When the seeds have been scorched (in ovens),* from that scorching *how should they revive* spring up? Even though the seed is there and has the necessary concomitants of earth and water, etc., there is no development into a sprout from the potentiality of a scorched seed, and so in the case of the taints also.

(Opponent) If so, why was this fifth state not given in the list? The sūtra should have read: scorched, dormant, thinned out, checked, active.

(Answer) No, because it does not apply to everyone. This fifth state of the taints is not common to all living beings, but is found in yogin-s alone, and for that reason it was not listed there.

In what way is it special? *In him alone* in one who is practising right vision *and not in others* are they scorched. *When his taints have dwindled away,* the yogin of right vision *is said to be skilful and in his final incarnation. In him alone and not in others is there the fifth state of the taints, that of scorched seed. Of his remaining taints, the seed potentiality is then scorched* like seeds of a grain such as barley which still exist but have had their germinating capacity scorched. *Even when confronting their objects they are not aroused,* for the saṃskāra remnant in the man of right vision is in a state like that of an arrow already loosed at the mark (to which no fresh impetus can be added).

> *Thinning out is explained thus: struck down by meditation on their opposites, the taints become thinned out.*
>
> *They are said to be checked when, intercepted again and again, they again and again become active in their own form. How does this happen? Because at the time of desire, anger is not seen; anger is not active at the time of desire. Then, desire, seen to be for one person, is not non-existent for others. Caitra is not indifferent to other women because he is in love with a particular woman. Rather, desire for her has possessed his mind, and its thought of the others is yet in the future, being at present dormant or thinned.*

The dormant state has been described, and also how there is no arousal of scorched seeds of taints in the yogin. Now *thinning out is explained thus: struck down* made powerless, enfeebled *by meditation on their opposites,* by meditation on their opposites, for instance by seeing the worthlessness of the body and so on, they are made powerless and become feeble, and the taints are said to be *thinned out.*

They are said to be checked when, intercepted again and again, they do not show themselves in the interval, when it is the turn of others to appear; then *they again and again become active* they rise up *in their own form,* in that very form, that very shape, in which they were perceived before.

Or (on another reading) if the word *checked* refers to the period of interception, then *they are not active in their own form,* in their manifest form in which they are seen before and after (the checked state).

He explains the point: *How does this happen? Because at the time of desire, anger is not seen; anger is not active at the time of desire,* their various forms and various mental processes being opposed. Anger is suppressed by the rise of desire and exists in another, unmanifest form, and this is what is called being checked.

Then, desire, seen to be for one person, is not non-existent for others. How is this? It is because in this case the conflict is between the objects. In the previous case anger was inoperative because of conflict with desire, but here it is mutual conflict between objects of desire. For a desire is attraction for a particular object – the desire is not then for some other object.

So *Caitra is not indifferent to other women because he is in love with a particular woman. Rather, desire for her has possessed his mind* in love with her. *Its thought of the others* of the other women *is in the future,* yet to come in particular manifestations of desire, *being at present dormant or thinned.*

(Opponent) Why is the commentator saying all this about desire seen to be for one person? He is just telling us what desire is: the mental process, whether now possessing the mind or yet to come, as distinguished by these differences of object, is nothing but desire.

(Answer) True, but that is not the context in which he is saying it. The context is explanation of the checked state, and that (discussion of the nature of desire) does not explain checking, nor is it relevant to the next topic, the active state. They do not need such a discussion.

All this is simply to fill in a possible gap, namely that it might be thought that there was no other state except the dormant, thinned out, and active states.

(Opponent) Indeed, it has been said that in so far as it does not possess the mind, so far it is dormant, and that a mental process struck down by meditation on the opposite, with its effect enfeebled, is called thinned. And it is declared that what is in possession of the mind, is active. Now what you called checked is supposed to be something which, having been perceived somewhere, (vanishes and then) is again perceived, like the course of the river Sarasvatī (which passes for a time underground). For when desire rises, anger is nowhere to be seen.

But then there is no quality to be called 'checked', because it is never something perceived.

(Answer) The reply is: if there is no state of being checked because it is not something perceived, then anger seen on one occasion ought not to exist inasmuch as on another occasion it is not perceived.

(Opponent) Be it so; it does not exist because it is not seen on the other occasion.

(Answer) Not so.

(Opponent) Why not?

(Answer) Because it was actually seen on the first occasion. If it is to be said that a taint does not exist when a different object is confronted, then it does not exist in the mind which possesses it. But an eye, because at some time it is not looking at an elephant, cannot be said not to exist when it is active in looking at a jar; for it clearly is there, looking at the jar. So he says, *desire, seen to be for one person, is not non-existent for others.*

Anger is seen to be checked when overcome by rising desire, as the course of the Sarasvatī (disappears for a time). Desire is dormant or thinned in regard to other objects (than the present focus), because it has the character of not being seen when confronting them.

(Opponent) Then what is the distinction between dormant and checked? In both cases they are invisible. There is no distinction.

(Answer) What was continuously visibly active is subordinated by another (taint) not fundamentally opposed to it, and so the first is not seen: this is the *checked* state, where seed has not been scorched.

The *dormant* state is when, though motivating causes are there, the taint has been subdued by its opponent – though the seeds have not been scorched – by which overpowering it has been reduced to a seed state.

(Opponent) If so, the words *it is dormant or thinned* are contradicted, because the activity, not now seen (in regard to the future object) is in fact being seen with a different object.

(Answer) Not so, because he is referring to desire for an object other than the one now in front. The particular quality of desire, in regard to a desirable object different (from its present focus) is the one which is dormant or thinned. It is not always inherently dormant or thinned, for it is still seen in certain directions. Whereas at the time of desire, anger is inherently dormant or thinned, and is not felt in regard to any object at all.

The commentary gives another example to illustrate the meaning of 'checked', because he wishes to point out two cases. One is when the relation of visible action (of a taint) has disappeared completely because it has been overcome by something incompatible, as in the example *anger is not seen at the time of desire.* The other case is when it appears only in regard to a particular object, and in regard to others is not seen to give rise to any effect. When Caitra is in love with one woman, his desire for other women is not visible; desire has taken possession of his mind in regard to her. In the case when it is seen directed to a particular object and there is nothing to be seen of it in regard to future mental process and its object – that is what is called checked.

(Opponent) Why is it not seen in regard to the other things?

(Answer) *It is dormant or thinned.* He is not discussing whether it is a case of dormancy or of thinning out; that is as the particular case may be. The point is, that it is not now seen because it is checked.

> *What possesses the mind in regard to an object is called active. These states are all included within the field of the taints.*

(Opponent) Is it a taint at all if it can be either checked or dormant or thinned or active?

(Answer) It is a valid point, but the states of checked and so on apply to them in their capacity as taints. Just as they are brought to an end by meditation on their opposite, so they are manifested by their particular manifesting causes.

What possesses the mind in regard to an object is called active.

(Opponent) Those that are dormant, thinned out or checked cannot have any effects, so they are not in fact taints. For what is dormant, thinned out or checked cannot, in the state of dormancy, inhibition or attenuation, effect any result. An enemy who has not been born cannot do any harm, nor can one bathe in a river where it has been intercepted. So let it be simply said that Ignorance is the field (of germination) of the subsequent ones; why all this about the dormant, thinned or checked, which cannot produce any results?

(Answer) This doubt the commentator meets in the words, *These states are all included within the field of the taints.*

(Opponent) *Is it a taint at all if it can be either checked or dormant or thinned or active?* It is not logical to divide them up in this way. Let a taint be simply the active, for apart from the active state no effect is produced.

(Answer) *It is a valid point,* but the refutation is given when it is said: *the states of checked and so on apply to them in their capacity as taints,* always retaining their quality of being taints. Since even in the state of being checked, the power to injure has not been lost, it is quite reasonable.

(Opponent) But at that time they are ineffective.

(Answer) Not so, and that is why the instruction is given to meditate on their opposites (to counter them in their subtle state). It is not that there is no need to act against an enemy who is nowhere to be seen, or who is asleep, or not yet born. In the scripture we hear that Indra for fear of his future enemy cut into seven pieces the embryo in Diti's womb.

And he himself declares the reason: *Just as they are brought to an end by meditation on their opposite – so they are manifested by their particular manifesting causes.*

Inasmuch as they are now manifested and again concealed and still again manifest in the future, so those in states like the dormant must be spoken of in order to give instructions on opposing them, because in these states the tainted nature has not yet been transcended.

Now he sums up:

> *All these taints are divisions of Ignorance. How so? In all of them, Ignorance alone prevails. Whatever is given a form by Ignorance, that the taints inhere in. They are felt at the time of deluded ideas; when Ignorance dwindles, they dwindle accordingly.*

So that *all these taints are divisions of Ignorance. How so?* Because *in all of them* I-am-ness and the rest, *Ignorance alone prevails,* flourishes, is seen to be predominant.

Whatever is given a form is determined *by Ignorance, that the taints* passion and the rest *inhere in,* they follow on that.

As, for instance, one sees the body of a woman, and though it is to be avoided, from self-will incited by Ignorance, he decides, 'This is to be enjoyed', and falls in love. The one who knows righteousness, deciding that this is illusion, is averse to it.

How is it that the taints inhere in it? *They are felt at the time of deluded ideas,* and hence they are divisions of Ignorance. So *when Ignorance dwindles, they dwindle accordingly*. The taints such as I-am-ness disappear as Ignorance disappears, for in the absence of Ignorance no taint can exist.

Now he explains what Ignorance is in itself:

Sūtra II.5

Ignorance is the conviction of permanence, purity, happiness and self in what are really impermanent, impure, painful and not self

(Opponent) But why does the nature of Ignorance have to be described?

(Answer) The commentator himself is going to discuss it in the passage beginning 'Ignorance is the root of the train of taints', and that is why its nature has to be taught here; unless the root of the train of taints is known, it cannot be uprooted.

Ignorance is the conviction of permanence in effects which are impermanent, as for instance the idea 'Eternal is the earth, eternal the heaven with its moon and stars, immortal are the shining ones.'

Then in the body of very repulsive impurity:

From its abode, from its origin, from its support, from its secretions, and from its end,
And because it has to be purified, the wise know the body as impure.
Thus (for the ignorant) there is conviction of purity in what is impure.

Ignorance is the conviction of permanence, purity, happiness and self in what are really impermanent, impure, painful and not self. In what way is this? *The conviction of permanence,* the deluded idea that there is permanence, *in effects which are impermanent, as for instance the idea 'Eternal is the earth, eternal the heaven with its moon and stars, immortal are the shining ones.'*

(Opponent) But we know from this very verse of the scriptures that these things like earth are permanent; how can it be said that they are mere effects (and therefore transient)?

(Answer) There is no mistake, because it is a question of relative permanence. In comparison with beings such as men, the earth and so on are indeed permanent, but the fact that they are effects and are not permanent is recognized by all proofs, and established in the holy texts by declarations like 'Heaven was not nor earth nor intermediate space'.

Then in the body of very repulsive impurity, the body in its impurity being a repellent seat of extreme afflictions, as it were a prison for the self. Its repulsive character is further described: *impure from its abode* from the fact of its time in the womb; *from its origin,* for the germ of the body is the white seed and the red; *from its support,* it is supported by wind, bile and phlegm, whose impurity is very well known; *from its secretions,* continual excretion of sweat, urine, and faeces; *and from its end* which is death, associated with the traditional impurity connected with a corpse.

(Opponent) Well, if the body is naturally impure, our attempts to keep clean are meaningless.

(Answer) He replies: *and because it has to be purified.* Inasmuch as methods of purification are prescribed by scripture purity is not natural to the body.

Or again, senses – the mind-sattva and others – are pure by their nature as sattva, and when they are contained in the body, it too becomes pure because of their purity. For we see that when it is not endowed with mind-sattva, etc., it is extremely impure.

So the wise know it as impure. This knowledge of the wise is mentioned to show that the idea of the body as pure is of a deluded intellect. Thus there is the conviction of pure in what is impure, held by a deluded mind.

> *The poet says, 'This girl, beautiful as the crescent moon, her limbs as if formed out of honey and nectar, her eyes like the petals of a blue lotus, sent forth from*

> *the moon as it were to refresh the world with her inviting glances' – how is there any real connection between these things? Thus in the impure there is an illusion of purity, and similarly conviction of good in what is not good, and profit in what is pointless.*
>
> *The conviction of happiness in what is painful will be described later, in the sūtra: 'Because of the sufferings caused by changes and anxieties and the saṃskāra-s of them, and from the clash of the guṇa-s, to the clear-sighted, everything is pain' (II.15). This conviction of happiness (where it does not exist) is Ignorance.*
>
> *Then the conviction of self in what is not self – either external accessories animate or inanimate, or in the body as the seat of extraverted experience, or in the mind which is an accessory to Puruṣa – such is the conviction of self in not self.*

The poet says, 'This girl, beautiful as the crescent moon, her limbs formed out of honey and nectar, her eyes like the petals of a blue lotus, sent forth from the moon as it were to refresh the world with her inviting glances' – how is there any real connection between these things? How should the body be really like these things? *Thus in the impure there is an illusion of purity, and similarly conviction of good in what is not good,* as in the case of ritual murderers (saṃsāra-mocaka), *and profit in what is profitless* as in the case of thieves.

The conviction of happiness in what is painful will be described later, in the sūtra (II.15): *Because of the sufferings caused by changes and anxieties and the saṃskāra-s of them, and from the clash of the guṇa-s, to the clear-sighted, everything is pain.* Ignorance is this conviction of happiness in saṃsāra, which is wholly pain.

> *Then the conviction of self in what is not self- either external accessories animate or inanimate* like cows or jars, *or in the body as the seat of extraverted experience, or in the mind which is an accessory to Puruṣa – such is the conviction of self in not self.*

(Opponent) But who is supposed to have this conviction of self in a mind which is not self? The conviction itself is in the mind.

(Answer) There is no anomaly, inasmuch as it has been said that Ignorance is a mental process of illusion. The mind it is, which supported by an acquired consciousness, arrogates to itself the conscious self, and by that confusion thinks, 'I am the seer, the hearer am I, this is mine'.

And on this it has been said: 'He who having accepted any thing manifest or unmanifest as his self, rejoices in its success and grieves at its reverses – he who thinks thus is a totally deluded mind.'

Ignorance has these four divisions. It is the root of the train of taints and of the karma-stock with its fruition.

And on this in this sense *it has been said: 'He who having accepted* having acknowledged *any thing manifest or unmanifest* anything from pradhāna through body and senses and so on down to the objects, either manifest, directly experienced, or unmanifest, something known from inference or authority, *as his self, rejoices in its success,* experiences something which is manifest or unmanifest by nature, as himself, so that he rejoices, he is thrilled, in its success, in its prosperity or glory, thinking of it as his own success, thinking 'in its success, I succeed; mine is this success', *and grieves at its reverses,* feeling 'This reverse is mine; it is I who have failed', *he who thinks thus is a totally deluded mind,* is Ignorant.

Ignorance has these four divisions.

(Opponent) But with the conviction of good in evil, and evil in good, there will be six divisions.

(Answer) No; those cases can fit into the four divisions.

(Ignorance) is the root the germ of growth *of the train of taints* of the continuous action of the taints ending with instinctive self-preservation *and of the karma-stock with its fruition* three-fold, as birth, death and experience. The sense is that Ignorance is the root of the entire saṃsāra.

(Grammatical Excursus on the Saṃskṛt compound avidyā)

And it (avidyā) should be known as a positive existent, as in the case of 'no-friend' (= positive enemy) and 'no hoof-mark' (= place impenetrable to cows).

And that avidyā (Ignorance) should be understood as a positive entity (vastu) that is different (antara) (from both knowledge and absence of knowledge), on the analogy of such phrases as 'no friend' (= enemy) and 'no hoof-mark' (= place impenetrable to cows).

(Opponent) But why does he say this, when he has already once said that avidyā is illusory knowledge, and thus a positive entity (and different from both knowledge and absence of knowledge)?

(Answer) The idea is this. The term avidyā (one might initially suppose) comprises a negative compound of the 'his man' (tatpuruṣa) type (in which one or more words qualify another word without themselves being inflected, and in which the referent, the person or thing ultimately denoted by the compound, lies within the meanings of the component words, and not outside them as in the case of a bahuvrīhi compound). Such a compound may have its last member as the principal one (i.e. as that which is the ultimate referent of the compound and of which the other member or members are only a qualification).

An example of such would be rājapuruṣa, 'the king's man' (where puruṣa = man is the last member of the compound and the referent). Or a compound of this class may have its first member as the principal. An example of this would be ardhapippalī, 'the half of a pepper' (Pāṇini II.ii.2) (where ardha = ardham = the half, taken as a noun, is the first member of the compound, and the qualified element, and the principal, and the referent, because we can speak of 'the half *of* a pepper' (cf. 'the man *of* the king') but not of 'a pepper *of* the half').

Here (in the compound a-vidyā, consisting of a- 'not' and vidyā 'knowledge') the first member (a- = 'not') may be taken as the principal one. But then all criteria (pramāna) for the meaning of vidyā (knowledge) are removed. And just where one would have expected (prasaṅga) the idea 'knowledge', there would arise – since there must be a meaning of some kind – notions of some other meaning (knowledge being negated). So there will be a meaning (namely 'not') of which the particular nature remains undetermined. As for avidyā having been said previously to be (something specific, namely) 'illusory knowledge', that should be regarded as a special technical term of the school.

Suppose it was a special technical term. What would be the harm? Well, on hearing the word avidyā there would be a doubt as to the meaning. The doubt would be of the form: 'Is the technical meaning (in the Yoga Sāstra) the same as the ordinary meaning in common speech, in accordance with the maxim, "It is to be understood that wherever possible words in the sūtras have the ordinary meanings that they have in the world"? Or should we understand something that is not the ordinary meaning of the word (aśabdārtha), as (in the case of a śāstrika phrase containing purely technical terms of grammar like) "guṇa and vṛddhi apply to ik (the short vowels) only"? So, as the meaning of the word avidyā would not be clear, it could not be put to practical use.'

(Since the assumption that the first element in the tatpuruṣa compound avidyā is the principal leads us nowhere) let us assume that the second element (vidyā) is the principal. They would be standing in apposition like 'blue' and 'lotus' in 'blue-lotus'. But here also there is a difficulty. For in the case of 'blue-lotus' a relation of qualifier and qualified between the two elements is intelligible (cp. Pāṇini II. 1.57), since the meanings of the words do not contradict one another. Here (however, this absence of contradiction is not the case, for) negation is expressed by the privative a- ('not') while vidyā expresses 'knowledge'. In such a case, if 'not' were the subordinate (and therefore the qualifier) in relation to the meaning of the second element in the compound ('knowledge'), the latter being the principal (and therefore the qualified and the referent), then the 'not' would abolish the meaning of that principal element (which was also the referent). And then its own existence as a subordinate element would be annulled, and the other element could not be the principal either.

For whatever has the function of negating (reading ni- for nir- throughout the passage) something, negates that object alone; it cannot negate its own relation as subordinate to that object. And if it did, the object of the negation would no longer be the principal (and the referent), for the same reason. Therefore, (in a negative tatpuruṣa compound) the subordinate element must be taken as subservient (vaśavartin) to the principal (and as unable to negate it). Hence (the meaning of the compound avidyā can be) only 'the absence (abhāva) of anything else *in* knowledge'. What is understood is 'mere knowledge', as the bare word 'not' always presupposes a positive (on which to operate, whether by way of negation or qualification).

Now, taking the earlier train of reasoning as the starting-point, the (conclusive) reply is given. 'And it (avidyā) must be understood as a positive entity like 'no friend' (= enemy) and 'no hoof-mark' (= thick forest impenetrable to cows)'.

As the term amitra ('no friend') is not 'absence of friend', nor 'mere friend', but the contrary of friend – an enemy; or again, the term agoṣpada (no hoof-mark) does not mean either 'absence of hoof-mark' or 'mere hoof-mark', but a place different from both of them; in the same way, avidyā is not 'right knowledge' or 'absence of right knowledge', but a cognition of a different kind, contrary to both of them.

He (Vyāsa) says now: *Just as no-friend (= enemy) is not an 'absence of friend',* implying thereby the idea 'as it would have been if it had been taken (as a negative compound) with the first member as principal, like 'the half of a pepper'.

Then he says, *nor (does no-friend mean) 'mere friend'.* As has already been explained, if the last element in a compound is the principal, the subordinate element must be subservient to it and cannot annul it. And so it has been said in the Nañ Vārtika (Mahābhāṣya II.ii.6 *ad init.),* '(If the last member of a negative compound were the principal, then) when one heard the words "Fetch a non-Brahmin" one would have the (absurd) idea of fetching a Brahmin.' In fact, if the last member of the compound is taken as the principal, the negative must always imply a positive. Such, therefore, is the case with 'no friend' (i.e. it is not a tatpuruṣa compound with either the first or the last member as principal, so it does not mean either 'absence of friend' or 'mere friend'). And such is the case with avidyā and certain other negative compounds also (such as a-nīti – immorality, and others).

And again (he says, proceeding to illustrate the matter from the example of a bahuvrīhi compound) *the term agoṣpada does not mean 'absence of hoof-mark' or 'a mere hoof-mark' but rather some positive entity (a place) that is different both from 'absence of hoof-mark' and from 'mere hoof-mark'.*

You will ask how that can be, when (in the compound agoṣpadam) all we hear is 'a mere hoof-mark' and 'its non-existence'. We reply: If we go by normal usage, we shall get the meaning 'no hoof-mark at all' (already implicitly rejected in considering amitra above). How so? Well, the meaning of 'not' is 'the contrary of existence' (= non-existence) and it asserts the non-existence of that to which it is applied.

So when we meet with the term agoṣpada (seen from our earlier arguments to mean something positive) three meanings are possible, namely: (1) something that might be, but is not, associated with a hoof-mark, (2) a mere hoof-mark, and (3) something positive, contrary to a hoof-mark.

Here, if the meaning had been 'a mere hoof-mark' there would have been no need to use the word 'not'. Even if you claimed that the word 'not' in such a case confirmed some other negation that had already been made about 'hoof mark', it would still be superfluous.

Then let us suppose that the word agoṣpada is used to mean something that might be, but is not, connected with a hoof-mark. But in this case the word 'not' could not be being used in its primary sense, as it would not be being used to say that a place was never *at all* visited by cows. For even if the place were visited by cows in the future, the term agoṣpada (understood in the loose sense now under consideration) would hold good throughout the three periods of time. Therefore, according to the principle, 'wherever it is possible for the word 'not' to mean 'not' (in the full sense), that is what it does mean', the two meanings – 'might be visited by cows but has not yet been' and 'merely visited by cows' – are rejected.

So (as the only remaining possibility) the term agoṣpada must mean a place contrary in nature to the places visited by cows.

But, you will ask, (if there is to be a compound at all, there must be a relation of qualifier and qualified, and) how can there be a relation of qualifier and qualified here (in the case of a-vidyā), as there is in the case of the blue-lotus, since avidyā is one entity, and existence and non-existence (represented by 'knowledge' and 'not') are contradictories? Admittedly, if the compound had been (a tatpuruṣa) meant only to assert the non-existence of knowledge, it would have been unintelligible. Hence the principle holds (here, as in a bahuvrīhi compound) that that *in which* the non-existence of something else is asserted is understood to be (a positive entity) different from that thing. And this is what the sūtra (Pāṇini VI.i.145) implies when it says: '(We have the form) goṣpada (and not gopada when the compound go-pada is used) to mean either "visited by cows" or "not visited by cows" or (when it is used to mean) "a measure" (pramāṇa) (of rainfall, namely "a puddle").'

Where the meaning is taken as 'not visited', the compound is understood as a bahuvrihi (where a negation does not negate the existence of the referent, as the latter lies *outside* the meanings of the words in the compound) (Pāṇini II.ii.24). 'Unvisited' means 'where no visitation (ever) occurs'.

And avidyā (though not a bahuvrīhi compound) is to be understood, in a similar way, as 'neither right knowledge, nor absence of right knowledge, but a (positive) cognition of a different kind, contrary to right knowledge'.

(End of excursus)

Sūtra II.6

The single selfhood, as it were, of the powers of seer and seeing is I-am-ness

Puruṣa is the power of seer; mind (buddhi) is the power of seeing. The taking on of a single nature as it were, by these two, is called the taint of I-am-ness.

Now the illusion called I-am-ness. *Puruṣa is seer,* his seeing being awareness, and he is a *power; seeing,* in the sense that by it something is seen, is also a *power,* whose nature is the determination of things by the mind (antaḥkaraṇa). *Of these two* powers of seer and seeing, whose natures are awareness and mental determination, *the single selfhood as it were:* single selfhood is the state where it is both one and this self; the word *iva, as it were,* shows that there is in fact absolute distinction between them. *The taking on of a single nature as it were is called the taint of I-am-ness.* That I-notion (aham-pratyaya) in which the distinction between mind (citta) and Puruṣa is not perceived, the notion 'he is this I', is the taint called technically I-am-ness. It was said earlier that what is called Ignorance is only illusory seeing, the conviction of self in the not-self of mind (antaḥkaraṇa) which is an accessory to Puruṣa. But here it is specified as I-am-ness, the seeing of mind (buddhi) and Puruṣa as not distinct, which as it were conflates them into a single nature.

When there comes about a failure, as it were, to distinguish between the experiencer and what is experienced, which are utterly distinct and nothing to do with each other, that is the condition for experience. But when the true nature of the two is recognized, that is Transcendental Aloneness. Then how could there be experience? So it has been said: 'Not seeing Puruṣa beyond the mind, distinct from it in such things as form, habitual character, and knowledge, he will make there a mental self out of delusion.'

On this it is said: *When there comes about a failure, as it were, to distinguish between the experiencer (bhoktṛ) and what is experienced (bhogya) which are utterly distinct and nothing to do with each other, that is the condition for experience.* The meaning is, that the cause of experience is the taint called I-am-ness. When there is an I-notion, there comes about the relation with pleasure, pain, etc., in the form 'I am pleased' or 'I am pained', and this is why it is so.

But when the true nature of the two mind (buddhi) and Puruṣa *is recognized,* in the discriminative awareness of their true nature in the form 'not I and mine' *that is Transcendental Aloneness (kaivalya)* with no mingling at all. *Then how could there be experience?* The cause is the undiscriminated I-notion taken as self, and the effect is experience; and when that cause is not there, neither is experience.

For unless sentience had been projected (adhyāropya) into the mind, there would be no recurrence of the fact of enjoyer or sufferer. The field of the I-notion is the location of the notions of pleasure and pain, and the location of 'I am an enjoyer' and 'I am a sufferer' is the same. In this way the egoity (ahaṅkāra) called I-am-ness (asmitā) is the cause of experience.

So it has been said: Puruṣa beyond the mind beyond the presence of the mind, *distinct from it* as being of different qualities, as being other than it. What those differences of qualities are, he explains:

in form by merely conforming to mental processes,
in habitual character by its witnessing of the mind,
in knowledge, as being of the nature of consciousness.

Or on another interpretation,

in form by the fact of its nature of purity and infinity,
in habitual character in that being immutable, it does not dissolve into any cause,
in knowledge in that it is the power-of-consciousness (citi-śakti) by nature.

In these qualities, it is distinct from mind (buddhi).

Then too, the mind is distinguishable from Puruṣa

in form as being essentially pleasure, pain and delusion,
in habitual character as essentially illumination, activity and fixity,
in knowledge as its essence is to determine all.

Not seeing Puruṣa thus *distinct* in mutually different form, habitual character and knowledge, *he will make there* in that mind *a mental self* a notion of self, *out of delusion (moha).* The seeing of mind and Puruṣa, which are utterly distinct in knowledge and habitual character and form, as inseparate as it were, to that extent illustrates I-am-ness.

But not seeing Puruṣa beyond, he makes in the mind a mental self; this is the Ignorance formerly described. Or if we take it that I-am-ness is a division of Ignorance, then the illustration stands as a whole. It is said that not seeing, he will make (the mental self), and it means that the cause of Ignorance is the failure-to-see the true nature of Puruṣa, and the cause of I-am-ness is the colouring of the mind as both seer and seen. But there is no seeing of Puruṣa himself because he is pure Seer-hood alone.

Sūtra II.7

Desire follows on (anujanma) pleasure

When one familiar with a pleasure now has a memory of it, his eagerness for the pleasure or for the means to it, that thirst or greed, is (called) desire.

Desire follows on (anujanma) is the consequence of (anuśayī) *pleasure.* To follow on means to arise afterwards. There are other readings of this sūtra and the next as 'the consequence (anuśayī) of pleasure' and 'the consequence of pain'. They read the sūtras as *Desire is the consequence of pleasure and hate is the consequence of pain,* meaning that the character of the one is to be a consequence of pleasure, and similarly with pain. In both readings the sense is simply following on, and that is its habitual character. So he will say, 'From righteousness, pleasure; from pleasure, desire' (comm. to IV.11).

As to the nature of this following on, he explains: *When one familiar with a pleasure,* knowing about it, *now has a memory of the pleasure* recalling previous experience of it, *his eagerness for the pleasure* the thrill *or the means to it,* in the shape of addiction to aloes and sandal and so on, *that thirst or greed, is desire.*

Sūtra II.8 Hate follows on (anujanma) pain

When one familiar with a pain now has a memory of it, that aversion towards the pain or what causes it, the desire to strike, the anger, is (called) hate.

Hate follows on pain, is the consequence of pain. Pain has been described already, as that by which living beings are struck down and which they struggle to end (comm. on I.31). *When one familiar with a pain* as in the previous explanation in regard to pleasure *has now a memory of the pain, that aversion towards the pain or what causes it* such as a robber, *the desire to strike* the will to hit back, *the anger, is hate.* It is all as explained under desire in the previous sūtra.

Sūtra II.9

With spontaneous momentum, instinctive even in a Knower, is self-preservation

The lust for life in every living being is in the form 'Let me not experience death', 'may I live'.

With spontaneous momentum instinctive even in a Knower, is self-preservation. Spontaneous because of what it is, pure Ignorance in the mind; *momentum:* ceaselessly operating to bear along, as a river is said to bear things along itself when it is seen that nothing is being done by any human agent. Or else, it is spontaneous because its very essence is to bear along perpetually. And this spontaneous momentum is instinctive *even in a Knower (vidvat),* even in one of right vision (samyagdarśana). The force of the word *even* is, that fear of death is logical only in the ignorant, who think of the self as destructible. It is illogical in those of right vision, who think that the self is indestructible. Just as this fear of death, proper in the more deluded minds which see the self as destructible, is instinctive, held to by them, and firm, so also it is instinctive even in the Knowers, though illogical in the light of their vision of the self as indestructible.

How is this fear of death instinctive in its sheer spontaneous momentum? From this fear of death, there is in all beings always the longing for life in the form 'Let me not experience death', 'let me not come to destruction', or lust for life in the form 'May I live', 'May I meet fortunate circumstances' and 'May I not be separated from them'. What the foolish always yearn for is, that they be not cut off from the chance of happiness.

> *This lust for life would not exist in one who had never experienced death; thereby experience of former lives is confirmed. The taint of self-preservation is seen in its spontaneous momentum even in a worm just born. The fear of death, not arising from present direct perception or inference or sacred authority, is essentially a vision of being destroyed, something causing destruction of self and its experience. It implies experience of the pangs of death in a previous life. This taint is instinctive in the least intelligent creature, and so too even in the knower of the first and last states. Why? For equally in the skilled as in the unskilled, there is this complex (vāsanā) of saṃskāra-s from past experience of death pangs.*

What do we conclude from the fact of this lust for life? *This lust for life would not exist in one who had never experienced death; thereby* by the fact of its existence *experience of former lives is confirmed.* What is being said is this: unless happiness had been experienced, no one would pray for it; without past experience of pain, there would be no desire to avoid it. Similarly though the pangs of death have not been (in this life) experienced by a man either directly or by inference, the fact of his lust for life points to experience of death previously, just as there can be no experience of birth unless there has been a birth. This is why the experiences of birth and death are taken to be without beginning. *This taint of self preservation is found even in a worm just born.*

Now as to the cause of this awarness of death: *the fear of death, not arising from present direct perception or inference or sacred authority, is essentially a vision of being destroyed, with destruction of self and its experience,* something causing destruction of self and its experience, and *implies experience of the pangs of death in a previous life. This taint is seen in the least intelligent creatures* such as worms *and so too even in the knower of the first and last states,* the first state being bondage and the last state being release (mukti), or else the states of birth and death. *It is instinctive. Why?* Why should it be instinctive in the Knower as in the unintelligent? He explains: *For equally in the skilled as in the unskilled,* the Knower and the ignorant, *there is this complex (vāsanā) of saṃskāra-s* of the fear of death *from past experience of death-pangs.*

It is going to be said, 'Rooted in taints is the karma-stock' (II.12) and 'While the root exists, it will bear fruit' (II.13). Therefore these taints are to be got rid of; they have been described with that in view. He will explain the means to diminish them: 'Their mental processes are got rid of by meditation' (II.11).

(Opponent) We do not know in which cases meditation applies. Is it when karma-s and taints are (already) scorched seeds, or does it apply in all cases?

(Answer) (The question is taken as answered in the next sūtra following:)

Sūtra II.10

In their subtle state, they are to be got rid of by dissolution in their source

When the yogin's mind has ended its involvement and dissolves, the five taints, now like scorched seeds, come to an end with it.

This sūtra is begun to distinguish the treatment of the cases: *In their subtle state, they are to be got rid of by dissolution in their source.* (The commentary adds:) *When the yogin's mind has ended its involvement and dissolves, the five taints, now like scorched seeds, come to an end with it.* What is being said is this: the taints, reduced to the sterility of fire-scorched seeds by the practice (abhyāsa) of right vision (samyagdarśana), come to their dissolution by reason of that very dissolution, that dissolving, of the mind which has wholly fulfilled the purposes of Puruṣa; so they do not need any practice of meditation (dhyāna). For as the saying goes, no fire is needed for what is already burnt, nor any grinding for what is powdered. The mind having fulfilled the purposes of Puruṣa has no reason to continue, and it spontaneously dissolves.

As to those which persist, though reduced to the seed state:

Sūtra II.11

Mental processes arising from them are got rid of by meditation

> *Mental processes from the taints are in manifest form (sthūla), and are first thinned out by the yoga of action; then they are to be got rid of by contemplation (prasaṅkhyāna), by meditation (dhyāna), until having thereby been made subtle, they are then made like scorched seeds.*

(Opponent) Which are the ones then which do need practices like meditation?

(Answer) *As to those which persist, though reduced to the seed state, mental processes arising from them are got rid of by meditation. Mental processes from the taints are in manifest form, and are first thinned out by the yoga of action,* consisting of tapas, self-study, and devotion to the Lord, this yoga being the opponent on the level of manifestation. Then from that thinning out they are reduced to the state of seed powers, when *they are to be got rid of by contemplation (prasaṅkhyāna), by meditation (dhyāna)* finely developed through constancy in right vision, which meditation is their great and mighty opponent, *until they have been thereby made subtle,* and more than that *have been made like scorched seeds,* until they have been made in fact no seeds at all.

> *As with washing clothes, first the surface dirt is scoured off; afterwards the deeper staining is removed by efforts with special means. In the same way the surface mental processes arising from the taints are lesser obstacles, but when subtle, they are great obstacles.*

What is the process like? *As with washing clothes, first the surface (sthūla) dirt is scoured off and afterwards the deeper (sūkṣma, subtle) staining* caused by oil and the like, *is removed by efforts with special means,* effective means such as alkalis; *in the same way the surface (sthūla) mental processes arising from the taints are lesser obstacles* which are overcome by practice of the yogic methods of tapas, self-study, devotion to the Lord, restraints and observances and the others; *but when subtle, they are great obstacles* to the steadiness of the light of right vision (samyagdarśana) created through the practices like tapas and self-study. They are great obstacles in view of their power as seeds.

Sūtra II.12

Rooted in taints is the karma-stock to be felt in present or future lives

That karma-stock of good and bad is produced from greed, delusion and anger. It is to be felt in the present or future lives.

(Opponent) Why strive to get rid of the taints?

(Answer) To this he says: *Rooted in taints is the karma-stock to be felt in present or future lives.* To say that the karma-stock is rooted in the taints means that its cause of origin is Ignorance and other taints. The karma-stock (āśaya), so-called because it is in stock (śaya) in the mind until (ā) it has brought forth its karma-fruit, is white or black in nature.

It, that is, its fruits, has to be *felt,* has to be experienced, in either the present life or a future one. The sūtra means that the karma-stock whose fruit has to be karmically experienced in lives present or future, has its root in the taints.

The karma-stock, of good or evil character, which comes to its consummation in a particular life and whose fruit has therefore to be felt in that life alone, is *karma-stock to be felt in the present life,* and when it is for another life, that is called the *karma-stock to be felt in future lives.*

The commentary now explains, that *that karma-stock of good or bad is produced from greed, anger and delusion,* pointing to the fact of its root in the taints. A stock of good karma may be produced out of greed: 'Let me enjoy a good reward either in heaven or here' – this is the spirit of such sacrifices as are performed from desire for heaven or desire for a son. Or it may be produced out of anger, as in the cases of Viśvamitra and Ambā, or out of delusion, as with Draupadī and Kumbhakarṇa. A stock of evil karma also may come from greed, as when they kill the leopard for its skin or the elephant for its tusks. And Karṇa told a lie out of greed to learn the science of weapons. It may come from anger, as with the murder of a Brahmin by Aśvatthāman in the Mahābhārata epic, or from delusion, as with those like ritual murderers (saṃsāra-mocaka), and Nahuṣa.

In each case there is a relation of both I-am-ness and Ignorance to the particular greed, anger or delusion. Why so? It is at the thought 'I have been insulted' that one becomes angry, at the thought, 'I am going to enjoy myself that one becomes greedy and with the thought 'I am confused' that one is deluded.

Ignorance too, characterized by deluded vision, is always involved, for without the presence of Ignorance, I-am-ness and the other taints cannot exist. Desire is sheer greed, whereas hate is anger; self-preservation is included simply under confusion (vimoha). But delusion (moha) is said to be Ignorance, because there is the same absence of discrimination. Desire and anger and delusion, independently of each other, are *occasions* for doing righteousness and unrighteousness, as he will say: *Preceded by greed, anger or delusion (to II.34).*

It the karma-stock arising from greed, anger and delusion, *is to be felt in the present life or in future lives.*

> *A stock of good karma, created by mantra, tapas and samādhi practised with keen intensity, or else perfected through devotion to the Lord, to a divine being, to a great seer (ṛṣi), or to a great saint, comes to fruition immediately.*

(Opponent) The karma-s are the same in their nature as cause, so how is it that some are to be felt in the present birth and some in future births?

(Answer) *A stock of good karma created by mantra, tapas and samādhi practised with keen intensity* with keen intensity of effort in application to them in their traditional forms, *or else perfected through devotion to the Lord, to a divine being, to a great seer (ṛṣi) or to a great saint:* the Lord has been described previously; a divine being means such as Āditya (the sun); great sages are those like Bhṛgu, and great saints are those whose minds delight in righteousness (dharma) and in knowledge (jñāna). Alternatively perfected merely through very intense devotion to these, *that karma-stock comes to fruition immediately* in that very birth, as with the boy Nandīśvara.

Then a stock of bad karma, repeated acts of injury, intensely tainted, done to terrified or sick or helpless beings, or done in betrayal of trust, or to great saints or ascetics, comes to fruition always immediately. As the boy Nandīśvara left his then human state and was transformed into divinity, and Nahuṣa, a prince among the gods, left that state of his and was transformed into animality.

Those in hell do not make any karma-stock to be felt in that present life of theirs.

Then a stock of bad karma, constantly *repeated acts of injury, intensely tainted* from excess of greed and other taints *done to terrified or sick or helpless beings or done in betrayal of trust, or to great saints or ascetics,* ascetics whose minds delight in righteousness and knowledge *comes to fruition* bears its fruit *immediately,* as with Nahuṣa.

In the world too, it is known from the Vṛkṣāyurveda (the science of forestry) that the interval up to the fruiting of trees corresponds to the particular latent potency (saṃskāra) of the seeds in the field. So with actions like going and cooking, experience shows that the nearness or remoteness of their fruit is according to the intensity or slackness of performance.

An example is given of a good karma-stock. *As the boy Nandīśvara* through perfection of his devotion to Maheśvara *left his then human state* a birth caused by very intensely tainted actions *and was transformed into divinity, and Nahuṣa* an example of bad karma-stock, *a prince among the gods, left that state of his* as a result of the karma-stock created by becoming involved in very intense illusion, and *was transformed into animality.*

Examples have already been given of how (results of) anger and so on have to be felt in corresponding lives either present or future. On the same principle, births resulting from involvement with taints like greed in mild or very feeble measure, with their good and bad karma-stock, are explained as having to be felt in future lives, as one would expect from experience in the world. So much for that.

In the case of those in hell, who have done actions such as murder of a Brahmin or sleeping with the wife of a teacher, which have merited hell for them and subjected them to its miseries, *they do not make any karma-stock to be felt in that present life of theirs* by which any fruit could be actualized.

(Opponent) How could those in hell originate karma, or such as animals, or divinities? The qualification for karma is in men (alone); we are told that it is this (earth) that is the stage for karma-action, not states like hell.

(Answer) Not so, for we see that Nahuṣa and others did make karma. And there is the scripture relating how Indra became guilty of killing a Brahmin by his slaying of Vṛtra, and how he engaged in yoga and other (penances).

As for the declaration that it is men who have the qualification for karma, and that the stage for karma-action is this world, that alludes to the speedy success in getting results. As it is said, 'speedily here in this world of men comes success born of action' (Gītā IV. 12).

In the tradition, there is the story about the insect seen by Vyāsa, which shows that there is karma even among animals. Furthermore, whatever has body and senses can perform action; in so far as they are accompanied by taints, actions of body, speech or mind must bring about results.

And for those who have got rid of taints, there is no karma-stock to be felt in future lives.

And for those who have got rid of taints who have right vision, *there is no karma-stock to be felt in future lives,* just because of the absence of taints. For there is no case where one freed from passion is born again. (But as to the present life) there may be a karmic result set going which seems to have been set off by karma arising from taints, because the latter was (indeed) the cause of it. Even for one who has got rid of taints, there is possibility of a karma-stock set going before he attained knowledge, which has to be felt in the present life because the results have begun to go into effect, as with an arrow released from the bow.

Sūtra II.13

While the root is there, it will bear the fruit of birth, life span and experience

While taints are there, the karma-stock will come to fruition, but not when the root of taints has been cut. It is like rice grains still encased in the husk, not

> *having been scorched, which are seeds with the power of growth; not so when they have been husked, or have been scorched.*

While the root is there, it will bear the fruit of birth, life span and experience. The root is the taint of karma. *While* this *root is there,* meaning while the taints are there, *it* the karma-stock of good and bad, born of greed and anger *will bear the fruit* will come to full fruition. What is that fruition? *birth, life span and experience.* With the words *While the root is there, the karma-stock will come to fruition, but not when the root of taints has been cut,* the commentator explains what is meant by the root. He then gives an example to show how while there are taints, the karma-stock will come to fruition: *It is like rice grains still encased in the husk, not having been scorched, which are seeds with the power of growth.*

> *So the karma-stock encased in taints grows to fruition; but not when the taints have been removed from it, or when the taint-seeds have been scorched. The fruition is of three kinds: birth, life span, and experience.*
>
> *Now an inquiry is made into different views on the subject.*

Even though still in the husk, if at some time the seeds have been scorched, they are without the power of growth. Again, without scorching, if the husk is removed they are incapable of growth. The example has been selected to act as a simile in both ways.

How so? *the karma-stock encased in taints grows to fruition,* enclosed in taints, like grains encased in the husk, *but not when the taints have been removed from it, or when the taint-seeds have been scorched.* As with husked rice grains, when the taints are removed, it does not grow to fruition.

For a yogin of right vision attained after destruction of his taints by the practices of yoga, and also for one whose taints have not been removed but, like unhusked rice whose fertility has been scorched away, have been made sterile, burnt by the fire of pure right vision alone, attained through the yoga practices – (for them) there is no growth (of the karma-stock) to maturity.

So it is that Vyāsa describes release (mokṣa) of the Sāṅkhya-s and of the yogin-s as different:

(Sāṅkhya)

'As seeds scorched by fire do not sprout any more,
So with taints scorched by the fire of knowledge:

The self meets them no more.'
(Mahābh, XII.204.16a,
Ś. Gītā Bh. XIII.23, Br.Su. Bh. 3.2.32)

(Yogin)
'Having gone beyond the yogic powers, the yogin is released.'
(Mahābh, XII.228.3k), and other such texts

In the present work too he will speak of Transcendental Aloneness (kaivalya) both for yogin-s who attained powers and for yogin-s who did not (i.e. Sāṅkhya-s) (comm. to III.55).

How many kinds of fruition are there? He answers, *The fruition is of three kinds: birth, life span, and experience. An inquiry is made into different views on the subject.* For what purpose? He points out that actions are done by a single living being in a single life which would merit incompatible results. As it is said: 'By ill actions done by the body, man goes to the state of plants; by those of speech, to that of birds and beasts; by those of thought, to birth in the lowest caste.' (Mahābh, XIII App. 15 1773).

(First question:) Does each single action cause a single life, or does a single action produce more than one life? The second question is: Do several actions bring about several lives, or do several actions actuate a single life?

In order to attain heaven, one will undertake more than one action, and there are groups of actions which will bring one to hell. Then too scripture says that a single action such as murder of a Brahmin causes more than one life, and tradition also says (Manu XII.55), 'The killer of a Brahmin goes to the wombs of a dog, a pig, an ass, a camel', and other such.

Now if actions which ought to cause life-circumstances incompatible in time and place were to fructify as a single life, then the properly contradictory nature of the fruitions would be lost. The karmic drive towards proper correspondence of results would be nullified.

If the lives are to be successive, still inasmuch as actions are innumerable, there would be nothing to determine which one among them should produce the next life, rather than others – that is to say, by which it should be caused and by which not. There would be no confidence among performers of action in regard to the results, and enthusiasm for pursuing man's highest goal (niḥśreyasa) would be destroyed.

If it be argued that some one of them operates as the cause and the others are destroyed, there is still the same difficulty, that there is nothing to determine which are to be destroyed and which remains operative.

If they are not to be destroyed, then there can be no release, because there will have been no opportunity for the working-out of that remainder. This is why the present inquiry is made, to show that the scriptures on karma and on the cessation of karma are meaningful.

Does each single action cause a single life? But one who desires heaven undertakes many actions for it. *Or does a single action produce more than one life?* This is the first question. As embracing the two alternatives, it forms a single question.

The second question is: Do several actions bring about several lives with compatible or incompatible fruits? *Or do several actions actuate a single life,* compatible or incompatible in fruits?

> *It is not that a single action is the cause of a single life. Why not? Between the innumerable remaining actions accumulated from time without beginning, and the actions of the present life, there is nothing to determine in what order their results will come, and so people will lose confidence, which is undesirable.*

What follows? *It is not that a single action is the cause of a single life. Why not?* There are so many actions that it would be impossible for each one to bring about a life. If from just one there was a life, then *between the innumerable remaining actions accumulated from time without beginning,* since saṃsāra is without beginning, each man in his individual lives has been piling up an incalculable amount of karma whether of compatible or incompatible fruit; between the remaining karma, all except what is now in operation, which remainder has been accumulated over so many lives that it is incalculable, *and the actions of the present life,* karma created in the present life which has not yet begun to produce its effects, *there is nothing to determine in what order their results will come,* whether what brings about the next future life is only some block of karma laid down in a previous life, or some block of karma of the present life – the order of fruition would not be certain.

And so people will lose confidence: they would be in doubt whether it would be karma of some previous life, whether bad or good, or else karma of the present life, bad or good, which would be going to fructify, and in such a quandary, no one would engage in a rite like the fire ceremony. The result would be despair, as even release would not be striven for. And that is an undesirable conclusion.

Now he rejects the second alternative of the first question:

> *Nor does a single action produce several lives. Why not? In each of these lives a number of actions will be done, each one of which would itself be a cause maturing into a corresponding life. There will be no scope for the fruition of all the actions. This too is undesirable.*

Now he rejects the second alternative of the first question. *Nor does a single action produce several lives. Why not?* Inasmuch as *in each of those lives a number of actions* are performed *each one of which would itself be a cause maturing into a corresponding life,* it is transformed into a life, and the effect is that *there will be no scope for the fruition of all the actions* other than the one which is actually producing its effect.

This too is undesirable. The absence of any control over the order of fruition of the karma is the same defect as before, and as an unacceptable conclusion is not to be allowed. But as to the fact that an action like Brahmin-murder does cause several lives, this is in the field of scriptural revelation, so that in the realm of such things as Brahmin-murder, it is to be accepted.

> *Nor do a number of actions cause that number of lives. Why not? The lives cannot be simultaneous, so it must be held that they come in succession, and that involves the same defect as before.*

Now the first alternative to the second question is refuted: *Nor do a number of actions cause that number of lives. Why* is that *not* accepted? He replies: *The lives cannot be simultaneous* for one who has not got divine powers, and so *it must be held that they come in succession, and that involves the same defect as before.* Whether it is one or several actions that actuate the lives, it is always the same difficulty, that there is nothing to determine the order of fruition and people would lose confidence.

Thus these alternatives are unacceptable, and now the approved conclusion is given:

> *A stock of karma good and bad, made to converge on a birth and death, in accumulated variety and in relations of dominance and subordination, is manifested by death; by one impulse, as a block, it makes a single birth. That*

birth has its life span by that karma alone: in that life span comes experience, by that karma alone.

Made to converge on a birth and death on a birth-and-death *a stock of karma good and bad,* the qualification 'which can be compatible as the cause of the circumstances of the new birth' is to be supplied; those which would be incompatible with the circumstances of the birth are to be felt in a future birth and their fruition is not yet determined. He will speak later about the three-fold distribution (viniyoga); here he is only speaking of the determination of a karma-stock of good and bad in so far as their fruits are not inconsistent with each other.

accumulated variety: it is so varied because it is a piling up of many karma-s of similar and dissimilar kind; *in relations of dominance and subordination,* one karma is dominant over another, but itself subordinate to yet another, so that though subordinate it is also dominant – in this way many karma-s are in relations of many different kinds.

manifested by death: as the conjunction of seed and field and potential (saṃskāra) is the cause of the manifestation of the being of the sprout, so is death the impelling cause of the manifestation of those karma-s which are not incompatible. And *by one impulse* becoming one single impetus *as a block* unified *it makes a single birth. That birth has its life span by that karma alone* which was manifested at the death; *in that life span comes experience by that karma alone* by which were created the birth and span of life. As by that same seed from which the sprout was sent forth, there come also the fruit and flowers and the rest.

It is declared that experience and life span come into operation by that karma alone, but it is not that no other cause of life span and experience and so on operates as to getting a son who will live, and the other objects of sacrifice for sons or cattle and other desires. Otherwise all scriptures and traditions would be vitiated. So when it is said *by that karma alone,* the point is only to remove any suspicion that having originated the birth, it might have had its effect and so cease.

This block of karma, as causing birth, life span, and experience, is declared to have three-fold fruition, and for this reason is called a one-life karma-block. But karma which produces a single result as an experience to be felt in the

> *present life is called of single fruition; or if two results, namely experience and life span, it is of double fruition; or if with three results, it is as with Nandīśvara and Nahuṣa.*

This block of karma, as causing birth, life span, and experience, is declared to have three-fold fruition namely three fruits, birth and the other two, *and for this reason is called a one-life (eka-bhāvika) karma-block* meaning that it converges on the one birth. *But karma which produces a single result as an experience to be felt in the present life is called of single fruition,* as for instance a sacrificial rite to get sons and property, *or if two results, namely experience and life span, it is of double fruition,* like a sacrifice first for life span and also for desires; *or if with three results, it is as with Nandīśvara and Nahuṣa.*

(Opponent) Surely it is inconsistent to say that in the cases of Nandīśvara and Nahuṣa it was a three-fold fruition experienced in the present life? The present life of Nandīśvara was a human state, and the (later) divine state of Nandīśvara, as also the (later) serpent state of Nahuṣa, were both future; for that original humanity of Nandīśvara is not to be classed as divinity, nor that original divinity of Nahuṣa as the serpent state. So how can these be a triple fruition felt in a present life?

(Answer) There is no inconsistency. In the two cases, the body perceived in that particular form was changed into another form. For Nandīśvara and Nahuṣa it was not as with others, whose change into another form of existence is by destruction of the particular body of that visible form and acquiring and entering another form of existence. So it is that these are cited as cases of triple fruition felt in the present life.

Thus the karma-block of three-fold kind is to be felt in the present life or in a future life. But what is to be felt in the present birth, of indeterminate fruition (a-niyata-vipāka) is sometimes of single fruition as causing experience, sometimes of double, as causing experience and life span, and sometimes of triple, as causing form of existence, life span, and experience, as in the cases of Nandīśvara and Nahuṣa.

But what is to be felt in a future life is of two kinds: of determinate fruition, and of indeterminate fruition. The determinate (niyata) fruition has been indicated in the passage beginning *A stock of karma good and bad, made by actions between birth and death, in accumulated variety and in relations of dominance and subordination, is manifested by death; by one impulse, as a* *block, it makes a single birth.*Indeterminate fruition is three-fold, as he now goes on to say.

> *Set going by experiences of taints and karma-s and their fruition (which form) saṃskāra-complexes (vāsanā); this mind has been massed in a block from time without beginning, as it were variegated, spread out in all directions like a fishing net with its knots. These vāsanā-s have many lives behind them.*

Here something is added about the block of saṃskāra-complexes (vāsanā) produced by the fruition of karma. *Set going by experiences of taints and karma-s and their fruition:* this means experiences of taints, experiences of karma-s, and experiences of their fruition; *saṃskāra-complexes* actuated by saṃskāra-s, *this mind (citta) has been massed in a block from time without beginning, as it were variegated* like a tent of wool and other materials *spread out* pervading *in all directions like a fishing net with its knots.*

Now in each single life, when the karma ripens, *saṃskāra-complexes with many lives behind them* are involved as accessories to it. For unless it were associated with a saṃskāra-complex, the attack in sudden fury (by the antelope father) on the infant masculinity of his new-born antelope son would be inexplicable. Nor could it come about merely from a saṃskāra impression of only one experience.

But *this karma-block,* created as the cause of birth and circumstances not incompatible between a birth and death, with its elements constituted as principal and subordinate, bringing about three-fold fruition, *is said to be of this or that single life.* It is not what is still to be felt in the present life, nor the indeterminate fruition in future lives, nor is it the saṃskāra-complexes.

He explains the nature of these last: *saṃskāra-s, the causes of memory, form complexes (vāsanā) which go back in time wihout beginning* because there is no beginning to saṃsāra whose nature is experience of taints and of karma-s and of their fruition.

But the karma-block of a single life previously mentioned has some elements exempt from fruition in that life. In what way? It *has a determinate and an indeterminate fruition.* What is the determinate fruition? What is manifested on death and brings about its effect. And this it is that forms the single life.

But what would cause incompatible birth and places and times, that has to be felt in future lives; being of opposite kind, its fruition is indeterminate. Why? Because it is opposed by the determinate fruition. They cannot be all in a single life because of the contradiction between them.

(Opponent) But it was said to be of a single life – *the karma-block of a single life.*

(Answer) That was only on the basis of the common point that it is all to be felt in a future life.

(Opponent) But it was said definitely that the karma-block, made to converge on a birth-and-death, in accumulated variety and in relations of dominance and subordination, manifested at death and massed in a block, makes a single birth; this is determinate, and that is now being contradicted. (But it must be determinate.) Why? Because death brings into manifestation all the previous karma, by breaking up the supporting container (ādhāra) of the karma-block and providing a new one. Suppose the container of the karma-block is human, it is also the substratum of divine and animal karma-blocks; when the container is broken, there will be no reason why one out of the divine or animal karma-blocks should manifest and not others, inasmuch as death is the common manifesting cause. For a light does not give up a segment of its illumination when it manifests its light.

(Answer) Not so, because it would take the meaning out of action. Actions of many kinds are performed, some in opposition to others. The same man who performs actions leading to heaven also engages in actions to acquire cattle and property, or action in the form of deeds of violence like the murder of a Brahmin, leading to the state of plants and so on. When this last is in the vegetable state or in hell, he cannot possess cattle or property. So the actions to acquire them would have become meaningless.

(Opponent) Let it be that (even in hell) he has the *happiness* of a property owner.

(Answer) When we speak of the desire for property, it does not mean desire merely for the happiness of having property; having the happiness of property is not the same as having the property itself. And it would vitiate all the scriptures. It would mean that the unseen worlds like heaven and hell were no more than subjective states of happiness or suffering, and that would contradict the sacred texts like 'From there, by the remainder of his karma' (Āpas. 2.2.2.3; Gaut. II.31), and the traditions, which declare that the remainder (of unfulfilled karma) does really exist. So not all the karma is manifested at death, because that *would* entail meaninglessness of some actions directly opposed to others. And if the scriptures about karma were meaningless, there would follow lack of interest in the scriptures on release also.

It is well known that there is variation among manifesting agencies: one may be manifesting while another is not. In the case of the eye making forms manifest, there is variation between the eye of the man Caitra and that of the owl, according to whether it is day or night. Though light ought to be equally a help for all eyes, to the owl's eye it is no help. Again, though the one body of a beautiful woman can produce happiness, or suffering, or delusion, yet in fact there is manifestation of only one of the three (in an individual case).

(Opponent) The difference there is due to things like karma, so the objection does not hold.

(Answer) But still not all the karma-s will manifest, because of the contradiction between them. If a field in which seeds have been sown is ploughed up, then even when causes like water are supplied to it, the seeds of competing types which may have been sown there will not all produce their sprouts and so on. So when the temporary human body supporting the karma-stock is broken up, there cannot be a simultaneous going into operation of the competing types of divine and animal karma-blocks.

Furthermore the manifesting agent of karma-s is not death alone, because we see that people aim at experiences to be felt in this present life.

(Opponent) There is manifestation of all those of which death alone is the manifesting agent.

(Answer) No, because of the opposition of divine and animal and human karma-blocks.

And there are different kinds of death: there is the present one and there are future ones. Because it has these distinctions, death does not manifest all the karma-s. There are contradictions which make distinct kinds of death, so that there are different deaths. For instance, the text, 'Whatever state of being he meditates on when he leaves the body at death' (to that he goes, Gītā VIII.6) differentiates death according to the differences of particular memory at that time. Therefore death does not make manifest all the karma-s; if it did, the distinctions made in it would become meaningless.

And the distinctions like memory (at death) would not alter or destroy what has been already accomplished, for memory is not an auxiliary to bring about destruction or alteration of accomplished karma. Memory should be independent. Consequently (on our theory) karma which has been engaged in is meaningful.

Moreover (on your theory) those who having died are now in the embryo state would have to have release (mokṣa), because there would be no operation of karma (before the birth).

(Opponent) In that state they might do actions which could have results.

(Answer) No, because that state is not yet equipped with senses. It is only when equipped with the senses that there can be operations and fruitfulness of action, and the state is not equipped with them.

(Opponent) It can be as in dream.

(Answer) No, because we do not admit any action there either. By the text 'Whatever he sees there, he is untouched by it' (Bṛhad. 4.3.15) scripture shows that there is no binding power in an action produced in the dream display. No one becomes a sinner just because his dreams show the senses engaged in something like Brahmin-murder.

(Opponent) He does, for penances are prescribed for wet dreams.

(Answer) No; the reason for the penance is the fact of emission of semen (not the content of the dream).

Even if it were admitted that states like that of the embryo can have a result like a dream state, still since there is no operation of the senses, the result itself is only on the level of dream, and there is no real action and agent. So the corollary of release (mokṣa, on exhaustion of karma) applies only to those who have been born from the womb.

Of these, the determination is only of the karma of determinate fruition due to be felt in a future life, but not of karma of indeterminate fruition due to be felt in a future life. Why? Because karma of indeterminate fruition due to be felt in a future life has three possible outcomes:

destruction of the created karma before fruition,
or merging into dominant karma,
or remaining for a long time in a state of repression by dominant karma already going into its determinate fruition.

Of these, destruction of the karma created but not yet fructifying is like the destruction of dark karma by the rise of bright karma in this very life.

So deaths do not make manifest all the karma-s, because there are distinctions among deaths, as he says: *Of these, the determination* the determination which was first spoken of by the commentary as what is created between birth and death, which produces the triple fruition (birth, life span and experience) *is only of the karma of determinate fruition due to be felt in a future life, but not of karma of indeterminate fruition due to be felt in a future life. Why? Because the karma of indeterminate fruition due to be felt in a future life has three possible outcomes.* What are they?

destruction of the created karma before its fruition, destruction of the karma which has not completed the normal course. This would be like the cancelling of created karma by such things as penances.

merging into the dominant karma. There is a blending with the dominant karma which is about to be felt in a determinate way; it is not set aside by the fruition of the dominant karma, but from within that, takes effect in the course of time. As when along with rice grains completely mature, some immature grains are sown, they produce only a small effect.

or else remaining in a state of repression by dominant karma already going into determinate fruition. The determinate fruition of the dominant karma is in the form of results already in operation; subdued by that, it remains repressed, because the place and time and causes are opposed to its own fruition. As when two antagonists fight, one of them is brought into a state of subjection, according to place and time and causes, to the active control of the other.

Of these, destruction of the karma created but not yet fructifying is like destruction by the rise of bright karma by the rise of the pure, consisting of tapas, self-study (svādhyāya), yoga, etc., and also of penances, etc., *of the dark karma* of impure nature, involving harm to others and so on, which had formerly possessed the mind; *in this very life,* not to be taken restrictively, for there can be destruction also of bad karma from action which had formerly possessed the mind in a previous life. As with people who have the disease of the nails (Manu XI.49) caused by sin (stealing, in a previous life); when (the sin is) recognized by such marks, its destruction is effected by a penance.

> *On which it has been said: 'karma-s are to be known as in pairs; one block made by the good cancels one made by the bad. Seek then to do good actions. Here it is that the sages instruct you on your welfare.'*

Then he explains by a citation from established authority, of another scripture: *On which it has been said: 'karma-s are to be known* by the man who is qualified as an aspirant *as in pairs* white and dark, in birth after birth. *One block made by the good* by good such as self-study *cancels* another block made by dark karma. Or *made by the good* may mean the block of white karma of a good man, which destroys the block of dark karma. *Seek* therefore *good actions* karma of the white, to make your own karma pure. Why should we do so? *Here it is* in this very life *that the sages (kavi)* who know the divisions of karma-s and their fruitions *instruct you* make known to you *your welfare* (śarma), your happiness (sukha), your peace (śānti).

> *Now the merging into dominant karma. On this it has been said: Suppose there is some slight blemish; removing it or thinking about it does not trouble the skilful one. Why not? Because there is for him so much other good fortune in which this will be submerged, that in heaven too it will make but little difference.*

Now the merging into dominant karma is illustrated. *Suppose there is some slight blemish* the traces of a very small fault. *removing it:* it needs removal but has not been removed; the sense is that the means for removing it is available to the one who is aware of it. *thinking about it* paying attention to it, thinking obsessively like the sinner in his distress, 'How did I come to do that sin? when shall I expiate it? I will never do that again', *does not trouble the skilful one* the knower (vidvat), well-versed in all aspects of karma and its fruition and the removal of defects and so on. This very small blemish is not able to reduce the far more numerous good results which are already in operation, or even if it should reduce them, it cannot introduce any effect of its own. Again, it cannot detract from the good karma itself. *Why not?* The spiritual aspirant feels that *because there is for him so much other good fortune* and thereby happiness *in which* great happiness *this* blemish *will be submerged, in heaven too it will make but little difference.*

> *Or remaining for a long time in a state of repression by dominant karma already going into determinate fruition. How is this? There, death is said to be indiscriminately the cause of going into manifestation only of karma-s due to be felt in a future life which are of determinate fruition, not of karma due to be felt in the present life, nor of karma of indeterminate fruition.*

Or remaining in a state of repression by dominant karma already going into determinate fruition. How is this? It is a difficult question.

(Opponent) *How is this* indeed! One feels it is reasonable that there should be subjection of one whose powers are ineffective to another whose power is effective, because the operation of the power derives from different causes. But here death is the manifesting cause of all karma-s alike; at death, all karma-s should go into operation, and it is not reasonable that there should be subjection to dominant karma. So let it be only the possibility of merging (and no other possibility).

(Answer) To this he replies: *Death is said to be indiscriminately the cause of going into manifestation only of karma-s due to be felt in a future life,* karma-s causing such place and time and fruitions and so on as are not inconsistent with each other, *which are of determinate fruition,* various karma-s of good and evil character; *but not of karma due to be felt in the present life* in the shape of sons, property and so on, *nor of karma of indeterminate fruition,* of that which is due to be felt in a future life, which has been explained above (as excluded by incompatibity).

> *But that which is due to be felt in a future life and is of indeterminate fruition may be destroyed, or merged, or for a long time may be put aside, as long as no compatible manifesting cause makes it appear.*
>
> *Since of that fruition itself the place and time and cause are not determinable, this course of karma is complicated and hard to know. It is not that the general rule about it fails because of an exception. The karma-stock of a single life is difficult to understand.*

But that which is due to be felt in a future life and is of indeterminate fruition may be destroyed, or merged, or for a long time may be put aside, set on one side, repressed, *as long as no compatible manifesting cause* some karma of similar kind, consonant with it, *makes it appear;* for a karma of compatible kind will bring it to fruition.

Since of that fruition itself, of that karma whose fruition is indeterminate, *the place and time and cause are not defined,* neither in what place or from what cause nor in what time the fruition of that karma will make its appearance, *this course of karma is complicated and hard to know.* It is *complicated* because of the various possibilities of destruction and merging and being repressed, *and hard to know* because in what time and in what place and by what cause the fruition will appear are undefined.

(Opponent) It was said that the karma due to be felt in a future life, manifesting at death, produces only a single life: *it makes only one life.* Now different possibilities are spoken of: destruction, merging, and a repressed state. The two statements contradict each other.

(Answer) No, because (the proposition) was later completed in the words *this is the determination of the determinate fruition due to be felt in future lives. For it is not that the general rule about it fails because of an exception,* because of our point about indetermination. Why does it not fail? Because, as it has been said, it is only that *the karma-stock of a single life is hard to understand,* not that it fails. The meaning is that it is not ruled out that karma of indeterminate fruition also should create a single life.

Or possibly the connection with the negative *not* is this: if one allows that the general rule does allow of an exception, the karma-stock of a single life will not be difficult to understand. So the exception operates as regards only one part of the general rule but not all, and thereby it is quite easy to understand the karma-stock as of determinate fruition in a single life.

There is another view. The subject here is what is to be understood about the course of karma and this exception says that the karma-stock of a single life is difficult to understand. The word *There* means: cause. Since there is no failure because of that exception to the causal general rule of the understanding of the course of karma which is the subject, the course of karma which is to be known should be known in that way alone. The phrase *hard to understand* means that it is supposed to be comprehensible only with pain and great effort.

Sūtra II.14

Their fruits are joy and suffering caused by virtue and sin

The birth, life span, and experience of which virtue is the causal agent are happy fruits; those of which sin is the causal agent are painful. What is inherently adverse is pain, so for the yogin even at the time of pleasure there is only pain, because even pleasure is adverse to the yogin.

Karma-stock has been further explained as: due to be felt in a present life, and due to be felt in future lives. Of it there are three fruitions: birth, life span, and experience. *Their fruits are joy and suffering, caused by virtue and sin. Joy* is happiness, *suffering* is pain. This pair of joy and suffering are the fruits of those (actions). Virtue and sin are also a pair, and these two are the respective causes. The causality of the two is a fact and so it is said that the causes are virtue and sin. *The birth, life span, and experience of which virtue is the causal agent are happy fruits; those of which sin is the causal agent are painful. What is inherently adverse is pain, so for the yogin even at the time of pleasure there is only pain, because even pleasure is adverse to the yogin.*

How so? The answer is:

Sūtra II.15

Because of the sufferings caused by changes and anxieties and the saṃskāra-s of them, and from the clash of the guṇa-s, to the clear-sighted, everything is pain alone

In every case, experience of pleasure is pervaded with passion-desire, deriving from some source conscious or unconscious; the karma-stock therefrom is produced by passion-desire.

How at a time when the object of experience is happiness, can it be pain? It has been said already (under II.5) that he is going to show that the experience of pleasure is pain. *The answer is* given now because in that place it was not explained. Because pain is the result of any action, and it has to be explained at length how it is reasonable that it (pain) should logically follow immediately on action.

Changes, anxieties and saṃskāra-s are to be understood separately; anxieties and saṃskāra-s are pain, and in addition to that pair there is change. These are pain alone, they cause pain, and *because of the sufferings caused by changes and anxieties and saṃskāra-s* caused by them, *everything is pain.* Why everything? Because the causes are taints, which can only bring about pain. Birth and life and experience, and the objects which cause the deposits of taints and so on, are causes of pain, and so it is that everything is pain alone.

Is it so to everyone? No. He says: *to the clear-sighted.* He who can distinguish the elements of taints, etc., is the one who sees clearly; it means that he recognizes the taints and karma-s and their maturing, and sees that they are causes which produce pain in everything, all being essentially the clash of the operation of the guṇa-s in changes and anxieties and saṃskāra-s. It is not so for others who do not have this clear vision, but for him it is all a fever of pain. Now when one becomes aware 'I am in that fever' as a fact in himself, even then one who is confused recognizes only this much: 'I am in pain.' If he were to discriminate further than that, he would think, 'This pain will also produce further pain.' Then he would be one who sees clearly, that all this is pain and has to be endured. So though at the time of suffering they see pain alone, those without clear sight do not realise that it will lead on to further pain in everything. Again, he who sees that change is a cause of pain is clear-sighted, one for whom all is pain.

He now explains how it is that there is painfulness in change: *in every case the experience of pleasure is pervaded with passion-desire (rāga).* By saying *in every case* he points to what is universally known by observation, since it is well known in the case of all living beings. Sons, cattle, gold and so on, attained after they have been striven for, constitute experience of pleasure. At the time of that experience the mind functions as passion, which is characteristic of the man who is feeling happy. This universal function is associated with taints and so causes virtue and sin. Pre-existing karma-stock is consumed as the result of karma-already-in-operation; on the occasion of experience, fresh karma is being piled up. So *while the root is there, the karma-stock whose root is the taints, comes to maturity,* that is, it happens.

> *So also when experiencing things which cause pain, he hates them, and he becomes bewildered; then there is a karma-stock created by the hate and illusion. Thus it is said: There can be no enjoyment of things without injury – built up on injury to others is the karma-stock of the body.*

So also when experiencing things which cause pain which are hostile to the current of pleasure, *he hates them,* and with his mind furious to protect his experience of pleasure, *he becomes bewildered,*and so it is that the *karma-stock is created by* is produced by, the previous operation *of hate and illusion.* Or it may be taken that hate and illusion themselves are the two functions which have created it.

Thus it is said: There can be no enjoyment of things none of this pleasure *without injury* without causing harm somewhere. As being a cause of destruction, enjoyment is itself described as a destroyer, inasmuch as it has the double effect. Even when one thinks, 'Let some other person also enjoy what is mine alone', the possibility of any enjoyment at all is dependent on wealth, the acquisition of which must certainly have caused pain to others. All the more will be the pain by the fact of having caused such suffering. Therefore *built up on injury to others is the karma-stock of the body;* from operation of that cause, the body goes forward.

Thus on each occasion of enjoyment, the karma-stock of desire, anger and illusion increases in so many ways. Experience of pleasure, characterized as it is by passion-desire, fever and illusion, and a correspondingly many-faceted karma-stock, is changing, and accordingly painful; this is what is called the painfulness of change. But for the one who sees all this clearly, even on the occasion of pleasure there is only pain, like a man eating rice and yogurt which he knows have been mixed with poison.

> *The pleasure in objects is said to be Ignorance. Pleasure is the calm from satisfaction of the senses by experiences. Pain is when there is no rest from agitation. Freedom from thirst cannot be attained by practice of sense experience. Why not? Because passions increase with application to sense enjoyments and skill of the sense-organs also increases. Therefore application to enjoyments is not a means to happiness. Surely the pleasure-seeker in the trap of sense-objects, sunk in a deep mire of pain, is like a man who running away from the scorpion's poison is bitten by a venomous snake. This which is in the end pain is counter-productive (but known as such) to the yogin alone, even on the occasion of pleasure.*

Furthermore, all is pain only, because pleasure in objects is in fact Ignorance. That experience of pleasure in objects is essentially an undiscriminating idea. On this he says, *The pleasure in objects is said to be Ignorance.*

(Opponent) Where has this been explained?

(Answer) It has been explained in this commentary in these words: 'When there comes about a failure, as it were, to distinguish between the experiencer and what is experienced, which are utterly distinct and nothing to do with each other, that is the condition for experience. But when the true nature of the two is recognized, that is Transcendental Aloneness. Then how could there be experience?' (comm. to II.6, p. 191). Again, it will be said later by the sūtra-author, 'Experience is an idea that fails to distinguish' (sūtra III.35). The ever-changing Ignorance makes everything baneful, and so pleasure in objects is itself a bane, because it contains the seeds of pain, as even the sweetest thing (is bitter) if it is known to cause illness. To explain what it means to say that pleasure in objects is Ignorance, he gives the verdict of the holy texts: *Pleasure is the calm from satisfaction of the senses by experiences.* The experiences are objects like sound; the senses experience them, and then there is a resulting satiety. As a result, a pacification of the senses, a state in the form of the idea 'There is nothing to cause disappointment or trouble', an absence of any defect; this is pleasure.

But pain is when there is no rest no relief *from agitation,* because of the presence of desire. On this it is said: 'There is no pain like thirst, no pleasure like freedom from thirst.' (Mahābh.XIII. App.15.3997, with atṛṣṇā instead of tyāga).

(Opponent) It is only by enjoyment that there can be freedom from thirst; that is the goal of enjoyment. Enjoyment becomes happiness.

(Answer) That is why he says: *Freedom from thirst cannot be attained by practice of sense experience. Why not?* He replies: *Because passions increase with application to sense enjoyments.* As it has been said:

Never is desire pacified by enjoyment of desires;

It increases all the more, as the sacrificial fire by the butter (oblations) poured into it. (Manu II.94)

Skills techniques in the practices of enjoyment correspondingly *increase in the senses.* Even though it may be that skill of the senses is preceded (normally) by skill in the mind, still it is seen that in eating and so on there is a skill in the sense organs too. *Like a man running away from the scorpion's poison, bitten by a venomous snake, is the pleasure-seeker trapped by objects,* caught by them, following after them, or obsessed with them, as a man's fear excited by a scorpion with its lesser venom brings him into a greater suffering, caught by the more virulent poison of a snake. So fleeing from this first merely apparent pain, which is in the end great pleasure (Gītā XVIII.37), frightened by the idea that it is painful, he becomes *sunk* in a boundless *mire of great pain.* In this way *this which is in the end pain, is counter-productive* as regards pleasure (and known as such) *to the yogin even on the occasions of pleasure.* Thus the yogin enjoys pleasure only with misgivings in his heart, for the karma which has yet to be experienced according to its quality is more powerful (than the occasion of pleasure). Therefore to the discriminating, all is pain.

What is the painfulness in anxiety? In every case, experience of anxiety is pervaded with aversion, deriving from some source conscious or unconscious; the karma-stock therefrom is produced by aversion.

Now the painfulness of anxiety (tāpa) is explained. A developing experience of pleasure becomes painful when its inevitable result is realized, through knowledge of its true nature, as does the pleasure of eating a sweet of yogurt and rice when known to be mixed with poison, in spite of the fact that its apparent nature does give a shade of pleasure sensation. Here again the painfulness is from the true nature of the thing, inasmuch as anxiety is inherently adverse.

> *Seeking means to pleasure by body, speech, and mind, he gets excited, and sets about helping or harming others. By that helping or harming of others he piles up virtue and sin. This karma-stock arising out of greed and delusion is called the pain of anxiety.*
>
> *What is the painfulness of saṃskāra? From experience of pleasure, there is a saṃskāra-stock of pleasure; from experience of pain, a saṃskāra-stock of pain. So the maturing of karma is experienced as pleasure or pain, and it again lays down a karma-stock. In this way the beginningless stream of pain, inherently adverse to him, distresses the yogin alone.*

Tormented by that pain, *seeking means to pleasure* refinements of various kinds, *he gets excited, and sets about helping or harming others.* Then *by that helping or harming of others he piles up virtue and sin.* This virtue and sin created by helping or harming others becomes *a karma-stock arising out of greed and delusion, the pain of anxiety* extending itself further and further. For the man who sees thus clearly, all is pain alone, as caused by involvement with objects.

Now he goes on to the pain of saṃskāra-s produced by experience of joy and suffering. *What* then *is the painfulness of saṃskāra? From experience of pleasure, there is a saṃskāra-stock of pleasure; from experience of pain, a saṃskāra-stock of pain.* Since pleasure and pain are pervaded by passion and hate, their respective saṃskāra-stocks too will be pervaded by passion and hate. *So the maturing of karma* in the form of birth, life span and experience *is experienced as pleasure or pain.*

The saṃskāra-stock of pleasure-pain experience is made up entirely of that experience, and so the saṃskāra-s as well as the experiences are entirely pervaded by passion and aversion. The respective saṃskāra-stocks become factors in action and experience, and in this way the saṃskāra-stocks become sources of pain. The dynamic character of saṃskāra is itself painful, and that is the painfulness of saṃskāra. For no one employs a means to an experience or action which he does not remember, and it is well known that memory depends on saṃskāra.

Even if a saṃskāra were not inherently painful, still to the man of clear sight who knows that it will cause pain, its very existence is itself pain, like the mere fact of having eaten poison (before any effect is felt). Thus as a result of change, anxiety and saṃskāra, everything indeed is pain. *In this way the beginningless stream of pain, inherently adverse to him, distresses the yogin alone.*

(Opponent) It is inherently adverse to the others also. Why does it not distress them?

(Answer) It does not distress the others, just because their minds are undiscriminating and calloused with every foulness of taints and so on. To them, the adverse quality is not the main thing. A man accepts on his head a fist-blow, even like a hammer, from his beloved. He puts up with the wetting and fouling by his baby son held to his chest. He feels he is moving in an ocean of joy and has no resentment at all in him. To him, it is not inherently adverse. So in the case of the undiscriminating man, he assents to the passion-desire and thereby increases it all the more.

(Opponent) The circumstances are the same for the yogin too, so why does it distress him?

> *Why? Because the knower is like an eyeball. As a thread of wool flicked on to the eyeball causes pain by its touch, but not on to other parts of the body, so these pains afflict the yogin alone, who is sensitive as an eyeball, and not another recipient of them. But that other is subjected again and again to pain brought on by himself, casting it off and then subjected again to what has been cast off again and again, with his mental processes from time without beginning shot through and through so to say with the various saṃskāra-complexes (vāsanā), taking on what he should avoid, namely 'I' and 'mine', born again and again – (on him) the three-fold sufferings, with causes both objective and subjective, flood down.*

(Answer) It afflicts him alone. *Why? Because the knower is like an eyeball.* The meaning is, that it afflicts him because of his purity and his withdrawal. The cause is not the same for him, inasmuch as he is a knower. He does not have an undiscriminating mind calloused with feelings of taints and so on, for he would not be a knower unless he had got rid of that calloused mind. So it is that it afflicts the knower alone, who is sensitive like an eyeball, and not the others.

On this he explains the difference between the knower and the ignorant by some examples. *As a thread of wool* though its touch is so light *flicked on to the eyeball, causes pain* because of the extreme sensitivity of the eyeball, so the pain afflicts the yogin whose consciousness is so refined and whose heart is so pure. The thread of wool lashed even very violently on to another member of the body will not cause pain by its contact. So the other recipient is not afflicted by pain, because his mind has become calloused with taints, like other limbs of the body which have hard skin.

He continues: *So those pains afflict the yogin alone, who is like the eyeball, and not another recipient.* He shows how the other recipient is like the other limbs of the body, in the next passage, beginning *But that other* and concluding with the words *the sufferings flood down. But that other is subjected to pain brought on by himself;* the effect of karma is brought on a man by way of mental process, the pain being induced by causes animate and inanimate; *subjected to pain again and again, casting it off* by leaving the body, and then in another place, having taken on another body, that pain which he had cast off emerges; *with his mental processes from time without beginning shot through and through so to say with various saṃskāra-complexes,* with Ignorance.

What is the character of this other? *Taking on what he should avoid, namely 'I' and 'mine'.* 'I' is something supposed, by illusion, in the body and senses and their qualities of action, attribute, and result; 'mine' is the idea of it in regard to externals, animate and inanimate. Both of these should be avoided, as they are wholly seeds which ripen into tainted karma. Without these two, passions, etc., and their karmic ripening cannot come about, so they are to be avoided, and this is a man who is taking on what he ought to avoid, namely 'I' and 'mine'.

Born again and again like one of the other members of the body in the simile, to be pursued by sufferings *with causes both objective and subjective,* objective in the form of a god or the elements of nature, and subjective, being that particular kind of cause; the sufferings result from both these kinds of cause.

Three-fold: the sufferings whether from external or the other causes are of three kinds, in that they are either past, future, or present. As the sūtra will say, 'To be escaped is the pain not yet come' (II.16). Or again, they are three-fold as being essentially taint, and karma, and its ripening, and again their triple painfulness is from change, or from anxiety, or from saṃskāra. So they are three-fold, and these *flood down,* they are the inevitable consequence.

> *Seeing that other one, and himself, and all beings, borne away by the stream of pain without beginning, the yogin takes refuge in right vision, destroyer of all pain.*

Seeing that other one, the undiscriminating recipient, *and himelf and all beings, being borne away by the stream of pain without beginning* submerged in that torrent of pain, *the yogin takes refuge in right vision, destroyer of all pain.*

(Opponent) But if he is a yogin, he must already have got right vision.

(Answer) One who is practising the yoga methods is a yogin even if he has not got right vision. The statement shows that yoga is the means to right vision.

Seeing that yoga and the fruit of yoga (powers) are all nothing but pain, he takes refuge in right wisdom. As the sūtra will say, 'From indifference to that too, the seeds of imperfection are destroyed, and there is Transcendental Aloneness' (III.50).

> *And from the clash of the operation of the guṇa-s, all is pain alone to the clearsighted man.*

And for another reason, all is pain to the clear-sighted man. What reason is that? *From the clash of the operations of the guṇa-s.*

(Opponent) Why has the teaching made a division between the reasons? It should have said simply, 'Because of changes, anxieties, saṃskāra-s, and clash of operations of the guṇa-s.'

(Answer) There is no mistake. Everyone knows experiences of pleasure and pain and the saṃskāra-complexes of them, and these are referred to in the phrase 'Because of the sufferings caused by changes and anxieties and saṃskāra-s'. But the man who has clear knowledge, which can distinguish their cause, becomes aware – in the perfection of his discrimination – of the clash of the operations as caused by the guṇa-s (in the mental processes), and this is a separate cause. But inasmuch as they are all painful and so causes of pain, they are put together in the one sūtra.

> *With their operations always tending to light or activity or fixity respectively, the guṇa-s are mutually dependent on each other. They produce ideas of just three kinds: peaceful, violent, and deluded. Because the operation of the guṇa-s fluctuates, the mind is a quick changer, as it is said. Each when predominant in operation and predominant as a mental idea, clashes with the predominance of the others, but when unmanifest, they co-operate with the predominant one.*

The guṇa-s are sattva, rajas and tamas; mental processes are formed out of them; there is pain from the clash of these. The guṇa-s are embodied in forms, like the inner organ of mind. As there is continual change of predominance among the guṇa-s, their operations clash; one of them is overcome by the rising up of another. Thus the operations of each of the three guṇa-s are every moment alternately suppressing the others or helping them to appear.

When among the three guṇa-s, which are inherently either happiness or pain or delusion respectively, a process belonging to one is in possession, it is not that there is no connection with the others. So the conclusion is this: when rajas arises, which is inherently pain, it is not to be taken that just because there is some pain, it must necessarily be pain only from a process of rajas. Sattva and tamas are there along with the rajas, and the painfulness is theirs too. And the rise and cessation of sattva and tamas follow from the operation of rajas, so that pain belongs to all of them.

He explains further: *With their operations always tending to light or activity or fixity respectively, the guṇa-s are mutually dependent on each other.* Although mutually clashing, they also act towards each other as helper and helped, like oil and wick and fire in a lamp. *They produce ideas of just three kinds, peaceful* of sattva, *violent* of rajas, *and deluded* of tamas. They go together as auxiliaries to each other. When a peaceful idea of sattva has arisen, it is at once overthrown by an upsurging thought of force, or rajas aided by tamas.

When some idea of force, a rājasik idea, comes to rise, supported by another guṇa, it is soon overcome by an idea of delusion, namely a tāmasik idea, supported by sattva, or else by a sāttvik idea supported by tamas. The idea of tamas in its turn is overcome by ideas of the other two, and similarly the sāttvik idea is overcome. Thus the guṇa-s have their rise and subjection and activity.

Why is this? *Because the operation of the guṇa-s fluctuates,* the essential nature of the guṇa-s shows in the forms of the mind, and *the mind is a quick changer, as it is said.*

(Opponent) Where is this said?

(Answer) In holy texts.

(Opponent) But why should the guṇa-s clash with each other?

(Answer) Because there cannot be more than one thing predominant in the one place, any more than in an inner room, darkness and light could be simultaneously predominant. There cannot be simultaneous predominance of the guṇa-s making up the form of the mind (antaḥkaraṇa) – in the shape of happiness, pain or delusion – either in their own forms as operational processes of light, activity and restriction, or as ideas of happiness and the others characterized by knowledge, etc.

The mental process is linked, along with the guṇa which is manifest, with the other two guṇa-s in their unmanifest forms, which do not clash because they are in the state of one evenness. As it is said, *each when predominant in operation and predominant as an idea clashes with the predominance (in operations and ideas) of the others, but when unmanifest, they co-operate with the predominant one.* When there is predominance (by sattva) in the form of happiness, there is no predominance (by rajas) in the form of pain or (by tamas) in the form of delusion. When the one is dominant, the others are not. So when the mental process of knowledge is predominant, that of the idea of greed is not so. When any one of them predominates the others do not.

> *So these guṇa-s come to form ideas of happiness, pain and delusion respectively, through the support of the other two, each one thus having the form of all. However the distinction is made between them according to which guṇa is then in the principal place.*

So these guṇa-s come to have the ideas of happiness, pain and delusion respectively through the support of both the others. The idea of happiness comes to sattva through the support of both rajas and tamas; rajas comes to have the idea of pain through the support of both sattva and tamas; tamas too comes by its ideas of delusion through the support of sattva and rajas. So each has the effect of all.

(Opponent) If so, how is the distinction made that this is a sāttvik idea and this of tamas and this of rajas?

(Answer) He says, *However the distinction is made between them according to which guṇa is then in the principal place.* The identification (as of a particular guṇa) is made or rejected according to whether it is predominant or subsidiary. Even in the scheme of the five elements, what is classified as 'earth' is also watery and fiery. There is this kind of clash of the guṇic processes and therefore all is pain to the clear-seeing man, as it has been said. The purpose is, that from (awareness of) this clash, there should come about the supreme detachment.

(Opponent) How is this purpose shown?

(Answer) A distinction was made in the sūtra, which first said 'because of the pain from changes and anxieties and saṃskāra-s' thus pointing to the pain-producing character of all thirst for things seen or heard about. But that has no relation to the supreme detachment, which is from the pain of things invisible.

But by adding 'and from the clash of the operation of the guṇa-s', he teaches the supreme detachment, namely detachment from the possession of qualities whether manifest or unmanifest. For there is pain from the very fact of mutually clashing guṇa processes. And when it is said here that each of them has the form of all, as either principal or subsidiary, the reference is to manifest and unmanifest qualifications. This is why the sūtra makes separate mention of the clash of the processes of the guṇa-s.

What produces this great mass of pain is Ignorance; what causes its annihilation is right vision.

As classics of medicine are in four parts: illness, cause of the illness, the healthy condition, and the remedy – so this work too has just four parts: saṃsāra, cause of saṃsāra, release, means of release.

Of these, saṃsāra with its many pains is what is to be escaped; the conjunction of pradhāna and Puruṣa is the cause of what is to be escaped; liberation (hāna) is the absolute cessation of the conjunction; right vision is the means to liberation.

From the fact of pain in change and anxiety and saṃskāra, it is demonstrated that the seed which *produces this great* as characterized by the guṇa-s and their qualities *mass of pain, is Ignorance, and what causes its annihilation is right vision* as its opponent. Since Knowledge (vidyā) is based on things as they really are, it is only Knowledge that causes the annihilation of Ignorance which is based on things otherwise than as they are, just as the correct view of the thing as it is, the moon single, abolishes the view of a false thing, the moon seen double.

As accompanied by the fundamental cause of pain, taints and karma-s and their ripening, all is pain, and so it has been shown. The one who suffers from that pain is the man of clear sight (vivekin), and as such he is the proper object of a work on right vision (samyagdarśana-śāstra) and not the other one, who 'accepts the very pain. He now seeks to illustrate the point by an example: *As classics of medicine are in four parts: illness, cause of the illness, the healthy condition, and the remedy.*

As the classics of medicine are divided for teaching purposes into four: illness, cause of illness, the normal state of health, and the treatment for that purpose, and it is called four-fold as having these four parts of illness, etc., so in this work of yoga. There is saṃsāra with its mass of pain; its cause is the conjunction of pradhāna and Puruṣa, arising from Ignorance; liberation from saṃsāra so caused is the purpose of a work on right vision (such as this one); and there is right vision itself. With these four, this too is a system of four parts. Again it is four-fold because its subjects are divided in the four ways.

In this (liberation) it is not that the true nature of the one who escapes has to be acquired or escaped from; that would mean that release would entail his destruction.

In this, it is not that the true nature of the one who escapes (has to be acquired or escaped from).

(Opponent) Here should have come the definition of the one who escapes, namely the sūtra 'The Seer is sight alone' (II.20).

(Answer) Not so. In order to explain the purpose of undertaking the work, saṃsāra has been described, with its taints and so on, all ending up in pain. The work is directed to that traveller-in-saṃsāra (saṃsārin) who by reason of the pain of saṃsāra has become a man of clear sight (vivekin). For such a man of clear sight the work is undertaken, and this was indicated in the first sūtra. Right vision alone is the goal of the work thus begun. This is therefore the right place, immediately following on the description of the pain of saṃsāra, to teach that the true nature of the one who escapes, namely Puruṣa, is not to be acquired or escaped from.

(Opponent) Why should it not be? Unless it is either acquirable or avoidable, it turns out to be nothing at all. In the world, happiness and what causes happiness are to be acquired, and pain and what causes it are to be avoided. So this Puruṣa too – being a thing – should have qualities on one side or the other.

(Answer) What would follow in that case? *release would entail his destruction.* If this had the character of something to be avoided, then it should be destroyed. And what would happen upon release? It would entail destruction of the self.

(Opponent) What is wrong with that?

(Answer) We shall explain what is wrong, in the Fourth Part, on Transcendental Aloneness (kaivalya). Moreover, since there is no other to be released, release would never come about.

(Opponent) Let it be that self alone is itself released from self.

(Answer) No. The action would be self-contradictory, and there cannot be a split in the very self. If self is to be what escapes from self which is to be escaped from, there will be yet another (escape), and so to an infinite regress. Each self which escapes would itself be escaped from. Nor can there be simultaneous existence of the two sides of the escape; and if they are to exist at different times, then they will not be self which is escaped from and self which escapes from it.

If it is accepted that the escaper is himself to be escaped from, there can never be the relation of escape, because there would be an infinite regress. In the infinite chain of escapers, it becomes meaningless for any escaper to strive for liberation at all, since he accepts that what he seeks to escape from is himself alone. There can be no resulting liberation, for the result sought by a man in bondage is not his own destruction, but release. Never does a man wish his own destruction, even when he sees that he is on the point of death. If this kind of escaper in the infinite chain did attain his purpose by destruction, he would not in fact be desiring true liberation, in the sense of attaining what liberation aims at.

As for the position that the one who escapes is eternal, this is what we are going to teach in the sūtra on the Seer in the Fourth Part on Transcendental Aloneness. Therefore what is to be escaped from is never Puruṣa but it is saṃsāra, the manifestation of the Great Principle and the rest, and full of pain. The point is, that Puruṣa has no such characteristics (as acquirability or avoidability); if it had such characteristics, it would imply a doctrine of its own perishability.

The doctrine that self is to be acquired would make it something caused. The teaching that it is eternal, denying both the other views (as acquirable or avoidable) – that is right vision.

(Opponent) Well, let it be something to be acquired, as a material object which causes happiness is acquired in order to get happiness.

(Answer) Not so.

(Opponent) Why not?

(Answer) *The doctrine that self is to be acquired would make it something caused.* If the relation is like that for acquiring material objects, and he is himself what is acquired, then the acquisition would be meaningless, because there is no other to acquire. A cloth is not acquired by the cloth itself; a thing has to be acquired by something else. And if another acquirer (of self by self) is supposed, there will be infinite regress, for he too will be acquired by another, and that one too by yet another.

Furthermore it would imply dependence on another. For a thing is acquired from something else which is its cause. Puruṣa will be taken as the cause of pradhāna consisting of sattva and the other guṇa-s, as the potter is the cause of acquiring the clay lump for a pot. But along with being the cause of acquiring pradhāna, this Puruṣa would (himelf) be acquired like pradhāna, and there would be the qualities like sattva in him also, because he would be something acquired like a lump of clay. So his acquisition of pradhāna would have nothing to give it any purpose.

(Opponent) Let it be acquired for the purpose of the Lord, or for mutual purposes among the Puruṣa-s.

(Answer) That would entail a whole mass of defects like being experienced, being unconscious, and being changeable. And therefore Puruṣa cannot have the qualities of pradhāna. And so he says, that the doctrine that self is to be acquired would make it something caused.

He is going to say that the cause is not of Puruṣa. If acquisition of it were causeless, the operations of pradhāna would be causeless. And nothing can be found that is for itself alone, for we do not find that lamps, etc., are for themselves alone.

Denying both the other views: rejecting both – that self is to be escaped from or that it is to be acquired – there follows *the teaching that it is eternal,* the doctrine of eternality of self. Even though pradhāna, which is something to be acquired, also has eternality, still as inherently changing, that (eternality) is not eternal. Pradhāna has defects like inherent plurality, impurity, Ignorance and dependence on another. If the Puruṣa-s were like that, there would be no release. Since bondage and release and their causes, Knowledge and Ignorance, must refer to the self, it would mean that bondage and release would be indistinguishable. So the doctrine of eternality is reached by rejecting both other views – that self is to be escaped from or that it is to be acquired – and *that is right vision.*

The four parts of this work are now explained:

Sūtra II.16

What is to be escaped is the pain not yet come

Pain which has passed, which has been exhausted by being lived through, is not in the category of the escapable, and present pain has attained its moment of experience and is not to be escaped in some other moment. So it is only pain not yet come, which afflicts the yogin sensitive as an eyeball, that is to be escaped.

Unless the patient too is included in the four-fold classification of disease, etc., the medical classic with its goal of health will not be complete in its four parts; here too, unless the one who escapes is included in the four-fold classification beginning with what is to be escaped, the work on right vision, whose fruit is release, will not be complete. Beginning with what is to be escaped, therefore, *The four parts of the work are now explained,* in what follows.

What is to be escaped is the pain not yet come. Pain which has passed which is gone, which belonged to a birth before the present one, which has been *exhausted by being lived through* and has passed away *is not in the category of the escapable.* It has died away simply of itself. *and present pain* in whatever life *has attained its moment of experience,* it has attained the state of being experienced in the course of the present moment; *that* pain *is not to be escaped in some other moment.* It goes of itself by being experienced, and there is no hope of escaping it in some other moment. *So it is only pain not yet come* pain in lives to come immediately after death *which afflicts the yogin sensitive as an eyeball, that is to be escaped.*

It is said to be escapable by right vision. The effort is to be made only that there should be no future births, not to inhibit present pain.

He identifies once again the cause of what can thus be escaped now:

Sūtra II.17

The Seer-Seen conjunction is the cause of what is to be escaped

The Seer is Puruṣa, witness of the mind (buddhi). The Seen is all objects (dharma) presented by mind-sattva.

It has been said that the work is set out in four parts. One part out of the four has been explained: what is to be escaped is the pain which has not yet come. Now the second part, which is the cause, the reason, of the pain is again identified.

(Opponent) But the cause of pain has already been pointed out, at the end of the summing up (in II.15) when it was said that Ignorance is the seed which produces that great mass of pain.

(Answer) True, but what was indicated there was only the bare nature of pain and the bare nature of its cause. In the statement of the bare nature of these, the causality has not been made clear, (as it now is in the words) *The Seer-Seen conjunction is the cause of what is to be escaped.*

The two-element compound Seer-Seen means the Seer and the Seen. The conjunction is of the Seer and the Seen. It could have been a three-element compound – the single word Seer-Seen-conjunction; the fact that the division is made into the separate elements (Seer-Seen, conjunction) is to confirm that the two are of a different class. The sūtra might have said: (conjunction of) experiencer and experienced (bhoktṛ-bhogya), or of thing and its owner, or of pradhāna and Puruṣa. But by the expression of Seer-Seen he wishes to show the conjunction as of those two elements and in no other way.

The Seer is Puruṣa, witness of the mind (buddhi) as is going to be explained. One who habitually witnesses is called a witness. He witnesses the mind (buddhi) which is the Seen, the mind (antaḥkaraṇa) in the form of ideas.

(Opponent) The Seen is simply objects like sound.

(Answer) It is to meet this objection that he adds, *The Seen is all objects (dharma) presented by mind-sattva.* Objects like sound are perceived not independently but only as presented by mind-sattva, being forms of ideas in the mind. If they were seen independently, it would mean that there would be some objects known to Puruṣa and some unknown, but reason (nyāya) establishes that objects are always known to Puruṣa. So it is that all objects are seen only as presented by mind (buddhi).

> *The seen object is like a magnet, which serves by mere proximity; by the fact of being seen, it belongs to Puruṣa its lord, whose nature is seeing, inasmuch as the seen object takes on the nature of an object of experience. Taking on as its own a different nature, though independent it is dependent on another, because it serves the purpose of another. The conjunction of the two powers, Seer and Sight, is beginningless and purposive. As the cause of pain, it is the cause of what is to be escaped.*

The seen object is like a magnet: it is like a magnet which serves by its action to create movement in the iron also. Because that (object) helps, as if it were a magnet, the two-fold purpose of Puruṣa, namely experience and release, *by the fact of being seen, it belongs to Puruṣa,* its lord, whose nature is pure consciousness (citi-svarūpa-mātra).

In what sense is it the property of Puruṣa? *It takes on the nature of an object of experience (karma-viṣaya).* In this compound karma-viṣaya, the element 'karma' has its sense of the grammatical object. The object is what becomes perceptible to that which is awareness (dṛṣi) by nature. To explain just how it is that it becomes objective, he says, *It takes on as its own a different nature.*

It takes itself to be of the nature of its own or another Puruṣa, and of the nature of objects like sound. It takes on itself the characteristics of their nature, taking the assumed characteristics of Puruṣa, or of objects like sound, to be its own being. When it takes on itself the nature of Puruṣa, then it assumes objectivity by the fact of being seen, and becomes a possession for the purpose of release. When it takes on itself the nature of objects like sound, it assumes objectivity by the fact of being seen, and becomes a possession for the purpose of experiencing in the world.

(Opponent) How can what is independent belong to another? What is independent does not look to anything else for its functioning. Even if that functioning does conform to a purpose of Puruṣa (by coincidence), it is a purely spontaneous functioning and nothing to do with serving Puruṣa. It is not reasonable that an independent and spontaneously acting thing should belong to another.

(Answer) *Though independent, it is dependent on another because it serves the purpose of another,* as carrying out the two purposes of Puruṣa. Therefore it belongs to that other. *The conjunction of the two powers, Seer and Sight, is beginningless.* He began with the pair Seer and Seen; now in summing up he speaks of the two powers as Seer and Sight. Since the conjunction of mind (buddhi) and Puruṣa comes into existence immediately on the rise of mind, it might be supposed that it had a beginning. It is to show how it has no beginning that he states that the conjunction is beginningless. Possessors of qualities (dharmin) being permanent, a relation between them would be permanent. Now the relation of the two powers of Seer and Seen is without a beginning, *and purposive,* since it is impelled by the purpose or goal of Puruṣa.

It follows that though the conjunction is thus beginningless, it will cease when the purpose ceases. A conjunction which is of the nature of possessors of qualities (dharmin), since it is from their very being, is not purposeful and so can only be eternal. But a conjunction which is only of passing qualities (dharma) will be passing. This conjunction of mind and Puruṣa is *the cause of what is to be escaped, the cause of pain.*

> *So it is said: by avoiding the cause that brings them together, there will be absolute prevention of pain. How so? Because we see that removing the cause of pain prevents pain. Just as there is vulnerability of the sole and sharpness of the thorn, and the prevention is either not treading with the foot on the thorn, or treading on it with sole protected. He who knows these two, adopts in practice a method of prevention, and adopting that method, does not experience the pain of being pierced.*
>
> *Why is he not pierced? By virtue of his knowledge of the three elements.*
>
> *Here rajas causes the hurt, and sattva it is which is hurt. Why so? Because sattva is in the position of object to the hurtful action.*

So it is said in the teaching *By avoiding the cause that makes them join;* the conjunction being of mind and Puruṣa, and its cause being Ignorance. How is it to be avoided? By making it disappear through its opponent, Knowledge, right vision the adversary of Ignorance. Therefore by avoiding the cause of their conjunction there will be *absolute* perfect *prevention of pain.* What is this (avoiding)? It is seeing rightly.

How is it so? A well-known example is cited: *just as there is vulnerability of the sole* because of its tenderness *and the sharpness of the thorn* from its nature as a hard point. The fact is well known that this particular conjunction is a cause of pain. *Prevention of the pain* of being pierced by a thorn *is either not treading* not stepping *with the foot on the thorn,* or if there is some reason for stepping there, *treading with the sole protected. He who knows these two* the vulnerability and the sharpness, or the two methods of avoidance, *he adopts in his life a method of prevention,* one of the two; *adopting that method, he does not experience the pain of being pierced* by a thorn.

In the present case, there are Puruṣa and pradhāna, which in its relation to sattva is compared to the thorn; the particular conjunction between these two, caused by Ignorance, is the cause of pain. The preventive measure is this: either disregard of seen objects, guṇa-s and their combinations which are particularizations of pradhāna alone, realizing through right knowledge that there is no good to be pursued, because Puruṣa is immutable, or else, experience by the mind-sattva, like one treading on a thorn, but shielded by right knowledge, of the objects such as sound which come uninvited, realizing that the karma of taking on a body must be known assuredly to bring about its fruits. Thus knowing the method of prevention, like the prevention of the pain of being pierced by a thorn, he does not incur the pain of saṃsāra.

How is it so? *By virtue of his awareness of the three elements.* It is awareness of pradhāna, Puruṣa, and their conjunction, these three, that shows the effectiveness of knowledge, for we see that one who is not aware of his sole and the thorn and their coming together is caused pain by his unawareness.

To explain: *Here rajas causes the pain;* pradhāna was compared to the thorn, as inflicting pain, but it is only through rajas, inherently painful as that is. As the object of rajas, *sattva alone is pained.* Like an axe chopping, any hurtful action has to have an object to operate on. *It is in the position of object to the pain caused by rajas.* Puruṣa the witness is not the object pained by rajas, for the painful effect is an object witnessed by Puruṣa. An axe does not operate on the woodman himelf, nor is the result mere cutting, but actual splitting some object like a piece of wood. Thus the apparent suffering of Puruṣa is the production of an effect in sattva the object; rajas is like the axe on wood, and sattva simply functions as something seen by Puruṣa.

Sattva being an object to it, the pain does not belong to the immutable, actionless knower-of the-field (kṣetrajña), because the object is something shown to him. But sattva being pained, Puruṣa conforming to that form, is pained likewise. He now goes on to explain the nature of the Seen.

So the pain does not affect Puruṣa because Puruṣa is *immutable,* being the Seer. Pain is modification of some object; for instance, the result of chopping is a change in the thing chopped, namely that it is divided into two. It does not affect the *immutable, actionless, knower-of-the-field (kṣetrajña)* whose immutability is to be established by the fact that it is always the witness of objects.

(Opponent) If Puruṣa is thus not pained, then it means that pradhāna will not be working for the purpose of Puruṣa, for it has just been said that there is (experience, namely) conformity to the mental process.

(Answer) To this he says: *because the object is something shown to him.* Objects are shown to him, who is unchanging and actionless. So *conforming to that form,* imitating that form of sattva the object of sight; the conforming to that form is when the mental idea (bauddha pratyaya) is in proximity to sight, and there is an appearance in the form of sight. Just as in proximity to lac, a crystal appears in the form of lac, so Puruṣa too *is pained*-figuratively.

He now goes on to explain the nature of the Seen. In the previous sūtra the order was Seer and Seen, so it might seem that the nature of the Seer should be explained first. But to understand what the Seer is, there must first be knowledge of what the Seen is. He is the Seer of what is seen distinct from himself, and it is as distinct from it that he is established as the Seer in himself. In order of importance, true, the Seer comes first as in the previous sūtra, but the present order is adopted for the definition.

Sūtra II. 18

With a constant tendency towards light, action, and fixity, the Seen consists of the elements and the senses, being for the purpose of experience and transcendence

Sattva tends towards light; rajas tends towards action; tamas tends towards fixity.

With a constant tendency towards light, action, fixity, the Seen consists of the elements and the senses, being for the purpose of experience and transcendence. Light and action and fixity. Light is placed first as being the most important. There is no particular reason for the order of the words fixity and action, as they both apply indiscriminately to many things. The word 'action' has in fact been put first in the compound.

With-a-constant-tendency (śīla) means with a tendency towards light and action and fixity (respectively). Light is illumination, and what has a constant tendency towards light is sattva.

(Opponent) But illumination is an action, and in that case how would a tendency to illumination be of sattva? It ought to be of rajas. And then, why should fixity of illumination be of tamas? Since illumination is the nature of sattva, it is fixed in that.

(Answer) No. The word for constantly tending towards – śīla – is not used about the simple nature of a thing. One does not say of a drummer that he constantly tends to be a drum, but that he constantly tends to play the drum. The word śīla – constantly tending towards – is never used apart from some functioning.

(Opponent) But fixity and light are the nature of tamas and sattva. The only force of the word śīla is to indicate their respective natures.

(Answer) The word does not refer to the whole nature. Here for instance in the case of rajas, its nature is pain, but it is said (only) that it constantly tends towards action, so the significance of the word śīla here is in connection with action. And the words fixity and light also have the sense of function.

(Opponent) But functioning is action, which must be of the nature of rajas alone.

(Answer) Not so, because it is accepted that the three guṇa-s have pradhāna as their common ground. If action were the very nature of rajas, there would be activity in pradhāna, the common ground of the guṇa-s. But the possession of activity is accepted only in the state of effect, not in the state of pradhāna (cause). So the word śīla, constantly tending, is not used in the sense of the (simple) nature of a guṇa.

> *Though distinct, these guṇa-s mutually affect each other. They change, they have the properties of conjunction and disjunction, they assume forms created by their mutual co-operation. Distinct from each other, they are identifiable even when their powers are conjoined.*

Though sattva and tamas do not tend towards action, they are associated with rajas which always does so, and through the action of rajas, fixity and illumination are described as activities, though in a figurative sense. That is what is meant by saying that sattva tends towards light and tamas towards fixity.

Of the three, the one with the constant tendency towards light is sattva. With the tendency to action, to go into operation, is rajas; with the tendency to fixity, to covering, to restriction, is tamas. *Though distinct, these guṇa-s mutually affect each other;* there is a distinction, some separation, between the guṇa-s even when mutually affecting each other.

Now it is explained in what sense the 'constant tendency to light' is said to be of sattva, and only that. Although from the influence of rajas-activity, sattva has the potentiality of revealing everything, yet that light is also restricted through the influence of tamas. Similarly the manifestation of activity by rajas is through the influence of sattva, but restriction of the activity is from the effect of tamas. The manifestation of fixity in tamas is from the influence of sattva, and its constant tendency towards fixity is from rajas. But the fixity is inherent in it, just as functioning is inherent in rajas, and light in sattva.

The mutual influence of the guṇa-s can thus be seen in the effects on others. *They have the properties of conjunction and disjunction:* the meaning of the Sanskrit compound is that they each possess these two properties, conjunction and disjunction. When some effect is beginning, they join together, with one guṇa predominant; they separate from one another, as another quality opposed to the first one arises.

They assume forms created by their mutual co-operation: the forms range from the Great Principle down to a clump of grass, and the sense is, that these forms whether of qualities (dharma) or possessor of qualities (dharmin) are taken on by guṇa-s in mutual co-operation. *Distinct from each other,* ultimately each is quite different from the others, *they are identifiable even when their powers are conjoined;*they are differentiated by their capacity to initiate and manifest wholly incompatible effects. On this it is said: 'when a particular effect is to begin, their component powers are absolutely commingled; when the effect has begun, the powers though indistinguishable separately can be identified (by inference from the effects).'

> *They deploy their respective powers, whether of similar or dissimilar kind. When one is predominant, the presence (of the others) is inferred as existing within the predominant one from the very fact of its operation as a guṇa.*

They deploy their respective powers, whether of similar or dissimilar kind: sattva is the element of similarity among sāttvik things; rajas is the element of similarity among rājasik things, and tamas among tāmasik things. But in relation to the other two, they are each elements of dissimilarity. The sense is, that the guṇa-s always tend to deploy their respective powers, whether of similar or dissimilar kind. For when an event is to begin, whether sāttvik or rājasik or tāmasik, no effect would be possible at all without all three guṇa-s deploying their respective powers.

> *When one is predominant, the presence (of the others) is inferred as existing within the predominant one from the very fact of its operation as a guṇa.*

(Opponent) In that case, since all co-operate with their different powers to produce a single effect, they will be equally important.

(Answer) When one is predominant, the presence is inferred of all of them. When in each successive event, the dominant one produces its particular effect, at that time the presence of the other two is explained to be subordinate. There cannot be predominance (prādhānya) of all of them at the same time, for if there were equal predominance (pradhāna) they would be simply pradhāna (defined as the state in which the guṇa-s are in equilibrium) and no effects would arise at all.

(Opponent) When some particular effect is produced under the dominance of one guṇa, how is the presence of the others known at all?

(Answer) By the very operation as a guṇa of the principal one, the presence in it of the others, though auxiliary, is implied. Unless the other two were there, comprised as auxiliaries in the principal one, its operation would not be possible. So from the fact of its operation, their existence is inferred.

> *They are effective as engaged in carrying out the purpose of Puruṣa. They serve by mere proximity, like a magnet. In the idea of any one of them, they all co-operate. They are what is meant by the word pradhāna.*

They are effective as engaged in carrying out the purpose of Puruṣa. The purpose of Puruṣa is two-fold: experience and transcendence. Whatever is to be done to implement it, that they are engaged in, and they are effective in producing the results. *They serve by mere proximity, like a magnet.* By the mere proximity of Puruṣa, they serve, in the form of change of ideas. *In the idea of any one of them, they all co-operate. In the idea,* the mental process, the knowledge, *of any one of them, they all co-operate* in its continuity, its fixity. *They are what is meant by the word pradhāna.* There is no other pradhāna apart from the three guṇa-s; the three when in the state of equilibrium are known by the one word pradhāna. When they are divided unevenly, they are called 'change' and have processes.

> *This is what is called the Seen. It consists of objects and senses. In its aspects as an object such as earth, it changes into physical and subtle forms, and in its aspect as senses like the ear, it changes into physical and subtle forms.*
>
> *It is not purposeless, but acts only in accordance with a purpose; it is for the purpose of experience and transcendence that this is seen by Puruṣa. Of the two-fold purpose, experience is the conviction that qualities desired and undesired are one's nature, there being no discrimination from them.*

This is what is called the Seen. It consists of objects and senses, of objects and senses separately; *in its aspect as an object such as earth it changes into subtle and physical forms:* existence as an object is of two kinds – subtle as subtle element (tan-mātra), and physical as particular objects. *it changes* it takes on that physical or subtle existence. *In its aspect as senses like the ear, it changes into subtle forms,* subtle in the form of 'I' (ahaṅkāra) and physical in the form of the ear, etc. *It* the Seen *is not purposeless,* for when there is activity, some purpose is always found. *It acts only in accordance with a purpose,* in line with one. What then is this purpose of the activity of the Seen? It is seen by Puruṣa for the purpose of experience and transcendence, being merely a means to them, as fire (is a means to cooking, warmth, etc.).

He describes the two, experience and transcendence. Of these, *the conviction of qualities, desired or undesired, as his own nature, without discriminating them, is experience, desired:* such things as contact with the fragrant sandalwood; *undesired:* those inherently unpleasant such as qualities in the form of contact with swords or thorns and so on; *conviction (of them) as his own nature:* in this way *without discriminating them.* In his idea of Puruṣa he fails to discriminate 'this is not Puruṣa, it is mind-sattva'. It is because the idea in his mind (bauddha pratyaya) overlooks the consciousness which it possesses. This as described is what is called experience of Puruṣa.

> *The conviction of the true nature of the experiencer as apart is called transcendence (apavarga). There is no other awareness (darśana) apart from these two. So it is said: 'But he who sees the three guṇa-s as the agents, and the Puruṣa, the fourth, as witness of their actions, seeing everything presented to him, does not suppose any awareness other than that.'*

Different from that mental idea (bauddha pratyaya), which is essentially experience, is the true nature of its witness, essential awareness, and *conviction of the true nature as apart is called transcendence,* for there is no further particularization of the one who has attained, after he has come to conviction of the true nature of the experiencer. For then he is one who is always established in his own nature; the conformity to the mental process was in the other state, namely a particularity.

There is no other third *awareness apart from these two.* Insofar as there is Ignorance, there are both the desired and undesired, and that is purely experience. But the nature of Puruṣa is not to be avoided nor to be chosen, and when that has been determined, then as has been said already, where is experience? Determination of Puruṣa is an idea opposed to the idea of the form of experience, characterized by Ignorance as that is. Apart from these two, there is no conceivable other third awareness.

So it is said: 'But he this seer with right awareness (samyagdarśin) *who sees the three guṇa-s* already described *as the agents* of all operations and their cessation *and the Puruṣa, the fourth,* as non-agent, being without any qualities of the guṇa-s *witness (sākṣin) of their actions* an overseer (upadraṣṭṛ) of the actions of the guṇa-s, like one who looks on as an overseer at successive actions, *seeing* aware as 'not I, not mine' *everything presented to him* displayed as objects to his sight by the guṇa-s in the character of minds (antaḥ-karaṇa), objects which are received by him only figuratively, taken as real in the form of mental ideas (buddhi-pratyaya) *does not suppose any other awareness than this.'* No other right vision is possible; he has the certainty that no other right vision can exist.

> *These two, experience and transcendence, are created by mind and function only in mind. How is it that they are attributed to Puruṣa?*
>
> *Just as victory or defeat encountered by the fighting men are attributed to the ruler because he experiences the effect of them, so bondage or release, happening in the mind alone, are attributed to Puruṣa, because he experiences the effect of them. In the mind alone are bondage, which is failure to fulfil the purpose of Puruṣa, and release, which is completion of that purpose. In this way perception and retention and knowledge and postulation and rejection and action and speech and determination-according-to-reason, and application to practice, are states of being, events in the mind, which are projected as real existences in Puruṣa.*

These two, experience and transcendence, are created by mind set going by mind *and function only in mind.*

(Opponent) *How is it that they are attributed to Puruṣa?* It is as if what has been done by one man is taken to be the work of another, as if the laundryman were supposed to have been the dyer of the clothes. How can it be that these two, existing in mind alone, are assigned to Puruṣa?

(Answer) *Because he experiences the effect of them,* as the perceiver of the ideas, correct or false.

He gives an example in illustration: *as victory or defeat encountered by the fighting men are attributed to the ruler because he experiences the effect of them, so bondage or release, happening in the mind alone, are attributed to Puruṣa, because he experiences the effect of them. In mind alone are bondage, which is failure to fulfil the purpose of Puruṣa, and release, which is the completion of that purpose.* Insofar as the mind thinks of experience and transcendence as needing something still to be done for fulfilment, it is bondage; release (mokṣa) is fulfilment of the purpose of Puruṣa. It is in mind alone that the fulfilment of the purpose (takes place), the completion of what was to be done. When it sees Puruṣa different from itself, unconnected with bondage or release, there is nothing more for it to do. That completion of what had to be done is what is called release of buddhi.

So perception and retention and knowledge and postulation and rejection and action and speech and determination-according-to-reason, and application to practice, are projected as real existences in Puruṣa. They are all the same as being merely ideas, so that they are qualities of mind existing in mind alone, created by mind, but taken to be real existences as projected in Puruṣa. Puruṣa perceives them and Puruṣa supports them – only in the sense that they are projected in Puruṣa.

Perception (grahaṇa) is reception of sounds, etc., by senses such as the ears. Not forgetting what has been perceived is *retention (dhāraṇa).* Determining the universal and particular in what is thus remembered is *knowledge* (vijñāna). Deliberating with a desire to reconsider a known particular is *postulation (ūha).* Exclusion (vyudasana) of qualities opposed to what has been proposed is *rejection (apoha).* Engagement with objects is *action (kriyā).* The mental process whose field is words is *speech (vacana).* Determination of the proof of any thing to be just such as it is in accordance with the relevant reasoning is *determination according to reason (yathā-nyāya-avadhāraṇa).* Practice (abhiyoga) again and again by the mind so that it does not waver from the right notion – this is *application (abhiniveśa).* These, beginning with perception, are existences projected in Puruṣa. *For he is the experiencer of their results* as the knower of the result of perception and of the others.

To determine the different phases of the three guṇa-s which make up the Seen, the following sūtra is presented:

Sūtra II.19

What particularizes itself, and what does not, what goes (liṅga, the Great principle) and what does not (a-liṅga, pradhāna), are guṇa-implementers

To determine the different phases the differentiation of the states of being *of the three guṇa-s which make up the Seen* whose nature has been described, *the following sūtra is presented; What particularizes itself and what does not, what goes and what does not, are guṇa-implementers.*

(Grammatical excursus on the peculiar reading of the sūtra: viśeṣāviśeṣa-liṅgamātrāliṅgā guṇaparvāṇaḥ instead of *viśeṣāviśeṣa-liṅgamātrāliṅgāni guṇaparvāṇi.)*

a-liṅga is a technical term for pradhāna, which does not go to dissolution (na liṅgati, see I.45), nor come from somewhere else. A masculine noun, a-liṅga, may be correctly derived from the root (liṅg, to go) by the extension (Mahābh. III.1.134) to any (qualified) root of the capacity of the pac- group roots to form a noun of agency by merely adding -a. The noun consequently assumes the appropriate gender (i.e. the masculine of an agent). Liṅga (not from a verbal root but in the conventional sense of) a mark (cihna) would be neuter (not masculine as here), and would point to an instrument (not an agent). Or else this may be taken as an adjectival compound (bahuvrīhi) meaning that there is no mark, no indication, of accessibility to direct perception, of that which is called pradhāna.

Thus what particularize themselves, and the others, are called parvan, derived (uṇādi iv.112) from pṝ to fill, because they fulfil (pālayanti) the purpose of Puruṣa by providing experience and transcendence, or else because they implement (pūrayanti) their own changes. The root pṝ takes the suffix -an to form a noun of agency (parvan), by the sūtra (Pā. hi.2.75) '(and these suffixes, including -an) are found affixed to other roots'. (As to its gender) the rule is that a noun ending in -n and not expressing agency is neuter, while if it does express agency it is of common gender. For instance merudṛśvan, one who has seen Meru, may be in the nominative merudṛśvā or merudṛśvanī.

Thus, what particularizes itself, and the others, are implementers. What implementers? They are guṇa-implementers.

There is however a reading of the sūtra by others: 'Particularized and unparticularized and liṅga-alone and without-liṅga are guṇa-implementations.'

Of these, space, air, fire, water, and earth are the elements, which are particularizations of the unparticularized subtle elements: sound, touch, form, taste, and smell. Ear, skin, eye, tongue, and nose are the mental sense-organs, and voice, hands and feet, organs of excretion and generation are organs of action; mind, the eleventh organ, is directed to everything. These are the particularizations of the unparticularized I-am-ness.

Of these, space, air, fire, water, and earth are the elements. Space is based on the subtle element (tanmātra) of sound; air is based on the subtle element of touch, and is characterized by sound and touch. Fire is based on the subtle element of form, and characterized by sound, touch, and form. Waters are based on the subtle element of taste, and characterized by the four: sound, touch, form, and taste. Earth is based on the subtle element of odour, and characterized by the five: sound, touch, form, taste, and smell.

(Opponent) Space is eternal. It is not a particularization of something that first appeared and later perished. Whatever appears, we see to be particularized and like earth, which first appears and subsequently perishes. So if space had a beginning it would be a particularization, first arising and subsequently perishing. And that is not so. Therefore space has no beginning. And if you say that its particularity is to be an absence which makes room (for other things), not so, because then the absence of other things, with forms, would also be eternal likewise. Space is eternal because it does not have the characteristic of non-eternality, being all-pervading like the Self and such things.

(Answer) No, for that would contradict scripture (āgama). It would be opposed to the scriptural text, From that, from this Self, space was created' (Taitt. 2.1). And it contradicts tradition.

(Opponent) The statement quoted is figurative, meaning merely that space became manifest.

(Answer) Not so, for that would mean that the subsequent statements of the creation of air etc. would also be figurative, because the same passage says that from space, air was created.

When you say of a thing which does not have the particularity of an origin that it is therefore not non-eternal, it comes to saying that because it is not particularized it is eternal. And it follows that what is particularized, is not eternal. And if so, since there is particularization as bondage and release and awareness and unawareness and so on in the self, etc., according to the Vaiśeṣika, it follows that their existence would be non-eternal, and his ultimate atoms and so on would also be non-eternal.

Time, place, space, and mind, are not all-pervading and not eternal, because like jars they are dependent on another (parārtha) and not self-sufficient (svārtha). Like jars, again, they have a beginning as being neither pradhāna nor Puruṣa. Similarly, space (ākāśa, with a beginning and so not eternal) is in the field of the external senses. It is an element like earth, and coming into conjunction with material things like earth which are not eternal, it partakes of their qualities. In medicine even it is said that an excess of space, like an excess of air, is something to be treated; expert physicians agree that excess of space (nabhas) is a symptom to be treated, which shows that it is classed among transient things.

These elements are *particularizations of the unparticularized subtle elements: sound, touch, form, taste, and smell.* They are particularizations as having various particular qualities, peaceful or violent or dull, etc. The subtle elements are unparticularized because they do not have such qualities.

Ear, skin, eye, tongue, and nose are mental sense-organs (buddhi-indriya) directed towards forming ideas (buddhi) of the objects like sound; their existence is inferred from the ideas of their respective objects. *Voice, hand and foot, organs of excretion and generation* are inferred as operators of the actions like speech.

(Opponent) There is no proof of the existence of voice and so on as separate organs.

(Answer) They are established from the scriptural texts. There are passages of scripture referring to the organs, such as 'Of all the Vedas, the organ of speech is the place of merging' (Bṛhad. Up. 2.4.11). And in the traditions everywhere there are directions and prohibitions to do or not do certain things, showing that ears and others are organs. The well-known maxim,

'No impulsive speaking, no fidgeting with hands or feet' (Manu IV.177) illustrates the point.

And then, voice and the other organs of the group are effective, like the eye. For in all the limbs we see the power of the (motor) organ going into operation, as in the case of sight. From birds to serpents and plants, there is always a mouth. *Mind the eleventh is directed to everything* to every object past future and present, and to the sense and motor organs.

These eleven sense-organs are *particularizations of the unparticularized I-am-ness;* I-am-ness is the feeling that I am, the idea 'I am'. This which is I-am-ness is characterized or indicated by the idea I am'; this the sixth of the unparticularized principles is the I-notion (ahaṅkāra).

These are the particularizations of the unparticularized.

This is the sixteen-fold transformation of the guṇa-s into particulars.

Of the guṇa-s sattva etc. without particularized form, *this is the sixteen-fold transformation.* Space has much sattva, air rajas, fire has sattva and rajas, earth has sattva and tamas. *(Water omitted – Tr.)* As being objects, there is some tamas in (all of) them, but their particularization is according to the principal guṇa. As luminous, all senses have much sattva, but the buddhi-senses with mind as the sixth are predominantly illuminators and so have much sattva. The action-senses have much rajas, being primarily action.

Now the six unparticularized. They are the subtle elements of sound, touch, form, taste, and smell, distinguished (respectively) by one, two, three, four, and all five, beginning with sound. The sixth unparticularized is pure I-am-ness.

These are the six unparticularized transformations of the Great principle, whose nature is pure being, which is bare form (liṅga- mātra). Beyond the unparticularized is that Great (self) which is pure being; supported in it, these fulfil their development to the limit.

And in the reverse process, they are supported in that Great (self) which is pure being, and go back to that pradhāna, the formless (a-liṅga) which is neither being-non-being (niḥsattāsattam), nor yet existent-non-existent (sadasat).

The six unparticularized are the subtle elements of sound, touch ... . Though the subtle element of touch has both characters (sound and touch), it is designated by the principal one (i.e. touch). The word *mātra* (in tan-mātra) is to rule out particularizations like peaceful, violent, and so on.

Distinguished by one, two, three, four, and all five characteristics: the distinction of the subtle element of touch is the character of having both sound and touch, and in this way each one has fewer characteristics than the one following it in the list.

The sixth unparticularized is pure I-am-ness (asmitā-mātra). In the list of the subtle elements beginning with sound, it stands sixth; it is the unparticularized (form) of the eleven sense-organs.

pure being, pure existence; *the bare form (liṅga-mātra, literally 'what goes')* the first form from the formless pradhāna, like the seed's becoming a sprout.

Of that whose nature, whose reality, is *Great,* beyond all particularizations and unparticularizations, *these are the six unparticularized transformations* of the guṇa-s like sattva, supported in the form called the Great. *Beyond* more subtle than the *unparticularized is the Great principle* called *bare form (liṅga-mātra); supported in that Great which is pure being* because of its greatness, supported in that which is their cause, they fulfil their development in the final particularizations like earth.

> *(And in the reverse process, they are supported in the Great self which is pure being, and then go back to the unmanifest pradhāna without form (a-liṅga), which has neither being nor non-being and is not existent-non-existent.) The Great Principle is a transformation of these (guṇa-s) into bare form, and their formless transformation has neither being nor non-being.*
>
> *The formless state is not caused by any purposefulness of Puruṣa; no purpose of Puruṣa brings it about, nor is there any purpose of Puruṣa in it. Hence it is classed as eternal.*

And in the reverse process when the unparticularized are dissolved, *they are supported in the Great self which is pure being* bare form (liṅga-mātra), *and then go back to the unmanifest.* What is that unmanifest?

neither being nor non-being without particularized or unparticularized;

not existent-non-existent: existent in the sense of being a slight development from the unmanifest; non-existent in the sense of being more subtle than the unparticularized. Existent-non-existent refers to the Great principle, which is both existent and non-existent in these senses. The unmanifest which has neither of the qualities is therefore not existent-non-existent.

The Great principle is the transformation of these guṇa-s like sattva *into bare form (liṅga-mātra);* supported in it, the unparticularized fulfil their development, and also go to dissolution.

The unmanifest *has neither being nor non-being, and is the formless (a-liṅga) transformation* of these guṇa-s. There is no transformation of the guṇa-s into any more subtle state, because as has been said: 'The scale of subtlety ends in pradhāna' (sūtra I.45).

Because it is formless, *The formless state is not caused by any purposefulness of Puruṣa;* no purpose of Puruṣa is an impelling cause of that formless state. The point is that there is no correlation of the formless state with any purpose of Puruṣa. He explains: *no purpose of Puruṣa brings it about.* Why is there no connection of that state with the purpose of Puruṣa? He says: *nor is there any purpose of Puruṣa in it* for it is self-sufficient; even to gods it cannot be known, as are known the Great principle and others.

That is why *it is classed as eternal.* For things like earth, which are subject to a purpose of Puruṣa, are seen to be non-eternal. But this state of pradhāna is not subject to any such purpose, and hence is classed as eternal.

> *But purposefulness of Puruṣa is a cause of the three differentiated states. This purpose being their final and efficient cause, they are classed as non-eternal.*
>
> *But the guṇa-s, conforming themselves to all qualities, neither perish nor are produced. The manifestations past and future, going and coming, which accompany the guṇa-s, make them appear as if they had the qualities of being produced and disappearing. It is as when it is said, 'Poor Devadatta! Why poor? Because his cows are dying.' It is only from the death of the cows that he is poorly off not that he himself has suffered harm.*

But purposefulness of Puruṣa is a cause of the three differentiated states particularized, unparticularized, and pure being; the states of the Great, etc., are subject to a purpose. *This purpose being their final and efficient cause, they are classed as non-eternal,* inasmuch as these states of the Great and the others come and go. *But the guṇa-s, conforming themselves to all qualities,* conforming to all changes *neither perish nor are produced.* As a snake conforms its length to its particular serpentine coilings, so the guṇa-s conform to the particularized and other states as what are considered to be lumps of earth and so on. As the snake does not dissolve when a coiled form dissolves, nor is produced when a particular coiled form is produced, so with the guṇa-s also. In the same way, when pots and trays of clay are destroyed or produced, the clay of which they are made is not thereby destroyed or produced.

The manifestations of qualities (dharma) *past and future, going and coming* (in the present) of these three kinds, *which accompany the guṇa-s* of which the guṇa-s are the causal material *make them appear as if they had qualities of being produced and of disappearing* – apparently arising and coming to an end, not that they really do so.

To give an illustration he says: *when it is said, 'Poor Devadatta! Why poor? Because his cows are dying', it is only from the death of the cows that he is poorly off, not that he himself has suffered harm.*A parallel case is given to illustrate the point. Just as in the case of Devadatta and his poverty, the 'wealth' of guṇa-s by the manifestations such as the Great principle which accompany them, and the variety caused by their clashing against each other and their separating, as also the 'poverty' when all that (variety) dissolves, are not any diminution or increase for the guṇa-s themselves.

> *Bare form (liṅga-mātra) is next to the formless (a-liṅga), and the differentiations from it do not depart from the sequence in their development.*

(Opponent) If every thing is an effect of pradhāna, why are not particularized or unparticularized produced directly (and not only after the Great principle)?

(Answer) *Bare form is next to the formless,* as the root of the tree is closest to the seed, and it is the root that is formed and differentiates first of all, not any of the later stages of the tree. So here the Great principle takes form in the pradhāna where it was concealed, and differentiates, becomes manifest, first, before the subsequent particularizations which are too remote. So he says that *they do not depart from the sequence.* They keep to the order, for one never sees anything which comes into existence out of its proper sequence.

> *The six unparticularized are formed in and differentiate out from the bare form (the Great principle), held to the due sequence of change; and in these unparticularized, the elements and sense organs are formed and differentiated. As has been said, there is no further principle beyond the particularized; they do not change further into any other principle. But there are changes of phase – of quality, of time-character, and of intensity – to be explained later.*

So the *six unparticularized* as described *are formed in and differentiate out from the bare form (the Great principle)* to which they are immediately proximate, *held to the due sequence of change, and in these unparticularized, the elements and sense organs are formed and differentiated.* In the subtle elements, the physical elements (bhūta) are formed and differentiated, as in the pure I-am-ness the senses along with the mind are formed and differentiated. *As has been said, there is no further principle beyond the particularized,* space and the others listed. The meaning is that there is no transformation into some further principle beyond the particulars. *They do not change further into any other principle.* What is called a principle is something common to all that supports life, lasting up to the cosmic dissolution (mahā-pralaya). Nothing like this appears beyond earth, etc., but there are changes of phase in accordance with the state of their quality (dharma) and time-character (lakṣaṇa) and state of intensity (avasthā): *there are changes of phase – quality, time-character and intensity – which will be explained later* in the Third Part.

The Seen has been explained. Now he takes up the determination of the true nature of the Seer.

Sūtra II.20

The Seer is sight alone; though pure, he looks on at the thoughts

'sight alone' means the power of the Seer alone, untouched by any qualification. This Puruṣa is the witness of mind. He is not like the mind, and not absolutely unlike it.

The Seen has been explained it has been determined. *Now he takes up the determination of the true nature of the Seer* by whom these objects are seen. *The Seer is sight alone; though pure, he looks on at the thoughts. The Seer:* Puruṣa aware of the Seen as it has been described. His definition is sight-alone; though pure, he looks on at the thoughts. Here are being presented the same two points previously described in the sūtras 'Then the Seer is established in his own nature' (I.3) and 'Otherwise, it conforms itself to the mental process' (I.4).

There is observation (anudarśana) of the thoughts in the mind (bauddha-pratyaya) by pure sight which is inherently immutable; from this fact the state of establishment in the true nature is exactly ascertained. *He looks on at the thoughts:* but here there is only an inference of existence. Why so? Because one finds that it is by something else, different from themselves, that seen objects like jars are perceived, and their revealers like lights, etc., are perceived separately. And thoughts, which reveal everything, are perceptible only by something different from themselves, so that they are known only as things seen, like jars and lights and so on.

Puruṣa, looking on at thought in the mind alone, sees only that, and never fails to see thought which is his object; he is therefore sight alone. The word 'alone' (mātra) is to reject all other qualities; it is used to exclude any idea that the Seer is equally the seat of desire and so on, which would contradict the fact that the Seer is sight. For the Seer-ship is simply of sight. This is what is meant by the words: *'sight alone' means the power of the Seer alone.* It is the seeing of the Seer that is his power, the power of the Seer. There is no other with the power of the Seer, and this power is the Seer himself. Now he explains further the meaning of the word 'alone'; *untouched by any qualification,* untouched by any qualification such as desire or the guṇa-s or the qualities of the guṇa-s.

He is the witness (prati-saṃvedin) of the mind: to witness is natural to him, in the sense that his essence is awareness of the mind's ideas. Now the commentator explains how it is to be understood that Puruṣa is witness of the mind, and sight-alone, and pure: *he is not like the mind, and not absolutely unlike.* This means that he is not of similar character to the mind, but neither is he absolutely devoid of its qualities. As to the dissimilarity, he adduces Puruṣa's nature of awareness, and his purity; and for his not being absolutely different, he adduces the fact that Puruṣa conforms to the mental process.

> *To some extent he is not like the mind. In what way? Because mind is changeable, in that an object is (sometimes) known to it and (sometimes) unknown. Its object, whether a cow or a jar, is known to it and also unknown, which shows its changeability. But the fact that the object of Puruṣa is always known shows clearly the unchangeability of Puruṣa. Why so? Because mind, which is by definition the object of Puruṣa, could not be (sometimes) known and (sometimes) unknown to him; hence the unchangeability of Puruṣa is established, in that his object is always known to him.*

(Opponent) How is it that he is not like the mind?

(Answer) *To some extent he is not like it.*

(Opponent) *In what way?* Why so?

(Answer) To show where the nature of Puruṣa is opposite to that of the mind he continues: *Because mind is changeable, in that an object is (sometimes) known to it and (sometimes) unknown.* He explains how this which is an object of the mind is known and unknown: *Its object, whether a cow or a jar, is known to it and also unknown,* known when mind is changed by that outer form, and unknown when it is not changed by the form.

If there were no changeability in it, the mind would be unchanging and always manifesting the object; the object would always be there for the mind. The fact that the object is known and (then) unknown shows the changeability of the mind; it is changeable because its object is known and (then) unknown, as with the eye depending on presence or absence of light.

With Puruṣa it is the reverse: the object is always known. Puruṣa's own object is only what is known to him always. So *the fact that the object of Puruṣa is always known shows clearly the unchangeability of Puruṣa.*

(Opponent) I am not convinced that it has been well established that the object of Puruṣa is always known. *Why* should this be *so?*

(Answer) He replies: *Because* – this word points to an established fact – *mind* namely the ideas of the mind *which is by definition the object of Puruṣa could not be (sometimes) known and (sometimes) unknown.* The mental idea can only be ever known, and it is just because his knowledge does not waver that it is certain that Puruṣa is apart. So Puruṣa always knows his object and therefore his unchangeability is established. The proposition is: Puruṣa is unchangeable; the reason is, because he always knows his object; the counter-instance is, unlike things like the mind.

(Opponent) But Puruṣa is aware of the object as determined by the mind, so the object will be known and unknown to Puruṣa as it is to the mind. What Puruṣa observes is what the mind determines, which is knownness or unknownness of the object. Therefore there will be changeability in Puruṣa too, because the object will be known and unknown to it, just as to the mind.

(Answer) The objection does not hold, for Puruṣa's object is the mind itself. The object for Puruṣa is only the mind in the form of an outer object, not that object in itself. So the object of Puruṣa is not known-and-unknown, because mind is always known to it, and accordingly there is no changeability in Puruṣa.

(Opponent) But some say: 'Puruṣa is aware of the object determined by the mind.' How can this be reconciled?

(Answer) But they too admit that Puruṣa is unchangeable. It comes down to what is being said in the words 'object determined by the mind'. When it is said that he is aware of the object in the form received as determined by the mind, it means that he is aware of the form of the mind. Otherwise it would follow that Puruṣa had all the mental qualities like changeability and existence-for-the-sake-of-another, and being a collaborator (with body, senses, and objects, etc.) and so on.

(Opponent) Unless he were changeable, he would have no vision at all.

(Answer) Not so, because it is vision that is the nature of Puruṣa. He who maintains that Puruṣa does change, must answer this: What is brought about by the change?

(Opponent) Seeing.

(Answer) This is refuted by the fact that seeing is the nature of Puruṣa, so no change is needed.

(Opponent) Then Puruṣa's awareness would not be experience, for experience is some modification.

(Answer) Then answer this: If so, Puruṣa would be impermanent by reason of having modifications, as are things like the body.

(Opponent) An internal modification would not be a cause of impermanence; the cause of impermanence is modification into another state of being.

(Answer) Then reply to this point: The state of modification is itself another state. The modification of an as yet unmodified thing is another state.

Once an object is accepted, there will be modification, and one cannot make such restrictions (of internal or external). Even with things which are changing (apparently only) internally, like diamonds and other jewels, there is still impermanance. The fact that objects are seen by a vision which arises from modification, cannot create a restriction in a permanent vision.

(Opponent) The knowledge does not arise from modification: it *is* modification.

(Answer) Then there should be knowledge in other things like the body, which also have modifications.

So it is established that Puruṣa is pure vision alone, and unchanging because he always knows his object. Although his nature is unchanging awareness, still, due to the presence or absence of mental ideas of seen objects, the statements are made: 'he sees', 'he will cause to see', 'he has seen'. These are like statements about its shining in the case of the sun (savitṛ) and other lights. The statement that the sun illumines, or will illumine, or is brightly illumining are designations according to the presence or absence of something illumined. The mind and other such things which are subject to purity (and other variations) are counter-examples. Thus it is not similar.

The mind is for-the-sake-of-another, inasmuch as it is a collaborator with body and senses and objects, whereas Puruṣa is self-sufficient (svārtha). Again, the mind determines what all the things are, and therefore consists of the three guṇa-s; as consisting of the three guṇa-s, it is unconscious. But Puruṣa as the overseer (upa-draṣṭṛ) of the guṇa-s is not like the mind.

(Opponent) Then he must be unlike it.

(Answer) Not absolutely unlike. Why not? Because though pure, he looks on at the idea. Looking on, he appears as if he were of its nature, though he is not of its nature.

It has been said: 'The changeless power-of experience which does not pass over, seems to have passed over into the changing object, falling onto the mental process. What is called the mental process of knowing is a taking on of the form of borrowed consciousness, by mere resemblance to the mental process, and not distinguished from it.'

The mind like ears, etc., *consists of the three guṇa-s because it determines all things* the totality of the objects, peaceful or violent or delusive. *But Puruṣa as the overseer (upa-draṣṭṛ)* is by reason of his witnesshood apart from the three guṇa-s. This is the proposition, and the mind, etc., are adduced as counter-instances, to show that as Puruṣa is apart from the three guṇa-s, he is not like the mind.

(Opponent) *Then he must be unlike it* and consequently will never come to experience, just because he is absolutely unlike the mind.

(Answer) The reply is: *Not absolutely unlike. Why not?* Your point is, that there is no reason to establish that the pure one, opposed to the nature of the mind, is not absolutely unlike the impure mental ideas. But this is not so, because it is established that he is witness of the mind and its ideas. *Because though pure, he looks on at the mental idea (bauddha-pratyaya), and* that perception of the mental idea is a demonstrated fact. When it is said that he looks on, the meaning is that he sees the mental idea which has assumed the form of the object. *Though he is not of its nature* not of the three guṇa-s, *looking on it, he appears as if he were of its nature,* as if of peaceful or violent or delusive character. So he is not absolutely different, because of his conformity in practice. It was said that Puruṣa would be explained as the witness of the mind, and this has now been done, and his resemblance (to the mind) has also been pointed out. As it is said in the scripture (tantra), *The changeless power-of-experience* the power-of-sight *which* as described already *does not pass over (into anything), seems to have passed over into the changing object* into the idea of the mind, having that as its object, *falling onto the mental process,* seeming to fall on to the mental process by its observation of it as a witness. It is from the power-of-sight (dṛk-śakti) that the mental idea gets its state of being an object when it arises.

Falling on to it as it perceives it, the power-of-experience is *taking on its form of borrowed consciousness,* acquiring its form of being endowed with consciousness, the form of being endowed with a Puruṣa, the form attained by that mental process, as a lump of glowing iron gets the form of being endowed with fire from being the object-of-sight, *by mere resemblance to the mental process* by its mere conformity to the mental process *and not distinguished from it,* this is *what is called the mental process of knowing (jña),* the mental process of pure knowing, being the mental process of mere perception (upalabdhi).

Sūtra II.21

The essence of the Seen is to be for the purpose of him alone

Since the Seen has its being as an object for Puruṣa, whose nature is sight alone, the essence of the Seen is to be for the purposes of him alone. It means that this is its true being. Therefore it has come to exist at all only through the being of that other, and when the purposes of experience and release have been effected, it is not seen by Puruṣa.

Him refers back to the Seer, sight alone, pure, whose self is as has been described; *for the purposes of him* means for him, for his sake, for his purpose, for which it becomes the object of sight. The purposes are either as experience or as release. *The essence of the Seen* means the essence of pradhāna, what it is in itself.

(Opponent) But this work is supposed to be setting out the four-fold field; why this irrelevancy?

(Answer) The goal is absolute cessation of suffering, and that is relevant.

(Opponent) But how can this absolute cessation of suffering you talk of come about through ascertaining that the Seen is for the purposes of Puruṣa?

(Answer) If it is realized that the nature of the Seen is only for his purposes, then when that purpose comes to an end completely, the Seen has fulfilled its purpose, and the Seen will end completely because there is nothing for it to do; there would be no goal for any activity by it. When a thing has in fact been done, there is nothing to make a new duty of it. But if the Seen were essentially self-sufficient (svārtha), then from that self-sufficiency it would again and again go into operation, and there would never be absolute cessation. This is why it is shown that it is only for the sake of Puruṣa.

The essence of the Seen is, that it is not self-sufficient, because the Seen is by definition something experienced, like a dish of rice, and because it is unconscious, and because it is something which collaborates (with body, senses and object). So he says, *Since the Seen has its being as an object for Puruṣa, whose nature is sight alone.* The word *iti* means 'since'. *The essence of the Seen is to be for the purposes of him alone. It means that this is its true being.* The raison d'être of pradhāna is only for the purposes of Puruṣa because it is in the position of object of sight, like a dish of rice.

Now he brings out what the sūtra intends to say: *Therefore* because it is limited to being for the purpose of Puruṣa *it has come to exist at all* as taking on the form of borrowed consciousness *by the nature of the other. When the purposes of experience and release have been effected, it is not seen by Puruṣa,* there being nothing to be effected apart from experience and release.

Losing its character, it comes to an end. Yet it does not end. How so?

Sūtra II.22

For one whose purpose has been effected, it is ended, but not for others, because it is common

> *In regard to a particular Puruṣa, the Seen is ended, but though it has come to an end, it is not ended for others, because it is common. For the skilful Puruṣa it comes to an end, but for the unskilful Puruṣa the purpose has not been effected, and for these it becomes their object of sight, given that nature by the nature of the other.*

In regard to a particular Puruṣa, one for whom the Seen has fulfilled its purpose, the Seen as an object would not be appearing: *Losing its character, it comes to an end. Yet it does not end* for all. *How so?* Why is this? There are many pradhāna-s, one for each Puruṣa, and it is only the one which has fulfilled its purpose that is to be regarded as being ended. *For one whose purpose has been effected, it is ended, but not ended for others, because it is common.* In regard to the Puruṣa for whom it has fulfilled its purpose by providing experience and release, so that the goal has been attained, in regard to that one Puruṣa there is no further impulse to action in the form of body and senses (kārya-karaṇa); *it is ended* since there is no character of being-nonbeing (i.e. the Great and its derivatives). *Though it is* said to be *ended* for him, it is not ended for others, because it is common. For those whose purpose has not been effected, it is not ended.

How is it not ended? *For the skilful Puruṣa it comes to an end;* by providing experience and then release, it has effected its purpose; *for the unskillful Puruṣa-s the purpose has not been effected,* it has not provided the experience and release which were to be provided, *and for these* unskilful ones *it becomes the object of sight;* they themselves being sight, it becomes the seen object of that sight, *given that nature by the nature of the other,* by the reflection (nirbhāsa) of Puruṣa in it. From this fact of being common, pradhāna is one alone, like the elements such as earth. But from the distinction of body and senses (kārya-karaṇa) it is certain that there is a variety of Puruṣa-s, and the difference between Puruṣa-s is also established from the fact of variety of happiness and suffering.

Therefore it is taught that the conjunction of the two powers of Seer and Seen is beginningless, because it is eternal. In this sense it has been said: There being a beginningless conjunction between the possessors of qualities (dharmin) and the qualities themselves, so between the qualities themselves, the conjunction is beginningless.

Therefore it is taught that the conjunction of the two powers of Seer and Seen is beginningless, because it is eternal. In this sense it has been said in the holy text (tantra): *There being a beginningless conjunction between the possessors of qualities (and the qualities themselves),* as there is a beginningless conjunction between the guṇa-s and Puruṣa-s, *so between the qualities themselves* from the Great Principle down to the body and senses *the conjunction* with Puruṣa-s *is beginningless,* the possessors being not separate from their qualities.

This sūtra is put forward with the intention of determining the nature of the conjunction:

Sūtra II.23

The conjunction causes awareness of the natures of the two powers, the property and its possessor

Puruṣa is the possessor who is joined to his own seen object for the purpose of seeing. Awareness of the seen object, arising from that conjunction, is experience; but awareness of the nature of the Seer is release.

The Seen has been determined; the Seer has been determined. It has been said that the conjunction of Seer and Seen is the cause of what-is-to-be-escaped, and now it has to be determined what sort of conjunction this is. The sūtra says, *The conjunction causes awareness of the nature of the two powers, the property and its possessor.*

The two powers, property and its possessor, are the mind and Puruṣa, and the conjunction *causes,* effects, awareness of their natures. That by whose existence the two natures – as of a face and mirror, as it were – are apprehended, is what causes awareness of the two natures.

Right knowledge (pramāṇa) of it is awareness of the nature of mind and of Puruṣa preceded by their conjunction, it being awareness of the nature of an object and its possessor, like the knowledge of the nature of the perceiving eye and the mirror. Awareness of pleasure and pain, such as the awareness of pleasure or pain from (fragrant) sandalwood or thorns, met with in the world of contrarieties, is preceded by conjunction causing pleasure and pain, from the fact that it is an awareness.

Puruṣa is the possessor who is joined to his own object to his own mind (buddhi) *for the purpose of seeing* for the purpose of seeing experience and release. The meaning is that the conjunction is through seeing alone. *Awareness* linked with seeing *of the Seen, arising from that conjunction is* not discriminated, and so is *experience; but awareness of the Seer,* being discriminated, *is release.*

In so far as the conjunction comes to an end when there is seeing and its result, seeing is said to be the cause of disjunction; and failure-to-see, as the opposite of seeing, is said to be the cause of conjunction. It is not that seeing causes release (mokṣa), because release is absence of bondage, simply from absence of failure-to-see. Seeing, namely knowledge, is said to bring about

Transcendental Aloneness (kaivalya) only in the sense that in the presence of seeing there is annihilation of failure-to-see which is the cause of bondage.

Inasmuch as the conjunction is linked to both seeing and the effect (of it), *the conjunction comes to an end when there is seeing and its result. Seeing is said to bring about Transcendental Aloneness only in the sense that seeing* as directed to Puruṣa *is said to be the cause of disjunction;* seeing that the guṇa-s and Puruṣa are different is called the cause of the disjunction of pradhāna and Puruṣa, because by that seeing, that effect comes to an end. Seeing truly what it is that brings into being saṃsāra and wanderer-in-saṃsāra (samsārin), removes the cause which conjoins the sufferer and the pain. What it sees is the true nature of sufferer and suffering, so it is like seeing the true nature of the cause of illness of a sick man.

Ignorance (a-vidyā) is the cause of joining the Seer to the Seen. As it is Ignorance that causes the pain-giving conjunction, it is like a false suggestion (mithyā-jñāna) of having been in contact with something harmful, which actually causes illness. The connection of Seer and Seen is preceded by illusory knowledge (mithyā-jñāna), and as causing pain, it resembles that (false idea) of having been in contact (with something harmful such as poison) in the case of a sick man. Inasmuch as *the opposite of seeing* the true nature of what is causing pain to the sufferer *is failure-to-see,* which sees it wrongly, *failure-to-see is said to be the cause of the conjunction,* meaning that its cause is Ignorance, and from the fact that the conjunction is pain-giving.

Inasmuch as seeing simply removes failure-to-see and brings about no other effect, *it is not that seeing causes release: release is absence of* painful *bondage simply* merely *from the absence of failure-to-see.* Nor is release something that has to be brought about apart from the absence of bondage, and this is why it is always accepted that release is eternal.

In the presence of seeing, in the presence of seeing directed to the field of Seer-Seen, *there is annihilation of failure-to-see* in that regard. For seeing and failure-to-see in regard to the same location are contradictories, like two areas of darkness and sunshine. In that sense *seeing is said to bring about Transcendental Aloneness (kaivalya)* as in the sūtra 'The means of escape is unwavering Knowledge-of-the-difference' (II.26).

What then is this failure-to-see?

(Opponent) Why, it has already been said that it is simply Ignorance, and on the analogy of negative forms like 'no friend' and 'trackless' it was explained as knowledge from illusion (viparyaya).

(Answer) True. But interpretations of a text are put forward by various parties to support their own ideas, and refuting views proposed by others is the best approach to confirming the views proposed by one's own side.

> *(1) Is it the involvement (adhikāra) of the guṇa-s?*
> *(2) Or is it the non-appearance of the mind (citta) as object for its owner whose nature is sight – namely, the absence of that seeing by which the object is known to its owner?*
> *(3) Is it the purposiveness of the guṇa-s?*

As to what this failure-to-see is, various views are now taken up for examination:

(1) Is it the involvement (adhikāra) of the guṇa-s? The general inquiry now comes down to specific questions. The involvement of the guṇa-s is their engagement (adhikṛti), their operation (pravṛtti).

(Opponent to this view) How can failure-to-see ever be supposed to be involvement of the guṇa-s?

(Answer by the proponent) From the sense of the compound, failure-to-see can certainly be involvement. In so far as there is operation of the guṇa-s, there is bondage, and the fact that the cause of bondage is Ignorance (a-vidyā) would be a strong confirmation of it. Then from the point of view of the words themselves, failure-to-see (a-darśana) is what is other than seeing (darśana), in which case there can be the supposition, because involvement of the guṇa-s is other than seeing.

(2) *Or is it the non-appearance of the mind (citta) as object for sight for its owner (svāmin) whose nature is sight?* Here the position is put forward on the basis of taking the first element (the negative a-) of the compound a-darśana (failure-to-see) as the principal element. *non-appearance of the mind:* before it appears, there is no seeing. As to what this so-called non-appearance is, he says further: *the absence of that seeing where the object* the mind *is known to its owner.* Failure-to-see is the absence of seeing that Puruṣa and the guṇa-s are different.

(3) *Is it the purposiveness of the guṇa-s?* The guṇa-s are purposive, acting for experience and release, and this is failure-to-see. Here the supposition relates to a concept (not to the words as such) of failure-to-see, and the point is that when something has a purpose, that purpose inevitably is fulfilled.

Now what is the fallacy in these views? The reply is: if failure-to-see were involvement in the guṇa-s, then knowledge (vidyā) would turn out to be useless. For in this view it would not become an opponent to failure-to-see. Knowledge and involvement not being in opposition, it would mean that there is no release, because the guṇa-s might come into operation again and again, by reason of the purpose which they have.

There is the same defect in the view that failure-to-see is the purposiveness of the guṇa-s, and also in the view of it as non-appearance of the mind, for absence of the mind will be absence of seeing, and if it (mind) is not actually there, knowledge cannot bring about its cessation. If it is not there, there is no place for its antagonist either.

> *(4) Is it Ignorance inhibited along with its mind, being the seed from which mind arises?*
>
> *(5) Is it manifestation of the saṃskāra of activity when the saṃskāra of stasis ceases? On this it has been said: 'If pradhāna were stasis alone, then anything functioning would not be pradhāna, because pradhāna should not be a cause of change; and if pradhāna were activity alone in functioning, again it would not be pradhāna because change would be perpetual. It gets its role as pradhāna by functioning in both ways, and only so. As regards other proposed causes, the same reasoning applies.'*

(4) *Is it Ignorance inhibited along with its mind, being the seed from which mind arises?* The proponent gives an alternative: distinction of a part of Ignorance as failure-to-see. In what way? Ignorance uninhibited is seen, and this is seeing. When inhibited, it is dissolved along with the mind into its *cause, being the seed from which mind arises,* the cause of that rise. That (inhibited) Ignorance is not seen, and there is therefore failure-to-see – that is the idea. But this view must certainly be defective in that it entails 'seeing' of the uninhibited state. But if it were amended to failure-to-see of both inhibited and uninhibited states, the conclusion would be unobjectionable.

(5) *Is it manifestation of the saṃskāra of activity when the saṃskāra of stasis ceases?* The connection with failure-to-see is not clear, but it may be explained thus: it is being said here that Ignorance inhibited along with its mind is

the seed from which mind rises, and it is implied that mind is inhibited in its own cause and then rises again. It is further implied that though the cause of the mind, it functions both in stasis and activity. The point was raised to make this clear. Stasis (sthiti) here means the saṃskāra which causes the state of equipoise of the guṇa-s. Then it says *when the saṃskāra of stasis ceases, manifestation of the saṃskāra of activity,* namely the saṃskāra going into operation in the form of the Great principle and the rest.

He illustrates what would be the defect if it functioned as stasis alone or as activity alone: *If pradhāna were stasis alone, then any thing functioning would not be pradhāna, because it would not be a source of change,* because (out of stasis) there would be no transformations in the form of the Great principle etc. But pradhāna is that from which originate (pradhatte) changes, and this not being such, would not be pradhāna.

If pradhāna were activity alone ever functioning in the form of change, then *change would be perpetual;* so it would not be a source (pradhātṛ) of change, and without that function, would not be pradhāna.

It gets its role as pradhāna by functioning in both ways in activity and in stasis *and only so* is pradhāna truly pradhāna. In fact *as regards other proposed causes* such as Puruṣa, a divine Lord (īśvara) or ultimate atoms (paramāṇu), *the same reasoning applies* reasoning on similar lines.

(6) Some hold that failure-to-see is the bare potential of seeing, for a holy text says that the activity of pradhāna is for the purpose of making itself known.

(7) Some say that Puruṣa with the power of knowing all, does not see before (pradhāna) goes into activity: the Seen with the powers of all effects and instruments is not then seen.

(6) The point is now illustrated: *Some hold that failure-to-see is the bare potential of seeing.* It is the potential of seeing in the unmanifest state, the seed as it were, the state where no sprout is yet manifest, and that is failure-to-see. Some hold this. On what authority? *A holy text (śruti) says that the activity of pradhāna is for the purpose of making itself known,* showing what it has to display. The failure-to-see is of this.

In this view, failure-to-see is a power essentially unmanifest, which when manifest is seeing. But as there would be no inherent opposition (between them), it would not be appropriate that failure-to-see should cease as a result of such seeing.

(7) Now another view: *Puruṣa with the power of knowing all* by its nature as a knower *before pradhāna goes into action, does not see* even though seeing is his nature: *the Seen pradhāna with the powers of all effects and instruments* and action *is not then seen* before going into operation, though in the final analysis existent. This is the state of failure-to-see of pradhāna and of Puruṣa.

Here too, for both of them, the earlier state alone is failure-to-see and the later one is seeing, so that the previous defect has not been touched.

> *(8) Some think of failure-to-see as a property of both. Though essentially of the Seen, dependent as it is on an idea in Puruṣa, seeing is as a property in Puruṣa. Though essentially not of Puruṣa, dependent as it is on an idea of the Seen, failure-to-see just appears a property in Puruṣa.*

(8) *Some think of failure-to-see as a property of both* pradhāna and Puruṣa. *Though essentially of the Seen,* not apart (from the Seen) *it is dependent on an idea in Puruṣa.* It is not seen by Puruṣa as such in his own nature, but it is seen by Puruṣa as distinct from his own nature, and the failure-to-see is a property of Puruṣa in the sense that it depends on an idea in Puruṣa. He clarifies the point: *Though essentially not of Puruṣa, dependent as it is on an idea of the Seen.* The idea of the Seen is knowledge, and it is dependent on that. How is it dependent? It is not seen by Puruṣa as such, but is seen by a co-operation dependent on an idea in the inner organ (antaḥkaraṇa). *This failure-to-see appears as a property of Puruṣa alone, though its essence is not (in fact) of Puruṣa;* so there can be no objection to taking it solely as a property of the Seen. All this has been for the sake of putting forward all the views.

> *(9) Seeing is knowledge, and that very knowledge is failure-to-see – so think some.*
>
> *These are the accepted views, and there are this many opinions about it.*

(9) *Seeing is knowledge, and that very knowledge is failure-to-see – so think some.* This idea assumes that the second element of the compound (a-darśana – failure-to-see) is the principal. Its defect has been exposed already under the sūtra on Ignorance (II.5).

These are the accepted views held by other schools *and there are this many opinions about it.* The point is, that the final conclusion is not to be determined by a majority verdict. Failure-to-see is properly defined as the cause of conjunction of mind (buddhi) and Puruṣa, because it is the opposite of seeing (the difference between them). The point has been made clear and need not be laboured.

The conjunction of each Puruṣa with the guṇa-s is the same; what is individual is the conjunction of the separate consciousness (pratyak-cetana) with its own mind.

Sūtra II.24

Its cause is Ignorance (a-vidyā)

This means the saṃskāra-complex (vāsanā) of illusory knowledge (viparyaya-jñāna).

The conjunction of each Puruṣa with the guṇa-s is the same. The conjunction of all of them with the guṇa-s is the same in each case. It is common, but *what is individual is the conjunction of the separate consciousness (pratyak-cetana),* the witness of the ideas of the mind (bauddha-pratyaya) *with its own mind.* And it is the failure-to-see by which this individual conjunction with its own mind comes about. *Its cause* the cause of the conjunction which makes it take the relation of possessor and possessed as its own true nature *is Ignorance; this means the saṃskāra-complex (vāsanā) of illusory knowledge (viparyaya-jñāna).*

(Opponent) But it has been said, 'Illusion is false knowledge based on an untrue form' (I.8), and it has been said that Ignorance is 'conviction of permanence, purity and happiness and self in what are really impermanent, impure, painful and not-self. How is it now said to be the saṃskāra-complex of illusory knowledge?

(Answer) It is not wrong to say so. As the effect of Ignorance, the saṃskāra-complex is spoken of as Ignorance itself. When all causes are dissolved and there is the state of sameness, the saṃskāra-complex of illusion again and again makes pradhāna go into function. Actual illusion is never a cause of the functioning because it does not exist before the rise of mind (buddhi), and so it is taught that it is the saṃskāra-complex of illusion which is the cause of the conjunction of pradhāna and Puruṣa.

Under the influence of the saṃskāra-complex of illusory knowledge, mind does not attain fulfilment of what it has to do, namely to know Puruṣa. While it has that involvement, again and again it revives. But in the culminating Knowledge of Puruṣa it attains fulfilment of what it had to do. With its involvement at an end, and failure-to-see gone, there is no cause of bondage and it does not revive again.

Under the influence of the saṃskāra-complex of illusory knowledge, mind does not attain fulfilment of what it has to do, it does not complete what it has to do, which is *to know Puruṣa,* as he says. For knowledge of Puruṣa is incumbent on the mind for its fulfilment, and the mind does not attain it *while it has that involvement* while that is incumbent on it; *again and again it revives* by the force of the saṃskāra-complex of illusory knowledge. But when it is fulfilled in Knowledge of Puruṣa, it attains its goal. He adds a further explanation:

With its involvement at an end, and failure-to-see gone, there is no cause of bondage. Failure-to-see alone is what binds, because karma and the fruition of karma have this as their root. When failure-to-see ceases, bondage ceases, being without its cause, *and it* (mind) *does not revive again.*

Here someone interrupts with the parable of the impotent man, who is asked by his simple-minded wife: 'O impotent Sir! My sister has a son, why not I?' He tells her, When I am dead, I will beget you a son.' So here, the Knowledge being present now does not cause the mind to cease, so what hope is there that it will do when it has disappeared?

To this, one who is near to being a teacher says in reply: 'But it is cessation of mind (buddhi) that is release. In the absence of its cause, failure-to-see, mind ceases, and that failure-to-see, cause of bondage, ceases through seeing. So it is cessation of mind (citta) that is release. Why then this needless confusion of his?'

Here someone interrupts with the parable of the man who is asked by his simple-minded wife: 'O impotent Sir! My sister has a son, why not I?' He tells her, 'When I am dead, I will beget you a son.' So here, the Knowledge being present now does not cause the mind to cease, so what hope is there that it will do so when it has disappeared?

(Opponent) The point is, that if Ignorance (a-vidyā) is the cause of the conjunction of mind and Puruṣa, and Knowledge (vidyā) makes Ignorance cease, then the rise of Knowledge ought to annul its opposite, Ignorance. But in fact Ignorance does not cease as soon as Knowledge arises. And if Ignorance thus does not cease when Knowledge is there, it will not cease when the Knowledge has perished, any more than there will be a son from an impotent man just because he is dead. And therefore Ignorance is not the cause of the conjunction.

(Answer) *To this, one who is near to being a teacher replies.* He is said to be only near to being a teacher in order to bring out the futility of the opponent's position. He interposes in reply: *In the absence of its cause, failure-to-see, mind ceases, and that failure-to-see, cause of bondage, ceases through seeing. Cessation of mind is release. Why then this needless confusion of his?*

It has been explained in detail that Ignorance is the cause of the conjunction of pradhāna and Puruṣa, that conjunction being itself the cause of suffering. It is by Knowledge that Ignorance ceases, and there should be no confusion about it. When it ceases, there must be a cessation of mind itself. Apart from Ignorance, there is no other cause of conjunction with mind, and therefore it is cessation of mind that is release.

As for the objection that buddhi does not cease to be immediately upon the rise of Knowledge, it is not valid. For the cause-effect relation is of more than one kind. For instance, carpenters and others build palaces; the palaces do not cease to be when the builders, their causes, have ceased work. And when a tree is broken, no special mark of that is immediately apparent (in the leaves). In the same way, while the saṃskāra-s, like a shot arrow in the air, have not yet exhausted themselves, for a time corresponding to the saṃskāra-s the mind continues its merely apparent existence. So the sacred text says, 'For him there is delay only so long (as he is not delivered from the body; then he will be perfect.' Chānd. VI. 14.2)

Pain that is to be escaped, conjunction as the cause of what is to be escaped, and the cause of the conjunction, have been declared. Now final release is to be spoken of.

Sūtra II.25

Without it, there is no conjunction, and that release is Transcendental Aloneness (kaivalya) of the power-of-sight

Without that failure-to-see there is no conjunction of mind and Puruṣa. That means absolute cessation of bondage. This is release (hāna), the Transcendental Aloneness of the power-of-sight. It is the state of detachment of Puruṣa, and no further conjunction with the guṇa-s. Then Puruṣa is said to be established in his own nature. Cessation of pain and disappearance of its cause is release.

The subject-matter of the work was said to come under four headings (on sūtra 1.1). Of these, one heading, compared to the illness (in medical works) has been explained as *Pain that is to be escaped,* in the words 'What is to be escaped is pain not yet come' (sūtra II.16). *Conjunction as the cause of what is to be escaped, and the cause of the conjunction, have been declared.* This is the second heading, corresponding to the cause of the illness. The cause of what is to be escaped has been described in detail as the conjunction of pradhāna and Puruṣa, along with Ignorance which is the cause of that. The elaboration of the explanations was to dispel any doubt as to the correct view.

Now final release (paraṃ hānam) corresponding to the state of health, the goal of the classics on release, *is to be spoken of.* The declaration that something is to be said is to bring the hearer's mind to concentration (samādhānam).

Without it, there is no conjunction, and that release is Transcendental Aloneness of the power-of sight. It refers back to the Ignorance already explained. *Without that failure-to-see* which is Ignorance *there is no conjunction of mind and Puruṣa* which is the cause of pain; *that means absolute cessation of bondage. This is release,* absolute cessation of bondage, Transcendental Aloneness of the power-of-sight Puruṣa. It is described further: *It is the state of detachment of Puruṣa, and no further conjunction with the guṇa-s.*

Having explained the meaning of the individual words, now he deals with the sentence as a whole. *The cessation of pain on disappearance of its cause is release. Then Puruṣa is said to be established in his own nature.* As it is going to be said (in sūtra IV.34): 'The power-of-consciousness established in its own nature.'

(Opponent) But while there is karma of indeterminate fruition still in existence, how can there be release? A new body will be formed by that karma of indeterminate fruition.

(Answer) No; it has been shown already how this is obviated. It was explained that the karma-s are made inoperative by the scorching of the seeds of taint (kleśa-bīja) by right Knowledge (samyag-darśana), as in the example of chaff, rice, and grain reduced to the state of scorched seeds, and so to sterility. So for the Knower (vidvat) there is no taking on of a new body, for there is nothing to cause it.

Now what is the means to obtain release?

The third division, corresponding to the healthy condition, has been dealt with, namely release (hāna), and now the fourth, which is comparable to the medical treatment, is to be taken up: *Now what is the means to obtain release?*

(Opponent) How can there be a means to obtain release? Release is not a thing which can be obtained, for it is simply cessation of bondage.

(Answer) You are wrong. For Ignorance to cease, something has to be done, with effort, as in the breaking of a fetter. Though release is not a *thing,* inasmuch as it is cessation of Ignorance in the presence of right Knowledge (samyak-khyāti), it is figuratively spoken of as something to be obtained.

Sūtra II.26

Unwavering Knowledge-of-the-difference is the means of release

Knowledge-of-the-difference is the idea that (mind-)sattva and Puruṣa are different. But this wavers, until illusory knowledge has ceased. When illusory knowledge is reduced to the condition of sterility like scorched seed, the sattva, cleansed of the taints of rajas, reaches the highest purity of consciousness of mastery; its flow of the ideas of Knowledge-of-the-difference becomes without taint.

Unwavering Knowledge-of-the-difference (viveka-khyāti) is the means of release. As to what that Knowledge-of-the-difference is which is being referred to, he says: *Knowledge-of-the-difference is the idea that (mind-)sattva and Puruṣa are different,* namely a correct awareness of where sattva and Puruṣa are similar and where they are distinct. *But this* Knowledge-of-the-difference *wavers* is not firm (sthira), is not effective, *until illusory knowledge (mithyā-jñāna) has ceased.*

As it is said:

As gold unrefined does not shine,
So the knowledge of an immature man attached to the world does not shine forth.

(Viṣṇusahasranāma 77)

And again:

Though the man who holds to desire and possession may have knowledge,
It does not sustain itself.

(Mahābh. XII.227.20)

But when illusory knowledge, like a scorched seed is reduced to sterility unable to produce any effect, *the sattva, cleansed of the taints of rajas* the taints themselves being rajas, it is now undefiled by any such impurity, *reaches the highest purity called consciousness of mastery;* it reaches the pure serenity of Knowledge (jñāna-prasād), and *its flow of the ideas of Knowledge-of-the-difference becomes untainted,* in which state this Knowledge is continuous.

This Knowledge-of-the-difference, unwavering, is the means to release. Thereby illusory knowledge is reduced to the condition of scorched seeds and unable to propagate any more, so Knowledge-of-the-difference is the path to release and the means of escape.

This Knowledge-of-the-difference thus untainted becomes *unwavering,* and when it is thus unwavering, *illusory knowledge is reduced to the condition of a scorched seed* because it is overcome *and unable to propagate any more,* just because it is like a scorched seed. So it is said:

As seeds scorched by fire do not sprout any more,

So with taints scorched by the fire of Knowledge; The self meets them no more.

(Mahābhārata XII.204,16a)

In the same way *Knowledge-of-the-difference is the path to release (mokṣa) and the means of escape (hāna).*

Sūtra II.27

Therein, the ultimate state of the Knowledge is seven-fold

The word Therein refers to the uprisen Knowledge (khyāti). Seven-fold: the Knowledge of the Knower-of the-difference, when no other ideas arise in the mind because the dirt of veiling impurity has gone, is of just seven aspects. They are:

(1) What is to be escaped has been fully examined and needs no more examining;

(2) The causes of what is to be escaped have dwindled away and need to be destroyed no more;

Now to show the characteristic conviction of his own experience in the man of right vision when that vision has awakened in him, he says: *Therein, the ultimate state of the Knowledge (prajñā) is seven-fold. The word Therein refers to* recalls *the uprisen Knowledge* the right vision now existing. *Because the dirt (mala) of veiling impurity has gone:* the veiling is merely impurity – taints and karma-s. They are dirt, and because that has gone, *no other ideas arise in the mind* no contrary ideas of other things such as 'mine' and 'I'. *Seven-fold:* he explains that *the Knowledge* the mind *of the Knower-of the-difference is of seven aspects.* Now he lists the seven divisions in order.

(1) *What is to be escaped has been fully examined:* suffering of every kind is what is to be escaped, and it has been known as such by conclusive proof, *and* the question of pain *needs no more examining.*

(2) *Its causes have dwindled away and need to be destroyed no more.* The plural indicates taints and karma-s both. There is not the smallest part of the taints and karma-s which has not been roasted by the fire of Knowledge and reduced to a scorched seed, and which would need to be further destroyed.

Here again it is to be called an ultimate state. There is nothing therefore to be destroyed in any idea, whether conformable or opposing, for its taints have dwindled away. Then the idea comes 'I am one who has done what was to be done', which is an idea marking maturity of right vision (saṃyagdarśana-paripāka), like the idea in one recovered from illness 'The cause of the illness has been destroyed and I am well: no more treatment.' Thus the second division of ultimate Knowledge has been explained.

> *(3) The samādhi of inhibition is release directly experienced:*
> *(4) Knowledge-of-the-difference, the means to release, has been perfected.*

> *These make up the four-fold freedom of Knowledge from anything left to be done.*

(3) *The samādhi of inhibition (nirodha samāpatti) is release directly experienced.* As it is close to release and of like form to release, the samādhi of inhibition is itself called release. The release is *directly experienced,* made the object of actual feeling. This is realized to be the final state of Transcendental Aloneness, the aloneness that was to be achieved. This is called the third aspect of the Knowledge which has reached its final state.

(4) *Knowledge-of the-difference, the means to release, has been perfected,* rightly and intensely practised. When the Knowledge which arises in the Knower-of-the-difference has attained conviction that right vision is established in truth, that is the fourth aspect of Knowledge.

These make up the four-fold freedom from anything left to be done. It is freedom of the Knowledge from anything to be done, from any duty. This is the fourfold freedom of Knowledge from anything to be done, that is, from anything to be done for the purpose of Puruṣa.

Or again, *freedom from anything to be done* can mean freedom, that is to say cessation, of anything to be done. He sums up by saying that this is the freedom from anything to be done, and it is four-fold.

> *But freeing of the mind is three-fold.*

Already described is the four-fold freedom from anything to be done, as being without any purpose of Puruṣa. Now comes cessation of the mind-guṇa-s. The freeing of the enlightened mind (Knowledge-mind) is dissolution of these, which had to fulfil the purpose of Puruṣa and now are without any purpose of Puruṣa. It is said to be three-fold.

(5) *Having discharged their involvement, the guṇa-s as mind turn, like rocks dislodged from the top of a mountain peak, towards dissolution in its own cause, and along with it come to rest.*
(6) *Nor having dissolved do they again make an appearance, since there is no purpose for them.*
(7) *In that state, beyond any connection with the guṇa-s, Puruṣa is said to be the light of his own nature alone, solitary and pure.*

(5) *The guṇa-s as mind (buddhi-guṇa)* sattva and the other two in their adopted form of mind, *having discharged their involvement* with nothing left for them to do, *turn towards dissolution.* Like what? *Like rocks dislodged from the top of a mountain peak.* As there is nothing left to do, they turn towards dissolution *in its own cause,* in the I-principle (ahaṅkāra) *along with it* along with their effect in the shape of mind, or else it may mean that mind along with its cause the I-principle comes to the causal state of being, where it is not manifest to the skilful Puruṣa, *and come to rest.* That is said to be the first freeing of the illumined mind (prajñā-citta).

(6) *Nor having dissolved do they again make an appearance* to Puruṣa, *since there is no purpose for them.* For, as has already been said, there is freedom from anything left to be done. This is called the second freeing of the illumined mind.

(7) *In that state* of dissolution of the guṇa-s with their purpose gone, *beyond any connection with the guṇa-s,* the connection with the guṇa-s which is a matter of the Seer and Seen, is transcended, and *Puruṣa is the light of his own nature alone,* in his own nature as sight alone and thus light, *solitary and pure,* is said to be the third freeing of the illumined mind.

The Puruṣa who sees this Knowledge in the seven-fold final state is called 'skilful'. Though it is the mind that is dissolved, he is said to be skilful, but only in the sense of being beyond the guṇa-s, freed.

The Puruṣa who sees, who perceives the indications that right vision has reached maturity by the *Knowledge in the seven-fold final state,* final in that it has reached the limit of stages and states, *is called 'skilful'.* The word 'skilful' is merely suggestive. *Though it is the mind that is dissolved* which comes to an end, *he is said to be skilful,* skilful only in the sense of becoming what he always was. Why skilful? He replies, *In the sense of being beyond guṇa-s.* For he who has transcended the guṇa-s is skilful.

Knowledge-of-the-difference, when perfected, is the means to release. Every perfection must have its own means, and so this topic is begun:

Sūtra II.28

From following up the methods of yoga, destruction of impurity and a growing light of knowledge up to Knowledge-of-the-difference

Knowledge-of-the-difference when perfected, Knowledge-of-the-difference when mastered, attaining its ultimate fruit in the seven-fold ultimate state of knowledge, *is the means to release. Every perfection must have its own means.* He introduces the subject of the means to perfection of Knowledge-of-the-difference: *From following up the methods of yoga, destruction of impurity and a growing light of knowledge up to Knowledge-of-the-difference.*

This does not mean to say that Knowledge-of-the-difference comes about from practice of the yoga methods alone; perfection in it is in fact only for those who begin with worship of a guru, and practice of virtue (dharma). What he wishes to say is, that without this yoga as a means, it does not come about. The practice of the yoga methods is not the means by itself, but it is only out of that practice that the perfection in Knowledge-of-the-difference comes about. And so it is said by the teacher(s): 'Yoga is for the purpose of knowledge of truth (yogas tattva-jñānā-'rtha).'

Eight yoga methods are to be given. From practising them, illusory knowledge with its five parts, whose nature is impurity, is destroyed and perishes. When it is destroyed, there is manifestation of right vision. In proportion to the practice done, the impurity is thinned out. In proportion to its destruction, the light of knowledge increases correspondingly. The increase is an experience of increasing refinement up to Knowledge-of-the-difference, up to the realization of the true nature of the guṇa-s and Puruṣa.

Practice of the methods of yoga which are to be given, leads to destruction of impurity, namely the taints. With their destruction there is light, illumination. How far does this light develop? *up to Knowledge-of-the-difference* it is added in explanation.

Now the Commentator gives an elaboration of his own to make it clearer. *Eight yoga methods are to be given. From practising them, illusory knowledge with its five parts is destroyed and perishes. When it is destroyed, there is manifestation of right vision (samyag-darśana),* like a light.

How does it come about? *In proportion to the practice done, the impurity is thinned out.* And so Manu has said:

By prāṇāyāma-s let him destroy defects (doṣa) of body;
By concentrations (dhāraṇā), the sins,
By dissociation (pratyāhāra), sense attachments,
By meditation (dhyāna), attributes not divine. (VI.72)

In proportion to its destruction, the light of knowledge increases correspondingly, like that of the sun at the end of the cold season. *The increase is an experience of increasing refinement* of perception. How far does it go? *up to Knowledge-of-the-difference.* He explains this: *up to knowledge of the true nature of the guṇa-s and Puruṣa.* The refinement ends only in the Knowledge of the difference between sattva and Puruṣa.

> *Following up the yoga methods is the cause of disjunction from impurity, as the axe is the cause of disjunction of what it cuts; but it is the cause of attaining Knowledge-of-the-difference, as dharma is the cause of happiness. And it is not a cause of anything else.*
>
> *How many kinds of cause are there listed in the authoritative books? They are said to be just these nine: Origination, maintenance, manifestation, modification, ideation, attaining, disjunction, alteration, sustaining – thus according to tradition, cause is of nine kinds.*

Following up the yoga methods is the cause of disjunction from impurity and also the cause of attaining Knowledge-of-the-difference. It is a cause, as in the cases of dharma and the axe; but here a single cause has the double effect. *It is not a cause of anything else.* In connection with this subject of cause, he sets forth the causes recognized by authority. *How many causes are there in the authoritative books?* He replies that *They are said to be just these nine,* which he gives by quoting a verse: *Origination, maintenance, manifestation, modification, ideation, attaining, disjunction, alteration, sustaining – thus according to tradition, cause is of nine kinds.*

> *An originating cause of knowledge is the mind. A maintaining cause is the fact that mind is for the purposes of Puruṣa, just as the body is kept going by food. A manifesting cause is illumination of a form so that there is knowledge of the form. A modifying cause of the mind is a new object, as the juxtaposition of fire causes cooking. An ideational cause is the knowledge of smoke causing knowledge of fire.*

To show the distinctions between them, he gives examples.

An originating cause of knowledge is the mind, for knowledge is a process of the mind, which is as water to the waves.

A maintaining cause is the fact that mind is for the purposes of Puruṣa. Mind is kept going by the fact of the purposes, namely experience and release, *just as the body is kept going by food.*

A manifesting cause is illumination of a form so that there is knowledge of that form. There is no perception of a form not made manifest by light.

A modifying cause of the mind is a new object. By juxtaposition of another object, the mind undergoes a change, *as the juxtaposition of fire causes cooking.* Fire is the cause of the change in form of what is cooked in the modification called cooking.

An ideational cause is the knowledge of smoke causing knowledge of fire. It is the cause of a fruitful idea of right knowledge. When it was said before that mind is an originating cause of knowledge, the meaning was simply that mind is the material cause of knowledge (irrespective of content).

> *The attaining cause of Knowledge-of-the-difference is following up the yoga methods; the same is the cause of disjunction from impurity. An altering cause is like a goldsmith with gold. Then with the one idea of a woman, Ignorance is the cause of delusion, the fact of painfulness is cause of aversion, the fact of happiness is cause of passion, and discriminative knowledge is the cause of unconcern. A sustaining cause is the upholding of the senses by the body, and that by them; and the elements of the bodies, and they mutually of each other, among all, whether animal, human or divine.*

The attaining cause of Knowledge-of-the-difference is following up the yoga methods, as righteousness is the attaining cause of happiness; *the same is the cause of disjunction from impurity,* as an axe is the cause of cutting off.

An altering cause is like a goldsmith with gold, for having demolished one form of the gold, he fashions something different like a dish, and then demolishing that new dish, he fashions something else, an ornament. This is called alteration.

Then with the one idea of a woman, Ignorance is the cause of delusion, the fact of painfulness is cause of aversion towards that same idea of a woman, *the fact of happiness is cause of passion, and discriminative knowledge is the cause of unconcern* without any idea of repulsion or attraction. Thus the single idea of the woman is, like gold taking many shapes, separated into many by the differences of delusion, painfulness, happiness, and unconcern.

Sustaining cause: sustaining is support, *as the senses by the body,* for without the body, the senses do not have any support, *and that by them,* the senses (in turn) become the cause that sustains the body. For the body is sustained through the operations of the senses.

Further, *the elements* such as space are the sustaining cause *of the bodies,* for the elements are, as the basis, the sustaining cause of bodies from Brahmā down to a post; *and they mutually* are causes of sustaining each other by way of reciprocal assistance, *among all* the categories *animal, human and divine,* the sustaining cause. Why? Because of their mutual dependence. The animal bodies are the sustaining cause of the human and divine, serving as beasts of burden, as givers of milk, and for sacrifices, etc. And the human bodies, by sacrifices and by domestication, sustain the divine and animal respectively; so too the divine sustain the other two by providing the cold and hot and rainy seasons.

Similarly all classes and stages of life are causes of sustaining each other by helping. The whole world is upheld by mutual co-operation.

> *These then are the nine causes; their potential capacity applies to the other things also. But following up the methods of yoga is a cause in only the two ways.*

It has been said that there are just the nine forms of causality, and others are rejected. *Their potential capacity applies to the other things also* in accordance with their respective potentialities. *But following up the methods of yoga is a cause in only the two ways,* as has been explained.

Now what are the yoga methods, by practising which there will be the two-fold effect (disjunction from impurity, Knowledge-of-the-difference)?

Now the methods of yoga are defined.

Sūtra II.29

Restraints, observances, posture, restraint of vital currents, dissociation, concentration, meditation, samādhi are the eight methods

(Opponent) But in other yoga scriptures there are only six methods – the ones from posture onwards. They say, 'The yoga of six methods is now expounded', and so on. For posture and those which follow it do directly help towards samādhi; not so the restraints and observances.

(Answer) The objection does not hold, because following the restraints and observances is the basic qualification to practise yoga. The qualification is not simply that one wants to do yoga, for the holy text says: 'But he who has not first turned away from his wickedness, who is not tranquil and subdued, or whose mind is not at rest, he can never obtain the Self (even) by knowledge' (Kaṭha 1.2.24). And in the Atharva text, 'It is in those who have tapas and brahmacarya, in whom truth is established' (Praś. Up. I.15), and in the Gītā, 'Firm in their vow of brahmacarya' (VI.14). So the restraints and observances are methods of yoga.

Of the two, restraint is mentioned first to emphasize its supreme importance. For it is everywhere recognized that restraint is of the highest importance. When a yogin is qualified by practising restraint and observance, he can go on to the posture and other steps. Becoming steady in each preceding one, he is able to master the next. But if he has not mounted the previous step, he cannot get on to a higher one.

And it is said elsewhere:

Mastery of a firm sitting posture, or other instructions of yoga, are not, in the case of distracted people; productive of yoga.

Getting rid of the defects, and samādhi – these two will certainly produce it, and nothing else will.

This verse is to emphasize the supreme importance of samādhi and abandonment of all defects; it is not meant to exclude posture and the other methods.

We shall now explain in their due order how each of these yoga methods is practised, and what its nature is.

We shall now explain in their due order how each of these restraints and the other methods *is to be practised, and what its nature is,* for they cannot be practised without knowing what they are.

Sūtra II.30

Of these, harmlessness, truth-speaking, no stealing, brahmacarya, not holding possessions, are the restraints

Of these, harmlessness means, in no way and at no time to do injury to any living being. The other restraints and observances are rooted in this, and they are practised only to bring this to its culmination, only for perfecting this. They are taught only as means to bring this out in its purity. For so it is said: Whatever many vows the man of Brahman would undertake, only in so far as he thereby refrains from doing harm impelled by delusion, does he bring out harmlessness in its purity.

Of these methods, first of all the restraints are described: *Harmlessness, truth-speaking, no stealing, brahmacarya, not holding possessions, are the restraints. Of these, harmlessness (a-hiṃsā) means in no way* in no capacity and in no fashion *to do injury to any living being,* to give pain to any being, whether immobile or active.

That harmlessness, most important among the restraints and observances, is to be practised in every capacity – body, speech and mind – he shows by saying, *The other restraints* truth-speaking and so on *are rooted in this,* they have harmlessness as their goal, have this as their purpose, *and they are practised only in order to bring this to its culmination, only for perfecting this.* Perfection in harmlessness is their culmination. He further explains: *They are taught only as means to bring this out in its purity,* to bring about harmlessness in all its purity. *For so it is said: Whatever many vows the man of Brahman would undertake, only in so far as he thereby refrains from harmful actions impelled by delusion,* rooted in violence and causing violence, *does he bring out harmlessness in its purity.*

> *Truth-speaking is said to be speech and thought in conformity with what has been seen or inferred or heard on authority. The speech spoken to convey one's own experience to others should be not deceitful, nor inaccurate, nor uninformative. It is that uttered for helping all beings. But that uttered to the harm of beings, even if it is what is called truth, when the ultimate aim is merely to injure beings, would not be truth. It would be a sin.*

Undertaking various vows of truth and the others, and also other vows not in conflict with them, the cause of one's doing harm becomes inoperative, inasmuch as one is withdrawn from the excitement which causes it; then in the absence of that cause, a very pure harmlessness arises. As, for instance, if vowed to a life of begging, occasions of injury like ploughing cease for him.

Truth-speaking is said to be speech and thought in conformity with what has been seen or inferred or heard on authority. That is truth. When there is knowledge arrived at through accurate means of knowledge, the communication of that knowledge just as it is to another by speech and mind is the very operation called truth-speaking. He continues: *The speech spoken to convey one's own experience to others should not be deceitful,* as when one states what one knows to be a fact, but this very truth is being spoken with the aim of tricking some other person. So Yudhiṣṭhira said, 'Aśvatthāman is killed – I mean the elephant.' *(The second sentence was spoken in a low voice, and the hearer believed it was his own son Aśvatthāman who had been killed – Tr.)*

Nor inaccurate, as when one speaks what is untrue in the belief that it is true, *nor uninformative,* inappropriate to enlighten the hearer, as when the speech is characterized by ambiguous expressions and inconclusive arguments, dark sayings or archaisms and the like.

That which is thus free from defects, and spoken with sincerity *uttered for helping all beings* makes truth glorious; *but that uttered to the harm of beings* though it may have the force of fact, does not amount to truthfulness. *even if it is what is called truth,* being without defect in what is said, *when the ultimate aim is merely to injure beings, that would not be truth,* for what is based on injuring others, even though free from the three defects of speech, does not amount to truth.

It would be a sin. And furthermore, by that hypocritical gloss of righteousness, the appearance of truthful utterance, the deceiver will come to regions of deep darkness. Therefore let one take care that his speech is for the welfare of all. As it is said:

> Let one speak what is true, let one speak what is kind, Let him not speak what is true but unkind;
> Let him speak what is kind and not untrue – That is the eternal righteousness.
>
> (Manu 4.138)

Stealing is the improper appropriation to oneself of others' things: refusal to do it, in freedom from desire, is non-stealing.

Stealing is the improper appropriation to oneself of others' things under the impulse of desire: *refusal to do it is non-stealing.* The stealing cannot exist in those whose desire has been cut off, and the refusal of that stealing arising from absence of the desire is non-stealing.

Brahmacarya is restraint of the sex organ and other senses.

Brahmacarya is restraint of the sex organ, the sexual and other senses, by a man who frees himself from urgings, whether verbal or mental, to break the vow.

Seeing the defects in objects involved in acquiring them, and defending them, and losing them, and being attached to them, and depriving others of them, one does not take them to himself, and that is not holding possessions.

Seeing the defects in objects involved in acquiring them and defending them, and losing them and being attached to them, and depriving others of them, one does not take them to himself, he does not appropriate them to himself, does not take them, *and that is not holding possessions.* It does not mean failure to appropriate them because of impossibility of doing so. The above are the restraints.

But these,

Sūtra II.31

When practised universally without qualification of birth, place, time, or obligation, they are called the Great Vow

For instance, harmlessness qualified by birth would be that of a fisherman, where he does injury to fish alone but to nothing else. It may be qualified by place, 'I will not kill anything at a place of pilgrimage', or by time, 'I will not kill on the fourteenth day,' 'I will not kill on an auspicious day'. Even where not limited in these three ways, it may be qualified by obligation. Harmlessness and the others are to be maintained all the time and in all circumstances and in regard to all objects without any conscious lapse. Restraints so practised are said to be universal, and are termed the Great Vow.

But these: this is to rule out the idea that qualifications like birth, place, and time, which distinguish other dharma-s, must apply to these also. Harmlessness and the other restraints, as they are undertaken by renunciates, are called the Great Vow. That is to say, they are called the Great Vow when practised regardless of birth and place and time, and universally. The Great Vow is one that is great, whose greatness lies in its universality.

To explain this universality he instances the particular case of harmlessness (a-hiṃsā) as universal. It might for instance discriminate between species, as a fisherman who does injury to fishes alone and not to others. This is doing injury to the fish species, and as his harmlessness is qualified in respect of fishes and not applied to the fish class, it is not universal.

It may be qualified by place. How? *'I will not kill anything at a place of pilgrimage',* such as Prayāg. Harmlessness at holy places, but not extending to places other than those, is not universal.

It may be qualified by time, 'I will not kill on the fourteenth day' and *'I will not kill on an auspicious day'.* As not extending to times other than the fourteenth day or auspicious days, this too is not universal.

Even where not limited in these three ways, it may be qualified by obligation, obligation being some rule of duty, as that one might catch fish only for offering to gods or Brahmins, and not otherwise; and as this makes the exception of the circumstances of the obligation laid down by his faith and so on, it is not universal. Again there are examples of warriors who resolve, 'I shall kill in battle only, and not off the battlefield', and this limits his harmlessness by obligation.

These restraints *harmlessness and the others are to be maintained* without any restriction as to species, such as the species already mentioned, or place or time or obligations, *all the time and in all circumstances and in regard to all objects* all living beings *without any conscious lapse,* unwaveringly; these are then *universal, and are termed the Great Vow.*

Sūtra II.32

Purity, contentment, tapas, self-study, and devotion to the Lord are the observances

> *Of these, external purity is attained by using earths and such like, and by purity of diet and so on also. The internal is washing away stains of the mind.*

Purity, contentment, tapas, self-study, and devotion to the Lord, are the observances. Of these, external purity is attained by using earths and such-like, this last phrase indicating water, *and by purity of diet and so on,* meaning foods such as butter and milk; the word *also* implies purity in seeing and listening.

This is the external purity. Now *the internal,* namely *washing away stains of the mind* such as desire and anger, by the waters of meditation (bhāvanā) on their opposites.

> *Contentment is being satisfied with the resources at hand and so not desiring more.*

As a result of the satisfaction with what is at hand, even though there may be some lack, he has the feeling, 'It is enough.'

> *Tapas is endurance of the opposites. The opposites are hunger and thirst, heat and cold, standing and sitting, complete silence and merely verbal silence. Vows are undertaken by them in accordance with their circumstances, (forms of fasting like) kṛcchra, cāndrāyāna, and sāntapana and others.*

Tapas is endurance of the opposites. The opposites are hunger and thirst, the desire to eat and desire to drink. To endure them is tapas, either as they occur naturally, or stimulated by reducing food and drink. *heat and cold,* either not relieved at all or relieved only partially; *standing and sitting:* in the tradition it says, 'Let him stand during the day and sit at night' (Gaut. Dh. Sū. 3.8.6., Manu XI.225 paraphrased); *complete silence and merely verbal silence:* in complete silence, nothing like hand-signs is allowed, whereas in the limited silence, indications by hands, etc., are permitted and it is only actual speech that is banned. *Vows are undertaken by them* by the yogin-s *according to their circumstances,* consistent with what is possible for them. To rule out what (abnormal forms of tapas) would be inconsistent with, for instance, the homa rite, or with their duties, he adds: *according to their circumstances.*

What are these vows? *kṛcchra,* for instance in the form sacred to Prajāpati: 'let him for three days eat once in the morning, for three days once in the evening, for three days live on unsolicited alms, and for three days fast' (Manu XI.212); *cāndrāyāna:* such as yavamadhya ('grain-waist', beginning with one mouthful a day and increasing by one mouthful up to fifteen and then reducing again), or pipīlikāmadhya ('ant-waist', beginning with fifteen and reducing to one and then) 'one by one let him increase his food' as the tradition says (Manu XI.217, 218); *sāntapana:* 'living on the urine of cows, cow dung, milk, sour milk, clarified butter and a decoction of kuśa grass, and fasting during one (day and) night, that is called sāntapana kṛcchra' (Manu XI.213). When this has been done three times it is a Great Sāntapana. The words *and others* are to include such fasts as Parāka (twelve days).

> *Svādhyāya (self study) is study of works on release (mokṣa-śāstra) or repetition of praṇava (OM).*

Svādhyāya (self study) is study of works on release (mokṣa-śāstra) such as the Upaniṣad-s.

(Break in the MS)

> *... (from devotion to God, as it has been said in I.29:) 'Realization of the separate consciousness and absence of obstacles.'*

(The lost portion of the text must cover repetition of OM as one of the methods of svādhyāya, a method stressed by the commentator in sūtras I.27–29, and his comments on devotion to the Lord, which may have been combined with the OM repetition. The practices have already appeared in the first sūtra of this Second Part, and were commented upon there. The comments in this place need not necessarily have been brief, for the remarks on tapas, which appear in the same place and also here, are quite different, though the Vyāsa here is short. Tr.)

To these restraints and observances -

Sūtra II.33

If there is obstruction by contrary ideas, meditation on their opposite

> *When in a Brahmin, contrary ideas arise, such as harming others (in forms like) 'I will kill him who offends me', 'I will tell lies about him', 'I will take his wealth for myself, 'I will take my pleasure with his wives', 'I will make myself master of all he has' – thus opposed by the blazing fire of the contrary ideas which carry him out of his path, let him meditate on the opposite of these: 'Roasted on the cruel fires of saṃsāra, I have sought refuge in the yoga path of causing fear to none. Yet this same I, having given up the contrary ideas, am taking to them again, acting like a dog. As the dog licks his own vomit, so am I taking again to what had been given up' – so should he meditate.*
>
> *The same procedure should be applied to the items of the other sūtra (on observances).*

If there is obstruction to these restraints and observances by contrary ideas (vi-tarka), namely opposing (vi-) notions (tarka), *let him meditate on the opposite of these* in the way which is to be explained, for unless they are countered, these ideas will cast the yogin into violence and other offences. *When in the Brahmin (yogin) the contrary ideas arise.* What sort of things are these ideas of violence and the rest, which are the ideas contrary to harmlessness and the other vows, and which are which? The idea contrary to harmlessness is violence: *'I will kill him who offends me.'* Then the thought, *'I will tell lies about him'* is the contrary idea which opposes truth. The idea contrary to not stealing is, *'I will take his wealth for myself,* and contrary to brahmacarya is *'I will take my pleasure with his wives',* and contrary to non-possession is *'I will make myself master of all he has'.* The point is to show how in each case he is led into violence and the other sins. The idea of taking another's wealth for oneself is caused by one's own attachment to that other's wealth, and becoming master of all he has is the desire to be a lord, with wealth and retainers like a prince or chief or minister.

Thus opposed by the blazing fire of the contrary ideas which carry him out of his path, let him meditate on the opposite of these: 'Roasted on the cruel fires of saṃsāra, I have sought refuge in the yoga path of causing fear to none. Yet this same I, having given up the contrary ideas like violence *am taking to them again, acting like a dog.'* This means that his action is like that of a dog, or that he who acts so is like a dog. Let him meditate on the likeness. This reinforces the point. 'I am like that man; why should I be like that? it is not yogic' – so should he meditate.

The same procedure should be applied to the items of the other sūtra (on observances) as well. The ideas contrary to purity – 'I will not practise purity' – and contrary to the other observances are to be looked at one by one in the same way. The commentary has described the principles only in relation to the restraints, because those are absolutely compulsory; the fault of omitting them is correspondingly grave, and they need special care.

Sūtra II.34

The contrary ideas, violence and the others, done or caused to be done or approved of, preceded by greed, anger or delusion, mild, medium, or intense – all result in endless pain and Ignorance. This is the meditation on their opposite

Of these, violence is taken as the example. It is threefold: done, or caused to be done, or approved. And each one of these too is threefold: from greed, as by one desiring meat and skin; from anger, as by one believing himself injured; from delusion, as by one who thinks that thereby he will acquire merit. Then greed, anger, and delusion are again threefold, namely mild, medium, and intense, so that violence has twenty-seven divisions. Again these three last have three further sub-divisions, mildly-mild, medium-mild, and intensely mild; then mildly-medium, medium-medium, and intensely medium; then mildly-intense, medium-intense, and intensely intense. In this way there are eighty-one sub-divisions of violence.

Now the sūtra shows what the contrary ideas are in themselves, the distinctions between them, the cause of their rise and their result:

The contrary ideas, violence and the others: this is what they are. *Done, or caused to be done or approved of,* are the distinctions; *preceded by greed, anger, or delusion,* shows the cause of their rise; *mild or medium or intense* means that the taint in them is either mild or medium or intense; *result in endless pain and Ignorance:* this is the meditation on their opposite, or it may be that the result is simply stated.

Of these, violence is taken simply to illustrate them all. It is of three kinds: done, caused to be done, or approved of. It is effected by one's own action, or caused to be done by employing an agent, or approved of, when what is done by others is assented to in one's own mind.

Each one of these too is three fold: from greed, as done or caused or approved by one desiring meat and skin, whereby a deer is killed; *from anger, as by one believing himself injured; from delusion, as by one who thinks thereby he will acquire merit.* There are thus these nine kinds, *and each of these too has three further sub-divisions. They are mild, medium and intense. Again these three last have three further subdivisions: mildly-mild, medium-mild, and intensely mild; then mildly-medium, medium-medium, and intensely medium; then mildly-*

intense, medium-intense, and intensely intense. In this way there are eighty-one sub-divisions of violence.

> *But with the distinctions of acting under orders, optional action and action in combination, in fact the varieties are innumerable, and there are also differences in the victims.*
>
> *The analysis is to be applied in the case of falsehood and other (breaches of restraints and observances).*
>
> *These contrary ideas result in endless pain and Ignorance; (let one practise) meditation on their opposite. So the killer deprives the victim of spirit, hurts him with a blow of a weapon, and then tears him away from life. Because he has deprived another of spirit, the supports of his own life, animate or inanimate, become weakened. Because he has caused pain, he experiences pain himself in hell or as an animal or a ghost. Because he has torn another from life, he goes to live in a life in which every moment he wishes to die, because the retribution as pain has to work itself right out, while he is panting for death.*
>
> *This reasoning should be applied- with just the necessary changes – to the other contrary ideas like untruth. Let one meditate on the unwelcome consequences, which follow like a shadow, of the contrary ideas, and let him not devote his mind to contrary ideas.*

Though there are the eighty-one divisions, in fact the varieties are innumerable because of further differences of action under orders, optional action, and action in combination. Take the difference as to orders. An officer gives orders to another, as from the king. Though himself only the king's officer, he is in charge and is said to be in charge. And all the officers either in a group or by choosing one, do the killing. Now it is the original commander who is said to be responsible for the killing done by the officers whether in a body or by one chosen. Then there are *differences in the victims,* as in the case of the executioner (who kills only a) man who has been condemned.

This analysis, the distinctions of done or caused to be done or approved of etc., *is to be applied in the case of falsehood and other (breaches of restraints and observances).*

The contrary ideas result in endless pain and Ignorance; they have endlessly as their result both pain and Ignorance. *Let one meditate on the opposite,* let him not turn towards them with his mind, but think: 'They endlessly result in pain, they endlessly result in Ignorance.'

Now he adduces the cruelty caused by the three fold operation of violence, to illustrate the distinction of results. *The killer deprives the victim of spirit,* by his murderous appearance and threats, he deprives the terrified victim of courage, *hurts him with a blow of a weapon, and then tears him away from life,* he ends his life.

Because he the killer *has deprived another of spirit, the supports of his own life, animate or inanimate,* either cattle or fields, etc., *become weakened. Because he has caused pain* as by blows of his weapon *he experiences pain himself in hell or as an animal or a ghost* according to the injury he has inflicted. *Because he has torn another away from life, he comes to live in a life* in a different mortal life *in which every moment he wishes to die, because the retribution as pain has to work itself right out,* it has inevitably to be experienced *while he is panting for death.*

Even if there should be an admixture of merit of some kind, so that the sin of violence is much reduced by a predominance of merit, still the life of happiness attained by the circumstance of merit will be a short one, because of the adverse association with violence.

This which has been said of violence *should be applied – with just the necessary changes – to the other contrary ideas like untruth. Let one meditate on the unwelcome consequences which follow like a shadow on the contrary ideas* like violence *and let him not devote his mind to contrary ideas.*

> *When the contrary ideas, escaped by meditation on their opposite, become of sterile quality, then the resulting divine powers so caused are an indication of the yogin's success.*

When the contrary ideas, escaped by meditation on their opposite, become of sterile quality: they have a quality, and that quality is sterility. When they have been cut off at the root and do not appear in the mind of the yogin, *then the resulting divine powers so caused* by rigid adherence to the restraints and observances *are an indication of the yogin's success.* The respective results of harmlessness and the others are evidence of success; success in yoga is determined by result alone. Furthermore as an incentive to the yogic practices, the divine power consequent on each is set out. Here is explained the particular sign of firmness in each one of the restraints and observances, a sign observable by direct perception, unlike the results of prescribed holy actions such as sacrifices. The sign of yogic success is given for each practice individually.

Sūtra II.35

With establishment of harmlessness, in his presence enmity is abandoned

> *This happens with all living beings.*

With establishment of harmlessness, when it is firm and clear of contrary ideas, *in his presence enmity is abandoned;* in the presence of that one who follows harmlessness, even natural enemies like snake and mongoose give up their antagonism.

Sūtra II.36

With establishment of truth, events confirm his words

> *When he says, 'Be righteous', that man becomes righteous; told by him, 'Do you attain heaven', that one attains heaven. His word is infallible.*

With establishment of truth, events confirm his words. When truth is firm in him, events confirm his words. The confirmation of the results of actions like sacrifices consists in the fact that they are actually attained, and it is to be understood that here these results follow something said by a truth-speaker. How so? *When he says* to an evil man, *'Be righteous',* from those words, *that man becomes righteous;* as when it was said by the gods, 'Let his mind delight in virtue' and Kuṇḍadhārārādhī became a righteous Brahmin (Mokṣadh. 271); *told by him, 'Do you attain heaven', that one attains heaven.* Just so Triśaṅku was told by Viśvāmitra, 'Attain heaven' (Viṣṇu Pur. etc.) and did attain it. It is unnecessary to cite many examples. *His word is infallible.*

Sūtra II.37

With establishment in non-stealing, all precious things come to him

From all directions precious things come to him.

With establishment in non-stealing, that is, desirelessness. What happens then? *From all directions precious things come to him,* to present themselves before him.

Sūtra II.38

With establishment in brahmacarya, attainment of energy

From that attainment, he draws out invincible good qualities from himself
And when perfected in it, he becomes able to confer knowledge on pupils.

With establishment in brahmacarya, attainment of energy. From that attainment of brahmacarya, *he draws out invincible good qualities,* he brings them out without limit *from himself.* He has irresistible energy for all good undertakings. The sense is, that he cannot be thwarted by any obstacle.

He becomes able to confer knowledge on pupils; to proper and virtuous pupils he can pass on his knowledge, as holy Vyāsa has enjoined.

Sūtra II.39

With firmness in not possessing property, clear knowledge of the conditions of birth

... becomes his. What is this birth? How does it take place? What do we become (after death), who shall we be and in what circumstances shall we be? Any such desire of his to know his situation in former, later and intermediate states is spontaneously gratified.

Clear knowledge of the conditions of birth: knowledge of how one is born. *What is this birth?* what is the truth about this birth of mine? *How does it take place?* by what process? *What do we become?* after death do we not exist, or do we exist?

Who shall we be and in what circumstances shall we be? Any such desire to know his situation in former, later and intermediate states past, future and present *is spontaneously gratified,* as a foreshadowing of right vision (samyagdarśana). Since he has no attachment to outer possessions, illumination of the field of his own self appears without effort on his part. But it does not in those who are fevered or depressed or craving for possessions, despite their efforts.

Now the observances are taken up:

Sūtra II.40

From purity, distaste for his own body and no intercourse with others

> *When by practising purity and seeing the defects in the body, he becomes disgusted with his own body, he becomes free from obsession with the body; seeing what the body essentially is, he has no intercourse with others. So seeing, the renunciate finds no purity in the body even after he has washed it with earth and water and other things; how should he engage in intercourse with the absolutely unpurified bodies of others?*

The perfections of the restraints have been stated, and *now the observances are taken up. From purity, distaste for his own body and no intercourse with others. When by practising purity and seeing the defects in the body, he becomes disgusted with his own body* he sees how contemptible the body is and becomes *a renunciate, free from obsession with the body.* Then *seeing what the body essentially is, he has no intercourse with others.* Even when he has washed clean his own body with clay and water and so on, he still does not find it pure, so how should he engage in intercourse with the unpurified bodies of others?

Furthermore,

Sūtra II.41

Purity of mind-sattva, cheerfulness, one-pointedness, conquest of the senses, and fitness for vision of the self

The words 'There arise' should be supplied at the beginning of the sūtra. There arises purity of mind-sattva, and from that arises cheerfulness; from that, one-pointedness; from that, conquest of the senses; and from that, fitness of mind-sattva for vision of the self which thus is attained from firmness in purity.

What else happens? *There arise purity of mind-sattva, cheerfulness, one-pointedness, conquest of the senses, and fitness for vision of the self.* As each earlier one becomes firm, the succeeding one appears. From purity *there arises purity of mind-sattva, and from that arises cheerfulness; from that, one-pointedness; from that, conquest of the senses; and from that, fitness of mind-sattva for vision of the self* It is all attained from firmness in purity, and it is this which is the perfection of purity.

Sūtra II.42

From contentment, attainment of unsurpassed happiness

So it is said: 'Whatever sex pleasure there may be in the world, whatever supreme happiness may be enjoyed in heaven, they cannot be accounted a sixteenth part of the happiness of destruction of craving.' (From a Pūrāṇa – Madhusudana)

So it is said: 'Whatever sex pleasure there may be here and now *in the world; whatever supreme happiness may be* that of gods and others *in heaven,* they are not to be compared with a *sixteenth part of the happiness of destruction of craving.'*

Sūtra II.43

From destruction of impurity by tapas, perfection of body and senses

As tapas becomes complete, it destroys the veiling taint of impurity; when the veiling taint is removed, there are perfections of the body like the ability to become minute, and perfection of the senses in such forms as hearing and seeing things which are remote.

From destruction of impurity by tapas, perfection of the body and senses. As tapas becomes complete, it destroys the veiling taint of impurity. The sense is that some particular practice of tapas has been perfected.

When the taint (mala) of that covering is removed, there are perfections of the body like the ability to become minute (aṇimā). The taints (mala) of the physical body, born of the conjugation of mother and father, of seed and womb and food, etc., are entirely removed by tapas. Thereby comes perfection of the body in such forms as becoming minute and so on. The taint which veils the senses by unrighteousness (a-dharma), etc., arising from their contact with the objects, is washed away by the rush of a stream of tapas. Then there is *perfection of the senses in such forms as hearing and seeing things which are remote.*

Sūtra II.44

From self-study, communion with the deity of his devotion

Gods, sages, and perfect beings to whom he is devoted come before the vision of the man intent on study of the self and give him their help.

Gods, sages, and perfect beings to whom he is devoted come to the vision of the man intent on study of the self and give him their help, in such ways as teaching.

Sūtra II.45

From devotion to the Lord, perfection in samādhi

The samādhi of one who has devoted his whole being to the Lord, is perfect. By this he knows unerringly whatever he desires, even in other places and times and bodies. The knowledge from that knows the thing as it really is.

From devotion to the Lord, perfection in samādhi. The samādhi of one who has devoted his whole being to the Lord, is perfect. By this perfection in samādhi *he knows unerringly whatever he desires. His knowledge (prajñā) knows the thing as it is (yathābhūta), even in other places and times and bodies.*

Having set out the restraints and observances, with their perfections, we go on to posture and the further steps.

Sūtra II.46

Posture is to be firm and pleasant

(Postures) such as the Lotus, the Auspicious, the Hero, the Svastika, the Staff, the Support, the Throne, the Curlew, the Elephant, the Camel, the Confirmed, the Favourite, and others.

Having set out the restraints and observances, with their perfections, we go on to posture and the further steps. Posture is to be firm and pleasant. It is to be both firm and pleasant. Let him practise a posture in which, when established, his mind and limbs will become firm, and which does not cause pain. Let it be a posture *such as the Lotus* posture; he will go on to give the names of postures well-known from other authoritative works (śāstra).

(First) let him go to a pure place, such as a cave in a holy mountain or an islet in a river, but not right beside a fire or running water, a place free from insects, without pebbles. Having sipped water in the traditional way, having bowed to the Highest Lord (parameśvara) the one ruler of the whole universe, and to the holy ones and to his own selfless teacher, master of yoga, let him lay a seat. On kusa grass he spreads an antelope skin, and on that a cloth, to prevent discomfort. In one of the mentioned places he should take his seat, facing east or north.

Of the seated postures, the Lotus posture is as follows. Let him bring in his left foot towards himself, and set it upon the right leg, and then the right foot over the left leg. Let him make firm his hips, chest and neck, and fix the gaze on the nosetip, like one dead or asleep, the lips closed like the cover on a round casket, the teeth not grinding against each other, the chin a fist's breadth away from the chest, and the tip of the tongue resting against the inside of the front teeth. The joined hands rest on the two heels in the position called Tortoise, or the reverential Brahma-añjali position. Once assumed, the posture is to be held steadily. When he has got beyond the initial effort at securing the proper disposition of body and limbs, this is called the Lotus posture.

The basic principles are the same with the other postures to be described, although each has its own special points. The posture in which he sits (simply) with the right foot over the left leg, and the right hand placed upon the left, is the Auspicious (bhadra) posture. The other points are the same (as in the Lotus).

The Hero posture is where one leg is bent (with the sole placed flat on the ground) and the other (leg from) knee (to toes) rests on the ground. In all these descriptions it is just the special points of the posture which are specified.

When the toes of the right foot are thrust between the left thigh and calf so that they are not seen, and similarly the toes of the left foot are concealed between right thigh and calf, the testicles resting comfortable (between the feet), this is the Auspicious or Svastika posture.

To attain the Staff posture, let one stretch out the legs with the ankles, toes and knees side by side like a staff.

The Support is so-called from the use of a yoga table as support, or a seat.

Stretching out the arms and putting them on the knees is the Throne posture. The Curlew, Elephant and Camel sitting postures look like the position of the curlew and the others when seated.

The Confirmed is some other arrangement which seems to be suitable to oneself; that seated posture in which one is not uneasy is called the Confirmed.

The Favourite posture: this is the one specially congenial to a sitter. The word 'others' (ādi) in the commentary indicates that there may be variations prescribed by a teacher.

Sūtra II.47

By relaxing effort and by samādhi (samāpatti) on infinity

The words 'it comes about' are to be supplied at the beginning of the sūtra. By withdrawal of effort, a posture is perfected, in which the limbs do not shift. Or when the mind is in samādhi on the infinite, the posture is perfected.

Now methods of mastering the posture are given. *By relaxing effort and by samādhi (samāpatti) on infinity – the words 'it comes about' are to be supplied.* The corollary is that the posture becomes completely firm. *By withdrawal of effort* after getting locked into position, or (when it is familiar) by not exerting effort at all; by this withdrawal of effort a *posture is perfected in which the limbs do not shift,* for it is effort that disturbs the limbs. So the posture thus becomes unmoving. *Or by samādhi (samāpatti) on infinity.* The universe is infinite, and the state of being infinite is infinity. When the mind attains samādhi on that which stands pervading all existence, *the posture is perfected* is made firm.

Sūtra II.48

From that, he becomes immune to the opposites

When a posture has been mastered, he is not overwhelmed by opposites like heat and cold.

From that, he becomes immune to the opposites. From that, from becoming firm in a posture. He gives an example of what he means: *not overwhelmed by opposites like heat and cold.*

Sūtra II.49

Prāṇāyāma is to sit in the posture and cut off the flow of in-breath and out-breath

The posture has been mastered. Now when he inhales outside air, it is called the in-breath (śvāsa); when he exhales the air from within, that is the out-breath (praśvāsa). Cutting off the flow of these two, so that they both cease, is prāṇāyāma.

He is now ready for prāṇāyāma. *Prāṇāyāma is to sit in the posture and cut off the flow of in-breath and out-breath. When* sitting in that posture made quite firm, *he inhales outside air, it is called the in-breath (śvāsa).* As water is sucked up through a tube by a continuous action, so by a continuous action through the two tubes of the nostrils, the external air is drawn in, in association with the downward-going current (apāna), and this drawing in is called the in-breath. Then *when he exhales the air from within,* in association with the operation of the upward-going current (prāṇa), its going out is *the out-breath.* Thus the two flows are distinguished. What then? He continues: *cutting off the flow of these two is* called *prāṇāyāma. Of this* -

Sūtra II.50

The external, internal, and fixating operations, practised in terms of place, of time and of number, become long and fine

Of these, stopping the flow after (a full) inhalation is the external; next, stopping the flow after (a full) exhalation is the internal. The third is the operation of fixation, not preceded by either of the other two, and effected by a single effort. As water thrown on a heated stone shrivels up on every side, so the flow of both ceases simultaneously. All three are practised in terms of place – by how far the field of each extends; in terms of time – how many moments each can be maintained; and in terms of number – how many inhalations and exhalations it takes till the first upstroke, and when that has been achieved, how many more till the second, and similarly how many more till the third

> *upstroke. These are called the mild, medium, and intense practice. Practised in this way, (the breath) becomes long and fine.*

Of this, of the three kinds *the external, internal and fixating operations, practised in terms of place, of time and of number, become long and fine.* There is an external operation, an internal operation, and a fixating operation. *Of these stopping the flow after (a full) inhalation is the external operation.* The operation in which the air from outside is taken in is the external operation, so it is called 'external', and others call it 'filling' (pūraka). *Next, stopping the flow after (a full) exhalation is the internal operation.* When the internal air is expelled away to the outside, it is the internal operation. Because it is internal air here, it is called internal, and others call it 'expulsion' (recaka).

But the third is the operation of fixation, not preceded by either of the other two neither the drawing in nor the exhaling *and effected by a single effort. As water thrown on a heated stone shrivels up on every side so* from a single effort, the operations of prāṇa and apāna simultaneously shrink to nothing and as he says, *the flow of both ceases.*

All three are practised in terms of place: in the external operation, the current drawn in is felt going through the space from the tip of the nose to the toes, and with the internal operation the expelled air is felt going through the space from the toes to the tip of the nose. In the operation of fixation it is felt pervading the body from the head to the soles of the feet. And again, its pervasion is measured by its range (the effect of breath on a hanging thread at a distance) of so many spans etc.

(They are) practised in terms of time – how many moments each can be maintained, how many moments the prāṇāyāma can be extended; *and in terms of number – how many inhalations and exhalations it takes* how many moments are counted to have passed *till the first upstroke.* The first up-stroke is when the held-in and excited airs first (rise up and) strike the head and cease there. This is the *mild practice.* Then, when the restrained air has risen in the up-stroke the first time, he counts how many exhalations it takes till the second up-stroke, and the prāṇāyāma taken to this point is said to be *medium.* Then the third one is practised by counting the number of inhalations and exhalations it takes till the third up-stroke. This practised to a third up-stroke is *intense.* Practised in this way by place, time and number, breathing lengthens out to extended periods, as the stages are mastered. The holy texts say that sages (ṛṣi) could prolong a breath for years. So it becomes *long.* And as the breathings become long and slow, they also become *fine.*

Sūtra II.51

The fourth prāṇāyāma comes when both external and internal fields have been felt into

The field of the external operation, as measured in terms of place, time, and number, has been practised and felt into. (The second prāṇāyāma) was practice in feeling into the field of the internal operation, as measured similarly. In both practices, the breath became long and fine. The fourth prāṇāyāma comes after the stages (mild, medium and intense) of these two practices have been gradually mastered, and it consists of cessation of both the operations. Whereas the third prāṇāyāma was stopping the breath without having previously brought to awareness the fields (of external and internal objects), the breath becoming long and fine simply by this practice according to place, time, and number; but the cessation in the fourth one comes only after having already brought to awareness those fields, feeling into them by gradually mastering the stages. This is what distinguishes the fourth prāṇāyāma.

The fourth prāṇāyāma comes when both external and internal fields have been felt into. The field of the external operation is the toes, etc., for the external air being drawn in, is felt pervading the inner regions. The field of the internal operation is earth and the other elements. The expiration outwards is felt pervading the earth and the other elements, as practised in terms of place, time and number. This fourth prāṇāyāma comes when both external and internal fields have been felt into.

The (first) practice was feeling into the pervasion of the field which is the object of the external operation, as measured by place, time and number; the second was feeling into the pervasion of the field which is the object of the internal operation, similarly. *In both practices, the breath became long and fine.* By feeling into the fields of the external and the internal objects, length and fineness of the breath come about, in both of them.

What follows? *After the stages (mild, medium, and intense) have been gradually mastered,* corresponding to the feeling into both operations of the breath, there is *cessation* of the flow of breath in both the external and internal operations, the flow of prāṇa (the upward and outward current) and apāna (the downward current).

(Opponent) The third and fourth prāṇāyāma-s are the same; one finds no distinction between the two.

(Answer) In the third one there is no prevous bringing to awareness of the fields; it is cessation of the breath by a single effort at cutting off the course of the breath. *The breath becomes long and fine by practising this alone, according to time, place and number. But the cessation in the fourth one comes after bringing to experience the fields of exhalation and inhalation* taken to the very limit, gradually mastering the stages, and this is the distinction between the third and the fourth.

Sūtra II.52

Thereby is destroyed the covering of the light

> *It destroys the karma which covers up Knowledge-of-the-difference in the yogin who has not practised prāṇāyāma. As it is declared: 'When the ever-bright sattva is covered over by Indra's net of great illusion, one is impelled to what is not to be done.' By the power of prāṇāyāma, the light-veiling karma binding him to the world becomes powerless, and moment by moment is destroyed. So it has been said: 'There is no tapas higher than prāṇāyāma; from it come purification from taints and the light of Knowledge.'*

Thereby is destroyed the covering of the light. It is karma by which the light is covered. *In the yogin who has not practised prāṇāyāma,* the Knowledge-of-the-difference is covered by *karma which covers up Knowledge-of-the-difference. It is declared* in another scripture that *when the ever-bright sattva is covered over by Indra's net of great illusion (mahāmoha), one is impelled to what should not be done.*(The mind) covered over by Indra's net of illusory knowledge (viparyaya jñāna) is impelled by the sattva-veiling karma to all that should not be done. *By practice of prāṇāyāma, the light-veiling karma binding him to the world becomes powerless, and* not merely does it become powerless, but it is *moment by moment destroyed. So it has been said: 'There is no tapas higher than prāṇāyāma; from it come purification from taints, and the light of Knowledge.'* (Cp. Manu VI.70, 72)

Sūtra II.53

Fitness of the mind for concentrations

Furthermore, simply from the practice of prāṇāyāma (comes fitness for concentrations). For it was said: 'Or by expulsion and retention of prāṇa.'

And there is something else from prāṇāyāma practice: *Simply from the practice of prāṇāyāma* comes *fitness of the mind for concentrations* which are to be explained. As has been said (sūtra I.34): 'By expulsion and retention of prāṇa' – from these two, steadiness of the mind is attained.

Now what is dissociation?

Sūtra II.54

Dissociation is when the senses, disjoined from their respective objects, assume as it were the nature of mind itself

When there is no conjunction with their respective objects, they assume as it were the nature of mind itself. When mind is inhibited, the senses are inhibited like the mind, without needing any other means for their subjection. As when the royal bee rises, the swarm rises, and when it settles they settle, so when the mind is inhibited the senses are inhibited. This is dissociation.

Now what is dissociation (pratyāhāra)? He introduces the exposition by way of a question. It is withdrawing the senses from their respective objects which is (the true pratyāhāra) among all the others. Next are given its characteristics: *Dissociation is when the senses, disjoined from their respective objects, assume as it were the nature of mind itself* The word *respective* refers to the particular objects like sound which are the fields of the corresponding senses like the ear. *Disjoined from their respective objects, the senses* which in the men of meditation are withdrawn from their objects as a result of seeing the defects in them *assume as it were the nature of mind itself* This means that they partake, as it were, of the form of the mind of the yogin.

On this it is said: *When mind is inhibited, the senses are inhibited like the mind, without needing any other means for their subjection* to conquer them. They are inhibited simply by inhibition of the mind. *As when the royal bee rises* – the unusual rājānam at the end of the compound instead of rājam is a Vedic form – *the swarm rises, and when it settles they settle, so when the mind is inhibited the senses are inhibited.*

Sūtra II.55

From that, supreme mastery of the senses.

Some hold that conquest of the senses means not being addicted to sound or other objects. Addiction (vy-asana) is attachment, in the sense that it impels (as-) him away (vy-)from his highest good. Such is addiction.

Some think that conquest of the senses means acceptance of what is not forbidden; it is approved sense-contact with the objects according to his own will. Others again say that conquest of the senses is to experience objects without desire or aversion, and void of pleasure or pain.

Jaigīṣavya holds that sense mastery is only the nonperception of objects resulting from one-pointedness. This mastery is the highest. When mind is inhibited, senses are inhibited; unlike the other conquests of the senses, yogins having practised this, do not have to look for further means.

Thus ends the Second part, on Means, of the Commentary by holy Vyāsa, compiler of the Vedas, on the Yoga Sūtra-s of holy Patañjali.

Some hold that conquest of the senses means not being addicted to sound or other objects, always abstaining from them, or not being attached to them. He explains what is meant by addiction (vy-asana): *addiction is attachment, in the sense that it impels (as-) him* wrenches him *away from (vy-)* association with *his highest good (śreyas). Such is addiction.*

Some think that conquest of the senses means acceptance of what is not forbidden; he says this is *approved* scripturally recognized *sense-contact with the objects according to his own will.* If he desire, he may engage in the things so long as they are not forbidden, or not (so engage). *Others again say that conquest* mastery *of the senses is to experience objects without desire or aversion, and void of pleasure or pain,* free from any idea that they are to be avoided or taken up. In the middle one (the previous view) actual desire and aversion are not ruled out; that is the distinction.

Now he puts forward the view which he favours:
Jaigīṣavya holds that sense mastery is only the non-perception of objects like sound *resulting from one-pointedness* of the senses from their conforming to the one-pointedness of the mind. *This mastery is the highest* out of all those which have been stated, in which *when mind is inhibited, senses are inhibited; unlike the other conquests of the senses* the masteries already mentioned, *yogin-s having practised this, do not have to look for further means* to attain mastery.

With this, the Second Part, on Means, of the sub-commentary by the holy Lord (bhagavat) Śaṅkara, who is a paramahaṃsa parivrājaka ācārya and pupil of holy Lord Govindapāda whose feet are to be worshipped, is complete.

Third Part:
GLORY

(Vyāsa bhāṣya:) The five outer methods of the means have been explained. Now dhāraṇā (concentration) is to be spoken of.

(Śaṅkara vivaraṇa:)
The five outer methods of the means to the cognitive (samprajñāta) yoga *have been explained.* Now the triad of dhāraṇā (concentration), dhyāna (meditation), and samādhi, the inner methods to that end, is explained. There is a division between inner method and outer method, and so the previous Part, the Part of the Means, was concluded with explanation of the outer methods. The triad of inner methods is now given separately from that, to preserve their unity. Presenting the inner methods as means immediately after explanation of the outer ones makes clear the connection of the Parts. Now in this Part the main topic is the glories, and therefore a new and separate Part is begun; the reason for the title is thus explained.

Dhāraṇā is to be spoken of As it comes next in order immediately after Dissociation (pratyāhāra), this is the proper place for it.

Sūtra III.1

Dhāraṇā is binding the mind to a place

Dhāraṇā is binding the mind to a place. It is binding the mind, as a purely mental process, to the navel circle, the heart lotus, the light in the head, the tip of the nose, the tip of the tongue, and other such locations; and to external objects.

Dhāraṇā (concentration) is binding the mind to one place. Binding to one place means binding it there, and it is the mind that is to be bound.

The commentator gives details, *binding to the navel circle* all the vital currents meet there in the form of a circle, so it is called the circle of the navel. On the form of the *heart lotus, the light in the head.*The door of the nāḍī nerve-channel of the head is radiant, and so it is called a light. To *the tip of the nose, the tip of the tongue, and other such locations, and to external objects,* such as the moon. To these the mind is bound.

The mental process (vṛtti) of that mind, held in those places without being dispersed, is called dhāraṇā, *as a purely mental process:* it functions simply as the idea of that place without any disturbance (vikṣepa).

Sūtra III.2

Continuity of the mind there is dhyāna (meditation)

Meditation is continuity of the idea of the meditation-object in that place – a stream of similar ideas untouched by any other idea.

Continuity of the idea in that place is meditation, in that place; for instance the navel circle and the other objects of dhāraṇā. *continuity of the idea of the meditation-object,* such as the place previously selected for meditation, means *a stream of similar ideas,* a stream of like ideas as a unity, a continuity of ideas *untouched* not disturbed *by any other idea* of opposite kind. That is dhyāna.

Whereas dhāraṇā is touched by other ideas imagined about the object, even though the mind has been settled on that object of meditation alone –

if made on the sun, its orbit and extreme brilliance are also the object of the concentration, for the mind is functioning on the location as a pure mental process – not so with dhyāna, for there it is only the stream of a single idea, untouched by any other idea of different kind.

Sūtra III.3

That same (meditation – dhyāna), when it comes to shine forth as the object alone, apparently empty of its own nature as knowledge, is called samādhi

> *That same (dhyāna), when it comes to shine forth in the form of the meditation-object alone, apparently empty of its own nature as an idea, and having entered the being of the meditation-object, becomes it – is called samādhi.*

That same, when it comes to shine forth as the object alone, apparently empty of its own nature as knowledge, is called samādhi. That same dhyāna, consisting of the idea-stream, having apparently (iva) given up being a stream of one idea *comes to shine forth in the form of the meditation-object* is radiant as the form of that object, *apparently empty of its own nature* of itself *as an idea* as perceiving, just as a clear crystal shines out as the material on which it has been placed, and is apparently empty of its own nature, and when *having entered the being of the meditation-object,* that being the cause of the thought, *becomes it,* that very dhyāna is samādhi.

(Opponent) But it was said previously (sūtra I.1 comm.): 'Yoga is samādhi', so samādhi should include all the methods. Yet here it is being taught that samādhi is but one of the methods of yoga. What has happened to the distinction between a method and the totality of all the methods?

(Answer) The answer is, that when it was said 'Yoga is samādhi' that was in regard to the particular point of fixing the mind. But here the particular point is the method whereby what was a stream of ideas becomes, from entering the being of the meditation-object, the very form of that object.

Sūtra III.4

The triad (held) at the one place is saṃyama

The triad – concentration, meditation, and samādhi – held at the one place, is called saṃyama. The triple means directed on to a single object is called by the technical name of saṃyama.

What has been explained as *the triad – concentration (dhāraṇā), meditation (dhyāna), and samādhi, held at the one place* brought to completion at a single location, is called *saṃyama.* So he says: *The triple means directed on to a single object is called by the technical name of saṃyama.*

The triad, thus perfected stage by stage, is for the purposes of this work called by the technical name of saṃyama. In the various passages, when it is a question of grasping something desired to be known, or mastering something desired to be mastered, it is taught that some appropriate saṃyama should be known, and in all these passages, saṃyama is the technical term used for the triad. For instance, it will be said (III. 16): 'From saṃyama on the three changes, knowledge of past and future', and (III.44): 'From saṃyama on their physical form, essential nature, subtle form, inherence, and purposefulness, conquest of the elements.'

Sūtra III.5

From mastery of that, the light of knowledge (prajñā)

From mastery of that saṃyama, there comes the light of knowledge. On whatever the saṃyama is set firm, of that very thing the samādhi-knowledge becomes firm.

From mastery of that, the light of knowledge. From mastery of that saṃyama from securing firmness in it, there is the power of manifesting the desired object, as if a light were being shone on it, *there comes the light of samādhi-knowledge. On whatever the saṃyama is set firm, of that very thing the samādhi-knowledge becomes firm.* By that light of samādhi-knowledge, which can illuminate anything even hidden or remote, the yogins see clearly what they have in mind, as if it were set on the palm of their hand.

Sūtra III.6

Its application is by stages

Its application is by stages. Its application the practice of that samādhi as it has to be done *is by stages:* external things are taken as objects of the meditation (dhyāna), and then internal things, and then such things as the three-fold changes of which he is going to speak (III. 16).

> *That saṃyama is to be practised by moving on to the next stage only when the first stage has been mastered. For if an early stage is not mastered, but missed out in favour of jumping on to the next stage, he will not attain saṃyama on the later stages at all. And without that, how will the knowledge-light ever arise?*

(But) for one who has mastered later stages, saṃyama practice on earlier stages such as telepathy would not be right. Why not? Because the purpose will have been attained already in another way.

That saṃyama is to be practised, to be done by the one rightly determined to master the stages *by moving on to the next stage only when the first stage has been mastered:* the yogin having fixed his meditation on some stage till he has attained saṃyama on it, goes on to the stage next after the saṃyama which he has mastered.

So when it is said (in III.44) that in saṃyama on elements like earth, the physical aspect, the essential nature, the subtle aspect, the inherent aspect, and the aspect of purposefulness are to be mastered in turn, it means that having performed saṃyama on the physical, the next saṃyama has to be on the essential only, which follows on the one that has been mastered. He should not pass over the essential nature and go on to the later aspects such as the subtle nature.

Why not? *Because if an earlier stage is not mastered, but missed out in favour of jumping to the next stage, he will not attain saṃyama on later stages* on subsequent stages *at all.* If, without having mastered the next in order, he tries to practise saṃyama on those that come later, he will not attain saṃyama on them, and that non-attainment will mean failure for him. *And without that* if he does not attain saṃyama on the later stages *how will knowledge-light ever arise?* For there would be nothing to bring it about: there can be no lamplight unless the oil, wick, and a flame are brought together.

For one who has mastered later stages a yogin who has mastered later stages such as (realization of) ātman, *saṃyama practice on earlier stages such as telepathy would not be right. Why not? Because the purpose* the later stages such as ātman-realization *will have been attained in another way,* quite different from such petty stages as telepathy. From things like telepathy there arises confusion, because their nature is absence of discriminative knowledge (viveka). For one whose saṃyama is on the later stages, to take the thoughts of others as object would mean to make a confusion in his own mind, though trained in yoga, and so it *would not be right.* For he will have already attained his purpose, ātman-realization, in a different way, by discrimination.

But others understand it as meaning that his purpose is telepathy, and that it is this which has been attained in another way. They say it is just by the higher stages such as ātman-realization that the aim, telepathy, is accomplished. But if this had been the meaning, it would have been said that saṃyama practice on earlier stages would not be needed, but not that it *would not be right.* The fact that the words *not right* are used implies that it is wrong.

> *As to the question: What stage is to come next after this one? On this, it is yoga alone that is the teacher. How so? It has been said*
>
> *Yoga is to be known by yoga;*
> *Yoga goes forward from yoga alone.*
> *He who is not careless in his yoga,*
> *For a long time sports in the yoga-s.*

As to the question: What stage is to come next after this one? – when one stage has been mastered, how is it to be decided what should come next? *On this, it is yoga alone that is the teacher.* 'Yoga' here means the attainment of saṃyama on the previous stage, and it is by that alone that one understands which is to be the next one.

How so? It has been said: Yoga is to be known by yoga. By the yoga which consists of the attainment of the previous saṃyama, the object of yoga which is to come next will be known. And this *Yoga,*saṃyama, *goes forward* becomes clear *from yoga alone,* from attainment of saṃyama on the previous stages alone.

Just as one blind from birth, ascending a flight of steps, from the feel of his foot on the first step knows confidently where the next one is, so *Yoga goes forward from yoga.*

Therefore he who knows this, *who is not careless in his yoga* who is restrained in *yoga., for a long time sports in the yogas,* in the fruits of yogic powers.

Sūtra III.7

Compared to the previous means, this triad is the direct means

Compared to the previously given five means beginning with restraints, this triad of concentration, meditation, and samādhi is the direct means to cognitive samādhi

Compared to the previous means, this triad is the direct means. Compared to the previously given five means beginning with restraints, this triad of dhāraṇā, dhyāna, and samādhi is the direct means to cognitive samādhi-yoga. In thus calling them the direct (literally, inner) means, he wishes to show that even though the previous ones may not have been perfected, effort should be made at these three.

Sūtra III.8

Even that is an indirect means as regards unseeded (yoga)

Even that triple method, though the direct means (to cognitive samādhi), is only an indirect method as regards the unseeded yoga. Why so? Because that comes about also without it.

Yoga can be effected even without going through the five-fold means of restraints, etc., from the mere accomplishment of the triad of concentration, meditation, and samādhi, by force of saṃskāra-s accumulated in a previous life, as in the case of the incorporeal gods, and those resolved into prakṛti.

But without that triad, yoga is not possible for anyone, because yoga is essentially associated with the operation of concentration and the other two. For the nature of yoga is perfection of the mind.

But when knowledge (jñāna) and detachment have been perfected, then there is no concern with concentration and so on. Thus we have cases of those like Maṅki and Piṅgalā who did attain full perfection from detachment alone.

Mastery of a firm sitting posture or other instructions of yoga, are not, in the case of distracted people, productive of yoga.
Getting rid of the defects, and samādhi – these two will certainly produce it, and nothing else will.

Even that is an indirect method (bahir-aṅga) as regards unseeded (yoga). Even that, though the direct means to seeded yoga, is an indirect means as regards unseeded yoga. Why so? Because that comes about also without it.

By discerning the distinction between mind-sattva and Puruṣa, the seedless yoga comes about, even in the absence of that triple direct means to the seeded; so the triad is only an indirect means (to the seedless). There are some who have exceedingly penetrating vision at their very birth, derived from saṃskāra-s (of past lives). In their case, unseeded samādhi will be produced by simple devotion to the practice of supreme detachment, and the idea of stopping (virāma-pratyaya), and they do not engage in concentration and meditation and samādhi. So it was said (Vyāsa on II.1): 'The yoga for a concentrated mind has been described; now he turns to how one of extravertive mind may become steady in yoga', and (I.19): '(It results from birth) in the case of the gods and of those who absorb themselves into nature.'

Now at times of inhibition of the mind, what then is that inhibitive transformation? For the mind is supposed to be something moving, as impelled by the guṇa-s.

Now at times of inhibition of the mind: it means at those times when the mind is inhibited by the practice of inhibition. The plural 'times' is used to show that it applies equally to mental processes whether of past, future, or present. At the time of inhibition, mind is imbued with the character of inhibition, and is (called) inhibited.

moving as impelled by the guṇa-s: as it consists of guṇa-s it is said to be impelled by guṇa-s. So he asks *what then is that inhibitive transformation?* There must inevitably be some transformation of the mind when it is inhibited from outer mental processes, because no inhibition could be postulated of a mind which was never transformed, but simply unchangeable like Puruṣa.

Sūtra III.9

The inhibitive transformation of the mind is when extravertive saṃskāra is overcome and the saṃskāra of inhibition is predominant, and mind itself is in a temporary state of inhibition

> *The extravertive saṃskāra is a characteristic of the mind: it is not of the nature of an idea. The saṃskāra of inhibition is also a characteristic of the mind itself. Of the two, there are subjection and predominance respectively (in the state of inhibition): extravertive saṃskāra-s are excluded and saṃskāra-s of inhibition are in possession. At the time of inhibition, the mind accords with the subjection and predominance. During the continuance of the change in the saṃskāra-s of the one mind, there is the inhibitive transformation.*

The inhibitive transformation of the mind is when extravertive saṃskāra is overcome, and saṃskāra of inhibition is predominant, and mind itself is in a temporary state of inhibition, extravertive: going out in various directions to function in the form of ideas in the mind; the saṃskāra laid down by that *is a characteristic (dharma) of the mind* its possessor (dharmin). *It is not of the nature of an idea.*

And the *saṃskāra* which is not an idea, *of* produced by *inhibition is also a characteristic of the mind itself* An extravertive saṃskāra, not being itself an idea, is not inhibited by inhibition of ideas. It is not overcome even though extravertive ideas may have been inhibited.

From inhibition of ideas, however, a saṃskāra of inhibition is laid down. *Of these two* the saṃskāra-s of extraversion and of inhibition, in the mind their possessor, *there are subjection and predominance respectively.*

(Opponent) Are the appearance of the one and disappearance of the other independent?

(Answer) No.

(Opponent) How is it then?

(Answer) *The saṃskāra-s of extraversion are excluded,* they are unable to bring about their effects *and the saṃskāra-s of inhibition are in possession.*

(Opponent) *At the time of inhibition,* does the mind accord with the subjection and predominance, as their possessor?

(Answer) The inhibitive transformation in the mind is when it accords with the subjection (of extravertive) and predominance (of inhibitive).

That *continuance* as explained *of the change in the saṃskāras of the one mind,* the change of saṃskāra-s by subjection of the extravertive and predominance of the inhibitive, comes about by exclusion of the extravertive, though there is still some connection, and predominance by the inhibitive because of their greater power, and this is called *inhibitive transformation.*

> *Then the mind, in the inhibition of samādhi, is declared to consist of saṃskāra-s alone.*

Then being inhibited from external ideas *the mind is declared to consist of saṃskāra-s alone.* As was said (I.18): 'The other follows on the practice of the idea of stopping, and consists of saṃskāra-s alone.' As this change terminates in inhibition, inasmuch as it makes for the absence of ideas, it is called the inhibitive transformation.

In cognitive (samādhi), though ideas do still exist, they are not being referred to here. Here it is only the fact of continued change of saṃskāra-s. Though there might also be samādhi when the consciousness is in the inhibited stage, that is not being referred to, but only the fact of inhibition. What is being spoken of is only saṃskāra-change, which occurs in the seeded condition (cognitive samādhi) as well. It is not a question of the ideas and one-pointedness of samādhi.

Sūtra III.10

It has a peaceful flow, by reason of the saṃskāra-s

From habituation of saṃskāra-s of inhibition, there comes about a peaceful flow of the mind. Beginning with the inhibitive saṃskāra, it lasts as long as it is not overcome by a saṃskāra of the character of extraversion.

It mind assuming the inhibitive change *has a peaceful flow, by reason of the saṃskāra-s. From habituation of saṃskāra-s of inhibition* in view of the habituation, the firmness, of the saṃskāra-s of inhibition *there comes about a peaceful flow* a calmness *of the mind.*

As to how long that peaceful flow lasts, he says: The peaceful flow which *begins with the inhibitive saṃskāra lasts as long as it,* the inhibitive saṃskāra, *is not overcome by a saṃskāra with the character of extraversion:* having been produced by extraversion, that saṃskāra will have the character of extraversion. The peaceful flow, however, arises from saṃskāra-s of inhibition.

Sūtra III.11

The destruction of the mind's dispersiveness, and rise of its one-pointedness, is the samādhi transformation

Dispersiveness is a characteristic of mind: one-pointedness also is a characteristic of mind. Destruction means disappearance: the rise of one-pointedness means its appearance. Because they are its characteristics, the mind conforms to each of them, since the mind possesses both the states as its own: it can be concentrated by the passing away (of extraversion) and coming forth (of one-pointedness). This is called the samādhi transformation.

Dispersiveness (sarvārthatā) of mind is its multifarious capacity for worldly experiences and also for release, that capacity being a characteristic of mind. It will be said (IV.23): 'The mind coloured by the seer and the objects of sight has all purposes (sarvārtham).'

one-pointedness also is a characteristic of mind. The sameness of the dying down and the following uprising process of a mind in samādhi is the *destruction of dispersiveness,* meaning its disappearance, for an existent thing never (really) perishes. *Rise of one-pointedness* means (similarly) its manifestation, for there is no coming to be of something which is non-existent.

the mind conforms itself to each of them destruction and rise *as they are its characteristics.* This sūtra goes with the previous one and is to be taken with it.

By a process of restriction (niyama), the mind, conforming to destruction of dispersion and rise of one-pointedness, changes so that samādhi is predominant. The conforming by mind to destruction of dispersiveness and rise of one-pointedness is the samādhi transformation. Predominance of samādhi in the state of one-pointedness may be defined as: that which in the state of one-pointedness illumines the object (of concentration).

He says: *That very mind conforming to the natural passing away and uprising* both inherent in it *of its two characteristics* dispersiveness and one-pointedness, *is concentrated. It is called the samādhi transformation* because samādhi is predominant in it.

Sūtra III.12

In that (samādhi) the sameness of the idea which has subsided and the newly risen idea in the mind is its transformation of one-pointedness

In the concentrated mind, the earlier idea having subsided, the next idea which rises is similar to it. The mind in samādhi assumes the form of both of them. This is repeated in just the same way till the breaking of the samādhi.

Of the mind which possesses that characteristic: this is the transformation of one-pointedness.

In that time of samādhi *the sameness of the idea which has subsided and the newly risen idea in the mind is its transformation of one-pointedness. In the concentrated mind* whose mental process is inhibited from going out *the earlier idea subsides* is subdued: *the next idea which rises* appears *is the same.* The concentrated mind means a mind in the state of samādhi, which is distinguished by concentration (samādhāna); *The mind in samādhi assumes the form of both* the ideas, the subsided and the newly risen. *This is repeated in just the same way:* the first idea having subsided, a further one of similar nature is born, and when that has subsided yet another rises, and when that too subsides, still another rises, and so *till the breaking of the samādhi,* up to the breaking of the samādhi by a saṃskāra of extraversion. *Of the mind which possesses the characteristic,* of assuming the form of subsidence and rise of similar ideas every instant, *this is the transformation of one-pointedness.*

Of these three transformations (inhibition, samādhi, and one-pointedness), the inhibitive transformation is the state where the mind is saṃskāra-s alone, as a result of inhibition of external mental processes (bāhya-vṛtti).

The samādhi transformation is from inhibition of external ideas (pratyaya), moving towards inhibition of all ideas but before total inhibition of ideas. For there will be no rise of one-pointedness at the later stage of inhibition of all ideas.

Then the one-pointed transformation is the similarity of the next thought to the one that has just subsided, which is possible only at the time of samādhi.

The three have been presented in an order so that a later one is interior to an earlier one.

(Opponent) What is the point of setting all these out?

(Answer) The purpose is meditation, on detachment. For it is all movement of the guṇa-s, and its character is nothing but change of guṇa-s. Also there is the purpose of teaching that knowledge of the past and future arise from saṃyama on the three transformations.

Sūtra III.13

By (analogy with) that, are explained the transformations of dharma, time-phase, and basis (avasthā) in the elements and in the senses

That just described mental transformation, in the form of dharma, time-phase and basis, is to be taken as extending to change of dharma, change of time-phase, and change of basis, in the elements and in the senses.

By (analogy with) that are explained the transformations of dharma, time-phase, and basis, in the elements and in the senses. That just described mental transformation – of what kind? – *in the form of dharma, time-phase, and basis* in the form of dharma, in the form of time-phase, and in the form of basis, *in the elements and in the senses* in physical elements like the earth and in the senses such as hearing where there is no change into a different principle (tattva). Change once recognized in the unsteadiness of mind, the *extension* is made to change in the elements and senses; difficult though it is to apprehend, it can be seen to be like the transformations of the mind in the three states of the yogin.

(Opponent) But the mental transformations that have just been described were: inhibition, samādhi, and one-pointedness, and not change of dharma, time-phase, or basis. So how can there be any extension?

(Answer) He shows how the latter have been covered too:

The repression and manifestation of the extraversion-inhibition pair in the dharmin (their possessor, the mind) is a transformation of dharma. The three time-phases of inhibition, corresponding to the three periods of time, are time-phase transformation. Putting aside the time-phase of the future, without leaving its dharma-hood, it comes to the present time-phase, where it is manifest as it really is: this is its second period.

The repression and manifestation in the dharmin the mind *of the extraversion-inhibition pair* of dharma-s *is a change of dharma.*

By referring to this difference between dharma-s, we have spoken of dharma-difference, and by referring to the repression and manifestation of the two dharma-s, extraversion and inhibition, we have assuredly spoken of changes of time-phase and basis.

How so? When from the present time-phase a dharma is changed to the time-phase of the past, it is repressed, and one which from the future phase is changed to the present phase, becomes manifest. From that reference to repression and manifestation, the slight change of basis at every instant has been indicated. As he says: *the three phases of inhibition are a time-phase transformation, corresponding to* presented along with *the three periods* past, future and present. Something that changes must inevitably have the three periods one after another. But an immutable in which they do not exist is called unchanging (kūṭastha).

This inhibition *putting aside the period of the future time-phase, comes to the present without leaving its dharma-hood* of inhibition, since no effect can originate which is not already existent. For if non-existent effects did originate, one thing would not have the three times, since there would be no three phases as determined by the three times. So he says: Without ever going away from its dharma-hood *it comes to the present time-phase, where* in which present phase *it is manifest as what it really is. This period is the second period* of inhibition – second in relation to the period of the future.

But when extraversion arises in the time-phase of the present, inhibition then enters its third period, the phase of the past, and this it is which comes to be its third period.

It is not separated from the time-phases of past and future.

In the same way, extraversion has three time-phases, as conjoined with the three periods. Putting aside the period of the present time-phase, without leaving its dharma-hood, it comes to the time-phase of the past. This is the second period for it. And it is not separated from the future and present time-phases.

Extraversion, having put aside the time-phase of the future in which it was held, comes to the time-phase of the present, without leaving its dharma-hood. And now, it functions in manifestation as its own true nature. This is its second period, and it is not separated from the past and future time-phases. Thus now there is inhibition, and now there is extraversion.

(Opponent) If this is so, then while it is still in the time-phase of the present, there is not a triple time-period of inhibition.

(Answer) To this he says: *It is not separated from the time-phases of past and future.* Why not? Because it is this which *is* future, present and past.

In the same way, extraversion has three time-phases, as conjoined with the three periods past, future and present; *putting aside the period of the time-phase of the present, without leaving its dharma-hood,* as was explained in the case of inhibition, when the dharma of the inhibitor was changing to the present period, *comes to the time-phase* the period *of the past. This is the second period for it,* for extraversion, taking the present as the first period. But in relation to the second, the third time-period itself will become second. *And it is not separated from the future and present time-phases.*

Again, *extraversion, having put aside the time-phase of the future in which it was held* by reason of a saṃskāra of inhibition, *comes to the time-phase of the present, without leaving its dharma-hood. And now, it functions in manifestation as its own true nature* in its proper operative or preventive capacities. *This is its second period* in relation to the future, *and it is not separated from the past and future time-phases.*

In this way the mind is disjointed from the dharma-pain of extraversion and inhibition. *Thus now there is inhibition, and now there is extraversion.* This is the change of time-phase of the mental dharma-s, extraversion and inhibition.

Similarly, change of saṃskāra-basis (avasthā) is described. At moments of inhibition, the saṃskāra-s of inhibition become powerful and the saṃskāra-s of extraversion are weakened. Such is the change of saṃskāra-basis of the dharma-s.

There is change for the dharmin (possessor) in his dharma-s, change for dharma-s in the time-phases of the three periods, change for the time-phases in the saṃskāra-basis.

Thus it is that the operation of the guṇa-s is never without changes of dharma, of time-phase and of saṃskāra-basis. The operation of the guṇa-s fluctuates. It is said that the essence of the guṇa-s is to cause activity. On these lines has to be understood the three-fold change in the elements and in the senses, arising from making a distinction between dharma and dharmin.

Similarly the change in saṃskāra-basis is described. What is it then? *At moments of inhibition* when inhibition is in the present phase *the saṃskāra-s of inhibition become powerful,* by the fact of its saṃskāra-s being powerful, inhibition itself dominates, *and the saṃskāra-s of extraversion are weakened,* with corresponding weakness of extraversion. Similarly, at the time of extraversion there is relative superiority of the extravertive saṃskāra-s and weakening of the inhibitive saṃskāra-s. *Such is the change of the saṃskāra-basis of the dharma-s,* which latter are conjoined from moment to moment with the strength, and corresponding weakness on the other side, of the basic saṃskāra-s.

He now shows which sort of change applies to which: *There is change for the dharmin (possessor) in his dharma-s,* as for example for the mind, their possessor, in its dharma-s like inhibition and extraversion; *(change) for dharma-s in the time-phases of the three periods,* as for mental dharma-s like inhibition in the phases of future, etc., *and change for the time-phases in the saṃskāra-basis,* as for the time-phases like the present in the strength and weakening of the saṃskāra basis.

Thus it is that the operation of the guṇa-s is never without never free from *changes of dharma, time-phase, and saṃskāra-basis.*

The operation of the guṇa-s fluctuates, and on that very point *it is said that the essence of the guṇa-s* sattva and the other two *is to cause activity,* being altogether causes impelling towards some operation. *On these lines has to be understood* in the light of the three-fold change in dharma, in time-phase, and in saṃskāra-basis which has been demonstrated, *the three-fold change in elements and in the senses, arising from making a distinction between dharma and dharmin.*

> *Ultimately however change is only one. Because the dharma is simply the nature of its dharmin, so it is merely a change of the dharmin that evolves by way of dharma-s. In this case a dharma at present in the dharmin has a different state in the time-periods. It is not that there is difference in the material substance. As when a vessel of gold is broken up and made into a different form, its state is different, but it is not that there is any difference in the material of the gold.*
>
> *An objector says: Your dharmin is (supposed to be) superior to dharma-s. (But if there were) any persisting entity, never changing from what it was previously, still it will have followed (at any rate) the difference of state between earlier and later: it would, in spite of its 'immutability' have been changing.*

Ultimately however change is only one. How so? *Because dharma is simply the nature of its dharmin (possessor),* for dharma has no separate existence in the absence of the dharmin, nor can there be any separate time-phase if dharma is excluded, nor can there be any separate existence of saṃskāra-basis without time-phase.

So it is merely the change of the dharmin that evolves by way of dharma-s by way of the triple distinction in dharma.

(Opponent) What then is the change of the dharmin? Is it not origination and destruction of what is absolutely non-existent previously?

(Answer) To this he says: *In this case, a dharma* for instance a jar *at present in the dharmin* namely the clay *has a different state in the time-periods of past, future and present,* there being difference in the notion of it: 'The jar is past, is present, is in the future' – (ideas) conceived of the jar which is present in the dharmin. The difference is simply between the dharma-s being manifest or being concealed. *It is not that there is difference in the material substance,* it is simply the clay material, another form of the dharmin.

Now he explains with an example: *As when a vessel of gold is broken up and is made into a different form* such as a bracelet *its state is different,* the difference being in the form of a svastika or a bracelet and so on, *but it is not that there is any difference in the material of the gold.*

An objector who professes the doctrine of origination from non-existence (asat-kārya-samārambhābhimānī) *says: 'Your (supposed) dharmin is to be superior to dharma-s* but it will be in fact a collection of dharma-s not yet existent, coming together one after another. There is no one dharmin persisting through the dharma-s past, future and present, yet apart from them. *(But if there were) any persisting entity* (which would in fact have to be) not superior to dharma-s, not apart from dharma-s, *never changing from what it was previously* with each successive change of the nature of the material, *still it will have followed* conformed to *(at any rate) the difference of state between earlier and later,* between the states of past, etc., and that would involve this contradiction: This dharmin which you postulate *would, in spite of its "immutability" have been changing* – in its supposed unchangingness, it would yet be changing.'

> *(Answer) This is no fallacy, because we do not take an absolute position. Everything in the three worlds passes away from its (state of) manifestation, and so there is no unchangeability, because this denies permanence. Though it has passed away, it exists, for its destruction is denied.*

(Answer) *This is no fallacy.* Why not? *Because we do not take an absolute position,* we do not take the position that the dharmin is absolutely unchanging, nor that it perishes absolutely. If the dharmin were absolutely unchanging, like the Self (ātman), then there would result the fallacy of unchangeability, because the dharma-s are not different from our dharmin. But we do not accept absolute unchangeability of the guṇa-s, which are the dharmin-s, for he is going to speak of the perpetual changeability of the guṇa-s.

Or again, we do not take a position of absolute difference or absolute non-difference as regards the dharma and dharmin. If there is absolute non-difference of the dharma-s from the persisting dharmin-s, it will result in unchangeability, whereas if it is absolute difference of the dharma-s, it would entail their absolute destruction. But neither absolute difference nor absolute non-difference is accepted by us, so there is no fallacy of unchangeability.

(Opponent) How is it that there is not unchangeability?

(Answer) To this he says: *Every thing in the three worlds passes away from its (state of) manifestation, and so there is no unchangeability.* Why not? *Because this denies permanence.* From the very fact that effects exist, permanence is denied.

(Opponent) Then the things are absolutely destroyed.

(Answer) To this he says: *Though it has passed away, its destruction is denied,* for the cause persists, and as the effect is no different from the cause, absolute destruction is certainly refuted. Now here it is said by some people:

(Opponent) This is a case of the fallacy of self-contradiction. How so? The modification passes away out of manifestation, for its permanence is denied; yet though it has passed away, it still exists, for its destruction is denied. So a reason has been given 'because permanence is denied' which is contradicted by the conclusion 'though passed away, the modification still exists'.

How can this be? Manifestation is coming to be what a thing is (ātma-lābha); passing (apāya) is its disappearance (pracyuti). If a modification, destroyed from being-what-it-is (ātma-lābha), (yet still) exists, it cannot be denied that it is permanent. Existence of the modification even when passed away out of manifestation has to be called permanence (on this showing).

What denies permanence is the disappearance of the modification from being-what-it-is; what disappears from being-what-it-is is impermanent; what exists does not disappear from being-what-it-is. Existence, and disappearance of being-what-it-is are two opposing qualities (dharma), and these two can not coexist. This reason, which having settled for a final conclusion goes on to negate that very same thing is what is termed a self-contradictory reason(ing).

(Answer) Our position has no such defect. As when something like a jar, though present, is not perceived (because it is) in an inner apartment, but cannot thereby be stated not to exist, inasmuch as it is made manifest by means of a light, so this triple world, coming together as causal relationship, is present but not clearly manifest, because it consists essentially of guṇa-s, but is made manifest by the impelling cause of the purposes of Puruṣa.

So it is that motion, on the destruction of its own saṃskāra and manifestation of the saṃskāra of stasis, according to causal association, goes out of manifestation. As when the light of a lamp is covered up, a jar and so on, though present, go out of manifestation because of the obscuring darkness, so here too the Great principle and the other qualities undergo creation and dissolution in the three time-periods, but not so sattva and the other two guṇa-s which possess those dharma-s.

So it is that the ultimate support of the Great principle and the rest, by sattva and the other two guṇa-s, does not have the quality of manifesting as a qualified thing (dharma-bhūta), but being a mass of altogether latent (niruddha) subtle dharma-s, is not perceived in the form of manifestation of physical dharma-s. Thus it was said: *Everything in the three worlds passes out of manifestation,* not that it passes away from the nature of the dharmin. And because it is permanent in its nature of dharmin, it is further said: *Though it has passed away, it exists.*

Thus there is a single dharmin of manifest form and also of potential form. As manifest it is transient, and as potential it is permanent, so how is there any contradiction? Devadatta, who is always seen going about in the course of his business, will not cease to be when his activity ceases: it is only the activity that has disappeared. So it is that the dharmin exists in the unmanifest state, as it is also observed in the state of manifestation; (when unmanifest) it is like a jar left in complete darkness.

Even the manifest thing is a dharmin in regard to its own various dharma-s; as dharmin it is taken as permanent, and as dharma-s it is transient. So among modifications (of prakṛti) there is no hard-and-fast distinction of dharma and dharmin, and it is quite acceptable that it should be inconclusive.

This does not contradict what was said: *it passes out of manifestation:* a reason was given, *because permanence is denied.* Nor is there contradiction in the words *though passed away, it exists.* The two statements refer to two different things. Nor does *because destruction is denied* conflict with *though passed away, it exists.* For Devadatta, though passed away from out-of-doors, still exists.

Now you might think: *exists* expresses permanence; then the assertion of permanence involves a contradiction with *because permanence is denied.* It is not so, because we do not accept the premise. We do not maintain permanence of manifestation, and this is the permanence that is being denied. We maintain that there are dharma-s both of potentiality and of manifestation, and that is how it is to be explained.

For one who does not see this, a further example may be given to remove the sense of a contradiction: the case of the blind man's mirror. It is like some blind man who, not realizing his own inability to see, procures a mirror for his own use.

Again, if you try to establish one side by saying that there is an illusory projection (adhyāropa) of permanence and transience, or manifestation and potentiality, on to the one locus, that cannot be a contradiction either, because it does not bring about a conflict (viparita). Why not? It was said *Though passed away, it exists ... because permanence is denied.* To say *because permanence is denied* comes down to saying *because of impermanence*; yet the existence of what has passed away asserts its permanence. The opposite of permanence is impermanence. But impermanence of one element is no reason for an impermanence (of the other, an assertion) which would contradict its permanence, and so bring about a conflict. For as it cannot in fact produce that undesirable conflict, it should not lead us to a contradiction.

You may insist that what has been termed denial of permanence should rather be called cessation from being-what-it-is (ātma-lābhāt pracyuti). Even so, this is simply a verbal difference, not a difference in meaning. Cessation from being-what-it-is, and impermanence, mean the same thing.

Then you may prefer the words 'because there is no possibility of permanence'; but in fact our phrase 'because permanence is denied' does express the meaning 'because there is no possibility of permanence'.

You may argue that this explanation of the meaning has been arbitrarily attributed (āropya), but to this we reply that the facts of permanence or impermanence are not maintained (absolutely) in the face of the difference between potential and manifest, and between dharma and dharmin.

By this reasoning we refute the charge of contradiction in the words: *Though it has passed away, it exists, for its destruction is denied.*

(Opponent) But how, on your theory, can you maintain the existence of something which, having passed out of manifestation, is not now being directly cognized (by the senses)? Inasmuch as it is not perceived, it does not exist, any more than a flower in the sky.

(Answer) The answer is, that non-cognizance (through the senses: anupalabdhi) is not conclusive, for there is cognizance by inference and by authority. What has manifested must have existed before it appeared, and out of that (pre-existence) it appeared. If it were non-existent it would never appear, any more than the horn of a hare. To allow existence of the non-existent, and non-existence of the existent, would mean that one could have no confidence in anything. Further, if non-existence is assumed from non-cognition, then the causes and accessories leading to the release of Selves could not exist or arise before they were cognized: so how could any of them ever be attained?

> *When it merges into its cause, it becomes subtle, and for that reason is not directly cognized. A dharma has changes of time-phase, present and past, in the three time-periods. Conjoined to the past time-phase, it is not disjoined from future and present. So what is present now is conjoined to the present time-phase but not disjoined from the past and future ones, and being joined to the future time-phase, is not disjoined from those of the present and past: as a man, though captivated by one woman, is not unattracted by others.*

'Of the non-existent (a-sat) there is no coming-to-be (bhāva); there is no not-coming-to-be of the existent,' says the holy text (āgama: Gītā II.16). Non-cognizance by the senses is no sufficient reason for (postulating) non-existence.

(Opponent) Well then, if the modification of the manifestation does exist, why is it not cognized?

(Answer) Though in the field of direct sense-perception, *when it merges into its cause, it becomes subtle, and for that reason is not directly cognized'*, the non-cognition is not because it is non-existent.

Now he goes on to speak of the change of time-phase of the objects and senses. *A dharma has changes of time-phase, present and past, in the three time-periods,* as a dharma is clay-lump, jar and so on, in the time-periods of the past and others. What is being said here?

Conjoined to the past time-phase, not that it has become non-existent. And *not disjoined from future and present,* the two other phases. The cause, the clay, is present, and even when the jar, etc. which are implicit in it are not perceivable, still the jar is thereby conjoined to the present time-phase. In the same way, the jar-which-is-to-be is the future of that clay, and in that sense we say 'It will be' – it is not disjoined from the future time-phase. *So what is present now is conjoined to the present time-phase, but not disjoined from the past and future ones, and* what is future *being joined to future time-phase, is not disjoined from those of the present and past.* A jar, being essentially clay in the past and future, is not disjoined from the other time-phases by the fact of its being clearly seen now.

(Opponent) How can a dharma conjoined to one time-phase not be disjoined from the other two?

(Answer) He gives a parallel instance of (being conjoined to one and yet) not being disjoined (from others): *as a man, though captivated by one woman, is not unattracted by others.* The passion for the others, however, is conjoined to the past and future times. It has been shown that this is because there is no destruction of the existent and no coming into being of the non-existent.

Here a difficulty is brought forward by others:

(Opponent) In the change of time-phase, everything is conjoined to all the phases, so there must be confusion of the time-periods (on your theory).

(Answer) This is the refutation: in the case of the dharma-s the fact of their being so does not have to be proved, and in the being-so of the dharma-s, the difference of time-

phase is also predicated. The present situation is not the only one. For (if it were, as the objector proposes) then this mind should never have the dharma of sexual passion, just because at the time of anger, sexual passion is not presenting itself.

Here a difficulty is brought forward by others:

(Opponent) *In the change of time-phase, everything* every dharma *is conjoined to all the phases, so there must be confusion of the time-periods.* How so? Because (on your theory) what is to be, is present now, and also past. There would be presence and futurity in the past, and pastness and futurity in what is present, and pastness and presence in what is future. Thus the time-periods would be mutually confused.

(Answer) *This is the refutation,* namely: *In the case of the dharma-s, the fact of their being so does not have to be proved.* In the case of a dharmin, say clay, its dharma-s – being a lump, being a jar, or being a dish – do not have to be proved to be so, namely different from other dharma-s, and *in the being-so of the dharma-s, the difference of time-phase is also predicated.* In the dharma-s being so and not otherwise, the difference of time-phase is also predicated as a fact.

How is this? For instance, when there is the stage of the clay lump, the jar conjoined to the future time is not present, nor is it past; and yet looked at as future clay-ness, it is not disjoined from the past and present.

So when conjoined to the present, it is not past nor yet future; and yet seen as a form of the dharmin, it is not disjoined from the past time-phase when it ceased to be, and from the future one where it comes into being.

Again, the past is conjoined to the past time and is not present nor future; and yet from the point of view of the manifestation of its clayness in direct experience, it is not unconnected with present and future.

It should be considered in its relationship with lumps and dishes and so on, and therefore he says: *The present situation is not the only one,* not the only time-phase of the dharma, for it has the three times, as has been explained. Thus the time-periods are not confused with each other.

For then (if the objection were valid) *this mind should never have the dharma of sexual passion)* the mind would be a dharmin free from passion, and no dharma of passion and the like, and the difference between them, could be established in it. The time-periods would be confused with each other. Why? *because at the time of anger, sexual passion is not presenting itself*

For at the time of anger, sexual passion does not present itself as if that were its own time, because at the time of anger, the passion is either past or future. So it is with anger at the time of passion. For if there were only the one time-phase – the present situation, in fact – then even at a time of anger, the sexual passion might present itself, or might not present itself, or else perhaps would never fail to be there even at any time of anger.

> *Moreover it is not possible for the three time-phases to be present at the same time in a single development; what would be possible is a sequence, each manifesting according to its particular causes. And it is said: 'The powers of the present form and the powers of development are in conflict, but the common elements (in the dharmin) co-operate with the dominating powers.'*
>
> *Therefore there is no confusion. When, for instance, sexual passion presents itself in relation to one person, it is not then non-existent in regard to other women. It is simply that it is continued in the common basis: in this sense it is existent at that time for that object. Time-phase also is to be explained on these lines.*

Moreover it is not possible for the three time-phases to be present at the same time in a single development of time, because of the contradiction (between them), *what would be possible is a sequence* a temporal sequence of the individual time-phases *each manifesting according to its particular causes,* the particular causes which bring about the jar, etc.

And it is said: 'The powers of present form and the powers of development are in conflict.' In the jar conjoined to the powers that have developed the present form, the powers which would develop the forms of lump and so on do not prevail because of the conflict between them; and so it is that the past and future forms, which are not in conflict since they conform equally to the dharmin, being *the common elements (in the dharmin), co-operate with the dominating powers.*

Therefore there is no confusion of the time-periods. For *When, for instance, sexual passion presents itself in relation to one person, it is not then non-existent in regard to other women.* What is it then? *It is simply that it is continued in the common basis* in the form of the mind, past or even in the future; *in this sense it is existent at that time for that object. The time-phase is explained on these lines.*

(Opponent) There is this doubt. The lump and the dish are past or future, and therefore do not exist in the jar state. They are in fact the past and future states of the dharmin called clay, and it is not a question of time-periods of lump and dish and so on.

> *It is not the dharmin that has the three time-periods, but the dharma-s that have them. They, defined by time-phase, are coming to particular states, and they are referred to as something different, because the thing is now in another state, not that it is another substance.*
>
> *It is like the single stroke, which in the hundreds place is 100, in the tens place is 10, and that same stroke in the units place is 1. Again, it is like the very same woman's being called mother and also daughter and sister.*

(Answer) The reply is: *It is not the dharmin that has the three time-periods, but the dharma-s that have them.* The dharmin called clay is not past or future by the pastness or futurity of the lump or dish. For in all these dharma-s, it conforms to what we recognize as clay. What then? It is the dharma-s, the clay-lump and so on, which have the three time-periods, as at the time of the pot we do not see the lump or the dish. So it is unquestionable that it is the dharma-s that have the conjunction with the three time-periods.

They the dharma-s *defined by the time-phase,* the clay lump and the others being marked out as being in one of the three time-periods *are coming to particular states* of strength or weakness, etc., *and they are referred to as something different,* as when a new pot has become old, *because the thing is now in another state, not that it is another substance* apart from the clay.

It is like the single stroke, which in the hundreds place namely the third place, the first two (units and tens) being vacant, *is 100; in the tens place is 10,* being in the second place with the units column empty; *and that same stroke in the units place is 1. Again, it is like the very same woman's being called mother and also daughter and sister,* from another point of view.

This is all simply difference of verbal notions arising from difference of state, but not from difference of dharma or of dharmin. And thereby, what is said by others to the effect that difference of verbal notion, time-phase, dharma, time and so on, is the cause of difference of effect and cause is shown to be fallacious.

> *As to change of state, it is said by some that this involves the defect of entailing immutability:*

> *(Opponent) The time-periods are determined by the functioning of the thing itself. When a dharma is not functioning as itself, then it is future. When it does so function, then it is present. When it has done so and has ceased, then it is past. As the dharmin-s are permanent, there will result immutability of dharma-s, time-phase, and state. This is the defect which is now put forward.*

As to the third change, *change of state, it is said by some that this involves the defect of entailing immutability (kauṭasthya).* What is this corollary of immutability?

(Opponent) *The time-periods* the present and the other two *are determined by the functioning of the thing itself* In what way? *When a dharma* a pot in the state of the lump *is not functioning as itself then it is future. When it does so function then it is present. When it has done so and has ceased, then it is past.* Here it is only the fact that the dharma has attained, or is now attaining, or will attain in the future, its innate functioning, becoming the dharmin as it really is, that establishes it in a state. And therefore, *as the dharmin-s* the guṇa-s *are permanent* because they can never be impermanent, *there will result immutability of dharma-s, time-phase, and state. This is the defect now put forward.*

> *(Answer) There is no such defect. Why not? Because even though a possessor of attributes (guṇin) may be permanent, there is variety from the clash between the attributes themselves. As any aggregate with a beginning, being purely dharma of imperishables such as sound, perishes – so the liṅga (Great principle), being purely a dharma of the imperishable guṇa-s, itself perishes. This is the technical meaning of change (vikāra).*

(Answer) *There is no such defect. Why not? Because even though a possessor of attributes may be permanent, there is variety from the clash between the attributes themselves.* Because of the variety of (degrees of) dominance or subjection among them, absolute immutability like the Puruṣa cannot be conceded to the guṇa-s. For the fact of change is generally accepted. Though they are ceaselessly changing, still no amount of mutual clashing leads to their becoming something else: so there is no immutability.

What is this variety of clashing? He says: *As any aggregate* like the body *with a beginning* having a cause *being purely a dharma* not other than the nature of that cause *perishes,* that dharma disappearing with the rise of another. Of what is the aggregate? He explains: *of imperishables like sound. So the liṅga* known as the Great principle, *with a beginning* having a cause *being purely a dharma, perishes* having become the nature *of the imperishable guṇa-s. This is the technical meaning of change (vikāra),* as being merely change of the dharma of the Great principle and the rest, and not of the guṇa-s. There is no destruction of the guṇa-s by their clashing variously: the guṇa-s are eternal by nature.

> *As an illustration of it: clay is a dharmin. Entering another form (a jar) from the lump form, it changes from that lump dharma. The jar form, having quitted the time-phase of futurity, now enters the present phase, and thus changes in the temporal sense.*
>
> *Then, the jar is every instant experiencing (change in) newness and age, and thus undergoes change of condition (avasthā). Condition is another dharma of the dharmin itself, and condition is another time-phase of the dharma also.*
>
> *Change is only one: a transformation of the substance, though analysed variously. The analysis should be applied to other things too.*

These changes of dharma, time-phase, and condition, do not overstep the bounds of the nature of the dharmin. The change is only one, which flows forth in all these particular ways: because change is disappearance of a preceding dharma, and rise of another dharma, in an enduring substance.

As an illustration of it: clay is a dharmin. Entering another form (a jar) from the lump form, it changes from that lump dharma. (The jar form, having quitted the time-phase of futurity, now enters the present phase, and thus changes in the temporal sense – omitted in the Vivaraṇa: Tr.)

Then, the jar is every instant experiencing (change in) newness and age, and thus undergoes change of condition (avasthā). Condition is another dharma such as a lump form *of the dharmin itself such*as clay in the sense that the dharmin comes to the condition of lump, dish, and other forms. *Of the dharma also,* the jar and so on, *the condition is another time-phase* such as the past. For it is that very jar, the dharma, which meets with the past, future, or present condition.

So *Change is only one … though analysed variously. The analysis should be applied to other things too,* to things other than the clay example – for instance, to body and senses.

These changes of dharma, time-phase and condition do not overstep the bounds of the nature of the dharmin. The change of the dharmin *is only one, which flows forth in all these particular ways,* namely change of dharma, time-phase, and condition. How is this? *because change is disappearance of a preceding dharma, and rise of another dharma, in an enduring substance,* and it is in this sense that the dharmin can be said to have change.

Sūtra III.14

What conforms to the subsided, uprisen, and indeterminable dharma-s is the dharmin

The dharma itself is the appropriate particularization of the mere potentiality of the dharmin. This potentiality of the dharmin is the dharma itself. It is inferred as an actual existence from the difference in effects to which it gives rise, one after another in the one (dharmin).

Of these, one that is visible is the present, exercising its own special function, and it is distinguished from other dharma-s which are either subsided or indeterminable. But when it accommodates itself to the common basis, being then simply the true nature of the dharmin, what is there to be distinguished, and by what?

What, then, is the dharmin? In an enduring basis, with the cessation of one dharma, another rises up, and this is called change. *What conforms to the subsided, uprisen, and indeterminable,* what is always conforming to the dharma-s, subsided, uprisen or indeterminable, which thus goes with them, by nature undivided in the divided, *is* determined to be *the dharmin. The dharma itself is the appropriate particularization of the mere potentiality of the dharmin:* it can change like the coils of a rope and so on, and *this potentiality* of circularity, etc. *of the dharmin is the dharma itself.*

So it exists in the dharmin, even when unmanifest: *it is inferred as an actual existence from the difference in effects to which it gives rise.* As when a lump of gold produces, at another place and another time, some effect like an earring, from the difference of effects one sees that this is manifesting to bring forth products dissimilar or similar; so in the dharmin it is inferred as an actual existence. *in the one* dharmin there are *one after another* dharma-s.

By these words he indicates that there are countless dharma-s in a single dharmin.

Of these, one that is visible is the present, exercising its own special function – for instance, carrying water; *and it is distinguished from other dharma-s which are either subsided or indeterminable. But when it accommodates itself to the common basis* the nature of the dharmin, *then being simply that true nature of the dharmin* having become the essential nature of the dharmin *what is there to be distinguished, and by what* could it be particularized? There is distinction only of forms corresponding to function, but not of something that is seen to have reverted to its cause – that is the point.

> *Those dharma-s of the dharmin which having been active have now ceased to function are the subsided: those that are in function are the uprisen, following on from their future time-phase. So also those that are past are following on from their present time-phase. Why should they not be following on (others in) the past? Because there is no before and after (there). There are priority and following on in the case of future and present: not so in the case of the past. So there is no following on by what is past. It is only the future which follows on the past.*

Now what are the dharma-s: subsided, uprisen, or indeterminable? *Those dharma-s of the dharmin which having been active have now ceased to function are the subsided; those that are in function are the uprisen, following on from their future time-phase.* So also *the past ones are following on from their present. Why should they not be following on (others in) the past?* It is a rhetorical question: they do not do so. *Because there is no before and after (there).* One who is behind another is his immediate successor, and the other one is first in relation to him. In this case, no one by himself can be first, since there is no one behind him. The past (dharma-s) then cannot follow on (others in) the past, *because there is no before and after (there). There are priority and following-on of future and present: not so in the case of the past. So there is no following-on by what is past.*

There is a reading (of the next sentence) which goes: 'It is only the future which follows on the present', but that would not be relevant to the context. So the reading must be: *It is only the future which follows on the past,* for that is to the point. How so? When a saṃskāra of extraversion is first overcome by a saṃskāra of inhibition, that saṃskāra of extraversion comes into the time-period of the past, having left the time-period of the present. But it is something yet-to-come-again in the future, which then becomes present, though not in direct sequence (from the past). This is why it is said that it is only the future which follows on the past.

> *What are the indeterminable (dharma-s)? Everything has the nature of everything.*

On this it has been said: every form of taste and the other sense qualities, being modifications of water and earth, are observed in plants, and these which are in the plants are in the same way in animals, and those of animals in plants. Thus everything, irrespective of genus, has the nature of everything.

How so? *On this it has been said: every form of taste and the other sense qualities, being modifications of water and earth, are observed in plants.* Just as the one quality of taste is met with in all sorts of forms – in, for example, sugar-cane and ginger, namely as sweetness and pungency respectively – so there is endless variety of colours such as whiteness or blackness, and so also with odours. *These which are in the plants are in the same way in animals,* as all the forms of taste and so on. When the plants are assimilated by them, all the forms of taste and colour, for instance, appear in the animals, *and those of animals in plants* which have assimilated them, in every form of taste and so on, as described by the science of forestry.

Also those of plants in plants, and of animals in animals. *Thus everything, irrespective of genus, has the nature of everything.* The three worlds exist on a finger's tip, and again: 'Brahmā created from his finger through its pores', and a hundred other such sacred texts and traditions confirm it.

> *Under the constraints of place, time, form, and cause, the essences do not manifest simultaneously. What runs through these dharma-s, manifest or unmanifest, is the dharmin which is their persisting support, and whose essence is both universal and particular.*

(Opponent) If everything has the nature of everything, then it should all be perceived everywhere, and there would never be the grief of separation from what is liked.

(Answer) In answer, he continues: *Under the constraints of place, time, form, and cause* there is restriction imposing constraint on place and so on, and so it is that *the essences* all the things *do not manifest simultaneously.* As some particular one, only on a particular occasion, at some place and time and in some form, they take a body corresponding to the causes such as dharma, as does for instance Rahu (the demon consisting of a head alone, who swallows sun and moon at eclipses). So it is that there are such things as grief at separation from what is liked. Since in each case the causes spread out to an incalculable extent, the (future) dharma-s cannot be determined.

What runs through these dharma-s, manifest or unmanifest, subsided or uprisen or indeterminable *is the dharmin which is their persisting support, and whose essence is both universal and particular.*

> *But for some (Buddhists) who hold there are dharma-s alone without any persisting support, there should be no experience. Why not? Because, when some action had been performed by one consciousness (vijñāna), how could another be made responsible in the sense of experiencing (its effects)? And there should be no memory: one person does not remember what was seen by another. And from the fact of recognition, it must be admitted that there is a permanent dharmin persisting through the dharma-changes. Thus there is no question of dharma-s alone, without any persisting support.*

But for some philosophers (= vijñāna-vādin Buddhist) *who hold there are dharma-s alone without any persisting support,* external or internal (ādhyātmika), and for whom there is supposed to be just knowledge alone: since his dharma-s are perishing at every instant, never attaining states of past, future and present at the same time, so that there cannot be any relation like experience-experiencer, *there should be no experience.*

He demonstrates why there would be no such relation. *Why not? When some action had been performed by one consciousness (vijñāna), how could another* consciousness, which would not have been the doer, *be made responsible in the sense of experiencing (its karmic effects)?* It is proper that the relation should be between the fruit and the agent who has intended it. It would be absurd to have one person the agent but someone else having responsibility for the fruit.

And there would be no memory: there would be no such memory as 'I have done what I had to do'. *One person does not remember what was seen by another:* Vasumitra does not remember what has been seen by Caitra. *And from the fact of recognition,* for we do recognize: 'that indeed is this.'

So *it is admitted* has to be accepted *that there is a permanent dharmin persisting through the dharma-changes.* It is not, however, that its true nature changes, for we realize, for instance, that it is still gold even when it conforms to the different shapes like ornaments. *Thus there is no question of dharma-s alone, without any persisting support.*

Sūtra III.15

Difference of sequence causes the differences of the changes

> *Difference of sequence causes the differences of the changes. If it is said that there can be only one change in one dharmin (the answer is): difference of sequence causes the differences of the changes.*
>
> *Thus with clay particles, there is the sequence of particle clay, lump clay, jar clay, shard clay, fragment clay. When one dharma follows immediately on another, it is its successor. When it is said that the clay lump is reborn as the jar, that is a sequence of dharma-change.*
>
> *The sequence of change of time-phase is, the jar's coming into the present from its future state, and the lump's going from the present to the past. There is no sequence from the past. Why not? Because there is immediate succession only when there is before and after, and there is none in the case of the past. Therefore the time-phase sequence is of the two times alone.*

Now the cause of the change-difference is given; it is when the differences are perfectly clear that it is possible to undertake a saṃyama meditation on the three changes.

For an idea about past and the others can only be produced by way of some indicatory mark, and not in any other way. *Difference of sequence causes the differences of the changes. If it is said that there can be only one change in one dharmin (the answer is):* there are dharma-differences among the dharma-s, etc., and for these differences there is a cause: *difference of sequence causes the differences of the changes.*

Sequence means immediate following, and change in it makes a difference. For each of the three sequences is observed to be marked off from the others. The dharma sequence is other than the sequences of time-phase and of condition; the time-phase sequence is other than those of dharma and of condition; and the condition sequence is other than those of dharma and time-phase. So the difference between them, thus clearly brought out, leads to the inference that sequence is the cause of the differences in the changes which are effects of sequence.

Thus there is the sequence, as regards a clay dharmin *of the clay particles* and the others listed; it changes according to the dharma-s, such as particle state, which do not appear simultaneously, but go into operation in sequence.

By using the word 'clay' with each, he demonstrates that it is the dharmin called clay which conforms to the dharma-s, such as particle, lump, jar, shard, and fragment, which are observably different from each other. The immediate successor to the particles is the lump; the immediate successor to the lump is the jar; the immediate successors to the jar are the broken pieces, and fragments are the immediate successors to the shards. So it is of dharma alone that there is *the sequence of particle clay, lump clay, jar clay, shard clay, and fragment clay:* this is a sequence of changes of dharma, not of time-phase, nor of condition. Then, *When one dharma follows immediately on another, it is its successor.* How is this? *When it is said that the lump is born again as the jar,* the sense is that the clay in the lump form becomes the jar. Figuratively they are non-different, and so it is said that the lump is reborn as the jar. It is not that the lump dharma does assume the nature of a different dharma. The succeeding dharma, called the jar dharma, destroys the lump dharma; having overcome it, it is born.

Dharma-change is of two kinds: change into something similar, and change into something dissimilar. When the lump is reborn as the jar, the dharmin called clay changes, in accordance with the dharma-s beginning with those of the jar, from the quite different lump, and this is a change of dharma-s which are dissimilar. But from the origin of the jar up to when it is broken, it changes only in accordance with the jar form alone, and this is change into the similar.

So with mind during inhibition. In the state of one-pointedness it changes in accordance with ideas similar in quality, as they are subdued and arise respectively; and mind also changes in accordance with dharma-s that are dissimilar, namely extraversion and inhibition. Then during periods of extraversion it undergoes change in accordance with ideas of dissimilar quality, namely peaceful, violent, or dull. All these are what is called the sequence of dharma-change.

Now he goes on to speak of the sequence of time-phase change. *The sequence of change of time-phase is the jar's coming into the present from its future state, and the lump's going from the present to the past,* corresponding to the rise of a dharma opposed to it. *There is no sequence from the past:* for the sequence of time-phase for the dharma was a time-phase immediately following on the present one, but there is no further time-phase following in immediate succession on a past one.

Why not? Because there is immediate succession only when there is before and after, and there is none in the case of the past. And therefore the time-phase sequence is of the two times alone, namely future and present. It is to show that there is no sequence in the past that he will say (in the sūtra III.52): From saṃyama on the instant and the two sequences of instants ...'

> *Then the sequence of change of condition: it is observed that a new jar in the end becomes old. It is inferred from the sequence which runs concurrently with the chain of moments, and has come into manifestation at the end. This third change is distinct from changes of dharma and of time-phase.*
>
> *While there is the difference of dharma and dharmin, these sequences take on their respective natures. In regard to another dharma, a dharma itself is a dharmin. But when from the highest standpoint it is shown that the non-different dharma is in the dharmin only figuratively, then this sequence appears as a simple unity.*

Then the sequence of change of condition: it is observed that a new jar in the end becomes old comes to its termination. *It is inferred from the sequence which runs concurrently with the chain of moments;*by the continuous erosion of its newness every moment, age will come upon it. And this at the very end, *has come into manifestation at the end.* But in the middle it is so subtle that it is not apparent, and so it is that in the middle stage the sequence is not observed, though it is there. It is to be inferred from the fact of its manifestation in the final stages: 'There must have been this sequence by which the ageing has brought about this final manifestation', for while the jar remained perfect, no ageing from moment to moment was observed. He will say (IV.33): 'The sequence is conjoined with every moment, (but) recognizable (only) at the very end.' So *this third change* of condition-sequence *is distinct* different *from changes of dharma or time.*

While there is difference of dharma and dharmin, these sequences take on their respective natures; so without difference of dharma and dharmin, there are no differences of sequence. *In regard to another dharma, a dharma itself is a dharmin.* Apart from guṇa-s, there is no dharma-dharmin relation.

In relation to unparticularized, the Great principle is the dharmin, and so with unparticularized in relation to particulars, and particulars in relation to quiescence or uprising. *But when from the highest standpoint it is shown that the non-different dharma is in the dharmin only figuratively, then this sequence appears as a simple unity.*

> *The dharma-s of the mind are two: observable and unobservable. Of these, the observable consists of ideas: the unobservable are things-in-themselves. The existence of the things-in-themselves is given to us through inference: inhibition, righteousness (dharma), saṃskāra-s, change; then life, activity, power. These are the dharma-s of the mind which are not open to observation.*

Now *The dharma-s of mind are two* of two sorts: *observable and unobservable,* perceptible and imperceptible. As to what they are, he explains: *Of these, the observable consist of ideas,* namely passion, aversion, delusion and so on. *The unobservable are things-in-themselves* existing in their own nature, but connected with effects.

And those imperceptible ones are just seven, existing functioning in their own sphere. How then are they known about? *The existence of the things-in-themselves is given to us through inference.* Their existence is known through the indications of their effects, but in themselves they are not accessible to any perception except divine perception. They are now listed:

Inhibition, dharma (righteousness), saṃskāra-s: inhibition has been explained already; righteousness means righteousness and unrighteousness both; saṃskāra-s, in the form of groups (vāsanā). *Change* is as defined above. Then he goes on: *life,* which comes to exist by a mental dharma characterized by the vital principle, engaging with all the senses in righteousness and the other purposes (of life), and this is what is called life, *activity,* functioning; *power,* potentiality, *are the dharma-s of the mind which are not open to observation,* not visible. This list of seven beginning with inhibition is given to describe the mental dharma-s which are not observable.

> *These (changes) are adduced as an object of saṃyama for a yogin who has acquired all the means for attaining the desired object (of knowledge of past and future).*

These three changes, in the form of dharma, time-phase, and condition, *are adduced as an object of saṃyama for a yogin who has acquired all the means,* who has become proficient in the whole range of them from restraint onwards, and whose saṃyama is very *firm, for attaining the desired object,* knowledge of what is past and future. Though three-fold, it is a single object of saṃyama.

Sūtra III.16

From saṃyama on the three changes, knowledge of what is past and future

From saṃyama on the changes of dharma, time-phase, and condition, knowledge of past and future things comes to the yogin. When dhāraṇā, dhyāna, and samādhi are made on the same thing, it is called saṃyama. By that, the three changes being directly perceived, there is produced knowledge of things past and future which are in them.

From saṃyama on the three changes, knowledge of what is past and future. The saṃyama is to be carried on up to the illumination of samādhi-prajñā.

Whatever object it is fixed on, it brings direct perception of that object as it really is. On whatever subtle or concealed or past or future or remote object the saṃyama is made, with the conscious intention to attain it, his purpose brings its fulfilment to the yogin.

From saṃyama on the changes of dharma, time-phase, and condition, knowledge of past and future things comes to the yogin. When dhāraṇā, dhyāna, and samādhi are made on the same thing, this is called saṃyama. By that saṃyama, *the three changes being directly perceived, there is produced knowledge of things past and future which are in them,* in the changes. Since all things are changeable by their conjunction with the past and the other changes, by making saṃyama on the three changes of all things, conjoined as they are with the three times, all things become directly perceived. And in that omniscient one who sees the uncertainty of what is inherently changing every moment, detachment is born.

Sūtra III.17

There is confusion from the mutual projection of word, meaning and idea on to each other. From saṃyama on their distinctness (comes) understanding of the cries of all beings

Now, another object for saṃyama is presented, directed towards word, meaning, and understanding. *There is confusion from the mutual projection of word, meaning, and idea on to each other. From saṃyama on their distinctness, understanding of the cries of all beings* is attained. Of these, what is word, and what again are the meaning and the idea? What is the cause of the confusion, and how are they to be distinguished?

> *With regard to these, speech has its function only in (uttering) letter-sounds. Hearing has as its field merely transformations of sound.*

With regard to these: what can be uttered by speech, and heard by ear, is word. The further point is examined, as to whether it is the voice alone, or apart from that. Bare utterance is not word. Why not? *speech has its function only in letter-sounds.* What is called speech is when the sense-organ is manifesting letter-sounds, depending on the eight places (of articulation), and fulfilling its purpose in mere manifestation of the letter-sounds. But it does not function to manifest a meaning, nor to manifest a word.

Nor is the sense of hearing of itself word, nor is word its special object. How so? Because *hearing has as its field merely transformations of sound,* and what is called sound may be either syllabic or non-syllabic. One particular transformation of it is of the nature of letter-sounds, a and so on; another would be the unintelligible sounds perceived in the cries of crows and other birds. The hearing being confined to making manifest merely transformations of sound, is not concerned with meaning and word.

> *A word, moreover, is something comprehensible by an idea binding together the tones (letter-sounds). They cannot combine (of themselves) because they cannot come together.*

(Opponent) Surely a word is simply what we can hear?

(Answer) No, because it must produce the notion of meaning; word is what causes meaning to be understood. What further is it? *A word, moreover, is something comprehensible by an idea binding together the tones.*

Tones are the sounds, objects of hearing, each of which ends after laying down a separate saṃskāra in the one attentive to them; the buddhi-idea which has been made to arise by the final sound is the buddhi-idea which binds together the tones. It originates from the saṃskāra which is laid down in the attentive mind from the binding together in sequence from the first sound onwards. What is grasped by that single buddhi(-notion) is the word. And since it is a matter of direct perception, as much as colours for instance, no other proof of it is needed.

(Opponent) But Revered (bhagavat) Upavarṣa says (that the word gauḥ – cow – is the letter-sounds g, au and a visarga (ḥ).

(Answer) It is not so, for (in mere letter-sounds) there is no expressiveness (of meaning). Why not? Because they cannot (of themselves) combine. *They cannot combine, because they cannot come together.* For at the time of pronunciation of g there is no au or ḥ; and at the time of pronunciation of the au there is no g, or ḥ; nor on the occasion of the operation of the visarga ḥ; are the other two there. Thus the letter-sounds cannot express (any meaning) because they cannot combine.

Just as there is no basis for simultaneous coexistence of the letter-sounds, in the same way their saṃskāra-s and memories, not being produced from them at the same time, cannot express (meaning) either. Another reason is that memory has a particular relation, applying only to some (previously) experienced object of its saṃskāra, whereas the (word-) notion is of something new.

To admit that saṃskāra-s had expressive power would contradict the accepted principles: 'Meaning is ascertained from word,' 'Relationship between things prior and things posterior is expressible by a verb,' and 'Dharma (right conduct) has (sacred) Word as its basis, so what is not based upon Word is to be disregarded.'

(Opponent) Still, capacity-to-be-a-word might be figuratively allowed to memory and saṃskāra, inasmuch as they consist essentially of the letter-sounds.

(Answer) Not so. The fact of consisting of letter-sounds as such amounts only to an unreal existence, (true only) if it were proved that letter-sounds are the word. (But they are not.) The world, because of indiscrimination, is under the delusion that the self is the body, etc., and so has this idea of it, though incorrect. But (popular opinion) is never a ground for taking something as an established fact.

Moreover, it is only with the operation of speech and hearing that the meaning is grasped, and this operation is necessary for them to have capacity-to-be-a-word as their essence. Now the final letter-sound does not express meaning because it is (only) a letter-sound like the first one, and it follows that memory-saṃskāra-s of final letter-sounds do not express meaning, because they are simply memory-saṃskāra-s like the memory-saṃskāra of the first one.

(Opponent) Suppose we say that the final letter-sound, with the aid of the saṃskāra-s laid down by the previous letter-sounds, expresses the meaning.

(Answer) Not so. Why not? Because that would entail that the meaning was produced simply from the pronunciation of the final letter-sound. How so? Because the hearer has (already) a mass of saṃskāra-s laid down by the letter-sounds g and so on uttered in days past, but the meaning would be recognized only from the utterance (today) of the final letter-sound.

(Opponent) Well, the pronunciation of the first letter-sound might have a limiting function?

(Answer) No. Since there is a time difference of the earlier ones from the last one, they cannot come into association to effect the restriction.

(Opponent) But for you too, when the letter-sounds do manifest the word, the earlier letter-sounds must have been pronounced as (progressively) limiting, so it is more reasonable that the expressive capacity be in the letter-sounds themselves rather than to propose (some entity like a sphoṭa meaning-flash) that is supposed to manifest the word.

(Answer) No. We only admit that the individual letter-sounds lay down their respective saṃskāra-s in the buddhi as their dharmin. For it is in the buddhi, where the saṃskāra-s of all the letter-sounds, uttered and then vanishing, have been progressively accumulated, that the word shines forth. This is the manifestation of the word by letter sounds – it is not that they act directly, like a light, on the word.

Nor is it any better (for you) to say that inasmuch as the saṃskāra-s are held in the same receptacle of buddhi as their dharmin-possessor, there is mutual co-operation between them, any more than in the case of memories, desires and aversion in regard to perception of things desired and undesired. It can never be supposed that the previous letter-sounds, or their saṃskāra-s have any association with the final letter-sound.

(Opponent) I too hold that the capacity of the letter-sounds to be a word is simply that they produce a buddhi-idea comprising the progressively accumulated saṃskāra-s produced by the letter-sounds in a defined order.

(Answer) Not so: that would contradict what has been admitted (by you). Insofar as it is an idea distinguished by the various saṃskāra-s, is this an idea of the meaning, or of the word? If it is of the meaning, then it turns out to be the word itself. Because what makes the notion of the meaning is that very thing. If it is of the word, then it would go against the principle: Meaning is ascertained from word.

So it has to be accepted that word is the object of a single idea apart from the letter-sounds. It follows that neither the final sound assisted by saṃskāra-s laid down by the previous letter sounds, nor memory, nor saṃskāra-s of them, have the expressive power. Because they all need something like an idea to help the saṃskāra-s.

(Opponent) In that case, why not the operation of the letter-sounds with the meaning, or word, as object?

> *Letter-sounds cannot possibly exist together, so essentially they have no concern with each other. Without amounting to and presenting any word, they appear and disappear. Individually, they are essentially non-verbal.*

(Answer) He says: *Letter-sounds cannot possibly exist together,* cannot possibly exist at the same time, because speech is a sequence. *So essentially they have no concern with each other,* they are not mutually co-operative since they have no connection of any kind. *Without amounting to and presenting any word,* not performing any function as a word, *they appear and disappear.* Neither individually nor collectively can they by any bodiless projection ever attain to being a word. *Individually, they are essentially non-verbal,* because they have no contemporaneous basis. Even as a combination their nature is still nonverbal, so what to say when they are separate parts of things established as not meaningful?

> *Still, each single letter-sound is full of potentialities for expressing all kinds of things: by the fact of mutual co-operation with other letter-sounds, it is endowed with all kinds of potential forms.*
>
> *A letter-sound is established by an earlier letter-sound as belonging to a particular formation, and an earlier one by a later one. Thus certain letter-sounds, assuming a particular sequence, are assigned by convention to a particular object. To that extent the particular letter-sounds have come to lose their power to express anything else. The g and au and ḥ are now indicating something having a dewlap.*

Still, each single letter-sound is full of potentialities for expressing all kinds of things, what is expressed being the words of the expression. And in the sense that it has the potentialities of manifesting the words, each one is full of those expressions, as the spokes are each drawn together in the hub of a wheel. For instance, the letter-sound g is full of the potentialities of indicating words like go (cow), varga (class), agni (fire), gagana (sky).

By the fact of mutual co-operation with other letter-sounds, as the word gauḥ is a co-operative interdependence of g, au, and ḥ, the word agni has the g co-operating with i and the others. So from joining up with various other letter-sounds as adjuncts according to the case, *it is endowed with all kinds of potential forms.*

A letter-sound is established by an earlier letter-sound as belonging to a particular formation, as indicating a particular word, *and an earlier one by a later one,* and one in the middle by both earlier and later ones.

Thus certain letter-sounds, assuming a particular sequence, being set in order in that specific sequence, *are assigned by convention to a particular object.* The conventional usage is: '*This,* inasmuch as its constituent elements are in *this* particular sequence, means *this* object.' By that convention as to the object, they are assigned to it.

By a convention as to letter-sounds, the actual word is conventionally agreed. For the word is a general conventional usage regarding a particular letter-sequence, an unambiguous function of the letter-sounds.

To that extent the particular letter-sounds have come to lose their power to express anything else since they are functioning solely to manifest one definite word expressing a particular object which has a dewlap, etc. (in the case of 'cow'); they have lost the other potentialities of manifesting other words. These powers of indicating other words are inoperative, are lost, because in the concentration (on the one word) those other particularities are subdued, and its are dominant. *The g and au and ḥ are not indicating something having a dewlap:* they are making manifest the word gauḥ (cow).

> *The single idea-flash of the letter-sounds in the recognized order of the sounds as assigned to their object by convention, is the Word, which is conventionally accepted as expressing what is to be expressed. That word is a simple unity. It is the object of a single idea, uttered with a single impetus, undivided, having no sequence and not of the nature of letter-sounds, brought into operation by the notion of the final letter-sound.*
>
> *When one person wishes to inform another, it is by the letter-sounds as spoken by speakers and heard by hearers, conforming to the saṃskāra-groups of the business of speech, to which no beginning can be ascribed. It is recognized by the minds of the people, who all regard it as something well-established.*

The single idea-flash (buddhi-nirbhāsa) the flash of the idea which is the unifier *of the letter-sounds in the recognized order of the sounds,* combined in a particular fixed sequence, which sequence is one with which they are potentially endowed, *as assigned to their object by convention* according to established rules, *is the Word,* the basis, what alone gives them their support, *which is conventionally accepted as expressing what is to be expressed* and not the letter-sounds, though it is conventionally accepted as through letter-sounds.

That word is a simple unity. A thing like a jar, though it is one, yet has parts, and so is found to be the object of a number of ideas: not so the word (for it).

It is the object of a single idea, perceived directly by all the world. The letter-sounds, being more than one, do not arise at the same moment, and never come to be the object of a single idea. But he who would reject by inference this unity of the (buddhi-) idea which is directly perceived, would be going against direct perception.

And so it is *uttered with a single impetus* with the awareness that the idea caused by the saṃskāra-s laid down, in the production of the letter-sound sequence, has reached completion. It is flashed out in an instant (jhaṭiti) in the final ideas as *(a thing) undivided* without having parts, and therefore *having no sequence, and not of the nature of letter-sounds, brought into operation by the notion of the final letter-sound.* The operation of the first letter-sound being passed along the line, it is only in the comprehension of the final letter-sound that it shines forth.

When one person wishes to inform another another mind, *it is by the letter-sounds as spoken by speakers and heard by hearers, conforming to the saṃskāra-groups (vāsanā) of the business of speech, to which no beginning can be ascribed. It is recognized by the minds of the people who all regard it as something well established,* and so goes on the beginningless whirling of the wheel of the world (saṃsāra).

Worldly life presupposes that it is from words that we understand what is intended, and so it is said that this is recognized by the worldly intelligences, impressed as they are with the saṃskāra-groups. There is erroneous understanding in those who are impelled to engage in goals purely of worldly business, that a word is as it were a (real) self.

Therefore, the word is distinct from its letter-sounds, because being grasped as a single idea (buddhi) it produces the notion (pratyaya) like a lamp, and because it is the cause of comprehension of an intended object, like a lamp and like the mind (buddhi). The letter-sounds are not the word because they are joined up in sequence by a single agent, and because they are (merely) instruments, like an axe or a carpenter's chisel and the like.

Now on this point, there is a view which is maintained by some:

(The verses which follow, and which Śaṅkara is going to criticize, re-interpret and finally amend, are from Kumārila's Ślokavārttika, XII. 131–136 – Tr.)

Neither letters nor sounds manifest any meaning-flash (sphoṭa) of word or sentence,
Because they (themselves) are manifestors, like the light of a lamp etc.
And from their mere existence, they are means - like a jar and such things;
Apart from worldly use, meaning is imaginable for them freely as one likes.
There is no sphoṭa-flash expressing the meaning, because it would (have to) be other than letter-sounds
Like a jar and such things; nor does this (statement) contradict perception, for no such dharmin is shown.
He who would deny that it is letter-sounds (which express the meaning) refuses what is directly experienced;

Since (the meaning) springs up immediately on the knowledge of the letter-sounds. He is like one denying the marks (of the hare) on the moon.
Arising from the letter-sounds, springing up immediately on the knowledge of them, is knowledge of the meaning;
What arises from a thing is like it, as for instance the knowledge of fire from smoke.
Again, g and the other letter-sounds express, like a lamp, the meaning such as gauḥ (cow);
For so it is firmly recognized, and so it has been previously.

Here it is being said: *Neither letters nor sounds manifest any meaning-flash (sphoṭa) of word or sentence.* Now neither word nor sentence is brought about just by itself. Since, then, no word or sentence is supposed to exist apart from the letter-sounds, and these do not manifest any meaning-flash of word or sentence, how is there any possibility of verbal communication between intelligent beings? And in any case, having spoken of a meaning-flash of word and sentence, to deny it now means that word and sentence have been accepted (as entities in their own right).

(Opponent) Let it be the meaning-flash as understood by others that is spoken of.

(Answer) That is making an issue of what is already settled (siddha-sādhyatā). It is not some other meaning-flash of the word and sentence (supposed) by another person which is being denied. He is denying any meaning-flash at all in any word or sentence.

(Opponent) Then let us say: The letter-sounds, set in their particular order, are what determines the meaning. What is denied is word and sentence (as such determiners).

(Answer) That too is wrong: it is self-contradictory.

(Opponent) Let us say that it is word and sentence apart from letter-sounds that are being denied.

(Answer) To have spoken of their being apart, though denying that they manifest meaning, shows that word and sentence have been accepted as existing apart.

(Opponent) Other people imagine them so, and that imaginary fact is what is being denied.

(Answer) Still, inasmuch as manifestation does occur, your argument fails.

(Opponent) Why?

(Answer) There are three possibilities. The letter-sounds:

> have the capacity to manifest a word apart from themselves; or
> have the capacity to manifest a word which is not apart from themelves; or
> have the capacity to manifest the meaning.

If they manifest what is apart from themselves, then they are not sufficient to themselves. If they manifest what is not apart from themselves, then nothing else is accomplished. In fact, manifesting capacity is only of something apart, not of what is not apart, just as in the case of the lamp. For a manifestor like a lamp is used to manifest other things, not to manifest itself. If self-manifestation were to be the purpose, there is after all self-manifestation by darkness too.

It being established that they manifest something apart from themselves, are they to manifest the word, or the meaning? Now a task such as carrying along a birch-tree, for example, which needs to be undertaken by a number, cannot be accomplished by only one among them. So the presentation of the meaning by just one of the letter-sounds is not possible, because it is something that has to be presented by a number.

Nor can it be said that the letter sounds, having laid down their respective saṃskāra-s, revive to reveal more and more, on the analogy of a man digging a well. Because the object is the single buddhi-idea of what is meant.

And just as the perishing consciousness (vijñāna) would not be able to lay down a saṃskāra for the consciousness that is to arise (immediately after it), as supposed in the Buddhist doctrine, because there is (for them) no persisting dharmin, so here there is no reciprocal relation between the letter-sounds, produced (as they are) at different times; for there is nothing to carry any force (effect) from each perishing earlier one to each subsequent one which is to arise. So the letter sounds do not manifest the *meaning.*

As the only alternative left, they are thus shown to be essentially manifestors purely of a *word,* which is apart from themselves. For us, this does not entail the flaw of the saṃskāra-s' having nothing to hold them. Because in the persisting conscious dharmin, aware of the continued incompleteness of the saṃskāra-s laid down successively by each precedent letter-sound, at the instant of the production of the last one there springs up in a flash the idea (buddhi) which is the undivided single idea intended.

If it is said that the letter-sounds manifest their own buddhi-idea, still that buddhi is only an instrument as regards comprehension of meaning; it is not the letter-sounds which bring about the result (in the hearer) by that instrumentality, because they have exhausted their efficacy in producing the instrumental buddhi. The operation in regard to the result belongs to the buddhi-idea alone, and the proof is that it is the word which operates to bring about that result. Since the comprehension of the meaning is distinct from the instrumental idea, expressiveness is not from the letter-sounds, though it is not denied that they are indirectly a means to the word.

So the verse cited above –

(Neither letters nor sounds manifest any meaning-flash
(sphoṭa) of word or sentence,
Because they (themselves) are manifestors,
like the light of a lamp, etc.)

- it should be amended to read:

Both letters and sounds manifest a meaning
ever distinct from themselves,
Because they (themselves) are manifestors,
like the light of a lamp, etc.

As generally recognized, the whole point of a thing like a jar is that it serves for something else: by its mere appearance it calls to mind its use for cooking, carrying, holding or whatever it may be. It is similarly true that what is wanted from letter-sounds is this: that from being there – like a jar – in their sequence, they serve to bring up a word distinct from themselves.

And from their mere existence, they are means – like a jar and such things:
Apart from worldly use, meaning is imaginable for them freely as one likes.

Whether it is a produced thing or an idea, however it may be, that from which the meaning is grasped, which is not composed of the rising and perishing letter-sounds because it is other than letter-sounds, is the meaning-flash (sphoṭa). Its effect must be accepted, because it is not comprised of letter-sounds. So the line

There is no sphoṭa-flash expressing the meaning,
Because it would (have to) be other than letter-sounds
(Like a jar and such things; nor does this (statement)
Contradict perception, for no such dharmin is shown.)

is contradicted by what any speaker accepts. And to argue *because it would be other than letter-sounds* establishes nothing about that other. A thing does not establish what is other than itself.

Furthermore, one who accepts the four-fold classification of words into nouns, verbal roots, prefixes and particles, has to accept that there must be something else, apart from the letter-sounds, to manifest the classes. For letter-sounds have no power to manifest classes of words: they manifest only classes of letter-sounds. Nor could there be a manifestation of a class considered as a whole, of which parts would be arising and perishing at different times. Even in cases where the parts are enduring, still the hands and feet and the rest do not make up corporeality without the body itself, so what to say of the case where they are not enduring?

(Grammatical Excursus)

(In what follows, homonyms are given to show that the same group of letter-sounds may produce widely different meanings: aśvaḥ can mean 'horse', or 'thou didst go' and so on. The structure of Saṃskṛt words is analysed to make related points. Translation is pointless because the English words would not exemplify what is meant. *Tr.)*

When it is said, for instance: 'aśvaḥ ayātam ayātam aśvaḥ bhavati tena mama vāyur vāyuḥ', the forms (aśvaḥ, ayātam, vāyuḥ' – homonyms) are the same, but mutually opposed as one of each pair belongs to the noun and the other to the verb class, a fact which letter-sound on its own cannot manifest.

If, when the word aśvaḥ is spoken, its a-ś-v-a-ḥ letters are manifesting as noun-class, they are different from manifestors of it as verb-class, which means that in the separate classes there is manifestation of separate things. This does not occur in a simple unity.

If it is supposed that it is by the context of the sense and juxtaposition with other words that it can be said 'Here it is a noun' and 'Here it is a verb', still, manifestation of the classes of noun and verb is by the context of the sense and so on, which letter-sound entirely on its own cannot effect. For a Brahmin on his own does not exemplify warrior status as well as his own Brahminhood.

It has to be accepted that there are many separate a-s and ś-s and v-s and so on. In the same way, words like 'cow' are quite separate. The facts that 'cow' is a word and 'horse' (aśva) is a word are well known, as are ma-ness and mā-ness and i-ness and ī-ness. So it is that a and so on manifest only universal classes of a-ness, etc., not the class differences of noun and verb of words like aśva.

So the word, distinct from the letter-sounds, has to be admitted as what manifests the universal of word-ness. Such being the case, the verses:

(He who would deny that it is the letter-sounds (which express the meaning) would be refusing what is directly experienced,
Since (the meaning) springs up immediately on the knowledge of the letter-sounds. He is like one denying the marks (of the hare) on the moon.

Arising from the letter-sounds, springing up immediately on the knowledge of them, is knowledge of the meaning:
What arises from a thing is like it, as for instance the knowledge of fire from smoke.)

should be amended to read:

He who would deny the sphoṭa meaning-flash following immediately on knowledge of the letter-sounds,
Would be refusing what is directly experienced. He is like one denying the marks (of the hare) on the moon.

Not arising from the letter-sounds is understanding of the meaning, which springs up instantly on the knowledge of them;

What arises from a thing is like it: as the understanding of fire is not from smoke (itself).

No instant arising has been shown without an idea to cause that understanding. If it is said that the mere succession is sufficient (cause), that would be casting doubt on an established truth (siddha-sādhyatā). For smoke alone is not a cause of the knowledge of fire: the cause is *knowledge* of the smoke (in the standard inference). What we are saying is this: as in cases such as smoke, so with the letter-sounds – something (else) is needed to help in the succession.

Nor could the g and au letter sounds combine, like (oil and wick in) a lamp, to manifest (the word gauḥ = cow) the meaning of the animal with the dewlap and horns. As they have no common time basis, it is clear that there will be no certainty about them. Even when they have the ḥ at the end, the common basis is still lacking. Letter-sounds have no contemporaneous basis for manifestation of meaning, whereas a lamp in its unbroken continuity holds evenly steady, and so provides a cause (for manifestation).

So this verse also -

(Again, g and the other letter-sounds express,
like a lamp, the meaning such as gauḥ (cow);
For so it is firmly recognized,
and so it has been previously.)

should read:

Again, g and the other letter-sounds do not express,
like a lamp, the meaning such as gauḥ;
For so it is firmly recognized,
and so it has been previously.

Again, letter-sounds like g do not act like a lamp to express gauḥ, because continuity is accepted (as needed for that), and they came (and went) before (the cognition).

Now comes the question of valid cognition. The letter-sounds do not express meaning, nor are they even a means of cognition (pramāṇa) of it, for they depend directly on a convention, like a numeral digit or an image (of a god such as Viṣṇu) and the like.

As the digit in the hundreds place, for instance, or the image of the god, are dependent on a convention, they illustrate merely the tradition; but they do not even approach giving valid knowledge in regard to what is meant by (the god) Viṣṇu, or one hundred, or another number.

Whereas valid cognition is something that does not depend on any convention, like for example a sentence or a lamp, which belong to the other category, and unlike letter-sounds, which can no more give valid cognition than an image. So, the letter-sounds manifest something distinct from themselves, which supplies the meaning; for they themselves are directly dependent on convention as much as a numeral digit or an image of Viṣṇu. That the sphoṭa meaning-flash does not depend directly on any such convention we have pointed out.

So who can refuse to accept the sphoṭa meaning-flash thus powerfully presented with these numerous arguments? This being now settled, the commentary goes on:

> *It is different from the idea of a convention, which is, that the binding together of just these (letter-sounds) as a particular group is expressive of a particular meaning. But convention has the nature of an illusory projection of word and meaning on to each other as memory-forms: 'This word* is *what is meant here, and what is meant here* is *this word; and the concept* is *what is meant and the word (for it).'*
>
> *Convention is this sort of mutual illusory projection. Because of the mutual projection, the word, meaning and concept are mixed up: cow is the word, cow is the meaning, cow is the concept (jñāna). He who knows the difference between them is an omniscient one.*

It a word *is different from the idea of a convention,* for the conventional idea is an inseparable conjunction of word, meaning and concept (jñāna). The difference of this from the sphere of the word has to be made out.

Convention is: that the binding together of just these, as a particular group, is expressive of a particular meaning, in the same way that this digit is 100, or again 1,000, or this image is Viṣṇu. *But convention has the nature of illusory projection (adhyāsa) of word and meaning on to each other as memory-forms,* and is not a (valid) cognition. For instance, 'This image is Viṣṇu, it indeed is the Four-armed (god)'. The concept is both, and both are the concept, with the concepts of the image and Viṣṇu projected on to each other.

So *'This word* is *what is meant here, and what is meant here* is *this word, and the concept (pratyaya)* is *what is meant and the word (for it).' Convention is this sort of mutual illusory projection (adhyāsa). Because of the mutual projection, the word, meaning and concept are mixed up:* cow *is the word,* cow *is the meaning,* cow *is the concept (jñāna).*

He who knows the difference between them, is an omniscient one. Because of the extreme difficulty of knowing the difference, no one who is not omniscient can experience them as different.

> *In every word there is the potentiality of a sentence: 'it exists'. When someone says 'tree', it is understood that it exists. For the object signified by a word cannot fail to exist. Nor can there be an action (expressed by a verb) without its factors-of-action.*

In every word there is the potentiality of a sentence: 'it exists'. When someone says 'tree', it is understood that it exists. For the object signified by a word cannot fail to exist. Why is this said? Because what he wishes to explain is the means of knowing the cries of all beings. Now 'cries of all beings' is in the field of meaning of sentences, not the field of meaning of words; for bare words, like bare letter-sounds, are meaningless, and do not amount to communication. Just as one aims at indicating a word by joining together letter-sounds with other letter-sounds, so with words too: the means of constructing a sentence is by looking to other words as well. So it is that validity is in the sentence alone, since there is no understanding of the object from the use of a word in isolation. Even where an isolated word (like the name Devadatta) is supposed to be its own context, still inevitably it is supplemented in the mind with the sense of existence, so that the word means 'It is Devadatta!' and so on; without context it is not intelligible.

In pralambate, paryāgacchati, abhyāgacchati and others of the same class, the karma-pravacanīya prefixes carry no significance at all. Then in the class typified by abhimanāyate, sumanāyate, durmanāyate, it is accepted that the prefix has an indicatory force. Also in such words as pratiṣṭhate, adhīte, etc. there is merely indicatory force and not direct denotation.

Nor can there be action (expressed by a verb) without its factors-of-action; in the simple context of action, some instrument, material or attribute is assumed.

Then, without fixed determination between base and suffix, the expression fails because of uncertainty. For instance, the word daridrātiḥ is understood by some as a complete word (dravya mātra). Yet daridra appears to be made up of nipāta and upasarga prefix elements; for we find drāti, nidrāti, daridrāti. So it must be said what the base is, whether drā or daridrā.

Those who take it to be daridrā, class the word drā as separate. In that case they read (the word) as its own bare letters, and to this 'zero-affixed' word they put on addition and augment as the affix. But others take (the word) to be with affix, getting the 'zero-affixed' word by lopping off the affix. In which cases it has to be said what the base is. And the point is no trivial one: once it has been determined to be a base, or else to be an affix, the force of the meanings, as base or affix, will be distinct.

Sometimes an upasarga prefix becomes part of the base, as for instance in a-saṅgrāmayata śūra, and in ataternaḥ, aḥ, asyāpatyamiḥ, iyān, adhunā, and so on, who is going to speak of the meaning of the base when there is no base? Then with agnicit, somasut, bhidā, chidā, atha, kati, amā, paca, paṭha and the like, who will speak of the meaning of the affix when there is no affix?

In such cases, who can imagine any meaningfulness of bases or affixes that are evidently not there?

(Opponent) Let it be so in these cases, but not elsewhere.

(Answer) You cannot have someone who is old in just half of the body.

Take the saying: Uddālaka-puṣpabhañjikā-pāram na Puṣpa-pracāyikā (the end of the game Crushing Uddālaka Flowers is not Flower-Gathering). What does the first member of the compound mean, and what the later? With words like pra-jñaḥ, saṃ-jña, without any context, what is the meaning of what?

With ṛṣabho, vṛṣabho, vṛṣah, udakam, udakumbhaḥ, kṣīrodaḥ, yāvo, yāvakaḥ, kūpaḥ, sūpaḥ, yūpaḥ, and so on, it has to be said which is the meaning of which. With dadhyaśāna, madhvatra and the like, what is the expressive word and what its limit?

Therefore in all cases, letter-sounds, bases, affixes, words, evidently unreal and without meaning, are simply means to sentences, which are without parts and evidently not unreal. These things are analysable out from the homogeneous partless sentence, when differentiated by illusory (mithyābhūta) letter-sounds, words, and intonations.

These things are not parts of the sentence. But inasmuch as they are means, they appear as if parts of it. When it comes to the result, they do not exist in it, so that they are unreal, like the stroke representing 100 and other numbers. In order to indicate a sentence which itself is not a thing uttered, they each take a particular form in conjunction with the sense organ, and then pass away. As they display differences of time of appearance and disappearance in their own order, they present the sentence itself as if it had a temporal succession, as if arising, as if disappearing, as if enduring, as if temporal, as if having differences – in these various forms.

So it is said, what is there of the sharp horn when it is abstracted from 'the horned hare'? It is a fancy (conjured up) just as the fancy of mirage water that attracts the thirsty deer is conjured up from the salty ground which is real, and a man from a post (mistaken for a man) or a post from a man, and silver from nacre.

As the mirage water and so on are in fact causes of one's coming to know the fact of the actual salty ground and so on, so letter-sounds, words, bases and affixes, being the cause of coming to know the actual meaning of the sentence, are discarded (similarly) when that is known. In some cases (the fancy) is removed (only) when the fact is reached, as with the mirage water, but in other cases it is purposefully intended (as a conventional fiction), as when from a number like 100 the digits are discarded (when the meaning is grasped), and as written letters in their forms standardized by convention are discarded from the letter-sounds a and so on (when they have been read). Now these are all accepted as being means to come to know the actual meaning; they do not thereby cease to be unreal. And so with words, etc.

He who acts independently with conventions of his own as to bases, suffixes, words, and letter-sounds, and the idea of the supposed written letters as other conventional means, and thinks that he comes to anything true in them by thus manipulating various methods of arriving at the meaning of sentences, is surely like a man who, wishing to see the moon during the rainy season, takes the cloud (indicated to him) as a pointer to the moon, as the moon itself.

As the sentence alone is real, so the meaning of the sentence is real; words, or word-meanings in isolation, do not amount to truth. Everything is inherently a universal and a particular, for there is no particular without a universal, nor a universal without a particular. When it is said 'cow', the implication is 'it exists'. Though the context is just that word in isolation, it is not an isolated word-meaning that is understood, but a sentence-meaning, a further meaning with the other words mentally supplied.

Therefore we hold this verse to be wrong:

The word-meanings (together) convey the sense,
when taken separately there would be a doubt;
Because certainty arises in (considering) the whole,
as with (the phrase): post-top-perch-crow. (Vā. Adhi. 363)

For it is clear that 'post', as a word-meaning in isolation, has not the meaning of a sentence. So there is wood, there is a post, there is a top, there is a crow – but unless account is taken of another word 'perch' supplied to 'at the top of the post', there is no idea of (what is meant by) the post-top-perch-crow (compound). Even supposing it is meant that these things are simply there, still the idea inevitably involves the extra word-meaning 'being'.

Therefore when even a sentence-meaning, standing by itself, is intrinsically dubious, how should word-meanings, which do not stand by themselves, reveal a sentence-meaning?

So the verse should be amended to

But the sentence conveys the sense,
when taken separately there would be a doubt;
Because certainty arises in (considering) the whole,
as with (the phrase): post-top-perch-crow.

And so:

By sentence alone is sentence-meaning spoken, for it is not something figurative made up by other things;
Because at the end there is the realization: 'It is so.' Treeness (is established) by the tree alone.

(Opponent) Treeness is not established by the word 'Palāśa!'.

(Answer) Quite true. By the sentence 'Palāśa!' the sentence-meaning 'Tree!' is not stated. For the object is different, one being the meaning of the sentence 'Palāśa!' as 'The palāśa exists' or 'The palāśa stands', and the other being the meaning of the sentence 'The tree'. And when a separate existence is accepted for words and letter-sounds, not having parts, how can it be imagined that a sentence made up of letter-sounds and words, which have no parts, should itself have parts? For it could not be made particular by any action of space, etc. So to insist on supposing that there are parts (in a sentence) is wholly unsound.

(Opponent) *'If in truth there are divisions into words and letter-sounds, it will be the same with the ultimate atoms,*

And so nothing will exist at all' – this is a frightener for children. (Vā. Adhi. 150)

(Answer) As we accept that the atoms themselves are nothing but dharma-s of sattva and the other two guṇa-s, (the opponent's) 'having cut them up, we affirm them' – this is a frightener for grown-ups.

(Opponent) Granted that in the case of an isolated word (there is understanding) from supplying something else to it, then what is the use of (ever) having a number of words?

> *There is confirmation (in the case of 'cooks') of the agent, instrument and object in a restrictive sense, namely as Caitra, fire and rice. We see an isolated word with the meaning of a sentence, for instance śrotriya (scriptural scholar) = knows the hymn by heart; lives = maintains the life-currents. There the word manifests as a sentence. The word has to be taken apart and parsed, to find whether it is here expressing an action, or an agent (in some cases). Otherwise, with words like bhavati (= in being, O Lady, it becomes), aśvaḥ (horse, thou didst go, etc.), ajāpayaḥ (thou didst conquer, goat's milk, etc.), where the form is common to both a noun and a verb, how can the distinction be made out?*

There is confirmation (in the case of 'cooks') of the agent, instrument, and object in a restrictive sense, namely as Caitra, fire, and rice. From the verbal form, the means is known, and this is confirmed by restriction among (possibly) understood objects: it is Caitra alone who is the agent, and fire alone that is the instrument, and rice alone that is the object.

The confirmation is purely by restriction of the meaning. *We see an isolated word with the meaning of a sentence, for instance śrotriya (scriptural scholar) = knows the hymn by heart.* The single word *śrotriya,* which is a description of a means (learning by heart) conveys the sense of the association of action and means as 'knows the hymn by heart'. So also *lives* is a word describing an action particularized by the indicated means for the action. The sentences 'knows the hymn by heart' and 'maintains the life-currents' are bringing out the meaning of the words 'śrotriya' and 'lives'.

So what is being said is that all words are ultimately meanings of other words, using the potentiality of making sentences, which is always there in all words.

Then in some places, by the mere verb, the means is indicated; elsewhere, by the mere noun, an action is declared. So it is said that the line between them is hard to determine.

The word has to be taken apart and parsed, to find whether it is expressing an action such as 'he lives' *or an agent* such as 'śrotriya', or 'kṣatriya' (warrior). *Otherwise,* if it is not analysed by abstraction from the sentence, then with words like bhavati or aśvaḥ or ajapayah, how will one parse them as verb or alternatively as agent, without having distinguished each from the noun or verb of the same form? 'O you, do you serve' – here bhavati (you, fern.) is a pronoun, but it can also be the form of the kṛt (present participle) suffix in the locative case: 'in being'; and bhavati as a verb means 'it comes to be', as a shoot from a seed.

'A horse (aśvas) goes' expresses a class; but in 'thou wentest (aśvas) to the village' the context is that aśvas is the second person singular of an aorist, of śu. In 'let the goat's milk (ajāpayas) be drunk', ajāpayas is a noun; in 'thou didst conquer (ajāpayas) the king', it is the second person singular of the imperfect of a causal form, of ji.

> *There is difference between word, meaning, and idea. When it is said for instance, 'The mansion shines-white (svetate)', the meaning is of action; in 'the white (svetaḥ) mansion', it is of an agent-subject. The meaning of it ('white') and the idea of it consist of action and agent. Why is this? Because of the association: 'this is that', which idea of their non-difference is called the convention.*

Between word, meaning, and idea, having shown how they are confused, the *difference* is now made out. *'The mansion shines-white (svetate)'* means an action; *'the white (svetaḥ) mansion'* is *an agent-subject.* From the fact of the thing's having action and agency, 'the white shines-white' displays both the sense of a verb and the sense of agent.

As the word consists of action and agent – in 'what is white, shines white; what shines white, is white', the one word is never without action and agent – so *the meaning* expressed by it *consists of action and agent, and the idea of* that meaning *consists of action and agent.* So the meaning consists of word and idea, and the idea too consists of word and meaning. *Why is this? Because of the association: 'this is that':* what the meaning is, that is the word; what the word is, that is the meaning and the idea; what the idea is, that is the meaning and the word – this sort of *idea of their non-difference* which is essentially memory, *is* what is *called the convention.*

But the white object has become the support of the word and the idea. Still, the word and idea do not correspond to it when it is being changed by its own changes of condition. So too the idea, and so too the word, do not change along with each other. Word changes in one way, meaning in another, and idea in yet another. So they are distinct. Out of the yogin's saṃyama on the distinctness, there comes to him understanding of the cries of all beings.

How is the distinction to be made? *But the white object* something like a mansion which has the quality white *has become the support of the word and the idea* as being expressible (by word) and being the content (of the idea). *Still, the word and idea* too *do not correspond to it when it is being changed by its own changes,* e.g. new or old; and it can exist when word and idea do not. *So too the idea* is not followed (in its changes) by the word or by the object (meant), for it goes on existing even when word and object do not. *So too the word* for the object meant, and the idea, are unstable. *Word changes in one way, meaning in another, and idea in yet another. So they are distinct.*

Out of the yogin's saṃyama on the distinctness: 'this is a manifestation of the nature of a sentence by convention out of letter-sounds; this is its meaning, and this the idea of that'; coming to direct perception of each in its own form as distinct word, meaning and idea, there comes understanding of the cries of all beings.

Sūtra III.18

From direct perception of the saṃskāra-s, knowledge of previous lives

From direct perception of the saṃskāra-s, knowledge of previous lives. The saṃskāra-s referred to here are the saṃskāra-groups called vāsanā, caused by memory and taints. The observable bring about fruition as righteousness and unrighteousness: the unobservable are mental dharma-s which have been laid down in previous existences as change, activity, inhibition, power, life, and righteousness. Saṃyama on these (two kinds) has the power to give direct perception of saṃskāra-s.

They can never be perceived apart from the place, time, cause, and experience: so it is with those associations that the yogin attains knowledge of previous births from direct perception of saṃskāra-s. This kind of saṃyama can be applied to other living beings also.

From direct perception of the saṃskāra-s, knowledge of previous lives. The saṃskāra-s referred to here are the saṃskāra-groups called vāsanā, both observable and unobservable, *caused by memory and taints.* The observable have begun to evolve the experience of the ripening of taints and karma as *mental dharma-s* caused by *righteousness and unrighteousness: the unobservable are mental dharma-s which have been laid down in previous existences,* performed in an absolutely endless chain of births, *as change, activity, inhibition, power, life, and righteousness,* as explained before (under III.15). *Saṃyama* made *on these* two kinds of saṃskāra-s *has the power to give direct perception of the saṃskāra-s.*

And because they go into operation associated with place, time, cause, and experience, when they are directly perceived it must also be in association with the particular place and so on. Therefore *They can never be perceived apart from the place, time, cause, and experience. So it is with those associations that the yogin attains knowledge of previous births from direct perception of saṃskāra-s.*

This kind of saṃyama can be applied to other living beings also: from the saṃyama on such saṃskāra-s of those whose births he wishes to know, the knowledge of their previous births comes to him.

To illustrate the result of this direct perception of saṃskāra-s, he now cites an ancient story.

(From here on there are some extended passages where the Vyāsa is simply repeated word for word by Śaṅkara, with hardly any comment. In extreme cases, the occasional word which is glossed is underlined, and the comment given below; the rest of the Vyāsa is not repeated. Tr.)

> *There is a story from scripture about this.*
>
> *The revered sage, Jaigīṣavya, by direct perception of his own saṃskāra-s, observed what had been his transmigrations through different births during ten world-periods, and realized the knowledge-born-of-discrimination (vivekajam jñānam). Then revered Āvatya assumed a human form, and came to ask him: 'Through ten world-periods you have known, with your clear purified mind, the pain of going through hells and animal existence, and again and again have been born among gods, and among men. Of which was there more – pleasure or pain?'*
>
> *Jaigīṣavya said to revered Āvatya: 'During my lives in the ten world-periods, I have known with my clear purified mind what it is to go through hell and animal existence, and again and again to be born among gods and men. Whatever I experienced, I account to have been all pain.'*
>
> *Revered Āvatya said: 'O one who has lived so long, are your mastery of nature, and that happiness of contentment known as supreme (sūtra II.42) also rejected as pain?'*
>
> *Revered Jaigīṣavya said: 'The happiness of contentment is supreme only in comparison with sense enjoyment. Compared to the happiness of Transcendental Aloneness (kaivalya) it is merely pain. Its quality of purity of mind is of the three guṇa-s. Any idea must be of the three guṇa-s, and rejected by me as something to be avoided.'*

(Vivaraṇa) ... *knowledge-born-of-discrimination* caused by detachment ...

> *'The pain of thirst runs through them like a thread. What is called real happiness is removal of the thread of thirst, is purity, freedom from constraint, and being well-disposed towards all.'*

How are the two forms of happiness to be compared? *The pain of thirst runs through like a thread. What is called real happiness* in contentment and mastery of nature *is removal of the thread of thirst, is purity, freedom from constraint, and being well-disposed towards all.*

Sūtra III.19

(From direct perception, through saṃyama) of his thought, knowledge of the mind of another

> *From saṃyama on his thought, direct perception of the thought, and from that, knowledge of the mind of another comes about.*

(From direct perception) of his thought, knowledge of the mind of another. From saṃyama on the thought of the other, *direct perception of the thought* of that other; with that direct perception *knowledge of the mind of another* who possesses that thought.

(Opponent) But if the ideas of someone else are directly perceived, will it not mean that the yogin will become an enjoyer when that other is happy, and a sufferer when he suffers?

Sūtra III.20

But not the subject of those ideas, because that was not the field of the saṃyama

> *He knows the idea which has been entertained. He does not know in what sort of subjective state that has been entertained, because that was not the only subject of the yogin's concentration. It was only the idea that was the subject of the concentration by the yogin's mind.*

(Answer) *But not the subject of those ideas, because that was not the field of the saṃyama. He* the yogin *knows the idea which has been entertained. He does not know in what sort of subjective state that*idea *has been entertained* by the other person. He does not know in what subjective state the other person's idea is held, whether it is happiness or suffering, so that he himself might become an enjoyer or a sufferer.

(Opponent) But if he does not know the subject, how would he know that the idea has been entertained there at all?

(Answer) He knows the general fact that it is entertained there, but not that it is entertained as something enjoyable, creating the subjective feeling of being an enjoyer. *It was only the idea that was the subject of the concentration by the yogin's mind.*

Sūtra III.21

From saṃyama on the form of the body, its potentiality of being seen is nullified. Being disjoined from the light of the eye, it disappears

> *From saṃyama on the form of the body, its potentiality of being seen is interrupted. When it is thus nullified, the body is disjoined from the light of the eye, and the yogin disappears. Similarly it is implied that he disappears from the field of other sense perceptions such as sound.*

From saṃyama on the form of the body, its potentiality of being seen is nullified. The form of the body refers to the yogin's own body, *its potentiality* of his body *of being seen* by the eyes of others *is nullified, interrupted,* is inhibited. As a result, the *light of the eye* of others is not in contact with the form of the body of the yogin, and *the yogin disappears. Similarly it is implied that he disappears from the field of other sense perceptions such as sound.* There is a power of hearing the yogin, and when this saṃyama is made on the sound, that power is nullified and so another person does not hear him. So it is to be understood in the case of touch and the other senses.

Sūtra III.22

Karma is rapid or slow. From saṃyama on it, or on omens, there comes foreknowledge of death

The karma which fructifies as life-span is of two kinds. Just as a wet cloth when spread out would dry in a shorter time, so is the rapid karma. And as the same cloth when screwed up would take a long time to dry, so is the slow. Or as fire in dry grass, with a following breeze, is carried everywhere and burns it up in a very short time, so is the rapid. And as the same fire, brought near to the pile of grass only gradually, would take a long time to burn it up, so is the slow. This karma which determines the length of life in one particular birth is of the two kinds: rapid or slow (in fructifying).

Karma is rapid or slow. From saṃyama on it or on omens, there comes foreknowledge of death. The karma which fructifies as life-span is of two kinds. What are they? That which having found an impelling cause brings its fruition quickly is rapid, but that whose flow is retarded will take a long time to bear fruit, and that is the slow.

Just as a wet cloth when spread out stretched out *would dry in a shorter time* more quickly, *so the rapid karma* which fructifies quickly as a life-span, and having done so, is extinguished. *And the same cloth when screwed up* not stretched out *would take a long time to dry, so the slow* gives the life-span over a long time.

Or as fire in dry grass, with a following breeze, with the wind behind it, *is carried everywhere and burns it up in a very short time, so the rapid* karma in a very short time will consume the life-span. *And as the same fire, brought near to the pile of grass only gradually, would take a long time to burn it up,* so the slow karma. *This karma which determines the length of life in one particular birth is of two kinds. From saṃyama on them there is knowledge of* one's own *final passing.* So too from saṃyama on the two kinds of karma of other people, comes knowledge of their passing. The purpose of knowing about one's passing is to create urgency in fulfilling human obligations.

Or from omens, they being of three kinds: relating to the person, relating to elemental spirits, and relating to the gods. Personal would be, for instance, when, on closing the ears, no humming sound is heard within, or on closing the eyes no light is perceived. Then elemental omens would be when one sees messengers of Death, or suddenly feels that departed ancestors have returned. Omens relating to the gods would be when one suddenly sees angels and so on, or when everything becomes confused.

From omens too, one knows the destined time of passing. *Or from omens* there comes knowledge of death, *they being of three kinds: relating to the person, relating to elemental spirits, and relating to the gods.*

He illustrates the personal ones: *when on closing the ears, no humming sound is heard within, or on closing the eyes, no light is perceived.*

And elemental ones would be when one sees messengers of Death, or suddenly feels that departed ancestors have returned.

Omens relating to the gods would be when he suddenly for no reason *sees angels and so on: or when everything becomes confused* that he sees and does. So the common word for ominous, namely ari-ṣṭha (standing as an enemy), is very appropriate, as when it is said: 'My vision became confused, which was a bad omen (ariṣṭha).'

Sūtra III.23

(From saṃyama) on friendliness and the others (compassion and goodwill, sūtra I.33) (there arise) powers

(From saṃyama) on friendliness and the others (compassion and goodwill) (there arise) powers. Friendliness, compassion, and goodwill are the three meditations (bhāvanā, sūtra I.33). Of these, he who practises meditation on friendliness towards happy beings obtains the power of friendliness; he who practises meditation on compassion towards the suffering obtains the power of compassion; he who practises meditation on goodwill towards those of virtuous conduct obtains the power of goodwill.

(Vivaraṇa repeats without comment.)

> *The samādhi which is produced from the meditation is saṃyama; from that, powers of unbounded energy arise. In regard to the habitually sinful, there is indifference (I.33) but not meditation. There is thus no samādhi on that, and therefore no power from indifference is mentioned, because there is no saṃyama on it.*

The samādhi which is produced from meditation (bhāvanā) on friendliness and the other two is *saṃyama* brought about by firmness in the meditations on friendliness and the others. *From that* saṃyama on friendliness and the others, *powers of unbounded energy arise. But in regard to the habitually sinful, there is indifference* to them *but not meditation, and so* because there is no meditation *there is no samādhi on that* indifference. *And therefore no power from indifference is mentioned, because there is no samādhi on it.*

Sūtra III.24

Powers like the power of an elephant (come from saṃyama) on them

> *From saṃyama on the power of an elephant, there comes to him the power of an elephant; from saṃyama on the power of the king of the birds (Vainateya), there comes to him that power of the king of the birds; from saṃyama on the power of the wind, there comes to him the power of the wind. Similarly in other cases.*

Powers like the power of an elephant (come from saṃyama) on them. A yogin endowed with the powers from meditation on friendliness, etc., comes to powers like those of an elephant, etc. if he makes saṃyama on them.

Sūtra III.25

By projecting the light of supernormal radiant perception (I.36) on to what is subtle, hidden or remote, (he comes to) knowledge of that

> *The supernormal perception referred to is one called Radiant (jyotismati), and when the yogin projects its light on to something subtle or hidden or remote, he discovers it.*

The supernormal perception referred to is the one called Radiant, and when the yogin projects focuses *its light* a ray of it *on to something subtle or hidden or remote, he discovers it.*

Sūtra III.26

From saṃyama on the sun, knowledge of the worlds

The worlds are listed as seven:

(1) *The terrestrial world, from the point called Avīci to the summit of Mount Meru;*
(2) *From the summit of Meru up to the Pole Star, being the world of stars called Antarīkṣa or intermediate region;*
(3) *Beyond that, the world of heaven, consisting of five planes beginning with the world of great Indra; then*
(4) *the Great world of Prajāpati, and then the three-fold world of Brahmā, namely:*
(5) *The Jana world (of divine beings),*
(6) *The Tapas world (of power),*
(7) *The Satya world (of truth).*

They are summarized in the verse.

The world of Brahmā three-fold,
Below it the Great world of Prajāpati,
Then that of great Indra –
all this is called heaven.
In the sky (intermediate region) are the stars,
And on earth, the creatures.

From Avīci one after another are six great hells constituted of earth, water, fire, wind, space, and darkness, and called respectively Mahākāla, Ambarīṣa, Raurava, Mahāraurava, Kālasūtra and Andhatāmisra; in these are born beings who are to suffer long lives of misery as a result of their karma. Then there are the seven nether words called Mahātala, Rasātala, Atala, Sutala, Vitala, Talātala, and Pātāla. Eighth is the region corresponding to this earth called Vasumatī, with its seven island continents, and in the middle the golden king of mountains called Sumeru. Its peaks on the four sides are of silver, lapis, crystal, gold. From the brilliant reflection of the lapis-lazuli, the sky to the south is the deep blue of a blue lotus leaf; the eastern is white, the western shining, and the northern yellow. To the south is the Jambu tree, whence that land is called Jambu-dvīpa. As the sun advances, day and night follow him exactly. To the north are three mountains, blue, white, and sharp-peaked, covering 2,000 leagues. Between them are three regions, each 9,000 leagues, called Ramaṇaka, Hiraṇmaya, and the Northern Kurus. To the south are the mountains regions called Niṣadha, Goldhorn, and the Snow-crags, each 2,000 leagues. Between them are three regions of 9,000 leagues each, called Harivarṣa, Kiṃpuruṣa, and Bhārata.

To the east of Sumeru is Bhadrāsava, bounded by the Mālyavat mountains; on the west, Ketumāla, bounded by the Gandhamādana range. In the middle is the zone of Ilāvṛta. Jambudvīpa is 100,000 leagues across, stretching out from Sumeru for 50,000 leagues in each direction. It is girdled by a salt sea double its extent. Then come the lands of Śāka, Kuśa, Kraunca, Śālmala, Magadha, and Puṣkara, each double the preceding, fringed with wonderful hills, and the seven seas of undulating surface like a mass of mustard seeds, with their waters of sugar-cane juice, of spirits, of butter, of curds, of cream, of milk, and of syrup. These lands encompassed by the seven seas and engirdled by the Lokāloka mountains are some 500,000,000 leagues across.

This whole configuration is contained within the cosmic Egg, and the Egg itself is a minute fragment of pradhāna, as it were a firefly in space.

In the lower worlds, in the sea, in the mountains, gods have their group abodes: Asuras, Gandharvas, Kinnaras, Kimpuruṣas, Yakṣas, Rākṣasas, Bhūtas, Pretas, Piśacas, Apasmārakas, Apsarases, Brahmarākṣasas, Kuṣmāṇḍas, Vināyakas. In all the lands there are righteous gods and humans. Sumeru is a pleasure-ground of the Thirty (gods), and in it are particular paradises: Miśravana, Nandana, Caitraratha, and Sumānasa. Sudharmā is the gods' assembly hall, Sudarṣana their castle, Vaijayanta their palace. The planets and constellations and stars move round the Pole Star like the sails of a windmill, and they revolve in circles above Sumeru. Six groups of gods dwell in the world of great Indra: the Thirty-three, the Agniṣvattas, the Yāmyas, the Tuṣitas, the Aparinirmita-vaśa-vartins, and the Parinirmita-vaṣa-vartins. All these have their desires fulfilled, and have the eight powers such as becoming minute. They live for an aeon, and delight in making love, in bodies assumed for the purpose, with the incomparable and compliant nymphs who form their train. In the Great world of Prajāpati there is a five-fold group of gods: Kumudas, Ṛbhus, Pratardanas, Añjanābhas, and Pracitābhas. These have mastery of the elements; their food is meditation (dhyāna); their lives are for a thousand aeons. In the Jana world, first of the Brahmā-worlds, there is a four-fold group of gods: Brahma-purohitas, Brahmakāyikas, Brahma-mahākāyikas, and the Amaras.

These have mastery over the elements and the senses. Each lives twice as long as those of the previous group. In the Tapas world, the second, there is a three-fold group of gods: Ābhāsvaras, Mahābhāsvaras, and Satya-mahābhāsvaras. These have mastery over the elements and the senses and prakṛti; each lives twice as long as the group before, their food is meditation, and their lives are chaste (ūrdhva-retas). Upwards there is no obstacle to their thought, and below there is no object obscure to them. In the third world of Brahmā, the Satya-world, there are four groups of gods: Acyutas, Śuddhanivāsas, Satyābhas, and Saṃjñāsaṃjñins. They build no dwellings but are grounded in themselves and maintain their order; they have mastery over pradhāna and live as long as there are creations. Of these, the Acyutas delight in savitarka dhyāna (meditation on the physical); Śuddhanivāsas in savicāra dhyāna (meditation on the subtle); Satyābhas in meditation on joy alone (ānanda-mātra); and the last group in meditation on I-am-ness alone.

All the seven worlds are in fact worlds of Brahmā. But the bodiless and those resolved into prakṛti, being in a state of release, are not classed as in the worlds. This all becomes capable of being directly perceived by the yogin who has made saṃyama on the sun-gate, and further on the other objects till all has been seen.

(The Vivaraṇa makes only a final comment:)

Making saṃyama on the sun, he directly surveys the whole extent of the worlds. But the commentator has explained what this would be on the accepted authority of the Purāṇa-s.

Sūtra III.27

(From saṃyama) on the moon, knowledge of the dispositions of the stars

> *If he makes it on the moon, he will apprehend the dispositions of the stars.*

(From saṃyama) on the moon, knowledge of the dispositions of the stars. Having come to know the extent of the worlds from saṃyama on the sun, *If he* then immediately *makes it on the moon, he will apprehend the dispositions of the stars.* From the sun-saṃyama the knowledge obtained is only of the extent of the worlds – the worlds and rivers and oceans and mountains spread out as described. But how the stars are disposed is not within its range. From the moon-saṃyama, however, there is understanding of the various dispositions of the stars.

Sūtra III.28

(From saṃyama) on the Pole Star, knowledge of their motions

> *Making saṃyama on the Pole Star, he would apprehend the motions of the stars. Then if he made saṃyama on the celestial chariots, he would come to know them.*

(From saṃyama) on the Pole Star, knowledge of their motions. And thereafter (after making the moon-saṃyama) immediately *Making saṃyama on the Pole Star, he will apprehend the motions of the stars* – how they converge and how

they separate. How at this time this planet is opposed by that one, and how it comes thus to be subdued, and then in that way it rises again – by these means he comes to know, for instance, the good and bad fortune of the living beings.

And similarly with other things. *If he made saṃyama on the celestial chariots, he would come to know them,* their various kinds, and courses, and all about them.

Sūtra III.29

On the navel circle, knowledge of the plan of the body

By making saṃyama on the navel circle, he apprehends the plan of the body. There are three humours (doṣa, which harm by excess): wind, bile, and phlegm. The corporeal elements (dhātu) are seven: skin, blood, flesh, fat, bone, marrow, and semen; the order of the list is, that each is exterior to the one which it precedes.

... *wind, bile, and phlegm,* and their proportions and their seats, etc. become knowable to him.

Then *The corporeal elements (dhātu) are seven,* in fixed relations of exterior and interior to each other. *Skin* is outside them all; next within is *blood,* and *then flesh,* and *then fat,* then *bone,* then *marrow,*and then *semen,* which is the most interior of all. *The order of the list is, that each is exterior to the one which it precedes.* Similarly he will come to know the plan of the nerves.

Sūtra III.30

At the pit of the throat, cessation of hunger and thirst

At the pit of the throat, cessation of hunger and thirst. Below the tongue is a cord; below the cord is the throat; below the throat is the pit. From saṃyama on it, hunger and thirst do not oppress him.

At the pit of the throat, cessation of hunger and thirst. Below the tongue is a cord, visible when the tongue is turned up; *below the cord is the throat; below the throat is the pit. From saṃyama on it, hunger and thirst do not oppress him.*

Sūtra III. 31

On the tortoise nerve, rigid steadiness

> *Below the throat-pit, in the chest, is a nerve-channel called the Tortoise. Having made saṃyama on it, he attains a state of rigid steadiness, like that of a snake or lizard (when gripped).*

Below the throat-pit, in the chest, is a nerve-channel called the Tortoise. Having made saṃyama on it, he attains a state of rigid steadiness, steadiness of the mind, *like a snake or lizard* which becomes absolutely rigid from being gripped by the neck.

Sūtra III.32

On the Light in the head, vision of the perfect ones

> *Within the hollow on the crown of the head there is a radiance (called) the Light. Having made saṃyama on it, there comes about the vision of the perfect ones moving between heaven and earth.*

On the Light in the head, vision of the perfect ones. Within the hollow on the crown of the head there is a radiance which is accordingly called the *Light.* From saṃyama on it *there comes about the vision of the perfect ones moving between heaven and earth.*

Sūtra III.33

By the prātibha supernormal knowledge too (he knows) everything

> *The supernormal knowledge called prātibha helps the yogin across, it being the first phase of knowledge-born-of-discrimination – like the glow of the sun at dawn. From this too the yogin-s know everything, namely from the rise of the supernormal knowledge called prātibha.*

By the prātibha supernormal knowledge too (he knows) everything. When the yogin makes saṃyama on the self (ātman), or is supremely devoted to the Lord (īśvara), the knowledge which rises spontaneously in his mind is *supernormal* and *helps him across, it being the first phase of knowledge-born-of-discrimination* which is going to be described.

like the glow of the sun at dawn: becoming to some extent visible at daybreak as the reddening, when it is about to rise. This is the first phase. *From this too the yogin-s know everything, namely from the rise of the supernormal knowledge of prātibha.*

Sūtra III.34

On the heart, awareness of the mind

> *In this city of Brahman is the small lotus which is the palace; in it is the consciousness. From saṃyama on it, awareness of the mind.*

On the heart, awareness of the mind. In this city of Brahman the body, *is the small* little *lotus,* the lump of flesh in the form of a lotus with its head turned down, *which is the palace,* like a palace in that it is the many-channelled meeting-place of the various nerves. *In it is the consciousness (vijñāna)* the mind (citta). *From saṃyama on it,* on the lotus which is strung on the tube that hangs in the lake of the breast, and which is the meeting-place of the life currents (prāṇa), comes *awareness of the mind* the sattva.

Sūtra III.35

Experience is an idea which does not distinguish between sattva and Puruṣa, though they are absolutely separate; by saṃyama on what-is-for-its-own-sake, (distinct) from what-is-for-the-sake-of-another, there comes knowledge of Puruṣa

Experience is an idea which does not distinguish between sattva and Puruṣa, though they are absolutely separate; by saṃyama on what-is-for-its-own-sake, (distinct) from what-is-for-the-sake-of-another, there comes knowledge of Puruṣa. Sattva is the mind (citta), *Puruṣa* is the experiencer (bhoktṛ); of these two which *are absolutely separate,* of absolutely opposed character and altogether separate existences, *an idea which does not distinguish them,* which takes them as the same, *is experience* of Puruṣa. *By saṃyama on what-is-for-its-own-sake* whose nature is pure consciousness, having distinguished it *from what-is-for-the-sake-of-another,* from sattva which by the idea of its being Puruṣa has the experience of being identical, *comes knowledge of Puruṣa.*

(Opponent) In what way is the mind-sattva for-the-sake-of-another, so that by making the distinction from it, saṃyama can be effected on what-is-for-its-own-sake?

(Answer) *Mind-sattva (buddhi-sattva) always tends towards light -*

> *Mind-sattva always tends towards light; equally bound up with it are the pair rajas and tamas. When they are mastered, mind-sattva is transformed by the idea that sattva and Puruṣa are different. That sattva is ever-changing; absolutely opposite in character is Puruṣa which is pure, different, for-its-own-sake, eternal, and pure consciousness by nature. Experience is an idea which does not distinguish between these two, although they are absolutely separate; (separate) because of the fact that Puruṣa has objects shown to it. This is the experience-idea which is something seen, because sattva is for-the-sake-of-another. Separate from that is the other idea, of Puruṣa's being pure consciousness by nature. From saṃyama on that is produced knowledge of Puruṣa.*

> *It is not that Puruṣa is seen by any idea of Puruṣa, which – because it is an idea – would be essentially mind. It is Puruṣa that sees the idea resting on his own self. And so it has been said: 'By what indeed would one know the knower?'*

Mind-sattva (buddhi-sattva) always tends towards light. Equally operative with sattva in the actualization of the purposes of Puruṣa, on the same basis and *bound up with it, are the pair Rajas and Tamas. When they are mastered,* when they have been subdued, *mind-sattva is transformed by the* yogin's *idea that sattva and Puruṣa are different.*

That sattva is ever-changing because it consists of the three guṇa-s, because it is transient, because it is for-the-sake-of-another, because it is not conscious; *absolutely opposite in character is Puruṣa, which is pure, different* being unchanging, *for-its-own-sake, eternal, and pure consciousness by nature.*

*Experience is an idea which does not distinguish between the two, although they are absolutely separate; (separate) because of the fact that Puruṣa has objects shown to it: this is the experience-idea.*Experience cannot be the other, unchanging one, because that has objects shown to it. *Sattva is for-the-sake-of-another,* so *experience,* which *is an idea* that does not distinguish, *is something seen* by Puruṣa. *Separate from that* from that figurative idea and its possessor *is the other idea of Puruṣa's being pure consciousness by nature,* the idea that Puruṣa alone is for-its-own-sake, since it has no change in it. *From saṃyama on that is produced knowledge of Puruṣa.*

(Opponent) But if Puruṣa is made the object of an idea, and Puruṣa is known by it, then Puruṣa ends up as for-the-sake-of-another.

(Answer) *It is not that by any idea of Puruṣa,* an idea with Puruṣa as object, which being an idea would be essentially mind-sattva, that being its quality, *Puruṣa becomes seen.* Because mind (buddhi) is not of itself conscious.

It is Puruṣa that sees the idea resting on his own self, a semblance of Puruṣa. The idea's resting on Puruṣa is in fact resting on a semblance of Puruṣa; it is not that the idea does rest on Puruṣa. As a mirror set before a face is changed to the form of the face, so the mind (citta) changed into the form of Puruṣa, a semblance of Puruṣa, is what is perceived by Puruṣa.

And so it is said: By what, indeed, would one know the knower? (Bṛhad. Up. 4.5.15). The meaning is, that Puruṣa does not come to the state of an object for anyone.

(Opponent) just as the sight, striking the surface of the mirror and reflected back, is the perceiver of the face, so Puruṣa too, striking against the mind (citta) and reflected back, should perceive its own self.

(Answer) No, because Puruṣa has no changes, and being unchanging, it has no possibility of going forth towards the mind, or returning from it.

Nor, as a matter of fact, does sight bring about perception of the face by being reflected. For the face is experienced as located within the perimeter of the mirror. The face itself however is not located in the mirror.

Moreover, it conforms to the mirror. For instance, a face reflected in a sword is seen to be long, but the face itself is not long. If the perception were really by the sight reflected back, it would be illogical that it conforms to the mirror.

Sūtra III.36

From that arise supernormal knowledge and hearing, touch, sight, taste, and awareness of events

> *From supernormal knowledge (prātibha) arises knowledge of what is subtle, hidden, or remote, in the past or future. From supernormal hearing comes hearing of divine sounds: from supernormal touch, he experiences touch of the perfect ones and others. From supernormal sight he perceives divine forms. From supernormal taste he experiences divine savours. From supernormal awareness of events (vārtā), he discovers the truth about worldly matters as they are.*

From that from samādhi (samādhāna) on what-exists-for-its-own-sake *arise supernormal knowledge (prātibha) and hearing, touch, sight, taste, and awareness of events. From prātibha supernormal knowledge* from the knowledge in the mind coming out of saṃyama on the self, comes *knowledge of what is subtle, hidden or remote, in the past or future. From supernormal hearing comes hearing of divine sounds: from supernormal touch* tactile awareness, *touch of the perfect ones and others. From supernormal sight* visual knowledge *he perceives divine forms; from supernormal taste* knowledge of that sense *he experiences divine savours. From supernormal awareness of events (vārtā)* with which he is concerned, comes knowledge of matters in the world, and from this *he discovers the truth about worldly matters as they are.*

Sūtra III.37

They are obstacles in samādhi, but perfections in the extravertive state

They – supernormal knowledge and the others – are obstacles when they appear in a mind concentrated. When they appear in a mind extraverted, they are perfections.

They are obstacles in samādhi, but perfections in the extraverted state. They – supernormal knowledge and the others – when they appear in a mind concentrated (samāhita) on Puruṣa *are obstacles,*because they are antagonistic to vision of Puruṣa. *When they appear in a mind extraverted, they are perfections:* they appear from saṃyama on Puruṣa, but not in a concentrated mind (samāhita citta) which is detached.

Sūtra III.38

From loosening of the cause of tying, and awareness of how the mind moves, the mind can enter another body

The mind is not (inherently) fixed, being constantly agitated. The point is, that it is held fixed in the body by the ties of its karma-stock. Loosening of that cause-of-tying comes about by force of samādhi; awareness of how the mind moves is from samādhi alone. From the thinning out of the karma-ties, and awareness of how his own mind moves, the yogin draws out the mind from his own body and installs it in other bodies.

As his mind flies out, the senses go with it. As the bees swarm after the flying royal bee and settle when it settles, so the senses follow the mind in its entry into another body, and are distributed there.

From loosening of the cause of tying, and awareness of how the mind moves, the mind can enter another body. Mind is not (inherently) fixed, being constantly agitated like a bell that has been struck, or the quivering scintillation of a mass of burning charcoal. *The point is, that it is held fixed in the body by the ties of its karma-stock,* so that it is confined to the body as its abode.

Karma is the cause of that tying. *Loosening of that cause,* the karma-stock's becoming loose, *comes about by force of samādhi. And awareness of how the mind moves is from samādhi alone. From the thinning out of the karma-ties, and awareness of how his own mind moves* – for instance, 'from this cause it is thrilled, or it is deluded, or it is disturbed on account of that cause' – this sort of awareness of the movements and real state of the mind, *the yogin draws out the mind from his own body and installs it in other bodies.*

As his mind flies out, the senses go with it, and it is by the operation of the senses in the other bodies that the functions like life-currents (prāṇa) appear there. *As the bees swarm after the flying royal bee and settle when it settles, so the senses follow the mind in its entry into another body, and are distributed there.*

Sūtra III.39

By mastering the upgoing vital current (udāna), he passes untouched over water, mud, thorns and so on, and at death he takes the upward course

> *Life is the operation of the totality of the senses, as prāṇa, etc. Its activity is five-fold. Prāṇa has its operation passing through the nostrils of the face as far as the heart; the samāna life-current, so-called because it evenly (sama) guides (āna), i.e. functions, as far as the navel; apāna is so-called because it guides (āna) down (apa), operating down to the soles of the feet; udāna leads upward (ūrdhvam), having its operation from the soles to the top of the head; pervading all is the vyāna life-current. Of them, prāṇa is the principal one.*
>
> *By mastering the udāna, he passes untouched over water and thorns and so on. Having mastered it, at death he takes the upward course.*

By mastering the upgoing vital current (udāna), he passes untouched over water, mud, thorns and so on, and at death he takes the upward course. Life is the operation of the totality of the senses, as prāṇa, etc.; living is the operation of all eleven senses. As a dovecot moves with the movement of the birds in it, so by the unitedly reinforced operation of all the senses without exception, the body is sustained; and that is its life. Of that life, controlled by the obligation to fulfil the purposes of Puruṣa, *the activity is five-fold,* differentiated into prāṇa (forward-going current), apāna (downward-going), vyāna (pervading), udāna (upward) and samāna (equalizing), *pervading all is the vyāna (vi-variously) life-current.*

Of them *prāṇa has its operation passing through the nostrils of the face as far as the heart. The samāna life-current, so-called because it evenly (sama) guides (āna), has its operation as far as the navel:* it functions as far as the navel region. *Apāna is so-called because it guides (āna) down (apa)* the urine and faeces, etc., *and* from the navel *operates down to the soles of the feet. Udāna is so-called because it leads upward (urdhvam)* in the body, *having its operation from the soles to the top of the head.*

Of them, prāṇa is the principal one. From mastering that, there follows mastery of apāna and the others. A method of mastering them is given in detail in Hairanyagarbha, but as their mastery follows from mastery of mind (manas), here no separate method is given. But from mastery of prāṇāyama they are also conquered. Here without concerning himself with describing particular methods of mastering them separately, he simply gives the result of conquering udāna. *He passes untouched over water, mud, thorns and so on;* the *and so on* extends it to e.g. a sword's edge, *at death he takes the upward course,* which will come about spontaneously.

Sūtra III.40

From mastery of samāna, blazing light

He who has mastered samāna effects an arousal of the fire and causes a blaze of light.

From mastery of samāna, blazing light. He who has mastered samāna effects an arousal of the fire (tejas) of the udāna (sic) fire which has its location in the samāna life-current, *and* as the performer of the act, the yogin thereby *causes* his navel to *blaze* with light.

Sūtra III.41

From saṃyama on the relation between hearing and space, divine hearing

Space is the basis of hearing and sound. So it has been said: 'Among hearers similarly placed, what is heard is the same for all.' That very fact is the mark of space. It is said to be by nature free from obstruction. So it is seen that things with a form are opposites of space, since they are clearly obstructions.

A sense of hearing is inferred from the perception of sound; among deaf and the not-deaf one perceives it and the other does not perceive it. Hence sound is the field of the sense of hearing alone. Divine hearing comes into operation in the yogin who has made saṃyama on the relation between hearing and space.

From saṃyama on the relation between hearing and space, divine hearing. What is this relation on which the saṃyama is to be made? He says: *Space is the basis of* all *hearing and sound.* As sound is the attribute of space, sounds have space as their basis. The relation between hearing and space is that there is nothing intervening between the hearing and the sound to which the hearing is directed.

So it has been said: 'Among hearers similarly placed: hearing is that by which something is heard, and those who are exercising it in the same place are the similarly-placed hearers. For them, *what is heard is the same for all':* it is in conjunction with one existent thing (space) which gives scope to it to spread, and which is by nature free from obstruction. *That very fact is the mark of space.*

It is said to be by nature free from obstruction. So it is seen of things with a form such as a jar, with the reverse character to that of space, *that they are opposites of space, since they are clearly obstructions,* and when there is no obstruction, as within a jewel such as a diamond, etc., there the space is (visible), from which *the all-pervasiveness of space is clear.*

Now he describes the mark of (the function of) hearing. *A sense of hearing is inferred from the perception of sound,* for *among deaf and not-deaf one perceives it and the other does not perceive it.* The reason for the not-deaf man's perception of the sound, and the other one's failure to perceive it, is in the sense of hearing.

Hence sound is the field of the sense of hearing alone, for it is not heard by the deaf. *Divine hearing comes into operation in the yogin who has made saṃyama on the relation between hearing and space.*

Sūtra III.42

From saṃyama on the relation between the body and space, followed by identification-in-samādhi (samāpatti) with the lightness of a thread, he travels through space

> *When there is the body, there is space. Its relation to the body is by the fact that it gives that scope to the body. When his saṃyama has mastered the relation between the two, if the yogin then makes identification-in-samādhi with light things, from cotton thread down to the ultimate atoms, he becomes light. He treads upon the waters with his feet, he walks on strands of spiders' webs, he goes on the sunbeams. Thereafter he takes any course through space as he wills.*

When there is the body, there is space. The necessarily inherent *relation to the body is by the fact that it* space *gives that scope to the body. When* a yogin's *saṃyama has mastered the relation between the two,* the necessarily inherent mutual relation between body and space, *if he makes identification-in-samādhi with light things, from cotton thread down to the ultimate atoms, he becomes light.* Having mastered the relation, he first attains the lightness of cotton. The yogin whose identification-in-samādhi (samāpatti) has mastered the relation between body and space, to practise the lightness which is first like cotton, *treads on waters with his feet,* and then going higher *walks on strands of spiders' webs,* and then becoming light as a spark from a firebrand *he goes on the sunbeams,* and then on the wind. *Thereafter he takes any course through space as he wills.*

Sūtra III.43

The Great Bodiless is a mental process (vṛtti) functioning exterior (to the body), and not imaginary; from this comes dwindling away of the covering of the light

A process of the mind (functioning) outside the body is the concentration (dhāraṇā) called Bodiless. If it comes to be (functioning) in some outside objects only as a process of a mind (still) wholly fixed in the body, it is called Imaginary Bodiless; but when it is the external process of a mind which has itself become external and unconnected with the body, it is Not-Imaginary. By the Imaginary, they practise for the Not-Imaginary, which is the Great Bodiless.

The Great Bodiless is a mental process (vṛtti) exterior (to the body), and not imaginary; from this comes dwindling away of the covering of the light. A process of the mind outside the body, which is produced resting on a definite object in another place, purely voluntarily, by the power of samādhi, *is the concentration (dhāraṇā) called the* Great *Bodiless.*

If it comes to be in some outside object *only as a process of a mind wholly fixed in the body,* in that case *it is called Imaginary,* because it is produced by a purposive imagination (saṅkalpa) of a mind fixed in the body, *but when* as a result of the power of samādhi causing loosening of the cause of the bodily ties *it is the external process of a mind which has itself become external and unconnected with the body, it is* said to be *Not-Imaginary.* With the Imaginary, the one who attains the exterior mental process is still limited by being restricted to the body; with the Not-Imaginary, his experience is not limited by restriction to the physical body as a basis.

Both of them are called Bodiless inasmuch as there is (in both) the idea 'outside', but the one which is Not-Imaginary is called the Great Bodiless.

By the Imaginary one, they practise for the Not-Imaginary Great Bodiless; practising continuity of the Imaginary meditation, they accomplish (finally) the Not-Imaginary.

By the Great Bodiless, yogin-s enter other bodies. By that concentration of the Great Bodiless, the covering of the mind-sattva, whose nature is light, is thinned away – the covering which is the triad of the taints and the karma-s and their fruition, rooted in rajas and tamas.

Sūtra III.44

From saṃyama on their physical form, essential nature, subtle form, inherence, and purposefulness: conquest of the elements

Here, the earths, having as particulars sound, etc., together with attributes like shape, etc., are defined as physical (sthūla).

Each one of the elements (bhūta) is five-fold: physical, essential, subtle, inherent, and with-a-purpose. *Here, the earths have as particulars sound, etc.:* sound, touch, form, taste, and smell. They are earth because of the operation of the subtle elements (tan-mātra) of the five kinds.

together with attributes like shape etc. In regard to the earths, these (attributes) are the shape, etc., which means shape, rough texture, impermeability, saltiness, rigidity, exclusiveness, endurance, dark colour.

Then, liquidity, clearness, subtlety, softness, weight, conservation, purification, adsorption, etc., are attributes of the watery.

Then the fiery are: rising, consuming, purifying, burning, cooking, lightness, brilliance, etc.

Then the gaseous are: transverse motion, purification, impulsion, strength, dispersion, etc.

The spatial are: omnipresence, non-displacement, permeability.

With these attributes such as *shape, etc., particulars are defined* in the classic for mundane purposes *as physical (sthūla).* So also the four-fold particulars of liquids such as taste, along with the attributes of subtlety, etc.; and the threefold particulars of fire such as colour, with the attributes of rising up and consuming, are also defined as physical.

Then the gaseous particulars of sound and touch, with (attributes such as) transverse motion, are physical.

And the particulars of space, with attributes like omnipresence, are physical.

This is called *the first* the physical *aspect of the elements.*

> *The second aspect is the universal, having a defined outline in the case of earth, liquidity for water; for fire, burning; for air (wind), impetus; omnipresence for space. This is technically called the Essential nature. Of the universal, sound and the rest are particulars. So it is said: 'Of these things, which are wholly comprised of one class, it is only the attribute that makes any distinction.'*
>
> *Material substance is an aggregate of universal and particular. For aggregation can be of two kinds: (either) where the distinction between the parts is abandoned, as for instance a human body, a tree, a herd, or a wood; (or) aggregation where the parts that make it up are still distinguished by name, as for instance (the collective) Both-gods-and-men, in which gods are one part and men are one part. Only with both can it be termed an aggregation.*

The second aspect, the essential nature, is now spoken of. It *is the universal* which, itself undivided, runs through the different earths, *having a definite outline in the case of earth.* Similarly the universal running through the watery tastes, etc. is *liquidity for water;* so too *for fire,* the universal running through fiery colour, etc. *is burning; for air,* the universal running through the touch and transverse motion, etc. is *impetus;* then the universal running through sound, etc. is *omnipresence for space. This is* the second aspect *called technically the Essential nature.*

Of that universal aspect, *sound and the rest are particulars. And so it is said: of these things, which are wholly comprised of one class* since sattva and the other two guṇa-s are running through them, *it is only the attribute (dharma) that makes a distinction.*

Material substance (dravya) is an aggregate of universal and particular. How so? *For aggregation can be of two kinds* established in two ways: *(either) where the distinction between the parts is abandoned,* in the sense that there is no idea of distinguishing them, *as for instance a human body, a tree, a herd, or a wood, (or) aggregation where the* different *parts that make it up* that comprise it *are still distinguished by name* both of them being specified, *as for instance (the collective) Both-gods-and-men, in which gods are one part and men are one part. Only with both,* with both the elements that make it up retaining their own distinctness *can it be termed an aggregation.*

> *What is meant here is both difference and non-difference, as when one can say of a grove of mango trees, or a society of Brahmins, simply 'mango-grove' or 'Brahmin-society'.*

> *This again is of two kinds: where the parts sustain their structure even when separated, and where the parts do not do so. An example of where the parts sustain their structure is an aggregate like a wood or a society; examples of where they do not sustain their structure are an organic whole, a body, a tree, or an ultimate atom. Patañjali (the Grammarian) says that a material substance is an aggregate made up of different parts which do not sustain their structure when separated.*
>
> *This is called the Essential aspect (svarūpa).*

What is meant here is both difference and non-difference of the two things, *as in* the expression *'a grove of mango trees'.* A meaning of difference is conveyed by 'of mango trees', and a meaning of non-difference by 'a grove'. The nominative and genitive in the phrase 'a grove of mango trees' refer to those two, non-difference and difference.

This aggregate *again is of two kinds: where the parts sustain their structure even when separated, and where the parts do not do so. An example of where the parts sustain their structure* remain self-sufficient, *is an aggregate like a wood or a society; examples of where they do not sustain their structure* do not remain self-sufficient in isolation, *are an organic whole, a body, a tree, or an ultimate atom.*For the ultimate atoms too have a structure inasmuch as they are the effects of the three guṇa-s and have defined form just as much as a jar. *Patañjali (the Grammarian) says that a material substance (dravya) is an aggregate made up of different parts which do not sustain their own structure when separated.*

This is called the Essential aspect (svarūpa), consisting of universal and particular.

> *Now what is their subtle aspect? It is the subtle element called tan-mātra, cause of the physical elements. The ultimate atom is a single part of it. This comprises universal and particular and is an aggregate made up of different parts which do not sustain their own structure when separated. All the subtle elements are similar in this respect.*

Now what is their subtle aspect? It is the subtle element called tan-mātra, cause of the physical elements. As it comes from the co-operation of a number of the ultimate atoms, *The ultimate atom is a single part of it* of the subtle element (tan-mātra). *This* too (the ultimate atom) *comprises universal and particular and is an aggregate made up of different parts which do not sustain their own structure when separated. All the subtle elements are similar in this respect.* So the subtle elements, free of particularity, and their component parts the ultimate atoms, *are the third* aspect of the elements, called the subtle aspect, and it is to be the object of saṃyama.

Because space arises from the operation of a subtle element, it has parts, and so is not eternal. Nor can space be perceived apart from sound, for there is no separation of dharma and dharmin.

(Opponent) With something like hair, the blackness goes and whiteness comes in its place. So things like blackness are attributes, going and coming in due order. But what does not go with the blackness and does not come with the whiteness is the material substance. Things such as space also have a real existence apart from attributes, because space, for instance, is separate from notions of sound.

(Answer) Not so, for the example does not show it. It is indeed the hairs, black and white themselves, which change according to the qualities such as blackness and whiteness. It has been said already that everything is of the nature of everything else (comm. to III.14). Attributes like whiteness are never found going and coming on an immovable support. The self-nature of a substance is not a question of taking off blackness and so on from it. It is said that substance is what is perceived by both sight and touch, and as colour and touch are of an organic whole, it is perceived by both sight and touch.

(Opponent) But colour is not perceived by touch, nor is touch perceived by sight; a material substance is what is perceived by both in the sense that 'what I am seeing, that it is that I am touching'. But what is perceived by the eye alone, and what is perceived by touch alone, is an attribute.

(Answer) Not so, for when there is a heap of things of different classes, like sesamum seeds and beans and barley, they cannot be made out separately: the heap is perceived by both sight and touch. The sight-touch perceiver grasps attributes only, because the two are external senses, like hearing; no 'class' apart from attributes is perceived. For it cannot be separated out to be perceived.

Even in something like a jar, the colour and touch that are perceived by one, in a mutual superimposition of the sight-touch pair, are only a limited (apprehension); for this colour-form may be also evil-smelling or sweet-smelling, for example.

So it is that in the absence of sound there can be no space, a product of tan-mātra-s. It has therefore a structure, and is not eternal.

> *Now the fourth aspect of the elements: the guṇa-s, ever tending towards knowledge, activity and stasis respectively, which tendencies are carried over into their effects, are what is meant by guṇa-inherence (in the elements).*

Now the fourth aspect of the elements: the guṇa-s ever tending towards knowledge, activity and stasis respectively, which tendencies are carried over into their effects, following on as the dharma-s of their effects, *are what is meant by guṇa-inherence (in the elements).* For they imitate them. This is the fourth aspect of the elements, called the guṇa inherence, which is to be made the subject of saṃyama.

> *Then their fifth aspect is Purposefulness: purpose of experience and purpose of release, both inherent in the guṇa-s. The guṇa-s being in the tan-mātra-s, in the elements, and in the transformations of the elemenets, everything is purposive.*

Then their fifth aspect is Purposefulness. It is explained as *purpose of experience and purpose of release,* and the two are both *inherent in the guṇa-s.* The purposefulness which runs through the guṇa-s as the purpose of experience and the purpose of release is the fifth aspect of the elements, the object of saṃyama described as Purposefulness.

The guṇa-s are inherent *in the tan-mātra-s, in the elements, in the transformations of the elements;* thus tan-mātra as the subtle aspect pervades elements and their transformations. Since the Essential aspect of the elements pervades the elemental transformations, *everything is purposive.*

The guṇa-s themselves have the purpose of experience and release, and they pervade everything else, so that by their purposiveness, all transformations of the elements also have purpose.

> *From saṃyama on the five elements in their five-fold aspects, there manifest: vision, and mastery over them. Having mastered these natural aspects of the*

elements, he becomes master of the elements. After that, the elemental powers follow his purposive will as a cow follows its beloved calf.

From saṃyama on the five elements in their five-fold aspects, the aspects already described, beginning with the physical, making saṃyama in the order given, first on the physical aspect, and when that has been mastered in the form of direct cognition (sākṣātkaraṇa), the yogin should immediately make saṃyama on the essential aspect. And so on to the subtle, then the inherence, and then on to the purposefulness, in due order. *(From that saṃyama) there manifest: vision* of them as they truly are, *and mastery over them. Having mastered these natural aspects of the elements,* the yogin *becomes master of the elements. After that, the elemental powers follow his purposive will as a cow,* the elemental powers being compared to a cow, *follows its beloved calf.*

Sūtra III.45

From it (the saṃyama) manifest a set of eight powers like becoming minute, and perfection of the body, with freedom from impediment for its (bodily) attributes

Of these powers, becoming minute is to be like an atom. Lightness – he becomes light; greatness – he becomes great; range – he could touch the moon with a fingertip; irresistible will – he can dive into the solid ground and move about there as if it were water; mastery – by this he can master the elements and elementals, and himself is not mastered by any others; sovereignty – he can will the production, absorption and disposition of them; omnipotence – his purposive idea becomes true, so that whatever that purpose, so the states of the elements and their natures become.

Now he describes the effects of saṃyama on himself. *From it, manifest a set of eight powers like becoming minute, and perfection of the body, with freedom from impediment for its (bodily) attributes. Of these,* what is *becoming minute?* It is to be *like an atom.* If he will, he is more subtle than the subtle. By that power he can enter anything, even a diamond, and so he cannot be seen by anyone.

Lightness – he becomes light, lighter even than such things as a cotton thread. By this power he can go anywhere without needing anything to support him.

greatness – he becomes great. He can extend as far as space, *range* – from this very earth *he could touch the moon with a finger-tip. irresistible will* – any desire he has comes to be as he desires; *he can dive into the solid ground and move about there* just as he wishes *as if it were water, mastery* – mastery of all worlds. *By this he can master the elements and elementals, and himself is not mastered by any others, sovereignty – he can will the production, absorption and disposition* the appearance, maintenance and dissolution *of them* the elements. *omnipotence* – in whatever he desires, the things become and remain as he wills. *His purposive idea becomes true, so that whatever that purpose, so the states of the elements and their natures become.*

> *Though he has the power, he does not create a reversal of (the nature of) things. Because they are as they are from the purpose of another omnipotent one before him.*
>
> *These are the eight powers.*

Though he this yogin *has the power, he does not create a reversal of (the nature of) things.* He does not make fire cold. Why not? *Because they* all things *are as they are from the purpose of another omnipotent one before him,* the Supreme Lord (parameśvara). A reversal by one who wished to reverse the order of things could not be without hate for that previous perfect one. Since the yogin is without impurity, he will not cause such a reversal, for his conduct is most excellent.

These eight powers, becoming minute and the rest, come about from mastery of the elements.

> *The perfections of the body will be described below. Freedom from impediments in the way of its attributes means: the earth with its hardness does not oppose the movements of the yogin, for his body can penetrate even rock; waters with all their wetness do not moisten the yogin; fire does not burn him with its heat, nor does the wind which makes all bow, move him; in space, which by nature obstructs nothing, he becomes hidden, becoming invisible even to perfected beings.*

The perfections of the body will be described below (sūtra III.46). Freedom from impediments in the way of its attributes means: there is no impediment by the attributes of the elements forming any obstruction in the way of the attributes of the yogin as described.

The earth with its hardness its particular attribute *does not oppose the movements of the yogin.* Why not? *His body can penetrate even rock. Waters with all their wetness do not moisten the yogin* though he stand in them a thousand years. *Fire does not burn him with its heat, nor does the wind which makes all bow, move him. In space, which by nature obstructs nothing,* even there where all is open, *he becomes hidden,* he becomes invisible. *He becomes invisible even to perfected beings.*

Sūtra III.46

The perfection of the body is grace, splendour, power, and diamond hardness

Grace means attractiveness; splendour means brightness; then it has unsurpassed power, and diamond hardness.

(No vivaraṇa comment)

Sūtra III.47

From saṃyama on their perception, essential nature, I-am-ness, inherence, and purposefulness, (comes) conquest of the senses

Sound and the others, comprising both universal and particular, are the sense-objects, and the operation of the senses on those objects is their perception (grahaṇa). The nature of the perception is not the universal aspect alone. If the particular instance (also) of its own object were not apprehended by the sense-organ, how would any object be accurately determined by the mind?

From saṃyama on their perception, essential nature, I-am-ness, inherence and purposefulness, (comes) conquest of the senses. All this is to be taken on the same basis as the earlier sūtra (III.44), except that pure I-am-ness is the particular corresponding to the tan-mātra-s in the case of the elements.

Sound and the others, comprising both universal and particular, are the sense-objects, and the operation (vṛtti) of the senses on those objects, which is essentially an apprehension of the particular, *is their perception (grahaṇa). The nature of the perception is not the universal aspect alone,* it is not the appearance in the mind simply of the universal aspect of sound etc. Why not? *If the particular instance (also) of its own object were not apprehended by the sense-organ,* if its own object-particular were not grasped, *how* indeed *would any object be accurately determined by the mind?* It could never be perceived.

The case is like the accurate determination, or failure of it, in the case of those free from the timira eye-disease, and those suffering from it. So there is no determination by the mind of any object which has not been apprehended by a sense-organ. It is on this operation (vṛtti) of the senses, whose essence is the particular, that the first saṃyama is to be made.

> *Next, the essential aspect: a sense is a substance which is a combination of universal and particular of the nature of light, whose parts are neither of them self-sufficient in isolation.*

Next, the essential aspect, the second aspect of the senses. It is *a combination of universal and particular of the nature of light:* the illumination of a particular object is the particular (application) of the senses, as lighting up the form of a particular like a jar is a particular application of a lamp. The universal is pure light. So *a sense is a substance which is (a combination) whose parts are neither of them self-sufficient in isolation.* Just as a universal like the quality of form has corresponding instances in things like physical objects, so a sense with its nature of light has a particular corresponding instance in the operation of perception, which is essentially a particular of the substance that is the sense. He should perform saṃyama on this, the second aspect of the senses.

> *The third aspect of them is the I-feeling, characterized as I-am-ness: it is a universal, and the senses are particular instances of it.*
>
> *The fourth aspect is the guṇa-s, which are determined as always tending towards light, activity and stasis respectively; the senses with I-feeling are a transformation of them.*

The fifth aspect is the purposefulness which runs throughout the guṇa-s.

The third aspect of them the senses *is the I-feeling, characterized as I-am-ness. Of that universal,* the I-feeling, *the senses* which are combinations whose parts are neither of them self-sufficient in isolation, and whose pervading aspect is perception, *are particulars.* The saṃyama is to be made on them.

The fourth aspect is the guṇa-s, which are determined as always tending towards light, activity, and stasis respectively. The senses with I-feeling are a transformation of them. Saṃyama is to be made on the guṇa-inherence.

The fifth aspect is the purposefulness which runs through the guṇa-s, with the corollary that purposefulness runs through everything, as explained previously.

From saṃyama on these five aspects of the senses, mastering them one by one in the order given till all five have been conquered, mastery of the senses appears in the yogin.

Then *saṃyama* is made *on these five aspects of the senses,* keeping strictly to the order; *mastering them one by one,* each separate one of the five *in the order given* keeping to the sequence, he conquers the five aspects. Then when *all five aspects have been conquered, mastery of the senses appears in the yogin,* with results to be described. Whereas what was previously said, 'From that, supreme mastery of the senses' (II.35) referred simply to mastery of the mental process of perception of objects, in the form of shutting out perception of them of any kind (through mental one-pointedness).

Sūtra III.48

From that, speediness as of the mind, independence of physical organs, and conquest of nature

From that (mastery of the senses), the body can travel with unsurpassable speed like that of the mind. Then, the senses can operate independent of a body in regard to any determined place, time and object.

Conquest of nature (pradhāna) is mastery of all effects of prakṛti-causes.

These three perfections are called Honey-formed, and they are acquired by conquering the five aspects (of the senses).

From that, speediness as of the mind, independence of physical organs, and conquest of nature (pradhāna). From that, from mastery of the senses *the body can travel with unsurpassable speed like that of the mind,* unsurpassable in that nothing can go faster than that. *Independence of physical organs* means that *the senses independent of a body,* dissociated from a body, *can operate in regard to any determined place* and determined *time and* determined *object. Mastery of all prakṛti-causes and their effects* means mastery of the eight prakṛti-s and their effects, and this *is mastery of nature.*

These three are called Honey-formed (madhu-pratīka) and they are acquired by conquering the five aspects (of the senses).

Sūtra III.49

Having simply the knowledge that (mind-)sattva and Puruṣa are different, one has omnipotence over all beings and is omniscient

One whose mind (buddhi-sattva) has been purified of the taint of rajas and tamas so that he is now in the highest purity and in the consciousness of mastery, firmly set simply in the knowledge that sattva and Puruṣa are different, has omnipotence over all beings.

As the essence of all, which all is essentially determination of guṇa-s, the guṇa-s in their entirety are presented to their Lord, the witness of the field, as the field of the seen – this is the meaning. Omniscience means instant discriminative knowledge of the guṇa-s which are the essence of all, whether determined as qualities subsided or uprisen or (as yet) indeterminable.

This perfection described is called Beyond Sorrow, and when he has attained it, the omniscient yogin whose taints and bonds have been thinned away, disports himself as a master.

Simply having the knowledge that (mind-)sattva and Puruṣa are different, one has omnipotence over all beings, and is omniscient. One whose mind-sattva has been purified of the taint (mala) of rajas and tamas by all kinds of means *so that he is now in the highest purity,* the highest clarity in an unbroken stream *and in the consciousness of mastery* in unsurpassed peace of pure knowledge – *he who is firmly set in the form of the simple knowledge that sattva and Puruṣa are different, has omnipotence over all beings,* over the whole aggregate of things at will.

As the essence of all the essence of the whole nature (prakṛti) and its transformations, *which is essentially determination of guṇa-s,* nothing but determinations of them transformed as causes and states such as buddhi, corresponding to qualities subsided or uprisen or indeterminable, *the guṇa-s in their entirety are presented to* are brought before *their Lord, the witness of the field (kṣetrajña)* who is sight alone, *as the field of the seen* as the field of experience – *this is the meaning.*

Omniscience means knowledge-born-of-discrimination (viveka-ja) arising *instantly* without stages, at the one time *of the guṇa-s, the essence of all, determined as qualities subsided or uprisen or (as yet) indeterminable.*

This perfection described, namely omnipotence and omniscience, *is called Beyond Sorrow, and when he has attained it, the omniscient yogin whose taints and bonds have been thinned away, disports himself as a master.*

Sūtra III.50

From indifference to that too, the seeds of imperfection are destroyed, and there is Transcendental Aloneness

> *When, in one who has become like this, the taints and karma-s are destroyed, there arises an idea of his (mind-)sattva which discriminates (as follows): sattva too is consigned to the side of what-is-to-be-escaped, and Puruṣa is unchanging and pure, quite different from sattva. In one who is thus indifferent to that (aforesaid perfection) too, whatever seeds of taint (kleśa) there may be, become like scorched rice-grains, incapable of germination, and they pass away along with the mind. When they have been dissolved, Puruṣa never again experiences the threefold suffering.*

From indifference to that too, the seeds of imperfection (doṣa) are destroyed, and there is Transcendental Aloneness. When, in one who has become like this omnipotent over all states of being, *the taints and karma-s are destroyed, there arises an idea of this (mind-)sattva which discriminates.* What sort of idea of this? He explains: *sattva too is consigned to the side of what-is-to-be-escaped* because of its transience and impurity and the fact that there are the two other guṇa-s, and so on, *and Puruṣa* without the attribute of sattva *is unchanging and pure* and so *quite different from sattva.*

In one who is indifferent to that omniscient overseeing of all states of being *too, whatever seeds of taint* in the shape of saṃskāra-groups (vāsanā) of Ignorance (avidyā) *there may be, become like scorched rice-grains, incapable of germination, and they* dissolving after having fulfilled their purpose, *pass away along with the mind* their seat. *When they have been dissolved, Puruṣa never again experiences the three-fold suffering* – relating to the inner self, etc. (to the elements, and to the gods).

> *When these guṇa-s, which manifest in the mind taints and karma-s and their fruition, have fulfilled their purpose and go back (into their root: pratiprasava), Puruṣa is absolutely disjoined from guṇa-s, and this is Transcendental Aloneness. Then Puruṣa is established in his own nature as pure power-of-consciousness.*

When these guṇa-s, which manifest in the mind as taints and karma-s and their fruition, have fulfilled their purpose and go back into dissolution, *Puruṣa is absolutely disjoined from guṇa-s, and this is Transcendental Aloneness. Then Puruṣa is established in his own nature as pure power-of consciousness.*

When it was said (in the sūtra) *From indifference to that too,* the word 'too' shows that Transcendental Aloneness arises from right vision (samyag-darśana) even though one may not have attained the yogic powers (aiśvarya).

Sūtra III.51

No reaction of attachment or pride in case of invitations from rulers of celestial realms, for undesirable consequences follow

The *realms* are divine regions like heaven, and their rulers are gods like Indra. There are invitations by them, such as: 'Noble Sir, pray take this seat ...' and so on. In such case, let him remember and understand the essential meanness of individual selfhood, and let him not react with *attachment or pride.* Reaction of attachment or pride will entail *undesirable consequences.*

There are four classes of yogin:

(1) the beginner (prathama-kalpika)
(2) in the Honeyed stage (madhu-bhūmika)
(3) with the light of knowledge (prajña-jyotis)
(4) one who has passed beyond all that was to be practised (ati-krānta-bhavanīya) Of these, the first is one who having roused the light of one of the supernormal perceptions of a divine object (I.35) is engaged in practising it;

The second has the truth-bearing knowledge (I.48);

The third has conquered the senses. He retains firmly all that has been actualized so far, and possesses the means for the accomplishment of what is still to be actualized;

The fourth is one who has passed through all that was to be practised, and whose sole purpose now is reversion of the mind. He has the seven-fold ultimate knowledge (II.27).

Of them, it is the Brahmin who has directly realized the Honeyed state, whose purity is seen by the celestial gods, and whom they allure into their realms.

There are four classes of yogin: the beginner, in the Honeyed stage, with the light of knowledge, and having passed beyond all that was to be practised. He will now describe them in the order given:

Of these, the first is one who having roused the light of one of the supernormal perceptions of a divine object having roused into operation one of the viṣayavatī functions such as the Radiant (jyotiṣmatī I.36) *is practising* is devoting himself to practice on it.

The second has the truth-bearing knowledge (I.48).

The third is one who has conquered the senses and retains firmly as is proper when something has been once attained *everything that has been actualized so far,* all that was to be actualized, and all that has been directly seen (in the case of knowledge) or mastered (in the case of the powers), *and who possesses the means for the accomplishment of what is still to be actualized,* what is to be realized directly (sākṣātkāra). The means for the accomplishment are: practice and detachment (I.12), and this is one who has them.

The fourth is one who has passed through all that was to be practised, and whose sole purpose now remaining *is reversion of the mind* the dissolution of the mind. *He has the seven-fold ultimate knowledge.*

Of them, it is the Brahmin who has directly realized the Honeyed stage the second stage, that of the truth-bearing knowledge *whose purity is seen (resentfully) by the celestial gods, and whom they allure into their realm,* saluting him with the words 'Noble Sir', as will now be described:

> *'Noble Sir! Do you take your seat here, do you enjoy yourself here. The pleasure is delicious, and delicious the girl. This elixir prevents age and death. Here is an aerial chariot, there a wish-fulfilling tree. The heavenly river Mandākinī, the perfect beings, and great sages, all give their blessings: the nymphs are without equal, and compliant. Sight and hearing are divine, and the body like a diamond. Your special virtues, Noble Sir, have merited all this. Do you take this high position, which is unfading, ever fresh, undying, and beloved of the gods.'*

But let him thus invited, meditate on the evils of that associationship:

> *Scorched by the fierce flames of saṃsāra, wandering in birth-and-death, I have just managed to obtain the lamp of yoga which destroys the blindness of taints. The winds of sensual things, wombs of craving, are its foes. How then can I, who have seen its light, be led astray by the mirage of these things of the senses, and make myself fuel for the burning fire of saṃsāra to flare up again? Farewell, you things like dreams, pursued by pitiable creatures!*

Thus confirming his purpose, let him practise samādhi on it. Giving up all association with them, let him take no pride in being thus solicited by the gods themselves. If he, through such pride, feels himself secure, he will forget that death has already grasped his forelock, and then carelessness – always to be guarded against as it seeks an opening – will enter and rouse the taints, with their undesirable consequences. By avoiding that association and that pride, what he has already practised becomes firm in him, and what he has yet to practise stands right before him.

(No Vivaraṇa comment)

Sūtra III.52

From saṃyama on the instant, and on the two sequences of instants, comes knowledge-born-of-discrimination

> *Just as the ultimate particle of matter is the atom, so the ultimate particle of time is the instant. Alternatively, an instant is (definable as) the time taken by an atom to pass from one point to the next one.*
>
> *A sequence is continuity of the unbroken flow of the instants in it. There is no real aggregation of the two: instants and their sequence. Hours and days and nights appear from mental aggregation.*
>
> *This time is empty of reality and has been set up by the mind, according to the nature of the words used. To the extravertive view of the people of the world, it merely seems to have reality. But the instant (itself) does have reality, being the support of the sequence. The sequence is essentially a continuity of instants.*

From saṃyama on the instant, and on the two (future and present; see under III.15) sequences of instants, comes knowledge-born-of discrimination. The commentary explains at length the instant and sequence: *(Just as) the ultimate particle of matter* from which no further subtraction can be made *is the (ultimate) atom, so the ultimate particle of time* smaller than the diminutions of the divisions set up by the world such as days and nights, until nothing more can be ground away *is the instant* which is an existent thing.

Or *Alternatively, an instant is (definable as) the time taken by an ultimate atom in motion to pass from one point to the next one.* The meaning is, that all time is instants.

The sequence – of instants – *is the continuity of the unbroken flow of these instants in it:* a flow, a continuity, which is unbroken, invariable, like a natural tendency of the instants in it. *There is no real aggregation of the two: instants and their sequence,* because there is no such thing as an instantaneous sequence, and an instant itself is but a single thing, so there can be no aggregation of them, no bringing together.

(Opponent) But if there is no aggregation of instant and sequence, how is it that the months and years and so on do in fact pass by?

(Answer) He replies: *The hours and days and nights arise from mental aggregation (buddhi-saṃhāra).* From a mentally conceived aggregation of instants and sequence, assumed by the mind from the assumption of, or relationship with, various positions, (taken) by the sun and other bodies. Thus time-difference is set up by the mind (buddhi).

For one whose mind (manas) is calm, flowing peacefully in a stream of the same idea, whose mind-sattva is established in the one-pointed state – though he has experience of time, an instant and a thousand ages are equal. This is not so in the extravertive mind. Then in dream too, in half an hour one's mind imagines that one has made a journey of several thousand leagues, which would take a full year to accomplish. Thus the aggregates of time are set up purely by the wonderful variety of mind (buddhi).

Even one who holds that there is an eternal absolute time apart still himself determines fastness and slowness etc. in accordance with the measure of some action, so that he cannot produce anything to indicate the existence of absolute time. The yardstick applied to an action whose measure is not yet known is, some action whose duration is already established; for instance (we say), 'He will sleep until the cows are milked' or 'He will study till the rice is boiled'. This is all that time is. Even if there were some eternal absolute (time), there could be no relation with that immutable, and it could not provide any firm basis against which to measure anything else.

(Opponent) It is time-in-action that is the firm basis for determination.

(Answer) Since it too would be acting, there would have to be something to determine its acting, and that would have to be done by some other time acting to determine it. And that would need yet another, so there would be an infinite regress. Moreover, if it were acting, it would follow that it was not eternal.

(Opponent) Let it be that time is what is measured simply by its operation.

(Answer) Other things too are measured simply by their operation, and there is no need to suppose time to be different. So it will have to be that time is simply action (as we say).

(Opponent) Well, time makes the determinations simply by the fact of existing.

(Answer) Everything else exists equally, so it should be just the same.

(Opponent) Your 'action-time' too is a mere logical construct (vikalpa).

(Answer) No, because everyone accepts the fact of action. When it is said 'slowly' or 'quickly', the idea is that it has been done with slack, or skilful, effort, and there is no reference to some outside time. So he says: *This time* in the shape of years and so on *is empty of reality and has been set up by the mind according to the quality of the words used:* moment, blink of an eye, day, night and so on are verbal constructs to which it conforms. *To the extraverted view of people of the world it merely seems to have reality.*

But the instant does have reality, it is actual, as is inferred from the fact that it is different in kind, *being the support of the sequence. The sequence is essentially a continuity of instants,* being caused by the idea (buddhi) of an unbroken flow of instants.

> *Yogin-s, experts in time, declare it to be that. Two instants do not occur together, nor is a pair of them a sequence, because it could not exist simultaneously with them.*

Sequence is immediate proximity of the following-on of the later, future, instant from the one that precedes it. Each one instant is present, with the earlier and later instants absent, and therefore there is no aggregation of them. But what are called instants gone, and instants yet-to-come, should be taken as being changes. At each instant the whole world experiences a change: all those qualities (dharma) are manifest as that instant.

Yogin-s, experts in time, declare it to be that instant. *Two instants do not occur together* so that they could be taken as an aggregate, for it is impossible for two instants to arise together in one possessor (dharmin). When the month Caitra begins, it begins at a single instant. Two instants do not occur together, *nor is a pair of them a sequence.* Why not? *Because it could not exist simultaneously with them*with the instants.

Sequence is immediate proximity of the following-on of the later, future, instant from the one that precedes it. Immediately proximate following-on of the later, future, jar from the clay lump would be a sequence. But a jar made of the clay lump on one potter's wheel is not in sequence with a clay lump on a different wheel.

Each one instant is present, with earlier and later instants absent; the earlier and later, past and future instants are not there, because it is simply the nature of the dharmin-possessor of the earlier and later: the dharmin is manifest as the present instant only. *Therefore there is no aggregation of them,* no aggregation of the instant and sequence.

But what are called instants gone and yet-to-come, past and future, *should be taken as being changes* of the dharmin, should be explained as changes of the dharmin. *At each instant the whole world experiences a change: all those qualities (dharma),* all things *are manifest as that instant,* manifest as the present instant.

When it was said above that there is no sequence from the past instant, the purpose was to rule out a sequence of sequences of them. For a sequence of sequences of instants entails reality of a sequence of instants, inasmuch as a sequence must be of a reality. And so to say 'From samādhi on the sequence and its instants' would not have been appropriate.

Therefore *From saṃyama on the instant and on the two sequences of instants* there is direct experience (sākṣātkaraṇa) of them, and from that, *knowledge-born-of-discrimination.* Inasmuch as all things are reckoned in instants and their sequences, when he discriminates these, he knows everything.

A particular field of the (omniscient) knowledge is now described.

Sūtra III.53

From this (knowledge) there is clear knowledge of two things (seemingly) equivalent because they cannot be distinguished by class, characteristic, or position

A difference in class may be the ground of differentiation, as for instance, 'This one is a cow, this one is a mare'. When the class is the same, a characteristic differentiates them: 'This cow has black eyes, that cow has lucky markings'. If there are two myrobalan fruits, of the same class and with the same characteristics, then difference in position may differentiate them: 'This is the front one, that is the one behind.' But if the fruit in front is moved, while the observer is attending to something else, to the position behind, then since the positions are as they were, he cannot detect rightly which is which; that (detection) would have to be through an infallible knowledge of truth, and so

> *it was said (in the sūtra above): From this – namely from knowledge-born-of-discrimination – there is clear knowledge (of the two fruits).*

What sort of things are knowable by that knowledge-born-of-discrimination? *A particular field of the knowledge is now described: From this there is clear knowledge of two things (seemingly) equivalent because they cannot be distinguished by class, characteristic, or position.*

A difference in class of the things *may be the ground of differentiation* of distinguishing the difference, *as for instance, 'This one is a cow, this one is a mare'.*

When they both belong to one class, so that there is no difference in class, then *When the class is the same, a characteristic (lakṣaṇa)* an indicatory mark (liṅga) may be what *differentiates them: 'This cow has black eyes, that cow has lucky markings.'*

When there is no difference of class, and no difference of characteristic, still a difference of position may be a ground for discerning the difference. *If there are two myrobalan fruits, of the same class and with the same characteristics, then a difference in position may differentiate them: 'This* fruit *is the front one, that is the one behind.'*

But if the fruit in front is moved – while the observer is attending to something else so that his mind is distracted – *to the position behind* and the rear one to the front position, *he will not be able to detect rightly which is which. That detection would have to come about by an infallible knowledge of truth* about the particular situation in question, since that is what is present. *And this is why it was said: From this -from the knowledge-born-of-discrimination – there is clear knowledge.* From the knowledge-born-of-discrimination attained by saṃyama on instant and sequence, there is clear knowledge about them.

> *How (can the difference possibly be known)? Its position at the instant of being the front fruit is distinct from the position at the instant of being the fruit behind. The two fruits are distinct in their respective experiences of their own point-instants. The difference of experience of the point-instants makes the difference between them.*

How is that? *Its position at the instant of being the front fruit* the position corresponding to being the front fruit *is distinct from the position at the instant of being the fruit behind,* the position corresponding to the fruit behind. *The two fruits* corresponding to the instant of being the front one and the one behind *are distinct in their particular experiences of their own point-instants,* having been affected by their positions at any given instant; at any instant their experiences are distinct, as they have been affected by the respective point-instants passed through. *The difference of experience of the point-instants makes the difference between them.*

> *This example illustrates how an expert yogin can, from the difference of their point-instants, get the idea of the difference between even two ultimate atoms, by his direct perception of the point-instant of the front atom, though it is identical in class and characteristic to the other atom; for when the one behind replaces it in that (front) position, the one that was behind is experiencing the front position at a different instant. In the case of the Lord and of the yogin, awareness of the distinction (between the two atoms) comes about from the difference between the instants.*

This example illustrates how an expert yogin can, from the difference of their point-instants, get the idea of the difference between – can distinguish – *even two ultimate atoms, by his direct perception (sākṣāt-karana) of the point-instant of the front atom, though it is identical in class and characteristic to the other atom,* by his direct perception of the instant coincident with its position as the front atom; *for when the one behind replaces it in that position* by coming to the front position, *the one that was behind is experiencing the front position at a different instant. In the case of the Lord and of the yogin, awareness of the distinction* – discrimination of the difference (between the two atoms) – *comes about from the difference between the instants.*

> *On this point, however, there are others who maintain that it is the ultimate particulars which alone make the idea of distinction. It is distinctions of location and characteristic, and distinctions of form, distance and class that are the causes of difference. To this it is said: 'since there is no difference of form or distance in the ultimate root-cause, there are no separate distinctions in the root' – thus Vārṣaganya.*

On this point, however, there are others who maintain that it is the ultimate particulars the permanent ultimate atoms *which alone make the idea of distinction,* so that saṃyama on instants and their sequences is irrelevant. As the particulars constituting for example a jar, make the idea of its difference (from other jars, etc.), so it should be particulars consisting of ultimate atoms that give the idea of its existence, and the idea of them as its true existence; they also make the idea of difference in what they rest in (āśraya).

As to this it has been said: *distinctions of location and characteristic, and distinctions of form, distance, and class are the causes of difference.* This was in fact said in regard to physical things, but of course the ultimate atoms are changing every instant. If the ultimate particulars had been stable, difference would be determinable, but this could not apply to things incessantly changing.

When the atom in front changes into the atom behind, and the one behind into the front one, there are then no fixed ultimate particulars, so that knowledge of the distinction between them could not be attained from them. Necessarily then it could come only from that Knowledge-born-of-discrimination produced by saṃyama on the instant and its sequences. For it has been shown that ultimate atoms are not permanent entities, and therefore it is the distinction of the instants alone that is to be sought by the mind of the yogin.

He demonstrates the truth of the transience of ultimate atoms by citing the view of another ācārya. *To this it is said: Since there is no difference of form or distance in the ultimate root-cause, there are no separate distinctions in the root – thus Vārṣaganya.* To propose a plurality of pradhāna-s, one for each Field-knower (kṣetra-jña), on the ground that there should be many separate pradhāna-s because each should be the object of one single Puruṣa-purpose, would be contrary to reason, in view of the fact that they could have no difference of form or distance or class.

So at the basis of the ultimate atoms too, no separateness can be supposed. Therefore the conclusion is: a single root. For it is not right that the distinctions of ultimate atoms should be permanent, for they have forms and colours and so on, so that they can only be impermanent, like a jar.

Sūtra III.54

Knowledge-born-of-discrimination, having all, and all times, for its object, is called Transcendent

It is called Transcendent in the sense that it flashes out spontaneously without any prompting from elsewhere. Having all as object means that there is nothing that does not become its object. With all times as its object, means that he knows them – past, future and present – in all their variety at all times. It grasps all at all times: without sequence, it arises in one instant. This is the culmination of knowledge-born-of discrimination; one ray of it is the yoga-light. What was begun in the Honeyed state now has its culmination.

Knowledge-born-of-discrimination, having all, and all times, for its object, is called Transcendent (tāraka). This is a peak of knowledge, attained by gods, ṛṣi-s, gandharva-spirits and so on. *It is called Transcendent,* inasmuch as this Knowledge-born-of-discrimination, as it is *said, flashes out spontaneously without any prompting from elsewhere.* It cannot be taught by another, nor by teaching can it be grasped as it is. So that has *all* things *as object,* which *means that there is nothing that does not become its object.*

And with all times as its object: all things *past, future and present, he knows them in all their variety* with all their particulars *at all times* with all their changes. *It grasps all at all times: without sequence, it arises in one instant,* instantaneously, and not in a sequence, as with us.

This is the culmination of Knowledge-born-of discrimination; one ray of it is the yoga-light. This very ray of knowledge is the yoga and light, or again it is the light of yoga. *What was begun* undertaken *in the Honeyed stage now has its culmination,* the culmination of discriminative-Knowledge (viveka-jñāna). The various forms of knowledge associated with travelling at the speed of thought and so on, culminating in discriminative-Knowledge, are one ray of this.

In one who has attained knowledge-born-of-discrimination –

Sūtra III.55

When the (mind-)sattva is like Puruṣa in purity, there is Transcendental Aloneness. So it is.

When the taints of rajas and tamas have been shaken off, the mind-sattva (buddhi-sattva), its seeds of taints scorched, becomes no more than the idea of the apartness of Puruṣa, and then it attains as it were purity like that of Puruṣa. The purity of Puruṣa means absence of experience being imputed to it. In that state there is Transcendental Aloneness, whether he has acquired the divine powers or has not, whether he is possessor of Knowledge-born-of-discrimination or he is not. For when the seeds of taints have been scorched, there is no dependence at all on any further knowledge. Through the purification of the sattva, the power and knowledge arising from samādhi-s are indeed attained, but the highest truth is this: by Knowledge, failure-to-see comes to an end, and when that ceases, there are none of the taints that have been described before. With no taints, there is no karma-fruition. In that state, the guṇa-s have finished with their involvement and no longer arise before Puruṣa as the Seen. That is the Transcendental Aloneness of Puruṣa when Puruṣa stands alone in his true nature as pure light. So it is.

This completes the third part, of the Glories, of the commentary by holy Vyāsa, compiler of the Veda-s, on the Yoga-sūtra of holy Patañjali.

The knowledge and power arising from yoga have been gone through and completed, and there are no knowledge and power beyond these. It was in reference to one who had attained the knowledge and power through yoga practice that it came to be said (III.50): *Indifference to that* becomes immediately Transcendental Aloneness; so here he says, *In one who has attained Knowledge-born-of-discrimination,*on cessation of extraverted vision, there is that Aloneness. How does he say this? *When the sattva is like Puruṣa in purity, there is Transcendental Aloneness.*

When the taints of rajas and tamas have been shaken off, the mind-sattva (buddhisattva), its seeds of taints scorched the ideas and saṃskāra-groups (vāsanā) having ceased within it, *becomes no more than the idea of apartness of Puruṣa,* being absorbed in the majesty of the idea of that apartness alone, *then it attains as it were purity like that of Puruṣa.*

Even though what consists of the three guṇa-s is of opposite nature to Puruṣa, and Puruṣa is of opposite nature to what is of the three guṇa-s, still inasmuch as it is transformed into the idea of the apartness of Puruṣa, it is said that it as it were attains a comparable purity.

In that state there is Transcendental Aloneness, whether he has acquired the divine powers or has not, whether he is possessor of Knowledge-born-of-discrimination or he is not, for in both cases there is the cause (of Transcendental Aloneness) which is nothing but cessation of Ignorance. *For when the seeds of taints have been scorched, there is no dependence at all on further knowledge.* He who sees rightly (samyagdarśin) realizes that everything consists of the three guṇa-s, and that this very idea is to be escaped from, as being of the three guṇa-s itself. And so he has no dependence at all on knowledge such as that of the Honeyed stage.

The yogic knowledge and power that have been described are a by-product brought about by way of the purity of (mind-)sattva, attained in the course of the pursuit of right vision (samyagdarśana). *But the highest truth is this: by Knowledge, failure-to-see comes to an end, and when that ceases, there are none of the taints that have been described before* such as I-am-ness, for their field is Ignorance. *With no taints, there is no karma-fruition,* as witness (sūtra-s II.12, 13): 'Rooted in taints is the karma-stock' and 'While the root is there, it will bear fruit'.

Therefore, this work has right vision alone for its goal, and glories of knowledge and power are not its purpose. *In this state, the guṇa-s have finished with their involvement, and no longer arise before the Puruṣa as the Seen. That is Transcendental Aloneness of Puruṣa, when Puruṣa stands alone in his true nature as pure light. So it is,* means that the Part has been completed.

With this is completed the Third Part, of Glories, of the sub-commentary by holy Lord Śaṅkara, who is a paramahaṃsa parivrājaka ācārya, and pupil of holy Lord Govindapāda whose feet are to be worshipped, on the commentary on the Yoga-sūtra-s of Patañjali.

Fourth Part:
TRANSCENDENTAL ALONENESS

(Śaṅkara vivaraṇa:)
In the First Part the main teaching was samādhi, and in the Second, the means to it were set out. In the Third Part were listed the forms of knowledge and power which are side-effects of the performance of the yoga methods, whose aim (however) is right vision (samyagdarśana), and they were disposed of with the comment of Jaigīṣavya: 'All that, is nothing but pain.' It was said (II.25) that escape from pain is absolute disjunction from guṇa-s. So it has just been declared: 'From indifference to that too, the seeds of imperfection are destroyed, and there is Transcendental Aloneness' (kaivalya) (III.50), and whether he has attained Knowledge-of-the-difference or has not attained Knowledge-of-the-difference, 'When the purity of mind-sattva and of Puruṣa is the same, there is Aloneness' (III.55). Now, that kaivalya has to be determined by refuting objections, and so this Part, on Transcendental Aloneness, is presented.

Then as means for that, the ways have to be explained of cutting off the saṃskāra-groups (vāsanā) accumulated over many previous births. Then another perfection (siddhi) not already given is taken up, to praise samādhi-perfections as an auxiliary to Aloneness. Criticism of some things in a category implies praise for the others in it. So when he will say: 'Of those, the mind whose perfections arise out of meditation has no karma-stock' (IV.6) and 'karma of yogin-s is not white nor black, but of others it is of three kinds', the intention to praise is clear.

Sūtra IV.1

Perfections (siddhi) arise from birth or from drugs or from mantra-s or from tapas or from samādhi

The perfections from birth are (enjoyed) in a different body. From drugs – such as an elixir of the demon realms; by mantra-s are attained levitation, the power of becoming minute and the other (seven); by tapas (are attained) such abilities as taking on any form, and going anywhere at will. The perfections from samādhi have been described.

The perfections from birth are in a different body, being attainment of another body in heaven or some similar region, by yoga or by other means. *From drugs – such as an elixir of the demon realms:* here the original body is not discarded, but by taking drugs like soma or the amalaka plant (some perfection is attained), *by mantra-s* being murmured *are attained levitation,* etc.; *by tapas (are attained) such abilities as taking on any form and going anywhere at will. The perfections from samādhi have been described* as already set out (in the Third Part).

The perfection which is from a specific cause is superior to the others. It is true of course that in the case of perfection of birth, the new body will have been supplied from the fact that a causal condition was set up in the past. But as regards that change into another birth, with a body that has not yet come into being, is that specific causal condition alone the material cause of it, or is there indeed something else?

Sūtra IV.2

The transformation into another life is implemented by prakṛti

The change of body and senses into another life, when they are transformed into the other life, is implemented by their prakṛti-natures. With the disappearance of the earlier transformation, the corresponding rise of the later transformation comes about by an integrating pervasion of the new parts.

With the disappearance of the earlier transformation, of the previous specific causal condition as established, *the corresponding rise of the later transformation comes about by an integrating pervasion of the new parts.* How so? Because from a cause of light import, there cannot come about a result of great import: from a raw lump of iron weighing 10 pala-s, can an 80–pala spearhead be produced?

> *The prakṛti-natures of the body and senses promote their respective forms, by implementing them in accordance with the motivating cause, of righteousness, etc.*

The prakṛti-natures of the body and senses promote their respective forms of body or of a sense organ, *by implementing them in accordance with the motivating cause, of righteousness (dharma), etc.* The word etcetera shows that unrighteousness (a-dharma) also is a cause.

(Opponent) It has been said that they promote their respective forms in accordance with the motivating cause of righteousness, etc. Does this cause, righteousness, etc., impel the prakṛti-natures, or does it not?

Sūtra IV.3

That cause is not the impelling drive itself, but it makes a breach in the retaining barrier of the natures, as does a farmer (for irrigation)

> *Righteousness, etc., though cause, cannot be the impelling drive of the natures. What happens, then? It makes a breach in the retaining barrier as does a farmer. The farmer, to irrigate a terraced field by flooding it with water from another (higher) field, does not take the water in his cupped hands, but makes a breach in its retaining barrier; when that is breached, the water pours into the lower field of itself. Similarly, righteousness breaches unrighteousness, the retaining barrier of the natures. When it is breached, the natures flow out into their respective forms.*

Righteousness, etc., though cause, cannot be the impelling drive of the natures. A cause cannot be powered, in a reversal of the cause-effect relation, by an effect like righteousness, which is merely a guiding cause. *What happens, then? It* the guiding cause, righteousness, etc. *makes a breach in its retaining barrier: when that is breached, the water pours into the lower field of itself. Similarly, righteousness breaches unrighteousness, the retaining barrier of the natures.* And unrighteousness too breaches the barrier which is righteousness. *When it is breached, the natures flow out into* implement *their respective forms.*

> *Then again, a farmer in his field cannot force the nutrients of water or earth into the roots of his grain. What does he do, then? He removes weeds like mudga, tinduka, gavidhuka and śyāmāka. With these gone, the nutrients enter, of themselves, the roots of the grain.*
>
> *So righteousness is a cause only as being simply annihilation of unrighteousness, because of the absolute opposition between its purity and the impurity (of the other); but righteousness is not an impelling cause of the activity of nature. Here there are the examples of Nandīśvara and others. Conversely, unrighteousness inhibits righteousness, entailing a transformation into impurity, as exemplified by such as Nahuṣa.*

Then again, a farmer in his field cannot force the nutrients of water or earth into the roots of his grain. What does he do, then? He removes from the roots of the grain *weeds like mudga, tinduka, gavidhuka and śyāmāka. With these gone, the nutrients enter, of themselves, the roots of the grain.*

So righteousness is a cause only as being simply annihilation of unrighteousness, and unrighteousness is similarly annihilation of righteousness, *because of the absolute opposition between its purity and the impurity (of the other); but righteousness is not an impelling cause of the activity of nature. Here there are the examples of Nandīśvara and others. Conversely, unrighteousness inhibits righteousness, entailing a transformation into impurity, as exemplified by such as Nahuṣa.*

(Opponent) Well, when a yogin projects several bodies, do they have one mind between them or a mind each?

This is something which has not been explained about the samādhi perfection.

Sūtra IV.4

The minds are projected from bare I-am-ness

Taking up this I-am-ness as the cause of the minds, he makes minds for the projections. Thus they have each a mind.

The minds are projected from bare I-am-ness (asmitā). Taking up this I-am-ness the I-notion (ahaṅkāra) *he* the yogin *makes minds for the projections* – projected minds, new, not formed by nature, and so independent of anyone. The word 'mind' is used as the example; senses and so on are also projected out of I-am-ness alone. *Thus they have each a mind* and senses.

Without mind and senses, a body would be almost a corpse, and meaningless. With just a single mind, there is no capacity for existence of auxiliary and principal, or differences in activity. But with the power, the creation of many bodies becomes possible to an individual consciousness (kṣetrajña). Difference in the instruments is needed for different activities of the secondary and principal.

But there are some who think that there will be a number of individual consciousnesses (kṣetrajña) corresponding to the separate bodies. Some of them urge that this is a doctrine of reaping the fruits of actions not committed. But others deny this, by asserting that the individual consciousnesses will have performed actions corresponding to their (present) situation.

How could the activities of several minds wait on the purposes of a single mind?

The answer is:

Sūtra IV.5

In the variety of activities, it is the one mind that impels the several minds

Though there is variety in their activities, it is one mind that impels all the minds which it has projected. From it come the differences in activity.

In the variety of activities, it is the one mind that impels the several minds. Though there is variety in their activities, it is one mind that impels all the minds which it has projected, as it were superintending the results in each different body.

And that complies with the will of the yogin. The other projected minds with their many different activities are obedient to the controller mind. *From it,* their bare activities are supervised, and further, *the differences in activity,* like the different activities which arise from the fact of one's being kind. So it is right that the activities of the projected minds should thus wait on the purposes of one mind.

Sūtra IV.6

Of those (minds with perfections), the mind whose perfections arise out of meditation (dhyāna) has no karma-stock

> *A mind is endowed with perfections in one of the five ways. Of those, only the mind whose perfections arise out of meditation has no karma-stock. Only of this one is there no such stock, no functioning of passion and the rest, and so there is no connection with good or ill, because the taints are eliminated from that yogin.*

Of those (minds with perfections) the mind whose perfections arise out of meditation (dhyāna) has no karma-stock. A mind is endowed with perfection in one of the five ways: by birth, drugs, mantra, tapas or samādhi. *Of those* among those, it is *only the mind whose perfections arise out of meditation* that *has no karma-stock.* It is free from any stock of taint or karma. *Only of this one is there no such stock, no functioning of passion and the rest, and so there is no connection with good or ill, because the taints are eliminated from that yogin.* As it has been said: 'Rooted in taints is the karma-stock' (II.12); he has no karma-stock because no taints are there.

> *But in others, a karma-stock is always found.*

But in the case *of others,* whose perfections arise from birth, etc., *a karma-stock is always found,* because the taints have not been eliminated.

Thus –

Sūtra IV.7

The karma of the yogin is neither white nor black; of the others, it is of three kinds

(Opponent) Why is it only for yogins that there is no karma-stock, while there is for others?

(Answer) Because *The karma of the yogin is thus neither white nor black; of the others, it is of three kinds.* This sūtra is a general statement covering the perfect and the imperfect.

(Opponent) But the previous sūtra too was just a general statement.

(Answer) No, because it had a purpose, namely to praise the perfections arising from samādhi; and praise of samādhi-perfections is not a general statement. On the contrary, through the reference there to meditation practice giving siddhi-perfections (parisankhyāna), it related to a special field; it was mentioned along with the undesirability of the four kinds of similar siddhi-perfections arising from birth, etc., so it is a praise of perfections arising from samādhi.

Furthermore, as intended to prohibit, for one seeking Aloneness, the means of obtaining these perfections by birth and so on, the previous sūtra had a special field. But this one is purely a general statement following on what was said in the previous sūtra.

> *There are four classes of karma. The black is of those of evil nature. Those actions which are achievable by external means are white-black. Inasmuch as their performance is by way of harming others and also being kind to them, a (corresponding) karma-stock is laid down.*

There are four classes of karma. The black is of those of evil nature, wicked souls who transgress the path of scripture and are very impure. *Those actions which are achievable by external means* to be effected by such means as a wife, son, cattle, or begging, *are white-black*. What are they? *Inasmuch as their performance is by way of harming others and also being kind to them, a (corresponding) karma-stock is laid down* since they involve a variety of taints, so they are black and white.

(Opponent) But actions like the jyotiṣṭoma rite are taught us from scripture, so they can be white only, never black.

(Answer) The answer is, Not so. For they are performed for a particular object, and so there are other considerations. They are in fact causes of both good and the reverse of good.

(Opponent) They are done with the idea of some result like heaven, so they will lead only to good.

(Answer) No, because the same argument would apply in the case of a man's rape of the wife of another; there too it should lead to good, because it is a longed-for desire.

(Opponent) Well, such actions as seizing another's wife entail sins like cruelty, and are prohibited, and occur under the impulse of passion and so on, so they are not the same thing.

(Answer) The same element is there. Selfishness is forbidden and so it leads to an undesired consequence. Taking life inevitably entails some cruelty, and so (animal) sacrifice must lead to both consequences, desired and undesired. The important point is that undesired consequences must follow because of the pain caused to others, for that is something prohibited.

It is an inescapable fact that without taking life (in sacrifices, etc.) one cannot come to experience the joy of heaven. And if this is so, jyotiṣṭoma and other such rites entailing giving pain have a dual nature.

(Opponent) What is forbidden is not the rites themselves, but to take life.

(Answer) Not so, because that comes to pass when they are performed.

Taking life is part of them. But those of your way of thinking should perform just the daily household rites, in which they would not be engaged in taking life. In fact they do them, and never omit them, and it is accepted that there is a causality from them.

Now if the action involving taking life is transferred (as merit) in heaven to another body, it would follow that there would never be release, for even though one abstained from selfish and forbidden actions, the results of what had been done in previous lives would be inescapable.

(Opponent) That is why the daily rites are done: to destroy that karma of previous lives.

(Answer) Not so, because no distinction can be made. There could not be anything to single out only those previous actions which have begun to produce undesirable effects as their fruit, but not those of desirable fruits. Since there must be the unseen (future) fruits, though one may perform only the daily rites, still he will not get release but will be reborn.

So it is established that even (those actions performed only for) desirable ends have the dual causality, because actions with external means take the form of both injuring and helping. It cannot be supposed that by the nitya rites the previously performed karmas of desirable fruit, such as jyotiṣṭoma, will come to an end, because there is no opposition between them. The non-opposition is because they are both of a pure nature, which is also confirmed in the holy texts.

Then again one may say that there are actions which should initiate more than one life, so that at the end of each successive life there will be various karmas-in-operation that remain over. So too since the karma of the present life perishes in giving the fruit of the present life, it is only the fresh desireful karma produced by the present life that initiates heaven, and also the suffering for taking life; there again it comes out as white-black.

We find, then, both the suffering concerned with taking life, and the joy known as heaven, and so the cause of the latter we infer to be of double nature. That being so, the prohibited acts of killing beings, performed in animal sacrifices like agnīṣṭomīya for the kratu rites, we infer to be black karma. The killing for the kratu rites, though something altogether undesirable, does secure the end.

(Opponent) If some holy texts are arbitrarily made out to be preliminary, and others the final ones, then those which exemplify the preliminary class become unauthoritative. Then arbitrarily some texts are made to contradict the very nature of the sacrificial rite, so that they rule out those texts on sacrifice.

(Answer) But the killing involved does not produce a contradiction; it is simply that there is a dual causality, like the dual causality in the case of simple eating, which gives both pleasure and also bodily sustenance. Again, bathing at a sacred place gives refreshment but has also a transcendental purpose. So the killing, though admittedly involving some undesirable result, never fails to bring about the great result of the kratu sacrifice.

(Opponent) Though they are to be done with external means, the daily rites (nitya) must be white karma when performed for themselves, and not in connection with any desire.

(Answer) Because they are indistinguishable from the same rites done with some desire, there is a defect in them. With all works of desire performed by the man of desire, there is a defectiveness of works-of-desire by the very association with desire; so there is the defect of Ignorance which causes desire and the rest, and this applies indiscriminately. All the daily rites have the dual nature. That there is Ignorance in the daily rites is shown by the fact that there is always something of which the performer has cause to repent (in the prayer at the end).

In any case, it is only an Ignorant man who performs actions at all: no action occurs to a Knower. For the Knower, the Puruṣa, does not conceive of any result apart from the state of his own true nature. The state of his nature exists alone, as cessation of all operations; thus no undertaking for any effect is appropriate to a Knower. Just so, one who is committed to a journey by land does not take to boats and so on, which are means of going by water.

(Opponent) In that case there is no distinction of the daily rites from rites performed specifically to get something desired.

(Answer) The daily rites are without defect when performed with the aim of doing away with action for any desired result.

Furthermore, if, when performing the daily rites, concentration in the form of right vision arises in the form: 'Why am I doing this?' or 'What is the result of this?' or 'What are the inherent defects in performance of these rites?' then that does make a distinction of the daily rites. But as to their both being white-black in essence, there is no distinction between these actions, inasmuch as there is the fact of having to be carried out with external means, and the involvement with giving pain to others. And so it has been said:

> *The white is of those who perform tapas, self-study, and meditation (dhyāna). For these, being a matter of the mind alone, are not concerned with outer means, nor do they give pain to others.*
>
> *The neither-black-nor-white karma is that of the renunciates (saṃnyāsin) – wanderers whose taints have faded away. Their karma is not white because they have renounced; it is not black because there is no cause for that.*
>
> *But for those of the other party, the fruit is of three kinds, as previously explained.*

The white class of karma *is of those who perform tapas, self-study (svādhyāya) and meditation (dhyāna). For these, being a matter of the mind alone, are not concerned with outer means* they do not look to outer means, *nor do they give pain to others.*

The neither-white-nor-black karma is that of the renunciates (saṃnyāsin), wanderers whose taints have faded away. They are occupying their last body, already existent before their realization. *Their karma is not white because they have renounced; it is not black because there is no cause for that,* there is no reason for it. Nor is it a mixture of white and black, because of the two facts: they have renounced external things, and there is nothing to cause it. So it is said:

> *When they depart who have not renounced, the fruit of their karma is of three kinds:*
> *Desirable, undesirable and mixed. But not so for the saṃnyāsin renouncers.*

But for those of the other party for the others who have acquired perfections by birth or drugs or mantra or tapas *the fruit is of three kinds* white, black and mixed *as previously explained,* for instance in the Second Part, in the sūtra 12: 'Rooted in taints'.

Sūtra IV.8

Therefore their consequent manifestation is of those saṃskāra-groups (vāsanā) that are compatible with it

Aloneness has been praised, and now the taints and karmas and saṃskāra-groups (vāsanā), which are causes of the obstructions to it, have to be set out. But the working of the taints, their antagonist, and their cessation, have already been described in detail. The next sūtra-s therefore are begun in order to explain similarly in detail the workings, the states, the antagonists and the cessation, of karma and of saṃskāra-groups, because it is when they cease that Aloneness is attained, and not otherwise.

> *Therefore, because there are the three kinds of result of the karmas, their consequent manifestation is of those saṃskāra-groups alone that are compatible with it. The fruition is like whatever kind of karma caused it; it is only saṃskāra-groups consonant with it that follow from the karma-fruition. The manifestation is of them alone. For when karma justifying heaven comes to maturity, there is no possibility for anything to bring into manifestation saṃskāra-groups producing birth in hell or as an animal or man, and it is only what are in accordance with a heavenly life that are manifested in that case. The argument is the same with birth in hell or in an animal or human state.*

Therefore for that reason *because there are the three kinds of result* black, white and mixed as explained before, *of the karmas* when they have matured into causal efficiency, *their consequent manifestation,* the result of that alone, *is of those saṃskāra-groups alone that are compatible with it,* of nature consonant with, and form similar to, the result.

It is explained: Among karmas which mature as divine, animal, or human birth, *the fruition is like whatever kind of karma caused it; it is only saṃskāra-groups consonant with it* the matured karma *that follow from* arise out of *the karma-fruition. The manifestation is of them alone.* This is because the fruition is of saṃskāra-s which are like the original karma. Just so a boy, seeing someone like his mother, runs after her. There is no manifestation of other saṃskāra-groups which would not be compatible.

For when karma justifying heaven comes to maturity, is just about to fructify, *there is no possibility for anything to bring into manifestation saṃskāra-groups producing birth in hell or as an animal or man,* since cause and effect must be of conformable nature, *and it is only what are in accordance with a heavenly life that are manifested in that case. The argument* the reasoning *is the same with birth in hell or in an animal or human state.*

When karma manifests as hell, the saṃskāra-groups in accordance with that karma are blazing up, but when animal karma matures, such saṃskāra-groups are repelled. The principle is the same for the human state. For the saṃskāra-groups of the respective kinds cannot come to fruition except in the company of those whose fruition is of similar kind. Neither do the saṃskāra-groups manifest their results at intervals in the fruition of other karma of comparable form which are in process of fructifying on their own account. Thus there is a beginningless cause–effect relation of karma and saṃskāra-group.

The saṃskāra-groups which are more remote, as having been laid down as members of a different class, or at different times, or at different places, are not in immediate proximity to karma that is now maturing. They are like remote friends and connections, and the nearer group has more effect than remoter ones. So there is no immediate consequence of very distant ones.

(Opponent) If it is so, one ends up with this conclusion: Suppose there is karma laid down a hundred aeons ago which should result in birth as a cat, while in the immediate past there is karma which would justify divine birth. From the opposition of the nearer saṃskāra-group of the divine, the causal potency which should manifest in a cat birth will not be actualized. The saṃskāra-groups of the cat karma, distant by a hundred aeons, would not be fulfilled because of remoteness, and it would have to be supposed that the karma which should have caused that fruition did not actualize it. The corollary would be that karmas and saṃskāra-groups are meaningless.

(Answer) To this he says:

Sūtra IV.9

Because there is sameness of form of memory and saṃskāra-s, there is consequent succession between them, even though separated by class and place and time

Fruition of karma in cat birth, for instance, is brought about by its own spontaneous drive, even if separated by a hundred classes or a hundred distances or a thousand aeons. Further, when the spontaneous drives towards actualization arise, very quickly they are made manifest, along with the saṃskāra-groups laid down for fruition as a cat, etc. Why? Because though they may be remote, a manifesting karma of the like kind has become an operative cause for them. So there is consequent succession.

Fruition of karma in cat birth, for instance, is brought about by its own spontaneous manifesting drive, its own manifesting capacity, even if separated by a hundred classes or a hundred distances or a thousand aeons.

(Opponent) The time-separation has been spoken of only by bringing difference of class. What is the point of the word 'time'?

(Answer) Even in one day there may be many little lives of such as insects. Time was mentioned in the sense that these are not (necessarily) in the distant past. Cat-karma fruition was shown to be impelled by its own spontaneous drive.

Further, when the spontaneous drives towards actualization arise, very quickly always rapidly *they are made manifest along with the saṃskāra-groups laid down for fruition as a cat, etc. Why so? Because though they may be remote, a manifesting karma of the like kind has become an operative cause for them.*

For karma causing the manifestation of a result in the form of a bull life does not become a cause of manifestation of a cat saṃskāra-group. They are not compatible, and a manifesting cause is always of compatible nature with its result. At the sight of a meal of something like tamarind, the tongue waters. *So* it is that *there is consequent succession* of the saṃskāra-groups, and their manifesting power is equal. Such being the case, there is no nearness or remoteness of saṃskāra-groups, because they are equally stored in the mind.

And why? Because memory and saṃskāra are of the one form. As were the experiences, so are the saṃskāra-s. And they are in the form of saṃskāra-groups (vāsanā). As the saṃskāra-groups, so are the memories. Memories are from saṃskāra-s. distanced as to class, place, and time. From memory again there are saṃskāra-s. so that these memories and saṃskāra-s are manifested in a concentration of power from the going-into-operation of the karma-stock.

And why? There is this further cause of consequent succession: *Because memory and saṃskāra are of the one form.*

It has been said before that manifesting karmas of the same class are the immediate cause of saṃskāra-groups. This is now taken further: *As were the experiences (anubhava), so are the saṃskāra-s.* As the ideas (pratyaya), so the saṃskāra-groups. *And they* the saṃskāra-s *are in the form of saṃskāra-groups. As the saṃskāra-groups, so are the memories.*

So it was said (comm. to I.11) in the passage which began: 'The thought, coloured by the thing known, shines out in the form of both the thing and the knowledge of it... .' *Memories are from saṃskāra-s, distanced as to class, place, and time. From memory again there are saṃskāra-s, so that these memories and saṃskāra-s are manifested in a concentration of power from the going-into-operation of the karma-stock.* It has been made clear that this going-into-operation of the karma stock is dependent on causal factors such as situation.

Thus there is a consequent succession because the causal chain is never cut even in the case of remote things. As the saṃskāra, so is the memory. From the fact that their drive to actualization is particular to each one, remoteness has no effect. From a saṃskāra, separated by even a hundred aeons, there is a memory of the same class, and so the causal succession is established.

Now he shows that owing to the beginninglessness of the saṃskāra-groups their fruition is a journey though a succession of countless wombs, describing this to create the feeling of detachment.

Sūtra IV.10

They are beginningless, because hope is eternal

This hope of self-preservation is seen in all, in such forms as 'May death not come' or 'May I survive'. It is not something spontaneous. Why not? How is it that there is fear of death, caused by memory of its hatefulness or of its pain, in a new-born animal which can never have had any experience of death? What is spontaneous would not need a cause.

They are beginningless, because hope is eternal. This hope of self-preservation is seen in all, in such forms as 'May death not come' or 'May I survive'. It is not something spontaneous, arising and developing of its own accord. *Why not? How is it that there is fear of death, caused by memory of its hatefulness or of its pain, in a new-born animal which can never have had any experience of death?* If it were spontaneous it would not have any impelling cause such as memories of pain: *what is spontaneous would not need a cause,* for the heat of fire which is spontaneous does not look to any cause for its effect.

The memory of an object that has never been experienced, whether desirable or undesirable, will never assail anybody. Even when a pleasant thing has been experienced, there is no desire for it unless it is recalled; and again, no aversion and fear are ever found for an experienced unpleasantness if it is not recalled. So in any new-born animal, there is observed immediately a hope of self-preservation, from termination of life never experienced here in this life. As this hope is eternal, we infer experience of the termination of a previous life. And before that, an earlier one, and then a still earlier. We thus infer the beginninglessness of the memory-saṃskāra-s and their causes, the experiences of life and death. From this, it is certain that the living being passes through many wombs. For that reason, the saṃskāra-group is hard to get away from; it cannot be escaped. Why not?

Inasmuch as this mind, coloured by beginningless saṃskāra-groups, under the impulse of a cause taking up some saṃskāra-groups only, goes into operation for the experience of Puruṣa.

Others hold that the mind, like lamplight contracting when put in a jar and expanding when set on a platform, assumes the size of the body; and thus there is an intermediate state. This (supposed) world-flow is the right one (they believe).

> *But the teachers say that it is only the mental process of the all-pervasive mind which contracts and expands.*

Inasmuch as this mind, coloured by beginningless saṃskāra-groups, under the impulse of a cause under the impulse of a karmic cause *taking up some saṃskāra-groups only* which have arrived at fruition of compatible effects from mature karma, *goes into operation for the experience of Puruṣa,* until it has completed its commitment.

As to this mind, *others hold that the mind, like lamplight contracting when put in a jar and expanding when set on a platform, assumes the size of the body* whether perhaps an elephant or a mosquito, as the light in a jar or on a platform and so on. And for this he gives further reasoning: *and thus* since there is the contraction and expansion, *there is an intermediate state.* In the interval after death and before the present birth, is the intermediate state. *This (supposed) world-flow,* the process by which one passes on, which also carries one beyond the body, the mind not being all-pervading *is the right one (they believe).*

But the teachers say that it is only the mental process (vṛtti) of the all-pervasive mind which contracts and expands. The word 'teacher' (ācārya) is used to promote reverence for what is being established. Although mind is all-pervasive, its fixity and movement, which are changes, occur by way of the senses; and in the yogic state, which is without the senses, there is the omniscience proper to its all-pervasive nature.

A fanciful idea of something outside experience, transcending the body, is not a valid cognition, because it is not perceived, any more than is the horn of a hare. A sacred text says: 'While he is in the body, there is no escape from pleasure and pain' (Chānd. VIII. 12.1), and another text: 'Who worships them as infinite (obtains an infinite world)'. (Bṛhad. I.5.13) teaches that the senses are all-pervasive.

> *The causes are of two kinds: external and internal. The external require means such as the body and actions such as praise and salutations and so on. (The internal are) those beginning with Faith. Thus it is said that the meditations on Friendliness and the others are for meditators their sports, independent of any external means, and productive of the highest dharma.*

Of the two, the mental cause is the stronger. Why? (Because after all,) by what could knowledge-detachment be overcome? Except by mental power, who could have devastated (like Uṣanas) the Daṇḍaka forest, or drunk up the ocean as Agastya did?

The contraction and expansion of the mental process (vṛtti) look to such causes as righteousness. *The causes are of two kinds: external and internal. The external require means such as the body and actions such as praise and salutations and so on.* What are the internal? He explains that they are *those beginning with Faith* (energy, memory, samādhi and prajña-knowledge – I.20). *Thus it is said that the meditations on Friendliness and the others (I.33) are for meditators their sports,* mental activities in which they engage *independent of any external means* not needing any external means but performed purely by mind alone, *and productive of the highest dharma.*

Of the two external and internal causes *the mental cause* the internal cause where mind is endowed with friendliness and the others *is the stronger. Why so? By what could knowledge-detachment be overcome?* Not by anything, is the meaning. Inasmuch as the whole class of the glories listed in the Third Part are accomplished by knowledge-detachment. *Except by mental power, who could have devastated (like Uṣanas) the Daṇḍaka forest, or drunk up the ocean as Agastya did?* So mental power alone is real power, and not the physical power. The holy text says: 'Therefore that of the mind is highest' (Mahānā. 79.12) and the Lord too has said:

Superior to the sacrifice with material things is the
knowledge-sacrifice, O Burner of the Foe;
All action without exception is perfected in knowledge.

(Gītā IV.33)

How then are these saṃskāra-groups destroyed?

(Opponent) They have been arising since time without beginning, so their destruction is not even remotely feasible. Yet unless they are destroyed, Transcendental Aloneness is not attainable.

Sūtra IV.11

They are held together by cause-effect-repository-focal-point. When these cease, they too cease

The compound 'cause-effect-repository-focal-point' is resolved into cause and effect and repository and focal-point. Since the saṃskāra-groups are held together by these, namely bound together by them, when the causes and the rest cease, the saṃskāra-groups also will cease along with them. And thereby the destruction of the saṃskāra-groups is effected.

> *As to cause: from righteousness, pleasure; following on (anuśayī) pleasure, desire. From unrighteousness, pain; following on pain, hate. From that, effort. Excited by that effort of speech and of body, he helps some and injures others. Then again from this, righteousness and unrighteousness. In this way there is a ceaselessly impelled revolving of this six-spoked wheel of saṃsāra. Ignorance is its driver. That Ignorance is the root of all taints.*

What is this *cause?* He explains: first of all, righteousness belongs to minds that are subject to Ignorance (avidyā). *From* that *righteousness, pleasure; following on (anuśayī) pleasure, desire.* Thus there is Ignorance, and from that itself unrighteousness, committing sin. *From unrighteousness, pain; following pain, hate. From that, effort* to restore the happiness and remove the pain as previously mentioned. *Excited by that effort of speech and of body, he helps some and injures others. Then again from this* helping and injuring, there come *righteousness and unrighteousness.* From these, pleasure and pain, and from them desire and hate, just as before; and so to effort again. *In this way there is a ceaselessly impelled revolving of this six-spoked wheel of saṃsāra.* It is turning every instant. *Ignorance is its driver,* as it were a young horseman making the chariot wheels whirl. *That Ignorance is the root of all taints:* the six-spoked wheel driven on by Ignorance is the cause of the saṃskāra-groups, for they are created by its turning.

When Ignorance is not there, then like any wheel whose lashings (that hold the wheel together) have given way, the wheel of Causes consisting of righteousness and the others collapses. With its collapse, the saṃskāra-groups, which arose from the turning of the six-spoked wheel, lose all their effectiveness.

> *As to effect: the coming into being of something by recourse to something else, is the effect of that something else. It is not that it was previously non-existent.*

As to effect, the coming into being of something by recourse to something else, is the effect of that something else. This too holds together the saṃskāra-groups, for when it is not there, they do not appear. It is effects like pleasure that lay down the saṃskāra-groups. *It is not that it was previously non-existent,* for nothing that is absolutely non-existent ever comes to be.

> *Mind still with its commitment is the repository of the saṃskāra-groups. For when the mind has fulfilled its commitment, the saṃskāra-groups have no repository and cannot maintain themselves.*
>
> *When some object comes forward and makes some saṃskāra-group manifest, that object is called its focal-point. In this way, all the saṃskāra-groups are held together by causes, results, repositories, and focal-points. When these are not there, the saṃskāra-groups based on them are not there.*

Mind still with its commitment, still having something it must do, and not yet clear of purposes of Puruṣa by Knowledge of his true nature as fulfilled, and without Ignorance, *is the repository of the saṃskāra-groups.* For it is in dependence on it that the causal wheel revolves. *For when the mind has fulfilled its commitment,* when there is no purpose of Puruṣa to be carried out, *the saṃskāra-groups have no repository and cannot maintain themselves.*

When some object comes forward and makes some saṃskāra-group manifest, that object is called its focal-point. In this way all the saṃskāra-groups are held together by causes, results, repositories, and focal-points. When these, causes and the others, *are not there, the saṃskāra-groups based on them are not there,* as when the parasol is taken away, no shadow is there.

The means of getting rid of them have been given in the Second Part. It was shown that when there is right vision (samyag-darśana), the saṃskāra-groups do not obstruct Aloneness, and when Ignorance goes, it is Aloneness that remains.

> *(Opponent) Of the non-existent there is no coming into being, and of the existent there is no destruction. As actual things, they (the saṃskāra-groups) will continue to be: how should they cease to exist?*

(Opponent) It has been said that when there is absence of these causes, there is absence of the saṃskāra-groups. But this is giving up your own previous conclusion. How so? Because that conclusion was: *Of the non-existent there is no coming into being* no arising *and of the existent there is no destruction.* Now the saṃskāra-groups do exist. *As actual things they will continue to be: how should they cease to exist?* The point is, that they certainly cannot cease to exist.

(Answer) The question is, what was meant by saying that when the causes, etc. are not there, the saṃskāra-groups are not there either, and again how there can be Transcendental Aloneness if there are still births caused by the saṃskāra-groups which (on this reasoning) cannot have ceased? He goes on to explain:

Sūtra IV.12

What are past and future do actually exist, but there is difference of time-phase in their dharma-s

So it is, but the commentator does not simply reiterate this conclusion, for he goes on to explain that when it was said that 'when the causes are nonexistent the saṃskāra-groups also are non-existent', it is not an absolute non-existence. What is it then? *Of the non-existent there is no coming into being; and of the existent there is no destruction. As actual things* inasmuch as they are facts, *they will continue to be; how should the saṃskāra-groups cease to exist?* The words allow some choice in interpretation, and the sense here is, that the saṃskāra-groups do not absolutely cease to be: they do actually exist, but as things in the past.

> *That whose manifestation is yet to come is future; that whose manifestation came (and went) is past; when a thing comes into operation, it is present. This triad is something knowable by knowledge. If it were not actually existent (in all three time-phases), then the knowledge of it would have in fact no object, and would not arise. Therefore, what is past and future does actually exist. If there is no potential result of action, whether that action aims at experience or it aims at release, it ends up as non-existent. Then why the prescriptions by experts directed towards a particular result, with that as motive?*

That whose manifestation is to come whose manifestation will come to be *is future,* like the jar-form in the lump state of the clay. The feeling 'It has been begun' when one takes up something which must be done is of future. *That whose manifestation came (and went) is past,* whose manifestation, in the form of perceptibility and acceptance as an object, came and passed away, as a smashed jar is said to be 'past'. If a means has to be resorted to for its manifestation, a thing will not be manifest now; if its manifestation has not gone, it is not past. What is it then? *When a thing comes into operation, it is present,*as a jar comes into operation in the use made of it.

This triad characterized by time-phases of past, future, and present *is something* which has the form of present dharma-s in a present dharmin, *knowable by knowledge* by proof, definite all over the world, and not wavering. How is this known? Because definite knowledge arises of it as an object. *If it were not actually existing (in all three time-phases) then the knowledge of it would have in fact no object, and would not arise,* just as (a purely verbal construct like) the horn of a hare never causes any definite knowledge to arise; and no objectivity is ever found that is not caused by the rise of knowledge of a definite fact. This knowledge holds in the field of general experience, as in the phrases, 'the jar will come to be' and 'the jar did exist'. So it is one thing which is joined with the three times, because it is the object of established knowledge.

Again, the knowledge of something like a jar, as past or future, is not knowledge of what is not a thing. With the words chosen, the knowledge is produced as a definite form, and it is as much knowledge of an object as the jar present. There is no vagueness in the meaning, and it can be inferred from indications, like the knowledge from the inference of fire from smoke.

Then again, a thing past or future becomes the object of an immediate idea at the sight of some indication, as something correctly inferred. *So what is past or future does exist.*

Furthermore, *If it* is held that *there is no potential result of action, whether that action aims at experience* of heaven as with sacrifices, *or it aims at release,* is concerned with release as in the case of samādhi, *it ends up as non-existent* like a hare's horn. For a hare's horn will never come to be – it is non-existent. Not so here. What is the position then? By sacrifices, life in heaven will come about, and by samādhi and the other methods, release (mokṣa). The expert and incontestable view is, that life in heaven, and release, do exist.

Therefore, if it were non-existent, *Then why* would the experts, not self-appointed, authorize or teach *the prescriptions by experts* in the form 'Do this and then that will happen' *directed towards a particular result, with that* result *as motive.* If it were non-existent, there would be no distinction between expert and non-expert as regards knowing what to do, and again the experts would have deluded views while the inexpert would be right.

Furthermore, experts themselves would not seek to get results if it were accepted that these were non-existent. And since non-existence has no distinctions in it, there could be no determination of causes; or again, everything would arise from everything. Nor could a cause even be employed; or if it were, the oilman could take the oil from sand – why should he need many sesamum seeds and so much effort? And the absolutely non-existent would produce what had never existed before, which is something never seen.

> *An efficient cause can bring to actuality a result already existent, but not produce what had not previously existed. A recognizable cause gives a particular aid towards what is effected; it produces something not indeed non-existent before.*
>
> *The dharmin consists of a number of dharma-s. Of it the dharma-s are in a particular condition according to the difference of time-phase. What is past or future is not like the present in manifestation as a substance. What is it then? The future has existence in its own nature as what is going to manifest; the past exists in its own nature as what has been experienced as manifest.*

So action, whether directed towards experience or towards release, is *an efficient cause* which *can bring to actuality a result* only which is *already existent, but not produce what had not previously existed.*For *a recognizable cause* by its very nature, *gives a particular aid towards what is effected,* as the cook when churning, etc. the thickened milk in a cooking-pot makes manifest the dadhi-curds in the form of the white substance; *it produces something,* the dadhi-curds *not indeed non-existent before.* So with all such action directed towards experience.

Then, *The dharmin consists of a number of dharma-s,* it has by nature a number of dharma-s. As a lump of gold has by nature the dharma-s of brooch or ring or other ornaments, whether latent or patent. *Of it* the dharmin *the dharma-s are in a particular condition according to the difference of time-phase,* corresponding to the difference of past time-phase and the others.

What is past or future is not like the present thing *in manifestation* endowed with manifestation, as for instance the ornament *as a substance* in the form of an effect, by its having come into operation. *What is it then? The future has existence in its own nature as what is going to manifest,* what is going to be; *the past exists in its own nature as what has been experienced as manifest* by a perceiver in the past.

> *It is only of the present time-phase that there is actual manifestation, but not of either the past or future phases. On the occasions of one time-phase, the other two never appear in the dharmin along with it.*

It is only of the present time-phase that there is actual manifestation, but not any manifestation *of either the past or future ones. On the occasions* at the time *of one time-phase, the other two never appear in the dharmin along with it,* because of the contradiction between them. These words rule out any mixing up of the times.

He who holds that past/future phases do not exist, will not find any difference of time-phase of dharma-s. Why not? Because for him there is no jar that will come to be, or that was in the past, since a jar is not potsherds, nor is it a clay lump. The dharma-qualities of the three time-phases would be fused with just one time-phase, that of the present as it occurs. Since (for them) a jar can only be the present one, they may indeed speak of it as past or future, but since there is nothing like a jar in the clay lump or in the potsherds – and in the clay itself there is no jar – so by 'the future jar' or 'the past jar' they would have to be referring to the clay lump, or the potsherds. It would be the same as saying 'horse' to mean a cow, or 'cow' to mean a horse.

(Opponent) Let us say that when we say past and future, we are referring to non-existence-before-coming-into-being, and non-existence-after-perishing.

(Answer) This is even worse, and still less acceptable. It is only as jar that there is the determination by the words 'the jar is past' or 'the jar is yet to come'. And on your theory, the potters would not say: 'The jars are past' or 'They will come to be.'

(Opponent) But no jar is perceived, in these cases.

(Answer) Neither are elephants or tigers perceived there, yet they are still said to be existent.

(Opponent) It is only because there has been a previous perception that they are said to be so.

(Answer) Not so. A jar for instance has also its various uses.

(Opponent) By the same reasoning as for the jar, those uses are non-existent.

(Answer) No, because there is nothing specific about non-existence. No relation of inherence, or acquired attribution, can be rightly supposed between existence and non-existence. What would show the jar to be nonexistent would not apply to its various uses; if it did, there would have to be some reality of your 'non-existent' at the far end of the relation.

(Opponent) Then let them be real.

(Answer) Then it has been accepted that the words 'future' and 'past' do represent facts.

(Opponent) Let the pieces of the potsherd-state, as generally accepted, be taken as the present jar in the future, because there is a relation between them: It is said, for instance, that life-currents (prāṇa) are the food which has been eaten.

(Answer) But here too, the jar would not exist in the clay lump, or in the potsherd fragments, any more than in the potter and his wheel and staff and cord. Since there is no distinction between the cases, there is no reason why the past jar should be identified in the fragments but not in the potter and his implements.

Nor could there be any relation between presently existing causes which produce things like jars, and the non-existent jars which are to be produced. And if the relation does not exist, it cannot function as an instrument to produce them.

(Opponent) There is no reason why it should not be the recognized intrinsic relation called samavaya, between what is produced and what effects the production.

(Answer) No, because that would require a relation, extrinsic or intrinsic, between contemporary things and things future to them. No relation between existent and non-existent is ever found, whether extrinsic or intrinsic.

Therefore, a relation is recognized between what is produced and the producer, so they must be existent; the effect exists before it actually occurs because it has a relation with other things, as in the familiar case of a jar. For it will become visible. And also it is visible, like a jar standing in an inner apartment: something to make it (visible to all) is needed, like a person to bring it out; and also some operation by that person.

Then again, general usage does not accept or intend, by the words 'past' and 'future', what is non-existent like a lotus in the sky. So what is past, and what is future, must actually exist.

So what exists in the three time-phases has not come out of non-existence. It is a manifestation of what already exists.

So what exists in the three time-phases has not come out of non-existence. What then? *It is a manifestation of what already exists.* Thus what is called the cessation of the saṃskāra-groups is in the nature of non-manifestation. They exist in their nature as guṇa-s, but they can have no effect, and there is no difficulty concerning the supposed impossibility of Transcendental Aloneness.

Now he wishes to explain further in what forms the dharma-s of past, future and present exist.

Sūtra IV.13

They are manifest or subtle, and consist of the guṇa-s

These three time-phases are present when of manifest nature. Past and future are essentially subtle, being the six Unparticularized. All this is, from the highest point of view, simply to be distinguished as a conglomerate of the guṇa-s, and so it says in the holy classic:

The ultimate form of the guṇa-s is not within the range of perception;

What can be perceived of it is but slight, like māyā.

They are manifest or subtle, and consist of the guṇa-s. These three time-phases coming up in the three forms of past, future and present, *are present* coming up in the present mode *when of manifest nature.* Their essence is, that they have become objects of public awareness. *Past and future are essentially subtle* and not objects of public awareness, *being* of the nature of *the six Unparticularized* (II. 19), their essence being I-am-ness and the other five. From these they take on (further) manifestation as the sixteen vikāra-changes (elements and organs) characterized by effect and cause.

All this, of the form of effect and cause (body and senses) in relation to the individual self, and essentially manifest, and also what is subtle in the form of the Unparticularized like I-am-ness and the others, and further what is the liṅga-mātra (= the Great principle, II.19) which is the subtle beyond the Unparticularized, all this world of sattva, rajas and tamas, ever tending towards light, activity and stasis respectively, *is from the highest point of view simply to be distinguished as a conglomerate of the guṇa-s,* as essentially guṇa-s, as consisting of the guṇa-s of sattva, rajas and tamas, which are ever tending towards light, activity and stasis, *and so it says in the holy classic:*

The ultimate form of the guṇa-s is not within the range of perception;

What can be perceived of it is but slight, like māyā.

Their ultimate form is freely arising in each separate thing, and in itself is *not within the range of perception,* not in the field of the senses; *what can be seen of it is* the conglomeration of disparate things disturbed by the clashing of the guṇa-s, *like māyā* but not just māyā. Like māyā, however, in its uncertainty. *Slight:* as being an insignificant and purely local change in the guṇa-s equally existing everywhere.

> *(Opponent) When everything is guṇa-s, how is it that a sound, for instance, is a single thing, with a single sense-organ (to perceive it)?*

(Opponent) When everything earth and all others *is guṇa-s, how is it that a sound* like that from a conch *is a single thing, with a single sense-organ* such as the ear, so that there is a single focal point for the mind? It ought not to be so: what is a product of triplicity should produce an idea which is triple.

And in the same way, there should be triplicity of each of the sense-organs. In which case, there would be no selectivity, because selection (in the case of hearing, for example) presupposes a single sound as perceived object and a single ear as perceiver. The same thing would apply to the object and sense-organ of touch and the other senses. Yet we do find selectivity.

(Answer) The reason is now to be given:

Sūtra IV.14

A thing is what it is by the fact of a unitary change

The guṇa-s are ever tending towards light, activity, and stasis respectively. When they have the nature of perception, a unitary change as an instrument (of perception) is the sense-organ of hearing. Then a unitary change in their nature as object is a sound, and that is the perceived sound. Then a unitary change of sounds and other objects of a class compatible with that form is an ultimate atom of earth, with the subtle element as component. Of these (atoms) are the unitary changes called earth, cow, tree, mountain and so on.

The guṇa-s are ever tending towards light, activity, and stasis respectively. When they have the nature of perception from predominance of light, essential awareness grounded in I-am-ness, *a unitary change as an instrument (of perception) is the sense-organ of hearing,* just as light comes out of the opposites oil, wick, and fire. The same applies to the skin and other sense-organs; there is an appropriate change into the sense-organ, by the guṇa-s combining to carry out the purpose of Puruṣa.

Then a unitary change in their nature as object, the nature of the guṇa-s with tamas predominant, *is a sound, and that is the perceived sound.*

With the other elements also it is to be harmonized, by similarly adding liquidity, heat, motility, and revealing – as they are compatible.

With the other elements also it is to be harmonized. Unitary change of sound, touch, colour, and taste, of a class compatible with liquidity, is an ultimate atom of water, with the subtle element of taste as component. Of these (atoms) is the unitary change of water.

The unitary change of sound, touch, and colour, of a class compatible with heat, is an ultimate atom of fire, with the subtle element of colour as component. Of these atoms the unitary change is fire, both the submarine fire and the light from firewood. The unitary change of sound and touch, of a class compatible with motility, is an ultimate atom of air, with the subtle element of touch as component. Of these atoms the unitary change is wind, and the seven Marut wind-gods. So the unitary change of sound, of a class compatible with revealing, is space.

On these lines it is all to be harmonized, as unitary change of things compatible brought together as liquidity, heat, motility and so on. So there is singleness of change, however many the things may be, and thus they form single objects, and there is something to give selectivity to it all as perceived and perception.

> *(Opponent) There is no object apart from consciousness (vijñāna): there is only consciousness apart from objects.*

(Opponent) This single object of an idea, such as a sound, does not exist at all. It is all simply displayed in consciousness, for the being of its being is consciousness. As to this being of its being, *There is no object apart from consciousness,* nor any separate being perceived from a separate consciousness, *There is only consciousness apart from objects,* a separate existence, perceived as separate.Thus we refute the theory of existence apart (from consciousness). For these reasons we assert that there is no object outside consciousness.

Here is the proof of it: there is no object perceived apart from consciousness, because apart from consciousness nothing is perceived, and objects are as consciousness itself. The conscious experiences of things in the waking state, being without any external objects, are simply consciousness, and so they are like the consciousness in the dream state. Or we could say that the objects imagined in consciousness during waking, as objects, are like those of dream. Again, whatever the objects, the consciousness is invariable, so that as consciousness it is like that of the dream state.

And in that case, what is there to trouble us? The Transcendental Aloneness (kaivalya) urged upon us, being outside the perception of Puruṣa, has no basis.

(Answer) As a pillar for example, though perceived, has no existence (on your theory), so vijñāna-consciousness similarly perceived, has no existence. That being non-existent, it would entail absence of any perceiving subject, for lack of proof. So of whom would there be the Aloneness (release – of which your school speaks)? By whom or what would the separation be seen, and again, by whom or what would the bondage or conjunction be asserted? In the absence of bondage, there would be no effort towards the attainment of the highest good (niḥśreyasa), and that result would not follow.

Furthermore, when it is said 'there is no object apart from consciousness', it means that the words consciousness and object have one and the same meaning, as if one were to say, 'combustion is fire'. In which case, consciousness is the perceived object and the perceiving subject both, so that the confrontation of object perceived and perceiving subject is a matter of mere words, and it is not denied that one thing can be both perceived object and perceiving subject. It would follow that Puruṣa too would be perceived object and perceiving subject. Then release too would be meaningless, and there would follow numerous other defective positions.

> *In this way they deny things as they are, holding that a thing is comparable to a dream object, no more than a form in consciousness, and not, in the final analysis, existent. In this way they are rejecting, on the basis of an essentially unproven logical construct, the thing standing before them in its own strength. How should their words have any credibility?*

So *in this way* by force of a mere show of reasoning, *they deny things as they are, holding that a thing is comparable to a dream object, no more than a form in consciousness, and not, in the final analysis, existent. In this way* by such a hypothesis *they* themselves *are rejecting,* denying this which they have admitted, by now saying 'it does not exist', *on the basis of an essentially unproven logical construct, the thing standing before them in its own strength. How should their words have any credibility?* For those who propagate denial of their own experience cannot be worthy of credence.

The proposition that there are no objects apart from vijñāna-consciousness contradicts direct perception. We should recognize that vijñāna-consciousness is an instrument of perception, by which we perceive an object, in the form of a worm for example. The consciousness which reveals it is the perceiver, and what is revealed is the object. Since perception arises from the two things, the object and consciousness which are distinct in character, there is no trace of anything apart (from them). So that your argument from non-perception of anything apart is unsound.

The fact of the form of the worm, etc. is not from consciousness alone. Out of the one consciousness there would not come both the revealer and the revealed, any more than out of a single light. When that one light is divided into two separate lights, we do not see one as illuminator and the other as illumined, because it is not possible that the two should be in either one separately. And it is the same in the case of consciousness.

Moreover, the Buddha's counter-argument undermines his own position. For you cannot propose that the very thing you desire to prove does not exist; and if it does exist apart from vijñāna-consciousness, then the jar and so on too must be taken to exist.

Even with knowledge of dream objects, inasmuch as they are perceived things, they are not without some objective basis.

To argue that knowledge has no object goes against perception and against normal usage. All knowledge has an object, just because it is knowledge; as there is knowledge of the bad arguments of the opponent and knowledge of the good arguments of one's own side. So it is fundamentally unsound to reason that such things as knowledge are without any object.

Why is it so unreasonable?

Sūtra IV.15

Since there is difference of the minds, while the object is the same, the two must be distinct categories

A single thing becomes an object of many minds, to which it is common. It is not dependent on any one mind, nor determined by a number of minds. The thing stands by itself. How so? The object is the same: there is difference of the minds.

Though the thing be the same, when the mind regarding it looks to righteousness, from that very thing there is knowledge of happiness. From that very thing, when the mind looks to unrighteousness, it is knowledge of pain. Similarly, looking to ignorance, it is delusive knowledge. From that very thing, looking to right knowledge, there comes unbiased knowledge. Therefore, object and knowledge are distinct categories, because they are different as object known and the knowledge of it; there is not even a trace of overlap between them.

Why is it so unreasonable that a perceived object should not exist? *Since there is difference of the minds, while the object is the same, the two must be distinct categories. A single thing* such as a son, *becomes an object of many minds,* the field of attention of a number of minds, *to which it is common,* the same. *It is not dependent on any one mind, nor,* just because it is not dependent on one mind, does it become *determined by a number of minds.*

The thing stands by itself, is established in self-dependence irrespective of minds. *How so? The object is the same,* the object such as a son is only one; *there is difference of the minds.* Though the son is a single object, there is plurality of the knowledge of the knowers. How is there this difference of the minds? The reply is: *Though the thing be the same, when the mind regarding it looks to righteousness, from that very thing there is knowledge of happiness* like that of mother and father in relation to the one son.

From that very thing such as a son, *when the mind looks to unrighteousness,* that is to say, is hostile, *knowledge of pain* will be entailed.

Similarly for the desire-dominated *looking to Ignorance, it is delusive knowledge. From that very thing* for instance, the son, for the yogin-s *looking to right knowledge, there comes unbiased knowledge,*without either rejection or possessiveness. For such animals as are beasts of prey, there is knowledge of it as food, and finally there is knowledge of the corpse of the son when it is abandoned (at the funeral rite).

If a thing were to be determined by the mind of one person, then the minds of the others would be coloured by the determination of that one mind, and this is not a reasonable idea, for we never find any whose knowledge is not circumscribed (by his own location). If the other minds were coloured by the determination of the one mind, then everyone would know everything equally, and we do not find this. *Therefore* it is not that the things are determined by mind, but that *object and knowledge are distinct categories, because they are different as object known and the knowledge of it; there is not even a trace of overlap between them.*

Something like a son, which becomes the object of knowledge of happiness, is not as such determined by that particular knowledge, because there are minds which are affected by it in quite different ways, just as a debating proposition appears to its proposer good, but to an opponent, defective. If the proponent and opponent, etc., were all simply vijñāna-consciousness, there would be collapse of means, ends and the rest of daily life.

(Opponent) Let it be that it is just other forms of knowledge that exist, apart from one's own vijñāna-consciousness.

(Answer) Suppose it were so. Then the thing, being the object of another's knowledge, is admitted to be a separate thing, and the argument becomes simply a matter of names. But the difference between object and subject needs no proof, and there is not even a trace of overlap between them.

(Opponent) If we accept your view that a thing is established in its own nature, then it ought not to be the focal point of differing ideas of happiness and so on (as it has been described just now).

(Answer) The reply follows:

> *A thing is a movement of the three guṇa-s, a functioning of guṇa-s. It is referred to minds according to their impelling cause such as righteousness or unrighteousness. The cause of an idea arising corresponding to what impels it is according to the particular nature of that (impulsion).*

A thing is a movement of the three guṇa-s, a function of guṇa-s. It is referred to minds as differences of happiness or pain, etc., *according to their impelling cause such as righteousness or unrighteousness,* inasmuch as they change and have various capacities. *The cause of an idea arising corresponding to what impels it* righteousness or another quality, *is according to the particular nature of that (impulsion).* In the case of an impulsion of something like righteousness, the thing such as a son becomes the cause of happiness, according to the nature of sattva. Where it is unrighteousness, it is cause of pain, according to the nature of rajas, and where it is a case of Ignorance, that same thing becomes a cause of delusion, according to the nature of tamas. In the case of Right Vision, that thing is a cause of unbiased knowledge, according to the nature of the thing as it is.

> *There are some who say: Existence of a thing is invariably concomitant with the knowledge of it, from the very fact that it is experienced, as happiness and so on. Ruling out the fact of common experience, they deny any actual (enduring) thing in the earlier and later moments.*

There are some others of the Buddhists, who accept the existence of external objects, *who say: Existence of a thing is invariably concomitant with the knowledge of it.* As vijñāna-consciousness arises and perishes every instant, with no permanent entity supporting it, in the same way it is only in conjunction with knowledge that an object is experienced and perishes, *from the very fact that it is experienced, as happiness and so on.* Just as experience in the form of happiness and pain, etc., arise and perish in conjunction with consciousness and are not common to all, so too objects such as jars originate and perish together in the same vijñāna-consciousness alone, as is shown by the fact that they are simply experienced.

They too, like the Vijñāna-vādin Buddhist, *ruling out the fact* that a *common* thing makes itself an object to various minds as happiness and other experiences, *deny any actual (enduring) thing in the earlier and later moments:* since its (existence is) appearance in one's own consciousness, in neither earlier nor later instants is any actual thing (to be supposed).

The actual nature of a thing, however, is not (mere) concomitance with vijñāna-consciousness, because there is the recognition 'That indeed (yesterday) is this (here and now)'. What arises and perishes in an instant, like vijñāna-consciousness, would not be recognized as 'That indeed is this'; for it is not thought 'That indeed is my vijñāna-consciousness here', but it is a thing that is cognized again, as 'That indeed is this'. While object and knowledge exist on the same occasion, still there has to be the distinction between them.

Nor is it a recognition arising from similarity. Because the object and subject arise and perish simultaneously. When it is established that some particular thing has been seen, the idea that arises at the sight of another thing which is similar to it, is: 'It is similar.' Or perhaps there is a desire: 'I hope to see something similar to it.' For when a thing is known to have perished on one day, no one will look forward to seeing it on the following day. Nor can the afore-mentioned desire be in the form 'someone very like me wishes to see it', for this is not what we find: everyone exerts himself for his own purposes, and is not seen to do so regarding those with whom he has no concern.

So the present object here and now is not just something concomitant with present knowledge here and now, because it is known also as an object in the past.

Again, what is past is not born and perishing concomitantly with past knowledge, because it is also known as an object now. Things known by knowledge past or future also exist now, because they are known as ideas in the present. What is here and now is the same in previous or later moments.

(Opponent) But there is uncertainty about them, as for instance the knowledge of happiness, pain and so on (described before).

(Answer) Not so, because it has also been shown that what is past or future exists in its own nature. In which case, happiness and so on do themselves exist in their own nature; the same reasoning applies when they are taken as the example.

(Opponent) There is not the feeling of happiness, etc., when a thing is in the time-phases of past or future as when it is in the form of the present.

(Answer) That is making an issue of what has been established already (siddha-sādhyatā): the bare existence of the boy is not his adulthood.

From here on it will be shown that it cannot be right that a thing should depend on mind for its existence. Would it depend on a single mind, or would it depend on several? As to dependence on a single mind, there is this to say:

Sūtra IV.16

It is not dependent on a single mind, for when it was not giving rise to valid cognition in that mind, what would it be?

> *If the thing were dependent on a single mind, when that mind was not focused on it, or was inhibited, the thing would not be in contact with it and would not be an object to any other mind either. So that thing would not produce any valid cognition, and would be essentially unknown. What would it be at that time? Again, why would it rise again to be connected with that mind? (Further) its parts which were not being cognized, would not exist. As the back would not exist, the front ought not to exist either.*

It is not dependent on a single mind, for when it was not giving rise to valid cognition in that mind, what would it be? To begin with, it is not dependent on a single mind, for supposing it were, *If the thing were dependent on a single mind, when that mind* on which the particular thing depended *was not focused on it,* when it was engaged with something else, *or was inhibited,* disappeared, *the thing would not be in contact with it,* with that mind which had valid cognition of it, *and would not be an object to any other mind either,* for it is supposed to be dependent on the single mind alone. *So that thing would not produce any valid cognition, and would be essentially unknown,* the mind that could know it being entirely inhibited. *What would it be at that time?* It could not be anything at all, for since it is known by that mind (alone), without the latter it would not come to exist through it.

(Opponent) The knowing mind is inhibited, so this too is inhibited similarly, because it is after all momentary. No further explanation is needed.

(Answer) Not so, because it would be the end of all worldly life, and also there would be nothing to determine what happened. 'This is fire: do not touch it. Take this, give that' – this sort of worldly exchange would be ended, because the thing would disappear along with its concomitant mind.

(Opponent) Something absolutely similar to it, produced in the chain (of instants of vijñāna-consciousness) would suffice for worldly life.

(Answer) Here again, who is to determine that from that very chain, there will be something which may be experienced as the same thing, and become the object of a further valid cognition? There is no ground for the determination.

In any case, as the thing depends on only the single mind, at the time of worldly life, what supports as an object a particular idea of the one party, will have no relation with ideas of the other party, for the thing is not supposed to be dependent on a plurality of minds. So when we are asked: 'Take this; give that!' how are we going to carry it out?

Nor would a pupil living with the teacher be able to co-operate in the passing on of instruction and so on. Thus a thing cannot be dependent on a single mind, for when the cognizing mind was absent or otherwise engaged, the (existence of) the thing would be undetermined.

Again, why would it the thing *rise again to be connected with that mind?* There is no reason why it should arise from that chain (of instants), as we have pointed out.

Further, *its* that thing's *parts which were not being cognized* not becoming the object of an idea of that single mind *would not exist.* For one part would be an object dependent on that mind, but another part would not be. Then *as the back would not exist, the front* which is before one *ought (logically) not to exist either.*

(Opponent) Well, on the principle of the Crow and the Palmyra Fruit (by a rare chance, the fruit falls from a high branch and kills the bird), a number of minds could come together simultaneously, so that the thing would emerge at the same time for them all.

(Answer) This is refuted by the point that if the back of a thing does not exist, then its front (logically) does not exist either. Nor could the sea of worldly affairs, made up of permanent relations, be navigated on the basis of chance conjunctions like the Crow and the Palmyra Fruit. All the defects in the contentions of the Consciousness-only doctrine are exactly the same here.

> *Therefore a thing is self-sufficient, common to all men, and minds, self-sufficient, function for their respective Puruṣa-s. From conjunction of the two comes perception, which is experience for Puruṣa.*

Therefore thus *a thing is self-sufficient, common to all men,* since the affairs of the world as a whole are feasible only on this basis, *and the minds function for their respective Puruṣa-s. From conjunction of the two* things and minds *comes perception, which is experience for Puruṣa.* So Puruṣa is the experiencer, mind is the instrument, and the thing is its field, namely the object; the categories of experiencer, instrument and object, are distinct.

(Opponent) How does experience of Puruṣa come from conjunction of mind and objects?

(Answer) He replies: For him who claims either that there is no thing apart from mind, or that the thing is wholly dependent on mind, there cannot be some objects known and some unknown. (However:)

Sūtra IV.17

According to whether the mind is coloured by it, a thing is known or unknown

According to whether that object causes a colouring of the mind corresponding to its existence, the thing is known or unknown. By whatever thing mind is coloured, that thing is known; by whatever thing it is not so coloured, that is unknown. And this colouring corresponds to a change of the mind. For mind is changed into the outer form when conjoined with that, through the channel of the senses.

As to what causes the change, he says:

> *The objects are comparable to a magnet, and the mind corresponds to iron. The object draws to itself and colours the mind. By whatever object the mind is coloured, that object is known; furthermore, another is unknown. From the fact that its objects have the character of being known and also not known, the mind must be changeable.*

The objects are comparable to a magnet like a magnet, *and the mind corresponds to iron,* being like iron in that when the object is near it, it is affected. The similarity of the object to a magnet is from its power to affect the mind simply by being near it. Thus *the object draws to itself and colours the mind,* which is changed into the form of the object.

By whatever object the mind is coloured, that object is known, and *furthermore, another* object, which does not colour the mind, *is unknown.*

So *From the fact that its objects have the character of being known and also not known, the mind must be changeable.* Here again, for one who maintains that the object is purely dependent on the mind, or else that it is mind itself, there will be either omniscience or else no knowledge of objects at all. For without knowledge, mind would not exist. But we do not find this, but rather that objects of the mind are known and also unknown. So there must be changeability of the mind, since its objects are not in a fixed state; and otherwise, relation with them is not feasible.

> *But to Him, that very mind is the object.*

But to Him, Puruṣa its Lord, the experiencer, *that very mind* whose objects are known and unknown *is the object* in the form of a mental process, for mind with its mental processes inhibited would not be an object.

Sūtra IV.18

To Him, the Lord, the mental processes are always known, from the fact of the unchangeability of Puruṣa

To Him, the Lord, Puruṣa, *the mental processes are always known.* There is direct perception of them, and it is unquestionable that they are always known as objects. Again, the mental processes, as directly perceivable, are in fact remembered as having been known directly, like a jar, and not on the basis of authority or of inference. In the same way their form is known exactly, and they are never objects of uncertainty. If the mental process were never directly perceived, then like outer objects, some of them would appear uncertain at some time. But never are any of them found to be in the realm of uncertainty.

(Opponent) Still, if an object is known at any time at all, it is said to be known.

(Answer) No mental process can occur which is not known by direct perception. Nor could one be inferred from a result, because it could not be determined what the result should be.

Since what is uncertain cannot be an object, and the mental processes are remembered purely as themselves, regardless of any object, they are always directly perceived. They are the perceiver's illuminator, instrument and manifestor, like a light. It is not that there is uncertainty (in perception) by the eye or other sense organ; there too there is direct perception. As things like jars are known by the special illumination of a light, so sounds are known through the ear by a special 'light' of its own, and so with the other senses and their objects.

And it cannot be argued that because this is not known in isolation, that is not a case of direct perception. The rays from two lamps are inseparably mingled with each other, and cannot be isolated as 'this ray is this one's, and that ray is that one's', yet we do not say that there is therefore no direct perception of them. In the same way here, a sense like the eye has a reciprocal relation with the external light which corresponds to it, and they are not known in isolation; but we cannot say simply on that ground that there is no direct perception. He who denies that the mental process must inevitably be directly perceived would surely deny himself too, for all perception depends on some mental process, and the 'light' of a perception of form depends on some idea.

And so he says: *To Him,* Puruṣa, *the mental processes are always known, from the fact of the unchangeability of Puruṣa.* That unchangeability is inherently eternal awareness, so it follows that they are always known as an object.

> *If the Lord, Puruṣa, were to change like the mind, then His objects – the mental processes – would be objects like those of the mind such as sound, which are known and unknown. The unchangeability of the Lord, Puruṣa, entails the perpetual knownness of the mind.*

If Puruṣa were to change like the mind, then His objects the mental processes would be objects like those of the mind such as sound, which are known and also *unknown.* The knownness and unknownness of universals such as sound should be understood as changes of the changing mind; in the same way, the knownness or unknownness of the objects of the senses correspond to changes of the senses. But not even one of the mental processes is sometimes known and sometimes unknown, for they are invariably nothing but known. And so *The unchangeability of the Lord, Puruṣa, entails the perpetual knownness of the mind* as process.

The proposition is, that Puruṣa is unchanging; the reason is, that its objects are always known; the example of the contrary is, mind and senses. Because we are dealing with a perceiver of objects, examples like freed Selves do not serve to refute the point that Puruṣa's objects are always known, because a freed Self does not have any objects.

> *(Opponent) There may be this possibility: mind alone will illumine itself and also illumine the object.*

(Opponent) There may be this possibility: mind alone, as both perceived and perceiver *will illumine itself and also illumine the object.* For mental processes themselves are self-cognized forms; they are like a lamp which causes to

shine both jars and other things as well as itself. Why should any Puruṣa be supposed, outside the mind, as a perceiver of the mental processes?

(Answer) The reply to this is:

Sūtra IV.19

It (mind) is not self-illumining, because it is itself something perceived

> *The other senses, and sound and so on, are not self-illumining. Just so the mind too is to be taken.*

It is not self-illumining, because it is itself something perceived. The other senses like the ear, *and* their objects *sound and so on are not self-illumining.* Neither the senses nor again their objects like sound are self-illumining, because they are themselves things perceived. *Just so the mind (manas) too is to be taken:* the mind (citta) is to be understood as not self-illumining, because it is something perceived.

(Opponent) Let it be like fire, which is self-illumining and also illumines objects. Perceivables like jars do indeed look to an outside illumination to be revealed as they are, but not so a light. As a light illumines itself and illumines objects, so let mind too be an illuminer in the same way; what need of a Self (ātman)? When people have a light, they do not fetch another light (to illumine that one).

And if a further perceiver is assumed, it would simply be an infinite regress. For it would follow that the vijñāna-consciousness would be perceived by something separate from it, and then there would be perception of that perceiver too by some other, and of that other by yet another. Furthermore, as the vijñāna-consciousness would itself be illuminative, there could be no complementary relation of principal and auxiliary with its own perceiver, any more than in the case of two lights. As therefore any assumed perceiver of vijñāna–consciousness is pointless; let it be that knowledge illumines itself and illumines others.

(Answer) You cannot with this very poor example repudiate the Self which is supported by the accepted canons of behaviour of the whole world. Why not?

> *Fire is not an example of it. For it is not that fire illumines a self-nature which is not (already) light. And light is seen, when there is a conjunction of the thing illuminated with its illuminator; and there is no conjunction in the simple nature of a thing.*

Fire is not an example of it, for it is not that fire illumines a self-nature which is not light. The example would be appropriate only if fire were not light, and if by itself alone, it were illumined like a jar. But it is not so, for fire is never not light.

And light is seen, when there is a conjunction of the thing illuminated with its illuminator; and there is no conjunction in the simple nature of a thing, for a conjunction is between two things, and a self-nature is not an illuminator unless there is some conjunction.

(Opponent) Still, fire does not need any other light, as does a jar.

(Answer) It is not something which can be illumined by another, and it has no form, like that of a jar, which could be so illumined. But it is not that thereby it is not seen by someone apart, for it is certainly perceived by the eye, which is apart from it in the same way.

A light will be brought to remove the darkness over an illuminable, like a jar; it is not that the jar is not illuminable. That the fire has no need of any other light has been declared by you yourself, when you said that there is no relation of principal and auxiliary between two lights. Though there is in fact a difference between the two lights, it is not because they are not illuminable that there is no relation of principal and auxiliary between them. So still less would there be any need for another light when there is no difference at all.

But the point of being perceptible to someone apart is not touched, because the two lights themselves are things seen, like a jar or other object. And thereby it is established that knowledge is known by something apart from itself, because it is something seen, like for instance the lights.

It is further established that knowledge is independent of any other instrument, because it is light by nature, as much as a lighted lamp. So there is no suspicion of any infinite regress.

(Opponent) If so, then as knowledge is inherently illuminating, and any perceiver of it will also be naturally an illuminator, there can be no mutual relation of principal and auxiliary between them, any more than between two lights.

(Answer) The point is not valid, because the Self (ātman) and knowledge are of different classes, as for instance the eye and a light.

(Opponent) But by the I-notion, the subject (pratyayin) knows the mind, in which case the very same thing has the character of both object and subject.

(Answer) Not so, because the mind consists of the three guṇa-s. In this case, the mind with tamas predominant depends on a distinct mental process consisting of sattva, like the body being scratched by the hand. In this case too, however, there is a separate perceiver of the object, a knower, which is Puruṣa. By the fact that the perceiver and perceived are of different classes, and that Puruṣa has no parts, we have refuted the contention that it is simply Puruṣa that is both the perceived object and the perceiver.

> *Furthermore, to say that mind is self-illumining would mean only that the mind is not a perceivable. As for instance: to say that space is self supporting means that it is not supported (by anything else). The whole activity of living beings arises from their awareness of the operations of their own mind: 'I am angry', 'I am afraid', 'My desire is for that one', 'My anger is against that one'. Unless there were perception of one's own mind, human activity would not be sensible.*

Furthermore, to say that mind is self illumining would mean only that the mind is not a perceivable, because the meaning of the statement that it is self-illumining is that it is not illumined, is not perceived, by another. It is not being said that it perceives itself. So an original word can have applications which give an opposite meaning to it, *As for instance, to say that space is self-supporting means that it is not supported,* that becoming the sense of the words. In the same way, 'Devadatta is sva-stha' (literally, self-standing) means that he is healthy, not that he literally stands in himself.

He now declares that the phrase in sūtra 19: 'because it is itself something perceived' shows that what was proposed, for no valid reason, would contradict direct perception, would contradict general usage, and would put an end to the affairs of life. *The whole activity of living beings arises from their awareness of the operations of their own mind: 'I am angry', 'I am afraid', 'My desire is for that one', 'My anger is against that one'.* Thus aware of, perceiving their own particular mind in operation, the discriminating are observed taking steps to get rid of anger, greed and so on. And in the same way, they perceive: 'My mind is clear', or perhaps impure, or bewildered. *Unless there were perception of one's own mind, human activity would not be sensible,* for when the mind has calmed the agitation, it is not sensible to say that we are not aware of it.

(Opponent) Allowing that point, but let the mind be self-illuminating and also illumining objects.

(Answer) The refutation is this:

Sūtra IV.20

They cannot both be clearly ascertained at the same time

They cannot both be clearly ascertained at the same time, for it takes some instants to discriminate objects, and it is not reasonable that it should then be discriminating oneself. Then again, when it clearly ascertains oneself, it is not then turned to objects, because it would take several instants to discriminate the self.

(Opponent) There is just a single discrimination – of both.

(Answer) No, because a discrimination has no parts. A mental operation which has no parts cannot reasonably illumine a number of things, as a light does. The light has different parts (rays), and so it can light up a number of things. But even our opponents do not think that knowledge has parts.

Further, acceptance that a single knowledge in a single instant should determine both, entails differentiation of action and agency. The determination of the two is an action, and what causes it is an agency.

> *It is not reasonable that there should be determination of both itself and another in a single instant, as the theorist of instants (kṣaṇa-vādin) holds, for he maintains that the origin of anything is itself action and is itself the agency.*

Why is it *not reasonable that there should be determination of both itself and another in a single instant, as the theorist of Instants (kṣaṇa-vādin) holds?* It is said by him, to establish his doctrine of Instants, that *the origin of anything* its coming into being *is itself action and is itself the agency.* This is his position. (But) differentiation of action and agency will shatter the doctrine that they are one instant, because the action-instant would have to be established by an agency.

> *(Opponent) There can be this view: an idea, naturally perishing (along with its instant), is known by another idea immediately afterwards in the same stream of instants.*

(Opponent) *There can be this view* of some of us: *an idea (buddhi) naturally perishing (along with its instant)* being extremely fragile, it perishes as it comes into existence, *is known by another idea* coming into being *immediately afterwards in the same stream of instants,* so that here the assumption of a permanently abiding Puruṣa is quite needless.

(Answer) The answer is:

Sūtra IV.21

If it is to be seen by another idea, further and yet further ideas will be required. And there will be confusion of memories

> *If the idea is to be seen by another idea, then by whom is that idea of the idea known? It would have to be known by another, and that too by yet another, endlessly.*

If it is to be seen by another idea, further and yet further ideas will be required. And there will be confusion of memories. If the idea the earlier idea which has perished of itself *is to be seen by another idea* which has arisen immediately afterwards in the stream of instants, *then by whom is that idea of the idea known?* The idea which knows the jar is here called the 'idea', and the idea for which it is itself an object is the 'idea of the idea'. By whom is that idea of the idea known, if there is no abiding knower? *It would have to be known by another, and that too by yet another, endlessly.*

And if the ideas of the ideas are not known, then the affairs of the world will collapse, because the saṃskāra-s of memory will not be available. There will be an exponentially proliferating string of ideas of the idea of the jar, all on the same level, but not the idea of the jar itself. As there is no end to the ideas of the idea of the jar, how would the idea of an object like a jar ever be definite?

There is this further difficulty: *And there will be confusion of memories.* The ideas of the idea, and their saṃskāra-s, will have the same form, so that one would get a confusion of memories.

> *As many as were the experiences of the ideas of the idea, so many would be the memories. As a result of that confusion, memory would not be specific. Everything is reduced to chaos by the Vaināśika Buddhists who explain away Puruṣa, who is the witness of the ideas. If they suppose the nature of an experiencer anywhere at all, they are going against (their own) logic.*
>
> *Some (of them) assume simple being, which having cast off this set of five skandha-groups, assembles others. After saying which, they shrink back from (declaring openly) that very thing (an enduring experiencer). And yet they still say: 'I will follow the life of brahmacarya under a teacher, so that there may be revulsion from the skandha-groups, freedom from passion, that they may not arise but be at peace.'*
>
> *The Sāṅkhya-s and Yoga-s and their followers (however) proclaim that by the word 'self (sva) they understand Puruṣa alone, the Lord of the mind, the experiencer.*

As many as were the experiences of the ideas of the idea, so many would be the consequent confused mass of *memories. As a result of that confusion* of the memories, *memory would not be specific,* in the form 'this memory is of that idea'. In the uncertainty, how could we carry on our lives? From the similarity of the forms, confusion of memories would result.

However much we might know of ideas of an idea, since there could be no memory of an idea of the self and its previous activity, we should all meet each other in bewilderment. If, to escape the infinite regress, we should stop at a separate idea somewhere, then that itself would be the *witness of the ideas.* And thus, though He (Puruṣa the witness) is so obvious, from the indication that the ideas are witnessed, *Everything* – the whole world – *is reduced to chaos by the Vaināśika Buddhists who explain away Puruṣa, who is the witness of the ideas.*

(Opponent) We get out of the difficulty of an infinite regress with our assumption of seed-bed consciousness (ālaya-vijñāna), which avoids the supposition of self (ātman).

(Answer) *If they suppose the nature of an experiencer anywhere at all, they are going against (their own) logic.* That seed-bed (ālaya) consciousness too is something to be known, and so there is an infinite regress; it involves the same difficulties already mentioned.

Some particular Vaināsika Buddhists *assume simple being* of the nature of an experiencer, but calling it instead 'simple being' (sattva-mātra), *which having cast off* thrown off *this set of five skandha-groups,* namely matter, feeling, perception, mental construction, vijñāna-consciousness *assembles* holds together *other* skandha-groups. *After saying which, they shrink back from (declaring openly) that very thing,* the assumption of a single being which is the fashioner of the past and future skandha-groups.

And yet they have another view which contradicts themselves. *They still say: 'I will follow the life of brahmacarya under a teacher so that there may be revulsion from the skandha-groups, freedom from passion, that they may not arise but be at peace'* and then they go on to deny the existence of that very being which they have just accepted. Calling it Vijñāna-consciousness-only, momentary, or Void, they deny self (ātman).

The Sāṅkhya-s and Yoga-s and their followers (however) proclaim that by the word 'self' (sva) they understand Puruṣa alone, the Lord of the mind, the experiencer.

In what way?

In what way do they understand the experiencer by the word 'self (sva)? In this way:

Sūtra IV.22

In assumption of its (the mind's) form on the part of the unmoving consciousness, is awareness of the idea of the self

In when there is *assumption of its (the mind's) form on the part of the unmoving consciousness,* there *is* comes to be *awareness of the idea of the self.* The *consciousness* is awareness, Puruṣa, which as it never changes, is unmoving. There is *assumption on the part of the consciousness,* though unmoving, *of its form. It* refers back to the familiar mind (citta), and *assumption of its form* means assumption of the form of that mind. In the assumption of its form by that consciousness, there comes to be *awareness of the idea of the self (sva).*

In the mind, there comes about a perception of the notion (bauddha-pratyaya) of the self. It is for this that the mind (buddhi) transforms itself into notions of objects like sound.

> *The power-of-the-experiencer does not change. Unmoving, it has as it were passed into the changing object, conforming to its function. The assumption of its form of borrowed consciousness by mere resemblance to the mental process, and not distinguished from it, is what is called the mental process of knowing. So it is said:*
>
> *Neither underworld nor mountain crevasse,*
> *nor darkness nor submarine depth,*
> *Is the secret cave in which is hidden the eternal*
> *Brahman:*
> *(But) it is the mental process when not discriminated –*
> *thus they teach.*

He makes it clear: *The power-of-the-experiencer (bhoktṛ-śakti)* the power-of-the-Seer as has been described *does not change. Unmoving* though it is, *it has as it were passed into the changing object* the idea in the mind (bauddha-pratyaya), as the field of the thinking subject, *conforming to its function,* conforming, as it were, perceiving it as its seer. An idea in the mind (bauddha-pratyaya), by merely arising becomes an object for it. The power-of-the-experiencer, perceiving it, conforms to that idea in the mind, the mental function (vṛtti).

The assumption of its form of borrowed consciousness, acquiring its form of being endowed with consciousness, the form of being endowed with a Puruṣa, the form attained by that mental process – as a lump of glowing iron gets the form of being endowed with fire placed near it – from being the object-of-sight, *by mere resemblance to the mental process* by its mere conformity to the mental process, *and not distinguished from it,* this *is what is called the mental process of knowing (jña),* the mental process of pure knowing, being the mental process of mere perception (upalabdhi). So it was said: 'Otherwise, it conforms itself to the mental process' (I.4), and further clarified with: 'Experience is the idea which does not distinguish (Puruṣa from mind-sattva)' (II.35).

The assumption of the form of the mind comes from the fact of difference between experiencer and experienced. Without a separate experiencer, there would be no reason for any appearance of mind alone as seer and seen. So it was well said that the followers of Sāṅkhya and Yoga understand by the word 'sva' the Puruṣa, while others, though in fact understanding it, yet shrink from admitting it.

So it is said – by mere resemblance to the process of the mind (buddhi-vṛtti) the 'knowledge' process is perceived in mind (buddhi) alone, and not outside it – *Neither underworld nor mountain crevasse, nor darkness nor submarine depth* nor any such thing, *Is the secret cave in which* cave *is hidden the eternal Brahman.* That secret cave is not the underworld or the other regions. As to that secret cave, where It is hidden: *It is the mental process,* it is in the secret cave of the mind (buddhi), the mental process called Self (ātman), called Brahman, *when not discriminated,* when it has not been separated out, when it is not discriminated from the process of the mind, *thus they teach,* those who can see the difference (vivekin).

Why is it then that Puruṣa assumes the form of the mind? Or again, is it that it (mind) is then experiencing its own buddhi, thus giving rise to the error of the Vaināśika Buddhists, who say that it is mind (citta) alone that is both object (grāhya) and subject (grāhaka)?

On that point, this is what is to be accepted:

Sūtra IV.23

Mind, coloured by Seer and seen, has the various purposes

Mind (citta) is coloured by an object cognizable to the mind, and by the fact of being (itself) an object, it is bound up with the subject, Puruṣa, by a mental function of belonging (to Him). It is this very mind alone that is coloured by the Seer and the seen. It assumes the appearance of object and subject, the unconscious becoming conscious. The mind, being insentient, essentially an object – conscious as it were, on the analogy of the crystal – is said to comprehend everything.

By that assumption of form by the mind, some have been misled into thinking: it is only mind which is conscious. Others hold that all this is mind alone, and that this world with its cows and jars and so on does not exist as self-sufficient. They are pathetic. Why? The basis of their delusion is the mind's appearance in all the forms.

But in samādhi-knowledge (prajña) the object of the knowledge is reflected in it (pratibimbī-bhūta), and from the fact of becoming the object of the meditation there, must be something other (than it).

Mind coloured by Seer Puruṣa *and seen* sound and the other objects, coloured by both, *has the various purposes (artha)* of Puruṣa, namely experience and release. *Mind (citta) is coloured by an object (artha)* something (viṣaya) which is comparable to a magnet, *cognizable to the mind, and by the fact of being an object* to Puruṣa, *it is bound up with the subject* (viṣayin) *Puruṣa,* next to it, *by the mental function (vṛtti)* a mental idea (mānasa pratyaya) *of belonging (ātmīya)* as being its object.

Bound up with Puruṣa as it is by way of a mental function of self-hood, and thereby coloured with the nature of the Seer, and coloured also by the objects like sound which it can cognize, *it is this mind alone* and not Puruṣa *that is coloured by Seer and seen.* He goes on to explain what is this colouring by Seer and seen: *It assumes the appearance of object and subject, the forms of conscious and unconscious.*

(Opponent) How is it possible that what is of itself unconscious becomes of conscious nature?

(Answer) It is possible. It is (only) seemingly conscious, from its eternal proximity to Puruṣa, and so those who cannot discriminate say that it is conscious. Not so with the objects, for they are inherently unconsciousness. That mind, however, is of itself unconscious is stated in the words that follow: The naturally unconscious becomes sentient.

> *The mind, being insentient, essentially an object, but conscious, as it were, on the analogy of the crystal, is said to comprehend everything.*

From that *By that assumption of form by the mind, some have been misled.* This taking on by the mind of that form has been a cause of delusion to the Vaiśeṣika-s. They, and others like them, whose minds have been bewildered by the magic trick (mahendrajāla) of the mind's conforming itself, say that *it is only that,* the mind, which *is conscious.* How so? Inasmuch as they think that consciousness produced by the conjunction of mind (manas) and Puruṣa is an attribute which is separable. But they have this distinction from the Vaināśika Buddhists: they hold to a permanent unitary dharmin.

Others Buddhists *hold that all this is mind alone, and that this world with its cows and jars and so on does not exist as self-sufficient,* that is to say, distinguished as common to the ideas (pratyaya) of everyone. In this way, they deny even their own experience. Thus deluded, these shallow Vaināśika thinkers *are pathetic.*

Why? The basis of their delusion is the mind's appearance in all the forms. This delusion of theirs does have some cause for it, not as in the case of the materialists (lokāya-tika), who have no ground for theirs, any more than the advocates of the Void (śūnya-vādin). These two last are simply engaged in deceiving people, and deserve no sympathy whatever. So it is rightly said of the previously mentioned pitiable ones that they are pathetic, because their delusion does have some basis.

Who then are undeluded? He replies: *In samādhi-knowledge (prajñā), the object of the knowledge is reflected in it (pratibimbī-bhūta), and from the fact of becoming the object of the meditation there, must be something other (than it).*

Perception in samādhi-knowledge (prajñā) means perception by an undeluded mind, for minds that are changeable (vikṣipta—comm. to I.1) are deluded. *In samādhi-knowledge,* undeluded, pure, discriminative, clear and profound, *the object of the knowledge is reflected in it* as it were in a spotless mirror, *and from the fact of* its *becoming the object of the meditation, there* in the samādhi-knowledge, which is the instrument, *is something other* than the samādhi-knowledge, which is essentially something produced by closeness to it, and is an action, and so forth.

> *If that (other) were itself to be merely the mind, how could the nature of the samādhi-knowledge be determined by samādhi-knowledge itself? Therefore this which is the object reflected in the samādhi-knowledge by which it is ascertained, is Puruṣa.*
>
> *As there is this distinction in nature between knower, knowing process and known object, those who realize that the distinction into three is innate – they see rightly, and Puruṣa is attained by them.*

If that other *were itself to be merely the mind, how could the nature of the samādhi-knowledge be determined by samādhi-knowledge itself?* There would be the absurdity of an action in its own self, so there is no way it could be determined. *Therefore this which is* something other than samādhi-knowledge, being *the object reflected in the samādhi-knowledge by which it is ascertained, is Puruṣa.* He is other than the object of the meditations of that samādhi-knowledge, being in fact the subject.

As there is this distinction in nature between knower, knowing process and known object, from the recognition of the difference between subject, instrument and object, inasmuch as an indivisible unity cannot be in successive instants a thing and then an agent and then an object, *those who realize that the distinction into the three is innate – they see rightly (samyagdarśin), and Puruṣa is attained* is reached *by them;* the context shows that this means that Puruṣa is known by them.

> *Why, again?*

Why again should there be a Puruṣa apart from the mind? It has already been proved by the fact that the mind is something seen, but now he intends to prove it by showing that this very mind must have a Lord, because it is a construct:

Sūtra IV.24

Though it is a mélange of countless saṃskāra-groups, it must exist for the purposes of another, because it is a construct

> *Though it is a mélange of countless saṃskāra-groups, it must exist for the purposes of another, namely experience or release of that other, like a house. For no construct exists as an end in itself*
>
> *The mind, being a construct – (what it effects) is done not for itself. For a happy mind is not for the purpose of happiness itself Nor is a mind with knowledge simply for the purpose of knowledge. Both are for the purposes of another.*

Though it is a mélange of countless saṃskāra-groups (vāsanā), it must exist for the purposes of another, because it is a construct. Even though that very mind is *a mélange,* implying that it causes delusion, *of countless saṃskāra-groups* laid down from time without beginning, still it recognizably exists *for another,* only *for the purposes of experience and release of that other, because it is a construct,* all construction being directed towards a purpose through the manipulation of effects, instruments, and objects. So *because it is a construct, like a house,* which is an illustration of how a construct like the mind exists only for another. *For no construct* is ever seen to *exist as an end in itself.*

Therefore *the mind, being a construct – (what it effects) is done not for itself. For a happy mind is not for the purpose of happiness itself,* nor for the purpose of a happy mind itself, *nor is a mind with knowledge simply for the purpose of knowledge* or for the sake of being a mind with knowledge. What are they for, then? The happy mind, or mind with knowledge, *Both are for the purposes of another.*

> *That other, which has as its purposes experience and release, is Puruṣa alone, not simply something else in a general sense as the Vaināśika may propose, for – as a construct – that too would exist only for the sake of another. This Other, however, is Puruṣa, not a construct but a particular.*

That other, which has as its purposes experience by a happy mind or a mind with knowledge, *and release, is Puruṣa alone, not simply something else in a general sense (as the Vaināśika may propose)* such as body or senses or objects. For the Vaināśika does not accept that a happy mind is for the sake of body or senses or objects – if he did, he would contradict his own position, for he accepts only vijñāna-consciousness as having the purpose of happiness and release. So he ought to accept that Puruṣa, apart from body, senses and objects, is the Other beyond vijñāna-consciousness, that has the purposes of experience and release.

If the *Vaināśika propose that it is something else in general terms* – if the Vaināśika in his delusion thinks that after all the purposefulness of constructs like houses is for some builder such as Devadatta, so that he does not need any particular Other, in that case he must answer this: Which other is to be taken in a general sense from among the ideas of body, senses, or objects? Is it all of them, or is it some one of them, or is it something of different class?

It is not to be taken in a general sense, for the Vaināśika himself does not accept that a generality could have a purpose directed towards experience or release. That would go against his own position. Neither does he maintain that aggregates like the body have purposes such as experience and release, because he supposes that such purposes must belong to a vijñāna (-consciousness) series.

Nor is what he calls the jñāna-knowledge series a unity, because it consists of instants; nor can the series have purposes of experience, because it is unreal, little more than a hare's horn. Nor again can he accept that it is someone out of the body and senses and so on, because he does not recognize purposefulness for experience or release in anything apart from the vijñāna-consciousness of his own system.

Nor is the body-senses 'aggregate' a reality for Vaināsika-s to which they could have recourse for providing a constructor's purpose for the mind. For how could something unreal have a purpose? Nor can you assert some construct of another kind, different from body and senses, etc.; for if you suppose some unseen one of a different kind with purposes of experience and release, that is just the Other we speak of. And this which is the Other in the construct situation cannot properly be something seen which is not the Self. Consequently the Other, having the purposes of experience and release, is not a construct.

What further? When it is said that mind is for the purpose of some constructor, it comes to saying that in the case of one who had attained his purpose, the mind would be for its own sake alone, since there would be no other as constructor. And if that were so, the absence of any example of self-sufficiency would refute your own position. He who thinks thus ends up saying the one thing, but in his heart the other one is making a disturbance, arguing that the position is refuted by the fact that senses like the eye exist only for the sake of some other.

(Opponent) They are for the sake of the vijñāna-consciousness.

(Answer) Vijñāna itself is a construct, so it too must exist for some other.

(Opponent) Vijñāna-consciousness consists of instants, so it is not a construct.

(Answer) It is; because something is seen apart from it, and you do not admit that that can be a thing-in-itself also consisting of instants. So that point too we refute.

So he explains: whatever *the Vaināśika may propose as* itself *the other in a general sense, that too being a construct would exist only for the sake of* yet *another.* Someone like Devadatta does not have a constructive purpose, because that would be acceptable to neither of us: for you do not accept anything apart from vijñāna-consciousness, and we do not look for any purposefulness apart from Puruṣa. Therefore, admitting that mere vijñāna-consciousness does not meet the case, it follows that *This Other, however, is Puruṣa, not a construct but a particular,* which has been established as self-sufficient.

The conclusion is, that the experiencer (bhoktṛ) is a conjunction (of the guṇa-s) with that self-sufficient One, caused by its own seen object, which is for the sake of that Other. Their disjunction is tantamount to release.

It has been said that the cause of the conjunction of the guṇa-s and Puruṣa is Ignorance, and that this ceases for the one who, seeking to know the Self, sees that One apart.

Sūtra IV.25

For him who sees that One apart, cessation of meditation on his own being

For him who sees that One apart, cessation of meditation on his own being. Puruṣa is apart (viśeṣa), not in the same category as manifest or unmanifest or universal, and he who *sees that one apart* is he whose vision always distinguishes Him clearly from manifest or unmanifest or universal. For him, once he has brought about the circumstances for release through right vision, *the meditation on his own being ceases.*

How is it known when there is this meditation on his own being? He replies:

> *As by the sprouting forth of grass in the rainy season, the actual existence of seed is inferred, so when someone is seen with a thrill, or perhaps tears, of joy, on hearing about the path to release, it is inferred that some good karma has been performed by him (at some time in the past), which is a seed of vision of the One apart, and which should lead him to release. For him, meditation on his own being begins of itself. When it is absent, then as has been said, from the defects of their character they have a taste for the prima facie (view of things), and a distaste for ascertainment (of the truth).*
>
> *Meditation on his own being is in the form: 'Who have I been (in past lives)? What happened to me? What is this world? How is it? What shall we become, and what is going to happen to us?' But it ceases for him who sees the One apart. Because this is all a display of changes of mind alone. Puruṣa, without Ignorance, is pure and untouched by qualities of the mind. For the skilful one, meditation on his own being ceases.*

For him who comes to see the One apart, *meditation on his own being,* which is the cause that should lead to Transcendental Aloneness, *begins of itself,* caused by karma of a previous life, or else by steadfastness in renunciation in this present one. And it goes on of itself, without instruction from a teacher. *When it* karma of this kind *is absent, then as has been said, from the defects of their character,* from having been joined with impure karma *they have a taste for the prima facie (view of things)* the opposite of right vision and the means to it, *and a distaste for ascertainment* right vision *(of the truth).*

What, then, is this meditation on his own being? It is: *'Who have I been (in past lives)? What happened to me? What is this world? How is it? What shall we become, and what is going to happen to us?' But it ceases for him who sees the One apart.* For when there is a desire to know something, and that thing is ascertained, the desire to know it ceases. Why should this be so? *Because this* 'Who shall we become?' and so on *is all a display of changes of mind alone* and not of Puruṣa. *Puruṣa, without Ignorance, is pure and untouched by qualities of the mind.* It is just for this reason that for him who sees the One apart, *For the skilful one, meditation on his own being ceases.*

Sūtra IV.26

Then the mind is inclined to discrimination, and is borne on towards Aloneness

> *His mind, that was inclined to objects, borne on to Ignorance, now in his case has changed, and is borne on to Aloneness.*

And when the vision of the One apart has arisen, *Then the mind is inclined to discrimination (viveka) and is borne on towards Aloneness (kaivalya). His mind that was inclined to objects,* on the slope towards objects *borne on to Ignorance,* taking its stand on Ignorance and turned to saṃsāra, *now in his case,* namely when there is vision of the One apart, *has changed and is borne on to Aloneness,* and is inclined to discrimination. So it is clear that a counter-current to the former stream is now flowing.

Sūtra IV.27

At intervals in it, other ideas arise from saṃskāra-s

> *His mind is being borne on towards discrimination, carried along on the current towards Knowledge-of the-difference. But at intervals, other ideas arise, in the form 'I am' or 'It is mine'. From where? From previous saṃskāra-s, whose seed-power is fading away.*

At intervals in it, other ideas arise from saṃskāra-s. His mind his consciousness of Puruṣa the Knower *is being borne on towards discrimination* further and further moving down towards discrimination, *carried along on the current towards Knowledge-of-the-difference (viveka-khyāti),* impelled by the stream towards the difference between Puruṣa and mind-sattva. *But at intervals,* in gaps of the current of discriminative ideas, *other ideas* of delusive character *arise, in the form 'I am' or 'It is mine'.*

From where do they come? *From previous saṃskāra-s* of an opposite kind laid down previously, *whose seed-power* in the form of taints, etc. *is fading away,* these other ideas arise.

Sūtra IV.28

The escape from these is like that described in the case of the taints

As the taints, reduced to scorched seeds, cannot germinate, so the previous saṃskāra-s, having become seeds scorched by the fire of knowledge, cannot bring forth ideas – this is the meaning.

The escape from these is like that described in the case of the taints. As the taints, reduced to scorched seeds, cannot germinate as was explained here previously (sūtra II.10): 'in their subtle state, they are to be got rid of by dissolution in their source', *so the previous saṃskāra-s* laid down by ideas in the form 'I am' and 'It is mine', *having become seeds scorched by the fire of knowledge (jñāna)* become unable to sprout forth, like scorched rice grains, *cannot bring forth ideas – this is the meaning.*

(Opponent) But saṃskāra-s of knowledge (jñāna) are not opponents (i.e. taints), so why should they not impel the mind to involvement (adhikāra)?

(Answer) *But those saṃskāra-s of right vision come to rest with the fulfilment of the mind's involvement.*

But those saṃskāra-s of right vision (samyagdarśana) come to rest with the fulfilment of the mind's involvement, they are dissolved along with their receptacle the mind, when its purpose has been fulfilled. They do not make the mind inclined to involvement, because knowledge is the opponent of Ignorance, the cause of involvement. Because they have no effect, they are not given attention, for when a thing is falling of itself, there is no point in searching for something to make it fall.

Sūtra IV.29

For one who is through and through a man of discriminative knowledge, but is not grasping over his meditation practice, there comes about the samādhi called Raincloud of Dharma

> *This Brahmin is not grasping over his meditation, and does not seek for anything even from that. Detached even from that, through and through he is a man of discriminative Knowledge alone.*
>
> *Because the saṃskāra-seed of taint is destroyed, for him no other ideas are created. Then, for that one, there comes about the samādhi called the Raincloud of Dharma.*

When a Brahmin has a mind moving towards Knowledge-of-the-difference, *For one, who is through and through a man of discriminative knowledge but is not grasping over his meditation practice (prasaṅkhyāna), there comes about the samādhi called Raincloud of Dharma. This Brahmin is not grasping over,* not seeking profit from *his meditation,* which is practice of discriminative vision, *and does not seek for anything even from that,* other than the special serenity of meditation practice. The word 'even' means that even in his meditation he has no desire for anything; he is *detached even from that* meditation, *through and through,* in everything, he has Knowledge-of-the-difference, *he is a man of discriminative Knowledge alone.*

Because the saṃskāra-seed of taint is destroyed, his body is as it were an empty house (Gītā V.13 and Śaṅkara Bh.), and *for him* who has his home in the serenity of Knowledge alone, *no other ideas are created. Then, for that one,* for that Brahmin who is through and through a man of discriminative Knowledge, there comes about the samādhi called: *Raincloud of Dharma.* It rains the supreme dharma called Transcendental Aloneness – hence this technical name.

Sūtra IV.30

From that, cessation of taints and karma-s

When that has been attained, Ignorance and the other taints are annihilated, with their roots. The karma-stocks, favourable and unfavourable, are destroyed and their roots killed. On cessation of taint and karma, the Knower is released while yet living. How so? Because the cause of coming-to-be is illusion. When illusion has faded away, no one is ever known to be born anywhere.

From that, cessation of taints and karma-s. When that samādhi called Raincloud of Dharma, corresponding to the maturing of right vision, comes about, *has been attained, Ignorance and the other taints are annihilated with their roots,* completely dissolved along with the saṃskāra-groups. *The karma-stocks favourable and unfavourable are destroyed and their roots killed,* They are cut off with their roots, the taints. *On cessation of taint and karma, the Knower is released while yet living. How so? Because illusion (viparyaya)* i.e. mithyā-jñāna, *is the cause of coming-to-be,* of birth. *When illusion has faded away, no one is ever known to be* (re-)born anywhere.

Sūtra IV.31

Then, with the infinity of knowledge free from all veiling taint, the knowable comes to be but a trifle

Then, knowledge is freed from all veils of taint and karma, and there is infinity of that knowledge.

Knowledge-sattva, which is infinite, (when) overcome and obscured by tamas, in places is set in motion by rajas. Thus stimulated, it can perceive. When it is freed from all veiling taints, there is infinity for it. With the infinity of knowledge, the knowable is but a trifle, like fireflies in the sky.

Then, with the infinity of knowledge free from all veiling taint, the knowable comes to be but a trifle. Then, with the Raincloud samādhi, *knowledge is freed from all veils of taint and karma,* born of rajas and tamas, *and there is infinity of that knowledge,* which is pure Knowledge-of-the-difference between mind-sattva and Puruṣa. How is it so?

Knowledge-sattva, which is infinite, (when) overcome and obscured by tamas, with the rajas taint suppressed, like a great waveless ocean, isolated, immutable – how could it be capable of perceiving anything? He replies: *in places* mind-sattva *is set in motion by rajas; thus stimulated,* as the vastness of the ocean surface is ruffled by the wind, *it can perceive.* There is no activity in sattva as such, for capacity for action is from rajas.

Then (*when it is freed from all veiling taints*) *there is infinity for it* mind-sattva, for there is nothing left to know: it is like the sun in the middle of a clear sky with all clouds dispersed and gone. *With the infinity of* that *knowledge,* there being nothing left to know, *the knowable is but a trifle, like fireflies in the sky.* As there is nothing to find out about fireflies in the sky, so there is nothing to be investigated now.

> *On which it has been said: 'The blind man pierced the gem; the fingerless man strung it on a thread; the neckless man wore it; the tongueless man praised it.'*

In the state of knowledge of the highest, there is total disappearance of illusion, and absence of any purpose of Puruṣa, and to show it, he presents this which has been said: '*The blind man pierced the gem, the fingerless man strung it on a thread, the neckless man wore it, the tongueless man praised it.*' (Taitt. Ār. I.11)

Though it is impossible for the blind man and his companions to pierce the gem or do the other things attributed to them, still through illusion it is made out that the blind man did pierce the gem. So also the relation of knowledge and what is knowable holds only in the state of illusion (viparyaya). Without illusion, the guṇa-s become void of all purposes of Puruṣa.

Sūtra IV.32

With that, the guṇa-s have fulfilled their purpose, and the succession of their changes comes to an end

With that, the guṇa-s have fulfilled their purpose, and the sequence of their changes comes to an end. For having fulfilled the purposes of experience and release, they cannot maintain themselves even a moment longer.

With that, the guṇa-s having fulfilled their purpose, the succession of their changes comes to an end. With that, with the Raincloud samādhi as cause, the guṇa-s of mind have fulfilled their purpose. Sattva and the other two are situated in the mind, and though they are impellers of body and senses, now their purposes have been fulfilled, for the purpose of Puruṣa has been fulfilled. These *guṇa-s have fulfilled their purpose* in the form of the stream of birth and death, *and the succession of their changes comes to an end. For having fulfilled the purposes of experience and release,* there is no purpose left for them. *They cannot maintain themselves even a moment longer.*

What is this succession?

It has been said that the succession of changes comes to an end. Now *What is this succession* of the guṇa-s, whose coming to an end has been described? To explain, he continues:

Sūtra IV.33

The succession is conjoined to each instant, (but) recognizable at the very end

The succession is conjoined to each instant, (but) recognizable at the very end. 'Conjoined to each instant' (pratiyogin) means that it is joined to each successive instant.

> *The succession is essentially the immediate following-on of the instants, recognized by the very end, the limit. Because no ageing of a cloth, which has not gone through a succession, comes about at the very end.*

The succession is essentially the immediate following-on of the instants, the immediate following-on of the instants is its essence, its very being, as has been explained (III.52). What then is the indication by which it is known? *By the very end of the change, its limit,* in the shape of the condition when it perishes, by that mark this, *the succession, is recognized.*

(Opponent) How is it recognized by the very end?

(Answer) *Because no ageing of a cloth, which has not gone through a succession,* which has not followed a succession, instant after instant, *comes about* (suddenly) *at the end,* the time of perishing. For no ageing of the cloth is seen in the bare existence of the thing. So it is inferred from the indication of the appearance of age; this succession is that by which this ageing has been brought about in the manifestation of the cloth.

(Opponent) If, then, there may be a succession that attains its limit, or that does not attain its limit, it is reasonable to speak of the guṇa-s having fulfilled their purpose and the succession of their changes coming to an end (IV.32). It follows that attainment or non-attainment of the limit should be allocated to permanence or non-permanence of succession (respectively). Of these two, succession is seen in the case of impermanent things like a cloth, but not in the case of permanent things. So there is a doubt whether the coming to an end of the succession of changes can apply in the case of the guṇa-s.

> *Succession is found in permanent things also. Permanence is of two kinds: the permanence-in-change (of guṇa-s) and immutable permanence (of Puruṣa-s). Permanence-in-change is when the essence of a thing is not destroyed in its changing. In both the cases, the nature is not destroyed and so there is permanence.*

(Answer) *Succession is found in permanent things also.*

(Opponent) What, everywhere?

(Answer) No. *Permanence is of two kinds: the permanence-in-change* of the guṇa-s, *and immutable permanence,* of Puruṣa-s.

(Opponent) Tell us how there can be permanence in the guṇa-s which are ever changing.

(Answer) *When the essence of a thing is not destroyed in its changing.* That whose nature is known by right knowledge (pramāṇa), is the essence of a thing. That in a thing which is not destroyed or made to vary, that is also permanence. So it is with the guṇa-s: their respective essences of happiness, pain and delusion, their respective characteristics of illumination, activity and stasis, are their nature which is not destroyed. So these too are permanent though changing.

In both cases guṇa-s and Puruṣa-s the nature is not destroyed, and so there is permanence. *Therefore, as change is observed among the permanent guṇa-s too, they both have, and have not, an end.*

> *Of the two, there is succession in guṇa-dharma-s such as the Great principle, which is perceivable at the end of the changes, so that it has a termination. But among the eternal guṇa-s, which are dharmin-s, it does not have a termination. Among the immutable eternals, freed Puruṣa-s established in their true nature alone, their existence as themselves is imagined to be experienced only in terms of a succession. As it is imagined on the basis of mere words, by assuming existence to be a process, it does not in fact have any termination.*

Of the two, there is succession in guṇa-dharma-s such as the Great principle, which is perceivable at the end of the changes, so that it has a termination, as with the body and so on. *But among the eternal guṇa-s, which are dharmin-s, it does not have a termination,* because they are eternal. *Among the immutable eternals, freed Puruṣa-s established in their true nature alone, their existence as themselves is imagined to be experienced only in terms of a succession,* which though it does not in fact exist in the freed Puruṣa-s, is imagined, as an approximation to the experience of freed Puruṣa-s. *As it is imagined on the basis of mere words, by assuming existence to be a process, it does not in fact have any termination.* From the point of view of the highest truth, the meaning is that there is no succession in Puruṣa-s, inasmuch as they do not change.

> *(Opponent) Now as regards this world, which functions in the guṇa-s whether as stasis or as activity, is there a termination of the succession or is there not?*
>
> *(Answer) This cannot be answered definitely. How is there any question that can be answered in absolute terms? For instance, Everyone born will die: will everyone who has died be re-born? can be answered by making a distinction. What distinction? The skilful one in whom Knowledge has arisen and whose craving has faded away will not be re-born; the others will be re-born.*
>
> *Then, Is human birth a superior one, or is it not superior? (The answer is:) In comparison with animals, it is superior, but in relation to Gods and sages, it is not.*
>
> *So this question (about the world) is not really answerable as a generalization without making a distinction – (for instance in the form) Is this world purely finite, or is it purely infinite? (The answer is:) For the skilful (yogin) the world has a termination, but not for others. The question (as put) was illegitimately limiting itself to one alternative: the question was not properly formulated.*

(Opponent) Now as regards this world, which functions in the guṇa-s whether as stasis in the form of pradhāna *or as activity* in the form of assuming change, *is there a termination of the succession or is there not?*

(Answer) This cannot be answered definitely. It cannot be asserted decisively that there is, nor that there is not. But by making a distinction, that in some cases there is and in some cases there is not, it can be answered.

How is there any question that can be answered in absolute terms without making a distinction? For instance, the answer *Everyone born will die* applies only to the Ignorant (a-jñānin).

(Opponent) But even the man of Knowledge must die.

(Answer) Not so, for the imagination of death is for the Ignorant alone, not for the Knower. So it is said: 'It is through illusion (mithyā) alone that the foolish say one dies.'

Will everyone who has died be re-born? can be answered by making a distinction, for there is no absolute answer.

(Opponent) *What distinction?*

(Answer) *The skilful one in whom Knowledge has arisen and whose craving has faded away will not be re-born; the others* who are Ignorant *will be re-born.*

Then, Is human birth a wholly *superior one, or is it not* wholly *superior?* is a question not answerable categorically. Only by making a distinction can it be answered. How so? *In comparison with animals, it is superior, but in relation to gods and sages, it is not* superior.

So this question (about the world) is not really answerable as a generalization, without making a distinction – for instance in the form *Is this world purely finite, or is it purely infinite?* is not answerable categorically because no account has been taken of bondage and release, but it is answerable by making a distinction: *For the skilful (yogin) the world has a termination, but not for others. So the question was illegitimately limiting itself to one alternative:* when it asked whether the world is purely finite, or purely infinite, the word 'or' was limiting it illegitimately to a single alternative. So *the question was not properly formulated* because it was in general terms without distinctions, like the other questions whether all that die will be re-born, and whether human birth is a purely superior one or not. It was thus proper to make the distinction when it was said: With that, the guṇa-s have fulfilled their purpose and the succession of their changes comes to an end (IV.32).

> *The termination of the involvement of the guṇa-s is what is called Transcendental Aloneness. Now its nature is to be determined.*

The termination of the involvement of the guṇa-s is what is called Transcendental Aloneness. Now its nature is to be determined. There are conflicting views about it. For some, it is absolute cessation of the chain of vijñāna-consciousness. But for others, it is a state of Puruṣa which is unconscious and simply subsists, having cut off its nine attributes of buddhi, desire, aversion, effort, pleasure, pain, righteousness and unrighteousness, with their saṃskāra-impressions. For others it is union (sa-yujya) with the Lord, and for others it is attainment of omniscience and other attributes equal to those of the Lord. Thus opinions are conflicting on what is meant by Transcendental Aloneness (kaivalya). Here then, to dispel the divergence of opinion, the true nature of Aloneness is determined:

Sūtra IV.34

Transcendental Aloneness is withdrawal of the guṇa-s, now without any purposes of Puruṣa; or it is the establishment of the power-of-consciousness in its own nature

That Transcendental Aloneness is withdrawal of the guṇa-s, whose essence is cause and effect, now that experience and release, the purposes of Puruṣa, are achieved and done with. Again, it is Puruṣa's power-of-consciousness established in its own nature, no longer bound up with mind-sattva, and alone, isolated: its permanence in that state alone is Transcendental Aloneness. OM.

Withdrawal is the flowing back from conjunction, and reduction to their cause, *of the guṇa-s, now without any purpose of Puruṣa,* though they are naturally ever-changing by assuming the nature *of cause and effect;* isolation of Puruṣa from being bound up with the guṇa-s *is Transcendental Aloneness.*

Or, it is the power-of-consciousness established in its own nature. Puruṣa's power-of-consciousness, not bound up with not involved with *mind-sattva, is alone, isolated; its permanence in that state alone is Transcendental Aloneness.*

(Opponent) How is it that there is difference of views about Aloneness, which is a unity? As to action there may be divergence, but not about a thing, because there cannot be division in the true nature of a thing. Aloneness too is a thing, so how can it be defined variously (as in the two definitions given in the sūtra as alternatives joined with *'or')?*

(Answer) It is quite allowable, because distinction is accepted in the case of cause and effect. There is difference on a basis of distinguishing cause and effect, but no division is being made in the true nature of the thing. When it is said there is changefulness of the guṇa-s, and that the involvement of Puruṣa by its conforming to the mental process, goes away as a result of a cause – namely the flowing back from conjunction of the guṇa-s which, though essentially cause and effect, are now without any purposes of Puruṣa- all that was a statement of the cause alone. The cause is the (current of) withdrawal, and first of all it was explained that this is Aloneness.

But second was, the specification of Aloneness in itself, uninvolved with the guṇa-s, as a result of the reverse current of the guṇa-s as cause. By ascertaining the truth that guṇa-s and Puruṣa are separate, and by showing up the claims to truth made by other doctrines, the different ideas of Aloneness have to be made clear.

The syllable OM is added as a blessing, so that, crowned with the mark of the Name of the supreme Lord, the work may be fruitful, and that there may be peace. So it is said, as it is in the Veda-s and the Āraṇyaka-s: OM.

(Salutations and colophon)

Whose expressive-word is OM, from whom is all action made fruitful, Who, himself without taints or fruition of karma, brings about everything as the fruit of actions,

Lord of lords, controller of preservation and coming into being and cessation of all creations, may he have regard to our good deeds and annul our bad.

He has given life to the three worlds.
A fraction of his unimaginable power became in this world the Fish and other avatāra-s reckoned to be ten;

Tormented by the continuous chain of the three sufferings arising from the taints, we go for refuge to Him who has Śeṣa (the cosmic serpent) as his couch.

Salutations to Patañjali, lord of yogin-s, lord of serpents (being an incarnation of Śeṣa) who by the power of the gem in his hoods lights everywhere on earth, in the sky, and in space,

who by (this) yoga has removed impurities of the mind, by (his) grammar those of speech, and by his (classic on) medicine those of the physical body – to that highest of sages, Patañjali, be this bow with my folded hands.

The sage Patañjali is supreme, by whom all the seekers of ends attain their highest good; the joy which he brings removes the three burning afflictions, by the Raincloud of Dharma (samādhi);

who to remove the heat of the Dharma-s of tainted action of those traversing the paths of worldly existence
appeared as the water-bearer of the yoga which leads to the
Raincloud of dharma – to that Ṛṣi Patañjali I bow down.

I bow down to him on whose countenance is a full moon, the teacher, the lord, who is not decorated with wealth and who is without the necklace of serpents, the incomparable Śaṅkara whose feet are to be worshipped.

With this, the Fourth Part, on Transcendental Aloneness, of the sub-commentary on the commentary to the yoga sūtra-s of Patañjali, by the holy Lord (bhagavat) Śaṅkara, who is a paramahaṃsa parivrājaka ācārya and pupil of holy Lord Govindapāda whose feet are to be worshipped, is complete.

This concludes the vivaraṇa sub-commentary.

www.ingramcontent.com/pod-product-compliance
Lightning Source LLC
Chambersburg PA
CBHW071113080526
44587CB00013B/1324
* 9 7 8 1 9 1 1 4 6 7 0 8 3 *